A Celebration of Literature and Response
Children, Books, and Teachers
in K–8 Classrooms

THIRD EDITION

Marjorie R. Hancock
Kansas State University

PEARSON

Merrill
Prentice Hall

Upper Saddle River, New Jersey
Columbus, Ohio

Library of Congress Cataloging-in-Publication Data

Hancock, Marjorie R.
  A celebration of literature and response : children, books, and teachers in K–8 classrooms / Marjorie R. Hancock.—
  3rd ed. p. cm.
  Includes bibliographical references and index.
  ISBN-13: 978-0-13-613394-0 (pbk.)
  ISBN-10: 0-13-613394-0 (pbk.)
  1. Children's literature—Study and teaching (Elementary) 2. Reader-response criticism. 3. Children—Books and reading. I. Title.
  LB1575.H36 2008·
  372.64'044—dc22

                    2007026378

Vice President and Executive Publisher: Jeffery W. Johnston
Senior Editor: Linda Ashe Bishop
Senior Development Editor: Hope Madden
Senior Production Editor: Mary M. Irvin
Senior Editorial Assistant: Laura Weaver
Production Coordination: Thistle Hill Publishing Services, LLC
Design Coordinator: Diane C. Lorenzo
Cover Designer: Kelly E. Donnelly
Cover Image: Jupiter Images
Production Manager: Pamela D. Bennett
Director of Marketing: David Gesell
Marketing Manager: Darcy Betts Prybella
Marketing Coordinator: Brian Mounts

This book was set in Souvenir by Integra Software Services. It was printed and bound by R. R. Donnelley & Sons Company. The cover was printed by Phoenix Color Corp.

Pearson Education Ltd.
Pearson Education Singapore Pte. Ltd.
Pearson Education Canada, Ltd.
Pearson Education—Japan

Pearson Education Australia Pty. Limited
Pearson Education North Asia Ltd.
Pearson Educación de Mexico, S.A. de C.V.
Pearson Education Malaysia Pte. Ltd.

                    10   17
                    ISBN-13: 978-0-13-613394-0
                    ISBN-10:   0-13-613394-0

Preface

I f books could be more, could show more, could own more, this book would have smells. . . .

It would have the smells of old farms; the sweet smell of new-mown hay as it falls off the oiled sickle blade when the horses pull the mower through the field, and the sour smell of manure steaming in a winter barn. It would have the sticky-slick smell of birth when the calves come and they suck for the first time on the rich, new milk; the dusty smell of winter hay dried and stored in the loft waiting to be dropped down to the cattle; the pungent fermented smell of the chopped corn silage when it is brought into the manger on the silage fork. This book would have the smell of new potatoes sliced and frying in light pepper on a woodstove burning dry pine, the damp smell of leather mittens steaming on the back of the stovetop, and the acrid smell of the slop bucket by the door when the lid is lifted and the potato peelings are dumped in—but it can't.

Books can't have smells.

If books could be more and own more and give more, this book would have sound. . . .

It would have the high, keening sound of the six-foot bucksaws as the men pull them back and forth through the trees to cut pine for paper pulp; the grunting-gassy sounds of the work teams snorting and slapping as they hit the harness to jerk the stumps out of the ground. It would have the chewing sounds of cows in the barn working at their cuds on a long winter's night; the solid thunking sound of the ax coming down to split stovewood, and the piercing scream of the pigs when the knife cuts their throats and they know death is at hand—but it can't.

Books can't have sound.

And finally if books could be more, give more, show more, this book would have light. . . .

Oh, it would have the soft gold light—gold with bits of hay dust floating in it—that slips through the crack in the barn wall; the light of the Coleman lantern hissing flat-white in the kitchen; the silver-gray light of middle winter day, the splattered, white-night light of a full moon on snow, the new light of dawn at the eastern edge of the pasture behind the cows coming in to be milked on a summer morning—but it can't.

Books can't have light.

If books could have more, give more, be more, show more, they would still need readers, who bring to them sound and smell and light and all the rest that can't be in books.

The book needs you.

G.P.

From *The Winter Room* by Gary Paulsen. Copyright © 1989 by Gary Paulsen. Reprinted by permission of the publisher, Orchard Books, New York.

Gary Paulsen's prologue to *The Winter Room* exemplifies the critical role that a reader plays in a transaction with a book. A celebration of literature, in all its glory, cannot take place without the reader. A book is printed text brought to life only when the reader brings smell to "*new potatoes sliced and frying in light pepper on a woodstove burning dry pine. . .*" (pp. 1–2). The reader turns words on the page into the sound of "*six-foot bucksaws as the men pull them back and forth through the trees to cut pine for paper pulp . . .*" (p. 2). Only a reader can envision and bring life to "*the new light of dawn at the eastern edge of the pasture behind the cows coming in to be milked on a summer morning . . .*" (p. 3). Books need the reader to create the sensory and emotional experiences carried by printed words on a page. Without a reader, literature cannot reach its potential. Literature must invite the personal perspective of the reader if the celebration is to begin.

A Celebration of Literature and Response invites you to participate in a celebration of quality children's literature and a celebration of responding to that literature. As a reader, you are invited to respond to thoughts and ideas in this text as you read. Share your questions, concerns, literacy memories, or book reading experiences through discussion. Record your innermost reactions, classroom connections, and personal responses to ideas shared in this text in a response journal or the margins of the text. Then, seek out the quality children's literature titles shared in this text and respond to them at your own level.

The premise of this textbook on children's literature is built around the transactional theory of reader response of Louise Rosenblatt, who supports the mutual interaction of the reader and the text during a literary event. This philosophy supports the belief that each reader forms a unique connection with a text *as* he or she reads. This perspective is a world apart from the traditional book reports I assigned during my early years of teaching or that you may have written in elementary school. Reader response theory encompasses a realm of response options that spontaneously and purposefully occur during and following the reading of a book. Therefore, this text not only surveys children's literature but introduces those aesthetic options teachers can present to encourage the reader to bring the text to life through personal response in the classroom. This text is a blend of literature and reader, of book and response, of teachers guiding and students responding. This textbook serves as a motivating introduction to the world of children's literature and the realm of children's responses as readers.

A Celebration of Literature and Response consists of five areas for celebrating children's books and readers.

Part I: Celebrating Literature, Response, and Teaching.   Chapter 1 introduces Louise Rosenblatt's transactional theory of reader response to literature and its impact on the way educators view readers and literature. Although her ideas have been available for almost 70 years, it is only during the past two decades that elementary teachers have conceptualized the natural connection between reading instruction and the potential of reader response to literature. Rosenblatt's legacy to literacy provides a foundational theory that encourages practitioners to open their classrooms to literature and to celebrate the natural responses of children to books. The second part of the chapter brings reader response to life as a developmental perspective on types of reader response to literature unfolds. Chapter 2 invites teachers to embrace children's literature as an instrument of response-based instruction. Readers investigate the definition of children's literature and reader response while clarifying a response-based teaching philosophy. Reasons for blending children's books and children's responses in the classroom provide convincing justification for assuming a response-based approach to teaching. Simulated visits to classrooms assist in visualizing the blending of literature, readers, teaching, and response in practice.

Part II: Celebrating Literature.   Six substantive chapters invite readers to appreciate the major literary genres and gain an understanding of literary elements and book selection criteria. Chapter 3 guides us through the picture book format of children's literature, building an awareness of the art and design of the picture book. Chapters 4, 5, 6, and 7 celebrate the genres of traditional literature/fantasy, poetry, realistic and historical fiction, and biography and informational nonfiction, respectively. Chapter 8 on multicultural and international literature across the genres provides a framework and numerous literary treasures that share ethnic and global cultures with children. Throughout each chapter, quality children's books are shared as illustrative examples. Special bibliographies in each chapter blend additional quality book titles from the past five years with contemporary titles from the first edition, and nostalgic classics that reflect the best aspects of each genre.

Part III: Celebrating Response Connections.   The five chapters in Part III form the heart of the text and the practical links sought by preservice and inservice teachers. They enrich the classroom repertoire of response-based activities through literature. These chapters contain teaching strategies for eliciting a developmental range of reader response and suggested literature that involves the reader in the literary experience. Concrete examples of activities with specific children's book titles abound. Chapter 9 begins with read-alouds and emerging response, and builds toward literature conversations as children grow in their ability to talk about books. Chapter 10 employs a developmental approach toward written response through journals. Chapter 11 celebrates literature as a model for writing by focusing on books that assist children as apprentices of the author's craft. Chapter 12 focuses on the expressive arts of drama, art, and music as outlets for reader response to literature. In Chapter 13, aesthetic response to nonfiction becomes a reality through planned informational responses.

Part IV: Celebrating Intertextual and Interdisciplinary Connections.
The integration of content area instruction is facilitated by blending the fictional and factual aspects of children's literature. Chapter 14 discusses the possibilities for literature-based integrated thematic instruction through "literature clusters" and "theme explorations." Step-by-step procedures for creating classroom investigations through literature are illustrated. This chapter includes a process for conceptualizing themes, selecting literature, and planning related activities. Several model literature clusters and theme explorations geared to three multiage levels are shared through graphic organizers, annotated bibliographies, and related language-based activities. In addition, technology connections to both fiction and nonfiction reflect the mutual benefits of linking literature to a technological world.

Part V: Celebrating Response Growth Through Assessment. Because authentic assessment is a key issue in the use of literature in the classroom, Chapter 15 addresses this issue with various assessment configurations. Included are a developmental response continuum, a rubric for literature response journals, checklists for literature discussions, and suggestions for paper and electronic portfolio documentation.

KEY FEATURES OF THE TEXT

A Celebration of Literature and Response features an abundance of resources and information to help you reach your teaching goals.

Literature . . .

- **Up-to-date literature.** The text emphasizes current literature with most books from the early 2000s through 2007. Practitioners seem energized by an introduction to new literature and are likely to implement new ideas with recent titles. Yet the text also weaves in familiar classic authors and titles in a Literary Legends feature so readers have their own past literature experiences from which to draw. The intention of the text is not to ignore the importance of quality literature through the years but to update the reader to the best of the new influx of quality published books.
- **Literature clusters.** In addition to the children's books cited within and at the end of each chapter, many chapters contain extended lists of recent children's books that emphasize a certain aspect of literature or provide additional response models for classroom use. They serve as a model for teacher design of other clusters on curricular or personal interest topics.
- **Developmental labeling of literature.** Bibliographies throughout the text contain the designation of **P** (primary, K–2), **I** (intermediate, 3–5), and **M** (middle school, 6–8) to assist teachers in age-appropriate use of literature. These designations indicate the level(s) at which the literature will best elicit response.
- **Multicultural and international literature.** Not only is multicultural children's literature woven throughout genre chapters and the entire text, but it is showcased in its own chapter that emphasizes selection criteria, outstanding

literature across cultures, and a framework for effective classroom inclusion. International children's literature is featured as an extended means of eliciting response through a global perspective.

- **Appendix.**   The appendix includes lists of book awards of interest to educators. All award information is current, well organized, and presented in a manner useful to preservice and inservice teachers as well as researchers in children's literature. This appendix is a quick reference to locate titles and authors for which the reader needs easy access.

. . . and Response

- **Reader response focus.**   Reader response to literature is not only discussed in introductory chapters but also integrated throughout the entire text. Each genre chapter concludes with connections to response-based chapters. Part III focuses on a developmental perspective across the spectrum of response options.
- **Links to the IRA/NCTE** *Standards for the English Language Arts.* Reader response to literature meaningfully links to several of the national standards to assist preservice and inservice teachers in aligning practice to mandated standards.
- **Authentic voices of response.**   Fresh examples of authentic responses to literature by children, preservice teachers, and inservice teachers are interspersed throughout the text to bring life to the idea of reader response to literature.
- **Interdisciplinary instruction.**   This edition suggests methods for selecting literature across genres to integrate instruction in multiage settings. The process and procedures for creating literature clusters and literature-based theme explorations are effectively articulated in a step-by-step format. An extended emphasis on nonfiction is evident in both the nonfiction genre and the nonfiction response chapters, which integrate the wonders of informational books into curricular areas through response.
- **Technology connections to literature.**   Technology enhances responses to and connections beyond literature through keypal literature circles and linking fact, fiction, and technological websites. Each chapter contains a feature titled Resources on the Web focused on technology-based connections to literature (Chapters 1–8) or technology-based response options (Chapters 9–15) to aid in integrating the power of literature and response with the strength of the new literacies.
- **Assessment focus.**   The text addresses assessment with a chapter that includes rubrics, checklists, response portfolios (both paper and electronic), and other response documentation strategies. The text addresses the important connections between assessment and response-based instruction while justifying the inclusion of literature in the classroom as an extension far richer and deeper than test data.

I hope that you, as the reader of this book, will interact with the words on the page and bring them to life through your own experiences with literature, with children, with teaching, and with the world around you. *Only you can bring this book to life.* Only readers can celebrate literature by bringing their own perspective to a book. I invite you to celebrate literature, not by merely reading about it but by experiencing it in your own unique way. This book is an invitation to access some of the hundreds of quality titles shared within these chapters, to read and respond to them on a personal level, and to share them with children across the spectrum of suggested response-based activities. Only then will the celebration of literature, response, and lifelong reading truly begin—both for you as a teacher and for the children you teach.

Acknowledgments

This textbook is the culmination of 10 years of elementary teaching in Illinois and 16 years of undergraduate and graduate teaching, supervision, and research at Kansas State University. The enthusiastic children, dedicated teachers, demanding professors, and outstanding professionals I encountered during my career made this book possible. Louise Rosenblatt deserves recognition for her conceptualization of a theory of reading literature that melds children and books together in a democratic classroom environment, encouraging each individual to connect personal experiences and innermost feelings to quality literature. Exploring her theory at the doctoral level began to answer so many questions I had as a teacher, thus planting the seed for this text and its successive revisions.

Authentic settings, real children, and dedicated teachers make this book believable. The preservice teachers of Kansas State University confirm my instructional philosophy as they confidently share successful response-based lessons in their practicum and student internship experiences. The teachers and children in USD #383, Manhattan/Ogden School, and USD #475, Geary County Schools, deserve thanks for supporting the infusion of countless literature-based lessons into their classrooms as part of the Kansas State University Professional Development School Partnership with each district. My graduate students and inservice participants across the state of Kansas shared children's literature and response-based ideas with their students and generously reported their enthusiastic results. Throughout the pages of this book are woven their reflections, their use of literature, and their own responses to children's books.

Special appreciation is due teacher researchers, graduate students, and practitioners for opening their classrooms to literature and reader response: Erin Jurand, Annie Opat, Diana Porter, Deb Shepek, and Stacy Tyler. I also deeply appreciate the responses of Cajsa and Adam Larson for their contributions to written response. I am so proud of Nathaniel Hancock, my grandson, for his oral and written responses as well. Thanks to Patrick Hancock, my talented English teacher son, for his features on literary legends in Chapters 1 through 8. Special thanks to Lotta Larson, my extraordinary doctoral student, for opening my eyes to technology connections through literature. Lotta is responsible for the technology chapter features, the CD database, and the instructor's manual aligned with this text. Thanks to these and many unmentioned educators for their contributions to responses and visions shared throughout the text.

I'd also like to thank the people at Merrill/Prentice Hall. Linda Bishop, my editor, helped create the original vision for my professional agenda in a challenging, yet fulfilling experience for this third edition. Hope Madden, my development editor, is a "special gift" from my editor to me. Hope gently nudges, strongly encourages, and definitely believes in the content and the completion of authoring a textbook. Hope is the reason that this textbook was revised in a timely and invigorated manner. Mary Irvin and the countless people who put this book into production were instrumental to its outcome. Angela Urquhart at Thistle Hill Publishing Services, in particular, checked citations and polished my writing with her expert editing staff.

My sincere thanks go to the professional reviewers who provided informed perspectives and opinions: Katrina Imison-Mázy, Purdue University; Bonnie Armbruster, University of Illinois at Urbana-Champaign; Shirley B. Ernst, Eastern Connecticut State University; Wendy Smith, Loyola College in Maryland; Ward A. Cockrum, Northern Arizona University; and Ruth Oswald, The University of Akron.

My deepest thanks to my children, Michael, Amy, and Patrick, for their understanding and encouragement during this project. Our mutual love of literature and respect for teaching have greatly influenced their professional lives as teachers themselves. I fondly dedicate the third edition of this text to Louise M. Rosenblatt, the respected theorist who provided the foundation of this text. Dr. Rosenblatt's passing in 2005 only made me more determined to continue carrying on her theoretical legacy to future K–8 teachers. Louise Rosenblatt will never be forgotten. Her philosophy and beliefs about reader response are timeless and now can be shared with the next generation of teaching professionals.

—*Marjorie R. Hancock*

Brief Contents

Contents

CONTENTS

PART IV
Celebrating Intertextual and Interdisciplinary Connections 377

PART V
Celebrating Response Growth Through Assessment 413

Note: Every effort has been made to provide accurate and current Internet information in this book. However, the Internet and information on it are constantly changing, so it is inevitable that some of the Internet addresses listed in this textbook will change.

PART I

Celebrating Literature, Response, and Teaching

The appeal of children's literature, the richness of reader response, and the satisfaction of quality teaching blend into a meaningful instructional philosophy in the K–8 classroom. Part I of *A Celebration of Literature and Response* challenges the reader to capture the very essence of the transaction between literature and response. Sam Sebesta (1997) promises this transaction is "a powerful potion, giving strength to the reader and the wish for more" (p. 545). As this celebration begins, elaborating the foundational knowledge that underlies this philosophy seems appropriate to appreciate fully the power of connecting readers, books, and teaching through reader response. Therefore, Part I of this text shares the theoretical and practical background needed to convey the innumerable benefits of teaching from a response-based perspective. Constantly linked to authentic literature, real classrooms, and energetic readers, these opening chapters provide the definitions, the theoretical perspective, and the practical connections necessary to proceed through this text with a flexible literary vision, a broadening response perspective, and a continuing celebration of the natural link between literature and readers.

The theoretical underpinnings of reader response to literature occupy the opening discussion of Chapter 1. The eloquent quotes and rich beliefs of Louise Rosenblatt (1978) convincingly capture the essence of aesthetic response. Practical connections to the world of real readers focus on modes of response to literature. They encourage developmentally appropriate responses across the language arts of reading, writing, listening, speaking, and visual representation. Children's book titles and related response modes weave their way throughout the text to constantly bring theory and practice together. At any age, readers' natural desire to share the literature with which they interact underlies the premise of reader response.

Chapter 2 begins with a definition of children's literature and convincingly presents a rationale for its inclusion in K–8 classrooms. Clarifying the concept of reader response through the perspectives of the reader, the text, and the context for response further contributes to an understanding of the uniqueness of each child in his or her interactions with text. This chapter transports the reader to the world of a literature-based classroom as it paints a portrait of teaching. It blends quality literature, meaningful response-based activities, and a variety of response options across both literary genres and curricular areas.

The introductory momentum of Part I provides the reader the information to most fully appreciate the philosophy, literature, and teaching connections of the remainder of the book. Part I provides basic background on literature and reader response, serves as the foundational link between theory, research, and practice, and highlights the natural link between literature, reader response, and teaching. Encouraging a celebration of both literature and reader response, these chapters issue an invitation to further investigate the unexplored boundaries of the interaction between books and readers in K–8 classrooms.

Rosenblatt, L. M. (1978). *The reader, the text, the poem: The transactional theory of a literary work*. Carbondale: Southern Illinois University Press.

Sebesta, S. L. (1997). Having my say. *The Reading Teacher, 50,* 542–549.

CHAPTER 1

Reader Response to Literature

From Rosenblatt's Theory to Classroom Practice

As if anticipating the arrival of a rock star, the entire Convention Center reverberated as participants of the 2004 National Council of Teachers of English Conference crowded into a small session room to celebrate the wisdom, impact, and democratic principles of Louise M. Rosenblatt—the visionary icon and initiator of reader response theory. The crowd greeted the theoretical genius—who was fast approaching her 100th birthday—with thunderous applause but immediately fell silent at the sound of the voice of the scholar who has had the greatest effect on the importance of literature in the classroom setting. Louise Rosenblatt spent her life teaching educators that our interactions with literature promise to change lives and society. Her theoretical works and engaging ideas radically changed teachers' thinking about the role of literature and literacy, teaching, and democracy.

On that memorable day in November 2004, Dr. Louise Rosenblatt's presence served as a reminder of the beliefs, the ongoing acceptance, the victory, and the renewed battle to retain literature as a showcase of the *reading process in America's classrooms. Accompanied to this session by her former doctoral students, now prestigious university professors, the panel served as a human reflection of over 70 years of generational commitment to the principles of literature as a foundation of democracy. Dr. Rosenblatt's theory gained acceptance and gathered momentum as she rooted its foundation in recognizable practice. Never were teachers left wondering—only experiencing—how the transaction between authentic literature and the individual reader created lifelong commitment to literacy and critical thought.*

On that same autumn afternoon, and everyday in classrooms across the country, children gather around their teachers to engage in treasured read-alouds or independent reading of contemporary and classic children's literature . Huddled closely on a reading rug of brilliant colors, children anticipate the charisma of the teacher's expressive voice as it blends literary text with the visual reflections of a well-selected book chosen for its potential to engage, expand, and extend unique reader response to a literary theme. Gathered in special comfortable reading zones, independent readers read a self-selected text and then take a moment to write a spontaneous response in a journal. Throughout the read-alouds, children spontaneously join in with predictable chants or repeated phrases. Alongside the independent reading, peers share exciting moments, random predictions, and immediate thoughts with those nearby. Children talk, draw, write, or create in response to the literary choices and, in doing so, bring the dream of Louise Rosenblatt to reality as each unique listener/reader personalizes his or her own response to literature, sharing within a community of readers and becoming future democratic citizens of the world.

Author's response to Louise Rosenblatt's message,
National Council of Teachers of English Conference,
November 2004.

In the past two decades, educators have simultaneously experienced a renaissance in the publication of children's literature and related philosophical trends that enriched and expanded the role of trade books in the classroom setting. Holistic philosophy, the reading–writing connection, and literature-based instruction provided momentum for the inclusion of children's literature during the entire school day. Not only does literature continue to be read aloud, but, in many dedicated classroom settings, it remains the heartbeat of the curriculum. Literature strives to retain the focus of both reading and writing programs and has ventured across curricular boundaries through interdisciplinary instruction. While confronting the challenges of legislative initiatives, high-stakes testing, standards accountability, and an increasing technology emphasis, literature holds its critical position in a literacy program focused on lifelong reading (Ayra et al., 2005).

This chapter shares Louise Rosenblatt's theory of reader response and connects its reality to authentic literature response of K–8 children. The first part of the chapter shares Dr. Rosenblatt's theoretical perspective in understandable terms, and the second part brings that theory to life through an examination of the seven patterns of response exhibited by children when they respond to literature. The link between theory and practice is a vital one for practitioners who seek a theoretical foundation to support quality literature-based connections in the K–8 classroom. The practical link to real books and real children ensures internalization of a response-based perspective by envisioning children's responses to literature.

LOUISE ROSENBLATT'S THEORY OF READER RESPONSE

> [T]here is in reality only the potential millions of individual readers of the potential millions of individual literary works. . . . The reading of any work of literature is, of necessity, an individual and unique occurrence, involving the mind and emotions of some particular reader. (Rosenblatt, 1938, 1955, p. 32)

Since its publication in 1938, Louise Rosenblatt's *Literature as Exploration* has provided the theoretical basis for research in the teaching and study of literature and has impacted the way literature is taught in school settings (Dressman & Webster, 2001). Acknowledged as the first book to support a reader response theory of literature, this masterpiece considers the personal, social, and cultural contexts of the reading act while showcasing the dynamics of the individual reader and the individual text as unique forces in the personal response to literature. Although supported by some teachers of college and high school literature for years, it has only been during the past decade that children's literature advocates have discovered the words of Dr. Rosenblatt as support for the inclusion of children's literature as a natural part of the elementary/middle-level curriculum (Cai, 2001). In her eloquent discussion of the role of the reader in the literary transaction, Dr. Rosenblatt supports teachers' desires to surround readers with quality children's literature experiences, resulting in the creation of lifelong readers whose emotions and empathy fostered by literature will reach beyond reading to influence their view of humanity.

For almost 70 years, the name of Louise Rosenblatt has been synonymous with the *transactional theory of reader response* to literature (Karolides, 1999). The theory focuses on the reciprocal relationship between the reader and the literature that results in individual responses to the text during and following engaged reading of literature. The interaction of the reader with the text is central to this theory as "a person becomes a reader by virtue of his activity in relation to the text" and "the text, a set of marks on the page, becomes the text of a poem . . . by virtue of its relationship with the reader" (Rosenblatt, 1978, p. 18). The resulting transaction occurs as the reader brings a wealth of life and literature experiences to the text and culminates in

Literary Legend

Reader Response to Literature

Louise M. Rosenblatt (1904–2005) provided the greatest theoretical influence to shape pedagogical practice in literature-based language arts instruction in the twentieth century. Her revolutionary approach to reading and the teaching of literature began with the 1938 publication of *Literature as Exploration*. She shared her transactional theory of reader response most clearly in 1978 in *The Reader, the Text, and the Poem,* which clearly articulated that the complex act of reading involves a unique transaction between the reader and the text. Her commitment to democracy, teachers, readers, and literature is evident through pedagogical practice across elementary, middle-level, secondary, and undergraduate/graduate college instruction.

Dr. Rosenblatt graduated from Barnard College in 1925 and received a doctorate in comparative literature from the Sorbonne in 1931. Her early teaching years were spent at Barnard College and Brooklyn College before she became a professor of English ed-ucation at New York University's School of Education (1948–1972). After her "retire-ment," she became a visiting professor at Rutgers and the University of Miami, yet her true impact was just emerging during this time. She received numerous awards from the National Council of Teachers of English and was elected to the International Reading Association Hall of Fame.

Dr. Rosenblatt's final book, *Making Meaning with Texts: Selected Essays,* was pub-lished just days before her death at age 100. Her fingerprints forever remain on class-room reading across all levels of instruction. She lived one of the fullest, richest, and most productive lives that educators have ever witnessed, and her legacy lies in those profes-sionals who continue to connect her theory to practice with readers in today's class-rooms. Her steadfast dedication to democratic principles, her principled belief in the value of personal response to literature, and the pure joy of reading itself mark the legacy of this respected theoretical icon.

Rosenblatt, L. M. (1978). *The reader, the text, the poem: The transactional theory of the literary work.* Carbondale: Southern Illinois University.

Rosenblatt, L. M. (1995). *Literature as exploration.* New York: Appleton-Century-Crofts (5th ed., Modern Language Association). (Original work published 1938)

Rosenblatt, L. M. (2005). *Making meaning with texts: Selected essays.* Portsmouth, NH: Heinemann.

a response that evokes the literary work of art as a truly personal experience for the reader.

The pinnacle of reader response results when the reader focuses an awareness on the very personal meaning that he or she is shaping. Then, and only then, will

FIGURE 1.1   Reader response to literature

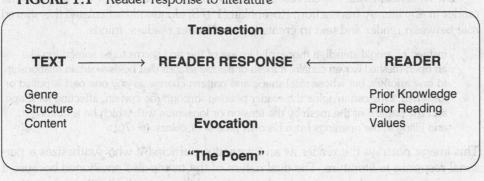

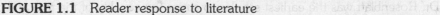

the reader create the aesthetically based literary work of art that Dr. Rosenblatt refers to as "the poem." The poem symbolizes the literary work of art created by the unique intervention of the reader. Figure 1.1 visually presents the ongoing process of reader response to literature. The reader draws on his or her own literature, life, and cognitive experiences. The "evocation of the poem" refers to the lived-through process of creating a unique perspective on the work while being guided by the text. As the reader continuously responds to the work, a constant stream of attitudes, ideas, and feelings runs through the participant's mind. Previous reading of literature and past personal experiences strongly influence the ongoing responses to a book. A simultaneous process occurs as the reader responds to the words on the page while at the same time drawing on unique experiences and knowledge to organize those thoughts. Out of this interaction, "the poem" is formed. As noted in the quote that opens this section, each reader thus evokes his or her own meaning from the same text, thereby prioritizing and encouraging the unique response to literature.

In *The Reader, the Text, the Poem* (1978), Dr. Rosenblatt artfully described the evolving balanced role of reader and text by likening the reading transaction to a play performed on a stage. Dr. Rosenblatt asks her readers to imagine a darkened stage with the author stage left, the reader stage right, and the book midway between them. The spotlight initially focuses on the author so that the reader and the text become almost invisible to the audience. In this scene, single meaning resides fully in the author's mind. Imagine the spotlight shifting next to the text with the reader and the author completely obscured. The reader remains in the shadow, his or her secondary role taken for granted while meaning lies solely in the printed word. After many years, however, the spotlight begins to move in the direction of the reader. The reader begins to gain importance as an active participant in the reading event. As the play ends, the spotlight focuses on all three characters—the reader, the author, the text. Dr. Rosenblatt's theory highlights the whole stage scenario as both the text and its creative author interact with the reader to create meaning.

Dr. Rosenblatt was the earliest scholar to stress the equality of the text and the reader in any literary transaction. Rosenblatt (1978) eloquently articulated this shared role between reader and text to create a vision in her readers' minds:

> Instead of a rigid stencil, a more valid image of the text seems to be something like an open-meshed woven curtain, a mesh of flexible strands that holds a certain relationship to one another, but whose total shape and pattern change as any one part is pulled or loosened. One can imagine the reader peering through the curtain, affecting its shape and the pattern of the mesh by the tension or looseness with which he is holding it, and filling in the openings from his own palette of colors. (p. 76)

This image portrays the reader as an interactive participant who synthesizes a personal response to literature. The dual nature of the text is also envisioned because it encourages personal responses by the reader while minimally limiting interactions within its own constraints. Sebesta (2001) simplified this scenario by stating, "The author isn't boss anymore, but neither is the reader. It's what they come up with together that makes the literary experience" (p. 245).

Although other writers have attempted to crystallize the reader's role in the literary transaction through the years (Bleich, 1978; Holland, 1968; Iser, 1978; Probst, 1984; Richards, 1929), it was Louise Rosenblatt's passionate words that painted a vivid portrait of the transaction between the reader and the text in the minds of elementary practitioners. Teachers were able to grasp Dr. Rosenblatt's complex theory, translate its distinctive message into instructional methodology, and share the wonder of natural response with readers of children's literature.

EFFERENT AND AESTHETIC RESPONSE

An awareness of the distinction between aesthetic and nonaesthetic reading is necessary if we are to understand transactional theory. Dr. Rosenblatt clearly differentiates between efferent and aesthetic reading, with the distinction lying in the primary direction or focus of the reader's attention.

In *efferent* reading, the reader's attention is focused primarily on acquiring information. This might be associated with the reading of Cheryl Bardoe's *Gregor Mendel* to investigate genetics, a close reading of Lynne Rae Perkins's *Criss-Cross* to gain familiarity with the varied cast of characters, or a reading of Robert Burleigh's *Seurat and La Grande Jatte* to obtain specific facts about the artist's life. This type of reading is designated efferent because it involves what is carried away from the reading event. In this case, genetic principles, the names and relationships of Perkins's complex cast of characters, and the accomplishments of a French artist would become the product of the reading experience. Equate efferent reading with the type of comprehension that is often asked for during basal reader or textbook instruction. The questions evoke only right or wrong answers, thereby cueing the reader to view reading as an information-gathering event.

In contrast, *aesthetic* reading is primarily concerned with the lived-through experience that occurs during interaction with the text. Aesthetic reading focuses on feelings and thoughts that flow through the reader's mind and heart as she or he reads. Aesthetic reading might be associated with repeated readings/viewings of

David Wiesner's *Flotsam* as a young boy discovers a vintage camera filled with images from the bottom of the sea. Or a reader may vicariously connect aesthetically with the emotional and personal survival of 10-year-old Lucky Trimble in Susan Patron's *The Higher Power of Lucky*. A reader/viewer may aesthetically relive the feelings of the spiritual and physical journey of Harriet Tubman in Carole Boston Weatherford's *Moses: When Harriet Tubman Led her People to Freedom* with vivid images by Kadir Nelson. This type of reading focuses more on the ongoing process of reading and viewing, the personal interaction, rather than the product of comprehension. The enjoyment of reading, involvement with the characters, and the single reader's emerging thoughts take priority over secondary details. Equate this with literature-based reading in which personal interaction with texts is encouraged through open-ended response prompts, response journals, or literature conversations. All interactions with the text are encouraged and valued as a targeted outcome of the active art of reading.

The terms *efferent* and *aesthetic* apply to a selective stance the reader adopts toward the literary text. The efferent stance pays more attention to the cognitive, the factual, the public, and the quantitative aspects of textual meaning. The aesthetic stance focuses on the affective, the emotional, the private, and the qualitative aspects of personal meaning. Efferent and aesthetic reading, however, should not be considered mutually exclusive of one another.

Although one important aspect of the reading event is the selection of a predominantly efferent or a predominantly aesthetic stance toward the text, Dr. Rosenblatt attests that most reading incorporates a continuous, unconscious fluctuation between these two stances. As noted in Figure 1.2, an accurate view of reader response lies on a continuum between the efferent and the aesthetic extremes, not on a distinct

FIGURE 1.2 Efferent and aesthetic response continuum

Efferent	←——————→	Aesthetic
Text focused	←——————→	Reader focused
Cognitive	←——————→	Affective
Final product	←——————→	Ongoing process
Comprehension	←——————→	Transaction
Factual	←——————→	Emotional
Information	←——————→	Enjoyment
Public understanding	←——————→	Personal connections
Quantitative aspects of meaning	←——————→	Qualitative aspects of meaning
Efferent	←——————→	Aesthetic

line between the two. At any moment during the reading process, the reader's stance can lie anywhere along this efferent–aesthetic continuum. Dr. Rosenblatt attests that most reading resides near the middle of the continuum and indicates a constant fluctuation between both extremes as characteristic of most readers. "No two readings, even by the same person, are identical" (Rosenblatt, 1994). Readers are simultaneously moving back and forth along the continuum as they read, blending information and sentiment, knowledge and connections to one's own experience.

For example, while discovering that Seurat was born in France in the 1800s (efferent), the reader might also identify his inventiveness and determination as admirable traits (aesthetic). At the same time, while becoming emotionally involved in a Harriet Tubman's flight to freedom (aesthetic), the reader might actually discover information about the Underground Railroad (efferent). Readers are not consciously aware of adopting one stance or the other. The reading experience remains a unique event in that some readers take on the aesthetic stance intuitively, whereas many, unfortunately, never learn to read aesthetically at all. Recognizing the differences between aesthetic and efferent reading while gaining an awareness of their interplay as part of the reading process serves as an important introduction to reader response theory and its connection to classroom practice. Teachers should clarify, model, and encourage both types of responses as readers interact with literature.

The shift in emphasis of reader response theory from the impact of the text alone to the dynamic interaction of the reader with it implies new priorities and procedures for the literature-based classroom. Dr. Rosenblatt's reader response theory suggests that students should not be subordinate to the literature but active participants in the reading process, making personal meaning and significance from the literature they encounter (Probst, 1984). Although theoretical differences are dispersed in ideas regarding the reader–text relationship, there is generally some consensus of thought on the following assumptions:

1. Meaning is not "contained" in the text but is derived from an interaction between the content and the structure of the author's message and the experience and the prior knowledge of the reader.
2. Readers comprehend differently because every reader is culturally and individually unique.
3. Examining readers' response to text is more valid than establishing one "correct" interpretation of text meaning. (Chase & Hynd, 1987, p. 531)

Louise Rosenblatt's theory has cast aside the isolated dominance of the text and directed the spotlight to the vital role of the reader whose response brings life to literature and literature to life (Hynds, 1989). A quote from Holland (1975) encompasses the spirit of reader response and the value of the reader in the literary transaction through a fairy tale illusion:

A literary text . . . consists only of a certain configuration of specks of carbon black on dried wood pulp. When these marks become words, when those words become images or metaphors or characters or events, they do so because the reader plays the part of a prince to the sleeping beauty. He [she] gives them life out of his [her] own desires. (p. 12)

FROM ROSENBLATT'S THEORY TO RESEARCH TO PRACTICE

Dr. Rosenblatt's lead in establishing the stature of the reader in the reader–text interaction has meaningfully provided the theoretical foundation needed for response-based, literature-focused instruction in the elementary/middle-level classroom setting.

Dr. Rosenblatt's theory of reader response supplied the theoretical basis of meaningful research studies conducted during the past 40 years. The attempt to reveal what thoughtful responses to literature take place in the mind of the reader has led researchers to focus on several dimensions of the response process. The diverse dimensions of response have been examined through both oral and written modes, across a variety of age groups, within a variety of genres, and through varied categorical schemes. Research has resulted in response categorization schemes (Hancock, 1993; Purves & Rippere, 1968; Squire, 1964) and affirmed the developmental nature of response (Applebee, 1978; Cullinan, Harwood, & Galda, 1983; Sebesta, Monson, & Senn, 1995). Other studies have documented reader stance as a basis for response (Cox & Many, 1992a, 1992b; Langer, 1990) and the dynamic role of the reader during the reading process (Many, 1991; Many & Cox, 1992). Case studies focused on the idiosyncratic nature of response (Fry, 1985; Galda, 1982; Hancock, 1991). Research conducted in classroom settings described patterns of response to literature (Hepler, 1982; Hickman, 1981; Kiefer, 1983; Yocum, 1987), and the height of reader response research—the 1990s—shared classroom-based research that reflects the strengths of response-based classroom practices (Altieri, 1995; Lehman & Scharer, 1996; Madura, 1995; Roller & Beed, 1994; Shine & Roser, 1999; Wollman-Bonilla & Werchadlo, 1995).

The current status of reader response research (2000–2007) identifies eight trends in reader response research, providing continued support for classroom-based reader response (Hancock, 2007). These trends and representative book or journal citations for further reading and discussion include the following:

1. Cultural diversity and response (Connor, 2003; Dressel, 2005; Lehr & Thompson, 2000; Louie, 2005; Martinez-Roldan & Lopez-Robertson, 2000). These studies involve both responses to multicultural literature as well as second-language learners' response to literature.
2. Reader responses of young children (Sipe, 2000, 2002; Sipe & Bauer, 2001). Researchers analyze responses of K–1 students to picture book read-alouds.
3. Response to nonfiction literature (Manduran, 2000; Pappas, 2006; Porter, 2006; Tower, 2002). These studies analyze efferent/aesthetic response to the growing body of quality biographical and informational nonfiction.
4. Literature discussion as response (Long & Gove, 2003; Malloch, 2002, 2004). The largest body of response research resides in studies of oral conversations about literature.
5. Critical literacy/reader response as comprehension (McLaughlin & DeVoogd, 2004). These studies focus on the level of meaning attained by readers through oral and written responses.
6. Multiple sign systems as response (Short, Kauffman, & Kahn, 2000; Whitin, 2005). Response expands beyond speaking and writing to include visual representation and multiple means of response.

7. Response and postmodern picture books (Goldstone, 2002; Lohfink, 2006; Panteleo, 2003, 2004; Serafini, 2005; Styles & Arizpe, 2001). Picture books featuring multiple dimensions of text and illustrations demand new research perspectives.
8. Technology connections to response (Carico & Logan, 2004; Larson, 2002, 2007). Online reading and response enters the realm of the "new literacies" providing a new venue for analyzing reader response.

The response-based ideas shared in this text are built from these quality research studies and provide a credible bridge between theory and research and practice for the teacher of literature and children.

PATTERNS OF RESPONSE TO LITERATURE

An appreciation for response to literature begins with theory but continues with an awareness of the wide range of responses that children exhibit as they interact with books. Janet Hickman (1980, 1981) observed and described patterns in elementary children's responses to literature as they occurred in the natural context of a K–5 school environment. Modes of response to literature observed by Hickman included (1) listening behavior, (2) contact with books, (3) the impulse to share, (4) actions and drama, (5) making things, (6) oral response, and (7) written response.

On one hand, much of what occurs in response to literature is unplanned and unrehearsed. On the other hand, many response-based activities are well conceived and planned by the teacher following the reading of a book. Teachers possess a great deal of power over children's response to literature (Hickman, 1983; Pantaleo, 1995). Through inclusion of teacher-selected books as read-alouds, effective incorporation of literature into the content areas, provision of easy access to literature, and management of opportunities for demonstrating these modes of response, teachers influence both the quantity and quality of the responses expressed by children. The teacher is indeed a powerful determiner of the response of children to the literature they read. That role can be nourished by an increasing awareness and knowledge of the possibilities and power of reader response. Learning to observe and encourage these variations in reader response opens a new view of literature in the classroom for both teacher and children.

The following discussion on modes of response to literature is based on the Hickman findings and further enhanced by professional observations of the interaction of children and books from kindergarten through eighth grade in real school settings. These patterns of response are presented in a gradual continuum moving from spontaneous response toward planned response activities initiated by the teacher. Acquiring an understanding of the potential of all varieties of response gains importance as teachers strive to build a strong response base and support a growing confidence in personal expression as they create lifelong readers. Much of this chapter serves as an overview to response topics that are discussed in greater depth in Part III of this text.

Listening Behavior

One of the most natural and observable modes of literature response is the behavior exhibited as literature is being read aloud to children. Listening behavior evidences itself in a child stretching to view an illustration, in the sound of spontaneous laughter, or in the chanting of a repetitive phrase. Listening behavior surrounds every library story hour, every home read-aloud event, and every classroom storytime. Because children learn to listen as they are learning to read (Lundsteen, 1990), listening behavior is developmentally the first mode of response to books. As parents, teachers, and caregivers, we often become too engaged in the act of reading aloud to actually notice this response. Awareness of its existence is the first step toward building an appreciation of response to literature.

Observe these rudimentary, but important, behaviors during read-alouds because they provide a developmental foundation for other modes of response. Human response mandates physical, spontaneous, and participatory response in a listener during a read-aloud event. Children nudge closer to Kevin Henkes's books to participate in the celebration of *Lilly's Big Day*, examine the contents of *Lilly's Purple Plastic Purse,* and applaud when Victoria forgets her lines in the school play in *Chrysanthemum.* Noting these natural occurrences in almost any uninhibited read-aloud setting convinces teachers of the importance of listening behaviors in establishing a groundwork for response.

Physical response.   Listening behavior evidences itself in where a child chooses to sit, the proximity of the child to the book, and listener movement during the read-aloud. Children stand, jump, and twirl without even planning these movements. Although physical response can be somewhat limited by adult direction and behavioral expectations, the importance of allowing for natural movement during a read-aloud is essential to capturing genuine response, particularly with younger children.

Doreen Cronin's *Wiggle* invites physical involvement in the antics of the doglike main character who models active movement throughout the entire book sharing. The same active invitation is extended by Julia Durango's *Cha Cha Chimps,* which encourages listening participants to engage in active movements through rhythmic chants alongside the read-aloud. Listening is not always a quiet activity but one that can welcome physical participation.

Spontaneous response.   This type of listening behavior includes the laughter, the tears, the facial expressions, the brief comments, and the applause that may interrupt or follow the read-aloud. Unplanned and unsolicited, these genuine reactions of listeners are worthy of recognition as a response to literature. Traditionally, the read-aloud was honored as a quiet episode, but an understanding of spontaneous response allows for individual reactions as they automatically occur within the listener.

A read-aloud of Norton Juster's *The Hello, Good-bye Window*, generates reactive stories of one's own grandparents' homes with memorable related visits.

A special window, a favorite room, or a special event surrounds the talk justified by the sharing of this title. Fifth graders, engrossed in a read-aloud of Karen Hesse's *Letters from Rifka,* begin scratching their heads as Rifka contracts ringworm. A sigh of relief and delight occurs as Rifka arrives in America and the tickling on her scalp is found to be the growth of new hair. The encouragement and valuing of spontaneous response make listening a more active process and the read-aloud an interactive event.

Participatory response. So many read-aloud choices for young children are predictable books with repetitive phrases and refrains. Joining in, chanting, clapping, and repeating provide a natural mode of listening behavior. No invitation is needed to bring about the participatory nature of response. It is inherent in the text and draws from the natural instincts of a child to become an active participant in a piece of literature.

Muncha! Muncha! Muncha! by Candace Fleming engages readers with the sounds of three hungry bunnies: "Tippy, tippy, tippy, pat! Muncha! Muncha! Muncha!" Cumulative predictable text follows a disgruntled Mr. McGreely trying to keep the rabbits from his vegetable garden. Light print on dark illustrations invites listeners to join in on the repeated refrains and "Muncha! Muncha! Muncha!" Humorous illustrations by G. Brian Karas turn a gardening melee into a participatory delight. Steve Jenkins and Robin Page's *What Do You Do with a Tail Like That?,* a nonfiction predictable book, can be read for purely animal information the first time, but it brings natural predictive participation on repeated readings. Built on rhyme and a cumulative display of well-tailed animals, the story invites listeners to join in at the ends of lines and become a part of predictable, informational text. Planned teacher read-aloud pauses allow for planned listener participation and rollicking classroom fun. Celebrating the natural invitations of books like these allows both teachers and children to appreciate the power of response that makes listening an active experience.

Contact with Books

Readers initiate their own response to literature through the multiple ways in which they make direct contact with books. Whether browsing in the library/media center, reading in a comfortable chair, or attending to books in their desks, contact with books tells observers something of a reader's interest, intent, and immersion in books. Contact with books includes reader choice as a response to literature. The self-selection of a book from the vast holdings of a library must be considered a genuine, personal response to literature.

Browsing and choosing. Observe children as they enter the inviting world of the library/media center or discover a fresh classroom display of themed book titles. Their wide-eyed faces light up at both brightly colored new books and at familiar favorites. Their fingers touch a shiny plastic cover, trace the words of the title, or fumble to turn a brightly illustrated page. Individual choice is a response to literature. In teachers' minds, response and choice should be synonymous with expressions of interest—the most obvious of children's responses to literature (Hickman, 1985). The act of selecting books for reading over those left for other readers involves scanning, decision making, and selecting—natural responses to literature. Sebesta and Monson (2003) report the complexity of reading interests and their important relationship to reading preferences.

Children's book preferences form an important aspect of reader response. Children often seek books by favorite authors, in preferred genres, or former read-alouds by the classroom teacher. For example, fifth graders couldn't wait to locate and read books by Walter Dean Myers after their teacher read aloud Sharon Creech's *Love That Dog*, in which a reluctant writer communicates with and meets the real Walter Dean Myers. The more familiar children become with literature, the more impact their literature schema has on their choices. Choice is a response that expands with the assistance of a knowledgeable teacher who immerses his or her students in literature.

The selection process warrants teacher observation and documentation. A fourth-grade student held a chapter book in each hand as the dismissal bell rang for lunch. His eyes journeyed from one cover to the other and back again. Finally, he placed one book back on the shelf and hurried to the scanner to check out *Brian's Winter.* When asked why he made that choice, he admitted that his teacher had read aloud *Hatchet* and he couldn't wait to read another book by Gary Paulsen. When asked about the book he returned to the shelf, he stated it would have been easier to read but that he had read it two times before and was ready for something new. Teachers can learn a great deal by asking children why they choose the books they do. As Hickman (1980) and Schlager (1978) discovered, teachers play a critical role in influencing reading choices. Their knowledge of and personal choices in literature can affect reader response exhibited through literature preferences of self-selected titles.

Attention to books.   Linger behind children as they leave the library or media center with their newly acquired selections. They hug them—Doreen Cronin's *Click, Clack, Moo: Cows That Type;* they clasp them to their bodies—Lois Ehlert's *Leaf Man;* they walk while reading them—Jack Prelutsky's *If Not for the Cat;* and they treat them like best friends—Pam Munoz Ryan's *Mud Is Cake.* Books even find their way to the cafeteria and the playground for the most dedicated readers. The attention children pay to books provides another avenue for response. Some children become so absorbed in a book that they simply don't hear the teacher calling them for the next activity. Many children experience that same commitment to self-selected books, especially on first acquiring them. They can't seem to get enough of the illustrations, the printed words, or the warm invitation a book extends to them as readers. The act of reading them over and over again or returning to a bookmarked chapter provides indications of this mode of response. Observe and celebrate this attention to literature within the context of the school day.

Proximity of books.   The location of books in children's lives provides another indication of literature response. Some children immediately stash books in a backpack for carrying home, whereas others use their desktop for immediate access. For some children a day never passes without a pile of library books perched on the corner of their desks. Keeping books close at hand indicates the desire and anticipation of the independent reading event and supports the long-term goal of creating lifelong readers. Teachers who fill their classrooms with literature and make it available to their students make literature accessible for independent reading throughout the day. Books kept close at hand reflect their value and importance in our daily lives.

The Impulse to Share

Although the reading event may be viewed as a personalized experience between the reader and the text, the act of reading dictates an almost instinctive need to share the textual event with others. The social aspects of response to literature surface as children exhibit an eagerness to share within their community of readers (Hepler & Hickman, 1982). Children, and even adults, cannot resist talking about books, making personal connections, rereading passages, or recommending a book to a friend. Reading was never meant to be an isolated incident in an elementary setting. Active minds and hearts demand opportunities to share unique characters, inspiring illustrations, and personal experiences related to books.

Reading together. Whether reading with a book buddy, partner reading, or round-robin reading in a small group, reading together elicits natural moments for reflection and sharing. Spontaneous thoughts and comments automatically spill forth as readers pause between read-aloud passages to allow for personalized comments. These responses range from predictions and explanations to wishes and wonderings, and their strength lies in the progression of interactive meaning-making that occurs during the reading of a text. Response must be considered on-task reading behavior, modeled by the teacher, and encouraged as a natural part of the ongoing reading process.

Telling about a book. Almost spontaneously, children begin to talk about the books they are reading. Although some teachers have incorporated a short time slot at the beginning or end of reading workshop to share books, younger children often choose to bring favorite literature to share for show-and-tell. Whether "telling" encompasses reading aloud a special passage or recounting the story itself to encourage others to read the book, telling is an important element of response. Jacqueline Woodson's *Coming on Home Soon* always elicits comments about moving, losing family, or waiting for the return of a loved one. Spreading the word about good reading material fulfills a natural impulse to share the excitement of a quality reading experience.

Teachers who realize the inherent need to share plan opportunities for book sharing as a part of their daily routine. A scheduled time following sustained silent reading is likely to overflow with descriptions of favorite parts, highlighted illustrations, and personal recommendations. Reading is social and the need to share its excitement and joy requires planned informal time in the course of the school day.

Sharing discoveries. "Look at this!" "Listen to this!" "Look what I found!" Comments like these are vigorously expressed during and following independent reading time in elementary classrooms. Children can't wait to share a character, an incident, an exciting illustration, or a fact-filled passage with anyone who will listen. The strength of this type of response lies in its genuine, extemporaneous nature. The masterful spontaneity that is reader response is often supported by read-ing partners who serve as listeners and sharers during these highly explosive response moments. Once again, it is the informed, response-conscious teacher who allows children to share these spontaneous thoughts. As children mature, these personal reactions can be recorded in a journal for sharing at a later time. If children are inhibited from sharing these discoveries as they occur, however, they begin to realize that a teacher values only those responses shared at the end of a book. The rich interactive nature of the reading process as it unfolds throughout a text can be lost if only retrospective response is encouraged.

RESOURCES ON THE WEB

The following websites host literacy-based lessons plans, online resources, and instructional ideas that may serve as inspiration and guidance for teachers looking for innovative and creative reader response–based activities.

ReadWriteThink

This site offers a wide selection of standards-based lesson plan and Internet resources. Use the search feature on this site to pinpoint specific grade levels or subject areas. For example, a keyword search of "reader response" or "literature response" will yield a multitude of response-based lessons plans. The high-quality site is a partnership of the International Reading Association (IRA), the National Council of Teachers of English (NCTE), and the MarcoPolo Education Foundation. http://www.readwritethink.org

TeachersFirst

TeachersFirst hosts a broad collection of lesson plans and Internet resources. Visitors may conduct a keyword search (e.g., "reader AND response" or "literature AND response") or search by subject ("reading," "language arts," or "literature"). Either way, the search will produce numerous lesson ideas and user-friendly resources. http://www.teachersfirst.com

Scholastic Teachers

The teacher section on the Scholastic website offers free lesson plans, online activities, and printable teaching tools. Browsers may locate lesson plans or online resources by subject ("reading" or "language arts"), grade levels, or keywords. http://teacher.scholastic.com/

Sharing connections. As children are exposed to more and more literature, they begin to connect each book to another title as they draw from their literature schema. For example, a second grader connected an independent reading of Amy Hest's *Mr. George Baker* with a teacher read-aloud of Eve Bunting's *A Wednesday Surprise*. When children make these higher level connections, they need to share their discovery with others for affirmation of their own response. Teachers who allow time for sharing as a natural response to reading provide the opportunity for this validation and expansion of thought. As this response phenomenon occurs foundationally in the primary grades, it builds into increasing self-confidence to discuss literature connections as the literary base expands across grade levels. Intertextual connections form an important response mode and are often indicators of those children who are destined to become lifelong readers.

Children also naturally connect books to their own lives. Teachers hardly close the back cover of a picture book before hands begin waving to share these natural connections. David, for example, couldn't wait to relate his story of hiding in a storm cellar during a tornado warning following the reading of Marcia Arnold's *The Bravest of Us All.* Stories of fear brought up an intertextual connection to Emily Arnold McCully's *Mirette on the High Wire.* Allowing a reasonable amount of time for sharing personal connections builds a foundation and confidence for future response. Children learn that response is valued and unique to the individual and move away from the "right" answer to a personal response to a question. This response principle provides a springboard for expanding developmentally appropriate response activities as the reader grows and matures in exploring other response options.

Actions and Drama

Being directly engaged and involved helps children identify with the literature they read. Besides focusing on vocabulary and aiding comprehension, action and drama include those children whose learning styles thrive on active immersion. Whether student initiated or teacher planned, puppet shows, improvisation, movement activities, and plays based on literature foster active comprehension and a deeper connection to literature.

Echoing the action.   Many books exist that invite children to become a part of the action of the story. In Nancy Van Laan's *Possum Come a-Knockin',* children take their cues from the dramatic actions of each perplexed family member as they whittle, knit, untangle, pound, hiss, and growl while a mischievous critter plays possum outside their door. Eric Carle's *From Head to Toe* encourages listeners to follow the movements of various animals. The question-and-answer format guarantees response as children proudly chant "I can do it!" as they replicate the movements. Listening skills cue children into applying their actions to accompany the active words of the literature texts.

Dramatic play.   Reenactment of fairy tales or folktales provides a means for dramatic play as response to literature. Acting out Jan Peck's *Way Far Away on a Wild Safari* reinforces sequencing as children develop a clearer sense of story. Dramatically reenacting Jan Brett's version of *The Mitten* allows for many characters to sequentially squeeze into a make-believe mitten and await a sneeze-induced explosion. Oral articulation and expressive talents are explored as this blend of language and drama expands the response capabilities of dramatic performers in the classroom.

Readers' theater.   Authentic literature that has been scripted into a readers' theater format is ideal for reading fluency, oral expression, and dramatic interpretation. The personalized expressive touch imposed on the original words of the text provide yet another dramatic response option. For example, Amy MacDonald's hilarious *Rachel Fister's Blister* readily translates into a readers' theater script. A multiplicity of characters allows for whole-class participation in the hectic efforts of the Fister family's attempt to relieve the hurt caused by the blister on Rachel's toe. Everyone's advice is enlisted until the wise Queen saves the day. Readers' theater scripts provide the words directly from literature while the readers' voices provide the dramatic response.

Artistic, Musical, and Constructive Response

Teachers often plan extension activities related to the arts following the reading of literature. Whether these take the form of drawings, multimedia presentations, musical accompaniment, or constructed models, they provide a hands-on approach to response and reach the child who may be less comfortable with the oral or written response options. The variety and meaningful connectedness to literature inferred from this response option provide a wealth of ideas for classroom extensions.

Visual representation.   Drawing or visual replication of a story, a single scene from a story, or a sequence of scenes appeals to the visual learner as a mode of response. Visual representation can reflect comprehension, emotions, attention to story detail, and personal interpretation of text. Kindergarten and first-grade response journals are delightfully filled with visual representations of story characters and actions. These drawings often serve as a springboard to oral and written language as they provide clues for what to say and what to write. Visual representations may serve as a rehearsal for later development of oral and written responses.

Constructions.   Many books inspire hands-on activities that extend the story into the realm of artistic response. Kristine O'Connell George's *Fold Me a Poem* inspires the folding of origami animals shared through poetic text; Paul Goble's *Storm Maker's Tipi* provides a model of the Plains Indians' habitat to be cut, folded, and assembled. Literature that suggests artistic construction allows the less verbal but manually talented child to excel in expression of response in this unique mode.

Tasting reading.   Just as the children in a primary classroom became engaged in the baking of their thundercake in response to Patricia Polacco's title, so too does literature often inspire the preparation and consumption of other culinary delights. While response takes on an active tone in this mode of response, literature provides a memorable experience through related cooking episodes. Lisa Campbell Ernst's fairy-tale variant, *Little Red Riding Hood: A Newfangled Prairie Tale,* naturally leads to the baking of Grandma's wheatberry muffin recipe imprinted on the endpapers. Marjorie Priceman's *How to Make an Apple Pie and See the World* takes the reader on a quest for the ultimate ingredients to put together the world's best apple pie. The gingerbread cookie recipe on Jim Aylesworth's *The Gingerbread Man* and the recipe for Elisa Kleven's *Sun Bread* create literature memories through taste experiences and provide variety in sharing response to these special books. Polly Horvath's humorous chapter book, *Everything on a Waffle,* and Nancy Willard's *The Moon & Riddles Diner and the Sunnyside Café* brim with authentic recipes.

Musical response.   Selecting classical background music for a read-aloud of Stephen Costanza's *Mozart Finds a Melody* or making rhythmic sounds on percussion instruments to accompany the reading of H. L. Panahi's *Bebop Express* are two ways in which musical response can be incorporated into the literature-based classroom. Judith Cherniak's *Carnival of the Animals* includes poems accompanied by Saint-Saens's music (CD included). The brilliantly colored artwork of Satoshi Kitamura seems to further enhance the lyrics and melody. A musical connection to literature can be found in many titles that incorporate song lyrics, including Mary Ann Hoberman's *Miss Mary Mack*. The music specialist can take an active part in extending this response mode into the classroom or the teacher can integrate the musical tones within the curriculum (Curtis, 2007). Note how this response style reaches yet another mode of expression for musically talented children.

Oral Response

As children listen to or read literature, their authentic responses may be conveyed through the oral response mode. This is typically the most common response mode as the voice of the reader longs to share and be valued for its individuality. Although spontaneous comments are valued, the mode of oral response tends to be more directed by teacher-initiated configurations or prompts. Response still remains genuine, but it takes on a more structured identity, allowing for a greater focus on the words of the reader.

Retelling/Storytelling. As teachers invite children to tell a story, their comprehension skills and attention to detail come into focus. Their sense of story, character, setting, and plot must organize their response while their own creativity is fostered and valued in the individualized sharing of a tale. Folktales and fairy tales work well with this response option because sequence and simple characterization provide structure for oral response. B. G. Hennessey's *The Boy Who Cried Wolf* presents a simple, sequentially structured story with a series of characters and a focused plot reminiscent of many traditional fairy tales. Retelling or, in a more creative mode, storytelling this tale from Russia provides children an opportunity to bring their own voices to a somewhat structured presentation. Ed Young's *I, Doko* and Margot Theis Raven's *Circle Unbroken* are tales simply sequenced and told by a storyteller—one a basket itself, one a grandmother—allowing primary and intermediate children to retell these tales. Yet the threads reinvite the continued retelling of the tale by the reader. Although oral response may be somewhat limited by the constraints of the tale, the words and emotions of the reteller provide much room for personalized response to the story.

Prompted response. To assist children in moving beyond spontaneous comments about literature, teachers construct response prompts to provide a more structured and directed approach to the oral response process. Response prompts can be defined as open-ended questions that elicit unique and individual response. Rather than limiting a child to a right or wrong answer, the prompts are posed in an effort to encourage individual interpretation and discussion. Here are three formidable prompts designed by Bleich (1978): What did you notice? How did this book make you feel? What does this book remind you of from your own life? As limiting as these three prompts may seem to be, they actually allow for freedom of expressive thought and foster developmental growth over time and across grade levels. Their power lies in their open-endedness, which allows each reader to bring personal interpretation to literature. When these prompts are applied to a poignant picture book text such as *Michael Rosen's Sad Book,* they produce a wide range of responses about friendship, loss, and rebirth of the human spirit. It is interesting to observe these same prompts used across age levels with the same book as the developmental characteristic of response becomes obvious.

Literature discussions. Oral response that builds from student-directed discussion groups (e.g., literature circles, book clubs) provides developmentally appropriate response outlets for students in intermediate/middle-level classrooms. Based on the idea of building from the articulated thoughts and ideas of others, literature discussions provide a format for free comments limited only by the bounds of the literature being discussed. The emphasis on student-generated talk driven by minimal teacher facilitation provides a setting for authenticity and unique expression. Generally used with the reading of chapter books, literature discussions elicit deep thinking in response to books across genres like these Newbery Medal and Honor titles: Alan Armstrong's *Whittington* (animal fantasy), Cynthia Lord's *Rules* (realistic fiction), and Cynthia Kadohata's *Kira-Kira* (multicultural historical fiction). Socially empowered response finds an audience within literature conversations.

Written Response

The written mode of response encourages the reader to capture and record her or his personal transaction with literature. Whereas oral response is fleeting, written response secures a permanent record of thoughts, opinions, feelings, and reactions during the act of reading. As children leave their egocentric selves behind, they are often more inhibited in sharing innermost responses to literature. The written response often becomes a means for private expression of thoughts.

Typically recorded in a journal format, written responses can ultimately be shared in discussion groups, exchanged with a reading partner, reflected on personally, or shared privately with a teacher. They can become an impetus for extended writing or effect the creation of an original work. Although the written response can begin in the primary grades, it is often viewed as a higher-level interaction with literature that reconstructs reading images and meaning into personalized thoughts on paper.

Literature journals. A literature journal is best described as a repository of wanderings, wonderings, speculations, questions, and explorative thoughts recorded during the reading process (Hancock, 1993). It allows the reader to make discoveries, let the mind ramble, and create room for the evolving text. Several names and adaptations exist for the reading journal, but all encourage spontaneous, honest written response to the literature children read.

- **Literature response journal.** This format allows for the free flow of thought throughout the entire reading process. Its unstructured format encourages the written recording of thoughts as they occur, rather than retrospectively following the reading event.

- **Dialogue journal.**   This format fosters continuous written dialogue between the reader and another respondent. Writing back and forth about a book being read creates a continuous conversation. The second respondent can be a peer, the classroom teacher, or another supervising adult (student teacher, paraprofessional, special education teacher). These responses read as letters between two readers.

- **Character journal.**   This format suggests a first-person interaction with the book by the reader assuming the guise of one of the book's characters. The "I" stance of the narrative creates strong involvement in the book and engages the reader with the persona of the character and the events.

- **Double-entry draft.**   This format suggests the journal be divided in two columns. Readers record direct quotes, lists, or other pertinent information on the left side, and then they record responses to these on the right side of each page.

- **Reading log.**   This format suggests a brief entry of the name of the book and author followed by a brief comment at the end of the book (picture book) or at the end of the day's reading (chapter book). More informal and less spontaneous, this writing is often kept in chart form as an ongoing process throughout the school year.

The freedom to write in most of these journals throughout the reading process preserves the spontaneous thoughts and interactions with the text. With practice and commitment to the response process, a full, rich range of written response can be revealed to most emotionally charged books. With teacher modeling of his or her own responses to a read-aloud on an overhead projector, children quickly acclimate themselves to the process. With strong teacher encouragement and frequent written feedback, children develop their own response styles and willingly internalize the written response process. Over time, the interplay between reading and written reflections slowly becomes a natural part of the reading process.

Literature as a model for writing.   Literature often serves as a springboard for extended writing activities that follow the format or genre structure of a book. Many researchers have pointed out the connections between reading literature and the writing process. Both Jane Hansen (1987/2001) and Donald Graves (1983/2003) pointed out the connections between the reading of quality literature and the production of quality writing. Golden (1984) demonstrated how readers draw on their concept of story during writing stories. A strategy for teaching story structure and its application to writing (Tompkins, 2008) includes the following suggestions:

- Focus on a single element of story structure or genre.
- Read literature emphasizing this element or genre.
- Discuss how the element was used in the genre read.
- Participate in prewriting activities that frame the element or genre (graphic organizers, retellings).
- Write stories incorporating the particular element or genre.

Sharing a *pourquoi* version of how a bear lost his tail may provide a model for students composing a parallel tale. Reading Jane Boulton's adaptation of *Only Opal: The Diary of a Young Girl* provides an inspiration for keeping a diary of one's own. Jon Scieszka's *The True Story of the Three Little Pigs* has inspired countless point-of-view fairy-tale creations. Literature as a model for writing serves a meaningful purpose as children internalize genre, literary elements, and the writing craft and begin to use these components in their own writing.

These seven modes of response are not exclusive, distinct, or isolated from one another. They tend to blend, overlap, and build on each other. Practitioners should never feel obliged to fit observations of children into one of these response modes. Although the categorical organization of this chapter creates a framework for exploring the possibilities, reader response does not warrant exclusive inclusion in a single area. Categories overlap because response naturally defies certain categorization. Although the categories tend to be presented in a continuum from student-initiated response to teacher-initiated response-based activities, any mode can be spontaneous and can be generated by the reader rather than the literacy facilitator in a classroom setting.

CLOSING THOUGHTS

The theoretical voice of Louise Rosenblatt speaks clearly to literature-based teachers. Dr. Rosenblatt's impact on both research and practice in the last decade is evidenced by the number of research studies and dissertations grounded in the transactional theory of reader response (Hancock, 2007). The impact of these studies evidences itself in the current content of university education courses, teacher inservices, and staff development seminars. Its impact is felt in the hearts of children as they build an endearing relationship with literature throughout the school day and across the school year. Its impact is seen in a teacher's decision to include trade books as a central core of the curriculum supported by a philosophy of natural learning. Literature-based classrooms form the ultimate tribute to the theoretical voice of Louise Rosenblatt that resounds clearly in elementary classrooms in which the individuality of the reader and the uniqueness of response are treasured commodities and desired outcomes of a democratic education (Pradl, 1996).

As Dr. Rosenblatt's theory enters the reality of the elementary/middle-level classroom, patterns of response to literature emerge. As teachers realize and explore the potential and the variety of modes of response to literature, they are better able to plan a balanced approach to response in the context of their literature-based curriculum. Response spans active participation, verbal acuity, the power of the written word, artistic creations, and the human need to share. Response addresses the varied learning styles of children and stirs creative minds and hearts. Response to literature moves children away from "correctness interpretation" and allows them the freedom to express the thoughts that linger in their hearts during and following a literature experience. Classrooms in which response to literature thrives are characterized by teachers valuing response as a factor in literacy growth (Martinez & Roser, 2003). When teachers provide opportunities for response, models of response, and receptiveness to response, children and literacy flourish.

This chapter has attempted to open your eyes to the possibilities of a response-based literature classroom. Subsequent chapters in this text further explore these natural modes of response to literature in greater depth. Valuing literature for literature's sake is central to a response-based teaching philosophy. Viewing literature as an avenue for response further allows for expression of a child's literary transaction with a book. As teachers attempt to bring variety, breadth, and depth to the natural response potential of children, an awareness of and understanding of several modes of response are essential for celebrating the response outcomes of a thriving literature-based classroom. Ultimately, the theory-into-practice link between Dr. Rosenblatt's transactional theory of reader response and the identified response modes of children evidences itself in the real classroom where engaged readers and quality books come together in a teaching/learning environment that supports quality literature and genuine response.

References

Altieri, J. L. (1995). Multicultural literature and multiethnic readers: Examining aesthetic involvement and preferences for text. *Reading Psychology, 16,* 43–70.

Applebee, A. N. (1978). *The child's concept of story: Ages two to seventeen.* Chicago: University of Chicago Press.

Ayra, P., Martens, P., Wilson, G. P., Altwerger, B., Jin, L., Laser, B., & Lang, D. (2005). Reclaiming literacy instruction: Evidence in support of literature-based programs. *Language Arts, 83,* 63–72.

Bleich, D. (1978). *Subjective criticism.* Baltimore: Johns Hopkins University Press.

Cai, M. (2001). Reflections on transactional theory as a theoretical guide for literacy and literature education. *The New Advocate, 14,* 19–32.

Carico, K. M., & Logan, D. (2004). A generation in cyberspace: Engaging readers through online discussions. *Language Arts, 81*(4), 293–302.

Chase, N. D., & Hynd, C. R. (1987). Reader response: An alternative way to teach students to think about text. *Journal of Reading, 30,* 530–540.

Connor, J. J. (2003). "The textbooks never said anything about . . ." Adolescents respond to *The middle passage: White ships/black cargo. Journal of Adolescent and Adult Literacy, 47*(3), 240–246.

Cox, C., & Many, J. E. (1992a). Reader stance towards a literary work: Applying the transactional

theory to children's responses. *Reading Psychology, 13,* 37–72.

Cox, C., & Many, J. E. (1992b). Toward an understanding of the aesthetic response to literature. *Language Arts, 69,* 28–33.

Cullinan, B. E., Harwood, K. T., & Galda, L. (1983). The reader and the story: Comprehension and response. *Journal of Research and Development in Education, 16,* 29–37.

Curtis, L. J. (2007). *The role of music in the literacy classroom: A kindergarten case study.* Unpublished doctoral dissertation, Kansas State University.

Dressel, J. H. (2005). Personal response and social responsibility: Responses of middle school students to multicultural literature. *The Reading Teacher, 58,* 750–764.

Dressman, M., & Webster, J. P. (2001). Retracing Rosenblatt: A textual archaeology. *Research in the Teaching of English, 36,* 110–145.

Fry, D. (1985). *Children talk about books: Seeing themselves as readers.* Philadelphia: Milton Keynes.

Galda, L. (1982). Assuming the spectator stance: An examination of the responses of three young readers. *Research in the Teaching of English, 16,* 1–20.

Golden, J. M. (1984). Children's concept of story in reading and writing. *The Reading Teacher, 37,* 578–584.

Goldstone, B. P. (2002). Whaz up with our book? Changing picture book codes and teaching implications. *The Reading Teacher, 55*(4), 362–370.

Graves, D. (2003). *Writing: Teachers and children at work.* Portsmouth, NH: Heinemann. (Original work published 1983)

Hancock, M. R. (1991). Literature response journals: Insights beyond the printed page. *Language Arts, 69,* 36–42.

Hancock, M. R. (1993). Exploring the meaning-making process through the content of literature response journals. *Research in the Teaching of English, 27,* 335–368.

Hancock, M. R. (2007). The status of reader response research: Sustaining the reader's voice in challenging times. In S. Lehr (Ed.), *Shattering the looking glass: Challenge, risk, and controversy in children's literature* (pp. 97–116). Norwood, MA: Christopher Gordon.

Hansen, J. (2001). *When writers read.* Portsmouth, NH: Heinemann. (Original work published 1987)

Hepler, S. (1982). Patterns of response to literature: A one-year study of a fifth- and sixth-grade classroom. *Dissertation Abstracts International, 43,* 1419A. (UMI 82-22100).

Hepler, S., & Hickman, J. (1982). "The book was okay. I love you"—Social aspects of response to literature. *Theory into Practice, 21,* 278–283.

Hickman, J. (1980). Children's responses to literature: What happens in the classroom. *Language Arts, 57,* 524–529.

Hickman, J. (1981). A new perspective on response to literature: Research in an elementary school setting. *Research in the Teaching of English, 15,* 343–354.

Hickman, J. (1983). Everything considered: Response to literature in an elementary school setting. *Journal of Research and Development in Education, 16,* 8–13.

Hickman, J. (1985). Looking at response to literature. In A. J. & M. T. Smith-Burke (Eds.), *Observing the language learner* (pp. 111–119). Newark, DE: International Reading Association and the National Council of Teachers of English.

Holland, N. N. (1968). *The dynamics of literary response.* New York: Norton.

Holland, N. N. (1975). *Five readers reading.* New Haven, CT: Yale University Press.

Hynds, S. (1989). Bring life to literature and literature to life: Social constructs and contexts of four adolescent readers. *Research in the Teaching of English, 23,* 30–61.

Iser, W. (1978). *The act of reading: A theory of aesthetic response.* Baltimore, MD: Johns Hopkins University Press.

Karolides, N. J. (1999). Theory and practice: An interview with Louise Rosenblatt. *Language Arts, 77,* 158–170. (Includes a complete bibliography of Rosenblatt's works)

Kiefer, B. Z. (1983). The responses of children in a combination first/second grade classroom to picture books in a variety of artistic styles. *Journal of Research and Development in Education, 16,* 14–20.

Langer, J. A. (1990). The process of understanding: Reading for literary and informative purposes. *Research in the Teaching of English, 24,* 229–260.

Larson, L. (2002). The KeyPal project: Integrating literature response and technology. *Kansas Journal of Reading, 18,* 57–62.

Larson, L. (2007). *A case study exploring the "new literacies" during a fifth-grade electronic reading workshop.* Unpublished doctoral dissertation, Kansas State University.

Lehman, B. A., & Scharer, P. L. (1996). Reading alone, talking together: The role of discussion in developing literary awareness. *The Reading Teacher, 50,* 26–35.

Lehr, S., & Thompson, D. (2000). The dynamic nature of response: Children reading and responding to *Maniac Magee* and *The Friendship. The Reading Teacher, 53,* 480–493.

Lohfink, G. (2006). *Fourth graders' responses to postmodern picture books in literature circles.* Unpublished doctoral dissertation, Kansas State University.

Long, T. W., & Gove, M. K. (2003). How engagement strategies and literature circles promote critical response in a fourth-grade urban classroom. *The Reading Teacher, 57,* 350–361.

Louie, B. Y. (2005). Development of empathetic responses with multicultural literature. *Journal of Adolescent and Adult Literacy, 48,* 566–578.

Lundsteen, S. (1990). Learning to listen and learning to read. In S. Hynds & D. L. Rubin (Eds.), *Perspectives on talk and learning.* Urbana, IL: National Council of Teachers of English.

Madura, S. (1995). The line and texture of aesthetic response: Primary children study authors and illustrators. *The Reading Teacher, 49,* 110–118.

Malloch, B. (2002). Scaffolding student talk: One teacher's role in literature discussion groups. *Reading Research Quarterly, 37,* 94–112.

Malloch, B. (2004). One teacher's journey: Transitioning into literature discussion groups. *Language Arts, 81*(4), 312–322.

Manduran, I. (2000). "Playing possum": A young child's responses to information books. *Language Arts, 77,* 391–397.

Many, J. E. (1991). The effects of stance and age level on children's literary responses. *Journal of Reading Behavior, 23,* 61–85.

Many, J. E., & Cox, C. (1992). *Reader stance and literary understanding: Exploring the theories, research, and practice.* Norwood, NJ: Ablex.

Martinez, M. G., & Roser, N. L. (2003). Children's responses to literature. In J. Flood, D. Lapp, J. R. Squire, & J. M. Jensen (Eds.), *Handbook of research on teaching the English language arts* (pp. 799–813). Mahwah, NJ: Erlbaum.

Martinez-Roldan, C. M., & Lopez-Robertson, J. M. (2000). Initiating literature circles in a first-grade bilingual classroom. *The Reading Teacher, 53,* 270–281.

McLaughlin, M., & DeVoogd, G. (2004). Critical literacy as comprehension: Expanding reader response. *Journal of Adolescent & Adult Literacy, 48*(1), 52–62.

Menon, S., & Hiebert, E. H. (2005). A comparison of first grader's reading with little books or literature-based basal anthologies. *Reading Research Quarterly, 40,* 12–38.

Pantaleo, S. (1995). The influence of teacher practice on student response to literature. *Journal of Children's Literature, 21,* 38–47.

Pantaleo, S. (2002). Grade 1 students meet David Wiesner's *Three Pigs. Journal of Children's Literature, 28*(2), 72–84.

Pantaleo, S. (2003). "Godzilla lives in New York": Grade 1 students and the peritextual features of picture books. *Journal of Children's Literature, 29*(2), 66–77.

Pantaleo, S. (2004). Young children and radical change characteristics in picture books. *The Reading Teacher, 58*(2), 178–187.

Pappas, C. C. (2006). The information book genre: Its role in integrated science literacy research and practice. *Reading Research Quarterly, 41*(2), 226–250.

Porter, D. (2006). *Oral and written responses of sixth graders to Orbis Pictus Award nonfiction in a curricular setting.* Unpublished doctoral dissertation, Kansas State University.

Pradl, G. M. (1996). Reading and democracy: The enduring influence of Louise Rosenblatt. *The New Advocate, 9,* 9–22.

Probst, R. E. (1984). *Adolescent literature: Response and analysis.* Columbus, OH: Charles E. Merrill.

Purves, A., & Rippere, V. (1968). *Elements of writing about a literary work: A study of response to literature* (Research Report No. 9). Urbana, IL: National Council of Teachers of English.

Richards, I. A. (1929). *Practical criticism: A study in literary judgment.* New York: Harcourt, Brace, and World.

Roller, C. M., & Beed, P. L. (1994). Sometimes the conversations were grand, and sometimes . . . *Language Arts, 71,* 509–515.

Rosenblatt, L. M. (1978). *The reader, the text, the poem: The transactional theory of the literary work.* Carbondale: Southern Illinois University Press.

Rosenblatt, L. M. (1994). The transactional theory of reading and writing. In R. B. Ruddell, M. R. Ruddell, & H. Singer (Eds.), *Theoretical models and processes of reading* (4th ed.) (pp. 1057–1092). Newark, DE: International Reading Association.

Rosenblatt, L. M. (1995). *Literature as exploration.* New York: Appleton-Century-Crofts. (5th ed., Modern Language Association) (Original work published 1938)

Schlager, N. (1978). Predicting children's choices in literature: A developmental approach. *Children's Literature in Education, 9,* 136–142.

Sebesta, S. L. (2001). What do teachers need to know about children's literature? *The New Advocate, 14,* 241–249.

Sebesta, S. L., & Monson, D. L. (2003). Reading preferences. In J. Flood, D. Lapp, J. R. Squire, & J. M. Jensen (Eds.), *Handbook of research on teaching the English language arts* (pp. 835–847). Mahwah, NJ: Erlbaum.

Sebesta, S. L., Monson, D. L., & Senn, H. D. (1995). A hierarchy to assess reader response. *Journal of Reading, 38,* 444–450.

Serafini, F. (2005). Voices in the park, voices in the classroom: Readers responding to postmodern picture books. *Reading Research and Instruction, 44*(3), 47–64.

Shine, S., & Roser, N. L. (1999). The role of genre in preschoolers' response to picture books. *Research in the Teaching of English, 34,* 197–254.

Short, K., Kauffman, G., & Kahn, L. (2000). "I just need to draw": Responding to literature across multiple sign systems. *The Reading Teacher, 54*(2), 160–171.

Sipe, L. R. (2000). The construction of literary understanding by first and second graders in oral response to picture storybook read-alouds. *Reading Research Quarterly, 35,* 252–275.

Sipe, L. R. (2002). Talking back and taking over: Young children's expressive engagement during storybook read-alouds. *The Reading Teacher, 55*(5), 476–483.

Sipe, L. R., & Bauer, J. (2001). Urban kindergarteners' literary understanding of picture story books. *The New Advocate, 14*(4), 329–342.

Squire, J. R. (1964). *The responses of adolescents while reading four short stories.* Champaign, IL: National Council of Teachers of English.

Styles, M., & Arizpe, E. (2001). A gorilla with 'grandpa's eyes': How children interpret visual texts—A case study of Anthony Browne's Zoo. *Children's Literature in Education, 30*(4), 261–281.

Tompkins, G. E. (2008). *Teaching writing: Balancing process and product* (5th ed.). Columbus, OH: Merrill/Prentice Hall.

Tower, C. (2002). "It's a snake, you guys!": The power of text characteristics on children's responses to information books. *Research in the Teaching of English, 37,* 55–88.

Whitin, P. (2005). The interplay of text, talk, and visual representation in expanding literary interpretation. *Research in the Teaching of English, 39,* 365–397.

Wollman-Bonilla, J. E., & Werchadlo, B. (1995). Literature response journals in a first-grade classroom. *Language Arts, 72,* 562–570.

Yocum, J. A. (1987). Children's responses to literature read aloud in the classroom. *Dissertation Abstracts International, 48,* 2300A. (UMI No. 87-26750)

Children's Books Cited [P] = K–2; [I] = 3–5; [M] = 6–8

Armstrong, Alan (2005). *Whittington.* Illus. by S. D. Schindler. New York: Random House. [I/M]

Arnold, Marcia (2000). *The bravest of us all.* Illus. by Brad Sneed. New York: Dial. [P/I]

Aylesworth, Jim (1998). *The gingerbread man.* Illus. by Barbara McClintock. New York: Scholastic. [P]

Bardoe, Cheryl (2006). *Gregor Mendel: The friar who grew peas.* Illus. by Jos. A. Smith. New York: Abrams (in association with the Field Museum).

Boulton, Judy (Adapter) (1994). *Only Opal: The diary of a young girl.* Illus. by Barbara Cooney. New York: Philomel Books. (From the diary of Opal Whiteley) [I]

Brett, Jan (Reteller) (1987). *Goldilocks and the three bears.* New York: Putnam. [P]

Brett, Jan (Reteller) (1989). *The mitten.* New York: Putnam. [P]

Bunting, Eve (1989). *The Wednesday surprise.* Illus. by Donald Carrick. New York: Clarion. [P]

Burleigh, Robert (2004). *Seurat and La Grande Jatte.* New York: Abrams. [I/M]

Burleigh, Robert (2005). *Toulouse-Lautrec: The Moulin Rouge and the city of lights.* New York: Abrams. [I/M]

Carle, Eric (1997). *From head to toe*. New York: HarperCollins. [P]

Cherniak, Judith (Ed.). (2006). *Carnival of the animals: Poems inspired by Saint-Saens' music*. Illus. by Satoshi Kitamura. Cambridge, MA: Candlewick. [I]

Costanza, Stephen (2004). *Mozart finds a melody*. New York: Henry Holt. [P/I]

Creech, Sharon (2001). *Love that dog*. New York: Joanna Cotler/HarperCollins.

Cronin, Doreen (2001). *CLICK, CLACK, MOO Cows that type*. Illus. by Betsy Lewin. New York: Simon & Schuster. [P]

Cronin, Doreen (2005). *Wiggle*. Illus by Scott Menchin. New York: Atheneum. [P]

Durango, Julia (2006). *Cha cha chimps*. Illus. by Eleanor Taylor. New York: Simon & Schuster. [P]

Ehlert, Lois (2005). *Leaf man*. San Diego: Harcourt. [P]

Ernst, Lisa Campbell (1995). *Little Red Riding Hood: A newfangled prairie tale*. New York: Simon & Schuster. [P/I]

Fleming, Candace (2002). *Muncha! Muncha! Muncha!* Illus. by G. Brian Karas. New York: Atheneum. [P]

George, Kristine O'Connell (2005). *Fold me a poem*. Illus. by L. Stringer. San Diego: Harcourt. [P/I]

Goble, Paul (2001). *Storm maker's tipi*. New York: Atheneum. [I]

Henkes, Kevin (1991). *Chrysanthemum*. New York: Greenwillow. [P]

Henkes, Kevin (1996). *Lilly's purple plastic purse*. New York: Greenwillow. [P]

Henkes, Kevin (2006). *Lilly's big day*. New York: Greenwillow. [P]

Hennessey, B. G. (Reteller) (2006). *The boy who cried wolf*. Illus. by Boris Kulikov. New York: Simon & Schuster. [P]

Hesse, K. (1992). *Letters from Rifka*. New York: Holt. [I/M]

Hest, Amy (2004). *Mr. George Baker*. Illus. by Jon J. Muth. Cambridge, MA: Candlewick. [P/I]

Hoberman, Mary Ann (1998). *Miss Mary Mack*. Illus. by Nadine Westcott. San Diego: Harcourt Brace. [P]

Horvath, Polly (2001). *Everything on a waffle*. New York: Farrar, Straus and Giroux. [I]

Jenkins, Steve, & Page, Robin (2003). *What do you do with a tail like that?* Boston: Houghton Mifflin. [P]

Juster, Norton (2005). *The hello, good-bye window*. Illus. by Chris Raschka. New York: Hyperion. [P]

Kadohata, Cynthia (2004). *Kira-Kira*. New York: Atheneum. [I]

Kleven, Elisa (2001). *Sun bread*. New York: Dutton. [P/I]

Lord, Cynthia (2006). *Rules*. New York: Scholastic. [I]

MacDonald, Amy (1990). *Rachel Fister's blister*. Illus. by Marjorie Priceman. Boston: Houghton Mifflin. [P/I]

McCully, E. A. (1993). *Mirette on the high wire*. New York: Putnam. [P]

Panahi, H. L. (2005). *Bebop express*. Illus. by Steve Johnson & Lou Fancher. New York: Amistad/HarperCollins. [P/I]

Patron, Susan (2006). *The higher power of Lucky*. Illus. by Matt Phelan. New York: Richard Jackson/Simon & Schuster. [I]

Paulsen, Gary (1987). *Hatchet*. New York: Bradbury. [I/M]

Paulsen, Gary (1996). *Brian's winter*. New York: Delacorte. [I/M]

Peck, Jan (2006). *Way far away on a wild safari*. Illus. by Valeria Petrone. New York: Simon & Schuster. [P]

Perkins, Lynne Rae (2005). *Criss-cross*. New York: Greenwillow/HarperCollins. [I/M]

Prelutsky, Jack (2004). *If not for the cat*. Illus. by Ted Rand. New York: Greenwillow. [P/I]

Priceman, Marjorie (1994). *How to make an apple pie and see the world*. New York: Knopf. [P/I]

Raven, Margot Theis (2004). *Circle unbroken: The story of a basket and its people*. Illus. by E. B. Lewis. New York: Farrar, Straus & Giroux. [I]

Rosen, Michael (2005). *Michael Rosen's sad book*. Illus. by Quentin Blake. Cambridge, MA: Candlewick. [I]

Ryan, Pam Munoz (2002). *Mud is cake*. Illus. by David McPhail. New York: Hyperion. [P]

Scieszka, Jon (1989). *The true story of the three little pigs as told by A. Wolf*. Illus. by Lane Smith. New York: Viking/Penguin. [I]

Van Laan, Nancy (1990). *Possum come a-knockin'*. Illus. by George Booth. New York: Knopf. [P]

Weatherford, Carole Boston (2006). *Moses: When Harriet Tubman led her people to freedom*. Illus. by Kadir Nelson. New York: Jump at the Sun/Hyperion. [I]

Wiesner, David (2006). *Flotsam*. New York: Clarion. [P/I]

Willard, Nancy (2001). *The Moon & Riddles diner and the Sunnyside Café*. Illus. by C. Butler. San Diego: Harcourt Brace. [P/I]

Woodson, Jacqueline (2004). *Coming on home soon*. Illus. by E. B. Lewis. New York: Putnam. [P/I]

Young, Ed (2004). *I, doko*. New York: Philomel. [P]

CHAPTER 2

Literature, Teaching, and Reader Response

Blending Books and Readers in the Classroom

When I recall early encounters with literature and first stirrings of response in my own literacy past, I remember only a few books during my childhood. Books were stored in the unfinished attic of our small four-room home. Through the dim light of a single ceiling bulb, I remember the sight, smell, and touch of the yellowed, Scotch®-taped pages of an incomplete set of Childcraft books—my first invitation to celebrate literature. I can still recall running my fingers along the black engravings on the orange textured covers as I longed to venture through three volumes containing ballads and poems, fairy tales, and animal stories—my first awakening to response to books. The desire to experience the richness of the words and the constant lure of story created a need to learn to read and uncover the magic between their covers.

My first years in elementary school turned me into a functional reader—a reader of basals, a master of worksheets. I learned to read through phonics, befriended Dick and Jane, and memorized sight word cards. I did what I was told, produced the right answers to comprehension *questions, remained in the middle group, and gradually became a fluent reader. In fact, I was able to climb the stairs to the attic and unlock the key to the words in those tempting Childcraft books.*

It wasn't until third grade, however, that I realized how literature, in stark contrast to instructional materials, would touch my own life and expand my view of reading. One special teacher, Mrs. Dunne, made learning an adventure that year. In a classroom of 50 students, she managed to infuse the crowded environment with engaged activities and motivating teaching techniques. What I remember most is Mrs. Dunne's voice as she introduced a daily literature read-aloud. Her rich invitation to literature and her compelling enthusiasm for reading blended with the exciting plots and memorable characters. First and foremost, I remember Gertrude Chandler Warner's The Boxcar Children, which ignited a response within me that has yet to be extinguished. Each day I anticipated the continuing adventures of Henry, Jessie, Violet, and Benny as they found treasures in the dump, shared creative meals on the blue tablecloth, and reunited with their loving grandfather. When Mrs. Dunne turned the final page of my first engagement with children's literature, she eagerly invited each of us to take a journey through those pages on our own. Not only did she permit me to take the book home, she told me about a wonderful place called the public library where similar journeys through literature awaited me.

That year in third grade I made a promise to myself. I pledged to become a teacher just like Mrs. Dunne with a passion for children and learning. I also vowed to cherish and read aloud literature in my own classroom with the same energy and fervor that Mrs. Dunne had read to me. My journey as a teacher at both elementary and college levels has provided me the privilege to take that journey and keep that promise while creating lovers of children's literature among both children and adults along the way.

As you think back on your own personal reasons for becoming a teacher, you may discover that your career goal is linked to children's literature. As readers attempt to recall their earliest responses to literature, it is often the memory of the read-aloud voice of a teacher that invades their thoughts. Many of our fondest memories of school and reading include the read-alouds that marked our invitation to celebrate literature through response: E. B. White's *Charlotte's Web*, Laura Ingalls Wilder's *Little House in the Big Woods*, Roald Dahl's *James and the Giant Peach*, or C. S. Lewis's *The Lion, the Witch, and the Wardrobe*. Fondest memories of school often flow toward weekly visits to the school library, documenting numbers of literature books read or dressing up as a book character. No matter what your literacy background, literature likely played a role in your decision to be a teacher.

The quality and role of children's literature in today's K–8 classrooms extend far beyond reading aloud, and reader responses far exceed mere record keeping. Literature currently pervades the curriculum as a resource for instruction, independent reading, and content area connections. Literature's richness is felt through narrative, expository, and poetic voices. It tugs on readers' heartstrings and whets their intellectual appetites as children naturally relate the relevancy of story and information to their own lives.

A Celebration of Literature and Response invites you as a teacher to embrace children's literature, to respond to it with both mind and heart, to make it an instrument of your teaching, and to share it with children in your classroom. What you take away from this textbook has the potential to touch children's lives, turn them into avid readers, and motivate them to continue their personal celebration of literature and response through a lifetime of reading. If your goal focuses on becoming a special teacher, including literature-based instruction in your classroom, and giving children the freedom to respond to literature in a personal way, then learning more about children's literature, children as readers, literature-based teaching, and reader response may be the most important step you take toward enriching your teaching prowess and clarifying your own educational philosophy.

This chapter serves as an invitation to preservice or inservice teachers to contemplate the connections between literature and teaching. Its purpose is to convince you that you need teaching, that teaching needs literature, and that literature needs children who respond to it and bring it to life. If our ultimate promise as educators is to create lifelong passionate readers, then our means to achieve that goal must be children's books that transcend, transform, transport, and translate printed words and vivid illustrations into memorable experiences that lead to a lifetime of reading enjoyment.

What is children's literature? Why teach with children's literature? What is reader response to literature? Why incorporate response to literature as a basis of a literature-based philosophy? These are the four critical questions this chapter addresses as you begin your journey or reaffirm your promise to link readers and books through the power of response to literature.

WHAT IS CHILDREN'S LITERATURE?

Children's literature can be defined as literature that appeals to the interests, needs, and reading preferences of children and captivates children as its major audience. Children's literature may be fictional, poetic, or factual, or a combination of any of these. The format that houses children's literature may be a picture book in which story blends with compelling illustrations or photographs for a visual and verbal adventure through story or factual content. Or the format may be a chapter book in which quality writing carries the story through a sequential unfolding of fictional plot or informational descriptions. Also referred to as trade books (in contrast to textbooks), children's literature provides appealing formats and motivating content to inspire children as they progress as emergent, novice, developing, and master readers.

Children's literature spans classic titles—Natalie Babbitt's *Tuck Everlasting,* Margaret Wise Brown's *Goodnight Moon,* and Robert McCloskey's *Make Way for Ducklings*—that have stood the test of time. Children's literature includes contemporary favorites—Kevin Henkes's *Kitten's First Full Moon,* Kate Di Camillo's *The Tale of Despereaux,* and Avi's *Crispin: The Cross of Lead*—that currently capture the attention of children. Children's literature also includes the newest books that grace bookstore shelves and school libraries—David McLimans's *Gone Wild: An Endangered Animal Alphabet* that inspires the alphabet with elegant graphic images, Jennifer Holm's Newbery Honor *Penny from Heaven,* or the *Orbis Pictus* Award *Quest for the Tree Kangaroo* by Sy Montgomery—all which still must undergo the careful scrutiny and approval of children. Children's books are honored on national award lists, receive children's choice awards, and reoccur in listings of notable books in language arts, social studies, and science. Children's literature has progressed in both quality and quantity during the last decade, and it has found credible acceptance both as independent reading material and as an instructional resource for both children and teachers.

The content of children's literature focuses primarily on the domain of childhood and early adolescence while including a wide variety of experiences that appeal to readers from elementary through middle school. Although content varies widely, it must appeal to the developmental level and natural interests of the individual reader. The following dimensions of content reflect a developmental approach to reading interests and evolving awareness of literature.

Appreciating the wonder of language. Children's literature captures and shares the wonder of the written word and the appeal of well-chosen language. Rhyme, rhythm, and repetition are the hallmark of books with appeal for the very young. Typically captured in poetic voice, young children can celebrate familiar Mother Goose characters or identify with everyday experience through a language-based adventure. Poetry collections and poem picture books contain words that roll off the tongue, create visual interpretations, and applaud the sounds of language. Picture storybooks eloquently select words and phrases that hold the interest of the listener on an enjoyable adventure through a book. Older readers focus on the use of word choice and literary devices as authors weave their stories through creative use of language. *Children's literature crafts words, creates images, and describes everyday objects in special ways.*

Sparking the imagination. Young children, in particular, enjoy books that whet their imaginative powers and allow them to venture into the realm of the impossible (Spencer, 2003). Evil stepmothers, beautiful princesses, and talking lions transport a child into a special place where the unbelievable seems real. Traditional tales typically have strong appeal to young readers as versions of *Rapunzel* by Paul

Zelinsky and *Cinderella* by Ruth Sanderson become a part of early childhood literary experiences. Literary tales of fantasy spark the imagination of older readers as well and transport them to worlds of talking animals or to kingdoms like Prydain that stretch their beliefs beyond reality. *Children's literature challenges creativity and ignites inventiveness in children.*

Reliving everyday experiences.   From going to bed (Kate Banks's *Close your Eyes*) to going to school (Michael Rosen's *Totally Wonderful Miss Plumberry*), from gaining an appreciation of family (Kate DiCamillo's *Because of Winn-Dixie*) to struggling to find acceptance (Patricia Reilly Giff's *Pictures of Hollis Woods*), children's literature honestly portrays the lives of children and preadolescents during those important years of growing up. Realistic fiction reveals experiences common to childhood and impending adulthood including those that challenge and define the nature of an individual. *Children's literature affirms real life and offers vicarious experiences from authentic situations while fostering empathy for the human condition.*

Revisiting the past.   Children's literature transports readers to historical places and settings or introduces characters placed in historical contexts. Historical fiction reveals the realities of historical circumstances (Deborah Hopkinson's *Under the Quilt of Night*), introduces flesh-and-blood characters (Pattie Mae in Sheila P. Moses's *The Return of Buddy Bush*), and shares unique perspectives about significant historical events (Nikki Giovanni's *Rosa*) that impact contemporary life. *Children's literature transports readers and transcends time while encouraging valid connections between the past and the present.*

Sharing lives and information.   Children's literature shares the lives of historical figures and the feats and triumphs of real everyday people through biography. From sports heroes (David Adler's *Joe Louis: America's Fighter*) to equal rights models (Russell Freedman's *The Voice That Challenged a Nation: Marian Anderson*), character and determination provide inspiration and direction in children's own lives. Nonfiction informational books extend the growing body of information about our world. Quality factual representations introduce the reader to the human fabric behind science (Carla Killough McClafferty's *Something Out of Nothing: Marie Curie and Radium*), a retrospective journey into an historical event (Jim Murphy's *An American Plague*), or an introduction to the arts (Caroline Desnoettes's *Look Closer: Art Masterpieces Through the Ages*). *Children's literature replays the triumphs and determination of renowned figures and shares an explosion of information and facts about the world in which we live.*

Although the content of recent children's literature is impressive and at times overwhelming to the adult reader, the quality of children's literature varies widely and should be a selective factor in determining the appropriateness of literature for children. Using children's books for enjoyment or instruction implies recognition of evaluative criteria and making certain that the best of children's books make their way into the lives of readers. Children's literature has certainly blossomed in content and quality since the days of *The Boxcar Children,* but it still possesses the potential to motivate children to become readers, to cause readers to reflect on the human condition, and to expand their knowledge of and perspectives on the world.

WHY TEACH WITH LITERATURE?

Teachers today are making countless instructional decisions daily based on the premise that children's books are effective instructional resources. Why are some teachers, districts, and schools committed to using children's literature in the classroom as they seek balance in their literacy programs? Why do some teachers believe in literature as a vehicle to achieve strong test scores as well as create lifelong readers? When we look at the high-quality books published for children, the visual appeal of their illustrations, and the enjoyment their stories bring readers, we can understand the lure of literature as the foundation of balanced literacy instruction. Somewhere between rigid prescriptive guides to instruction and the passionate lure of literature, "the goals of literacy and literature instruction must meaningfully intersect" (Roser, 2001, p. 233). The reasons go far beyond the appeal of the book. The support begins in the early literacy environment and progresses throughout the school years as literature affects language development, reading achievement, and writing in literature-rich classroom settings. Classic and recent research (Ayra et al., 2005; Galda & Cullinan, 1991; McGee, 1992; Tunnell & Jacobs, 1989) affirms the benefits of using literature as a foundation of literacy instruction both in the home and in the classroom.

Literature fosters home literacy.   The convincing argument for the use of children's literature for literacy instruction and teaching curricular content begins with the early years in the home. For more than 30 years, studies of emergent literacy have documented the important role of literature in children's reading achievement, social interactions, and the rites of passage into a literate world (Teale & Sulzby, 1986). Children who are read to at home develop highly positive associations with books. Their perception of their parents' attitude toward reading is an important influence on their own attitudes toward reading. The pleasant bond developed between reader and listener provides memories of warm, loving experiences later associated with the reading act. Marie Clay (1979) attests that being read literature early and often develops familiarity with the conventions of print. Studies consistently point to positive relationships between the number of books in a home and a child's reading ability (Durkin, 1966; Lamme, 1985) and the relationship between being read to at an early age and success in reading at school (Durkin, 1974). Even in a technological age, establishing a literature habit, acquiring a sense of story, and nurturing a love of read-aloud literature will never die if introduced by a loving parent in a safe home environment (Hancock, 2000). All signs point to literature as a key to early literacy and continued literacy growth.

Literature enhances language development.   If literature can have such an impact in the home environment, it seems logical that immersion in literature can have similar positive influences in the early school environment. Reading and listening to a variety of books increase interest and motivation in learning to read (Mendoza, 1985). The language of literature assists in language development while children feed their "linguistic data pool" (Harste, Woodward, & Burke, 1984) from encounters with stories. Exposure to quality writing through literature leads to a wider oral and written vocabulary as a child matures.

Literature aids comprehension.   Stories provide a way for children to make sense of their world. As they connect their own lives to a story, children begin to sort out the complexities of daily life (Pardo, 2004; Wells, 1986). Knowledge about narrative structure is a benefit to children acquainted with literature. Knowing that a story has a beginning, a problem, a resolution, and an end begins to provide a visual framework of how a story works. Research acknowledges that informational text also sets up early expository schema and that reading aloud and responding to nonfiction is also valid to a child's early sense of understanding how text works (Vardell, 2003). Because a meaning-centered approach to literacy must be supported by continued growth in understanding, literature provides the necessary support for that process.

Literature provides a writing model.   Reading literature as a model of quality writing is linked to success in writing proficiency. Exposure to narrative through the use of literature results in more elaborate language structure by those exposed to literature compared with those exposed to basal stories (Eckhoff, 1983). The sense of story developed during early reading provides the framework for the structure of story. Reading and discussing literature as the author's craft makes children more aware of their own authorship (Hansen, 1987/2001).

Literature inspires inquiry within and across disciplines.   Literature can focus on subject matter associated with the traditional disciplines. Many teachers enhance instruction by including a related piece of children's literature as motivation for the prescribed curriculum. Literature not only has the potential to answer questions, but it can also incite learners to ask even more. Inquiry-based learning often begins with literature and exposure to a single title but continues on an adventure of connections among books (Short, 1993). The natural connections between literature and the engagement of a curious reader begin the inquiry process that may evolve from a single discipline but expand to an interdisciplinary study. Even in a technological society, "literature transcends time and place and cultures and helps us to review the past, interpret the present, and envision the future" (Bishop, 2000, p. 73).

Literature creates readers.   Availability and choice of books, time spent with books, and a supportive, enthusiastic teacher are essential elements for creating readers. Children need time to look at books, to listen to books, to respond to books, to read independently, and to reflect on the reading experience. Galda (2001) reminds teachers that reading books helps children learn things they need to know to become a reader. Children's books provide opportunities for meaningful practice or reading skills and strategies. Reading good books actually turns children into avid readers. This remains one of the most valid arguments for literature-based instruction.

Observations of successful literature-based classrooms indicate that the teacher plays a key role in creating the literature-rich environment that supports literacy (Hepler, 1982; Hickman, 1981). The teacher is the orchestrator of a setting that provides books, choice, time, and support so that children are encouraged to connect with books. A teacher who supports literature as the basis of literacy and curricular instruction provides an effective entry into literacy and also puts children one step closer to becoming lifelong readers.

Why literature? Literature provides a passport to the world of reading by serving as a motivating means to acquire the strategies and fluency needed to comprehend text. Literature creates excitement and enjoyment about the reading process by transporting the child to worlds of fact and fantasy. Literature provides a model for writing both story and information by providing strong support for the author's craft. Robert Probst (2000) describes literature as "invitations to a passionate engagement with human experience" (p. 8). Literature simply creates readers. Bernice Cullinan (1992) claims teachers have the "joyful responsibility of handing these treasures on to children . . . we can fill children's baskets of memory with beautiful language and life experiences with the books we share with them. The memories will last a lifetime" (p. 430).

WHAT IS READER RESPONSE?

Reader response to literature describes the unique interaction that occurs within the mind and heart of the individual reader throughout the literature event. Although the theoretical foundation of reader response is grounded in the work of Louise Rosenblatt (see Chapter 1), this initial discussion will assist you in understanding the components of reader response within a literature-based teaching philosophy. The three components of reader response include (1) the reader, (2) the literature, and (3) the context for response (Galda, 1988). A visual model of the components contributing to response to literature (Figure 2.1) serves as a visual representation that links children's literature, the reader, and the response environment. Reader response to literature is affected by who we are as readers, the books we select to read, and the broad and narrower contexts that surround the reading event. As these components define the dynamic act of reading, they blend into the unique transaction of reader response to literature. Looking at each of these factors more closely emphasizes the complexity of reader response to literature and clarifies the many factors that contribute to the individuality of response.

Reader Response: The Reader

Readers, young and old, actively engage with literature. Who we are and what we have experienced in our lives influence our responses to books. The places we've traveled, the people we've met, the books we've read, and the values we hold determine how we interact with the literature we read. Jane Yolen (1985) aptly focuses on the crucial role of the reader when she states,

FIGURE 2.1   Components of response: Reader, text, context

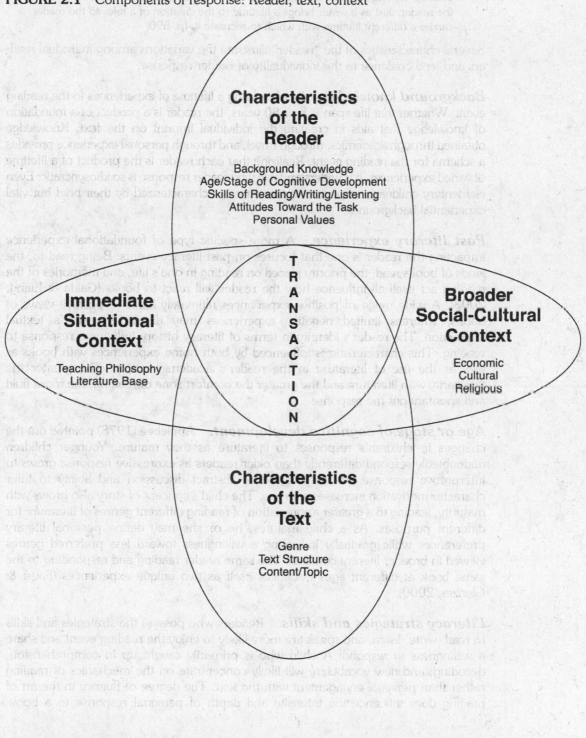

Characteristics of the Reader

Background Knowledge
Age/Stage of Cognitive Development
Skills of Reading/Writing/Listening
Attitudes Toward the Task
Personal Values

Immediate Situational Context

Teaching Philosophy
Literature Base

TRANSACTION

Broader Social-Cultural Context

Economic
Cultural
Religious

Characteristics of the Text

Genre
Text Structure
Content/Topic

There is no real story on the page, only that which is created between the writer and the reader. Just as a writer brings a lifetime to the creation of a tale, so the reader carries a different lifetime with which to recreate it. (p. 590)

Several characteristics of the "reader" illustrate the variations among individual readers and lend credence to the individuality of reader response.

Background knowledge. Readers bring a lifetime of experiences to the reading event. Whether that life span is 8 or 80 years, the reader is a product of a foundation of knowledge that aids in creating the individual imprint on the text. Knowledge obtained through academics, through travel, and through personal experience provides a schema for the reading event. Realizing that each reader is the product of a lifetime of varied experiences, it is understandable why reader response is so idiosyncratic. Even elementary children's responses to literature are characterized by their brief but vital experiential backgrounds.

Past literary experience. A more specific type of foundational experience impacting the reader is one that focuses on past literacy events. Being read to, the kinds of books read, the priority placed on reading in one's life, and memories of the reading act itself all influence how the reader will react to books (Galda & Liang, 2003). A wide range of positive experiences ultimately leads to positive views of books, whereas limited negative experiences may distort a reader's textual interaction. The reader's identity in terms of literacy history influences response to reading. This characteristic is influenced by both home experiences with books as well as the use of literature in the reader's academic setting. The greater the familiarity with literature and the greater the comfort zone of reading, the more fluid and spontaneous the response.

Age or stage of cognitive development. Applebee (1978) pointed out the changes in children's responses to literature as they mature. Younger children undoubtedly respond differently than older readers as expressive response grows to interpretive response and the degree of abstract discussion and ability to infer character motivation increases with age. The child's concept of story also grows with maturity, leading to a greater appreciation of reading different genres of literature for different purposes. As a child matures, he or she may define personal literary preferences while gradually indicating a willingness toward less preferred genres viewed in broader literary contexts. The same reader reading and responding to the same book at different ages evidences itself as two unique experiences (Faust & Glenzer, 2000).

Literacy strategies and skills. Readers who possess the strategies and skills to read, write, listen, and speak are more likely to enjoy the reading event and share a willingness to respond. A child who is primarily caught up in comprehension, decoding, and new vocabulary will likely concentrate on the mechanics of reading rather than personal engagement with the text. The degree of fluency in the art of reading does influence the intensity and depth of personal response to a book.

Children who struggle with receptive and communication skills, however, are still quite capable of response to literature, although the depth and variety of their responses may be somewhat encumbered.

Attitudes toward the task. Just as in any learning situation, motivation for both reading and responding can come from outside and within the reader. A new book self-selected or chosen by a teacher creates a natural motivation for most children, but a love of reading and a desire to share depends on intrinsic motivation (Serafini, 2004). The natural desire to read and transact with a book leads to genuine response; resistance may limit response, but does not prevent it from occurring (Edmunds & Rausermann, 2006).

Personal morality and values. Readers are a reflection of their ethical backgrounds because their lives are grounded in varying concepts of acceptable and unacceptable behavior. Moral background becomes an influential part of response to the actions and decisions of characters in literature. Readers measure the right and wrong of characters against their personal value systems. These comparisons typically find their way into the responses of all children and affirm or refute their internal belief systems.

These six reader characteristics illustrate the multiple factors that create the unique reader who is a critical part of the response process. As teachers realize the various components of the reader that affect response, they gain a deeper understanding of why the literary responses children share reflect such a diversity of thought.

Reader Response: The Literature

Textual characteristics also impact the response of readers to literature. An examination of how text selection influences response allows teachers to value the importance of self-selected or teacher-selected texts in the response process. The following text characteristics impact reader response.

Genre. The genre of the selected literature influences the content and intensity of the transactional response. All literary genres are capable of eliciting reader response, but some genres (and specific books within a genre) naturally influence intense aesthetic response. Realistic fiction, for example, is both a preferred genre for middle elementary readers and a genre that elicits intense response. If the genre is one preferred by the reader, response is likely to be more genuine, honest, and comfortable. Nevertheless, a variety of literary genres should be shared with readers in an attempt to develop reading tastes and their own response capabilities (Hancock, 2007).

Text structure. Narrative, expository, and poetic text structures each influence response in a unique way. Children often respond to a book with a particular structure in that writing mode. For example, responses to a book of poetry may actually be the writing of one's own poem modeled from the pattern, topic, or structure of the text. Narrative writing, in contrast, often results in first-person responses. Straightforward expository writing may elicit efferent facts but is often tempered by narrative sharing of personal reactions to those facts.

Literary elements.   Various literary aspects of the text itself may influence response. An author's writing style can influence response as a story unfolds in a positive or negative framework. Characterization, particularly the age of the main character, can influence character identification and a reader's interest in the story. Point of view can influence the reader's emotional distance from the text. First person draws the reader closer to the character and story outcome; third person may help the reader take a detached, objective stance toward story events. Even the lead-ins and endings of both entire books and individual chapters impact response in that they encourage readers to predict outcomes or extend the story in their own minds.

Content / Topic.   The story or informational content between the covers of a book strongly influences response. If the content is aesthetic and touches the reader's life in a personal way (divorce, sports competitions, friendship), the response is likely to be more spontaneous and genuine as children make connections between their own lives and that of the character. If the topic of an informational title is self-selected, the response is likely to build on the background knowledge or interest in the topic that initially led the reader to the book.

The nature and quality of response depend on the text to which the reader responds. If the teacher selects the text, issues of genre, text structure, literary quality, and topic interest must be considered. If the child chooses a text for independent reading and response, not just any title will do. There are indeed books whose inherent aesthetic nature leads to a richer emotional response to literature. These are the titles that are recognized and highlighted throughout this entire text—books with special features that naturally cause them to elicit response through a variety of outlets.

Reader Response: The Context

The context or setting for response to literature involves a dual perspective. First, the context for response includes the broad social-cultural context of a child's life, which forms the foundation of response. A child's family's socioeconomic status, cultural or ethnic background, or religious beliefs set the stage for the kinds of responses a child chooses to share. Connections between a book and one's own life become apparent in this broader context of response. The reader as a product of environmental surroundings brings a personal context to the reading event.

The second contextual perspective on response focuses exclusively on the immediate situational context of the classroom, which includes the philosophy of the teacher, the literature-based focus, and the valued, respected expression of individual response in the classroom setting.

The context in which reader response is generated influences the ways in which readers choose to respond. Teachers whose beliefs are grounded in holistic philosophy are likely to align literature-based instruction with their whole-to-part learning philosophy. They select instructional methodology that includes reading workshops containing a critical response component. These teachers value self-selection, independent thinking, and genuine response. Children need not seek the "right" answer but are encouraged to bring original thoughts to their written responses or oral discussion groups as books are shared. The context surrounding the invitation to respond must genuinely support originality of thought, interpretation, and connections if an honest response is to occur. A context built on valued individualism and personal reaction allows the optimal context for reader response.

As the reader, the text, and the context overlap to form a personal response to literature, teachers recognize and appreciate the varying individual perspectives that blend into textual response. The most fulfilling aspect of response to a teacher is the variety of responses that cross his or her path during oral or written sharing. Unlike worksheets keyed to tallying specific correct answers, reader response encourages the individual to encounter the text in a one-on-one engagement and to share the spontaneous, distinctive reaction with the text. Nurturing the uniqueness of the reader, valuing the traits of the text, and acknowledging the importance of the context for response allows response to emerge and flourish over time.

What is reader response? Reader response implies the unique, individual connection between a reader and children's literature in the context of a teaching or learning environment. No two readers have the same response to the same text. Reader response to literature encourages the expression of independent thoughts, personal reflections, and emotional engagement during and following the reading event.

WHY A READER RESPONSE VIEW OF LITERATURE AND TEACHING?

For the past decade, many elementary/middle-level teachers have incorporated a response-based view of children's literature in their classrooms. In these literature-based settings, children may write in journals as they read, talk about books with peers, or express personal meaning through the expressive arts. Enjoying reading is a hallmark of this approach, although becoming a fluent reader maintains its importance. In this approach to literacy instruction, several factors typically appear as priorities or characteristics.

- Instruction is primarily *literature based* because it is accomplished through real children's books with a balance of time spent on real reading and some time spent on reading instruction itself.
- Instruction is *child centered* with choice an honored aspect of the program. Topics and purposes are keyed to children's interests and needs, and authenticity sparks motivation both for readers and lifelong learners.
- Instruction is *integrated* with the language arts as listening, speaking, writing, viewing, and visual representation become outlets for response to literature.
- Instruction is *balanced* with the strategies and skills being applied and practiced in the *authentic context of literature.*

A response-based view of children's literature focuses on two major assumptions. First, the stance a child assumes as a reader fluctuates between aesthetic (pleasure/personal connections) and efferent (details/information). This premise assumes reading is a dynamic process featuring changing purposes as a reader interacts with the unfolding text. Second, individual meaning is personally constructed from an engaged, reflective encounter with literature. Because literature is absorbed by unique readers, multiple interpretations of texts are encouraged and honored as each literature experience is personalized. This view of reading stretches beyond testing personal recollections by answering a series of questions at the end of a story or attending to details as an indication of reading ability or prowess. Internalizing this theoretical perspective leads to an invigorating style of teaching and learning literacy in K–8 classrooms.

Reader response to literature evidences itself in many observable ways in real classroom settings. Even to a novice observer, the use of literature as the basis of literacy instruction provides an indication of a response-based program. Recognizing sustained silent reading, writing during reading, and periodic book discussions are first signs of the implementation of this approach. Looking beyond the literature, however, the more informed observer might recognize chanting, the shared book experience, dramatic reenactment, reading workshops, literature response journals, and literature circles as indicators of a response-based teaching philosophy.

Why would a teacher choose to adopt this philosophy in light of high-stakes testing, increased accountability, and a move toward a more "balanced" approach to literacy? Dixie Spiegel's (1998) retrospective report on the implementation of reader response activities and the simultaneous growth of readers provides a framework for a discussion of the positive aspects of this type of instruction. The results of a decade of implementation of reader response in the elementary/middle-level classroom point to a number of reasons for its continued inclusion in literacy instruction. As you continue to read, place yourself in the role of the reader and recall your own instructional experiences, attitudes toward reading, and personal connections to literature during your own K–8 learning experience. At the same time, place yourself in the role of teacher and reflect on your own literacy goals and outcomes for your students.

Experiencing reading success.   Perhaps the most satisfying outcome of a response-based approach to literacy is the feeling of accomplishment children exhibit as readers. Self-confidence often lacking in more traditional classrooms abounds here. Even children who struggle with reading feel glimmers of success as their own growth is documented rather than being compared to the average reader at a designated grade level. As valued meaning makers, each child feels the importance of the unique viewpoint he or she brings to the literature. Increased success leads to growing contributions to literature circles and expansion of written responses. The confidence of believing in oneself as a reader and a learner may provide the greatest impetus to continuing learning outside the classroom.

Meeting diverse needs.   Because a response-based approach requires literature across all literary genres as a resource for teaching, there is "something for everybody," and the gap between quality literature, reading preferences, and reading ability is narrowed. Classrooms are filled with diverse readers with different abilities, tastes, and interests. Finding the right book for the right child at the right moment only becomes possible when selecting from thousands of fiction and nonfiction titles rather than being restricted by a single textbook or anthology as a resource for learning. The sheer numbers of quality books cry out for inclusion not only in the literacy program but as a basis for instruction across curricular areas.

Becoming risk takers.   Because a response-based classroom includes sharing one's own interpretation of literature, readers become risk takers whose unique opinions are valued. Students use their own writing and speaking voices as they contribute to literature journals and discussions. Instead of responses matching those of a teacher or a teacher edition of a textbook, reader response broadens the scope of acceptance as a springboard for continuing conversations about literature. Students learn to validate their thinking, to support their contentions with details from literature, and to express themselves articulately without the threat of intimidation. The risk taking fostered in a response-based approach extends beyond the classroom as critical thinking and decision making become lifelong learning processes.

Assuming responsibility for learning.   Readers gain a sense of responsibility for selecting literature and for fulfilling the demands of a response-based agenda. Because their audience often includes peers, students seem even more responsible for reading books, constructing meaning, recording reflective responses, and explaining an interpretation. Children learn to value and share their own voice in response to the books they read. The small group aspects of response-based instruction, especially literature circles, promote responsibility in ways that are absent from traditional methodologies.

Making personal connections. A response-based approach to teaching encourages the ownership of literature through personal connections to one's own life, other pieces of literature one has read, or to the world beyond one's own life. A reader becomes a part of a book and gains a vested interest in the reading process when he or she can connect to it in a personal way. For example, children can relate characters' feelings and experiences to occurrences in their own lives (loss of a pet, loss of a friend, personal struggles, personal successes). When that connection is made, the book forms a bond with the reader and the act of reading becomes a more satisfying experience. When students share their own personal connections to literature, they share a part of themselves, assume the role of expert, and bring credibility to their discussion. Readers can also connect to characters' situations, moral dilemmas, and decision making. Characters as role models help readers realize they are not alone in their personal situations. These opportunities are greatly minimized when instruction is limited to textbooks. Personal connections to literature create lifelong readers who feel the sense of kinsmanship, friendship, and identity with characters that face circumstances not unfamiliar to their own.

Encouraging higher-level thinking. Reader response to literature moves the reading process from a passive encounter to an active partnership in creating meaning throughout the entire reading encounter. Response-based activities often solicit a reader's response throughout the reading process instead of waiting for a retrospective view at the completion of the text as in the case of traditional book reports. This type of ongoing thinking, constant reflection, and monitoring of emotions serves as a model for a lifetime of reflective thinking during the reading process. Although student response may be documented through response journals or periodic literature circles, the message of "read–reflect–respond" gradually becomes a natural part of the reading process, even when response is no longer required outside of the school setting. Students actually begin to think about the author's message rather than focusing only on the unfolding of events. Greater involvement with literature leads to a deeper interaction with story, characters, and theme. Internalizing the response process results in continued higher-level considerations over time.

Understanding reading as a process. A response-based approach implies active involvement with literature. Sharing responses with peers builds the realization that meaning making is individualized and an ongoing process throughout the entire literary encounter. Predicting, connecting, evaluating, identifying, and relating constitute active reading strategies that exhibit themselves throughout the response process. The constructive nature of meaning making also provides opportunities to weigh others' opinions against one's own viewpoint. Reader response fosters listening skills and makes room for altering one's own meaning as evidence and different viewpoints are shared.

Appreciating literary quality.   Literature as a basis of reader response affords readers the opportunity to expect quality in the books they read. Teachers who use a response-based approach to instruction bring familiarity with children's literature classics to their classrooms while keeping abreast of current high-quality children's books. They read professional journals, collaborate with their library/media center specialist, and seek literature that matches skills, strategies, and topics taught in the curriculum. Because literary elements form a part of literary discussions, readers demand the high quality of many of the teacher-selected books introduced during read-aloud sessions. Sharing quality authors and illustrators with children provides a model for quality reading. If valuable time is to be spent reading, then reading the highest quality literature becomes an important lifelong consideration.

Why should a teacher want to incorporate a reader response approach in K–8 classrooms? Teachers who incorporate reader response approaches to literature issue lifelong invitations to children to engage in reading and researching through literature. Children acquire many admirable traits as readers, reflective thinkers, and decision makers through a steady diet of response. Their ability to share their own responses while accepting the opinions of others transcends the school setting. If your educational outcomes focus on creating readers that read outside the walls of your classroom and beyond the hours of the school day, then you have the opportunity to learn more about literature and response in the coming chapters. Learning more about literature, about readers, and about reader response can set the stage for the philosophy you share in your classroom.

BLENDING LITERATURE, TEACHING, AND READER RESPONSE IN THE CLASSROOM

What does children's literature, literature-based instruction, and a reader response philosophy look like in a real classroom? Perhaps this evolving discussion of its multiple benefits has excited you about children's literature and the importance of designating reader response as the core of your teaching philosophy. Yet an observational "visit" to a first-grade, a third-grade, and a sixth-grade classroom might more clearly visualize this philosophy in action. As you reflect on the following teaching/learning scenarios, picture the classroom arrangement, sense the immersion in literature, grasp the role of the teacher, and revel in the motivation of the students as they engage in literature-based reader response through quality teaching.

A first-grade teacher's journal entries provide an outstanding example of literature and reader response as the basis of instruction with young children. Read this primary teacher's reflective journal to begin to internalize the importance of literature, the freedom of children to respond, diverse opportunities for a variety of responses, the enthusiasm that fills this classroom, and the philosophy that drives this instruction.

Literary Legend

Children's Literature in the Classroom

Charlotte Huck (1922–2005) spent a lifetime bringing children and books together by integrating children's literature across the curriculum. Her vision for the connectedness between children and books was articulated in 1961 in *Children's Literature in the Elementary School,* now in its 9th edition. Her belief that every teacher and librarian has the responsibility to share rich literature experiences with children has empowered members of our profession to open classroom doors to the enjoyment of quality books.

Charlotte Huck received three degrees from Northwestern University interspersed with authentic teaching experience in Missouri and Illinois. She joined the education faculty at Ohio State University in 1955, with only a single undergraduate children's literature course to teach. Dr. Huck created a nationally respected master's and doctoral program in children's literature. Inviting graduate students into her home, the "attic rats" emerged in teacher education institutions across the nation to spread the literary spirit and classroom message of their mentor.

During her career, Dr. Huck was a member of the Newbery and Caldecott award committee, chaired the Caldecott committee, awarded the prestigious Arbuthnot Award for a distinguished professor of children's literature, and elected to the IRA Reading Hall of Fame. Upon her "active retirement" in 1986, she turned to writing her own children's books as well as continuing activities related to children and books. Charlotte Huck's legacy continues through each child who feels the magic of literature penetrate his or her heart when introduced quality literature by the dynamic voice of a classroom teacher or school librarian.

Huck, C. (1961). *Children's literature in the elementary school.* New York: Holt, Rinehart & Winston.

Huck, Charlotte (1989). *Princess Furball.* Illus. by Anita Lobel. New York: Greenwillow.

Huck, Charlotte (1996). *Toads and diamonds.* Illus. by Anita Lobel. New York: Greenwillow.

Huck, Charlotte (1998). *A creepy countdown.* Illus. by Jos. A. Smith. New York: Greenwillow.

Huck, Charlotte (2001). *Black bull of Norraway: A Scottish tale.* Illus. by Anita Lobel. New York: Greenwillow.

Kiefer, B. Z., with Hepler, S., & Hickman, J. (2007). *Charlotte Huck's children's literature* (9th ed.). Boston: McGraw-Hill.

During the first week of school, one of the books I read to the children was Eileen Christelow's Five Little Monkeys Jumping on the Bed. *They knew the chant from kindergarten. Today as they were working on a math activity that had monkeys pictured in one section, they began chanting "Five little monkeys . . ." with rhythm and expression. The book is on our library table—they love to read it during their free time.*

The children loved Jan Brett's Berlioz the Bear. *They started clapping when the bee stung the hindquarters of the mule. I also read Brett's* The Owl and the Pussycat *and* The Mitten. *They were so enthusiastic over Jan Brett's illustrations. The book fair didn't have Brett's* The Wild Christmas Reindeer, *but we can order it. . . . I did!*

I used a lot of poetry today. After lunch as we were getting ready for storytime I taught the children the poem "I Eat My Peas With Honey" since we had peas for lunch. I also read a pizza poem by Ogden Nash—we had pizza, too! After school I wrote the poems on chart paper, but I have a problem. Where am I going to hang all these poems? We'll see how the children like them . . . maybe they will have an idea about where they should be displayed.

Today I introduced Jan Brett's Goldilocks and the Three Bears, *which lends itself to acting out so we plan to work on that aspect of response. This will be a different approach to responding for us. Some of the children volunteered to bring in items for the performance. I didn't remind them or write a note, but they remembered. What fun they had (me, too) as they acted out the story. I discussed with them that acting out, making a puppet play, etc., were ways to "respond" to the stories we read. This helps us understand the story better.*

First-Grade Teacher's Reflective Journal

Every journal entry is filled with the joys of literature and response. Children revel in literature-based opportunities. They have become risk takers whose choices are honored and whose ideas become the basis for instruction. With 30 years of teaching experience, this educator has turned her love of literature and her belief in the value of response into an active classroom philosophy. Literature, authors, language, and language arts surround the children with the motivation and materials to become readers. Books become familiar companions, language becomes an alliterative escapade, writing becomes a challenge, and the expressive arts are valued as a mode of response. This teacher is an artist, a crafter of language, and an orchestrator of response with her students. She believes in literature and response as a means of inviting her students into the world of reading.

Ideally as children progress in school, their eagerness for reading gains continuous momentum. Traditional programs may offer routine and regimented schedules with little freedom for choice, self-expression, or variety. Inclusion of literature-based components, even in a standards-based classroom, however, provides the necessary reminders of the lifelong joy of literature. Peering into an exemplary third-grade response-based classroom affords a view of an energetic approach to literacy.

On entering Mr. Lowell's third grade, I am immediately awakened to a rich blend of books, readers, and response. Within four brightly painted walls lies a wealth of titles from all genres displayed in a variety of configurations. An author study table featuring Roald Dahl catches my eye, but I am quickly distracted by a thematic study displaying a myriad of titles related to "An Exploration of Change." My visual sense notes books across genres ranging from A Circle of Seasons *by Myra Cohn Livingston, to* Many Thousand Gone *by Virginia Hamilton, to* Letting Swift River Go *by Jane Yolen. A huge mural sweeping the length of the back of the classroom contains a map of the United States with colored thumbtacks holding labels of book titles set in various venues of our country. I note Ruckman's* Night of the Twisters *in Nebraska, Bartone's* Peppe the Lamplighter *in New York, and Boulton's* Only Opal *in the Pacific Northwest.*

Moving my focus from books to response, I find delight in the colorful mobiles hanging from the ceiling that depict all of the beloved characters of Beverly Cleary.

Literature webs cover open wall spaces; sculptures of dinosaurs next to a copy of Rohmann's Time Flies *fill the shelf below the windows. Organized in plastic crates are response journals that include reading graphs of books of varied genres. A castle of cardboard is accompanied by David Macauley's* Castle *and homemade pig puppets complement Steven Kellogg's newest version of* The Three Little Pigs.

My attention flows to the readers who quietly fill the open and isolated spaces of the room. Some children choose the solitude and familiarity of their desks; others seek the comfort of pillow-filled corners and a carpeted, wooden loft. Children read—some with piles of picture books at their sides, others with a single chapter book in their lap. Children read—many slowly digest captions and illustrations in nonfiction selections while others cling to every word the author offers. I have entered the classroom at DEAR time (Drop Everything and Read). I mentally applaud the on-task behavior of children who are not reading because they have to but because they want to and are given choice in their selections for 20 minutes of enjoyment tailored to their needs. I know that the literature-based philosophy I am witnessing is not confined to this part of the day but woven throughout the entire curriculum. The evidence of response displayed indicates a full-time commitment to literature in the lives of children.

Author Observational Notes

This classroom scenario exemplifies the phrase "littered with literacy" and evokes the principles of response-based instruction in an intermediate elementary classroom. Reading of authentic literature, freedom of choice, encouraged risk taking, and literature as the focus of cross-curricular instruction evidence themselves in all directions. The room reflects active engagement in literature throughout the school day and provides motivation and access to literature throughout the school year.

By the time readers reach middle school, the configuration for response-based teaching through literature is typically implemented in the reading workshop format. The three essential components of a reading workshop include the literature itself, response to literature through the language arts, and literature conversations. As independence thrives with approaching adolescence, group work becomes the hallmark of reader response and interactive discussions, and collaborative response-based projects dominate the reading period. A scenario from a sixth-grade classroom sets the stage for the workings of this response-based approach at this level.

Ms. Lopez has chosen a "survival" themeset of literature for her nineteen middle-level readers. With groups of six, six, and seven students, she has selected three titles from which they may choose: Paula Fox's Monkey Island, *Felice Holman's* Slake's Limbo, *and Gary Paulsen's* Brian's Winter. *After a brief, energetic book talk about each on Friday, she allowed students to rank their choices for reading workshop. Satisfied students, most of whom receive their first choice this Monday morning, get to the business of reading. Typically, 30 minutes of the 1-hour workshop is devoted to reading, 15 minutes to recording response, and 15 minutes to literature circles or whole-class conversations. The students show familiarity with the schedule so little time is wasted on organization.*

After reading for 30 minutes, Paul's group decides on an illustrated timeline to share their thoughts on Brian's Winter. *Keith suggests a response journal in chronological order of the unfolding plot for* Slake's Limbo. *Meredith encourages her group to choose sketches with captions for a single event from each chapter of* Monkey Island. *Obviously, this teacher encourages a variety of modes of response and provides for individual differences among groups. The last portion of class time today is spent as a whole-class discussion focusing on the type of survival faced by each book's character. Before class closes, reading assignments for the following day are determined by the group with an agreement to share responses in literature circles the next day. Ms. Lopez reminds students that contractual forms for response are due on Wednesday.*

Although the reading workshop pattern will likely continue for almost 2 weeks, responsibility apparently lies with the readers and their sharing of thoughts, opinions, and reactions to daily reading through peer discussion. When the reading of the books is completed, individuals plan to share their response projects within the group and then more extensively with the entire class. On a daily basis, the momentum of the literature provides the impetus to read while the positive reaction to talking about books with peers sustains the discussion process.

Author's Observational Notes

The independence, freedom, and responsibility of the reading workshop format makes it ideal for preadolescent readers who tend to thrive in its apparently unstructured nature. Yet daily routines actually keep this format quite structured, and readers remain highly accountable for learning. The modeling of organization, talk about books, and high expectations maintained by the teacher as facilitator make the reading workshop highly effective when blending literature, written/oral/artistic response, and book discussion.

These virtual classroom visits highlight the potential effectiveness of literature-based instruction across grade levels. As children's literature and reader response blend through the strong philosophy of literature-based teaching, children appreciate quality literature, express unique response to the books they read, and build a foundation for a lifetime of quality reading. These scenarios are indicative of the quality teaching and learning occurring in schools across the nation when literature, teaching, and reader response blend in a unified philosophy. These classrooms can serve as models for your own teaching environment in which a constant flow of quality literature, a variety of reader response options, and a teaching philosophy supporting literature blend into effective practice supporting the goal of creating lifelong readers.

CLOSING THOUGHTS

The blending of quality children's literature, eager readers, and response to literature as part of a balanced literacy program results in rich engagement in the act of reading. Children's literature comes to life only when books and readers interact. This textbook celebrates both the wonder of children's literature and the empowerment of individual readers as they relate to the interconnections of children's literature, aesthetic teaching, and reader response. Connecting literature and reader response becomes the basis of literacy instruction both within and beyond the school. To gain a clearer understanding of the links between children's literature, teaching, and reader response, you are enthusiastically invited to do the following:

- Seek out and respond to the quality children's literature presented between the covers of this text.
- Apply the connected response-based activities in a classroom setting, either at the elementary/middle level with children or in the college classroom.
- Explore and observe the full spectrum of response options across literary genres and curricular content areas.

The teacher who possesses and implements a response-based, literature-focused philosophy of teaching serves as a catalyst for authentic reader response and the creation of lifelong readers. You are invited to anticipate the continuing celebration of children's literature and reader response as they gently weave their way through the succeeding chapters of this text and into your teaching philosophy and current or future literature-based classroom.

References

Applebee, A. (1978). *The child's concept of story: Ages two to seventeen*. Chicago: University of Chicago Press.

Ayra, P., Martens, P., Wilson, G. P., Altwerger, B., Jin, L., Laser, B., & Lang, D. (2005). Reclaiming literacy instruction: Evidence in support of literature-based programs. *Language Arts, 83*, 63–72.

Bishop, R. S. (2000). Why literature? *The New Advocate, 13*, 73–76.

Clay, M. M. (1979). *Reading: The patterning of complex behavior* (2nd ed.). Auckland, New Zealand: Heinemann.

Cullinan, B. E. (1992). Whole language and children's literature. *Language Arts, 69*, 426–430.

Durkin, D. (1966). *Children who read early*. New York: Teachers College Press.

Durkin, D. (1974). A six-year study of children who learned to read in school at the age of four. *Reading Research Quarterly, 10*, 9–61.

Eckhoff, B. (1983). How reading affects children's writing. *Language Arts, 60*, 607–616.

Edmunds, K. M., & Rauserman, K. L. (2006). What teachers can learn about reading motivation through conversations with children. *The Reading Teacher, 59*, 414–424.

Faust, M. A., & Glenzer, N. (2000). "I could read those parts over and over:" Eighth graders rereading to enhance enjoyment and learning with literature. *Journal of Adolescent & Adult Literacy, 44*, 234–239.

Galda, L. (1988). Readers, texts, and contexts: A response-based view of literature in the classroom. *The New Advocate, 1*, 92–102.

Galda, L. (2001). High stakes reading: Articulating the place of children's literature in the curriculum. *The New Advocate, 14*, 223–228.

Galda, L., & Cullinan, B. E. (2003). Literature for literacy: What research says about the benefits of using trade books in the classroom. In J. Flood, J. M. Jensen, D. Lapp, & J. Squire (Eds.), *Handbook of research on teaching the English language arts* (pp. 529–535). New York: Macmillan.

Galda, L., & Liang, L. M. (2003). Literature as experience or looking for facts: Stance in the classroom. *Reading Research Quarterly, 38*, 268–275.

Hancock, M. R. (2000). The survival of the book in a megabyte world: Children's literature in the new millennium. *Journal of Children's Literature, 26*, 8–17.

Hancock, M. R. (2007). *Language arts: Extending the possibilities*. Upper Saddle River, NJ: Merrill/Prentice Hall.

Hansen, J. (2001). *When writers read*. Portsmouth, NH: Heinemann. (Original work published 1987)

Harste, J., Woodward, V., & Burke, C. (1984). *Language stories and literacy lessons*. Portsmouth, NH: Heinemann.

Hepler, S. (1982). *Patterns of response to literature: A one-year study of a fifth- and sixth-grade classroom*. Unpublished doctoral dissertation, Ohio State University.

Hickman, J. (1981). A new perspective on response to literature: Research in a classroom setting. *Research in the Teaching of English, 15*, 343–354.

Lamme, L. (1985). *Growing up reading*. Washington, DC: Acropolis Books.

McGee, L. M. (1992). Focus on research: Exploring the literature-based reading revolution. *Language Arts, 69*, 529–537.

Mendoza, A. (1985). Reading to children: Their preferences. *The Reading Teacher, 38*, 522–527.

Pardo, L. S. (2004). What every teacher needs to know about comprehension. *The Reading Teacher, 58,* 272–280.

Probst, R. (2000). Literature as invitation. *Voices from the Middle, 8,* 8–15.

Roser, N. L. (2001). A place for everything and literature in its place. *The New Advocate, 14,* 211–221.

Serafini, F. (2004). Images of reading and the reader. *The Reading Teacher, 57,* 610–617.

Short, K. G. (1993). Making connections across literature and life. In K. E. Holland, R. A. Hungerford, & S. B. Ernst (Eds.), *Journeying: Children responding to literature* (pp. 284–301). Portsmouth, NH: Heinemann.

Spencer, M. M. (2003). What more needs saying about imagination? *Reading Research Quarterly, 38,* 546–551.

Spiegel, D. L. (1998). Reader response approaches and the growth of readers. *Language Arts, 76,* 41–48.

Teale, W. H., & Sulzby, E. (1986). *Emergent literacy: Reading and writing.* Norwood, NJ: Ablex.

Tunnell, M. O., & Jacobs, J. S. (1989). Using "real" books: Research findings on literature-based reading instruction. *The Reading Teacher, 42,* 470–477.

Vardell, S. M. (2003). Using read-aloud to explore the layers of nonfiction. In R. Bamford & J. Kristo (Eds.), *Making facts come alive: Choosing quality nonfiction literature K–8* (2nd ed., pp. 151–167). Norwood, MA: Christopher-Gordon.

Wells, G. (1986). *The meaning makers: Children learning language and using language to learn.* Portsmouth, NH: Heinemann.

Yolen, J. (1985). The story between. *Language Arts, 62,* 590–592.

Children's Books Cited [P] = K–2; [I] = 3–5; [M] = 6–8

Adler, David (2005). *Joe Lewis: America's fighter.* Illus. by Terry Widener. San Diego: Harcourt. [P/I]

Avi (2002). *Crispin: The cross of lead.* New York: Hyperion. [I]

Babbitt, Natalie (1975). *Tuck everlasting.* New York: Farrar, Straus and Giroux. [I/M]

Banks, Kate (2002). *Close your eyes.* Illus. by Georg Hallenslebin. New York: Farrar, Straus & Giroux. [P]

Bartone, Elisa (1993). *Peppe the lamplighter.* Illus. by Ted Lewin. New York: Lothrop, Lee & Shepard. [P/I]

Boulton, Jane (Adapter) (1994). *Only Opal: The diary of a young girl.* Illus. by Barbara Cooney. New York: Philomel. [I]

Brett, Jan (1987). *Goldilocks and the three bears.* New York: Putnam. [P]

Brett, Jan (1989). *The mitten.* New York: Putnam. [P]

Brett, Jan (1990). *The wild Christmas reindeer.* New York: Putnam. [P]

Brett, Jan (1991). *Berlioz the bear.* New York: Putnam. [P]

Brett, Jan (1991). *The owl and the pussycat.* (by Edward Lear) New York: Putnam. [P]

Brown, Margaret W. (1947). *Goodnight moon.* Illus. by Clement Hurd. New York: Harper & Row. [P]

Christelow, Eileen (1989). *Five little monkeys jumping on the bed.* New York: Clarion. [P]

Dahl, Roald (1961). *James and the giant peach.* Illus. by Nancy E. Burkert. New York: Knopf. [I]

Desnoettes, Caroline (2006). *Look closer: Art masterpieces through the ages.* New York: Bloomsbury. [P/I]

Di Camillo, Kate (2000). *Because of Winn-Dixie.* Cambridge, MA: Candlewick. [I]

Di Camillo, Kate (2003). *The tale of Despereaux: Being the story of a mouse, a princess, some soup, and a spool of thread.* Illus, by Timothy Basil Ering. Cambridge, MA: Candlewick. [P/I]

Fox, Paula (1991). *Monkey island.* New York: Orchard. [I]

Freedman, Russell (2004). *The voice that challenged a nation: Marian Anderson and the struggle for equal rights.* New York: Clarion. [M]

Giff, Patricia Reilly (2002). *Pictures of Hollis Woods*. New York: Wendy Lamb/Random House. [I]

Giovanni, Nikki (2005). *Rosa*. Illus. by Bryan Collier. New York: Henry Holt. [P/I]

Hamilton, Virginia (1993). *Many thousand gone: African Americans from slavery to freedom*. Illus. by Leo and Diane Dillon. New York: Knopf. [I/M]

Henkes, Kevin (2004). *Kitten's first full moon*. New York: Greenwillow. [P]

Holm, Jennifer (2006). *Penny from heaven*. New York: Random House. [I]

Holman, Felice (1974). *Slake's limbo*. New York: Scribner's. [I]

Hopkinson, Deborah (2002). *Under the quilt of night*. New York: Atheneum. [I]

Kellogg, Steven (1997). *The three little pigs*. New York: Morrow. [P/I]

Lewis, C. S. (1961). *The lion, the witch, and the wardrobe*. New York: Macmillan. [I]

Livingston, Myra Cohn (1982). *A circle of seasons*. Illus. by Leonard Everett Fisher. New York: Holiday House. [P/I]

Macauley, David (1977). *Castle*. Boston: Houghton Mifflin. [I/M]

McClafferty, Carla Killough (2006). *Something out of nothing: Marie Curie and radium*. New York: Farrar Straus Giroux. [I/M]

McCloskey, Robert (1941). *Make way for ducklings*. New York: Viking. [P]

McLimans, David (2006). *Gone wild: An endangered animal alphabet*. New York: Walker. [I/M]

Montgomery, Sy (2006). *Quest for the tree kangaroo: An expedition to the Cloud Forest of New Guinea*. Photographs by Nic Bishop. Boston: Houghton Mifflin. [I/M]

Moses, Sheila P. (2006). *The return of Buddy Bush*. New York: McElderry. [I/M]

Murphy, Jim (2002). *An American plague: The true and terrifying story of the yellow fever epidemic of 1793*. New York: Clarion. [I/M]

Paulsen, Gary (1996). *Brian's winter*. New York: Delacorte. [I]

Rohmann, Eric (1994). *Time flies*. New York: Crown. [P/I]

Rosen, Michael (2006). *Totally wonderful Miss Plumberry*. Illus. by C. Lee. Cambridge, MA: Candlewick. [P]

Ruckman, Ivy (1984). *Night of the twisters*. New York: Crowell. [I]

Sanderson, Ruth (2002). *Cinderella*. New York: Little, Brown. [P/I]

Warner, Gertrude Chandler (1942). *The boxcar children*. Morton Grove, IL: Albert Whitman. [P/I]

White, E. B. (1952). *Charlotte's web*. New York: Harper & Row. [P/I]

Wilder, Laura I. (1932/1953). *Little house in the big woods*. New York: Harper & Row. [P/I]

Yolen, Jane (1992). *Letting swift river go*. Illus. by Barbara Cooney. Boston: Little, Brown. [P/I]

Zelinsky, Paul (1997). *Rapunzel*. New York: Dial. [I]

PART II

Celebrating Literature

The wonder and enjoyment of children's literature reside in the variety of ways in which books convey a story. Some stories emerge from the realm of make-believe; others ground themselves in the reality of everyday life. As some tales unfold through the art of the storyteller, others relate information in descriptive ways. Some stories share the lives of real people; other books build on the delight of words and rhyme. It is this variety that helps literature reach every reader with satisfaction. At the same time, it is this variety that creates a need for advocates of children's literature to organize literature using a common scheme as a basis for literary discussion.

To categorize and discuss efficiently the large number of children's books in print today, literary genres serve as a framework and an organizational scheme for classifying children's literature. Books that have a great deal in common with each other are placed in a literary genre according to similar traits. When books with these similar literary characteristics form a group, that group is called a literary genre (Darigan, Tunnell, & Jacobs, 2002).

Differentiation often begins with the two formats of a book: picture books or chapter books. Picture books (Chapter 3) are particularly distinguished because of their blend of art and text. They can contain stories from any genre. Literary genres are the organizational scheme for discussion in this part. They include traditional tales and modern fantasy (Chapter 4), poetry (Chapter 5), realistic and historical fiction (Chapter 6), and biography and informational books (Chapter 7). In addition, multicultural literature and international literature that flow across each genre are discussed in Chapter 8.

To celebrate the variety of children's literature, the next six chapters showcase picture books, the seven literary genres for children, and multicultural/international literature. The discussion for each genre defines it, lists characteristics of the genre, denotes categories of books within the genre, and discusses the benefits of the genre as part of a well-rounded literacy program. Reader response connections to each genre are summarized after each genre is presented. For extensive connections, see Part III of this text.

The literary genre approach to presenting literature provides the most consistent organizational scheme used when studying or discussing children's literature (Pavonetti, 1997). Although an issues approach or an inquiry approach to children's literature may be used, a general knowledge of literary genres supports practitioners who surround their students with a blend of high-quality books from the entire literary realm.

Darigan, D. L., Tunnell, M. O., & Jacobs, J. S. (2002). *Children's literature: Engaging teachers and children in good books.* Upper Saddle River, NJ: Merrill/Prentice Hall.

Pavonetti, L. (1997). Conversations among colleagues: A master class in teaching children's literature. *Journal of Children's Literature, 23,* 66–69.

CHAPTER 3

The Art of the Picture Book
Blending Illustration and Text

"You have two 'hello-goodbye' windows at your house, Grandma. One is on the front porch. You know . . . sometimes I hide and ring the doorbell and you have to look out the window to see who it is. Then, when I leave, you stand by the window as we pull down the driveway and say goodbye by waving. The second window is in the kitchen—the doors out to the patio. You can watch me play basketball or soccer while you cook dinner. I look inside once in a while to see what you are cooking. In fact, we eat dinner at the kitchen table just like they do in the story. If I stay overnight, I can see my reflection in the windows, just like the girl in the story.

I like the big pictures filled with color. They seem so real even if the colors spread over the lines. That's how I color! My favorite pages are the two that show the night sky with all the stars. They remind me of sitting on your front porch watching the fireworks on the Fourth of July."

Seven-year-old's oral response to *The Hello, Goodbye Window* by Norton Jester, Illustrated by Chris Raschka (2006 Caldecott Medal Award)

The picture book is a celebration of both text and art. The words that tell a story enhanced by artful illustrations blend into a magical experience (Hoppe, 2004). Kevin Henkes, the May Hill Arbuthnot Honor Lecturer for 2007, author/illustrator of *Kitten's First Full Moon* (2005 Caldecott Award), *Chrysanthemum, Lilly's Purple Plastic Purse,* and *Lilly's Big Day,* celebrates the wonder of the picture book format for children's literature.

> The great thing about a successful picture book is you can't have great illustrations without a great text, and you can't have a great text without great illustrations. . . . The art form of the picture book is, in fact, all thirty-two pages—pictures and words—working together. (Henkes, 1992, p. 39)

In this chapter, the term *picture book* is used as an umbrella term to denote the broad group of books containing illustrations and, in most cases, words. Its broad terminology includes baby/board books, ABC books, engineered books, counting books, concept books, wordless books, picture storybooks, and transitional books (Lynch-Brown & Tomlinson, 2002). The term *picture storybook,* however, is a more specific term and used in this text to refer to books that primarily convey stories through both the art of illustrating and the art of writing. Picture storybooks span several genres and appeal to readers of all ages. Most picture books published are picture storybooks so the blending of language and art is showcased during this chapter discussion. Distinguishing between the two terms becomes more significant as one becomes more acquainted with children's literature.

This chapter begins a celebration of children's literature by focusing on the popular picture book format. The picture book houses well-composed text and exceptional artwork across all literary genres. From Lisa Cline-Ransome's *Quilt Alphabet* (ABC) to Eric Kimmel's *Anansi and the Magic Stick* (traditional tale), from Lynn Curlee's *Seven Wonders of the Ancient World* (informational) to Douglas Florian's *Mammalabilia* (poetry), picture books thrive on the harmonizing of energetic text and imaginative art into this creative, cherished format. Picture books also address the art of visual literacy and its potential to assist with comprehension and aesthetic understanding (Kiefer, 1995).

The Caldecott Medal, named in honor of the nineteenth-century English illustrator Randolph Caldecott, is awarded each year to the artist of the most distinguished American picture book for children. Artists such as Chris Raschka, Kevin Henkes, Mordecai Gerstein, Eric Rohmann, David Weisner, David Small, Mary Azarian, Paul Zelinsky, David Wisniewski, and Emily Arnold McCully have won this prestigious award for illustration. The appendix contains a list of these winning illustrators and their books. Several honored award-winning books are mentioned throughout this chapter.

Besides highlighting quality picture books, this chapter includes discussions of the role of picture books in visual literacy; types of picture books available for reader enjoyment, delight, and response; the impression and importance of book design; art media, graphic techniques, and artistic style; the power of illustration to blend with well-written text to tell a story; and evaluative criteria for and potential response for picture books This chapter also serves as background for a study of the literary genres

(Chapters 4 through 7) and multicultural/international literature (Chapter 8), which use the picture book as well as the chapter book formats to share both narrative and expository writing.

THE PICTURE BOOK AND VISUAL LITERACY

Children today grow up in a visual world surrounded by a barrage of images on computer monitors, across Internet sites, on television and movie screens, and throughout their environment. The term *visual literacy* implies a level of discrimination that can sort through this constant deluge of visual images in an attempt to develop a personal sense of discretionary viewing and judgment. The illustrations in picture books naturally invite active participation in viewing. With the abundance of picture books available to children at home, school, bookstores, and libraries, it becomes increasingly important for children to develop a sense for judging quality and establishing personal taste in book illustration.

Many adults actually believe that children's books are "wasted" on children. Teacher comments on recent Caldecott award-winning illustrations including Paul Zelinsky's *Rapunzel* and David Wisniewski's *Golem* have been directed at their "lack of appeal" to children. Yet children tend to be more attuned to detail and more aware of their perceptions than adults give them credit. Jacobs and Tunnell (1996) believe that as readers get older they tend to be "dulled by overload or by the real and imagined expectations our educational system have imposed on us which alter the way we view images" (p. 34). Children often learn to ignore their own personal reactions and the details in illustrations to fulfill narrowly focused views of learning. In becoming less aware, they become less sensitive to the differences in the art of the picture book and less discriminating in the process of developing personal tastes.

In *The Potential of Picture Books,* Barbara Kiefer (1995) describes visual literacy for children as the ability to "discriminate and interpret what they see. This process involves their attention, their recognition, and finally their understanding" (p. 8). Teachers, parents, and librarians play a crucial role in helping children develop the ability to "see" through picture book illustrations. By enriching discriminatory abilities and encouraging the development of personal taste in visual imagery in picture books, children can attain independence of expression and response. To accomplish this, however, teachers must learn more about children's book illustrations, including style, medium, and design as well as more about the illustrators themselves. Enhancing visual literacy through picture books begins with a fresh view of illustrations through a child's eyes.

Picture books possess the potential for children to become discriminators of personal tastes in art. If all they view are cartoons, all they will appreciate are cartoon-like drawings. If, however, a knowledgeable, open-minded teacher, parent, or librarian attends to the choices, comments, and exuberance they exhibit toward a variety of illustrations, individual tastes can be cultivated. Teachers have long recognized the potential of picture books to develop reading and writing literacy. Now picture books stand poised to elicit the intellectual and emotional response of children to art. Picture books provide an exceptional means of cultivating visual literacy and artistic

Literary Legend

Picture Book Author/Illustrator

When it came to creating picture books, no amount of research was too much for **Robert McCloskey** (1914–2003). In creating his Caldecott Award–winning *Make Way for Ducklings,* McCloskey lived with 16 ducks in his New York City apartment to assure that his illustrations would accurately capture the movement and the spirit of real ducks. In treating picture books as a serious art like any other, McCloskey opened the door to this exciting medium for countless other serious artists and storytellers. Born in Hamilton, Ohio, McCloskey would use his childhood years as the setting for his first picture book *Lentil.* Starting out during the years of the Great Depression as an aspiring painter of everyday American life, McCloskey welcomed picture books as an opportunity to find an audience for his artwork and to express his knack for storytelling. Readers are pulled into his books by the engaging illustrations, but the good-natured stories keep them coming back.

From his utterly plausible and lifelike ducks and bears, to colorful Maine landscapes, to Jackson Pollock–like experiments using the inside of a whale's belly as the canvas, McCloskey always managed to merge a child's wondrous outlook with the discipline and dedication required for successful artistic endeavor. Just as Robert McCloskey's influence on picture books is lasting, his unforgettable ducklings have gained permanence as bronze sculptures in public parks in both Boston and Moscow. In creating his classic picture books, this small-town Ohio boy made an impact still felt around the world.

(1940). *Lentil*. New York: Viking Press.

(1942). *Make way for ducklings*. New York: Viking Press.

(1943). *Homer Price*. New York: Viking Press.

(1949). *Blueberries for Sal*. New York: Viking Press.

(1951). *The Centerburg tales*. New York: Viking Press.

(1953). *One morning in Maine*. New York: Viking Press.

(1958). *Time of wonder*. New York: Viking Press.

(1963). *Burt Dow, deep water man*. New York: Viking Press.

appreciation in an increasingly visual world. This chapter strives to share more about the art of the picture book with those who choose to work with children so their own visual literacy, as well as that of their students, can be extended through better informed picture book experiences.

TYPES OF PICTURE BOOKS

The picture book format includes many different types of books that appeal to the very young, to emergent readers, to older readers, and even to adults. Defining and discussing these books in sequence by age of reader to which they appeal emphasizes the breadth of the picture book format and the size of its audience, and it allows discovery of and distinguishing among the wide range of categories of picture books.

Baby/Board Books

First books for babies receive increasing importance as continuing research points out connections between early reading to children and later academic success (Teale, 1986). These books are manufactured of thick cardboard, plastic, or cloth to withstand the wear and tear of eager hands. Many classic titles have taken on the board book format as the quality and popularity of these books have increased. Titles currently in board book format include Leo Lionni's *Let's Play* and Byron Barton's *My Car.* They serve as important lap-sitting experiences as young hands begin to turn the pages, eager fingers point to bright colors, and a sense of story begins to take hold. Independent exploration with these books fulfills a need for a young child to discover the world of books. Response is typically in the form of physical book exploration tempered by spontaneous sounds of delight from the youngest bibliophiles. Quality baby/board books emphasize patterns or familiar associations to encourage verbal interaction between an adult and a child. Figure 3.1 lists just a sampling of colorful, sturdy titles available for the very young.

Mother Goose and Nursery Rhymes

The rhythm, rhyme, and predictability of Mother Goose and traditional nursery rhymes explain why these remain an appealing type of picture book for young children. Mother Goose books are often read over and over again as children begin to value and appreciate the sound of language. These books serve as outstanding language models for children as they begin to experiment with language by attempting to repeat the well-loved rhymes. The illustrations in these books often have strong appeal to young children as characters like Old King Cole, Little Boy Blue, and Peter, Peter Pumpkin Eater come to life on the page. New, colorful editions of Mother Goose rhymes continue to be published, such as Jane Yolen's *This Little Piggy and Other Rhymes to Sing and Play* and Jane Chapman's *Sing a Song of Sixpence*, but some of the classic editions bring the same exuberant response from children. Arnold Lobel's *Book of Mother Goose* (1997), for example, is a reissue of a popular 1986 title by Random House. Response is typically in the form of language repetition and physical delight (smiles, clapping, pointing) as children begin to recognize familiar characters and related language as valued friends. The best collections include a wide variety of rhymes thematically organized for sharing and indexed by both titles and first lines. Figure 3.1 lists additional versions of these rhyming traditions.

Engineered/Participation Books

Pop-up books, flap books, and toy books are included in the engineered or participation book category. Like board books, these books beg active involvement. The difference is that they are usually delicately produced and require special care. These are likely to appeal to grandparents as much as children but often are intricate enough to discourage child engagement. *Cookie Count: A Tasty Pop-Up* by Robert Sabuda incorporates

FIGURE 3.1 Book Cluster: Books for the very young

First Books [All P]

Barton, Byron (2001). *My car.* New York: Greenwillow.

Brown, Marc Tolan (1998). *Marc Brown's favorite finger rhymes.* New York: Dutton. (Board book)

Brown, Margaret Wise (2002). *Give yourself to the rain: Poems for the very young.* Illus. by Terri Weidner. New York: Simon & Schuster.

Brown, Margaret Wise (2002). *My world of color.* Illus. by Loretta Krupinski. New York: Hyperion.

Carle, Eric (1999). *The very clumsy click beetle.* New York: Philomel.

Henkes, Kevin (2004). *Lilly's chocolate heart.* New York: Greenwillow. (Board book)

Hoban, Tana (1993). *Black on white.* New York: Greenwillow. (Board book)

Hopkins, Lee Bennett (Ed.) (1998). *Climb into my lap: First poems to read together.* Illus. by Kathryn Brown. New York: Simon & Schuster.

Hurd, Thatcher (1998). *Zoom city.* New York: HarperCollins. (Board book)

Jenkins, Emily (2006). *Hug, hug, hug!* Illus. by Tomek Bogacki. New York: Farrar. (Board book)

Liao, Jimmy (2006). *The sounds of color: A journey of the imagination.* New York: Little, Brown.

Martin, Bill Jr., & Archambault, John (1993). *Chicka Chicka ABC.* Illus. by Lois Ehlert. New York: Simon & Schuster. (Board book)

Oxenbury, Helen (1995). *I see.* Cambridge, MA: Candlewick Press. (Board book)

Rathmann, Peggy (1997). *Goodnight gorilla.* New York: Putnam. (Board book)

Rockwell, Anne (1999). *Bumblebee, bumblebee, do you know me?* New York: HarperCollins.

Ryder, Joanne (2002). *Big bear ball.* Illus. by Steven Kellogg. New York: HarperCollins.

Rylant, Cynthia (2001). *Good morning, sweetie pie and other poems for little children.* Illus. by Jane Dyer. New York: Simon & Schuster.

Shannon, David (2002). *Duck on a bike.* New York: Blue Sky/Scholastic.

Simmons, Jane (2002). *Quack, Daisy, QUACK!* Boston: Little, Brown.

Siomades, Lorianne (2001). *The itsy bitsy spider.* Honesdale, PA: Boyds Mills. (Board book)

Wells, Rosemary (1997/1973). *Noisy Nora.* New York: Dial.

Wells, Rosemary (1998). *Max's breakfast.* New York: Dial. (Board book); see also *Max's bath, Max's bedtime, Max's birthday, Max's first word, Max's new suit, Max's ride,* and *Max's toys.*

Yolen, Jane (2000). *How do dinosaurs say goodnight?* Illus. by Mark Teague. New York: Blue Sky/Scholastic.

Yolen, Jane (2000). *Off we go!* Illus. by Lauren Molk. New York: Little, Brown.

Yolen, Jane (2003). *How do dinosaurs get well soon?* Illus. by Mark Teague. New York: Scholastic. (Board book)

Yorinks, Arthur (1996). *Frank and Joey eat lunch.* Illus. by Maurice Sendak. New York: HarperCollins. (Board book)

Zemach, Margot (2001). *Some from the moon, some from the sun: Poems and songs for everyone.* New York: Farrar, Straus and Giroux.

Mother Goose and Nursery Rhymes [All P]

Ada, Alma Flor, & Campoy, F. Isabel (2003). *¡Pio peep! Traditional Spanish nursery rhymes.* English adaptations by Alice Schertle. Illus. by Vivi Escriva. New York: HarperCollins.

Cabrera, Jane (2001). *Old Mother Hubbard.* Illus. by Sarah Catherine Martin. New York: Holiday House.

Chapman, Jane (2004). *Sing a song of sixpence: A pocketful of nursery rhymes and tales.* Cambridge, MA: Candlewick.

FIGURE 3.1 Continued

Dyer, Jane (1996). *Animal crackers: A delectable collection of pictures, poems, and lullabies for the very young.* Boston: Little, Brown.

Grey, Mini (2006). *The adventures of the dish and the spoon.* New York: Knopf.

Lobel, Arnold (1997). *The Arnold Lobel book of Mother Goose.* New York: Knopf/Random House. (Former title: *Random House book of Mother Goose*)

Opie, Iona A. (1996). *My very first Mother Goose.* Illus. by Rosemary Wells. Cambridge, MA: Candlewick Press.

Opie, Iona (Ed.) (1999). *Here comes Mother Goose.* Illus. by Rosemary Wells. Cambridge, MA: Candlewick Press.

Pinkney, Brian (Adapter) (2006). *Hush, little baby.* New York: Amistad/Greenwillow.

Stevens, Janet, & Crummel, Susan (2001). *And the dish ran away with the spoon.* Illus. by Janet Stevens. San Diego: Harcourt.

Wells, Rosemary (2004). *My kindergarten.* New York: Hyperion.

Yaccarino, Dan (2003). *Dan Yaccarino's Mother Goose.* New York: Random House.

Yolen, Jane (Ed.) (2006). *This little piggy.* Illus. by Will Hillenbrand. Musical arrangements by Adam Stemple. Cambridge, MA: Candlewick.

artistic cutouts and pop-ups of a bounty of sweets created through intricate paper engineering. Jan Pienkowski's *Pizza!* contains flaps to open and tabs to pull in an amazing movable feast. These books provide see-through, changeable, dimensional, movable illustrations with which a child may interact.

Books that beg to be shared with children and invite active involvement with the book itself fit the category of participation books. Participation books engage readers in tracing shapes with their fingers, sliding pages to uncover colorful images, or lifting flaps to reveal instant surprises. Titles that are meant for exploration by young children include Eric Carle's insect quartet (*The Very Hungry Caterpillar, The Very Quiet Cricket, The Very Busy Spider, The Very Lonely Firefly*) and Lois Ehlert's *Hands.* For older children, books like Robert Sabuda and Matthew Reinhart's *Encyclopedia Prehistorica: Sharks and Other Sea Monsters* and Kyle Olmon and Tracy Sabin's *Castle: Medieval Days and Knights* offer hours of enjoyment and lots of information. By becoming actively involved with books, an eagerness for books and an interest in reading begin to evolve. Response exhibits itself through active engagement and the related early language and social talk that results from the interactive nature of parent–child participation with these books.

Alphabet Books

Although initially associated with young children, today's alphabet books have appeal across all age levels. Their unique designs and simple, effective text combine to teach far more content than the ABCs. Widely used as books in thematic explorations, they cover a wide variety of topics and transmit an extensive amount of information. In addition to illustrations and a consistent organizational pattern, alphabet books generally have a uniform short format. Those focused around a specific concept or theme can be characterized as informational.

Pictures, format, content, and text form the structure of an alphabet book. The illustrations are the inherent feature of these books as artists create intriguing and interesting visual displays built on single letters. David Pelletier's *The Graphic Alphabet,* for example, promotes visual inquiry by using graphic design to illustrate the letterform while retaining the natural shape of the letter as well as representing the meaning of the word. To accomplish this, snow rests on the peaks of an "M" for mountain, a sideways "D" resembles a devil, and a brilliant red "R" echoes a rip across the page, all showcased on a stark black background. Imaginations are ignited in Henry Horenstein's *A is for . . .?* as black-and-white close-up photography encourages children to predict the animal from the visual clue.

Most alphabet books have a predictable organizational manner, are concise, and rarely exceed a 26-letter presentation. Anita Lobel's *Away from Home* shares boys' names and exotic places in alliterative fashion just as *Allison's Zinnea* shares girls' names paired with exotic flowers. In many cases, the content extends beyond the features of letter identification, letter–sound correspondence, and object identification traditionally associated with these books. In *The Turn-Around, Upside-Down Alphabet Book* by Lisa Campbell Ernst, the emphasis is on the imaginative visual images created by each letter as the book is physically turned. The wide range of content complexity makes alphabet books usable with many age groups. Alphabet book text is typically written in poetic form, but narrative and expository text often appear in themed alphabet books. Beyond their traditional use with emergent and beginning readers, alphabet books provide valuable information to readers of all ages. Chaney (1993) suggests alphabet books can provide students with:

1. An introduction to or an overview of a theme exploration (Chris Demarest's *Firefighters A to Z*)
2. A stimulus for further research (Lynn Cheney's *America: A Patriotic Primer*)
3. Oral and written language development (Bill Martin and John Archambault's *Chicka Chicka Boom Boom*)
4. Multicultural awareness (Virginia Stroud's *The Path of the Quiet Elk: A Native American Alphabet Book*)

Whereas young children tend to respond to alphabet books through their predictable nature as in George Shannon's *Tomorrow's Alphabet* or through ties to phonemic awareness as in Peter Catalanatto's *Matthew A. B. C.,* response from older children is often in the form of inquiry piqued by oral comments on visual or textual representations. In selecting an ABC book, consider the appropriateness of the theme, print, and presentation style for the developmental level of the child. Figure 3.2 represents a cross-section of alphabet books for all ages and on all topics.

Counting/Number Books

In their simplest form, counting books present material in a predictable, sequenced format that appeals to the young child. Numbers and/or number words are teamed with illustrations or photographs of correctly numbered objects. Christopher Wormell's

FIGURE 3.2   Book Cluster: Alphabet books [all P/I]

Aylesworth, Jim (1992). *Old black fly.* Illus. by S. Gammel. New York: Holt.
Azarian, Mary (2000). *A gardener's alphabet.* Boston: Houghton Mifflin.
Barron, Rex (2000). *Fed up! A feast of frazzled foods.* New York: Putnam.
Cox, Paul (2001). *Abstract alphabet: A book of animals.* San Francisco: Chronicle.
Darling, Kathy (1996). *Amazon ABC.* New York: Lothrop, Lee & Shepard.
Demarest, Chris (2005). *Alpha Bravo Charlie: The military alphabet.* New York: McElderry.
Ernst, Lisa Campbell (1996). *The letters are lost.* New York: Viking.
Ernst, Lisa Campbell (2004). *The turn-around, upside-down alphabet book.* New York: Simon & Schuster.
Fleming, Denise (2002). *Alphabet under construction.* New York: Henry Holt.
Floca, Brian (2003). *The racecar alphabet.* New York: Atheneum.
Horenstein, Henry (1999). *Arf! Beg! Catch! Dogs from A to Z.* New York: Cartwheel/Scholastic.
Hepworth, Catherine (1992). *ANTics!: An alphabet anthology.* New York: Putnam.
Hyman, Trina Schart (1980/2000). *The alphabet game.* New York: SeaStar.
Inkpen, Mick (2001). *Kippers A to Z: An alphabet adventure.* San Diego: Harcourt Brace.
Isadora, Rachel (1999). *A B C pop.* New York: Viking.
Jonas, Ann (1990). *Aardvarks, disembark!* New York: Greenwillow.
Lear, Edward (1999). *An Edward Lear alphabet.* Illus. by Vladimir Radunsky. New York: HarperCollins.
Lear, Edward (2005/1871). *A was once an apple pie.* Illus. by Suse McDonald. New York: Orchard.
Lester, Mike (2000). *A is for salad.* New York: Putnam.
Lobel, Anita (1990). *Allison's zinnea.* New York: Greenwillow.
Lobel, Anita (1994). *Away from home.* New York: Greenwillow.
MacDonald, Ross (2003). *Achoo! Bang! Crash! The noisy alphabet.* New York: Roaring Brook.
Markle, Sandra (1998). *Gone forever!: An alphabet of extinct animals.* New York: Atheneum.
Martin, Bill Jr., & Archambault, John (1989). *Chicka chicka boom boom.* Illus. by Lois Ehlert. New York: Simon & Schuster.
McDonell, Flora (1997). *Flora McDonell's ABC.* Cambridge, MA: Candlewick Press.
Metropolitan Museum of Art (2002). *Museum ABC.* Boston: Little, Brown.
Palotta, Jerry (2004). *The beetle alphabet book.* Watertown, MA: Charlesbridge.
Paul, Ann Whitford (1991). *Eight hands round: A patchwork alphabet.* Illus. by Jeannette Winter. New York: HarperCollins.
Pelletier, David (1996). *The graphic alphabet.* New York: Orchard Books.
Pinto, Sara (2003). *The alphabet room.* New York: Bloomsbury USA.
Rose, Deborah Lee (2000). *Into the A, B, sea: An ocean alphabet.* Illus. by Steve Jenkins. New York: Scholastic.
Shannon, George (1996). *Tomorrow's alphabet.* Illus. by Donald Crews. New York: Greenwillow.
Slate, Joseph (1996). *Miss Bindergarten gets ready for kindergarten.* New York: Dutton.
Slate, Joseph (2001). *Miss Bindergarten takes a field trip with kindergarten.* Illus. by Ashley Wolff. New York: Dutton.
Stroud, Virginia (1996). *The path of the quiet elk: A Native American alphabet book.* New York: Dial.
Viorst, Judith (1994). *The alphabet from Z to A (with much confusion on the way).* Illus. by Richard Hull. New York: Atheneum.
Wells, Rosemary (2006). *Max's ABC.* New York: Viking.
Wells, Ruth (1992). *A to Zen: A book of Japanese culture.* Illus. by Yoshi. Saxonville, MA: Picture Book Studio.
Wildsmith, Brian (1962). *Brian Wildsmith's ABC.* New York: FranklinWatts.
Yorinks, Arthur (1999). *The alphabet atlas.* Illus. by Adrienne Yorinks and Jeanyee Wong. New York: Winslow.

Teeth, Tales, and Tentacles introduces numbers via animal characteristics through colorful woodblock prints. The response to these books includes counting aloud, pointing to objects, and making number–print associations. Quality oral language results from the interactive nature of the counting book.

Although this type of picture book was traditionally associated with young children, it, too, like the alphabet book, has stretched its use to older children as well through expanded mathematical concepts. Loreen Leedy's *Follow the Money* invites the reader on the journey of a quarter from the bank through a series of daily transactions. David Schwartz's *If You Hopped Like a Frog* provides thought-provoking comparisons if humans had the physical capabilities of animals. Steve Jenkins's *Actual Size* and *Prehistoric Actual Size* provide concepts of authentic size of today's wildlife and prehistoric dinosaurs.

An additional dimension to counting books includes picture storybooks that actually use numbers in a variety of ways to carry the plot. Jeanette Winter's *Josephina* portrays a Mexican artist who created her world *(un sol, dos angeles, tres casas)* through colorful clay images. Daniil Kharms's *First, Second* sequences its plot by ordinal number while prompting the reader to problem-solve along with the whimsical characters. The ending actually encourages written response by suggesting a sequel of a new series of adventures by the imaginative reader.

As literature has expanded beyond counting across curricular boundaries to mathematics, more books of this type have been published. Consider the appeal of the theme and the simplicity or complexity of the mathematical concept in selecting these books for children. Figure 3.3 represents a sample of some of these beginning and early math concept titles.

Concept Books

As curiosity and wonder fill the eyes of young children and their unquenchable thirst for knowledge abounds, the inclusion of concept books in their reading repertoire can assist in creating a knowledge base of essential conceptual information that can be used to expand their understanding of their surroundings. Concept books share shapes, colors, sizes, and objects with children in creative picture book formats. Illustrations initiate natural interaction for child/parent/teacher.

The author/photographer Tana Hoban is synonymous with bold, clear concept books that teach children about common aspects of their world. In *Just Look,* children peer through open circles on black pages to identify objects and animals through close-up and wide-range photographs. Stephen Swinburne's challenge of *What's Opposite?* and Ed Emberly's striking black background and colored shapes on *The Wing on a Flea: A Book About Shapes* engage children in early book encounters while building the parental bond through the lap-reading experience. Lois Ehlert's *In My World* uses die-cut shapes to enumerate familiar items from the natural world (bugs, worms, frogs, leaves). The brief accompanying text provides both action and description while encouraging the child to predict before turning the page. The response to concept books results in a heightened interest and inquiry as exhibited by speculations and questions.

FIGURE 3.3 Book Cluster: Counting books [all P/early I]

Arnosky, Jim (1999). *Mouse numbers: A very first counting book*. New York: Clarion.

Baker, Keith (1999). *Quack and count*. San Diego: Harcourt Brace.

Bang, Molly (1997/1983). *Diez, Nueve, Ocho*. Trans. by Clarita Kohen. New York: Greenwillow.

Bloom, Valerie (1996). *Fruits: A Caribbean counting poem*. Illus. by David Axtell. New York: Holt.

Brooks, Alan (1996). *Frogs jump: A counting book*. Illus. by Steven Kellogg. New York: Scholastic.

Cronin, Doreen (2006). *Click, clack, splish, splash: A counting adventure*. Illus. by Betsy Lewin. New York: Atheneum.

Demarest, Chris (2002). *Smokejumpers one to ten*. New York: McElderry.

Donaldson, Julia (2006). *One Ted falls out of bed*. Illus. by Anna Currey. New York: Henry Holt.

Edwards, Pamela Duncan (2000). *ROAR! A noisy counting book*. Illus. by Harry Cole. New York: HarperCollins.

Falwell, Cathryn (2001). *Turtle splash! Countdown at the pond*. New York: Greenwillow.

Geisert, Arthur (1996). *Roman numerals I to MM*. Boston: Houghton Mifflin.

Grover, Max (1995). *Amazing & incredible counting stories! A number of tall tales*. San Diego: Harcourt Brace/Browndeer Press.

Grover, Max (1996). *Circles and squares everywhere!* San Diego: Browndeer/Harcourt Brace.

Haskins, Jim, & Benson, Kathleen (1996). *Count your way through Ireland*. Illus. by Beth Wright. Minneapolis, MN: Carolrhoda. (*Count your way* series includes Africa, Arab world, Brazil, Canada, China, France, Germany, Greece, India, Israel, Italy, Japan, Korea, Mexico, and Russia.)

Hoberman, Mary Ann (1997). *One of each*. Illus. by Marjorie Priceman. Boston: Little, Brown.

Hutchins, Pat (2000). *Ten red apples*. New York: Greenwillow.

Johnson, Stephen (1998). *City by numbers*. New York: Viking.

Kharms, Daniil (1996). *First, Second*. Trans. from the Russian by Richard Pevear. Illus. by Marc Rosenthal. New York: Farrar, Straus and Giroux.

Lobel, Anita (2000). *One lighthouse, one moon*. New York: Greenwillow.

Lyon, George Ella (1998). *Counting on the woods: A poem*. Photographs by Ann W. Olson. New York: DK Publishing.

Martin, Jr., Bill, & Sampson, Michael (2001). *Rock it, sock it, number line*. Illus. by Heather Cahoon. New York: Henry Holt.

Merriam, Eve (1993). *12 ways to get to 11*. Illus. by Bernie Karlin. New York: Simon & Schuster.

Millich, Zoran (2005). *City 1 2 3*. Tonawanda, NY: Kids Can Press.

Morales, Yuyi (2003). *Just a minute: A trickster tale and counting book*. San Francisco: Chronicle.

Moss, Lloyd (1995). *Zin! zin! zin!: A violin*. Illus. by Marjorie Priceman. New York: Simon & Schuster.

Nikola-Lisa, W. (1996). *One hole in the road*. Illus. by Dan Yaccarino. New York: Holt.

Pomeroy, Diana (1996). *One potato: A counting book of potato prints*. San Diego: Harcourt Brace.

Rankin, Laura (1998). *The handmade counting book*. New York: Dial.

Reiser, Lynn (2006). *Hardworking puppies*. San Diego: Harcourt.

Saul, Carol P. (1998). *Barn cat: A counting book*. Illus. by Mary Azarian. Boston: Little, Brown.

Sierra, Judy (1997). *Counting crocodiles*. Illus. by Will Hillenbrand. San Diego: Gulliver/Harcourt Brace.

Wells, Rosemary (2000). *Emily's first 100 days of school*. New York: Hyperion.

Winter, Jeanette (1996). *Josephina*. San Diego: Harcourt Brace.

Wormell, Christopher (2004). *Teeth, tales, and tentacles: An animal counting book*. Philadelphia: Running Press.

Wordless Picture Books

Picture books without words allow the illustrations to tell the story on their own. The words to the story and the voice of the storyteller lie in the viewer's mind or are manufactured orally in the discussion with an adult or peer participant. Wordless picture books provide an opportunity for children to use picture clues to create the story. The opportunities for language development are rich and varied as children attempt orally to impose their developing sense of story on the illustrations.

Visual "readers" may eloquently project their feelings for Barbara Lehman's *Museum Trip* and *The Red Book*, both of which invite verbal story to outstanding illustrations. Paul Fleischman's *Sidewalk Circus* also tells a story through pictures, leaving the articulation of the plot to the reader. Eric Rohmann's *Time Flies,* for older children, occurs in a natural history museum when dinosaurs seem to come to life as a bird enters their domain. David Wiesner's *Sector 7* depicts a class trip to the Empire State Building where a boy is befriended by a cloud who escorts him to a celestial cloud factory. Fantasy illustrations invite children to invent their own text. These books beg for spoken or unspoken words to accompany eloquent visual representations.

Responses to wordless picture books come in the form of oral stories to accompany the pictures. Young children's stories can be dictated to older students; older children might also write the text to share with their younger counterparts. Wordless books invite a language experience—oral or written—that reminds us that meaning resides within the illustrations in the intentional absence of the text. Emily Arnold McCully's *Four Hungry Kittens* and Jacqueline Preiss Weltzman's and Robin Preiss Glasser's *You Can't Take a Balloon into the Museum of Fine Art* both invite text in both simple and complex formats. Small in number but high in creative oral and written responses, these books supply the illustration yet rely on the reader's imagination for the story.

Picture Storybooks

The type of picture book generally associated with the term *picture book* is the picture storybook. The picture storybook shares a story with the reader through well-written text that is blended with effective illustrations. In contrast to a picture book, the continuity between the language and the illustrations takes on even more importance as pictures help tell the story, showing action, character expressions, well-defined settings, and plot development. The stories within the covers of a picture storybook can belong to almost any literary genre, including realistic fiction (Eve Bunting's *Smoky Nights*), historical fiction (Elizabeth Fitzgerald Howard's *Virgie Goes to School with Us Boys*), traditional tale (David Wiesner's *The Three Pigs*), modern fantasy (Paul Fleischman's *Westlandia*), biography (James Cross Giblin's *The Amazing Life of Benjamin Franklin*), and informational books (Judith St. George's *So You Want to Be President?*). Reader response to picture storybooks truly engages personal response modes as children react individually to the unfolding of spellbinding, humorous, or captivating stories. The majority of picture books published each year are picture storybooks, hence the tendency to simply refer to them as picture books. The term *picture storybook* as used in this text carries a stronger connotation regarding the blending of story and illustration, which places special demands on both the author and the artist.

My Great Aunt Arizona by Gloria Houston is a picture storybook that shares the life, love, and hugs of a special teacher. The story is told through pictures that brightly portray a one-room school, Aunt Arizona's braids wound round her head, and her precious hugs. The words are well chosen and arranged repetitively at times for special effect. It is the unraveling of the story enhanced by visual characterization that makes this a classic picture storybook. *The World's Greatest Elephant,* written by Ralph Helfer and illustrated by Ted Lewin, is another showcase for combining splendid words and vivid pictures based on a true story of the lifelong friendship between a boy and an elephant. The opening invitation to join this adventure is enhanced by single- and double-page art that takes the reader on many incredible adventures filled with danger and survival.

The picture storybook dominates the read-aloud selections in early elementary classrooms. They are the perfect length (5 to 10 minutes) for read-aloud time. Through the oral reading of picture storybooks, emergent readers develop a sense of story, an appreciation for language, and an awareness of illustrations as a support and a means to enhance the text. Picture storybooks abound on library and classroom shelves, making them choices for independent reading of familiar favorites as well as reading challenges for new selections. The perfect blend of illustrations and the language of story brings hours of enjoyment to the literacy classroom each day.

Picture Books for Older Readers

Although the picture book format has been linked to young children and emergent readers, some picture book titles are intended for older readers and even adults. Because picture books have typically been housed in elementary (K–5) libraries or in the juvenile collections of public libraries, these special creations are often lost to the very audience for whom they were intended. The use of picture books in middle-school (grades 6–8) classrooms is no longer shunned but encouraged because they provide a stimulus for older children to become more effective readers (Bainbridge & Pantaleo, 2001).

The *postmodern* picture book (Goldstone, 2004; Panteleo, 2004) is gradually gaining acceptance as a subgenre of the picture book with multiple story lines, narrators, and perspectives. Unexpected formats like David Macauley's *Black and White* can present challenges in text structure, multiple meanings, and opportunities for critical analysis (Ansley, 2002). Kevin O'Malley's *Once upon a Cool Motorcycle Dude* and David Weisner's *Three Pigs* provide examples of this unique visual literacy picture book connection that promotes higher-level thinking and unique response (Lohfink, 2006).

Picture books for older readers provide efficient read-alouds, powerful genre models, and exemplary models of narrative and expository writing. In fact, the changes in postmodern picture books can help readers make sense of an increasingly complex world (Goldstone, 2001/2002). Books like Barbara Kerley's *The Dinosaurs of Waterhouse Hawkins* and *Walt Whitman: Words for America* as well as Diane Stanley's *Michaelangelo* read well even at the middle-school level.

With a growing knowledge of children's literature, a teacher will readily recognize the content, reading level, and amount of text that tends to support the designation of picture books for older readers. Figure 3.4 designates those titles especially applicable to the interests and curricular focus of older students (grades 6–8).

FIGURE 3.4 Book Cluster: Picture books for older readers [all I/M]

Avi (2003). *Silent movie.* Illus. by C. B. Mordan. New York: Atheneum.

Bildner, Phil (2005). *The shot heard 'round the world.* Illus. by C. F. Payne. New York: Simon & Schuster.

Burleigh, Robert (1999). *Hercules.* Illus. by Raul Colon. San Diego: Harcourt Brace.

Burns, Khephra (2001). *Mansa Musa: The lion of Mali.* Illus. by Leo & Diane Dillon. San Diego: Gulliver & Harcourt Brace.

Fritz, Jean (2001). *Leonardo's horse.* Illus. by Hudson Talbott. New York: Putnam.

Heide, Florence Parry, & Gilliland, Judith Heide (1999). *The house of wisdom.* Illus. by Mary Grandpre. New York: DK Ink.

Kerley, Barbara (2001). *The dinosaurs of Waterhouse Hawkins.* Illus. by Brian Selznick. New York: Scholastic.

Mannis, Celeste D (2003). *The queen's progress: An Elizabethan alphabet.* Illus. by Bagram Ibatoulline. New York: Viking.

Marsalis, Wynton (2005). *Jazz ABZ: An A to Z collection of jazz portraits.* Illus. by Paul Rogers. Cambridge, MA: Candlewick.

McKissack, Patricia, & McKissack, Frederick (1994). *Christmas in the Big House, Christmas in the Quarters.* Illus. by John Thompson. New York: Scholastic.

Mitchell, Stephen (Reteller) (2002). *Hans Christian Andersen's The Nightingale.* Illus. by Bagram Ibatoulline. Cambridge, MA: Candlewick.

Myers, Walter Dean (2003). *Blues journey.* Illus. by Christopher Myers. New York: Holiday House.

Polacco, Patricia (2000). *The butterfly.* New York: Philomel.

Rosen, Michael (2005). *Michael Rosen's sad book.* Illus. by Quentin Blake. Cambridge, MA: Candlewick.

Ross, Stewart (1997). *Charlotte Bronte and Jane Eyre.* Illus. by R. Van Nutt. New York: Viking.

Shakespeare, William (Retold by Ann Keay Beneduce) (1996). *The tempest.* Illus. by G. Spirin. New York: Philomel Books.

Sis, Peter (1996). *Starry messenger.* New York: Farrar, Straus and Giroux.

Sis, Peter (1998). *Tibet: Through the red box.* New York: Farrar, Straus & Giroux.

Stanley, Diane (1996). *Leonardo Da Vinci.* New York: Morrow. (Orbis Pictus Award, 1998)

Stanley, Diane (2000). *Michaelangelo.* New York: Morrow.

Stanley, Diane (2002). *Saladin: Noble prince of Islam.* New York: HarperCollins.

Stockton, Frank R. (2004). *The bee man of Orn.* Illus. by P. J. Lynch. Cambridge, MA: Candlewick. (DVD included)

Van Allsburg, Chris (1991). *The wretched stone.* Boston: Houghton Mifflin.

Van Allsburg, Chris (1993). *The sweetest fig.* Boston: Houghton Mifflin.

Wiesner, David (1991). *Tuesday.* New York: Clarion. (Newbery Medal, 1992)

Wiesner, David (1999). *Sector 7.* New York: Clarion.

Willard, Nancy (1991). *Pish, posh, said Hieronymous Bosch.* Illus. by Leo & Diane Dillon. San Diego: Harcourt.

Wisniewski, David (1997). *Golem.* New York: Clarion. (Newbery Medal, 1998)

Transitional Picture/Chapter Books

Picture books particularly designed for independent reading are regarded as easy-to-read books. More text and fewer illustrations are common in this format. Because the text in many picture books is beyond the independent reading level of the reader, children need access to some books that build confidence in their own ability to read yet retain the enjoyment of reading authentic literature. Limited vocabulary, simple plot, and a balance of words and pictures characterize easy-to-read books. Several books by Dr. Seuss that contain rhyming and repetitive elements fit this category. They fill a specific purpose in children's literature by ensuring success as emergent readers achieve the response of "I can read!" through the challenge and excitement of reading real books. In response to this growing body of literature, the American Library Association created the Theodor Seuss Geisel Award for these transitional books that invite early readers into the world of reading. *Henry and Mudge and the Great Grandpas*, written by Cynthia Rylant and illustrated by Sucie Stevenson, was the first recipient of the award in 2006.

Some children outgrow some picture books and long to tackle full-length chapter books. This can be a big step and a formidable task for second- and third-grade students. The transitional picture/chapter book, however, typically has several short chapters, uses simplified vocabulary, and incorporates illustrations intermittently (at least every other page) to offer comprehension clues and entertainment to the child transitioning toward the chapter book format. Even the dimensional size approaches that of a chapter book. Several children's authors have written transitional books that allow young independent readers to transition from the world of picture books to the world of chapter books. Jessie Haas's *Runaway Radish* consists of five chapters with partial page pencil sketches by Margot Apple on most of the 56 pages. Tedd Arnold penned *Hi! Fly Guy*, which blends cartoon art and a wonderful friendship. Suzanne Bloom created *A Splendid Friend, Indeed,* celebrating the relationship between a goose and a polar bear. Claudia Mills targets an emergent reader audience with the classic *Gus and Grandpa* series. Teachers praise these books as an important milestone on the journey toward lifelong reading. Besides being a transition between picture and chapter books, they also serve as ideal formats as readers transition from oral to written response explorations. Figure 3.5 lists increasing welcome additions to transitional picture book offerings as children strive to read earlier and find comfort and success with these titles.

ARTISTIC DESIGN IN PICTURE BOOKS

The interplay of a picture book's text and illustrations achieves an optimal blend of literacy components, and the design of a book extends visual literacy to another dimension (Giorgis & Johnson, 2001). Book design reaches beyond the visual and verbal aspects of the picture book. A book's overall design is what intrigues children about a book in the first place. Design includes the book's size and shape, the book jacket, the endpapers, the front matter, the lettering, and the placement of art and text on the page. Design is one of the factors that attract the child to a selection for

FIGURE 3.5 Book Cluster: Transitional picture/chapter books [all P/early I]

Arnold, Tedd (2005). *Hi! Fly guy.* New York: Cartwheel/Scholastic.

Barrows, Annie (2006). *Ivy and Bean.* Illus by Sophie Blackall. San Francisco: Chronicle. (Series)

Bloom, Suzanne (2005). *A splendid friend, indeed.* Honesdale, PA: Boyds Mills.

Brisson, P. (1997). *Hot fudge hero.* Illus. by D. C. Bluthenthal. New York: Holt. (Redfeather book)

Brown, L. K. (1997). *Rex and Lilly schooltime.* Illus. by Marc Brown. Boston: Little, Brown.

Calmenson, S., & Cole, J. (1997). *Rockin' reptiles.* Illus. by L. Munsinger. New York: Morrow.

Cutler, Jane (2005). *Rose and Riley come and go.* Illus. by Thomas F. Yezerski. New York: Farrar. (Series)

Danziger, Paula (2001). *What a trip, Amber Brown.* Illus. by Tony Ross. New York: Putnam (*A is for Amber* series)

de Paola, Tomie (2001). *Meet the Barkers: Morgan and Moffat go to school.* New York: Putnam (*Meet the Barkers* series).

DiCamillo, Kate (2006). *Mercy Watson fights crime.* Illus. by Chris Van Dusen. Cambridge, MA: Candlewick. (Series) See also: *Mercy Watson to the rescue*; *Mercy Watson goes for a ride.*

Hoban, L. (1996). *Arthur's back to school day.* New York: HarperCollins.

Howe, James (2001). *Pinky and Rex and the just-right pet.* Illus. by Melissa Sweet. (*Pinky and Rex Ready to Read Series*). New York: Atheneum. See also *Pinky and Rex and the perfect pumpkin* (1998); and *Pinky and Rex and the school play* (1998).

Howe, James (2006). *Houndsley and Catina.* Illus. by Mary Louise Gay. Cambridge, MA: Candlewick. (Series)

Jacobson, Jennifer R (2006). *Andy Shane and the pumpkin trick.* Illus. by Abby Carter. Cambridge, MA: Candlewick. (Series) See also: *Andy Shane and the very bossy Dolores Starbuckle.*

Krensky, Stephen (2001). *Arthur and the goalie ghost.* Illus. by Marc Brown. (Arthur Good Sports series) Boston: Little, Brown. See also: *Arthur and the best coach ever* (2001); *Arthur and the recess rookie* (2001); *Arthur and the seventh-inning stretcher* (2001); and *Arthur and the race to read* (2001).

Kvasnosky, Laura M. (2006). *Zelda and Ivy: The runaways.* Cambridge, MA: Candlewick. (Series) See also: *Zelda and Ivy and the boy next door; Zelda and Ivy: One Christmas; Zelda and Ivy.*

McDonald, M. (1997). *Beezy.* Illus. by N. Poydar. New York: Orchard Books.

McDonald, M. (1998). *Beezy magic.* Illus. by N. Poydar. New York: Orchard Books.

Mills, Claudia (2001). *Gus and Grandpa at basketball.* Illus. by Catherine Stock. New York: Farrar, Straus & Giroux. See also: *Gus and Grandpa and the two-wheeled bike* (1999); *Gus and Grandpa ride the train* (1998); *Gus and Grandpa at the hospital* (1998); *Gus and Grandpa and the Christmas cookies* (1997); and *Gus and Grandpa* (1997).

Regan, Dian Curtis (1999). *The friendship of Milly and Tug.* Illus. by Jennifer Danza. New York: Henry Holt. (Redfeather chapter book)

Rylant, Cynthia (1999). *Some good news.* Illus. by Wendy Halperin. (The Cobble Street Cousins series) New York: Simon & Schuster. See also: *A little shopping* (1998).

Rylant, Cynthia (2000). *Henry and Mudge and Annie's perfect pet.* Illus. by Sucie Stevenson. New York: Simon & Schuster. See also: *Henry and Mudge and the snowman plan* (1999); *Henry and Mudge and Annie's good move* (1998); *Henry and Mudge and the starry night (1998); Henry and Mudge and the sneaky crackers* (1997); and *Henry and Mudge and the bedtime thumps* (20 titles in series).

FIGURE 3.5 Continued

Rylant, Cynthia (2001). *Mr. Putter & Tabby feed the fish.* Illus. by Arthur Howard. San Diego: Harcourt Brace. See also: *Mr Putter & Tabby paint the porch* (2000); *Mr. Putter & Tabby toot the horn* (1998); *Mr. Putter & Tabby row the boat* (1997); *Mr. Putter & Tabby fly the plane* (1997).

Rylant, Cynthia (2001). *Poppleton in winter.* Illus. by Mark Teague. New York: Scholastic. See also: *Poppleton has fun* (2000); *Poppleton in fall* (1999); *Poppleton in spring* (1999); *Poppleton forever* (1998); *Poppleton everyday* (1998); and *Poppleton: Book one* (1997).

Rylant, Cynthia (2005). *The lighthouse family: The turtle.* Illus. by Preston McDaniels. New York: Simon & Schuster. (Series) See also: *The storm; The whale; The eagle.*

Silverman, Erica (2005). *Cowgirl Kate and Cocoa.* Illus. by Betsy Lewin. San Diego: Harcourt Brace.

Stevenson, James (1996). *Yard sale.* New York: Greenwillow.

Stevenson, J. (1997). *Heat wave at Mud Flat.* New York: Greenwillow.

Stevenson, J. (1997). *The Mud Flat mystery.* New York: Greenwillow.

Stevenson, J. (1998). *Mud Flat April fool.* New York: Greenwillow.

Stevenson, J. (1999). *Mud Flat spring.* New York: Greenwillow.

Stevenson, J. (2000). *Christmas at Mud Flat.* New York: Greenwillow.

Van Leeuwen, Jean (2005). *Amanda pig and the really hot day.* Illus. by Ann Schweninger. New York: Dial.

independent reading as well. An attractive cover in compelling color with unique lettering invites students inside a book to explore both pictures and story. The blend of a picture book's text, illustrations, and elements of design results in a greater overall effect than any one of these components can achieve separately.

Book Size and Shape

Most picture books conveniently fit into an 8½ by 11-inch format. These books tell compelling stories, feature award-winning presentations, and efficiently fit on library shelves. Occasionally, however, the text or illustration of a picture book lends itself to a special format. Awareness of these special instances and speculation about design decisions may help children understand the challenging tasks of the art director in negotiating book design. Articulating reasons for special book formats is in itself a response to literature.

Louise Borden's *The Day Eddie Met the Author* is slightly undersized to 7¼ by 9¼ inches to represent the size of a traditional writing composition book. The snapshot-like pastel and watercolor art of Stephen T. Johnson captures the love between Katie and her grandma in Lenore Look's *Love as Strong as Ginger.* The 8 by 8½-inch format effectively frames each illustration in a scrapbook-like format. Fred Marcellino's illustrations for *The Tale of Little Babaji* (1996) update the text of Helen Bannerman's *The Tale of Little Black Sambo* (1899). Those who remember the original book format will recall its similar compact size, with the updated, unstereotyped new version set in India. The diminutive format still effectively captures the strength of four tigers as they melt into butter yet manages to be large enough to hold a plate of "a Hundred and Sixty-nine" pancakes for Babaji.

Just as undersized formats can be useful, oversized formats can prove necessary if they hold special creations that require additional space. The premier artwork of Kadir Nelson in Carole Boston Weatherford's *Moses: When Harriet Tubman Led her People to Freedom* requires the 11 by 12-inch format to capture the dramatic episodes and flowing text in this fictional story focuses on the Underground Railroad. The bright, bold collage illustrations in Lois Ehlert's *Waiting for Wings* requires the choice of a large format (12¼ by 10¼ inches) to hold the striking constructed shapes and brilliant-colored designs inspired by butterflies and flowers. This masterpiece combines flowing text and informational identification pages to blend both narrative and expository formats within a single book. The dome-shaped top of Jean Fritz's *Leonardo's Horse* encases an historical overview of Leonardo da Vinci's dream of creating a larger-than-life bronze horse. A space in which to share such a large figure posed a problem, but the construction of a dome-shaped studio gallery provided the solution. This book's unique shape echoes the artistic dominance of the horse and even showcases the text in an usual format.

Book Jackets

A book jacket serves to protect a book and to provide information about its content, its author and/or illustrator, and its special features. Even more, the illustration on the front cover of the book jacket serves as an invitation to open the book and explore. The illustration on the back cover may serve as a reason to reflect, relive, or relate the book to one's own experiences. We actually teach a lesson in visual literacy when we ask children "What do you think this book is about?" before a read-aloud session. Children provide answers to that question by paying attention to initial cues on the book jacket that ignite engagement in literature. The book jacket does, in a sense, initiate the first response to a book.

Many book jackets contain wraparound art that provides a continuous poster-like scene from front to back. Jerry Pinkney's watercolor jacket brings life and meaning to Patricia McKissack's *Goin' Someplace Special.* The front cover introduces the reader to Tricia Ann dressed in a flower-patterned turquoise dress confidently smiling while she waits for the bus. The wraparound to the back of the book features Tricia's humble but warm, inviting home that foreshadows the love and support of family. Even before reading the text, the viewer joins in the anticipation of Tricia's journey to "someplace special" and appreciates the energetic simplicity of growing up in a house full of love.

JoEllen McAllister Stammen's jacket illustration of Cristina Kessler's *Jubela* highlights the love of a baby rhinoceros and his protective mother. As the wraparound cover is opened to its full perspective, the viewer perceives the size, dominance, and security provided by an animal mother on the African plains. The total book jacket effect is to emphasize the adoptive mother–child relationship that provides the theme in this true story from Swaziland.

A book jacket may also have separate, but related, illustrations on the front and the back. Kevin Hawkes's watercolor cover illustration for Michelle Knudsen's *Library Lion* gently showcases the lion overseeing the reading of young children. The back cover, however, focuses more humorously on the lion's tail joyfully dusting the library shelves.

Library Lion

MICHELLE KNUDSEN illustrated by **KEVIN HAWKES**

Between these covers lies the delightful tale of a lion, so well suited to the library, who breaks the library "quiet" rules to get help for Miss Merriweather, the librarian.

E. B. Lewis's gentle watercolor artwork invites the reader into the dream of independent, spirited Virgie in Elizabeth Fitzgerald Howard's *Virgie Goes to School with Us Boys*. Virgie's eager smile and sparkling eyes reflect her goal of gaining an education during the Reconstruction era when few girls attended school. The background reveals the backs of her five brothers as they carry their lunch pails on their way to school. The back cover provides a small watercolor of a similar scene, but now Virgie tags along as her dream of attending school becomes reality. This simple, detailed final portrait summons the reader to reflect and revisit the story of Virgie's goal and the power of education to make that dream come true. These separate front and back artworks are, in their own way, very special because they house important story content between their contrasting picture frames.

Endpapers

Endpapers serve a utilitarian function in that they attach the pages of a book to its casing. But they also provide an interesting transition from the exterior to the interior of a book. Initially, they may go unnoticed as the reader's momentum moves him or her toward the text. An astute teacher, however, can open children's eyes to these effective connecting links between book covers and text. Evidencing awareness, sharing discovery, and revealing connections to the text formulate responses to literature.

In their simplest forms, endpapers are colored illustration-free paper. Even then, their colors are chosen to enhance the book jacket or to express a mood or feeling. Red endpapers emphasize the red roses that symbolize freedom and justice in Angela Johnson's *A Sweet Smell of Roses*. The black, white, and gray illustrations of Eric Velasquez carry the symbolic touch of red throughout the story. The reader can almost taste and smell the luscious gingerbread in the rich cinnamon-brown endpapers in Jim Aylesworth's retelling of *The Gingerbread Man*. A delicious tangerine-orange shade provides color for the endpapers of Alma Flor Ada's traditional tale of *The Three Golden Oranges*. The solid black endpapers of Andrea Davis Pinkney and Brian Pinkney's *Ella Fitzgerald* are embossed with a swirled texture reflecting the material of an elegant dress actually worn by the jazz virtuosa.

Many illustrators plan for endpapers that complement the story or the artwork that graces the book's interior. In *My Dad,* Anthony Browne uses subdued golden plaid endpapers crisscrossed with yellow lines to foreshadow and recall the admiration of a son for his dad who wore a bathrobe with this same colorful plaid pattern throughout the entire book. Ian Falconer's *Olivia Forms a Band* heralds red polka dots on white background to replicate one of Olivia's outfits in the story. The endpapers of Deborah Noyes's *Hana in the Time of the Tulips* showcase Bagram Ibatoulline's acrylic landscape of the Dutch countryside and windmill. These meaningful connections between story and endpapers make them worth noting, sharing, and responding to prior to or following a book reading experience. Once readers are made aware of their special connection to the book, they are certain to stop and note them independently as they begin their reading journey.

Front and Back Matter

In examining the visual qualities of a picture book, children become adept at discovering the importance of what comes before and after the text. The front matter includes the pages between the front endpapers and the first page of text. Besides supplying important copyright and publication information for adults, these pages often introduce prospective readers to the story's mood, character(s), setting, theme, or content. They may also provide important background regarding the origin of the story or insights into the illustrations. Most recently, this information is more often shared as back matter, pages at the book's conclusion that provide additional information to the reader.

Title page. The title page introduces the reader to the book, showcases the full title, and distinguishes the author and/or illustrator and the publisher. The title page is commonly housed on a single page but can extend across two pages as a double-page spread. Children can easily be made aware of its importance as a page to be examined before the reading of a story. Insights into the story can be gleaned by examining the illustrations on the title page, and the importance of differentiating author, title, and publisher can be confirmed.

David Wiesner uses a single-page title page in classic style in *The Three Pigs*, the 2002 Caldecott Medal title. The three pigs, each shown from a different perspective, carry loads of straw, twigs, and bricks to build their homes as simple text reveals the title, the author/illustrator, and the publisher. A double-page spread by Mo Willems invites the reader into the simple world of *Knuffle Bunny: A Cautionary Tale* through four framed portraits that introduce the reader to the cartoon-like characters—mom, dad, baby, and Knuffle Bunny—and to the photographed story setting—home, front porch steps, and laundromat. Speculating on this illustration initiates predictive reader response prior to actual textual exposure.

Dedication page.   Dedications typically appear after the title page or opposite or on the same page with the copyright and publishing information. The new trend is to include them on the final page of the book, which also contains publishing information. A dedication usually expresses appreciation to someone closely associated with the author or illustrator, but it can also add a statement reflecting a message related to the text. For example, Patricia Polacco touchingly dedicates *Thank You, Mr. Falker* to a former teacher who helped her overcome her dyslexia and to realize the sweetness of reading. In Phil Bildner's *Shoeless Joe and Black Betsy,* illustrator C. F. Payne dedicates his effort "To the memory of Vada Pinson and all the other great ball players who thrilled wide-eyed kids like me. May there be a day I can visit Coopertown and find Joe Jackson and Pete Rose where they belong—in the Hall of Fame." Sometimes a dedication takes the form of an acknowledgment, such as John Bierhorst's recognition of his retold tales told in the Hopi pueblos of Arizona in *Is My Friend at Home? Pueblo Fireside Tales.*

Author's notes.   Another recent trend in picture books is to include additional information about the background for the book on a special page, either at the beginning, but more commonly following the story. As children realize that authors often get ideas for stories from their own lives (or lives of others), these notes provide assurance that even commonplace events and people can give rise to stories. D. B. Johnson's portrayal of an adventurous spirit in *Henry Hikes to Fitchburg* is supplemented by an author's note about Henry David Thoreau, on whose life and habits this story was based. Penda Diakite's *I Lost my Tooth in Africa* contains an author's note explaining the origin of the tale, and her father's, Baba Wague Diakite, artist note. Teachers should read these author's notes following the read-aloud of the book and encourage rereading with the newly acquired information as rich contextual background.

Borders

Some illustrators choose to use borders around their illustrations to artistically complement the main illustrations. Others incorporate borders to predict forthcoming happenings or to reveal an ongoing story taking place alongside the illustrations but related to the text. The creative use of borders enhances artistic presentation but can also extend meaning beyond the visual and verbal aspects of the book.

Pamela Patrick's simple yet effective quilt-patterned frames encase the text of Richard Ammon's *Amish Horses* and *An Amish Year.* A thin-lined red or green frame surrounds each page, further highlighting the quilt pattern and the realistic illustrations. Brian Pinkney's variations on palm trees, flowers, and vines provide the background border for Robert San Souci's text in *Cendrillon: A Caribbean Cinderella.* The borders link the tropical setting to the text and provide eye-catching frames for the reader.

The masterful crafting of borders for import beyond the text is synonymous with the work of Jan Brett. Her classic retelling of *The Mitten* (1989) introduced the reader to the use of borders to review and predict events in the story. As Brett cleverly packed animals in the mitten one by one, she used mitten-shaped cutouts in the right and left borders of double-page spreads to review the previous mitten inhabitant and preview the impending occupant. She continues her border artwork in *Comet's Nine Lives* (1996) as frames made of shells, rope, and sealife encase each of a Nantucket cat's adventures. *The Hat* (1997) further capitalizes on this border characteristic of Brett's artistry. Sometimes the borders of a book go undetected, but knowledge of their inclusion makes the discerning eye aware of their role in book design.

Lettering and Type

Type selection involves three critical decisions for the book designer or illustrator. The first choice of font selection is an important one because today more than 6,000 type fonts are available for printed text. The right choice of type to match an historical period, a story genre, or a mood or setting can add to successful presentation. The second choice includes size of type. Considerations of the age of the intended audience and of format size are primary factors in this decision. Finally, the choice of dark type on a light background or light type on a dark background must be made. The combined effect of these three decisions provides an added dimension to the overall conceptualization of the picture book.

Color and size of type is an exaggerated and unique feature of Jon Scieszka's *The Stinky Cheese Man and Other Fairly Stupid Tales.* In the main fairy-tale retelling, the type begins with five characters per inch, reduces to nine characters per inch, and ends with type that is three characters per inch. The one-page retelling of "Jack's Story" ranges from 4 red characters per inch to an almost unreadable 28 black characters per inch as the story suggests continued repetition at the bottom of the page. Throughout the text, varying type reflects the humor of the tale—even the dedication is printed upside down.

In a nostalgic portrayal of the childhood of Booker T. Washington, Marie Bradby's text meshes with Chris Soentpiet's art in a meaningful way in *More Than Anything Else.* From sunup to sundown, the type is black set on the pure white background of the saltworks where Booker and Papa arduously labor. Throughout most of the book, however, the type is rendered in yellow with dark backgrounds reflecting the light of the kerosene lanterns, candles, or fireplace on the faces and setting of the story. This technique is particularly effective in the book's final illustration in which Booker learns to write and read his name. Margie Palatini's *The Web Files* humorously uses a typewriter-like font that replicates the style of a detective report. In Marjorie Priceman's *Hot Air: The (Mostly) True Story of the First Hot-Air Balloon Ride*, the text begins traditionally but gradually floats across the page as the animals react to their balloon ride. These types of design decisions combine to make a picture book into a work of art.

Use of Space

The location of text in relation to illustrations is another aspect of book design. Text can appear on the same side of the page or it can be alternated from right side to left side intermittently. Text can appear in the upper right and the lower left on each double-page spread or it can be alternated according to the illustrator's needs. In *Tea with Milk*, Allen Say chooses to place the text effectively on the left-hand page of his picture book while the right-hand page holds his masterful watercolor cultural representations. Jean Craighead George's text blends into Thomas Locker's landscape art and almost begs to be printed on the upper left of most pages in *To Climb a Waterfall*. The sky or treetops seem aptly to house the text for this well-crafted book. Occasionally, the text is moved to a rock or a stream, but the artwork itself seems to provide a place effortlessly for the text. Much of James Cross Giblin's *The Amazing Life of Benjamin Franklin* echoes the two column spread of the newspaper—the *Philadelphia Gazette*—which Franklin began. In *Fly!* by Christopher Myers, the text is placed in the white centerfold of each page while the illustrations span the remainder of the space.

No single design element alone makes an outstanding picture book. It is the effective blending of all of these design elements

RESOURCES ON THE WEB
Picture Books
The Internet offers a wide variety of picture books for children of all ages. Teachers may introduce these sites to an entire class on a large screen by connecting a computer and projector or by letting students explore the books at individual desktop or laptop computers.

Picturing Books: A Website About Picture Books
This is an outstanding resource where students and teachers can explore the anatomy of a picture book (borders, endpapers, dual image covers, etc.), a picture book timeline, and a picture book glossary. The site also includes information about artistic media and style and how to select and evaluate picture books. There are also many links to author/illustrator sites and other sites that promote the use of picture books. *http://picturingbooks.imaginarylands.org/*

Storyline Online
Members of the Screen Actors Guild Foundation (such as Melissa Gilbert, Jason Alexander, and Haylie Duff) read aloud well-known children's picture books in a series of online streaming videos. While the actor or actress reads the story, the authentic book illustrations are shown in the video. *http://www.storylineonline.net/*

International Children's Digital Library
The International Children's Digital Library (ICDL) is a project of the University of Maryland's Human-Computer Interaction Lab. The ICDL currently contains about 800 books, in a myriad of languages, for children ages 3 through 13. Although the majority of books are picture books, chapter books are available for older readers. It's a strictly online resource; works cannot be downloaded or printed. *http://www.icdlbooks.org/*

Caldecott Medal Home Page
Visit the Caldecott Medal home page (American Library Association) to learn more about the Caldecott Medal selection process, and past and present Caldecott Medal and Honor books.
http://www.ala.org/ala/alsc/awardsscholarships/literaryawds/caldecottmedal/caldecottmedal.htm

Picture Book Authors and Illustrators
Robert McCloskey
Horn Book Radio Review: interview with Robert McCloskey
http://www.hbook.com/exhibit/mccloskeyradio.html

Kevin Henkes
Official site of Kevin Henkes *http://www.kevinhenkes.com/*
KidsReads.com – *http://www.kidsreads.com/authors/au-henkes-kevin.asp*

(continued)

with exquisite illustrations and powerful text that creates a cohesive whole. Then, and only then, does the picture book appeal to the eye and stir the imagination of the reader. Open any Caldecott award-winning title (see appendix) and note how several of these design techniques blend into an integrated whole—the picture book. Equally as important in the creation of a picture book is the text itself, which eloquently carries the story through well-chosen words, focus and organization, sentence flow, and the presence of an author's voice to engage the reader. As teachers and students open their eyes to an awareness of the intricate blending of book design and text, they grow both in their appreciation of the artistic qualities of the picture book and in their ability to respond to the quality of well-written text.

ARTISTIC STYLE IN PICTURE BOOKS

The style of an illustration is revealed by the way in which the artist uses the elements of art and the chosen media to create a visual image. Style results from a blend of color, line, and shape with the media choices an illustrator selects. Style is a result of all the decisions an illustrator makes in producing a final product, likened to placing a signature on a work of art. Illustrators typically become identified with a particular style, especially by children, although many choose to continue to explore, experiment, and extend their artwork during their emerging careers.

Six basic styles of art are recognized in children's book illustrations, just as they are in museum art. These include realism, surrealism, expressionism, impressionism, folk art, and cartoon art. With guidance and modeling, children can learn to recognize the characteristics of each of these styles and respond to illustrations by discussing the illustrator's style.

Realism. Realism or representational art incorporates a natural reproduction of people, nature, and objects as they actually appear in the real world. Allen Say's representations of his ancestors in *Kamishibai Man* appear lifelike; their facial expressions and authentic forms bring reality to the viewer's eyes. In Patricia and Frederick McKissack's *Christmas in the Big House, Christmas in the Quarters,* John Thompson brings contrasting personalities to life from both sides of plantation life—slaves and masters—as they prepare for their holiday celebration. Ruth Sanderson's realism invades the oil paintings of the traditional tale, *Cinderella.* Mike Wimmer's paintings capture living, breathing growing-up, family, and presidential portraits in Frank Keating's *Theodore.* Almost photographic in their quality, realistic illustrations bring true-to-life qualities to characters, settings, and scenarios in literature.

Surrealism.   In children's illustrations, surrealism skews realism in its attempts to represent the mingling of the unconscious with the dreamlike qualities of imagination. The haunting paintings of Rafal Olbinski in John Gruen's *Flowers & Fables* not only illuminate the text but suggest further unfolding of tales to children. A spectacular world of whimsical paradoxes and playful contradictions abound in J. Patrick Lewis's *BoshBlobberBosh: Runcible Poems from Edward Lear.* Illustrated in a surrealistic style by Gary Kelley, incongruencies of flying fish, noseless faces, and abstract beauties fill the pages. Quint Buchholz's *The Collector of Moments* challenges the artistic eye with snow elephants in Canada, circus-decorated Venetian doorways, and penguins at a railway station. Children, perhaps more than adults, enjoy responding to and making sense of the fantastical portrayal of dreamlike states in surrealistic illustrations.

Expressionism.   The use of bright colors and figures that are a bit disproportionate in giving form to strong inner feelings while presenting a modified or distorted reality characterize expressionism. Faith Ringgold's characters in *Tar Beach* represent this style of art through characters and a rooftop setting. With an emphasis on inner feelings, the bright colors and unique angles and perspectives of Susan Guevara's illustrations in Gary Soto's *Chato's Kitchen* also represent this stylistic mode. D. B. Johnson's characters in *Henry Builds a Cabin* and its sequels are recognized as expressionistic by children because of the vivid colors, exaggerated gestures, and extreme facial expressions. Expressionism has become an increasingly popular mode of illustrator style.

Impressionism.   Impressionism characteristically prioritizes light, movement, and color over definition of detail. Emily Arnold McCully captures the essence of this style in both her Caldecott award winner, *Mirette on the High Wire,* and her more recent *Marvelous Mattie: How Margaret E. Knight Became an Inventor.* Either a light or dark background illuminates each illustration and dramatically allows rich watercolors to blend history, culture, and a fine story. Michael Foreman offers impressionistic renderings of village and mountain life in *Mia's Story: A Sketchbook of Hopes and Dreams* with pastel blues and greens as seasonal sunlight and snow reflect off the mountain's surface.

Folk art.   The childlike characteristic of folk art causes it to appear flat and lack a sense of proportion. Claire Nivola's folk art in *The Forest* is well suited to a saga of a mouse who must leave home to explore the forest and overcome his fear. A touch of folk art is seen in Wendell Minor's historical renderings in *Yankee Doodle America: The Spirit of 1776 from A to Z.* Q for Quakers, for example, shows a vivid portrayal of rural farmers who believed in religious freedom. A more traditional style of folk art is found in Will Moses's adaptation of Washington Irving's *Rip Van Winkle* with diminutive characters interspersed throughout the book.

Cartoon art.   The cartoon style appeals to children so it is not surprising that some of children's favorite illustrators create in this style. Tomie de Paola is the

Impressionism prioritizes light, movement, and color over details. *Mia's Story, copyright © 2006 by Michael Foreman. Reproduced by permission of the publisher, Candlewick Press, Inc., Cambridge, MA, on behalf of Walker Books Ltd., London.*

master of cartoon art as evidenced in *Strega Nona: Her Story* and *Tom* as well as countless other creations. His memorable characters are easily recognized and loved by young children. Great respect was gained for the cartoon art style when the Caldecott award was given to Peggy Rathmann for *Officer Buckle and Gloria* and a Caldecott honor to Betsy Lewin in Doreen Cronin's *Click Clack Moo, Cows That Type*. The humor of the characters, the bright bold colors, and the movement created have made these favorites with teachers and children alike. Kevin Henkes brings delightful mice to life, and Steven Kellogg has mesmerized children for decades with his own cartoon-like characters. Cartoon art has reached the informational genre as children delight in Bruce Degen's art in Joanna Cole's *The Magic School Bus and the Science Fair Expedition* and Gene Barretta's *Now & Ben: The Modern Inventions of Benjamin Franklin*. Popular with children, the bright colors and stark pen and ink outlines of this style focus reader/viewer attention and permanently etch these characters in children's hearts and minds.

As children are drawn to and recognize the art of favorite illustrators and the characteristics of styles of artistic expression, their interest and curiosity in children's book illustrations will deepen. A teacher does not have to be an art expert to respond aesthetically to the picture book (Kiefer, 1995b). This quality artwork serves as an introduction to the real world of art as connections between the world of children's picture books and the broader world of art become apparent.

ARTISTIC MEDIA IN PICTURE BOOKS

Examining the media illustrators use to create their works of art can help children understand and appreciate the pictures while encouraging them to respond by using these media in their own artistic explorations (Elleman, 1994). Information on media may be located on the copyright page or in the illustrator's biographical notes on the book jacket. If this information is not available, children can be encouraged to speculate by using clues from the techniques they have learned from previous illustrated books. Response to illustrations may include why an illustrator chose a particular medium and what effect is achieved through that medium. Children can compare this book with other titles by the same artist to see if the same medium was used.

Six basic art media are repeatedly found in children's book illustrations. These include oil paints, watercolors, graphite pencils, acrylics, pastels, and gouache. More commonly today, mixed media abound in children's book art and refer to the blending of these and other types of media for a special, unique effect. Relating each medium and mixed media to distinguished artists will help differentiate them as children become aware of their characteristic features.

Oil paints dominate the deep rich illustrations of Thomas Locker in more than 20 picture books. Originally an adult landscape artist, Locker brought his painterly techniques to children's books, most recently those dealing with science. In Locker's Images of Conservationists series, Locker and Joseph Bruchac share *Rachel Carson: Preserving a Sense of Wonder* through landscapes, wildlife, and personal portraits. In *Sky Tree: Seeing Science Through Art* with Candice Christiansen, Locker paints 12 portraits of the same tree as it passes through the seasons of the year and explains how light affects each depiction. Because children are rarely exposed to oils, Locker's artwork, besides being enjoyed for its inherent quality, can also serve as an introduction to the art of the great masters. James Ransome's oil paintings in *Under the Quilt of Night* by Deborah Hopkinson capture the risk of those who chose to seek freedom via the Underground Railroad. Deep purples surround dark faces as the night envelops the flight to freedom.

Oil paints richly capture the Rembrandt style of the 1500s in Holland. Hana in the Time of Tulips, *text copyright © 2004 by Deborah Noyes, illustrations copyright © 2004 by Bagram Ibatoulline. Reproduced by permission of the publisher, Candlewick Press, Inc., Cambridge, MA.*

Watercolor, a commonly used medium in picture books, has the power to portray a variety of moods from whimsical and lighthearted to serious and downcast. Jerry Pinkney performs magic with his use of watercolors both to portray the classic *The Little Red Hen* and to capture the spirit of the young boy in Billie Holiday's *God Bless the Child*. Watercolors add lip-smacking appeal to James Stevenson's *Corn Chowder,* making his illustrations taste just as good as his poems. Vivid tones and blended colors provide a celebration for viewers. Brad Sneed's watercolor caricatures in Marsha Diane Arnold's *The Bravest of Us All* and Robert Andrew Parker's historical portrayals in Louise Borden's *Across the Blue Pacific: A World War II Story* reflect the ability of watercolor to flow across the page and outside the lines.

Chris Van Allsburg's graphite drawings for *The Mysteries of Harris Burdick* and *Jumanji* often come to mind first when looking for connections to this medium. Vera B. Williams contrasts two sisters in *Amber Was Brave, Essie Was Smart* with colored line drawings. Kevin Henkes's gouache and colored pencil drawings in the 2005 Caldecott Medal title, *Kitten's First Full Moon*, match the simplicity of the story in which a kitten seeks a bowl of milk. A slight pink blush, hardly visible to the viewer, overrides the graphite drawings.

Pastel drawings are made with compressed colored chalk that blends well and works best on rough paper. Pastels form the foundation of illustrations by Lisa Campbell Ernst whose *Stella Louella's Runaway Book* incorporates an ink outline and pencil cross-hatching to complement the pastel drawings. Thomas B. Allen also uses pastels to color his charcoal-drawn illustrations in George Shannon's *Climbing Kansas Mountains*, which combine the rough tinted paper and blending of charcoal and pastels that have become the hallmark of Allen's many illustrated children's books.

Acrylic and gouache are two newer media that have added variety to the illustrator's palette. Jeanette Winter uses pure acrylic to tell the tsunami true story of *Mama*, in which a baby hippo loses his mama but finds a new home and a new mama. Well-defined line and deep rich color exemplify the potential of this media. Brian Selznick's use of acrylics in Rosemary Wells's *Wingwalker* effectively capture the Dust Bowl/Depression era. Gouache, in contrast, is a method of painting with opaque colors. Chesley McLaren uses gouache in Shana Corey's *You Forgot Your Skirt, Amelia Bloomer!* as the medium captures the lighter, freer alternative to the heavy petticoats of the mid-1800s.

More artists are introducing mixed media or new media to children's book illustrations. The reverse side of the title page often includes a small print reference to the type of media used to produce the illustrations. For example, Giselle Potter blends pencil, ink, gouache, gesso, and watercolor in Roni Schotter's *The Boy Who Loved Words*. David Wiesner's Caldecott Medal title, *The Three Pigs,* was executed in watercolor, gouache, colored inks, pencil, and colored pencil. With each new publishing year, experimental media bring rich color, texture, and dimension to children's books.

GRAPHIC TECHNIQUES IN PICTURE BOOKS

Beyond selecting media with which to present their images, illustrators must choose creative techniques to transmit the visions carried in their minds. These techniques include woodcuts, scratchboards, engravings, collage, cut paper, and digitally generated art. Recognition of these art techniques is also important because they bring unique responses from children instilled by their own special characteristics.

Woodcuts give a strong and powerful impression as the boldness and depth of black highlights this intricate technique. Mary Azarian, the 1999 Caldecott Medal recipient, skillfully uses crafted tinted woodcuts to capture the rural Vermont landscape and the rugged characters in Jacqueline Briggs Martin's *Snowflake Bentley*. Azarian's woodcuts also effectively capture the play of the moon on the landscape in Penny Pollock's *When the Moon Is Full: A Lunar Year* and Leslie Conner's *Miss Bridie Chose a Shovel*. Beckie Prange's hand-colored woodblock art graces the pages of Joyce Sidman's *Song of the Water Boatman and Other Pond Poems*.

Engravings are a related technique that add a sense of permanence and strength to book illustrations. Barry Moser chose to use them for Patricia MacLachlan's *What You Know First*. Both the author and illustrator chose photographs from their own family albums to serve as models for these intricate artworks. The engravings proved to be an effective choice for sharing nostalgic memories of childhood and home. John Lawrence incorporates vinyl engravings in *This Little Chick* as bold lines and color mark the simplicity of barnyard characters.

The scratchboard technique has become the specialty of Brian Pinkney. Scratchboard uses a white board covered with black ink into which a drawing is scratched with a sharp tool. Pinkney adds color with oil pastels or oil, wiping away any excess. This technique was most recently demonstrated in Andrea Davis Pinkney's two books, *Duke Ellington* and *Ella Fitzgerald*. The use of light and shadow is particularly noteworthy as are the attention to detail, both facial expressions and bodily movement. Beth Krommes perfects the colorful, detailed scratchboard technique in Joyce Sidman's *Butterfly Eyes and Other Secrets of the Meadow*. Children have been informally exploring this technique for years in school as they covered pieces of paper with black crayon and scratched out a drawing with a sharp object.

Collage is an artistic composition made by gluing different materials onto a surface. The master of paper collage is Eric Carle, whose 35 years of book illustrating reflect his ability to bring paper to life. He prepares his own colored tissue papers by using various brushes to splash or splatter, or by fingerpainting acrylic paint onto the tissue paper. The prepared paper is then cut or torn into shapes as needed and glued onto white illustration board. Carle's animals are particularly impressive as overlapped tissue paper giraffes, elephants, and roosters fill the page. Carle's insect quartet employs this technique with a caterpillar, a spider, a cricket, and a lightning bug. Because this technique has become the hallmark of his work, his illustrations are perhaps the most recognizable by young children, including *Mister Seahorse*. Ezra Jack Keats and Leo Lionni also effectively represent early masters of collage.

Cut paper layering is related to collage but requires an even sharper eye for defining detail. David Wisniewski has been honored for this technique for *Golem*, the 1997 Caldecott Medal book. This artist uses colored paper for his cut illustrations, which are held together with double-stick photo mounts. To achieve depth between pieces of paper, he uses double-stick foam tape or places thicker matboard behind layers of paper. He uses a precise bladed knife and often uses between 800 and 1,000 blades to complete 16 illustrations in one book (Cummings, 1995). *Golem* represents the apex of Wisniewski's picture book career. His cuttings of the city of Prague and the dominant monster-like Golem creatively fill the book's pages with varying perspectives and dramatic action. Double-page spreads provide a panoramic unfolding of events, and the deep brown, black, red, and orange-toned papers aptly reflect the story elements. The cut of the paper is so acute that one can almost feel its sharpness. *Golem* blends the high drama of an eloquently retold story with the dramatic flair of the cut paper technique to form an award-winning picture book.

Digitally illustrated books are appearing on the market with greater frequency as this technology becomes available to book illustrators and publishing houses. The illustrations for Audrey Wood's *Alphabet Adventure* were digitally generated by Bruce Wood resulting in vivid colors and dimensional art. Russell Benfanti's *Hide, Clyde!* introduces the young reader to a small chameleon through digital paintings while offering the additional option of an *ipicturebook* that can be downloaded to a portable, desktop, or handheld PC. Uncertainty and disagreement have arisen over this technique's acceptance as authentic book illustration, yet children will be drawn to its vivid color, cartoon-like design, dimensional possibilities, and the potential of software to contribute to their own book illustrating attempts.

Golem blends the dramatic flair of cut paper with the splendid retelling of an eloquent tale of Prague.
Jacket from Golem *by David Wisniewski. Copyright 1996 by David Wisniewski. Reprinted by permission of Clarion Books/Houghton Mifflin Company. All rights reserved.*

Each illustrator brings special talents and choices to the art of the picture book. The variety of choices blended with unique artistic talents makes children's book illustrations an outstanding topic for response by both adults and the children with whom they share these works of art (Kiefer, 1989).

EVALUATING QUALITY PICTURE BOOKS

Picture books are a child's first invitation into the world of literature and the potential start of a lifelong adventure with reading. Quality time spent during the reading/listening event should be accompanied by the highest quality literature. Although children should be encouraged to choose their favorite books to be read and reread, adults must be responsible for selecting a pool of quality literature from which endearing favorites may grow. The following straightforward criteria adapted from John Stewig's *Looking at Picture Books* (1995) assist teachers, librarians, and parents in identifying the best of the world of the picture book so listeners and readers alike can engage in quality verbal and visual literary experiences.

Criteria for language in picture books:

- The author uses a variety of rich familiar and unfamiliar words to embrace the reader/listener's understanding of what they know and extend them toward what they have yet to learn.
- A variety of sentence structures introduces readers/listeners to sentence types as well as adding interest to the text.
- The author creatively uses literary devices to captivate the reader/listener. These may include repetitive words, phrases, or sentences that engage children in the text.
- The text invites reader response through participating, noticing, relating, or expressing feelings.

Criteria for art in picture books:

- The artist uses an original idea that allows the viewer to see something familiar in a new way or to introduce something not ever seen before.
- The art captivates the viewer because of style, medium, sequence, or placement on the page.
- The art enhances or extends the text, creating a greater understanding of the words through artistic images or additional details not mentioned in the text.
- The art invites viewer response through noticing, discussing, pointing, relating to text, discovering details, or expressing feelings.

In addition, picture books should be written about topics children find interesting. Adult enthusiasm can play an especially important role in introducing quality picture books to children. The ultimate evaluative criteria for a picture book is whether children will be engaged, entertained, and encouraged to continue on their lifelong reading adventure.

BENEFITS OF PICTURE BOOKS

Picture books provide an open invitation into the world of reading. Their absorption and appreciation as read-aloud windows into the world of literature inspire young children to become readers. The impetus provided by picture books joins forces with the natural desire to become a reader. The impact of early picture books on the understanding of how text and pictures work to create story provide a springboard into the reading process. The list of benefits is virtually endless, but here are a few valuable contributions:

- Picture books provide the foundation for developing a sense of story—beginning, middle, and ending.
- Picture books introduce the basic elements of narrative including character, setting, and plot.
- Picture books induct the reader into the interplay of text and illustration because both contribute to comprehension and personal response—the ultimate goals of reading.
- Picture books provide a compact vehicle for early reader response to literature and the power of making a book one's own through personal connections.
- Picture books blend the power of the text with the appeal of the visual image as an entry-level introduction to literacy.
- Picture books create childhood memories of familiar books and characters that last a lifetime.

READER RESPONSE TO PICTURE BOOKS

Picture books provide a strong impetus for early response to literature through the use of prompts. Asking children how the story makes them feel, what it reminds them of from their own life, and what they notice about the story opens wide possibilities to response before, during, and after the book has been read aloud. Most picture storybooks are also the perfect length for the 5- to 10-minute read-aloud time designated by teachers. Allowing time for response to both the story and the illustrations makes for a richer read-aloud experience. Picture books abound on the library and classroom shelves, making many of them fine choices for independent reading by second- and third-grade students. Book buddies from upper grades long to share picture storybooks, especially of their own childhood favorites, with kindergartners and first graders. The perfect blend of illustrations and the language of story brings hours of enjoyment to the literacy classroom each day.

Readers respond to picture books through written journals, through illustration, and through oral conversations. Young children carry repetitive text and familiar characters with them to their world of play. Readers respond to picture books by recognizing familiar authors and illustrators and forming early preferences for genres and artistic style and visual representation. Building a repertoire of favorite authors and titles leads the reader toward further reading choices. The picture book provides the impetus for the emerging reader's lifelong journey into literature.

CLOSING THOUGHTS

The world of picture books encompasses books for all ages and titles across all genres. The art of the picture book lies in the blend of its words and its illustrations. Children, however, do not always recognize the beauty of the language of the text and the special types of illustrations without the guidance of a knowledgeable teacher. The more teachers learn about illustration, the more children will respond to the visual aspects of a book. The more teachers point out exceptional language, the more children will warm to the special word choices of an author. Early impressions of literature and reading begin with motivating readings and presentations of quality picture books. As children learn more about the blending of language and art, they develop their own artistic and literary tastes as they develop into readers.

Classroom time is precious, and the books we choose to share as teachers can directly influence student motivation and attitude toward reading and literature. Because so many picture books are published each year, teachers need to evaluate selectively the ones they choose to use in their classrooms. An awareness of book design and format, a sense of quality writing, a knowledge of various art media, styles, and techniques, and a feel for the response potential of the book help in making informed decisions about which picture books to share with children. Over time, teachers should expose children to a variety of illustrators whose artistic styles combine with well-written text and blend into the extraordinary aesthetic experience that is the picture book.

References

Ansley, M. (2002). "It's not all black and white": Postmodern picture books and new literacies. *Journal of Adolescent & Adult Literacy, 45,* 444–457.

Bainbridge, J., & Pantaleo, S. (2001). Filling the gaps in text: Picture book reading in the middle years. *The New Advocate, 14,* 401–411.

Chaney, J. A. (1993). Alphabet books: Resources for learning. *The Reading Teacher, 47,* 96–104.

Cummings, P. (Ed.). (1995). *Talking with artists: Volume two.* New York: Simon & Schuster.

Elleman, B. (1994). Illustration as art. *Book Links, 3,* 28–31.

Giorgis, C., & Johnson, N. J. (2001). Gaining insights into picture book illustration and design. *Journal of Children's Literature, 27,* 62–63.

Goldstone, B. P. (2001/2002). Whaz up with our books? Changing picture book codes and teaching implications. *The Reading Teacher, 55,* 362–370.

Goldstone, B. P. (2004). The postmodern picture book: A new subgenre. *Language Arts, 81,* 196–204.

Henkes, K. (1992). The artist at work. *The Horn Book Magazine, 68,* 38–47.

Hoppe, A. (2004). Half the story: Text and illustration in picture books. *The Horn Book Magazine, 80,* 41–50.

Jacobs, J. S., & Tunnell, M. O. (1996). *Children's literature, briefly.* Upper Saddle River, NJ: Merrill/Prentice Hall.

Kiefer, B. Z. (1989). Picture books for all the ages. In J. Hickman & B. E. Cullinan (Eds.), *Children's literature in the classroom: Weaving Charlotte's web* (pp. 75–88). Needham Heights, MA: Christopher Gordon.

Kiefer, B. Z. (1995a). *The potential of picture books: From visual literacy to aesthetic understanding.* Upper Saddle River, NJ: Merrill/Prentice Hall.

Kiefer, B. Z. (1995b). Responding to literature as art in picture books. In N. L. Roser & M. G. Martinez (Eds.), *Book talk and beyond: Children and teachers respond to literature* (pp. 191–200). Newark, DE: International Reading Association.

Lohfink, G. (2006). *Responses to postmodern picture books in a fourth-grade literature circle.* Unpublished doctoral dissertation, Kansas State University.

Lynch-Brown, C., & Tomlinson, C. M. (2002). *Essentials of children's literature* (4th ed.). Boston: Allyn & Bacon.

Panteleo, S. (2004). Young children and radical change characteristics in picture books. *The Reading Teacher, 58,* 178–187.

Stewig, J. W. (1995). *Looking at picture books.* Fort Atkinson, WI: Highsmith Press.

Teale, W. H. (1986). Home background and young children's literacy development. In W. H. Teale & E. Sulzby (Eds.), *Emergent literacy: Writing and reading* (pp. 173–205). Norwood, NJ: Ablex.

Children's Books Cited [P] = K–2; [I] = 3–5; [M] = 6–8

Ada, Alma Flor (1999). *The three golden oranges.* Illus. by Reg Cartwright. New York: Atheneum. [P/I]

Ammon, Richard (2000). *An Amish year.* Illus. by Pamela Patrick. New York: Atheneum. [I]

Ammon, Richard (2001). *Amish horses.* Illus. by Pamela Patrick. New York: Atheneum. [I]

Arnold, Marsha Diane (2000). *The bravest of us all.* Illus. by Brad Sneed. New York: Dial. [P/I]

Arnold, Tedd (2005). *Hi! Fly guy.* New York: Scholastic/Cartwheel. [P]

Aylesworth, Jim (1998). *The gingerbread man.* Illus. by Barbara McClintock. New York: Scholastic. [P]

Bannerman, Helen (1996). *The tale of Little Babaji.* Illus. by Fred Marcellino. New York: HarperCollins. [P]

Barretta, Gene (2006). *Now & Ben: The modern inventions of Benjamin Franklin.* New York: Henry Holt. [I]

Barton, Byron (2003). *My car.* New York: Harper Festival. [Board Book]

Benfanti, Russell (2002). *Hide, Clyde!* New York: Little, Brown/ipicturebooks. [P]

Bierhorst, John (Reteller) (2001). *Is my friend at home? Pueblo fireside tales.* Illus. by Wendy Watson. New York: Farrar, Straus and Giroux. [P]

Bildner, Phil (2002). *Shoeless Joe & Black Betsy.* Illus. by C. F. Payne. New York: Simon & Schuster. [I/M]

Bloom, Suzanne (2005). *A splendid friend, indeed.* Honesdale, PA: Boyds Mills Press. [P]

Borden, Louise (2001). *The day Eddie met the author.* Illus. by Adam Gustavson. New York: McElderry. [I]

Borden, Louise (2006). *Across the blue Pacific: A World War II story.* Illus. by Robert Andrew Parker. Boston: Houghton Mifflin. [I/M]

Bradby, Marie (1995). *More than anything else.* Illus. by Chris Soentpiet. New York: Orchard Books. [P/I]

Brett, Jan (1989). *The mitten.* New York: Putnam. [P]

Brett, Jan (1996). *Comet's nine lives.* New York: Putnam. [P]

Brett, Jan (1997). *The hat.* New York: Putnam. [P]

Browne, Anthony (2000). *My dad.* New York: Farrar, Straus and Giroux. [P]

Buchholz, Quint (1997). *The collector of moments.* New York: Farrar, Straus and Giroux. [I/M]

Bunting, Eve (1994). *Smoky nights.* Illus. by David Diaz. San Diego: Harcourt. [P/I]

Carle, Eric (1968). *The very hungry caterpillar.* New York: Philomel Books. [P]

Carle, Eric (1984). *The very busy spider.* New York: Philomel Books. [P]

Carle, Eric (1990). *The very quiet cricket.* New York: Philomel Books. [P]

Carle, Eric (1995). *The very lonely firefly*. New York: Philomel Books. [P]

Carle, Eric (2004). *Mister Seahorse* New York: Philomel Books. [P]

Catalanatto, Peter (2002). *Matthew A. B. C.* New York: Atheneum. [P]

Chapman, Jane (2004). *Sing a song of sixpence; A pocketful of nursery rhymes and tales*. Cambridge, MA: Candlewick Press. [P]

Cheney, Lynn (2002). *America: A patriotic primer*. Illus. by Robin Preiss Glasser. New York: Simon & Schuster. [P/I]

Cline-Ransome, Lisa (2001). *The quilt alphabet*. Illus. by James Ransome. New York: Holiday House. [P]

Cole, Joanna (2006). *The magic school bus and the science fair expedition*. Illus. by Bruce Degen. New York: Scholastic. [I]

Conner, Leslie (2004). *Miss Bridie chose a shovel*. Illus. by Mary Azarian. Boston: Houghton Mifflin. [P/I]

Corey, Shana (2000). *You forgot your skirt, Amelia Bloomer!* Illus. by Chesley McLaren. New York: Scholastic. [I/M]

Cronin, Doreen (2001). *Click clack moo, cows that type*. Illus. by Betsy Lewin. New York: Simon & Schuster. [P]

Curlee, Lynn (2002). *Seven wonders of the ancient world*. New York: Atheneum. [I/M]

Demarest, Chris (2001). *Firefighters A to Z*. New York: McElderry. [P]

de Paola, Tomie (1993). *Tom*. New York: Putnam. [P]

de Paola, Tomie (1996). *Strega Nona: Her story*. New York: Putnam. [P]

Diakite, Penda (2006). *I lost my tooth in Africa*. Illus. by Baba Wague Diakite. New York: Scholastic. [P]

Ehlert, Lois (1997). *Hands*. San Diego: Harcourt Brace. [P]

Ehlert, Lois (2001). *Waiting for wings*. San Diego: Harcourt. [P/I]

Ehlert, Lois (2002). *In my world*. San Diego: Harcourt. [P]

Emberly, Ed (2001). *The wing on a flea: A book about shapes*. Boston: Little, Brown. [P]

Ernst, Lisa Campbell (1999). *Stella Louella's runaway book*. New York: Simon & Schuster. [P]

Ernst, Lisa Campbell (2004). *The turn-around, upside-down alphabet book*. New York: Simon & Schuster. [P/I]

Falconer, Ian (2006). *Olivia forms a band*. New York: Atheneum. [P]

Fleischman, Paul (1999). *Westlandia*. Illus. by Kevin Hawkes. Cambridge, MA: Candlewick. [P/I]

Fleischman, Paul (2004). *Sidewalk circus*. Cambridge, MA: Candlewick. [P/I]

Florian, Douglas (2000). *Mammalabilia*. San Diego: Harcourt Brace. [P/I]

Foreman, Michael (2006). *Mia's story: A sketch-book of hopes and dreams*. Cambridge, MA: Candlewick. [P/I]

Fritz, Jean (2001). *Leonardo's horse*. Illus. by Hudson Talbott. New York: Putnam. [I/M]

George, Jean Craighead (1995). *To climb a waterfall*. Illus. by Thomas Locker. New York: Philomel Books. [I]

Giblin, James Cross (2000). *The amazing life of Benjamin Franklin*. Illus. by Michael Dooling. New York: Scholastic. [I/M]

Gruen, John (1996). *Flowers & fables*. Illus. by Rafal Olbinski. San Diego: Harcourt Brace. [I/M]

Haas, Jessie (2001). *Runaway Radish*. Illus. by Margot Apple. New York: Greenwillow. [P/I]

Helfer, Ralph (2006). *The world's greatest elephant*. Illus. by Ted Lewin. New York: Philomel. [P/I]

Henkes, Kevin (1991). *Chrysanthemum*. New York: Greenwillow. [P]

Henkes, Kevin (1996). *Lilly's purple plastic purse*. New York: Greenwillow. [P]

Henkes, Kevin (2004). *Kitten's first full moon*. New York: Greenwillow. [P]

Henkes, Kevin (2006). *Lilly's big day*. New York: Greenwillow. [P]

Hoban, Tana (1996). *Just look*. New York: Greenwillow. [P]

Holliday, Billie, & Herzog, Arthur (2004). *God bless the child*. Illus. by Jerry Pinkney. New York: HarperCollins. [P/I]

Hopkinson, Deborah (2002). *Under the quilt of night*. Illus. by James E. Ransome. New York: Atheneum. [I]

Horenstein, Henry (1999). *A is for . . .? A photographic alphabet of animals*. San Diego: Harcourt Brace. [P]

Houston, Gloria (1992). *My great aunt Arizona.* Illus. by Susan Lambe. New York: Harper-Collins. [I]

Howard, Elizabeth Fitzgerald (2000). *Virgie goes to school with us boys.* Illus. by E. B. Lewis. New York: Simon & Schuster. [I]

Irving, Washington (1999). *Rip Van Winkle.* Illus. by Will Moses. New York: Philomel. [I/M]

Jenkins, Steve (2004). *Actual size.* Boston: Houghton Mifflin. [P/I]

Jenkins, Steve (2005). *Prehistoric actual size.* Boston: Houghton Mifflin. [P/I]

Jester, Norton (2005). *The hello, good-bye window.* Illus. by Chris Raschka. New York: MDC Books/Hyperion. [P]

Johnson, Angela (2005). *A sweet smell of roses.* Illus. by Eric Velasquez. New York: Simon & Schuster. [I]

Johnson, D. B. (2000). *Henry hikes to Fitchburg.* Boston: Houghton Mifflin. [P/I]

Johnson, D. B. (2002). *Henry builds a cabin.* Boston: Houghton Mifflin. [P/I]

Keating, Frank (2006). *Theodore.* Illus. by Mike Wimmer. New York: Simon & Schuster. [I]

Kerley, Barbara (2001). *The dinosaurs of Waterhouse Hawkins.* Illus. by Brian Selznick. New York: Scholastic. [I/M]

Kerley, Barbara (2004). *Walt Whitman: Words for America.* Illus. by Brian Selznick. New York: Scholastic. [I/M]

Kessler, Cristina (2001). *Jubela.* Illus. by JoEllen McAllister Stammen. New York: Simon & Schuster. [P]

Kharms, Daniil (1996). *First, second.* Translated from the Russian by Richard Pevear. Illus. by Marc Rosenthal. New York: Farrar, Straus and Giroux. [I]

Kimmel, Eric (2002). *Anansi and the magic stick.* Illus. by Janet Stevens. New York: Holiday House. [P/I]

Knudsen, Michelle (2006). *Library lion.* Illus. by Kevin Hawkes. Cambridge, MA: Candlewick. [P/I]

Lawrence, John (2002). *This little chick.* Cambridge, MA: Candlewick. [P]

Leedy, Loreen (2002). *Follow the money.* New York: Holiday House. [P]

Lehman, Barbara (2004). *The red book.* Boston: Houghton. [P/I]

Lehman, Barbara (2005). *Museum trip.* Boston: Houghton. [P/I]

Lewis, J. Patrick (1998). *Boshblobberbosh.* Illus. by Gary Kelley. San Diego: Harcourt Brace. [I/M]

Lionni, Leo (2003). *Let's play.* New York: Knopf. [Board Book]

Lobel, Anita (1990). *Allison's zinnea.* New York: Greenwillow. [P/I]

Lobel, Anita (1994). *Away from home.* New York: Greenwillow. [P/I]

Lobel, Arnold (Illustrator) (1997). *Book of Mother Goose.* New York: Random House. [P]

Locker, Thomas, with Candice Christiansen (1995). *Sky tree: Seeing science through art.* Illus. by Thomas Locker. New York: HarperCollins. [I]

Locker, Thomas, & Bruchac, Joseph (2004). *Rachel Carson: Preserving a sense of wonder* (Images of Conservationist series). Golden, CO: Fulcrum. [I]

Look, Lenore (1999). *Love as strong as ginger.* Illus. by Stephen T. Johnson. New York: Atheneum. [P/I]

Macauley, David (1990). *Black and white.* Boston: Houghton Mifflin. [I/M]

MacLachlan, Patricia (1995). *What you know first.* Engravings by Barry Moser. New York: Joanna Cotler Books/HarperCollins. [I]

Martin, Bill, Jr., & Archambault, John (1989). *Chicka chicka boom boom.* Illus. by Lois Ehlert. New York: Simon & Schuster. [P]

Martin, Jacqueline Briggs (1998). *Snowflake Bentley.* Illus. by Mary Azarian. Boston: Houghton Mifflin. [P/I]

McCully, Emily Arnold (1992). *Mirette on the high wire.* New York: Putnam. [P]

McCully, Emily Arnold (2001). *Four hungry kittens.* New York: Dial. [P]

McCully, Emily Arnold (2006). *Marvelous Mattie: How Margaret K. Knight became an inventor.* New York: Farrar, Straus & Giroux. [I]

McKissack, P. C. (2001). *Goin' someplace special.* Illus. by Jerry Pinkney. New York: Atheneum. [P/I]

McKissack, P. C., & McKissack, F. L. (1994). *Christmas in the big house, Christmas in the quarters.* Illus. by John Thompson. New York: Scholastic. [I/M]

Mills, Claudia (2001). *Gus and Grandpa at basketball.* Illus. by Catherine Stock. New York: Farrar, Straus & Giroux. [P]

Minor, Wendell (2006). *Yankee doodle America: The spirit of 1776 from A to Z.* New York: Putnam. [I/M]

Myers, Christopher (2002). *Fly!* New York: Jump at the Sun/Hyperion. [I]

Nivola, Claire (2002). *The forest.* New York: Farrar, Straus and Giroux. [P/I]

Noyes, Deborah (2004). *Hana in the time of the tulips.* Illus. by Bagram Ibatoulline. Cambridge, MA: Candlewick. [I/M]

Olmon, Kyle (2006). *Castle: Medieval days and knights.* Illus. by Tracy Sabin. New York: Orchard. [I/M]

O'Malley, Kevin (2005). *Once upon a cool motorcycle dude.* Illus. by Scott Goto, Carol Heyer, & Kevin O'Malley. New York: Walker. [I /M]

Palatini, Margie (2001). *The web files.* Illus. by Richard Egielski. New York: Hyperion. [I/M]

Pelletier, David (1996). *The graphic alphabet.* New York: Orchard Books. [P/I]

Pienkowski, Jan (2001). *Pizza! A yummy pop up.* Cambridge, MA: Candlewick. [P]

Pinkney, Andrea Davis (2000). *Duke Ellington: The piano prince and his orchestra.* Illus. by Brian Pinkney. New York: Hyperion. [I/M]

Pinkney, Andrea Davis (2002). *Ella Fitzgerald: The tale of a vocal virtuosa.* New York: Hyperion. [I/M]

Pinkney, Jerry (2006). *The little red hen.* New York: Dial. [P]

Pollaco, Patricia (1999). *Thank you, Mr. Falker.* New York: Philomel. [I/M]

Pollock, Penny (2001). *When the moon is full: A lunar year.* Illus. by Mary Azarian. New York: Little, Brown. [P]

Priceman, Marjorie (2005). *Hot air: The (mostly) true story of the first hot-air balloon ride.* New York; Atheneum. [P/I]

Rathmann, Peggy (1995). *Officer Buckle and Gloria.* New York: Putnam. [P]

Ringgold, Faith (1991). *Tar beach.* New York: Crown. [P/I]

Rohmann, Eric (1994). *Time flies.* New York: Crown. [P/I]

Rylant, Cynthia (2005). *Henry & Mudge and the great grandpas.* (*Henry & Mudge* series). New York: Greenwillow. [P]

Sabuda, Robert (1997). *Cookie count: A tasty pop up.* New York: Simon & Schuster. [P]

Sabuda, Robert, & Reinhart, Matthew (2006). *Encyclopedia prehistorica: Sharks and other sea monsters.* Cambridge, MA: Candlewick. [I /M]

Sanderson, Ruth (2002). *Cinderella.* Boston: Little, Brown. [P/I]

San Souci, Robert D. (1998). *Cendrillon: A Caribbean Cinderella.* Illus. by Brian Pinkney. New York: Simon & Schuster. [P/I]

Say, Allen (1999) *Tea with milk.* Boston: Houghton Mifflin. [P/I]

Say, Allen (2004). *Kamishibai man.* Boston: Houghton Mifflin. [P/I]

Schotter, Roni (2006). *The boy who loved words.* Illus. by Giselle Potter. New York: Schwartz & Wade Books. [I]

Schwartz, David (1999). *If you hopped like a frog.* Illus. by James Warhola. New York: Scholastic. [P/I]

Scieszka, Jon (1992). *The stinky cheese man and other fairly stupid tales.* Illus. by Lane Smith. New York: Viking. [P/I]

Shannon, George (1993). *Climbing Kansas mountains.* Illus. by Thomas B. Allen. New York: Bradbury. [P]

Shannon, George (1996). *Tomorrow's alphabet.* Illus. by Donald Crews. New York: Greenwillow. [P]

Sidman, Joyce (2005). *Song of the water boatman and other pond poems.* Illus. by Beckie Prange. Boston: Houghton Mifflin. [I]

Sidman, Joyce (2006). *Butterfly eyes and other secrets of the meadow.* Illus. by Beth Krommes. Boston: Houghton Mifflin. [I/M]

Soto, Gary (1995). *Chato's kitchen.* Illus. by Susan Guevara. New York: Putnam. [P]

Stanley, Diane (2000). *Michaelangelo.* New York: HarperCollins. [I/M]

St. George, Judith (2000). *So you want to be president?* Illus. by David Small. New York: Philomel. [I]

Stevenson, James (2003). *Corn chowder: Poems.* New York: Greenwillow. [I]

Stroud, Virginia (1996). *The path of the quiet elk: A Native American alphabet book*. New York: Dial. [I]

Swinburne, Stephen R. (2000). *What's opposite?* Honesdale, PA: Boyds Mills Press. [P]

Van Allsburg, Chris (1981). *Jumanji*. Boston: Houghton Mifflin. [I]

Van Allsburg, Chris (1984). *The mysteries of Harris Burdick*. Boston: Houghton Mifflin. [I/M]

Weatherford, Carole Boston (2006). *Moses: When Harriet Tubman led her people to freedom*. Illus. by Kadir Nelson. New York: Jump at the Sun/Hyperion. [I/M]

Wells, Rosemary (2002). *Wingwalker*. Illus. by Brian Selznick. New York: Hyperion. [I]

Weltzman, Jacqueline Preiss (2002). *You can't take a balloon into the Museum of Fine Arts*. Illus. by Robin Preiss Glasser. New York: Dial. [I]

Wiesner, David (1999). *Sector 7*. New York: Clarion. [I]

Wiesner, David (2001). *The three pigs*. New York: Clarion. [P/I]

Willems, Mo (2004). *Knuffle bunny: A cautionary tale*. New York: Hyperion. [P]

Williams, Vera B. (2001). *Amber was brave, Essie was smart*. New York: HarperCollins. [P/I]

Winter, Jeanette (1996). *Josephina*. San Diego: Harcourt Brace. [P/I]

Winter, Jeanette (2006). *Mama: A true story in which a baby hippo loses his mama during a tsunami, but finds a new home, and a new mama*. San Diego: Harcourt. [P]

Wisniewski, David (1996). *Golem*. New York: Clarion. [I/M]

Wood, Audrey (2001). *Alphabet adventure*. Illus. by Bruce Woods. New York: Scholastic. [P]

Wormell, Christopher (2005). *Teeth, tails, and tentacles: An animal counting book*. Philadelphia, PA: Running Press Book Publishers. [P/I]

Yolen, Jane (Ed.) (2006). *This little piggy and other rhymes to sing and play*. Illus. by Will Hildebrand. Musical arrangements by Adam Stemple. Cambridge, MA: Candlewick. (CD included) [P]

Zelinsky, Paul O. (1997). *Rapunzel*. New York: Dutton. [P/I]

CHAPTER 4

Traditional Tales and Modern Fantasy
The Domain of Imagination

> **COYOTE**
>
> Coyote . . . wise.
> Coyote was swift, like the wind.
> Coyote . . . brown.
> Coyote was sly, tricky, fast, old; he was cool and quick to me.
> Coyote . . . the hunter.
> Coyote was the catcher of rabbits and squirrels.
> Coyote . . . smart.
> Coyote was strong, fast, smart, a team worker and a wise guy.
> Coyote . . . old.
> Coyote has memories, but falls asleep and dreams of a new life, a new world.
>
> Third-grade class poem written in
> response to Nancy Wood's *Old Coyote*

Traditional literature and fantasy dwell in the domain of imagination. Whether tales are told by word of mouth or written down for readers to savor, their origin lies in the imagination of those who originally created them. "Fantasy is storytelling with the beguiling power to transform the impossible into the imaginable, and to reveal our own 'real' world in a fresh and truth-bearing light (Marcus, 2006, p. 1).

This chapter honors the inspiration of the storyteller whose tales were eventually recorded and the inventive genius of the creator of the fantastic who dreams the impossible yet causes the reader to linger on the possible.

Traditional tales and fantasy transport the reader to worlds inhabited by talking animals, fairy princesses, and monumental heroes. They introduce the reader to memorable characters from the far corners of the world and issue invitations to embark on heroic quests. Acknowledging the otherworld of this imaginative domain results in a true appreciation of the creative genres of traditional literature and fantasy.

TRADITIONAL LITERATURE

No one can be sure where and when stories originated. They were carried by the mesmerizing voices of storytellers as they moved from country to country. While interested listeners absorbed the details of each story, new retellers were likely to share their own versions with unique details to suit their own tastes, reflect their own cultures, and reach their own audiences. The oral tradition of communicating these tales from country to country lasted for centuries before the stories were finally recorded in print.

According to Jane Yolen (1981) in *Touch Magic: Fantasy, Faerie, and Folklore in the Literature of Childhood*, folk or traditional literature possesses two major functions. The most basic function is "to provide a landscape of allusion" (p. 15). Beginning with the first story a child hears, he or she builds a repertoire of stories filled with heroes and monsters, heroines and helpers, and even tricksters who manage to outwit even the wisest foes. As children hear more stories and tales, they become linked as their literary landscape is broadened and stretched with memorable characters who form the framework for further literary encounters. "Stories lean on stories" (p. 15) and a growing sense of familiarity is necessary as preparation for appreciating the literature children will encounter in their lifetimes as readers. The second function of folklore is "to provide a way of looking at another culture from the inside out" (p. 16). Superheroes and heroines of today spring from a need within our culture to replicate the glory and strength of characters of the past. Robin Hood, Anansi the spider, Sir Lancelot, and Sweet Betsey from Pike stem from the gods and goddesses of Greek, Roman, and Norse mythology. "Stories lean on stories, culture on cultures" (p. 16). Old stories and honored characters bridge the past and the present while providing the background needed for understanding ongoing encounters with literature.

The historical and cultural heritage of traditional tales is the birthright of children today. Yet traditional tales no longer seem to be an assumed rite of childhood. If children are denied access to the legacy of traditional stories, they will lack the essential literary insights and visions expressed through oral language for hundreds of years. This chapter celebrates the oral and written legacy of the genre of traditional tales and discusses titles that can be shared with children for their enjoyment and response.

Traditional literature includes those stories that originally passed to listeners through the oral tradition of storytelling. They are not attributed to individual authors but are usually associated with the groups of people or cultures in which they originated. Ted Lewin's *The Storytellers* builds a sense of the oral tradition as words weave stories and stories take flight around the world. Although the oral tradition came first, the act of writing down a story actually performed its own magic on this genre as tales gained permanence through print. Traditional tales include folktales, fairy tales, fables, myths, and legends. This vast heritage of traditional tales finds written expression today in continued retellings that emphasize old values through their modern adaptations, especially in the picture book format. Traditional tales, in this text, also include the modern fairy tale because it echoes the resounding voice from the art of long ago storytelling.

Characteristics of Traditional Tales

Traditional tales can be divided into different types, but they all possess some commonalities because they were shared orally for centuries.

Like a kaleidoscope, a folktale is made up of large and small units—motifs—incidents that, like bits of colored glass, are picked up as the tale travels from story to story, from country to country, from culture to culture. Shake up the folktale kaleidoscope, and these motifs arrange themselves in an infinite variety of usable and attractive forms (Yolen, 1981, p. 17).

The following characteristics of traditional tales reflect the storytelling tradition from which they were generated:

- **Simple story structure.**   The beginning quickly identifies the setting and characters and introduces the problem. The middle builds the action through a series of conflicts moving toward a climax. The ending resolves the problem and brings closure to the story. Niroot Puttapipat's brief retelling and illustration of *The Musicians of Bremen* reveals the simple story of a donkey, a dog, a cat, and a rooster who play to a band of robbers while traveling to Bremen to become musicians.

- **One-dimensional characters.**   The characters in the stories usually possess a single dominant characteristic, typically good or evil, that makes them easy to identify (handsome prince, wicked stepmother). B. G. Hennessey's retelling of *The Boy Who Cried Wolf* focuses on a bored shepherd who ignorantly attempts to make life more interesting for himself and the townspeople.

- **Indistinct settings.**   Settings are inexplicit because the tales traveled from country to country. "Once upon a time . . . ." and "Long ago in a far away land . . . ." tend to reflect the secondary nature of setting to the story itself. Ruth Sanderson's *Cinderella* finds herself in the chimney corner where she sits quietly among the cinders.

- **Succinct language.**   Standard beginnings and endings encase simple, patterned motifs, typically in threes. Complicated descriptions are avoided. Repeated chants or refrains economize on total words. The opening line of Jim Aylesworth's *Aunt Pitty Patty's Piggy*, for example, reflects utter simplicity: "Once upon a time, Aunt Pitty Patty took her little niece Nelly to the market" (n. p.). Piggy's stubborn repeated phrase, "No, no, no, I will not go!" (n. p.) weaves a predictable journey throughout the text.

- **Predictable themes.** Good triumphs over evil, hard work and effort breed success, and brains outwitting brawn encompass themes that are likely to prevail. Candace Fleming's *Gator Gumbo* features an aging alligator who makes a pot of spicy-hot gumbo and tricks a lazy possum, otter, and skunk as they unsuspectingly become meat for mama's gumbo recipe.
- **Happy endings.** ". . . and they lived happily ever after" keeps the young listener/reader satisfied and motivated to revisit this genre. Hans Christian Andersen's classic *The Ugly Duckling* translated from the Danish by Anthea Bell and illustrated in vivid watercolors by Robert Ingpen portrays an awkward bird's ridiculing, rejection, and shunning only to discover that the beauty he sought was within his swanlike appearance all along.

As these characteristics become familiar to children, they are likely to emerge as a natural part of their oral or written response to traditional tales.

Types of Traditional Tales

To assist in classifying the wide realm of traditional tales, four groups are identified as a basis for discussion. As teachers introduce traditional literature to their students, they should include examples from each of these traditional literature subgenres. Building a strong foundation across this genre prepares readers for a lifetime of appreciation of literature.

Folktales. Folktales originated from the lives and daily happenings and imaginations of the common folk. They form the most numerous type of traditional tale and one that has remained popular through the centuries. Although all traditional literature might be considered folktales, this category is used to describe several common types of folktales with their identifying characteristics:

- **Cumulative tales.** Based on built-on phrases, these tales encourage children to join in as new lines are added to a repeated refrain. The constant rhythm, simple plot, and humor tend to make this popular fare with the youngest children. Paul Galdone's *The Gingerbread Boy* invites participation as children quickly learn the repeated refrains. Perhaps the most famous cumulative tale is Jeanette Winter's depiction of *The House That Jack Built*.
- **Beast tales.** These tales of talking animals with human characteristics are likely to include a competition between animals. Cleverness and sharp wit typically triumph over size and physical prowess. Robert San Souci's *Pedro and the Monkey* tells the Puss-in-Boots variant of a farmer in the Philippines irritated by a monkey who stole his corn. After capturing him, the kind-hearted Pedro releases the monkey, and, in return, the monkey promises to arrange for Pedro to marry the daughter of a rich landowner. As the reader wonders how a monkey can accomplish that feat, the storyteller reveals how cleverness leads to fulfillment of a promise.
- *Pourquoi* **tales.** These tales give unscientific explanations of why things are the way they are in the natural world. The name comes from the French word

pronounced "por-quah," meaning "why." Lois Duncan's *The Magic of Spider Woman* reveals the reason why the Navajo blanket contains spirit trails that reflect the belief of keeping balance in our lives. Wandering Girl must overcome her passion to create the most beautiful blanket in all the world as Spider Woman shares a lesson with her. Lore Segal shares brief *pourquoi* tales in *More Mole Stories and Little Gopher, Too*.

- **Nonsense tales.** These tales focus on a simple-minded character whose lack of common sense leads him or her toward a series of silly mistakes. Also known as noodlehead or numbskull tales, the simpleton often travels through life surviving on luck rather than brains. Margie Palatini tells how *The Three Silly Billies* creatively devise a way to include other familiar tale characters to help pay the toll over the troll bridge.

- **Trickster tales.** Often a type of natural creature, the trickster outwits all other creatures in the story. Some tricksters are prankish or crafty; others are wise and generous in their actions. Jim Aylesworth's *The Tale of Tricky Fox* portrays a seemingly cunning character who plays on the curiosity of humans to achieve his end while learning an important lesson. Verna Aardema's *Anansi Does the Impossible* challenges Anansi the spider, the ultimate trickster, to enlist the help of his wife to buy back folktales from the sun. Eric Kimmel shares more of the famed trickster in *Anansi and the Magic Stick*. Lapin can't resist playing tricks on Bouki in three Cajun tales in Sharon Arms Doucet's *Lapin Plays Possum*. Virginia Hamilton memorably gathered an entire array of these cunning characters in *A Ring of Tricksters: Animal Tales from America, the West Indies, and Africa*.

Because traditional tales, including folktales, have their origin in the oral tradition, they were carried by word of mouth to the far corners of the world. Different versions of traditional tales span the globe and deserve recognition. Figure 4.1 shares only a sampling of recently published traditional tales from around the world. They span continents and cultures, but all have one commonality—they tell a good story. Whether read aloud or retold in the voice of the storyteller, these tales not only bring the traditional tale genre to children, they bring the world to readers as well.

Fairy tales. Often identified as a type of magical folktale, the fairy tale contains dominant elements of magic and enchantment. Although often placed in the genre of modern fantasy, they are included here as a type of folktale because they are commonly told through storytelling. Recent interest in fairy-tale variants has renewed interest in this subgenre in elementary classrooms.

Along with shouldering an honored role in literary history, fairy tales maintain a unique place in child development. Bruno Bettleheim (1977) has long supported the role of fairy tales in satisfying emotional needs. In *The Uses of Enchantment*, he analyzes several tales in detail to relate how they enable children to cope with the reality of their emotions in their world. The fine line and personal connections between fairy tales and reality has been further explored by Favat (1977) who parallels components of fairy tales and the concepts of reality in 6- through 8-year-olds, a peak period of interest in these tales.

FIGURE 4.1 Traditional tales around the world

Africa

Aardema, Verna (1996). *The lonely lioness and the ostrich chicks.* Illus. by Yumi Heo. New York: Knopf. (Masai tale) [P]

Berry, James (1996). *Don't leave an elephant to go and chase a bird.* Illus. by A. Grifalconi. New York: Simon & Schuster. (Ghana, Trickster tale) [P/I]

Bryan, Ashley (2003). *Beautiful blackbird.* New York: Atheneum. [P]

Burns, Khephra (2001). *Mansa Musa: The lion of Mali.* Illus. by Leo & Diane Dillon. New York: Gulliver. [I/M]

Diakite, Baba Wague (2003). *The magic gourd.* New York: Scholastic. [P]

Gershator, Phillis (1998). *Zzzng! Zzzng! Zzzng! A Yoruba tale.* Illus. by Teresa Smith. New York: Orchard. [P]

McDermott, Gerald (1992). *Zomo the rabbit: A trickster tale from West Africa.* San Diego: Harcourt Brace. [P/I]

Paye, Won-Ldy (2002). *Head, body, legs: A story from Liberia.* Illus. by Julie Paschkis. New York: Henry Holt. [P]

Australia/New Zealand

Bishop, Gavin (1996). *Maui and the sun: A Maori tale.* New York: North-South Books. (Trickster tale) [P/I]

China

Casanova, Mary (2000). *The hunter: A Chinese folktale.* Illus. by Ed Young. New York: Atheneum. [P/I]

Chang, Margaret, & Chang, Raymond (1997). *The beggar's magic.* Illus. by D. Johnson. New York: McElderry Books. [P/I]

Demi (1990). *The empty pot.* New York: Holt. [I]

Demi (1996). *The dragon's tale and other animal fables of the Chinese zodiac.* New York: Henry Holt. [I]

Kimmel, Eric (1999). *The rooster's antlers: A story of the Chinese zodiac.* Illus. by YongSheng Xuan. New York: Holiday House. [I]

Poole, Amy Lowry (1999). *How the rooster got his crown.* New York: Holiday House. [P]

San Souci, Robert D. (1998). *Fa Mulan.* Illus. by Jean & Mou-Sien Tseng. New York: Hyperion. [I]

Tompert, Ann (1996). *The jade horse: The cricket and the peach stone.* Illus. by W. Trang. Honesdale, PA: Boyds Mills Press. [P/I]

Yep, Laurence (1997). *The Khan's daughter: A Mongolian folktale.* Illus. by J. & M. Tseng. New York: Scholastic. [I]

Young, Ed (1998). *The lost horse: A Chinese folktale.* San Diego: Harcourt Brace. [P]

Japan/Korea/Vietnam

Bodkin, Odds (1998). *The crane wife.* Illus. by G. Spirin. San Diego: Gulliver/Harcourt Brace. [P/I]

Johnston, Tony (1990). *The badger and the magic fan: A Japanese folktale.* Illus. by T. de Paola. New York: Putnam. [P]

Kajikawa, Kimiko (2000). *Yoshi's feast.* Illus. by Yumi Heo. New York: DK Ink. [P]

Martin, Rafe (1996). *Mysterious tales of Japan.* Illus. by Tatsuro Kiuchi. New York: Putnam. [I/M]

Paterson, Katherine (1990). *The tale of the Mandarin ducks.* Illus. by L. & D. Dillon. New York: Lodestar. [I]

San Souci, Daniel (1999). *In the moonlight mist: A Korean tale.* Illus. by Eujin Kim Neilan. Honesdale, PA: Boyds Mills. [I]

Wada, Stephanie (2005). *Momotaro and the island of ogres.* Illus. by Kano Naganobu. New York: Braziller. [I/M]

FIGURE 4.1   Continued

India

Martin, Rafe (1985). *Foolish rabbit's big mistake.* Illus. by Ed Young. New York: Putnam. [P]
Martin, Rafe (1998). *The brave little parrot.* Illus. by Susan Garber. New York: Putnam. [P]

Middle East

Balouch, Kristen (2000). *The king and the three thieves: A Persian tale.* New York: Viking. [P/I]
Demi (1997). *One grain of rice: A mathematical folktale.* New York: Scholastic. [I/M]
Henderson, Kathy (2006). *Lugalbanda: The boy who got caught up in war.* Illus. by Jane Ray. Cambridge, MA: Candlewick Press. (ancient Iraq) [I]
Johnson-Davies, Denys (2005). *Goha the wise fool.* Illus. by Hag Hamdy and Hany. New York: Philomel. [P/I]
Souhami, Jessica (1999). *No dinner! The story of the old woman and the pumpkin.* New York: Marshall Cavendish. [P]
Yolen, Jane (1996). *Little mouse & elephant.* Illus. by John Segal. New York: Simon & Schuster. [P]

Russia

Martin, Rafe (2000). *The language of birds.* Illus. by Susan Gaber. New York: Putnam. [I]
McCaughrean, Geraldine (2000). *Grandma chickenlegs.* Illus. by Moira Kemp. Minneapolis, MN: Carolrhoda. [I]
Polacco, Patricia (1993). *Babushka Baba Yaga.* New York: Philomel Books. [P/I]
Sanderson, Ruth (2000). *The golden mare, the firebird, and the magic ring.* Boston: Little, Brown. [I]
San Souci, Robert D. (1998). *A weave of words.* Illus. by R. Colon. New York: Orchard Books. (Armenia) [I]
San Souci, Robert D. (2000). *Peter and the blue witch baby.* Illus. by Alexi Natchev. New York: Doubleday. [I]
Vagin, Vladimir (2000). *Peter and the wolf.* From the symphony by Sergei Prokofiev. New York: Scholastic. [P/I]

Eastern Europe

Philip, Neil (2001). *Noah and the devil: A legend of Noah's ark from Romania.* Illus. by Isabelle Brent. New York: Clarion. [I]
Prose, Francine (2000). *The demon's mistake: A story from Chelm.* Illus. by Mark H. Podwell. New York: Greenwillow. (Czechoslovakia) [I]
Sturges, Philemon, & Vojtech, Anna (1996). *Marushka and the month brothers.* Illus. by A. Vojtech. New York: North-South Books. (Czechoslovakia) [P/I]

Western Europe

Dasent, George Webb (Translator) (2005). *East o' the sun and west o' the moon.* Illus. by P. J. Lynch. Cambridge, MA: Candlewick Press. (Norway) [I/M]
Del Negro, Janie (2005). *Willa and the wind.* Illus. by Heather Solomon. Marshall Cavendish. (Norway) [P/I]
Kimmel, Eric (1996). *Count Silvernose: A story from Italy.* Illus. by Omar Rayyan. New York: Holiday House. [I]
Hodges, Margaret (1996). *Molly Limbo.* Illus. by E. Miles. New York: Atheneum. (Scotland) [P/I]

(continued)

FIGURE 4.1 Continued

Huck, Charlotte (2001). *The black bull of Narroway: A Scottish tale.* Illus. by Anita Lobel. New York: Greenwillow. [P/I]

Lunge-Larsen, Lise (1999). *The troll with no heart in his body and other tales of trolls from Norway.* (Originally told by Peter Christen Asbjornsen and Jorgen Engebretsen Moe). Illus. by Betsy Bowen. Boston: Houghton Mifflin. [I]

Orgel, Doris (2004). *The Bremen town musicians and other animal tales from Grimm.* Illus. by Bert Kitchen. New York: Roaring Brook Press. (Germany) [P]

Poole, Amy (2005). *The pea blossom.* New York: Holiday House. (Denmark) [P/I]

Sierra, Judith (2000). *The beautiful butterfly: A folktale from Spain.* Illus. by Victoria Chess. New York: Clarion. [P]

Souhami, Jessica (2002). *Mrs. McCool and the giant Cuhullin: An Irish tale.* New York: Henry Holt. [P]

Stewig, John (2001). *Mother Holly: A retelling from the Brothers Grimm.* Illus. by Johanna Westerman. New York: North-South Books. [P]

Williams, Marcia (2007). *Chaucer's Canterbury tales.* Cambridge, MA: Candlewick Press. (England) [I/M]

Caribbean

Ada, Alma Flor (1993). *The rooster who went to his uncle's wedding.* Illus. by K. Kuchera. New York: Putnam. (Cuba) [P]

Hamilton, Virginia (2000). *The girl who spun gold.* Illus. by Leo & Diane Dillon. New York: Scholastic. [I/M]

Hausman, Gerald (1998). *Doctor bird: Three lookin' up tales from Jamaica.* Illus. by A. Wolff. New York: Philomel Books. [P/I]

Jaffe, Nina (1996). *The golden flower: A Taino myth from Puerto Rico.* Illus. by E. Sanchez. New York: Simon & Schuster. [P/I]

Montes, Marisa (2000). *Juan Bobo goes to work: A Puerto Rican folktale.* Illus. by Joe Cedpeda. New York: Morrow. [P/I]

San Souci, Robert D. (1995). *The faithful friend.* Illus. by Brian Pinkney. New York: Simon & Schuster. [I]

Mexico

Camboy, F. Isabel, & Ada, Alma Flor (2006). *Tales our abuelitas told: A Hispanic folktale collection.* Illus. by Felipe Davales, Vivf Eseriva, Susan Guevara, & Legla Torres. New York: Atheneum. [P/I]

Ehlert, Lois (1997). *Cuckoo: A Mexican folktale/Cucú: Un cuento folklórico.* Translated by Gloria Andujar. San Diego: Harcourt Brace. [P/I]

Gollub, Matthew (1996). *Uncle snake.* Illus. by L. Martinez. New York: Tambourine/Morrow. (Pourquoi) [P/I]

Marcantonio, Patricia Santos (2005). *Red ridin' in the hood and other cuentos.* Illus. by Renato Alarcao. New York: Farrar, Straus & Giroux. [I]

McDermott, Gerald (1997). *Musicians of the sun.* New York: Simon & Schuster. [P/I]

Mora, Pat (2005). *Dona Flor: A tall tale about a giant woman with a great big heart.* Illus. by Raul Colon. New York: Knopf. [P/I]

Rockwell, Anne F. (2000). *The boy who wouldn't obey: A Mayan legend.* New York: Greenwillow. [I]

FIGURE 4.1   Continued

Collected Tales From Around the World

Climo, Shirley (2005). *Monkey business: Stories from around the world*. Illus. by Erik Brooks. New York: Henry Holt. [I/M]

Doherty, Berlie (1998). *Tales of wonder and magic*. Illus. by J. Wijngaard. Cambridge, MA: Candlewick Press. [I/M]

Oberman, Sheldon (2006). *Solomon and the ant and other Jewish folktales*. Honesdale, PA: Boyds Mills Press. [I/M]

Sherman, Josepha (1996). *Trickster tales: Forty folk stories from around the world*. Illus. by David Boston. Little Rock, AR: August House. [I]

Walker, Paul R. (1997). *Little folk: Stories from around the world*. Illus. by J. Bernardin. San Diego: Harcourt Brace. [I]

See Chapter 8, "Multicultural and International Literature," for examples of traditional tales of the African American, Native American, Asian American, and Hispanic American cultures.

Fairy tales are typically the realm of elves, fairies, witches, wizards, magicians, and fairy godmothers. Magical objects touch their hands in the forms of wands, branches, or pixie dust. Transformations and spells of enchantment dominate their plots as princes turn into frogs and princesses fall into timeless sleep. These tales of magic, wonder, and the supernatural capture young children's attention as they are carried into a world of towering castles, talking mirrors, glass slippers, and magical beans. The imaginative and dreamlike qualities of fairy tales and the allusions made to them in everyday life identify them as an essential part of a child's literary background.

Retellings of popular fairy tales have created masterpieces of storytelling and illustration in recent years. Paul Zelinsky's Caldecott award–winning retelling of *Rapunzel* is a tribute to the importance of well-told tales in the literary lives of children. Drawing on elements from early French and Italian art, Zelinsky blends stunning oil paintings with a powerfully written version of this Grimm fairy tale. Zelinsky previously blended retelling and art successfully in *Rumpelstiltskin* and teamed with Rika Lesser for a retelling of *Hansel and Gretel*. Trina Schart Hyman has also resurrected traditional fairy tales in inviting realistic formats through *Little Red Riding Hood*, and Angela Barrett eloquently portrayed the *Beauty and the Beast* in Max Eilenberg's retelling through her romantic watercolors.

Several fairy tales have been expanded to full-length chapter book formats with great appeal to older readers. Robin McKinley's *Beauty: A Retelling of the Story of Beauty and the Beast* captures the essence of love. Just as in the original version, Beauty's growing admiration for the beast releases him from the spell and turns him into a handsome prince. Donna Napoli's *Zel* extends the Rapunzel story through the alternating voices of Rapunzel, her mother, and the prince while revealing the psychological motivations of the characters. On a lighter note, Gail Levine's *Ella Enchanted*, a Newbery honor book, introduces Ella of Frell who struggles against a childhood curse that forces her to obey any order she receives. Margaret Peterson Haddix's *Just Ella* begins with Ella betrothed to Prince Charming but suffocating

MAX EILENBERG ILLUSTRATED BY ANGELA BARRETT

under the restrictions and expectations of a princess. The latest Cinderella adaptation is Diane Stanley's *Bella at Midnight* which preserves its fairy-tale magic while adding ample variety in the guise of an intelligent, assertive heroine.

Fairy-tale variants are modern fairy tales that are slight alterations of original tales and provide a different perspective through character, details, setting, or ending. Jon Scieszka's ground-breaking point-of-view variant called *The True Story of the Three Little Pigs* is told from the perspective of A. Wolf. David Wiesner's *The Three Pigs* won the Caldecott Medal in 2002 for its unique artistic extension of this tale. *The Wolf's Story* by Toby Forward tells "what really happened to Little Red Riding Hood." A traditional fairy tale like E. Nesbit's *Jack and the Beanstalk* takes on a new twist as female heroines rise to the challenge of independent problem solving and resourcefulness (Marshall, 2004) in Mary Pope Osborne's *Kate and the Beanstalk* and *The Brave Little Seamstress.* Chapter 11 discusses in detail how these fairy-tale variants can become a springboard for response-related writing activities.

Fables. Fables tell a simple story that teaches a moral lesson or emphasizes a universal truth. Animal characters carry the action of these brief tales with the moral commonly stated at the tale's end. Aesop's fables are the best known collection of fables in the world with Arnold Lobel's award-winning *Fables* providing an outstanding format for younger children. Ed Young's *Seven Blind Mice* also provides a colorful means to introduce fables to students. Michael Morpurgo's *The McElderry Book of Aesop's Fables* and Jerry Pinkney's *Aesop's Fables* introduce readers to the verbal morals and visual lessons inspired by these traditional stories. Paul Rosenthal's *Yo, Aesop! Get a Load of These Fables* and Jon Scieszka and Lane Smith's *Squids Will Be Squids: Fresh Morals, Beastly Tales*, in contrast, provide a

Literary Legend

Fairy Tale Creator

To read the fairy tales of **Hans Christian Andersen** (1805–1875) is to discover a sense of his own fairy-tale life, to hear his distinctive storytelling voice, and to experience the disappointments and joys of life's unpredictable journey. Revisiting his early life, his personal and professional struggles, his lifelong pursuit of fame, and his ultimate recognition as an international celebrity and creator of 156 fairy tales pays tribute to this inventor of the fairy-tale genre.

As a penniless child, Hans was a loner, busy reading, listening to his father's stories, singing, and playing with his toy theater. At 14, with no money or invitation, he bid farewell to Odense and made his way to the city of Copenhagen to seek his fame. Knocking on the doors of prominent citizens, he was fortunate to meet Jonas Collins, a director of the Royal Theater who sponsored his career. In 1835 H.C. Andersen published his first four fairy tales in a paper booklet: *The Princess and the Pea, The Tinderbox, Little Claus and Big Claus, and Little Ida's Flowers*. Most of Andersen's greatest tales were written between 1835 and 1848, and many of his tales reveal aspects of his own life in some guise. Unrequited love (*The Steadfast Tin Solider*), a duckling who becomes a swan (*The Ugly Duckling*), a starving, freezing street girl rescued from the cold (*The Little Matchgirl*)—all reflect aspects of Andersen's own life.

The recent celebration of 200 years of Hans Christian Andersen enabled adults and educators to introduce his timeless treasures to yet another generation of listeners and readers. Countless anthologies, translations, retellings, and illustrated editions of Andersen's fairy tales rekindle our recognition of his effortless gift of language, the sadness and grief of characters, and the ultimate joy and surprise in life's journey—"the most beautiful fairy tale" of all.

(1999). *The little match girl*. Retold and illus. by Jerry Pinkney. New York: Dial.

(2002). *The nightingale*. Retold by Stephen Mitchell. Illus. by Bagram Ibatoulline. Cambridge, MA: Candlewick.

(2003). *The stories of Hans Christian Andersen: A new translation from the Danish* by Diana Crone Frank and Jeffrey Frank. Illus. by Vilhelm Pedersen and Lorenz Frolich. Boston: Houghton Mifflin.

(2004). *Tales of Hans Christian Andersen*. Edited and translated by Naomi Lewis. Illus. by Joel Stewart. Cambridge, MA: Candlewick.

(2004). *The little mermaid*. Translated by Anthea Bell. Illus. by Lisbeth Zwerger. New York: Minedition.

(2004). *Thumbelina*. Retold and illus. by Brad Sneed. New York: Dial.

(2005). *The ugly duckling*. Translated by Anthea Bell. Illus. by Robert Ingpen. New York: Minedition.

lighthearted, updated approach to these traditional bits of Aesop's wisdom. All maintain the essence of lessons to be learned and applied to life. The Aesop Prize for folktales and other traditional tales is now awarded to recognize the power of the traditional literature genre (MacDonald, 2006).

Myths. Myths are stories that explain the origins of the world and its natural phenomena. Similar to *pourquoi* tales, myths feature Roman, Greek, or Norse gods and goddesses who control human fate from a heaven-like setting. Myths that are collected and ordered logically present a mythology of the entire universe. Because myths seem more abstract, they are generally popular with upper elementary students. Myths also encompass cultural creation tales as evidenced by Virginia Hamilton's *In the Beginning: Creation Stories from Around the World*. Creation tales depict the struggle to form the earth from darkness and chaos. Leach (2001) reports an explosion of creation myths across continents and cultures in the past decade.

Anne Rockwell's *The One-Eyed Giant and Other Monsters from the Greek Myths* shares the ever-popular myths of the Cyclops, Medusa, the Minotaur, and Sylla. *Favorite Norse Myths* retold by Mary Pope Osborne include "How Thor Got His Hammer" and "The Golden Apples." *The Illustrated Book of Myths: Tales and Legends of the World* retold by Neil Philip shares tales from around the globe with timeless universal stories that form our literary heritage. Many of these tales are accumulated in collections and are most appropriately shared with intermediate-grade and middle-school students.

Legends. Legends share the stories of extraordinary deeds accomplished by real or supposedly real heroes and heroines. Legends describe the daring feats of a person of lowly status whose good deeds or heroic quest is eventually rewarded with a high position. Heroes or heroines are often accompanied by a wise mentor who directs or guides them through unexpected challenges. Although their journey may be entered into with trepidation, their self-determination and inner confidence allow these heroes and heroines to succeed. Eric Kimmel's retellings of *The Hero Beowulf* and *Blackbeard's Last Fight* are believably illustrated by Leonard Everett Fisher. Trina Schart Hyman, the highly respected illustrator of legends and tales, realistically depicts royalty in Margaret Hodges's *Merlin and the Making of the King*. M. T. Anderson's *The Serpent Came to Glouster*, Robert Burleigh's *Hercules*, and Michael Morpurgo's *Sir Gawain and the Green Knight* are a few examples of legends that span time and settings.

Tall tales are legends in which seemingly common people with exaggerated character traits accomplish unbelievable tasks. American tall tale heroes parallel our country's historical expansion and include Steven Kellogg's *Pecos Bill,* the Texas cowboy; Lynne Bertrand's *Granite Baby;* and Caroline Arnold's *The Terrible Hodag and the Animal Catchers* from the lumber camps of Wisconsin. Tall tale heroines have gained increasing recognition through Pat Mora's *Dona Flor: A Tall Tale of A Giant Woman with a Great Big Heart* and other tales featuring females in assertive roles.

EVALUATING QUALITY TRADITIONAL TALES

The following expectations for quality traditional literature assist in evaluating and selecting books from this wide-ranged literary genre.

- The story should be appropriate to the developmental age of the children who will read and enjoy it.
- The oral storytelling style of the original tale should be preserved in the book retelling as evidenced in an oral read-aloud.
- The integrity of the original culture of the tale should be retained through authentic names, cultural terminology, and cultural authenticity of language elements.
- The illustrated versions of traditional tales should be of high quality and provide assistance in interpreting story, plot, characters, and theme.
- An author's note or introduction should explain the origin of the tale and its connections across cultures and locations to reinforce the source of traditional tales.

When these standards are applied to Baba Wague Diakite's *The Hatseller and the Monkeys*, we view a traditional tale suited for an introduction to the folktale genre for young children. The succinct writing and appealing African phrases beg to be delivered through an oral read-aloud in a storytelling voice. The vibrant ceramic tile illustrations bring Ba Musa, the monkeys, and all the plants and creatures of the fertile African countryside vividly to life. Chains of monkeys frame each page, keeping children's eyes and ears focused on the evolving story. An author's note explains the source of the story in his own life and the versions of the tale shared around the world. Spontaneous responses include cheering, jeering, and satisfaction with the outcome.

BENEFITS OF TRADITIONAL TALES

Traditional tales have been handed down through the oral tradition for centuries, yet they retain their ability to entertain their audience. Bowman (2004) points out the importance of folklore as an extraordinary teaching tool. During this time of growing cultural diversity, traditional tales serve important purposes in the lives of children.

- Traditional tales carry on the strong oral tradition of storytelling.
- Traditional tales provide an important introduction to simple story structure as repeated readings contribute to comfort and confidence through the predictable nature of the tales.
- Traditional tales provide a resource for classroom storytelling by teachers or retellings by children.
- Traditional tales provide an added dimension to a child's cultural literacy as she or he experiences tales from around the world.
- Traditional tales provide moral models for children as the struggle between good and evil is applied to incidents in their own lives.

READER RESPONSE TO TRADITIONAL TALES

Reader response connections to traditional literature hold a wide range of possibilities because of the broadness of this literary genre. Traditional literature begs to be shared through retellings or storytelling with older children. The familiarity of plot and dialogue often assists in puppet presentations or dramatic improvisations. Children often respond to the moral themes of these tales as evidenced in both oral and written response. Fairy-tale variants, in particular, serve as springboards to ideas for writing one's own variant by changing a single aspect of the story—character, setting, ending. Tall tales and myths are also enthusiastically embraced as models for writing in these particular formats.

Mostly, however, children respond to good stories. Children love repeating the memorable lines of the characters in imitative voices. They readily share their favorite characters, how they would have approached a problem, or their opinions on the outcomes. Teachers should allow time before, during, and after reading for voices to surface. Traditional tales do not require prompting, just freedom to respond naturally and spontaneously. Teri Lesesne (2001) provides a wealth of titles and ideas for responding to recent traditional tales.

Traditional tales provide a background of the oral heritage of literature that should become a part of a child's literary repertoire. An abundance of quality picture books originated from a variety of cultures and shared over a variety of times supplies the reader with extensive access to this literary genre. Although initiation to this genre generally occurs in the home setting, teachers must be certain that children have opportunities to listen to, retell, and internalize these oral treasures in the school setting. A study by Mello (2001) reports powerful responses to oral storytelling of traditional tales which "furnish students with a broader cultural lens to view the world." (p. 548). The fairy tales, Greek myths, and tall tales we read as children are seldom forgotten. Often reread, powerfully retold, and

---

RESOURCES ON THE WEB
Fairy Tales

Many online resources can assist teachers and students as they read and discuss fairy tales. Use these sites to access multiple copies of the same fairy tale or locate difficult-to-find fairy tales that are no longer easily accessible in print. Students may enjoy the related games and online activities.

Hans Christian Andersen Odense City Museums
In the Hans Christian Andersen section of the Odense City Museums website, you can find information about three Andersen museums: The Hans Christian Andersen Museum, Hans Christian Andersen's Childhood Home, and Hans Christian Andersen in Vingårdsstræde. Browsers can also view the museum's digital collections, where it is possible to study the writer's original manuscripts, his pictorial artwork, and portraits of him and his acquaintances. Plenty of information about Andersen's life and work as well as the objects in the museum collections is provided. *http://www.museum.odense.dk/H_C_Andersen.aspx*

Hans Christian Andersen Fairy Tales and Stories
This site presents a bibliographical information chronology, and the complete stories of H. C. Andersen. Other features include the H. C. Andersen postage stamp collection, virtual bookstore, and annotated links to other H. C. Andersen websites. *http://hca.gilead.org.il/*

Folklore, Fairy Tales, and Mythology Electronic Texts
Edited and/or translated by Dr. Ashliman from the University of Pittsburg, this is an excellent resource of multiple versions of traditional tales. For example, the site contains over 15 versions of Cinderella originating from across the world. Related links to other online resources are also included. *http://www.pitt.edu/~dash/folktexts. html*

Fairy Tales
Maintained by the University of Maryland, this site features a large collection of fairy tales by many different authors. The stories are printable in plain text format. *http://www.lib.umd.edu/ETC/ReadingRoom/Fiction/FairyTales/*

always cherished, traditional literature holds a special place in a child's literary experience.

MODERN FANTASY

Modern fantasy is characterized by a single element or set of complex elements that only exist in the imagination. The imaginary element provides the bridge that separates fantasy from realism. Fantasy suspends the reader's belief as he or she enters a new world or accepts a scientific impossibility in our own world. The conceptualization of fantasy reveals author ingenuity as imaginary settings, magical dimensions, and heroes and heroines possessing incredible powers compel the reader to transcend reality and willingly partake of a fanciful tale (Cruz & Pollock, 2004). Great fantasies can even reveal new insights into the world of reality.

In Jane Yolen's (1997) introduction to her collection of fanciful short stories, *Twelve Impossible Things Before Breakfast*, she shares her experience with fantasy writing.

> You fill the tale with creatures or people who never existed, or you take a spin on stories that are well-known and loved. And all the while you talk about the fantastic, you are actually writing about the real world and real emotions, the right-here and the right-now. It is a kind of literary displacement, a way of looking at what worries both writer and reader by glancing out of the corner of one's eye. (p. x)

Fantasy describes books in which magic causes impossible and wondrous events to occur. Fantasy tales can be set in our own everyday world or in a "secondary world" somewhat like our own. The existence of the magic cannot be explained but certainly can be savored. The narrative storytelling of the fantasy genre is magical in its ability to enchant readers and draw them past the boundaries of the reality of their world and into the inexplicable magic of another (Kurkjian, Livingston, Young, & Avi, 2006). Fantasy, however, does not escape reality but illuminates it by transporting readers to a world different from their

KidsFunCanada.com
This is a fun, interactive site with games, e-learning modules, and activities related to fairy-tale stories by the Grimm Brothers, Hans Christian Andersen, and other classic tales. Children can listen to the story or Turn off the sound and read the text independently.
http://www.kidsfuncanda.com/en/

Grimm's Fairy Tales
National Geographic brings a dozen of Grimm's classic fairy tales to this website, including Cinderella, The Bremen Town-Musicians, and Rapunzel. All stories include beautiful illustrations; some incorporate audio so students can listen to the story. Additional site features include maps, information about the Grimms, kids' activities, and extensive links to related websites.
http://www.nationalgeographic.com/grimm/

Fantasy Authors
Lloyd Alexander
Kidsreads.com—Lloyd Alexander
http://www.kidreads.com/authors/au-alexander-lloyd.asp
Children's Literature: Meet Authors & Illustrators
http://www.childrenslit.com/f_lloydalexander.html

J. K. Rowling
J.K. Rowling Official Site
http://www.jkrowling.com/
Scholastic: Meet J.K. Rowling
http://www.scholastic.com/harrypotter/author/

Kate DiCamillo
Kate DiCamillo.com
http://www.katedicamillo.com/

T. A. Barron
T. A. Barron Official Website
http://www.tabarron.com/tabarron/

own while demonstrating truths that persist in both worlds. Lynn (1995) describes fantasy as "imaginative, fanciful, visionary, strange, otherworldly, supernatural, mysterious, frightening, magical, inexplicable, wondrous, dreamlike, and, paradoxically, realistic" (p. xxv). A natural yearning for a sudden glimpse of something strange and different may lead the reader to a truer sense of reality.

Through the years, fantasy has played a vital role in popular children's literature. E. B. White's *Charlotte's Web* transported the reader into the world of talking animals, Natalie Babbit's *Tuck Everlasting* caused deliberation on the consequences of eternal life. J. R. R. Tolkein's *The Hobbit* enthralled the reader with Bilbo Baggins and an introduction to the world of Middle Earth; Lloyd Alexander transported participants to Taran and five incredible chronicles of the pigkeeper turned hero in *The Book of Three*. Some of the most memorable books from childhood are fantasies often read aloud by teachers or parents: Lewis Carroll's *Alice Through the Looking Glass,* Kenneth Grahame's *The Wind in the Willows*, Roald Dahl's *James and the Giant Peach*. Once introduced to the realm of fantasy, children are likely to approach this genre with anticipation and excitement.

The fantasy genre gained momentum with readers with the introduction of J. K. Rowling's *Harry Potter and the Sorcerer's Stone* to the United States. Anticipation of its six sequels (*Harry Potter and the Chamber of Secrets, Harry Potter and the Prisoner of Azkaban, Harry Potter and the Goblet of Fire, Harry Potter and the Order of the Phoenix, Harry Potter and the Half-Blood Prince*, and *Harry Potter and the Deathly Hallows*) has ignited young readers' imaginations and developed unquenchable thirst for the fantasy genre. Hogwarts School, the Quidditch broom, and witchcraft and wizardry have even intrigued adult readers. Mark West (2000) reminds fantasy advocates that although some controversy has accompanied the series, the fantasy genre, stretching back to Frank Baum's (1900) *The Wonderful Wizard of Oz*, has always been a target for potential censorship. Yet fantasy ultimately grants children the freedom to exercise their imaginations and to rekindle and experience the joy of visual response during reading.

Types of Fantasy

Important variations exist among the different types of fantasy that make subgenre classification both challenging and valuable. The breadth of the fantasy genre is intriguing as imagination enters the world of people, places, situations, and things. Because most fantasies are continuing quests or adventures, the trend in the fantasy genre has been to produce books as a trilogy, quartet, or series that follows a character through many adventures in a distinctive secondary imaginative world of magic. Figure 4.2 lists and elaborates on many fantasy series books, old and new, that will motivate children to become engaged in fantasy books.

Although most of their titles are high fantasy, they also include animal fantasy and toy fantasy, two of the fantasy types discussed in this section. Because this is a genre often unfamiliar to or forgotten by unimaginative adults, it becomes even more important for them to build their own awareness of books in this genre.

Literary Legend

Fantasy Author

Born in Philadelphia, **Lloyd Alexander** (1924–2007) developed an early affinity for Arthurian legends. His childhood memory of using a trash can lid for a shield and his uncle's cane as Excalibur displays the sort of heroic longing seen in many of his fictional creations. As a teenager, Lloyd decided he wanted to be a writer, a decision that appalled his parents, who did not read books. After attempting a variety of ill-suited jobs, Lloyd joined the army. His interest in Welsh mythology has its roots in a training assignment in Wales during World War II. Years later, this land and its legends would serve as a source of inspiration for Alexander's greatest fantasy creation—the land of Prydain and the five novels that chronicle the adventures of an Assistant Pig-Keeper who longs for adventure and finds it. The final Prydain novel, *The High King,* was awarded the Newbery Award in 1969.

After writing seven years before getting a book published, and writing for adults in the beginning, Alexander turned to writing for young readers, and most of his books belong to the fantasy genre. Drawing from mythologies from all corners of the world, his novels are a unique blend of fantasy, realism, and comedy working together to explore what it is that makes us human. At first glance, strange lands and unfamiliar names might seem daunting for young readers, but Alexander's characters—ranging from bean-counters and orphans to magicians and kings—immediately draw everyone in. Whether using his uncle's cane or a mere pen, Lloyd Alexander's imagination has, for a lifetime, created so much that is remarkable.

(1964). *The book of three.* New York: Henry Holt.

(1965). *The black cauldron.* New York: Henry Holt.

(1966). *The Castle of Llyr.* New York: Henry Holt.

(1967). *Taran wanderer.* New York: Henry Holt.

(1969). *The high king.* New York: Henry Holt.

(1991). *The remarkable journey of Prince Jen.* New York: Dutton.

(1995). *The Arkadians.* New York: Dutton.

(1999). *Gypsy Rizka.* New York: Dutton.

(2002). *The rope trick.* New York: Dutton.

Animal fantasy.   Perhaps the most popular read-alouds from the fantasy genre, animal fantasies showcase animals who possess human qualities in addition to their natural characteristics. They are personified with human emotions, they reason through complex situations, and they communicate with other animals. Famous stars of rodent fantasies, for example, include Beverly Cleary's adventurous *Ralph S. Mouse,* E. B. White's diminutive *Stuart Little,* Robert O'Brien's widowed Mrs. Frisby, courageous

FIGURE 4.2 Book Cluster: Fantasy series books

THE CHRONICLES OF PRYDAIN by Lloyd Alexander. New York: Holt. [I/M]

(1964). *The book of three.* Taran, a young pigkeeper, and Gwydion, a warrior, battle
the Horned King.

(1965). *The black cauldron.* Taran and Gwydion plan to destroy the black cauldron of the Lord of the
Land of Death. (Newbery Honor book)

(1966). *The castle of Llyr.* Taran and Gwydion rescue Princess Eilonwy, who has been kidnapped by
the wicked steward.

(1967). *Taran wanderer.* Taran, grown to a young man, journeys through Prydain
seeking his identity.

(1968). *The high king.* The final struggle of the people of Prydain against the Lord of the Land of Death.
(Newbery Medal, 1969)

WESTMARK TRILOGY by Lloyd Alexander. New York: Dutton. [I/M]

(1981). *Westmark.* Theo and Mickle turn the tables on Cabbarus, the king's evil minister, when he tries
to gain control of the throne.

(1982). *The kestrel.* Theo becomes a bloodthirsty warrior defending his love, Queen Mickle of Westmark.

(1984). *The beggar queen.* Westmark is overthrown by ex-minister Cabbarus, forcing a resistance
movement.

THE GREAT TREE OF AVALON by T. A. Barron. New York: Philomel. [I/M]

(2004). *Book One: Child of the dark prophecy.*

(2005). *Book Two: Shadow on the stars.*

(2006). *Book Three: The eternal flame.*

THE LOST YEARS OF MERLIN EPIC by T. A. Barron. New York: Philomel. [I/M]

(1996). *The lost years of Merlin.* A young boy washes ashore on the coast of ancient Wales with no
memory until an awakening of his power and his second sight identifies him as Merlin, destined to
be the greatest wizard of all time.

(1997). *The seven songs of Merlin.* Merlin encounters his mother and discovers the dark
side of his powers.

(1998). *The fires of Merlin.* Merlin encounters fire in the form of an ancient dragon and discovers the
power to heal is greater than the power to destroy.

(1999). *The mirror of Merlin.* The young wizard gains a greater understanding of his powers and his
humanity while discovering a magic mirror that can alter one's fate.

(2000). *Wings of Merlin.* Merlin gains mastery over his powers as he strives to save his homeland and
all the people he loves from destruction.

**THE ARTHUR SEEING STONE TRILOGY by Kevin Crossley-Holland. New York:
Arthur Levine/Scholastic. [M]**

(2001). *The seeing stone.* Book One. Young Arthur de Caldicot's and King Arthur's lives intertwine
during this pageant of characters and life in the Middle Ages.

(2002). *At the crossing places.* Book Two. The tales of Camelot, Arthur and Guinevere and the Knights
of the Round Table mirror life during the time of the Fourth Crusade.

(2004). *King of the middle march.* Arthur de Caldicot witnesses the horrors of the Fourth Crusade as
well as the downfall of King Arthur's Court.

FIGURE 4.2   Continued

THE SPIDERWICK CHRONICLES by T. Diterlizzi and H. Black. New York: Simon & Schuster. [I/M]

(2003). *The field guide: Book one.*
(2003). *The seeing stone: Book two.*
(2003). *Lucinda's secret: Book three.*
(2004). *The ironwood tree: Book four.*
(2004). *The wrath of mulgarath: Book five.*

INKHEART TRILOGY by Cornelia Funke. New York: Scholastic/Chicken House. [I/M]

Characters have the ability to "read" characters out of classic books and into today's world while
   readers are able to transport themselves into the world of fictional books.
(2003). *Inkheart.*
(2005). *Inkspell.*
(2007). *Inkdeath.*

REDWALL SAGA by Brian Jacques. New York: Putnam. [M]

(1987). *Redwall.* Matthias Mouse defends Redwall Abbey from rats with plans to enslave mice.
(1988). *Mossflower.* (Prequel) Martin the Warrior battles wildcat Tsarmina for peace in the Woodlands.
(1990). *Mattimeo.* Matthias's son, enslaved by a fox, is rescued by his father while his mother saves
   the abbey.
(1992). *Mariel of Redwall.* The daughter of Joseph the bellmaker becomes a warrior in quest of Gabool.
(1993). *Salamandastron.* Martin's sword is stolen and the castle is attacked by Ferahgo the Assassin.
Additional titles in this series include *Martin the Warrior* (1994), *The Bellmaker* (1995), *Outcast of Redwall*
   (1996), *The pearls of Lutra* (1997), *The long patrol* (1997); *Marlfox* (1999); *Lord Brocktree* (2000);
   Taggrung (2001); *Triss* (2002); *Loamhedge* (2003); *Rakkety Tam* (2004); and *High Rhulain* (2005).

EARTHSEA QUARTET by Ursula Le Guin. New York: Parnassus/Atheneum. [M]

(1968). *A wizard of Earthsea.* Ged, studying wizardry, accidentally conjures up a terrifying creature that
   threatens the existence of the world of Earthsea.
(1971). *The tombs of Atuan.* Ged invades the forbidden labyrinth of Atuan, forcing Tenar to make a
   choice. (Newbery Honor book, 1972)
(1972). *The farthest shore.* Ged and Prince Arren make a journey into the Shadow Kingdom of the
   dead.
(1990). *Tehanu: The last book of Earthsea.* Tenar heals both an abused child and Ged, who lost his
   magical powers in a struggle to save the world.

THE CHRONICLES OF NARNIA by C. S. Lewis. New York: Macmillan. (Suggested reading order) [I]

(1955). *The magician's nephew.* Digory and Polly borrow an uncle's magic rings and are transported to
   Narnia, just as Aslan is singing it into existence.

(continued)

FIGURE 4.2 Continued

(1951). *The lion, the witch, and the wardrobe.* Many years later, four children stumble through a magic wardrobe into Narnia where they struggle to break the White Witch's enchantment.

(1954). *The horse and his boy.* Shasta and Aravis and their talking horses flee into Narnia.

(1951). *Prince Caspian: The return to Narnia.* The four children help Aslan restore Prince Caspian's throne.

(1952). *The voyage of the Dawn Treader.* Sailing to World's End in search of seven missing noblemen.

(1953). *The silver chair.* Aslan sends Eustace and Jill on a quest to free Prince Rilian.

(1956). *The last battle.* Aslan calls all creatures who love Narnia to battle against the forces of evil.

THE WIND ON FIRE TRILOGY by William Nicholson. Illus. by Peter Sis. New York: Hyperion. [M]

(2000). *The wind singer.* Twins Kestrel and Bowman set off to find the key to the long-defunct wind singer, which was once the source of happiness and harmony in Aramanth.

(2001). *Slaves of the mastery.* Aramanth is destroyed and the separated twins embark on parallel journeys to fight for the freedom of their people.

(2002). *Firesong.* Led by their prophetess mother, Bowman and Kestrel travel with the Manth people to their promised land.

MAGIC TREE HOUSE BOOKS by Mary Pope Osborne. Illus. by Sal Murdocca. New York: Random House. [P]

This fantasy series for young readers focuses on children transported by their magic tree house to historical periods and events.

(2006). *Night of the new magicians.* (Paris, World's Fair 1889) #35

(2005). *Season of the sandstorms.* (Ancient Baghdad) #34

(2005). *Carnival at candlelight.* (17th-century Venice) #33

(2004). *Winter of the ice wizard.* #32

(2004). *Summer of the sea serpent.* #31

(2003). *Haunted castle on hallow's eve.* #30

HIS DARK MATERIALS TRILOGY by Philip Pullman. New York: Knopf. [I/M]

(1996). *The golden compass.* Lyra Belacqua, accompanied by her daemon, Pantalaimon, sets out to prevent gruesome scientific experiments on children in the Far North.

(1997). *The subtle knife.* Lyra and her daemon help Will Parry in his search for his father and a magic knife.

(1999). *The amber spyglass.* Lyra and an intriguing cast of characters bring a startling resolution to their quest.

(2003). *Lyra's Oxford.* Lyra is back at Oxford, but her peace is shattered by a demon.

FIGURE 4.2 Continued

PERCY JACKSON AND THE OLYMPIANS by Rick Riordan. New York: Hyperion. [I/M]

Perseus Jackson joins demigods at Camp Half-Blood on Long Island and embarks on several adventures and dangerous challenges in the footsteps of Greek gods.
(2005). *The lightning thief: Book one.*
(2006). *The sea of monsters: Book two.*
(2007). *The titan's curse: Book three.*

HARRY POTTER SERIES by J. K. Rowling. Illus. by Mary Grandpré. New York: Scholastic. [I/M]

A young boy with a great destiny proves his worth and develops his prowess while attending Hogwarts School of Witchcraft and Wizardry.
(1998). *Harry Potter and the sorcerer's stone.*
(1999). *Harry Potter and the chamber of secrets.*
(1999). *Harry Potter and the prisoner of Azkaban.*
(2000). *Harry Potter and the goblet of fire.*
(2003). *Harry Potter and the order of the phoenix.*
(2005). *Harry Potter and the half-blood prince.*
(2007). *Harry Potter and the deathly hallows.*

THE TIME WARP TRIO by Jon Scieszka. New York: Viking. [P/I]

Joe, Fred, and Sam perform heroic deeds during their humorous time travel adventures.
(2000). *See you later, gladiator.* Illus. by Adam Macauley.
(2001). *Sam Samurai.* Illus. by Adam Macauley.
(2003). *Me, oh Maya!*
(2004). *Da wild, da crazy, da Vinci.*
(2005). *Oh say, I can't see.*

DRAGONOLOGY CHRONICLES by Dugald A. Steer. Cambridge, MA: Candlewick. [I/M]

Daniel and Beatrice encounter adventures under the tutorage of Dr. Ernest Drake undermined by the evil dragonologist, Ignatius Crook, who is determined to steal the powerful Dragon's Eye jewel that controls the fate of all dragons.
(2006). *The dragon's eye: Volume One.*
(2005). *Dragonology handbook: A practical course in dragons.*

LORD OF THE RINGS TRILOGY by J. R. R.Tolkien. Boston: Houghton Mifflin. [I/M]

(1965). *The fellowship of the ring.* Frodo Baggins inherits a magic ring from Uncle Bilbo and begins a journey to protect it from the powers of evil. Set in Middle Earth.
(1965). *The two towers.* Frodo and Sam take the ring to the borders of the Dark Kingdom while the Company of the Ring battle the wizard Saruman and his goblin army.
(1965). *The return of the king.* Frodo and Sam bring the ring to Mount Doom where it is destroyed to help the forces of good win over the Dark Lord.

Animal fantasy invites the reader to view reality through the eyes of a personified creature.

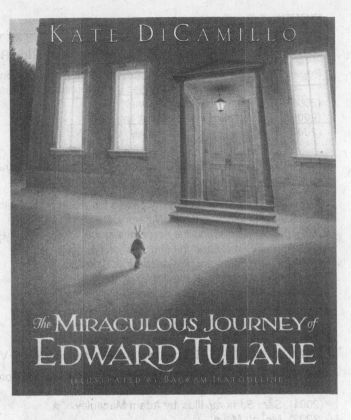

Miss Bianca in Margery Sharp's *The Rescuers*, and the melodramatic survivor in William Steig's *Abel's Island*. These endearing creatures possess humanitarian ideals and engage in challenging encounters in a quest for a better life for themselves or their owners. In its most effective form, animal fantasy permits the reader to view life through the eyes of an animal while gaining a clearer perspective on one's own values.

Kate Di Camillo's Newbery medal *The Tale of Despereaux: Being the Story of a Mouse, a Princess, Some Soup, and a Spool of Thread* showcases a mouse in love with music, stories, and a princess named Pea. Yet he is banished to a dungeon teeming with rats including the archenemy, Roscuro. Stunning pencil illustrations by Timothy Basil Ering spark the imagination of the listener/reader as an imaginative tale seeks reality in the mind's eye. *Poppy* and *Poppy's Return* epitomize the strengths of the animal fantasy as Avi skillfully humanizes the deer mouse heroine who is forced to confront a bully owl, who claims that he alone protects the mouse community. Poppy reflects the best of both animal and human worlds as she embarks alone on her dangerous quests. Tor Seidler creates another trend in heroic rodents through Montague Mad-Rat, set in urban New York, in *A Rat's Tale* and personifies his jealous adversary in its sequel, *The Revenge of Randall Reese-Rat*. These quality animal fantasy read-alouds in both homes and classrooms serve as a strong introduction to the fantasy genre.

An extremely popular series of animal fantasy is the Redwall Saga series by Brian Jacques. In the original *Redwall* (1987) Matthias Mouse defends Redwall Abbey against marauding rats bent on enslaving the peaceful mice in residence there. Prequels and sequels (see Figure 4.2) engage other rodent heroes and heroines in bravely fought battles against animal foes. Other classic animal fantasies that deserve special recognition include Dick King-Smith's *Babe: The Gallant Pig*, Robert Lawson's *Rabbit Hill*, and Robert O'Brien's Newbery award winner *Mrs. Frisby and the Rats of NIHM*. Traditionally, these titles have served as an invitation to the broader world of fantasy literature.

Humorous fantasy. Talented authors introduce readers to humorous and exaggerated tales, including those with fast-paced, comedic plots, bizarre characters, and amusing incidents. Roald Dahl, a master of humorous fantasy, introduces the *BFG* (big friendly giant) who kidnaps Sophie and delivers her to Giant Country where "human beans" provide a steady diet for the inhabitants. In *Matilda*, Dahl introduces a brilliant first grader who triumphs over her parents and Miss Trunchbull, the school principal. Sid Fleischman's *By the Great Horn Spoon* and *Mr. Mysterious and Company* and several titles by Margaret Mahy and Daniel Pinkwater bring a smile to new fans of the funny side of fantasy. J. K. Rowling's enthralling *Harry Potter and the Sorcerer's Stone* and its subsequent series read-alikes, including Eoin Colfer's *Artemis Fowl*, promise to keep the genre alive for years to come.

Magic adventure and toy fantasy. Fantasy can transport the reader to a world of strange happenings in which unearthly wonders surprise and delight. Imagine a world in which toys come to life, miniature people go about their daily lives, and strange occurrences confront the imagination. Memorable members of this extraordinary group of literary characters include Carolyn Bailey's *Miss Hickory*, a country doll with an applewood twig body and hickory nut head, Susan Cooper's ancient and mischievous Scottish spirit named *The Boggart*, Mary Norton's diminutive *The Borrowers*, and Sylvia Waugh's family of life-sized cloth and kapok rag dolls in *Mennyms Alone*. The newest addition to the world of toy fantasy is Kate Di Camillo's *The Miraculous Journey of Edward Tulane*, the tale of an arrogant lost china rabbit whose homeward journey takes him from a watery grave to the hands of a fisherman's wife to the care of a hobo and his dog to the hands of a dying girl. With every person he touches, Edward's heart grows a bit softer. Enhanced by the color plates of Bagram Ibatoulline, this handsome book provides the ultimate toy fantasy read-aloud.

Cornelia Funke has become one of today's most beloved authors of magical stories for children. *Dragon Rider* tales a boy and a dragon on a quest that takes them to magical lands with marvelous creatures finding their own courage along the way. A fold-out colored map in the middle of the book brings visual geography to a magical adventure. For older readers, *The Thief Lord* brings two orphaned brothers, Prosper and Bo, to Venice where they meet the Thief Lord, the leader of runaway children, seeking to steal a magical wooden ring.

A popular series in this fantasy subgenre is the Magic Shop books by Bruce Coville. A magical ring (*The Monster's Ring*), a dragon's egg (*Jeremy Thatcher, Dragon Hatcher*), a talking amphibian (*Jennifer Murdley's Toad*), and a mysterious skull

(*The Skull of Truth*) have lured many intermediate readers to the fantasy genre. Lynne Reid Banks's *The Indian in the Cupboard* and its subsequent series follows a toy Indian and a boy on harrowing western adventures. Nominated consistently for children's choice awards, fantasy series provide yet another tempting invitation into the fantasy genre.

Ghost fantasy.   The world of the supernatural encompasses ghosts, mystery, and unexplainable happenings. A popular author of the supernatural world is Mary Downing Hahn whose books are consistently nominated and honored on children's choice lists. Her books take the reader to the borders of the supernatural in *The Doll in the Garden* and *A Time for Andrew*. Although ghost fantasy is popular reading, it is important to steer children toward quality selections. These mildly chilling stories do not include horror and often contain amusing rather than horrifying elements. With a touch of ghostly humor, Sid Fleischman's *The Midnight Horse* introduces Touch and his ghostly friend, the Great Chuffalo, who work together to foil the dastardly deeds of Judge Henry Wigglesforth. Tales of ghosts and the supernatural fascinate readers of all ages.

A more serious approach to this subgenre is David Almond's *Skellig* in which Michael discovers a strange creature beneath the spider webs in a crumbling garage. Almond's eerie but masterfully written novels, including *Kit's Wilderness* and *Heaven Eyes*, celebrate the magic that is part of our past and present lives. With scrutiny in selection, these titles appeal to both intermediate- and middle-level readers.

Time travel fantasy.   Time shift fantasy is based on characters who readily shift from a particular moment in the present to a point in someone else's past. Characters begin a story in their own safe world, yet find themselves instantly transported to another time, having changed places with an individual from the period. The new place can be a parallel universe, existing at the same time, or a historical world, dispatching them to a situation from the past.

Primary-level readers can "get hooked" on time travel through Mary Pope Osborne's Magic Tree House series. Young readers are instantly transported to the Middle Ages, Egypt, the Ice Age, feudal Japan, Pompeii, or ancient China through brief, easy-to-read time travel fantasy. In Jon Scieszka's humorous Time Warp Trio series (*The Good, the Bad & the Goofy; Knights of the Kitchen Table; The Not-So-Jolly Roger*) Joe, Fred, and Sam travel through time using a magic book given to Joe by his magician uncle. Easy-to-read humor makes these a popular choice as children grow into full-length chapter book time travel.

Dan Gutman's *Shoeless Joe and Me: A Baseball Card Adventure* follows Joe Stoshack from a baseball card to 1919 to meet baseball great Joe Jackson and try to prevent the fixing of the World Series in which Joe was implicated. Other titles in the series include encounters with Babe Ruth, Jackie Robinson, and Honus Wagner. Interspersed with authentic photographs and newspaper clippings, these time travel books draw a commendable fine line between fantasy and realism. Janet Lunn's *The Root Cellar* finds Rose opening a vine-covered root cellar door to enter the Civil War era, 100 years in the past. The strength and determination she requires during this trying time serve her well on her return to the present. Opening the door as a symbol of the Passover seder steals Hannah away to a Polish village during the Holocaust of the 1940s in Jane Yolen's *The Devil's Arithmetic*. Susan Cooper's *King of Shadows* transports Nat Field from London's new Globe theater to 1599 where he is seemingly trapped in Elizabethan England. Cooper's newest *Victory* follows two lives across the Atlantic Ocean 200 years apart, yet connected by Vice-Admiral Lord Nelson in 1805. Although time travel fantasy titles often cross the line toward the historical fiction genre, they do possess the identifying characteristic of travel across time with a return, enriched and informed, to the present.

High fantasy. Heroic, dramatic quests are the hallmark of the popular high fantasy as readers are transported to secondary worlds with names like Narnia, Earthsea, or Prydain. These secondary worlds are close enough to reality to allow identification yet far enough away to suspend reader belief. The main characters of high fantasy often possess lofty ideals and noble codes of honor that assist them on their searches and challenging missions. Their complex plots provide a formidable task for readers as heroes weave their way through intricate adventures against formidable foes. The never-ending battle between good and evil also forces the reader to confront philosophical truths along the adventurous journey.

The adventures of high fantasy often continue through several volumes (see Figure 4.2). The roots of high fantasy trace back to L. Frank Baum's 14 titles of *The Wizard of Oz* (1900) series (extended to 53 by additional authors), thus providing a century of high fantasy to children. Once a reader finds an adventure to follow, his or her imagination is fed through several sequential titles. The Narnia Chronicles of C. S. Lewis, for example, contain seven books; Lloyd Alexander's Prydain Chronicles number five. Once aware of classic high fantasy, readers easily look to new fantasy titles like Philip Pullman's *The Golden Compass, The Subtle Knife*, and *The Amber Spyglass* and favorite authors like Anne McCaffrey or Robin McKinley. T. A. Barron's powerful *The Lost Years of Merlin* begins a series epic following a young boy from the day he washes ashore on the coast of Wales to his ultimate destiny as the great wizard, Merlin. Throughout these five titles, Barron's readers perceive an added dimension to Arthurian lore as they discover the hero within themselves, perhaps still dormant, yet waiting to be revealed. Barron's newest series, *The Great Tree of Avalon: Child of the Dark Prophecy*, is about an ancient tree planted by Merlin to connect heaven and earth. Coming under attack, the fate of this kingdom lies in the hands of three young people. High fantasy bestows the power to turn dreams into reality as readers vicariously experience the challenge of the quest for heroic excellence.

Science fantasy. Set in a future world, science fantasy balances scientific fact and probabilities with fiction. Such books often raise questions about the future, causing readers to reflect on the direction of their values and their world. Historically, this subgenre has been graced with titles including Madeline L'Engle's *A Wrinkle in Time* and John Christopher's *The White Mountains* series, often referred to as science fiction. With an increasing emphasis on story over scientific fact, the term *science fantasy* seems more appropriate for children's literature.

Science fantasy gained momentum and respect as a subgenre of fantasy with the publication of Lois Lowry's *The Giver*, winner of the 1994 Newbery Medal. Jonas lives in a seemingly idyllic, peaceful world as he awaits the Ceremony of the Twelve during which he will be assigned his life's work. His role as Receiver of the Memory designates him not only the keeper of events but of feelings as well. Jonas comes to understand the fullness of human experience with its pain, joy, and color through the current Giver. Beginning to question the orderliness of his own existence and the price humanity has paid for a tranquil life, Jonas escapes with Gabriel, a foster child, and begins a journey that may result in his demise or return him to his lost humanity. Jonas's people lacked choice, but Lowry bestows this precious gift on her readers as she challenges them to ponder the future of their civilization. Lowry revisits this theme in *Gathering Blue, Messenger,* and *Gossamer.* These richly rewarding science fantasies instilled new life in an often forgotten genre for children.

EVALUATING QUALITY FANTASY

Although the number of books in the fantasy genre is smaller than in other genres, guidelines for quality must still be applied in choosing the best fantasy to share with children. Standards include these:

- Fantasy convinces the reader of the possibility of the improbable. Readers must suspend belief and all that they know of reality and willingly enter the world of the impossible.
- Fantasy effectively establishes a setting that is original in both time and place. Authors of fantasy must create ingenious, creative worlds.
- Fantasy is compelling and well written with action and well-developed plausible characters and language that reflects the extraordinary world in which it occurs.
- Fantasy continuously makes the fantastic element believable throughout the story. The element must remain central to the story, and all details must remain consistent with the characteristics of the fantastic element.
- Fantasy creates belief in the unbelievable while maintaining a balance between imagination and what we perceive realism to be.

BENEFITS OF FANTASY

Fantasy fuels the imagination and begs readers to move beyond the real world into an imaginary world where anything is possible. Perhaps the greatest contribution of fantasy to literature lies in its ability to challenge and develop a child's imagination. Children are encouraged to pretend, to visualize, and to dream what might be. Too often today, imaginations are limited to the visual images children are bombarded with through television and movies. When the literary words create a vision of a new world and paint a portrait of a hero or heroine who captures the imagination, fantasy has achieved its primary goal.

Fantasy provides an escape from reality as readers are invited to take on the heroic characteristics of a person from a realm outside our own world. Identifying with the improbable not only entertains but causes the reader to consider the deeper possibilities of an extraordinary world. Often the realities of life—abuse of power, life and death, justice under the law—are couched in fantasy and provide a reason to reflect on morality, values, mortality, community, society, and the larger world.

READER RESPONSE TO FANTASY

An excellent connection and introduction to reader response to fantasy for younger students is picture books that border on fantastic worlds. Looking at the realm of the impossible makes read-alouds magical and calls for imaginative responses. Books like Donna Jo Napoli's *Albert* and Catherine Ann Cullen's *The Magical, Mystical, Marvelous Coat* draw young eyes and ears into the world of fantasy. Brian Jacques's *The Great Redwall Feast* is a picture book introduction to the abbey and creatures of Redwall and an inspiring invitation to future readers of the Redwall Saga series as reading ability and developmental maturity stretch.

Young children's responses will likely blur the probable and the possible, revealing their belief that such settings and possibilities do exist. They enjoy suspending belief and often respond as if the book is a real-world experience. Although young children may respond to fantasy only as an adventure story, their ability to accept and revel in the presence of magic and impossibility may actually pave the way for continuing selection of books in this genre as they grow. Young children share an openness to accepting the fantastic more readily that they can then transfer to developing literary tastes.

With intermediate readers, response builds on the genre of fantasy as the innermost thoughts, reflections, and judgments find an audience with a teacher, peer, or literature conversation group. Young people can find adventure, humor, or nonsense in fantasy. They may also reflect beyond this level to a richer experience of sensing inner truths surrounding the entertaining tale. Begin with read-alouds of picture books like Nancy Wood's *Mr. And Mrs. God in the Creation Kitchen* or *How the Tiny People Grew Tall*. The text and illustrations tantalize the imagination and serve as a springboard for response. Middle-school readers will enjoy a read-aloud of Robin McKinley's romantic tale of *The Stone Fey*. This illustrated brief fantasy serves as a special invitation to respond to the fantasy genre.

Journals work well with fantasy because time travel and heroic adventures in strange settings inspire participation in the text through writing. Artistic responses enable the reader to draw the secondary world of which they have momentarily been a part of and to envision the hero or heroine in his or her glory in a triumph over insurmountable challenges. Of all the genres, fantasy may be the most untapped resource for response and needs to be further considered and explored to truly uncover its potential.

CLOSING THOUGHTS

Traditional tales and fantasy offer entertainment and escape while providing involvement, ideas and insights, and clarification of feelings and values. One of the special qualities of traditional tales and fantasy literature is that they invite the reader to share the hero or heroine's hopes, struggles, and triumphs and end on a note of hope for the future. Stories that illuminate, delight, and refresh are the type that create readers. Those who work with children need to make a special effort to share books from these genres with both young and older readers. Jane Yolen (1981), writer of numerous books of fantasy, fairies, and folklore invites participation in these genres.

Knowing that, that magic has consequences, whether it is the magic of wonder, the magic of language, or the magic of challenging a waiting mind, then it is up to the artist, the writer, the storyteller [or the teacher] to reach out and touch that awesome magic. Touch magic—and pass it on. (p. 91)

References

Bettleheim, B. (1977). *The uses of enchantment: The meaning and importance of fairy tales.* New York: Vintage.

Bowman, P. B. (2004). "Oh, that's just folklore": Valuing the ordinary as an extraordinary teaching tool. *Language Arts, 81*, 385–395.

Cruz, M. C., & Pollock, K. B. (2004). Stepping into the wardrobe: A fantasy genre study. *Language Arts, 81*, 184–195.

Favat, Andre (1977). *Child and tale: The origins of interest* (NCTE Research Report No. 19). Urbana, IL: National Council of Teachers of English.

Kurkjian, C., Livingston, N., Young, T., & Avi (2006). Worlds of fantasy. *The Reading Teacher, 59*, 492–503.

Leach, A. N. (2001). The earth's birthday story: Creation myths in children's books. *Journal of Children's Literature, 27*, 43–48.

Lesesne, T. S. (2001). Spinning stories: Tales for all our students. *Journal of Children's Literature, 27*, 64–69.

Lynn, R. N. (1995). *Fantasy literature for children and young adults: An annotated bibliography* (4th ed.). New Providence, NJ: R. R. Bowker.

MacDonald , M. R. (2006). The Aesop prize: Folktales and more. *Book Links, 15*, 54–58.

Marcus, L. S. (Ed.). (2006). *The wand in the word: Conversations with writers of fantasy.* Cambridge, MA: Candlewick Press.

Marshall, E. (2004). Stripping for the wolf: Rethinking representations of gender in children's literature. *Reading Research Quarterly, 39*, 256–270.

Mello, R. (2001). Cinderella meets Ulysses. *Language Arts, 78*, 548–555.

West, M. (2000). Fantasy literature for children: Past, present, and future tensions. *Journal of Children's Literature, 26*, 35–39.

Yolen, J. (1981). *Touch magic: Fantasy, faerie, and folklore in the literature of childhood.* New York: Philomel Books.

Children's Books Cited: Traditional Literature [P] = K–2; [I] = 3–5; [M] = 6–8

Aardema, Verna (1997). *Anansi does the impossible: An Ashanti tale.* Illus. by Lisa Desimini. New York: Atheneum. [P/I]

Andersen, Hans Christian (2005). *The ugly duckling.* Translated by Anthea Bell. Illus. by Robert Ingpen. New York: Penguin/minedition. [P/I]

Anderson. M: T. (2005). *The serpent came to Gloucester.* Illus. by Bagram Ibatoulline. Cambridge, MA: Candlewick Press. [I/M]

Arnold, Caroline (2006). *The terrible hodag and the animal catchers.* Illus. by John Sandford. Honesdale, PA: Boyds Mills Press. [P/I]

Aylesworth, Jim (Reteller) (1999). *Aunt Pitty Patty's piggy.* Illus. by Barbara McClintock. New York: Scholastic. [P]

Aylesworth, Jim (Reteller) (2001). *The tale of tricky fox: A New England trickster tale.* Illus. by Barbara McClintock. New York: Scholastic. [P]

Bertrand, Lynne (2005). *Granite baby.* Illus. by Kevin Hawkes. New York: Melanie Kroupa/Farrar, Straus & Giroux. [P/I]

Burleigh, Robert (1999). *Hercules.* Illus. by Raul Colon. San Diego: Harcourt Brace. [I/M]

Diakite, Baba Wague (1999). *The hatseller and the monkeys.* New York: Scholastic. [P/I]

Doucet, Sharon Arms (2002). *Lapin plays possum: Trickster tales from the Louisiana bayou.* Illus. by Scott Cook. New York: Farrar, Straus and Giroux. [I]

Duncan, Lois (1996). *The magic of spider woman*. Illus. by Shonto Begay. New York: Scholastic. [I]

Eilenberg, Max (Reteller) (2006). *Beauty and the beast*. Illus. by Angela Barrett. Cambridge, MA: Candlewick Press. [P/I]

Fleming, Candace (2004). *Gator gumbo*. Illus. by Sally Anne Lambert. New York: Farrar, Straus & Giroux. [P/I]

Forward, Toby (2005). *The wolf's story: What really happened to Little Red Riding Hood*. Illus. by Izhar Cohen. Cambridge, MA: Candlewick Press. [I]

Galdone, Paul (1984). *The gingerbread boy*. Boston: Clarion. [P]

Haddix, Margaret Peterson (1999). *Just Ella*. New York: Simon & Schuster. [M]

Hamilton, Virginia (1988). *In the beginning: Creation stories from around the world*. Illus. by Barry Moser. New York: Harcourt Brace. [I/M]

Hamilton, Virginia (1997). *A ring of tricksters: Animal tales from America, the West Indies, and Africa*. Illus. by Barry Moser. New York: Blue Sky/Scholastic. [I/M]

Hennessey, B. G. (2006). *The boy who cried wolf*. Illus. by Boris Kulikov. New York: Simon & Schuster. [P]

Hodges, Margaret (2004). *Merlin and the making of the king*. Illus by Trina Schart Hyman. New York: Holiday House. [I]

Hyman, Trina Schart (Reteller) (1983). *Little Red Riding Hood*. New York: Holiday House. [P/I]

Kellogg, Steven (1986). *Pecos Bill*. New York: Morrow. [P/I]

Kimmel, Eric A. (Reteller) (2002). *Anansi and the magic stick*. Illus. by Janet Stevens. New York: Holiday House. [P]

Kimmel, Eric A. (2005). *The hero Beowulf*. Illus. by Leonard Everett Fisher. New York: Farrar, Straus & Giroux. [I]

Kimmel, Eric A. (2006). *Blackbeard's last fight*. Illus. by Leonard Everett Fisher. New York: Farrar, Straus & Giroux. [I]

Lesser, Rika (Reteller) (1984). *Hansel and Gretel*. Illus. by Paul O. Zelinsky. New York: Dodd/Mead. [P/I]

Levine, Gail C. (1997). *Ella enchanted*. New York: HarperCollins. [I/M]

Lewin, Ted (1998). *The storytellers*. New York: Lothrop, Lee & Shepard. [P/I]

Lobel, Arnold (1980). *Fables*. New York: Harper & Row. [P]

McKinley, Robin (1978). *Beauty: A retelling of the story of Beauty and the beast*. New York: Harper & Row. [I/M]

Mora, Pat (2005). *Dona Flor: A tall tale about a giant woman with a great big heart*. Illus. by Raul Colon. New York: Knopf. [P/I]

Morpurgo, Michael (Reteller) (2004). *Sir Gawain and the green knight*. Illus by Michael Foreman. Cambridge, MA: Candlewick Press. [I/M]

Morpurgo, Michael (Reteller) (2005). *The McElderry book of Aesop's fables*. Illus. by Emma Chichester Clark. New York: Margaret K. McElderry Books. [P/I]

Napoli, Donna J. (1996). *Zel*. New York: Dutton. [M]

Nesbit, E. (2006). *Jack and the beanstalk*. Illus. by Matt Tavares. Cambridge, MA: Candlewick Press. [P/I]

Osborne, Mary Pope (1996). *Favorite Norse myths*. Illus. by Troy Howell. New York: Scholastic. [I/M]

Osborne, Mary Pope (2000). *Kate and the beanstalk*. Illus. by Giselle Potter. New York: Atheneum. [I]

Osborne, Mary Pope (2002). *The brave little seamstress*. Illus. by Giselle Potter. New York: Atheneum. [I]

Palatini, Margie (2005). *The three silly billies*. Illus. by Barry Moser. New York: Simon & Schuster. [P/I]

Philip, Neil (Reteller) (1995). *The illustrated book of myths: Tales and legends of the world*. Illus. by Nilesh Mistry. New York: Dorling Kindersley. [I/M]

Pinkney, Jerry (Reteller) (2000). *Aesop's fables*. New York: SeaStar. [I]

Puttapipat, Niroot (2005). *The musicians of Bremen*. Cambridge, MA: Candlewick Press. [P]

Rockwell, Anne (1996). *The one-eyed giant and other monsters from the Greek myths*. New York: Greenwillow Books. [I/M]

Rosenthal, Paul (1998). *Yo, Aesop! Get a load of these fables*. Illus. by Marc Rosenthal. New York: Simon & Schuster. [I]

Sanderson, Ruth (2004/1985). *Cinderella*. New York: Dutton. [P/I]

San Souci, Robert D. (1996). *Pedro and the monkey*. Illus. by Michael Hays. New York: Morrow. [P/I]

Scieszka, Jon (1989). *The true story of the three little pigs by A. Wolf as told to Jon Scieszka*. Illus. by Lane Smith. New York: Viking/Penguin. [I]

Scieszka, Jon, & Smith, Lane (1998). *Squids will be squids: Fresh morals, beastly tales*. New York: Viking. [I/M]

Segal, Lore (2005). *More mole stories and little gopher, too*. Illus. by Sergio Ruzzier. New York; Farrar, Straus & Giroux. [P]

Stanley, Diane (2006). *Bella at midnight*. Illus by Bagram Ibatoulline. New York: HarperCollins. [I/M]

Wiesner, David (2001). *The three pigs*. New York: Clarion. [P/I]

Winter, Jeanette (2000). *The house that Jack built*. New York: Dial. [P]

Young, Ed (1992). *Seven blind mice*. New York: Philomel Books. [P]

Zelinsky, Paul O. (1986). *Rumpelstiltskin*. New York: Dutton. [P/I]

Zelinsky, Paul O. (1997). *Rapunzel*. New York: Dutton. [I/M]

Children's Books Cited: Modern Fantasy

Alexander, Lloyd (1964). *The book of three*. New York: Holt. (See additional titles in the Prydain Chronicles). [I/M]

Almond, David (1998). *Skellig*. New York: Delacorte. [M]

Almond, David (2000). *Kit's wilderness*. New York: Delacorte. [M]

Almond, David (2001). *Heaven eyes*. New York: Delacorte. [M]

Avi (1995). *Poppy*. Illus. by Brian Floca. New York: Orchard Books. [I]

Avi (2005). *Poppy's return*. Illus. by Brian Floca. New York: HarperCollins. [I]

Babbitt, Natalie (1975). *Tuck everlasting*. New York: Farrar, Straus and Giroux. [I]

Bailey, Carolyn (1946/1962). *Miss Hickory*. Illus. by Ruth Gannett. New York: Viking. [I]

Banks, Lynne Reid (1981). *The Indian in the cupboard*. Illus. by Brock Cole. New York: Doubleday. [I]

Barron, T. A. (1996). *The lost years of Merlin*. New York: Philomel. [I/M]

Barron, T. A. (2004). *The great tree of Avalon: Child of the dark prophecy*. New York: Philomel. [I/M]

Baum, Frank (1900). *The wonderful wizard of Oz*. Chicago: Hill. [I/M]

Carroll, Lewis (1865/2005). *Alice through the looking-glass*. Illus. by Helen Oxenbury. Cambridge, MA: Candlewick Press. [I]

Christopher, John (1967). *The white mountains*. New York: Macmillan. [I]

Cleary, Beverly (1982). *Ralph S. Mouse*. Illus. by Paul Zelinsky. New York: Morrow. [P/I]

Colfer, Eoin (2001). *Artemis Fowl*. New York: Hyperion. [I/M]

Cooper, Susan (1993). *The boggart*. New York: McElderry Books. [I]

Cooper, Susan (1999). *King of shadows*. New York: McElderry. [I/M]

Cooper, Susan (2006). *Victory*. New York: McElderry. [I/M]

Coville, Bruce (1982). *The monster's ring*. San Diego: Harcourt Brace. [I]

Coville, Bruce (1991). *Jeremy Thatcher, dragon hatcher*. San Diego: Harcourt Brace. [I]

Coville, Bruce (1992). *Jennifer Murdley's toad*. San Diego: Harcourt Brace. [I]

Coville, Bruce (1997). *The skull of truth*. San Diego: Harcourt Brace. [I]

Cullen, Catherine Ann (2001). *The magical, mystical, marvelous coat*. Illus. by David Christiana. Boston: Little, Brown. [P]

Dahl, Roald (1961). *James and the giant peach*. Illus. by Nancy E. Burkert. New York: Knopf. [P/I]

Dahl, Roald (1982). *BFG*. Illus. by Quentin Blake. New York: Farrar, Straus and Giroux. [P/I]

Dahl, Roald (1988). *Matilda*. Illus. by Quentin Blake. New York: Viking. [P/I]

DiCamillo, Kate (2003). *The tale of Despereaux: Being the story of a mouse, a princess, some soup, and a spool of thread*. Illus. by Timothy Basil Ering. Cambridge, MA: Candlewick Press. [P/I]

DiCamillo, Kate (2006). *The miraculous journey of Edward Tulane*. Illus. by Bagram Ibatoulline. Cambridge, MA: Candlewick Press. [P/I]

Fleischman, Sid (1963). *By the great horn spoon*. Illus. by Eric Von Schmidt. Boston: Little, Brown. [P/I]

Fleischman, Sid (1990). *The midnight horse*. Illus. by Peter Sis. New York: Greenwillow. [I]

Fleischman, Sid (1997). *Mr. Mysterious and company*. Illus. by Eric Von Schmidt. New York: Greenwillow. [P/I]

Funke, Cornelia (2002). *The thief lord*. Translated from German by Oliver Latsch. New York: Scholastic/Chicken House. [I/M]

Funke, Cornelia (2004). *Dragon rider*. Translated from German by Anthea Bell. New York: Scholastic/Chicken House. [I]

Grahame, Kenneth (1908). *The wind in the willows*. Abridged and illus. by Inga Moore. Cambridge, MA: Candlewick Press. [P/I]

Gutman, Dan (2002). *Shoeless Joe and me: A baseball card adventure*. New York: Harper-Collins. [I]

Hahn, Mary Downing (1989). *The doll in the garden: A ghost story*. Boston: Houghton Mifflin. [I]

Hahn, Mary Downing (1994). *A time for Andrew: A ghost story*. Boston: Clarion. [I]

Jacques, Brian (1987). *Redwall*. (Redwall Saga series). New York: Putnam. [I/M]

Jacques, Brian (1996). *The great Redwall feast*. Illus. by Christopher Denise. New York: Philomel Books. [P/I]

King-Smith, Dick (1985). *Babe: The gallant pig*. Illus. by Mary Rayner. New York: Crown. [I]

Lawson, Robert (1944). *Rabbit hill*. New York: Viking. [I]

L'Engle, Madeline (1962). *A wrinkle in time*. New York: Farrar, Straus and Giroux. [I]

Lowry, Lois (1993). *The giver*. Boston: Houghton Mifflin. [I/M]

Lowry, Lois (2000). *Gathering blue*. Boston: Houghton Mifflin. [I/M]

Lowry, Lois (2004). *Messenger*. Boston: Houghton Mifflin. [I/M]

Lowry, Lois (2006). *Gossamer*. Boston: Houghton Mifflin. [I/M]

Lunn, Janet (1983). *The root cellar*. New York: Scribner's. [I/M]

McKinley, Robin (1998). *The stone fey*. Illus. by John Clapp. San Diego: Harcourt Brace. [M]

Napoli, Donna Jo (2001). *Albert*. Illus. by Jim LaMarche. San Diego: Harcourt Brace. [P/I]

Norton, Mary (1953). *The borrowers*. Illus. by Beth and Joe Krush. New York: Harcourt Brace. [I]

O'Brien, Robert C. (1971). *Mrs. Frisby and the rats of NIHM*. New York: Atheneum. [I]

Pullman, Philip (1996). *The golden compass*. New York: Knopf. [I/M]

Pullman, Philip (1997). *The subtle knife*. New York: Random House. [I/M]

Pullman, Philip (2000). *The amber spyglass*. New York: Random House. [I/M]

Rowling, J. K. (1998). *Harry Potter and the sorcerer's stone*. New York: Scholastic. [I/M]

Rowling, J. K. (1999). *Harry Potter and the chamber of secrets*. New York: Scholastic. [I/M]

Rowling, J. K. (1999). *Harry Potter and the prisoner of Azkaban*. New York: Scholastic. [I/M]

Rowling, J. K. (2000). *Harry Potter and the goblet of fire*. New York: Scholastic. [I/M]

Rowling, J. K. (2003). *Harry Potter and the order of the phoenix*. New York: Scholastic. [I/M]

Rowling, J. K. (2005). *Harry Potter and the half-blood prince*. New York: Scholastic. [I/M]

Rowling, J. K. (2007). *Harry Potter and the deathly hallows*. New York: Scholastic. [I/M]

Scieszka, Jon (1991). *Knights of the kitchen table* (Time Warp Trio series). Illus. by Lane Smith. New York: Viking. [I]

Scieszka, Jon (1991). *The not-so Jolly Roger* (Time Warp Trio series). Illus. by Lane Smith. New York: Viking. [I]

Scieszka, Jon (1992). *The good, the bad, & the goofy* (Time Warp Trio series). Illus. by Lane Smith. New York: Viking. [I]

Seidler, Tor (2000). *A rat's tale*. Illus. by Brett Helquist. New York: Farrar, Straus and Giroux. [I/M]

Seidler, Tor (2001). *The revenge of Randall Reese-Rat*. Illus. by Brett Helquist. New York: Farrar, Straus & Giroux. [I/M]

Sharp, Margery (1959). *The rescuers*. Illus. by Garth Williams. Boston: Little, Brown. [P/I]

Steig, William (1976). *Abel's island*. New York: Farrar, Straus and Giroux. [I]

Tolkien, J. R. R. (1938). *The hobbit*. Boston: Houghton Mifflin. [I/M]

Waugh, Sylvia (1996). *Mennyms alone*. New York: Greenwillow Books. [I]

White, E. B. (1945). *Stuart Little*. Illus. by Garth Williams. New York: Harper & Row. [P/I]

White, E. B. (1952). *Charlotte's web*. Illus. by Garth Williams. New York: Harper & Row. [P/I]

Wood, Nancy (2004). *Old coyote*. Illus. by Max Grafe. Cambridge, MA: Candlewick. [P/I]

Wood, Nancy (2005). *How the tiny people grew tall: An original creation tale*. Illus. by Rebecca Walsh. Cambridge, MA: Candlewick Press. [P]

Wood, Nancy (2006). *Mr. and Mrs. God in the creation kitchen*. Illus. by Timothy Basil Ering. Cambridge, MA: Candlewick Press. [P]

Yolen, Jane (1990). *The devil's arithmetic*. New York: Viking/Penguin. [I/M]

Yolen, Jane (1997). *Twelve impossible things before breakfast*. San Diego: Harcourt Brace. [I/M]

CHAPTER 5

Poetry
The Power and Pleasure
of Language

> **ANIMAL HAIKU**
>
> Long, scaly, sharp teeth,
> Scary, hungry, and massive.
> Suspicious reptile.
> (Crocodile)
> Monstrous, waving ears
> Slow pace with heavy, big feet
> King of the jungle.
> (Elephant)
> Flitty, flighty wings
> Colorful and bright insect
> Translucent airplane.
> (Dragonfly)
> Long ears on the floor,
> Slow moving four shortened legs
> Brown and white delight.
> (Bassett hound)
>
> Second grade haiku written in response
> to Jack Prelutsky's *If Not for the Cat*

Poetry is an invitation to celebrate language and emotions. Poetry delights our funny bones, touches our hearts, titillates our senses, and heightens our awareness. Poetry with its focus on reflection and emotion is "necessary nourishment for the soul" (Bownas, McClure, & Oxley, 1998, p. 48). Extending and intensifying everyday experiences, poetry enhances and enriches our appreciation for the power of words to capture the essence of objects, thoughts, and feelings. Poetry should be a valued part of a child's everyday life, both in and out of school (Fletcher, 2002).

Poetry naturally invites a response from children. The effective language selectively chosen for sound and meaning, the structured patterning of words, and the flow of those words from our lips make active response a natural tendency rather than an option. Poetry demands response from our total being as it engages our intellect, emotions, senses, and imaginations. Poetry has the power to open doors so children can expand their views of the world while celebrating even the commonplace as a fresh experience.

THE ELEMENTS OF POETRY

Poetry is more than an emotional experience. The essence of poetry lies in its selective language. Eve Merriam, honored children's poet, shared that she sometimes spent weeks looking for precisely the right word to capture her thoughts in her poems.

The elements of poetry are essentially language related. There is no emphasis on plot or character, neither setting nor point of view. There is, however, language—in all its glory and with all its propensity to capture objects, emotions, and thoughts. The elements of poetry include rhythm, rhyme and sound, imagery, figurative language, and shape and spacing. When children unpeel the onion skin of poetry, they are exposing and feasting on the language that surrounds the poetic experience.

Children should be made aware of the elements of poetry, but not be required to analyze them. These language elements are shared to heighten adult awareness of the wonders of this genre and to assist them in selecting the best to share with children. A knowledge of the language impact on poetry impacts one's attitude toward poetry, the way it is read, and the manner in which it is shared. For poetry to become a steady diet across the curriculum and throughout the school day, teachers must feel a sense of wonder in its language roots.

Rhythm

Rhythm can be described as the flow of language that creates a sense of movement in the listener. Poetic rhythm can best be detected through a read-aloud in which the reader's voice captures the hand-clapping or foot-stomping pattern of words. Children respond naturally to rhythm because poems possess a music of their own that invites response. Classic poems often contain this trait, but so, too, do some new ones. Listen to the simple, yet obviously present rhyme of "A Wish" by Tim Myers's fresh voice in *Dark Sparkle Tea and Other Bedtime Poems*.

Literary Legend

Memorable Poet

Eve Merriam (1916–1992) believed that poetry should be shared, enjoyed, and read aloud by families, friends, and children. Born to Russian parents in Philadelphia, Pennsylvania, Eve developed a fascination with rhyme and alliteration that she carried with her throughout life. In 1981, she deservedly won the NCTE Award for Excellence in Poetry for Children. Her more than 20 books of poetry for children are filled with poems that are sometimes humorous, sometimes serious, and often both at the same time. Aware that children are often confused by poetry, Merriam wrote many poems that can serve as lessons to help make this unique art more approachable.

Whether writing nonsense rhymes or poems that addressed social issues including war, racism, and pollution, Eve Merriam infused every line with her characteristic love of language and its endless possibilities. As her poems spoke to thoughts and realities that are part of children's everyday lives, they occasionally became targets for censorship. In particular, *The Inner City Mother Goose* was controversial for its realistic portrayal of urban problems, and *Halloween ABC* for the darker tone of its poems. In spite of these challenges, the innovation of using children's poetry as a forum to discuss social issues will prove to be, along with her delightful wordplay, among her most lasting contributions to literature.

(1962). *There is no rhyme for silver*. Illus. by Joseph Schidelman. New York: Atheneum.

(1966). *It doesn't always have to rhyme*. New York: Atheneum.

(1969). *Catch a little poem*. New York: Atheneum.

(1969). *The inner city Mother Goose*. Illus. by Lawrence Ratzin. New York: Simon & Schuster.

(1970). *Finding a poem*. New York: Atheneum.

(1985). *Blackberry ink*. Illus. by Hans Wilhelm. New York: William Morrow.

(1986). *Fresh paint: New poems*. New York: Macmillan.

(1986). *A sky full of poems*. New York: Yearling.

(1987). *Halloween ABC*. Illus. by Lane Smith. New York: Simon & Schuster.

(1989). *A poem for a pickle: Funnybone verses*. Illus. by Sheila Hamanaka. New York: William Morrow.

A WISH

I wish I could see,
as night comes on,
how the deer who hide
all day long
are not so shy
when shadows come,
hungry enough
not to turn and run,
but step from the trees,
nervous and peering –
then lower their heads
and feed in the clearing.*

Rhyme

Just as children respond to rhythm, so, too, do they respond to the rhyme created by the words. Rhyme is the "sing-songedness" of the chosen words painstakingly selected by the poet. As children are engaged in first experiences with poetry, it is the rhyme of the poems that can build a positive response to the genre. The well-loved rhyme and rhythm of Mother Goose, like those shared in Iona Opie's *My Very First Mother Goose* or Jane Chapman's *Sing a Song of Sixpence*, are actually a strong introduction to this poetic element. Jack Prelutsky's title poem from *The Frogs Wore Red Suspenders* provides delight for the tongue and the ear.

Rhyme is related to the sound of words, and certain literary devices are well suited to creating the sounds that result in rhyme. Alliteration, the repetition of initial consonant sounds, can be effective in creating rhyme. For example, Lew Sarett's "Four Little Foxes" begins, "Speak gently, Spring, and make no sudden sound. . . ." Similarly, assonance is the repetition of vowel sounds that typically results in internal, rather than external, rhyme. David McCord's "The Pickety Fence" uses wonderful, imaginative word choices like *pickety, clickety, lickety,* and *rickety* to repeat the same sound and establish internal rhyme that appeals to the ear and eye.

Imagery

Language can create sensory experiences for children as it arouses their senses of sight, touch, taste, smell, and sound. Descriptions of a lofty buffalo, a scaly snake, blackberry jam, an evergreen forest, or a chirping cricket can stimulate the sensory images children create in their minds. Words vividly paint pictures for children—pictures that open the door to discovery of everyday things in the complex world. Constance Levy's collection titled *SPLASH! Poems of Our Watery World* bursts with imagery. Picture this . . .

---

*"A Wish" from *Dark Sparkle Tea and Other Bedtime Poems* (p. 29) by Tim Myers. Boyds Mills Press, 2006. Reprinted with permission of Boyds Mills Press, Inc. Text copyright © 2006 by Tim Myers.

FULL MOON ON MIRROR LAKE

Tonight
on this still,
smooth lake
high
in its forest place,
the wandering,
wondering moon
becomes acquainted
with his face.*

Figurative Language

Because words are vital to creating images in a poem, poets often rely on literary devices to assist them in economizing on words, yet creating sensory images that appeal to children. Poets may compare two like objects so the connection of one to the other adds meaning for the reader. When writers use the words *like* or *as* to make a comparison, the literary device is called a *simile*. In a *metaphor*, the poet refers to another object as if it were the object or idea. For example, John Frank portrays the wind the season of winter as a thief in his collection, *A Chill in the Air: Nature Poems of Fall and Winter*.

THIEF

The winter wind's a clever thief:
He'll join with you in play,
Then slip his hand inside your coat
And steal the warmth away.†

It is not so important for children to distinguish between these two forms of figurative language. Their importance lies in teacher recognition of figurative language so children may be drawn to and respond to these types of comparisons.

Personification casts inanimate objects and animals in a human light. Children typically recognize this literary device because they personify some of their own possessions during play. In the simple "Toaster" from *The Kitchen Talks*, Shirley Mozelle personifies this favorite kitchen appliance as a jack-in-the-box.

Shape and Spacing

The arrangement of words on the page is one of the simple, yet important distinguishing features between poetry and prose in the eyes of children. Stanzas, indentations, variations in line length, centering, margins, and shape are all features children notice when they begin to read poetry independently. These elements also influence children as

*"Full Moon on Mirror Lake" from *SPLASH! Poems of Our Watery World* (p. 24) by Constance Levy. Published by Orchard Books, an imprint of Scholastic Inc. Copyright © 2002 by Constance Kling Levy. Reprinted by permission.

†Reprinted with the permission of Simon & Schuster Books for Young Readers, an imprint of Simon & Schuster Children's Publishing Division from *A Chill in the Air* by John Frank. Text copyright © 2003 by John Frank.

The varied arrangements of words on the page is a distinguishing feature of poetry for children.

Cover from Toasting Marshmallows: Camping Poems *by Kristine O'Connell George. Jacket illustration copyright © 2001 by Kate Kiesler. Reprinted by permission of Clarion Books, an imprint of Houghton Mifflin Company. All rights reserved.*

writing models when they begin to compose their own poems. Examine the placement of words in "Tent" by Kristine O'Connell George from her collection titled *Toasting Marshmallows: Camping Poems.*

TENT

First,
smooth dirt.
No rocks or roots.
Next, sharp stakes, poles,
strong nylon rope. Shake, snap.
Billow, *whoof*, settle. Tug. Pull taut.
Our tent is up! Blooming, bright orange.*

Rhythm, rhyme, language, and shape all combine to create the total response to a poem. Children may react to isolated elements, but it is the response to the whole that creates emotion in the reader. Adults should never make poetic elements the objective of sharing poetry. Children should have an opportunity to hear a poem, to respond to a poem, and to relate a poem to familiar poems, but never to analyze a poem. Teachers, however, need to be aware of these poetic elements so they may select only the best poems to share with children.

---

*"Tent" from *Toasting Marshmallows: Camping Poems* (p. 4) by Kristine O'Connell George. Text copyright © 2001 by Kristine O'Connell George. Reprinted by permission of Clarion Books, an imprint of Houghton Mifflin Company. All rights reserved.

FORMS OF POETRY

Just as with other literary genres, poetry can be classified to better discuss the variation in the poetic genre. Forms of poetry are useful to adults to ensure they select poems that expose children to all variations in form. Although terminology may be shared with children, it is not necessary for them to recognize form. Enjoyment of poetry, in any form, should be our outcome in sharing this genre with children.

Narrative Poems

Popular with children, narrative poems tell a story. In reading classic poems like *The Night Before Christmas* or *The Midnight Ride of Paul Revere*, the poetic elements merge with story to create reading pleasure. Kevin Crossley-Holland's *Once Upon a Poem* overflows with favorite poems that tell stories for children of all ages, including Eugene Field's "Wynken, Blynken, and Nod," Lewis Carroll's "Jabberwocky," and Alfred Noyes's "The Highwayman." M. T. Anderson's poem tells the tale of *The Serpent Came to Gloucester,* which begins:

> It was on a day when the sun was bright,
> When the limpets were thick on the rocks,
> When the seagulls would squack
> And would talk and would fight
> For the fish laid to dry on the docks.
>
> It was on a day when we washed all our clothes,
> When we hung them to dry on the frame
> Of a little rowboat that would soon be mine.
> It was on that day that the serpent came —*

Children are likely to respond to this narrative by continuing to read the rhyming saga and linger on the reality of this narrative based on a true incident in Massachusetts in the early 1800s.

Lyrical Poetry

Lyrical poetry is descriptive poetry that energizes an object, scene, or feeling through language that reflects a songlike quality. Lyric poems don't read, they *sing* their way into our minds and hearts. In a traditional sense, several of Robert Louis Stevenson's poems from *A Child's Garden of Verses* create a melodic quality that keeps them in our minds. A newer collection of summer poems for children, *Summersaults* by Douglas Florian, captures that songlike quality of a warm evening, particularly in "Summer Night," through the sounds of bullfrogs, crickets, mosquitoes, and cicadas.

Limericks

Particularly popular with children, this nonsense verse is a formula poem. The five-line poem (first line rhymes with second line, third and fourth line rhyme, fifth line

*From The Serpent Came to Gloucester, text copyright © 2005 M. T. Anderson. Illustrations copyright © 2005 Bagram Ibatoulline. Reproduced by permission of the publisher Candlewick Press, Inc., Cambridge, MA.

rhymes with first and second lines) is a humorous statement that creates a character, a setting, an ironic twist. Although Ogden Nash is considered the grand master of this poetic form, Arnold Lobel took it on more recently in *The Book of Pigericks*, limericks about pigs across the United States. X. J. Kennedy's *Brats* humorously uses the limerick form to tell tales of famous brats that surround our lives. In *Exploding Gravy: Poems to Make You Laugh*, a collection of varied poem formats, Kennedy tickles the reader's funnybone through a limerick:

HOOKED ON BOOKS

A remarkable man of Bound Brook
Likes to hang up his coat on a hook,
But what makes him of note
Is he keeps on his coat
While he dangles, absorbed in a book.*

Children do enjoy responding to limericks by writing them. Because they are nonsense, almost any topic works, and the rhyme scheme is straightforward and achievable for intermediate-grade students.

Free Verse

Gaining increasing popularity and deserved respect as a poetic form, free verse has no discernible pattern. Free verse flows freely on the printed page and does not contain the rhyme that children typically associate with poetry. Children who listen to free verse read aloud will be released from the rhymed poem stereotype. Void of external rhyme, free verse does contain an internal rhythm that makes it read well aloud. Sample the sound of "He," a riddle describing a fox, by Joyce Sidman in *Butterfly Eyes and other Secrets of the Meadow*.

HE

trots
through
meadow-gold grass
in Dawn sun
    furred
    mysterious
a word
    hunting
    its own
meaning
Who is he?†

---

*"Hooked on Books" from *Exploding Gravy: Poems to Make You Laugh,* by X. J. Kennedy (p. 80), published by Little, Brown and Company. Copyright © 2002 by X. J. Kennedy. Reprinted by permission of Curtis Brown, Ltd.

†"He" from *Butterfly Eyes and Other Secrets of the Meadow* by Joyce Sidman. Text copyright © 2006 by Joyce Sidman. Reprinted by permission of Houghton Mifflin Company. All rights reserved.

Haiku

A deceptively simple form of poetry, haiku originated in Japan in the 13th century. In its purest sense, haiku contains 17 syllables in three lines (5 syllables/7 syllables/ 5 syllables) focusing on a season or a symbol of a season. Many haiku writers today write about almost any topic from the natural world and do not necessarily adhere to the original syllable formula. In spite of their simple form, haiku share complex ideas for deeper reflection. J. Patrick Lewis (1995) in an introduction to his original haiku collection, *Black Swan White Crow*, believes, "The best haiku make you think and wonder for a lot longer than it takes to say them" (n.p.). Because haiku elicit reflection, they provide effective poetry to share for reader response connections.

Readers enjoy the flow, simplicity, and natural connection of haiku from Jack Prelutsky's *If Not for the Cat* in poems that describe a beaver and a jellyfish. Reflection and response flow naturally from the listener. Ted Rand's watercolor art provides essential visual balance for each haiku—revealing, eye-pleasing, and quietly satisfying. Also discover striking black-and-white photographs of city streets by Henri Silberman paired with haiku for older students selected by Paul Janeczko in *Stone Bench in an Empty Park*.

Concrete Poetry

Sometimes the message of a poem is not only delivered through its words but through the visual presentation of the words on the page. Concrete poetry is poetry that carries a portion of its meaning through its shape. Once children are visually introduced to this kind of poetry, they want to write their own. Initial emphasis on meaning must supercede the drawing or the poetic flavor will be lost. Joan Bransfield Graham pairs her concrete poetry with the visual displays of Nancy Davis in *Flicker Flash*.

Other concrete poetry may be located in J. Patrick Lewis's *Doodle Dandies: Poems That Take Shape*. Paul Janezcko's selected poetry for *A Poke in the I* and Joyce Sidman's *Meow Ruff* are presented as concrete poems. This style is captured by the visual presentations by Chris Raschka in the book jacket, the table of contents, as well as the portrayal of the 30 poems.

Acrostic poetry is a type of concrete poetry because it uses the alphabetical structure of a word to creat the language structure of the poem. The well-chosen words in the alphabetical poems of Jennifer Belle blend with the reknowned art of David McPhail in *Animal Stackers*.

> **L**onely, or
> **A**re there any gentlemen bugs to
> **D**ate?
> **Y**ou look
> **B**eautiful in your
> **U**nusual dotted dress at the
> **G**arden party.*

Teachers should share all types of poetry with their students, exposing them to the breadth and depth of this genre. A copy of Paul Janeczko's *A Kick in the Head: An Everyday Guide to Poetic Form* should reside on every teacher's desk as a model of countless forms of poetry. The library typically abounds with poetry books and anthologies, making poetry books accessible for classroom independent reading, poet displays, or integration with themed units. Teachers need to document or record the types of poetry they select, keeping an eye on balance and variety as they share this inspiring genre with children.

TYPES OF POETRY COLLECTIONS

Besides categorizing poetry by its form, poetry can also be discussed in general terms by focusing on its organization or content. This classification ranges from comprehensive collections to specialized collections by a single author. The increased publication of poetry books for children necessitates an additional means to view the breadth and depth of this genre.

---

*From *Animal Stackers* by Jennifer Beale. Copyright © 2005 by Jennifer Beale. Reprinted by permission of Hyperion Books for Children. All rights reserved.

Comprehensive Anthologies

Anthologies are collections of children's poems that contain a large number of poems from many well-known poets. Anthologists select poems, gain permission to reprint them, and arrange them in a meaningful format. Most teachers like to keep a poetry anthology on their desk so they can locate a poem on a topic during a teachable moment. Two of the most useful in print are *Sing a Song of Popcorn*, edited by Beatrice Schenk de Regniers, and *The Random House Book of Poetry for Children*, edited by Jack Prelutsky. One of the most recent anthologies, although not quite as comprehensive, is *A Jar of Tiny Stars: Poems by NCTE Award-Winning Poets*, edited by Bernice Cullinan, which offers a collection of poems selected by children from the offerings of David McCord, Aileen Fisher, Karla Kushkin, Myra Cohn Livingston, Eve Merriam, John Ciardi, Lillian Moore, Arnold Adoff, Valerie Worth, and Barbara Esbensen. Caroline's Kennedy's selections in *A Family of Poems* encourages poetry reading across contemporary/classic and form/style.

Other anthologies focus on an extensive number of poems with a single theme. Jack Prelutsky's *The Beauty of the Beast: Poems from the Animal Kingdom*, Lee Bennett Hopkins's selections in *My America: A Poetry Atlas of the United States*, and Catherine Clinton's selections in *I, Too, Sing America: Three Centuries of African American Poetry* provide recent examples of themed collections.

Specialized Collections

A trend in poetry publication has been to produce shorter collections of poems on a specific topic. Either authored by a single poet or collected from the works of several poets, the narrower scope and reduced number of poems truly suit the style of thematic, interdisciplinary instruction teachers are sharing in classrooms. Lee Bennett Hopkins carries a reputation as a respected anthologist whose selections in *Hoofbeats, Claws, & Rippled Fins: Creature Poems* catch the interest of young poetry lovers. Kate Kiesler's *Wings on the Wind: Bird Poems* pairs creatively with Dorothy M. Kennedy's *Make Things Fly: Poems About the Wind*. On a more reflective note is Georgia Heard's *This Place I Know: Poems of Comfort* compiled following the terrorist events of September 11, 2001, and Eloise Greenfield's *When the Horses Ride By*, a tribute to children during times of war.

Many strong themed collections authored by a single poet belong to Douglas Florian. *Insectlopedia* presents a swarm of insect poems; *In the Swim* blends poetry with creatures of the sea. *On the Wing* focuses on creatures of the air; *Mammalabilia* poetically portrays creatures of the land. A new collection by Julie Larios, *Yellow Elephant: A Bright Bestiary* creates a themed animal/color series of poems with excellent word choice and vivid illustrations by Julie Paschkis.

YELLOW ELEPHANT

Yellow elephant
In the jungle sun,
In the day's yellow heat,
Trumpeting her song
And galumphing along.

Oh,
I think no other animal can
(I know a mosquito can't)
glow in the jungle sun
like a wild-eared
yellow elephant.*

Specialized collections like these carry poetry into thematic explorations across the curriculum.

Poem Picture Books

A special showcase for a single poem is a picture book format in which the text of the poem is blended with striking illustrations for both a visual as well as an oral reading experience (Glazer & Lamme, 1990). The poem picture book, a "story in verse" (Isaacs, 2003), continues to gain recognition as *ellington was not a street* by Ntozake Shange unfolds with poetic text and the premier artwork of Kadir Nelson. Diane Siebert's *Mississippi* has language that flows across the page like the river that flows across the heart of our country. Younger children may be engaged by Cynthia Jabar's watercolor impressions of Rachel Field's *Grace for an Island Meal*. Angela Johnson's poetic text in *Those Building Men* blends with the art of Barry Moser, which captures the strength and courage of the constructors of the transcontinental railroad. Traditional poems often take the format of poem picture books. The historical period art of Christopher Bing adds vision and depth to E. L. Thayer's *Casey at the Bat* and Longfellow's *The Midnight Ride of Paul Revere*. Children eagerly join in with the poetic text prompted by cues from the lushly detailed illustrations, creating a strong introduction to the traditional sounds and visions of poetry.

SORTING POETRY BY CONTENT

Humorous Verse

The poetry collections with the highest circulation rate are works of humorous verse. The placement of the poem surrounded by the space on the page often invites even reluctant readers to browse and sample the varied fare of children's humorous poets. Shel Silverstein (*A Light in the Attic; Falling Up*) and Jack Prelutsky (*A Pizza the Size of the Sun*) never fail to bring a smile to children's faces even at the mention of their names. Jim Aylesworth's contribution to the simplicity of humorous poetry is *The Burger and the Hot Dog*, which includes "So Pretty!"—imaging an orange's attraction to a lemon.

Nature Poetry

Children's natural curiosity can open their eyes to well-selected poems whose words paint the wonders of nature. Whether integrating these with a science unit or merely

---

*Text excerpt from "Yellow Elephant" in *Yellow Elephant: A Bright Bestiary* by Julie Larios, illustrated by Julie Paschkis. Text copyright © 2006 by Julie Larios. Reprinted by permission of Harcourt, Inc.

sharing them as good poetry, nature poems restore our sense of wonder. Penny Pollock's *When the Moon is Full: A Lunar Year* shares the wonders of the full moon as it casts its spell on each month. Exquisite woodcuts by Mary Azarian bring the scenes to life.

SEPTEMBER

The Harvest Moon

Squirrel rests in an ancient oak,
tail wrapped round her like a cloak,
looking over the moonlit field
where Mother Earth's generous yield
of endless acorns, nuts, and seeds
is quite enough to meet all needs.

*September marks the final gathering
of most crops. This is celebrated
in many cultures.**

Versatility in Poems

Some poets write poems about a wide variety of experiences and topics. Although difficult to classify, these poets should be honored for the versatility they bring to the poetic genre. Eve Merriam's *Blackberry Ink*, David McCord's *One at a Time*, Nancy Larrick's *Mice Are Nice*, Alice Schertle's *Keepers*, Janet Wong's *Knock on Wood*, and Barbara Esbensen's *Dance with Me* share poetic talent that demands appreciation. They write poems about daily experiences, nature, animals, and feelings while spanning many poetic forms.

This same variety weaves its way across curricular areas. J. Patrick Lewis's *A World of Wonders* and *Monumental Verses* and Lee Bennett Hopkins's collection of *Wonderful Words* provide delectable language treats as poetry enhances social studies and language arts instruction.

EVALUATING QUALITY POETRY

One of the best ways of evaluating poetry is to read it aloud. If the words flow and create excitement within you, if the poem appeals to your senses, if the poem makes you stop and reflect long after it is over, if a phrase or word keeps recurring in your mind, then perhaps you have found a special poem.

Joan Glazer (1997) cites five basic criteria that distinguish great poems from good poems. These criteria reflect standards to apply when assessing a poem:

- A fresh or original view of the subject is presented.
- Insight or emotion is shown or felt.

---

*"September: The Harvest Moon" from *When the Moon Is Full* by Penny Pollock. Copyright © 2001 by Penny Pollock (text); copyright © 2001 by Mary Azarian (illustrations). By permission of Little, Brown and Co.

- Poetic devices are used effectively.
- Language is used effectively.
- The voice or persona within the poem appears to be sincere. (p. 278)

Children come to school with a natural appreciation for the rhyme, rhythm, and sounds of language. Teachers need to capitalize on that tendency by selecting poems that appeal to those natural preferences. As children develop as listeners and readers, teachers need to deepen their poetic appreciation with a variety of poetic forms and surround them with the best of the genre.

One of the areas with which to begin the decision-making process in poetry selection is to consider the poetry reading preferences of children. Studies of primary (grades 1–3) students' preferences (Fisher & Natarella, 1982), of intermediate (grades 4–6) students' preferences (Terry, 1974), and middle-level (grades 7–9) students' preferences (Kutiper, 1985) confirmed the findings of Terry's (1972) original study, some of which are shared here:

1. The narrative form of poetry was popular with readers of all ages; free verse and haiku were the most disliked forms.
2. Students preferred poems that contain rhyme, rhythm, and sound.
3. Children most enjoyed poetry that contained humor, familiar experiences, and animals.
4. Younger students preferred contemporary poems.
5. Students disliked poems that contained visual imagery or figurative language. (Kutiper & Wilson, 1993, p. 29)

A library circulation study of poetry books reinforced these findings as humorous titles by Silverstein (*A Light in the Attic, Where the Sidewalk Ends*), Prelutsky (*The New Kid on the Block, Something Big Has Been Here*), and Viorst (*If I Were in Charge of the World and Other Worries*) revealed the highest school circulation figures (Kutiper & Wilson, 1993). The rhyme, rhythm, humor, and narrative form of these student-selected poems align with children's designated preferences.

The findings of these studies do not imply that teachers should prioritize children's likes over dislikes in sharing poetry. The implication for teachers is to initiate poetry exposure with student preferences and gradually bridge those experiences toward those poetic forms that they typically avoid. If we limit children's exposure to poetry to a few popular poets, the rich possibilities of this genre will be left unexplored and unappreciated. Teachers may include poetry in interdisciplinary studies, provide classroom poetry collections, and read aloud poetry on a regular basis. The greater the diversity of poems, the more opportunities for response to and appreciation for this genre to develop.

This chapter includes many quality poetry collections and poets within its pages, and the list given in Figure 5.1 adds even greater depth to a poetry repertoire. Both classic poets who have gained recognition through the years and contemporary poets whose books have special appeal for today's children are included in this list. In addition, professional articles continue to update teachers' knowledge of quality poetry (Chance, 2001; Crawford et. al., 2001; Hade & Murphy, 2000; Kurkjian, Livingston, Young, & Fletcher, 2006; Nelson, 2005).

FIGURE 5.1   Book Cluster: Additional poetry to share

Classic Poetry

Ciardi, John (1962). *You read to me, I'll read to you.* Illus. by Edward Gorey. Philadelphia: Lippincott. [P/I]

Fisher, Aileen (1969). *In one door and out the other: A book of poems.* Illus. by Lillian Hoban. New York: Crowell. [P/I]

Fleischmann, Paul (1988). *Joyful noise: Poems for two voices.* Illus. by Eric Beddows. New York: Harper. [I/M]

Greenfield, Eloise (1978). *Honey, I love, and other love poems.* Illus. by Diane & Leo Dillon. New York: Crowell. [P/I]

Hoberman, Mary Ann (1991). *Fathers, mothers, sisters, brothers: A collection of family poems.* Illus. by Marylin Hafner. Boston: Joy Street Books. [P/I]

Hopkins, Lee Bennett (1990). *Good books, good times!* Illus. by Harry Stevenson. New York: Harper-Collins. [P/I]

Kennedy, X. J., & Kennedy, Dorothy J. (Compilers) (1982). *Knock at a star: A child's introduction to poetry.* Illus. by K. A.Weinhaus. Boston: Little, Brown. [P/I]

Kuskin, Karla (1972). *Any me I want to be.* New York: Harper & Row. [P]

Larrick, Nancy (1985/1968). *Piping down the valleys wild.* Illus. by Ellen Raskin. New York: Delacorte. [P/I]

Livingston, Myra Cohn (1982). *A circle of seasons.* Illus. by Leonard Everett Fisher. New York: Holiday House. [P/I]

McCord, David (1977). *One at a time: Collected poems for the young.* Illus. by Henry B. Kane. Boston: Little, Brown. [P/I]

Merriam, Eve (1964). *It doesn't always have to rhyme.* Illus. by Malcolm Spooner. New York: Atheneum. [P/I]

Moore, Lillian (1982). *Something new begins: New and selected poems.* Illus. by Mary Jane Dunton. New York: Atheneum. [P/I]

O'Neill, Mary (1989/1961). *Hailstones and halibut bones.* Illus. by Leonard Weisgard. New York: Doubleday. [P/I]

Prelutsky, Jack (1984). *The new kid on the block.* Illus. by James Stevenson. New York: Greenwillow Books. [P/I]

Silverstein, Shel (1974). *Where the sidewalk ends.* New York: Harper & Row. [P/I]

Viorst, Judith (1982). *If I were in charge of the world and other worries: Poems for children and their parents.* Illus. by Lynne Cherry. New York: Atheneum. [I]

Willard, Nancy (1981). *A visit to William Blake's Inn: Poems for innocent and experienced travellers.* Illus. by Alice & Martin Provensen. San Diego: Harcourt Brace. [P/I]

Worth, Valerie (1972). *Small poems.* Illus. by Natalie Babbitt.New York: Farrar, Straus and Giroux. [P/I]

Contemporary Poetry

Adolph, Arnold (2000). *Touch the poem.* Illus. by Lisa Desimini. New York: Scholastic. [I]

Carlson, Lori M. (Ed.) (1994). *Cool salsa: Growing up Latino in the United States.* New York: Holt. [M]

Cherniak, Judith (Selector) (2005). *Carnival of the animals: Poems inspired by Saint-Saens' music.* Illus. by Satoshi Kitamura. Cambridge, MA: Candlewick. (CD included) [I/M]

English, Karen (2004). *Speak to me (and I will listen between the lines).* Illus. by Amy June Bates. New York: Farrar, Straus & Giroux. [I]

George, Kristine O'Connell (2002). *Swimming upstream: Middle school poems.* Illus. by Debbie Tilley. New York: Clarion. [M]

(continued)

FIGURE 5.1 Continued

George, Kristine O'Connell (2004). *Hummingbird nest: A journal of poems.* Illus. By Barry Moser. San Diego: Harcourt. [I]

Grandits, John (2004). *Technically, it's not my fault: Concrete poems.* New York: Clarion. [I/M]

Havill, Juanita (2006). *I heard it from Alice Zucchini: Poems about the garden.* Illus. by Christine Davenier. San Francisco: Chronicle. [I]

Jackson, Rob (2006). *Animal mischief.* Illus. by Laura Jacobsen. Honesdale, PA: Boyds Mills Press. [P/I]

Janeczko, Paul B. (1998). *That sweet diamond: Baseball poems.* Illus. by Carole Katchen. New York: Atheneum. [I/M]

Levy, Constance (1998). *A crack in the clouds and other poems.* Illus. by Robin Bell Corfield. New York: McElderry. [I/M]

Lewis, J. Patrick (2006). *Once upon a tomb: Gravely humorous verses.* Illus. by Simon Bartram. Cambridge, MA: Candlewick. [I]

Mozelle, Shirley (2006). *The kitchen talks.* Illus. by Petra Mathers. New York: Henry Holt. [P]

Nye, Naomi Shahib (Ed.) (2000). *Come with me: Poems for a journey.* Illus. by Dan Yaccarino. New York: Greenwillow. [M/P/I]

Pomerantz, Charlotte (2005). *Thunderboom! Poems for everyone.* Illus. by Rob Shepperson. Asheville, NC: Front Street. [P/I]

Prelutsky, Jack (2002). *Scranimals.* Illus. by Peter Sis. New York: Greenwillow. [I]

Schertle, Alice (1999). *A lucky thing.* Illus. by Wendell Minor. San Diego: Harcourt Brace. [I]

Sidman, Joyce (2005). *Song of the water boatman and other pond poems.* Illus. by Beckie Prange. Boston: Houghton Mifflin. [I]

Spinelli, Eileen (2004). *In our backyard garden.* Illus. by Marcy Ramsey. New York: Simon & Schuster. [I]

Stevenson, James (2003). *Corn chowder.* New York: Greenwillow. [I]

Wong, Janet (2000). *Night garden: Poems from the world of dreams.* Illus. by Julie Paschkis. New York: McElderry. [P/I]

See additional multicultural poetry listed in Chapter 8, "Multicultural and International Literature."

BENEFITS OF POETRY

The value of poetry is measured by the overall emotional impact and the creative use of language of the poems. Poetry touches the mind and the heart through the senses and the wonder of words. The benefits of poetry are far reaching and as varied as children's poetry is itself.

- Poetry should be fun and provide pure enjoyment for children. Word play, rhyme, repetition, and humor open the door to the world of poems.
- Poetry helps children see everyday things through a new lens. The words and music of poetry provide a sense of wonder and understanding for children.
- Poems provide a mirror of one's literary heritage. Childhood rhymes reflect our cultures, our times, and our family values.
- Poetry provides the sounds of language through choral reading, dramatic readings, or group presentations.
- Poetry provides a brief moment of respite from a hectic personal or classroom day. The brevity and succinctness of poetry transitions well in classrooms and establishes a link between the academic and the aesthetic curriculum.

READER RESPONSE TO POETRY

Response to poetry with young children takes the form of oral response as children repeat words, phrases, and rhymes that capture their language sensations (Bownas et al., 1998). Choral reading experiences bring appreciation to the sounds of poetry as large and small groups use voice to project the poetic emotions beyond the printed page (Apol & Harris, 1999). Paul Janeczko's selected poetry in *Dirty Laundry Pile: Poems in Different Voices* provides poems just screaming to be read aloud.

Children can also respond to poetry, especially poem picture books, through art. Drawing what you see when you listen to a lyrical poem or sketching an interpretation of a haiku usually reflects differences in how words and images are perceived. Groups or individuals can create an anthology of favorite poems by selecting and documenting the work of popular poets during theme explorations. Selecting poems that relate to the sea during an ocean theme, for example, brings together a vast array of quality poetry.

Elster (2000) reports that children and teachers use a wide repertoire of strategies (summary, performance, text-to-life connections) when they read and respond to poetry. Poetry engages the imagination of readers and provides opportunities for readers to apply a variety of personal response and meaning-making strategies.

The written response to a poem through personal interpretation, literary analysis, or self-created poetry is not encouraged until children have learned to love poetry. In most cases, the reader must be immersed and drenched in poetry long before the written assignment of a poem occurs. Poetry must speak enjoyment to the reader before it can become the writing model. Although poetry and writing can be addressed as response (see Chapter 11), it is far more important to savor its word choice, its texture, its emotions, and its ability to inspire reflection during the early stages of appreciation. When appreciation takes hold, the time may be ripe for the written response through self-created poetry.

Meanwhile, teachers can support responses to poetry on a daily basis through an interactive poetry session in the classroom. Rather than turning these experiences into lessons, they should occur spontaneously as the rich experience of poetry unfolds.

- Read aloud and savor poetry regularly.
- Linger over the language of poetry to appreciate wordcrafting.
- Invite children to participate in poetry by joining in on repeated phrases or responding to rhythm or rhyme through movement.
- Read aloud a few poems from a collection, inviting children to venture through the rest of the collection on their own.
- Encourage children to select favorite poems and share orally during poetry-sharing sessions.
- Build a repertoire of poems so children can compare, discuss, respond, relate, recall, and develop personal tastes in poetry.
- Share poet studies to build familiarity with quality writers in this genre.
- Provide opportunities for choral reading of poetry for individual, partner, book buddy, small group, or whole-class performances.
- Add the aesthetic dimension of poetry across the curriculum.
- Build appreciation for languages and dialects of other cultures through multicultural poetry.
- Appreciate the universality of poetry to address common objects, emotions, and themes through the power of language.

One of the most respected children's poets, Eve Merriam, makes a suggestion on relishing the joy of poetry in selected lines of "How to Eat a Poem."

> Pick it up with your fingers and lick the juice
> that may run down your chin.
> It is ready and ripe now, whenever you are.*

Savor the flavor and message of poetry as you select and share the wealth of this genre with children of all ages.

CLOSING THOUGHTS

This chapter celebrates the genre of poetry through which well-chosen words invite readers to ponder, observe, smile, reflect, or laugh. Young children "take to poetry as naturally as breathing, and . . . [poetry] is as essential to their well-being as air that

---

*Excerpt from "How to Eat a Poem" by Eve Merriam from *Jamboree Rhymes for All Times* by Eve Merriam. Copyright © 1962, 1964, 1966, 1973, 1984 Eve Merriam. Used by permission of Marian Reiner.

is clean" (Schliesman, 1998, p. 35). Older children attach to poetry as both readers and listeners. A wealth of recent innovative poetry in single-poet collections and anthologies celebrates opportunities to engage readers beyond their early years toward poetic experiences for a lifetime. Regardless of the age of the child, remember that meanings in poems lie in the individual hearts and minds of the reader. Myra Cohn Livingston (1990), children's poet/author/anthologist, articulately supports the uniqueness of poetic response:

> There is no poem that can live, come alive, without a reader. The reader, the listener, breathes into each work of art his own experience, his own sensitivity, and re-creates it in meaningful terms. (p. 207)

Response to poetry makes way for the diverse emotions, delights, challenges, and understandings it stirs within the individual child. Response to poetry creates life-long lovers of language, words, and the poetic genre.

References

Apol, L., & Harris, J. (1999). Joyful noises: Creating poems for voices and ears. *Language Arts, 76*, 314–322.

Bownas, J., McClure, A. A., & Oxley, P. (1998). Talking about books: Bringing the rhythm of poetry into the classroom. *Language Arts, 75*, 48–55.

Chance, R. (2001). Beyond Silverstein: Poetry for middle schoolers. *Voices from the Middle, 9*, 88–90.

Crawford, K., Hartke, J., Humphrey, A., Spycher, E., Steffan, M., & Wilson, J. (2001). The aesthetic power of poetry. *Language Arts, 78*, 385–391.

Elster, C. A. (2000). Entering and opening the world of a poem. *Language Arts, 78*, 71–77.

Fisher, C. J., & Natarella, M. A. (1982). Young children's preferences in poetry: A national survey of first, second, and third graders. *Research in the Teaching of English, 16*, 339–354.

Fletcher, R. (2002). *Poetry matters.* New York: HarperCollins.

Glazer, J. I. (1997). *Introduction to children's literature* (2nd ed.). Upper Saddle River, NJ: Merrill/Prentice Hall.

Glazer, J. I., & Lamme, L. L. (1990). Poem picture books and their uses in the classroom. *The Reading Teacher, 44*, 102–109.

Hade, D. D., & Murphy, L. (2000). Voice and image: A look at recent poetry. *Language Arts, 77*, 344–352.

Isaacs, K. T. (2003). Stories in verse. *Book Links, 12*, 10–15.

Kurkjian, C., Livingston, N., Young, T., & Fletcher, R. (2006). A pickle barrel of poems. *The Reading Teacher, 59*, 598-608.

Kutiper, K. (1985). A survey of the adolescent poetry preferences of seventh, eighth, and ninth graders. Unpublished doctoral dissertation, University of Houston.

Kutiper, K., & Wilson, P. (1993). Updating poetry preferences: A look at the poetry children really like. *The Reading Teacher, 47*, 28–35.

Livingston, M. C. (1990). *Climb into the bell tower: Essays on poetry.* New York: Harper & Row.

Nelson, P. (2005). Could you and your students use a poetry getaway? *The Reading Teacher, 58,* 771–773.

Schliesman, M. (1998). Poetry for every child. *Book Links, 7*, 35–39.

Terry, A. (1972). A national study of children's poetry preferences in the fourth, fifth, and sixth grades. Unpublished doctoral dissertation, Ohio State University, Columbus.

Terry, A. (1974). *Children's poetry preferences: A national survey of upper elementary grades* (NCTE Report No. 16). Urbana, IL: National Council of Teachers of English.

Children's Books Cited [P] = K–2; [I] = 3–5; [M] = 6–8

Anderson, M. T. (2005). *The serpent came to Gloucester*. Illus. by Bagram Ibatoulline. Cambridge, MA: Candlewick. [I/M]

Aylesworth, Jim (2001). *The burger and the hot dog*. Illus. by Stephen Gammell. New York: Atheneum. [P/I]

Belle, Jennifer (2005). *Animal stackers*. Illus. by David McPhail. New York: Hyperion. [P]

Chapman, Jane (2004). *Sing a song of sixpence: A pocketful of nursery rhymes and tales*. Cambridge, MA: Candlewick. [P]

Clinton, Catherine (Ed.) (1998). *I, too, sing America: Three centuries of African American poetry*. Illus. by Stephan Alcorn. New York: Houghton Mifflin. [I/M]

Crossley-Holland, K. (Selector) (2004). *Once upon a poem: Favorite poems that tell stories*. Illus. by Peter Bailey, Sian Bailey, Carol Lawson, & Chris McEwan. New York: Scholastic/Chicken House. [P/I/M]

Cullinan, Bernice E. (Ed.) (1996). *A jar of tiny stars: Poems by NCTE award-winning poets*. Honesdale, PA: Wordsong/Boyds Mills Press & National Council of Teachers of English. [P/I]

de Regniers, Beatrice Schenk (Ed.) (1988). *Sing a song of popcorn*. Illus. by Nine Caldecott Medal artists. New York: Scholastic. [P/I]

Esbensen, Barbara Juster (1995). *Dance with me*. Illus. by Megan Lloyd. New York: Harper-Collins. [P/I]

Field, Rachel (2006/1924). *Grace for an island meal*. Illus. by Cynthia Jabar. New York: Farrar, Straus & Giroux. [P]

Florian, Douglas (1996). *On the wing*. San Diego: Harcourt Brace. [I/M]

Florian, Douglas (1997). *In the swim*. San Diego: Harcourt Brace. [I/M]

Florian, Douglas (1998). *Insectlopedia*. San Diego: Harcourt Brace. [I/M]

Florian, Douglas (2000). *Mammalabilia*. San Diego: Harcourt Brace. [I/M]

Florian, Douglas (2002). *Summersaults*. New York: Greenwillow. [P/I]

Frank, John (2003). *A chill in the air: Nature poems of fall and winter*. New York: Simon & Schuster. [P]

George, Kristine O'Connell (2001). *Toasting marshmallows: Camping poems*. Illus. by Kate Kiesler. New York: Clarion. [I/M]

Graham, Joan Bransfield (1999). *Flicker flash*. Illus. by Nancy Davis. New York: Houghton Mifflin. [P/I]

Greenfield, Eloise (2006). *When the horses ride by: Children in the times of war*. Illus. by Jan Spivey Gilchrist. New York: Lee & Low. [I/M]

Heard, Georgia (Selector) (2002). *This place I know: Poems of comfort*. Illus. by 18 renowned picture book artists. Cambridge, MA: Candlewick. [P/I/M]

Hopkins, Lee Bennett (Selector) (2000). *My America: A poetry atlas of the United States*. Illus. by Stephen Alcorn. New York: Simon & Schuster. [P/I/M]

Hopkins, Lee Bennett (Selector) (2002). *Hoofbeats, claws & rippled fins: Creature poems*. Illus. by Stephen Alcorn. New York: HarperCollins. [P/I]

Hopkins, Lee Bennett (Selector) (2004). *Wonderful words: Poems about reading, writing, speaking, and listening*. New York: Simon & Schuster. [P/I]

Janeczko, Paul (Selector) (2000). *Stone bench in an empty park*. Photographs by Henri Silberman. New York: Orchard. [I/M]

Janeczko, Paul (Selector) (2001). *Dirty laundry pile: Poems in different voices*. Illus. by Melissa Sweet. New York: HarperCollins. [P/I]

Janeczko, Paul (Selector) (2001). *A poke in the I: A collection of concrete poems*. Illus. by Chris Raschka. Cambridge, MA: Candlewick. [P/I/M]

Janeczko, Paul (Selector) (2005). *A kick in the head: An everyday guide to poetic form*. Illus. by Chris Raschka. Cambridge, MA: Candlewick. [P/I/M]

Johnson, Angela (2001). *Those building men*. Illus. by Barry Moser. New York: Scholastic. [I/M]

Kennedy, Caroline (Selector) (2005). *A family of poems: My favorite poems for children*. Illus. by Jon J. Muth. New York: Hyperion. [P/I/M]

Kennedy, Dorothy (Ed.) (1998). *Make things fly: Poems about the wind*. Illus. by Sasha Meret. New York: McElderry. [P/I]

Kennedy, X. J. (1986). *Brats*. Illus. by James Watts. New York: Atheneum. [I]

Kennedy, X. J. (2002). *Exploding gravy: Poems to make you laugh*. Illus. by Joy Allen. Boston: Little, Brown. [I]

Kiesler, Kate (Selector) (2002). *Wings on the wind: Bird poems*. Illus. by Kate Kiesler. New York: Clarion. [P/I]

Larios, Julie (2006). *Yellow elephant: A bright bestiary*. Illus. by Julie Paschkis. San Diego: Harcourt. [P/I]

Larrick, Nancy (1990). *Mice are nice*. Illus. by Ed Young. New York: Philomel Books. [P/I]

Levy, Constance (2002). *SPLASH! Poems of our watery world*. Illus. by David Soman. New York: Orchard. [I]

Lewis, J. Patrick (1995). *Black swan white crow*. Woodcuts by Chris Manson. New York: Atheneum. [I]

Lewis, J. Patrick (1998). *Doodle dandies: Poems that take shape*. Illus. by Lisa Desimini. New York: Atheneum. [P/I]

Lewis, J. Patrick (2002). *A world of wonders: Geographic travels in verse and rhyme*. Illus. by Alison Jay. New York: Dial. [I]

Lewis, J. Patrick (2005). *Monumental verses*. Washington, DC: National Geographic. [I/M]

Lobel, Arnold (1983). *The book of pigericks*. New York: Harper & Row. [P/I]

Longfellow, Henry Wadsworth (2001). *The midnight ride of Paul Revere*. Illus. by Christopher Bing. Brooklyn, NY: Handprint. [I/M]

McCord, David (1977). *One at a time*. Illus. by Henry B. Kane. Boston: Little, Brown. [P]

Merriam, Eve (1985). *Blackberry ink*. Illus. by Hans Wilhelm. New York: Morrow. [P]

Moore, Clement C. (1980). *The night before Christmas*. Illus. by Tomie de Paola. New York: Holiday House. [P]

Mozelle, Shirley (2006). *The kitchen talks*. Illus. by Petra Mathers. New York: Henry Holt. [P/I]

Myers, Tim (2006). *Dark sparkle tea and other bedtime poems*. Illus. by Kelley Cunningham. Honesdale, PA: Boyds Mills Press. [P/I]

Opie, Iona (Ed.) (1996). *My very first Mother Goose*. Illus. by Rosemary Wells. Cambridge, MA: Candlewick Press. [P]

Pollock, Penny (2001). *When the moon is full: A lunar year*. Illus. by Mary Azarian. Boston: Little, Brown. [P/I]

Prelutsky, Jack (Ed.) (1983). *The Random House book of poetry for children*. Illus. by Arnold Lobel. New York: Random House. [I/P]

Prelutsky, Jack (1984). *The new kid on the block*. Illus. by James Stevenson. New York: Greenwillow Books. [I]

Prelutsky, Jack (1990). *Something big has been here*. Illus. by James Stevenson. New York: Greenwillow Books. [I]

Prelutsky, Jack (1996). *A pizza the size of the sun*. Illus. by James Stevenson. New York: Greenwillow Books. [I]

Prelutsky, Jack (Selector) (1997). *The beauty of the beast: Poems from the animal kingdom*. Illus. by Meilo So. New York: Knopf. [P/I]

Prelutsky, Jack (2002). *The frogs wore red suspenders*. Illus. by Petra Mathers. New York: Greenwillow. [I/P]

Prelutsky, Jack (2004). *If not for the cat*. Illus. by Ted Rand. New York: Greenwillow. [P/I]

Schertle, Alice (1996). *Keepers*. Illus. by Ted Rand. New York: Lothrop, Lee & Shepard. [I]

Shange, Ntozake (2004). *Ellington was not a street*. Illus. by Kadir Nelson. New York: Simon & Schuster. [I/M]

Sidman, Joyce (2006). *Butterfly eyes and other secrets of the meadow*. Illus. by Beth Krommes. Boston: Houghton Mifflin. [P/I]

Sidman, Joyce (2006). *Meow Ruff: A story in concrete poetry*. Illus. by Michelle Berg. Boston: Houghton Mifflin. [P]

Siebert, Diane (2001). *Mississippi*. Illus. by Greg Harlin. New York: HarperCollins. [I/M]

Silverstein, Shel (1974). *Where the sidewalk ends*. New York: Harper & Row. [I]

Silverstein, Shel (1981). *A light in the attic*. New York: Harper & Row. [I]

Silverstein, Shel (1996). *Falling up*. New York: HarperCollins. [I]

Stevenson, James (2000). *Cornflakes: Poems by James Stevenson*. New York: Greenwillow. [I]

Stevenson, Robert Louis (1885/1947). *A child's garden of verses*. Illus. by Tasha Tudor. New York: Oxford University Press. [P/I]

Thayer, Ernest Lawrence (2000). *Casey at the bat: A ballad of the Republic sung in the year 1888*. Illus. by Christopher Bing. Brooklyn, NY: Handprint. [P/I/M]

Viorst, Judith (1982). *If I were in charge of the world and other worries*. Illus. by Lynne Cherry. New York: Atheneum. [I/M]

Wong, Janet (2003). *Knock on wood: Poems about superstitions*. Illus.by Jule Paschkis. New York: McElderry. [I]

CHAPTER 6

Realistic and Historical Fiction
The Boundary of Reality

When I read about Jane's new ideas about Sabrina Starr, I could just see her brain working. I just want to tell her to keep writing and not to let anyone stop her. When Mr. Dupree told her that the book was lousy, I just wanted to slap him! It made Jane so upset and hurt, but I do think some good came out of it. She learned that there will be some people that don't understand her writing or think that it's lousy. But if you are a true writer, like Jane, you won't give up.

Overall, I loved this book and I liked how it switched off to different characters. I also liked how each of the four sisters were so unique. Each one had her special talents. I don't have any sisters, but I have two best friends. We all have different qualities, but that just makes our friendship stronger. I think this is the same for the Penderwick sisters. I hope Jeanne Birdsall has a sequel because I would love to read further tales on the Penderwicks.

Sixth-grade response to Jeanne Birdsall's *The Penderwicks:*
A Summer Tale of Four Sisters, Two Rabbits,
and a Very Interesting Boy (National Book Award, 2006)

Realistic stories about people like themselves set in both contemporary or historical times appeal to children as readers. The ability to identify with a character challenged by contemporary problems or surrounded by historical events engages the reader in literature. Fiction provides a realistic view of people and issues while keeping the reader at a safe distance from their actual occurrence. Realistic fiction set in contemporary times addresses the commonalities of family, friendship, humor, and growing up. On a more serious side, realistic fiction addresses hardships, cruelties, and problems that face society and touch children's lives. Historical fiction, in contrast, transports the reader to historical contexts in which heroism and courage become real attributes of character. Universal problems set in historical times and circumstances cause readers to make connections to their own lives today.

This chapter on the fictional genres of realistic and historical fiction covers literature that contains truth but keeps the reader distanced from the harsh realities that life poses in both contemporary and historical times. The book becomes an opportunity to experience life, either yesterday or today, and learn that we are not alone. Characters in realistic and historical fiction face challenges and frustrations, succeed and fail just like the reader. Perhaps the genres with most appeal to independent readers, realistic fiction and historical fiction play an important role in engaging and developing lifelong readers.

CONTEMPORARY REALISTIC FICTION

The genre of realistic fiction contains stories that reflect contemporary life, take place in familiar settings, and present common situations with which the reader can identify. Grounded in the common perception of what life is really like, realistic fiction strives for a balance between reality (realism) and make-believe (fiction). Quality realistic fiction can be so true to life that it often contains issues that face children in their everyday lives.

The protagonists in realistic fiction face real-life problems (abuse, divorce, illness, disability, drugs, death), confront them, and mature from the life experience. Readers can gain insights into challenging situations they are facing or may face while learning about handling the problem with determination, forethought, and control. Because realistic fiction is a reflection of our society, the types of problems faced by the main characters change with time. Whereas the heroes and heroines of the 1970s may have faced divorce, foster homes, and death, today's characters face those challenges as well as abuse, terrorism, drugs, AIDS, and their own sexuality. Because societal changes warrant changes in realistic fiction, at any given time some number of books in this genre will be considered controversial and possibly even subject to censorship, particularly in a school setting (Dresang, 2003). The issues of selection and censorship are discussed later in this chapter.

Realistic fiction is the most popular genre of children's literature with readers. When children walk into the library/media center and ask for a mystery, an adventure, a humorous story, or a sports story, they are actually requesting realistic fiction. Its popularity lies in the reality and believability of characters, situations, and settings. Children often read these books as if they are real and their responses reflect their involvement with the story. When children can slip into a character's life because it parallels their own or that of their peers, they are more inclined to read a book.

A study (Hancock, 1996), inviting updating, analyzed state children's choice book awards based on the votes of the children who either read nominated books independently or had nominated books read to them. The most popular children's choice books between 1985 and 1995 were all realistic fiction and included *Shiloh* (20 state awards), *There's a Boy in the Girl's Bathroom* (17 state awards), *Maniac Magee* (14 state awards), and *Hatchet* (12 state awards). The most popular children's choice authors included respected writers of realistic fiction including Mary Downing Hahn (26 state awards for 6 titles), Phyllis Reynolds Naylor (24 state awards/4 titles), Louis Sachar (21 awards/2 titles), Lois Lowry (18 awards/7 titles), and Jerry Spinelli (17 state awards/3 titles). In fact, almost half (48%) of all state children's choice awards between 1985 and 1995 were received by works of contemporary realistic fiction. These findings provide further support for the popularity of this genre, particularly with children who are independent readers of chapter books.

Types of Realistic Fiction

Because realistic fiction covers such a broad range of contemporary life situations, this genre is commonly divided into narrower categories for discussion. Three major categories posed by Kiefer, Hickman, and Hepler (2007) with major subthemes comprehensively reflect all contemporary realistic fiction.

The first category, "Becoming One's Own Person," covers the transition from being a child and growing into an adult. The nurturing warmth of the traditional family, challenging relationships within the family, the role of extended families, and living through families in transition provide realistic themes about the role of family in growing up. Jack Gantos's *Jack Adrift,* James Howe's *Totally Joe*, Ruth White's *Buttermilk Hill*, Sharon Creech's *Walk Two Moons*, and Stephanie Tolan's *Surviving the Applewhites* address growing up in less than perfect circumstances. Realistic fiction also includes stories of living with others including the struggle for peer acceptance and the importance of friendship. Readers of classics like Katherine Paterson's *Bridge to Terabithia*, Jerry Spinelli's *Maniac Magee*, and the Newbery Medal title, Lynne Rae Perkins's *Criss Cross*, witness the struggle for acceptance and the bond of strong relationships. Titles in this category hold the contemporary reader's interest, connect to one's own life, and touch the human heart with their sincerity and authenticity.

The second category of "Coping with Problems of the Human Condition" includes the challenges of physical disabilities and mental disabilities, growing old,

Literary Legend

Realistic Fiction Author

As a child, **Beverly Cleary** (1916–) grew bored and frustrated with the uninteresting learn-to-read school texts. As an adult, working as a children's librarian, she took note of the many children who were unable to find themselves portrayed in the books that lined the shelves. Determined to remedy the situation, Beverly Cleary made it her mission to create compelling, realistic characters—Ramona, Ellen Tebbits, and Henry Huggins—who brought books to life and made reading fun. Although the problems of the adult world, such as a parent's loss of a job or divorce, occasionally appear, her books are most noteworthy for consistently capturing a child's perspective through everyday events. In particular, the mischievous and inventive Ramona has given all children a character to identify with since her first appearance in 1955.

Cleary gained belated critical recognition by winning the Newbery Award for *Dear Mr. Henshaw* in 1984, but the true measure of her impact is reflected by the more than 35 statewide awards her books have earned as a result of their continued popularity with young readers. For so many readers, Cleary's books were the first chapter books they ever read, and the thrill of that initial discovery of such vivid characters continues to be passed down to children and grandchildren.

(1951). *Ellen Tebbits.* Illus. by Louis Darling. New York: William Morrow.

(1954). *Henry and Ribsy.* Illus. by Louis Darling. New York: William Morrow.

(1968). *Ramona the pest.* Illus. by Louis Darling. New York: William Morrow.

(1977). *Ramona and her father.* Illus. by Alan Tiegreen. New York: William Morrow.

(1978). *Henry Huggins.* Illus. by Louis Darling. New York: William Morrow.

(1979). *Ramona and her mother.* Illus. by Alan Tiegreen. New York: William Morrow.

(1981). *Ramona Quimby, age 8.* Illus. by Alan Tiegreen. New York: William Morrow.

(1983). *Dear Mr. Henshaw.* Illus. by Paul Zelinsky. New York: William Morrow.

(1984). *Ramona forever.* Illus. by Alan Tiegreen. New York: William Morrow.

(1988). *A girl from Yamhill: A memoir.* New York: William Morrow.

(1991). *Strider.* Illus. by Paul O. Zelinsky. New York: William Morrow.

(1999). *Ramona's world.* New York: William Morrow.

and death and dying. Virginia Hamilton's *Bluish* put the reader in honest, empathetic touch with a leukemia victim in a wheelchair. Kimberly Holt's *Dancing in Cadillac Light* poignantly reveals a special understanding between a granddaughter and an aging grandfather. Cynthia Rylant's *Missing May*, Sharon Creech's *Chasing Redbird*, and Barbara Park's *Mick Harte Was Here* address coping with the aftermath of the death of a loved one. The last decade has revealed a broader interest in writing and reading titles reflecting the realities faced by characters with disabilities (Landrum, 2001; Landrum, 1999/2000; Swartz & Hendricks, 2000). Figure 6.1 lists criteria for selecting books on these issues and shares other examples of quality literature that address these important realities of life.

FIGURE 6.1   Book Cluster: Realistic fiction—Coping with problems of the human condition

Criteria for Selecting Books Incorporating Disabilities or Chronic Illness

- Promotes empathy, not pity and depicts acceptance, not ridicule.
- Emphasizes success rather than, or in addition to, failure.
- Promotes positive images of persons with disabilities.
- Assists children's growth in understanding of the disability while modeling respect.
- Promotes an attitude of "one of us" rather than "one of them."
- Utilizes language that stresses person first, disability second (e.g., Mark who is deaf).
- Depicts person with disability in real settings, activities, or occupations.

Adapted from Blaska (1996).

Physical Disabilities

Konigsburg, E. L. (1996). *The view from Saturday.* New York: Atheneum. [I/M]
    A sixth-grade teacher, a paraplegic, helps four students develop a special bond as they compete in an Academic Bowl competition.
McMahon, Patricia (2000). *Dancing wheels.* Boston: Houghton Mifflin.(Paraplegic) [I]
Mikaelsen, Ben (1998). *Petey.* New York: Hyperion. (Cerebral palsy) [I/M]
Paulsen, Gary (1991). *The monument.* New York: Delacorte. [M]
    Rocky is self-conscious of the braces on her leg until a remarkable artist who comes to her small town to design a monument changes her life.
Platt, Chris (1998). *Willow king.* New York: Random House. [I/M]
    Katie, a physically challenged 13-year-old, saves a crippled foal and nurses him back to health and eventual championships.
Spinelli, Jerry (1997). *Crash.* New York: Scholastic. (Paralysis) [I/M]
Tolan, Stephanie (1997). *Who's there?* New York: William Morrow. (Mute)
White, Ruth (1997). *Belle Prater's boy.* New York: Scholastic. (Visually impaired) [I/M]

Learning Disabilities

Banks, Jacqueline T. (1995). *Egg-drop blues.* Boston: Houghton Mifflin. (Dyslexia)
Gantos, Jack (1999). *Joey Pigza swallowed the key.* New York: Farrar, Straus and Giroux. [I]
Gantos, Jack (2000). *Joey Pigza loses control.* New York: Farrar, Straus and Giroux. [I]

(continued)

FIGURE 6.1   Continued

Gantos, Jack (2002). *What would Joey do?* New York: Farrar, Straus and Giroux. [I]
Tashjian, Janet (1997). *Tru confessions.* New York: Henry Holt. (Developmentally delayed) [I/M]

Mental Disabilities

Conly, Jane L. (1993). *Crazy lady!* New York: HarperCollins. [M]
   As he comes to terms with his mother's death, Vernon finds comfort with the neighborhood
   outcasts, a woman with alcoholism and her son, a child with mental retardation.
Fleming, Virginia (1993). *Be good to Eddie Lee.* Illus. by Floyd Cooper. New York: Philomel
   Books.(Picture book) [P/I]
   Christy considers Eddie, a child with Down syndrome, a real pest. But when he follows her into the
   woods, he shares special discoveries with her to indeed show he is a special person.
Fox, Paula (1997). *Radiance descending.* [I] New York: D.K. Inc. Note: Dorling Kindersley changed their
   name to D.K. Ink.
   Paul scarcely is able to accept his 7-year-old brother, who has Down syndrome. With the love of
   his grandfather and neighbors, Paul is able to recognize the qualities that make Jacob a special
   person.
Haddon, Mark (2003). *The curious incident of the dog in the night-time.* New York: Doubleday. (Autism)
Holt, Kimberly W. (1998). *My Louisiana sky.* New York: Henry Holt. [I/M]
   After her grandmother's death, 12-year-old Tiger Ann Parker struggles to accept her parents, who
   have mental disabilities. She soon realizes their love and personal capabilities contribute to her
   sense of family and home.
Philbrick, Rodman (1993). *Freak the mighty.* New York: Blue Sky/Scholastic. [M]
   Max, who has a learning disability, and his brilliant friend Freak, born with a birth defect, combine
   forces to make a powerful team.
Philbrick, Rodman (1998). *Max the mighty.* New York: Scholastic. [I/M]
Wood, June Rae (1992). *The man who loved clowns.* New York: Putnam. [I/M]
   Delrita loves her Uncle Punky but sometimes feels ashamed of his behavior because he has Down
   syndrome. Her developing understanding of love and loss creates two memorable characters.
Wood, June Rae (1995). *When pigs fly.* New York: Putnam. (Down syndrome) [I/M]

Chronic Illness/AIDS

Holt, Kimberly Willis (2001). *Dancing in Cadillac light.* New York: Putnam. (Alzheimer's disease) [I/M]
Nelson, Theresa (1994). *Earthshine.* New York: Orchard Books. [M]
   Slim's father has AIDS and she learns to deal with the anger and guilt that diminish her own spirit.
   A support group and Isaiah, whose mother has AIDS, help Slim cope as her father moves closer
   to death.
Porte, Barbara A. (1994). *Something terrible happened.* New York: Orchard Books. [I/M]
   When Gillian's mother dies of AIDS, she returns to her deceased father's family in Tennessee to
   deal with death. Her biracial ancestry brings her a new understanding of herself as a stable family
   helps her cope.

The final category focuses on "Living in a Diverse World" and addresses racial and ethnic diversity, stories about minorities, and stories set in the context of world cultures. Beverly Naidoo's *The Other Side of Truth* shares the realities of apartheid; Walter Dean Myers's *Monster* presents a realistic view of urban life in America. Andrew Clements's *The Jacket* confronts the issues of racism and quick judgments and reminds the reader of lingering prejudices in society. Suzanne Fisher Staples's Newbery Honor book, *Shabanu: Daughter of the Wind,* and *Under the Persimmon Tree* take the reader to the desert culture of Pakistan and Afghanistan and their expectations within our modern world. This category is elaborated on in Chapter 8 on multicultural and international children's literature.

These three categories are especially, but not exclusively, applicable to maturing readers in the upper elementary and middle schools through realistic fiction chapter books. Although these subgenres form a comprehensive scheme with which professionals can organize children's realistic fiction, younger children are more apt to relate to the realistic fiction genre through a simplified scheme that addresses children's choices and favorites. It is important to be knowledgeable about the higher level categorization scheme, but teachers may find intermediate elementary students more highly motivated by the simple terminology of the following popular categories.

Family stories.   Most children share the common life experience of having a family. Although the configuration of that family differs, it supports, loves, and nurtures the child in a way that makes a difference in his or her life. Jeanne Birdsall's *The Pendericks: A Summer Tale of Four Sisters, Two Rabbits, and a Very Interesting Boy*, a Newbery Honor title, captures the nostalgic spirit of family life. Beverly Cleary's timeless Ramona series (*Ramona's World*) and Lois Lowry's classic Anastasia books, including *Zooman Sam,* humorously invite us into the Quimby and Krupnik families for a taste of sibling life. For primary readers, Megan McDonald updates family life for younger readers through her *Judy Moody, M. D.,* and *Stink: The Incredible Shrinking Kid* family series. Children thrive on stories that share the joys, challenges, and sadnesses of growing up as a member of the unit they call family.

School stories.   Stories that take place in school bring a universal setting to young readers. Here the cast of characters includes a special teacher, classmates, the class bully, the custodian, the principal, and the projects and celebrations that fill the school year. Andrew Clements's popularity in this subgenre has produced *Frindle, The Janitor's Boy, The Landry News, The School Story,* and *Lunch Money.* These titles continue to be nominated and win state awards, attesting to the appeal of school stories to intermediate readers. The close connections to children's own lives make these titles not only popular read-alouds but books that children choose on their own again and again.

Animal stories.   Few readers can encounter an animal story without wiping away a tear as our affinity with animals puts response at an emotional high. Sharing love and receiving loyalty in return provide a major theme of these books, but it is typically the character who grows because of his or her encounter with an animal

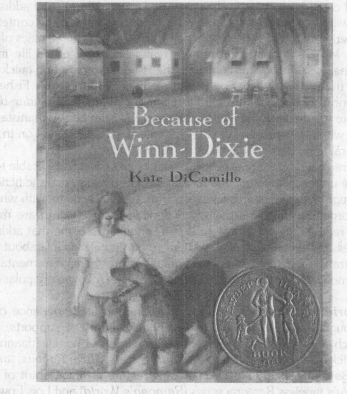

friend. Phyllis Reynolds Naylor's *Shiloh* trilogy, John Gardiner's *Stone Fox,* and Wilson Rawls's *Where the Red Fern Grows* are timeless stories that reach the response core of the reader. Karen Hesse's *Sable* and Kate Di Camillo's *Because of Winn Dixie* are newer titles that add to this beloved subgenre.

Adventure/survival stories. Survival stories hold powerful appeal to students in the middle grades. Without adult assistance, characters encounter situations that require quick thinking, problem solving, and inner strength. Reflecting on their ordeals, they realize that they have grown, not only in physical prowess but in confidence and independence. Gary Paulsen's survival quartet (*Hatchet, The River, Brian's Winter,* and *Brian's Return*) fosters response discussion on qualities and kinds of survival. Kirkpatrick Hill's *Winter Camp,* Will Hobbs's *Down the Yukon,* and Ben Mikaelsen's *Touching Spirit Bear* reflect the strong reader attraction to the adventure story.

Humorous stories. Humorous realistic fiction finds characters involved in amusing predicaments that are solved in clever ways. Books like Phyllis Reynolds Naylor's *Roxie and the Hooligans* and Polly Horvath titles, including *The Pepins and Their Problems,* serve to introduce younger readers to the realistic fiction genre.

Especially appealing to transitional readers, each chapter often stands alone as an episode in the life of the character.

Serious stories.   Stories that focus on societal issues fit this category. Betsy Byars's *Cracker Jackson,* for example, addresses the issue of domestic abuse; Ruth White's *Belle Prater's Boy* seeks the answers to a mother's disappearance. These are the stories of which aesthetic response can become the focus as they attempt to identify the reader with flesh-and-blood characters within the context of real-life issues.

Mysteries.   During some stage of a young reader's life, mystery has a role in motivating reading. Whereas generations of readers were raised on Nancy Drew and the Hardy Boys as supersleuths, today's readers have greater variety and quality. Cynthia DeFelice's character, Allie Nichols, takes us on adventures in *The Ghost and Mrs. Hobbs, The Ghost of Fossil Glen*, and *The Ghost of Cutler Creek*. A new series by Tracy Mack and Michael Citrin, Sherlock Holmes and the Baker Street Irregulars, provides a first title—*The Fall of the Amazing Zalindas*—which possesses the intriguing, fast action plots that hook readers. *Chasing Vermeer* by Blue Balliett blends art and mystery for the intermediate reader. Perhaps this subgenre exists to introduce young readers to realistic fiction and, after a time, send them off to explore the genre further.

    The genre of contemporary realistic fiction is indeed diverse in that it shares situations that are real and characters who must respond with maturity to deal with the real world of growing up. This most popular genre among school-age readers is a thriving one and naturally invites reader response.

Considering Literary Elements in Realistic Fiction

Works of children's realistic fiction must adhere to the high standards of the use of literary elements applicable to all quality fiction. Literary elements appropriate for discussion and evaluation in children's literature include plot, character, setting, theme, and point of view. Although all literature justifies mention of these elements, it is in the narrative form of contemporary realistic fiction where these elements may best be modeled. Examining the complexity of story structure begins with the recognition of these five literary elements in the context of authentic literature. The beginnings of children's writing are grounded in the use of these elements throughout quality literature. In the following discussion, a recent example of realistic fiction, Kate Di Camillo's Newbery Honor title, *Because of Winn-Dixie,* is used to exemplify each element.

Plot.   Plot is the sequence of events that occurs to characters in situations in the beginning, middle, and end of a story. Conflict is the tension within the plot between a character and nature, a character and society, between characters, or even *within* the character. The unfolding conflict and ultimate resolution are what keep readers reading. Plot development occurs when the problem and conflict are introduced, continues as roadblocks are placed in the face of the character, reaches a high point when the problem is about to be solved, and concludes with the solution of the problem and removal of roadblocks at the end of the story (Tompkins, 2005).

For example, the beginning of *Because of Winn-Dixie* transports the reader to the small southern town to which India Opal Baloni has just moved with her preacher father. Opal not only faces the continuing longing for her mother, but she must make new friends in yet another attempt to find a place she can call home. Adopting a ragged mutt named Winn-Dixie helps her in making friends with the eccentric characters in the town. The plot resolution occurs when Opal comes to realize that she has much for which to be grateful and is ready to move on from past memories to making a new life in her new home.

Setting.   Although setting is often described as where the story takes place, setting can also include dimensions of location, weather, time, or time period (Tompkins, 2005). Some stories have backdrop settings, barely sketched; others have specific well-described locations. In realistic fiction, the time frame of the story focuses on a contemporary setting over a relatively short time span.

The setting for Di Camillo's *Because of Winn-Dixie* is the steamy, sultry town of Naomi, Florida, a small community showcasing a Winn-Dixie supermarket, the Herman W. Block Library, Otis's Pet Store, and a variety of eccentric inhabitants. The Open Arms Baptist Church attempts to instill a growing community spirit in this southern town while it reluctantly opens its arms to the new preacher and his daughter. The loss of India Opal's mother at age 3 provides background for the reader of the melancholy, lonely life of the reverend and his daughter continually leaving friends and memories behind in their mobile life.

Character.   Characters in realistic fiction are those involved in the story. The main characters are fully developed; supporting characters are minimally portrayed. Authors develop characters through appearance, action, dialogue, and monologue (Tompkins, 2005). Award-winning realistic fiction is often remembered because of unforgettable characters and personal growth.

India Opal Baloni is portrayed as a lonely 10-year-old prone to making unusual friends. After picking up a dog and naming him after the local grocery store, Opal also befriends mysterious Gloria Dump, storytelling librarian Fanny Block, and guitar-strumming Otis before coming to terms with her peers, Sweetie Pie and Stevie and Dunlap Dewberry. Opal longs to hold on to the memories of her mother, so the preacher fills her with a list of 10 things about her mama. While finding her place in her new home, Opal realizes that she and her dog, Winn-Dixie, are instrumental in building a permanent place for a future with those who embrace her engaging spirit. Kate Di Camillo creatively showcases minor characters to allow the reader to see the personal skills of Opal in bringing lonely but kind individuals together.

Theme.   Theme is the underlying meaning or message of a story that encompasses truths about human nature and/or society. Usually dealing with the character's emotions or values, themes are either openly stated or implied in a character's actions. Friendship, courage, responsibility, truth, and justice are common themes used in children's literature (Tompkins, 2005).

The theme for *Because of Winn-Dixie* focuses on the loss of a loved one and the role of inner strength to persevere and the power of friends in building a new life. "Mama . . . I know ten things about you, and that's not enough. . . . He misses you and I miss you, but my heart doesn't feel empty anymore. It's full all the way up" (pp. 177–178). A tender canine becomes the instrument that draws Opal to newfound friends, leading her to realize just how much she has reason to be thankful.

Viewpoint. The focus of the narrator determines the believability of the plot and the reader's understanding of the story. In children's literature read by intermediate-and middle-level readers, the first-person point of view and the omniscient view are most commonly used. A story told through the eyes of the main character using the narrative "I" is first person. The narrator is both an eyewitness and a story participant. The omniscient viewpoint, in contrast, sees and knows all. The author informs the reader of a character's thoughts and feelings (Tompkins, 2005).

In *Because of Winn-Dixie,* the author shares every action, feeling, and thought of India Opal through a first-person perspective. Opal describes her early encounters with townspeople and her evolving friendships and intriguing episodes with them. Opal pours out her heart through the author's well-chosen words, thus tugging at the heartstrings of the reader. The first-person voice brings the reader even closer to the main character, vicariously feeling her loss and her recovery during the story.

These five literary elements—plot, character, setting, theme, and viewpoint—are well defined and modeled in quality realistic fiction. These elements become the basis of the criteria for evaluating quality realistic fiction for children and positively influence readers as writers of fiction.

Realistic Fiction Series Books

Because of this genre's appeal to young readers, realistic fiction often appears in the form of series books. Series books are formula fiction written with predictable plots, standard characters, and simplified writing style. Their predictable formulas may stretch a plot over several titles, describe different characters in similar situations, or carry the same character through different situations. These books with simple variations provide comfort in "their confirmation of previous expectations" (Nodelman, 1992) and the security of knowing that the story goes on even as the final page is turned.

Although literary experts typically view series books as a "lesser" type of literature, generations of young readers have thrived on a comforting familiarity within these titles. Grandparents may have grown up on a steady diet of the Bobbsey Twins or Tom Swift series; many of today's parents enjoyed a steady diet of Nancy Drew and Hardy Boys mysteries. Many college students might eagerly admit their attachment to Encyclopedia Brown (Donald Sobol), the Sweet Valley Twins (Francine Pascal), or the Baby-Sitters Club (Ann Martin) series. Many ardent adult readers attribute their zest for reading to their emerging adolescence when series books presented predictable characters and absorbing plots that built confidence in oneself both as a reader and as a person. Nodelman (1992) speculates that learning basic story patterns as the foundation of all fiction builds a schema for the divergent patterns in the quality literature that lies beyond the series book.

Fortunately, several recognized children's authors have taken on the task of writing books in a series. Betsy Byars, Newbery Award medalist, introduces the Herculeah Jones mystery series, in which a budding spy helps his private investigator mother solve a series of intriguing cases. Newbery medalist Phyllis Reynolds Naylor presents Alice McKinley (*Alice-in-Between, Alice in Lace*) as she takes on the task of growing up female in an all-male household. The gravitation of quality authors into the realm of series books has recently brought a more positive view to this aspect of the realistic fiction genre.

Figure 6.2 presents a listing of both contemporary and classic series realistic fiction books that are likely to find their way into the self-selected readings of

FIGURE 6.2 Book Cluster: Realistic fiction series books

Cameron, Ann

Julian and Henry series, New York: Knopf. [I]
  (1981). *Stories Julian tells.*
  (1986). *More stories Julian tells.*
  (1995). *The stories Huey tells.*
  (1997). *More stories Huey tells.*
Gloria series. Illus. by Lis Toft. New York: Farrar, Straus & Giroux. [I]
  (2000). *Gloria's way.*
  (2001). *Gloria rising.*

Danziger, Paula

The Amber Brown series, New York: Putnam. [I]
  (1994). *Amber Brown is not a crayon.*
  (1995). *Amber Brown goes fourth.*
  (2001). *What a trip, Amber Brown.*
  (2002). *It's a fair day, Amber Brown.*
  (2002). *Get ready for second grade, Amber Brown.*
  (2003). *Amber Brown is green with envy.*
  (2004). *Second grade rules, Amber Brown.*
  (2005). *Orange you glad it's Halloween, Amber Brown?*

Lowry, Lois

Anastasia Krupnik series, Boston: Houghton Mifflin. [I]
  (1979). *Anastasia Krupnik* and numerous other titles including
  (1986). *Anastasia has the answers.*
  (1987). *Anastasia's chosen career.*
  (1991). *Anastasia at this address.*
  (1992). *Attaboy, Sam!* (Anastasia's brother)
  (1995). *Anastasia, absolutely.*
  (1996). *See you around, Sam.* (Anastasia's brother)
  (1999). *Zooman Sam* (Anastasia's brother)

FIGURE 6.2 Continued

McDonald, Megan

Judy Moody series. Illus. by P. Reynolds. Cambridge, MA: Candlewick. [I]
    (2000). *Judy Moody was in a mood. Not a good mood. A bad mood.*
    (2001). *Judy Moody gets famous.*
    (2002). *Judy Moody saves the world.*
    (2003). *Judy Moody predicts the future.*
    (2004). *Judy Moody: The doctor is in!*
    (2005). *Judy Moody declares independence.*
    (2006). *Judy Moody: Around the world in 8 1/2 days.*

Stink Series
    (2005). *Stink: The incredible shrinking kid.*
    (2006). *Stink: The incredible galactic jawbreaker.*

Naylor, Phyllis Reynolds

Alice McKinley series, New York: Atheneum. [I]
    (1985). *Agony of Alice* and numerous other titles including
    (1994). *Alice in-between.*
    (1995). *Alice the brave.*
    (1997). *Outrageously Alice.*
    (1999). *Alice on the outside.*
    (2002). *Simply Alice.*
    (2003). *Patiently Alice.*
    (2003). *Alice in Blunderland.*
    (2004). *Including Alice.*
    (2004). *Lovingly Alice.*
    (2005). *Alice on her way.*
    (2006). *Alice in know.*

Hartford Boys/Malloy Girls series, New York: Delacorte. [I]
    (1993). *The boys start the war.*
    (1993). *The girls get even.*
    (1994). *The boys against the girls.*
    (1998). *The girls' revenge.*
    (1999). *A traitor among the boys.*
    (2000). *A spy among the girls.*
    (2002). *The girls take over.*
    (2003). *Boys in control.*
    (2004). *Girls rule!*
    (2005). *Boys rock!*

Shiloh Trilogy. New York:Atheneum. [I]
    (1991). *Shiloh.*
    (1996). *Shiloh season.*
    (1997). *Saving Shiloh.*

intermediate and middle-school students. School librarians, classroom teachers, and parents should be aware of their appeal and their ability to "hook" readers on reading. As mentioned in Chapter 2, readers' choices are genuine responses to literature. Because these books awaken readers to the enjoyment of reading, the continuing selection of titles in a series is indeed a valid form of reader response.

EVALUATING QUALITY REALISTIC FICTION

Because realistic fiction is such a popular genre, it does require careful scrutiny for inclusion in the classroom or library/media center. Realistic fiction reflects the social conditions of our times, so the issues addressed and the situations rendered may create controversy in a school setting. Criteria to locate quality titles in this genre include the following:

- Realistic fiction must, first and foremost, share a good story that engages readers so much that they actually care about the outcome of the book.
- Realistic fiction must embrace realistic characters, situations, and settings that reflect life in a believable way.
- Character development forms an integral part of the story. The characters must grow and learn about themselves during the course of the book.
- The plot must be fresh and carry the reader into a challenging situation that requires problem solving or reflections on moral or value issues.
- Realistic fiction must maintain an optimistic view of our lives in spite of the problems that surround the story. The reader must be left with the message that people do have control over their lives and problems can be overcome, dealt with, and solved.
- Realistic fiction should reflect a balance of the different subgenre types and incorporate both males and females as protagonists who face problems with determination and courage, regardless of the eventual outcome.

BENEFITS OF REALISTIC FICTION

Although it seems somewhat redundant to enumerate the strengths of this genre, the following list emphasizes why it plays such an important role in both reading for pleasure and personal/social development of the reader.

- Realistic fiction invites the reader to gain insights into themselves and their peers in the context of realistic relationships and problems that form the core of our lives.
- Realistic fiction fosters reader engagement and understanding because situations and events are familiar to the reader. This factor actually contributes to the popularity of this genre.
- Realistic fiction presents a model of confronting life experiences in which the reader serves as a spectator as characters cope with contemporary issues.

- Realistic fiction provides readers with a safe distance from unknown areas while building reader awareness of their existence. Rather than sheltering, realistic fiction invites readers to observe and empathize with the problems of others that may never touch their own lives.
- Realistic fiction depicts life in other cultures set in geographic regions around the world, allowing for a broader perspective on viewing the world.

READER RESPONSE TO REALISTIC FICTION

Realistic fiction provides sound support for reader response through literature response journals, character journals, and literature conversations. Some of the richest personal responses are elicited from realistic fiction. Responses to living through the experiences of others reflect an empathy and preparedness for confronting problems in one's own life. The real world of growing up is a challenge, but realistic fiction books provide a connection to that world so readers experience the fact that they are not alone with the problems they face.

The written response is perhaps the strongest mode gleaned from interactions with realistic fiction (see Chapter 10). Because of the private nature of written reader response, the reader is more confident sharing connections with his or her own life as literature and reality bridge a challenging time in a young person's life. Realistic fiction holds the key to better understanding oneself and others as the realities of contemporary life confront us.

HISTORICAL FICTION

Historical fiction is realistic fiction set in the historical past. Although the story is imaginary, characters and events introduced could really have occurred in this historical context. Based on historical facts, the story is skillfully blended with historical settings, historical figures, and historical events. Not only does historical fiction convey a sense of the period, but it shares a rousing story that actually could have taken place. Figure 6.3 provides a sequenced list of quality historical fiction grouped by historical period.

The Ballad of Lucy Whipple by Karen Cushman exemplifies the true-to-life characters, historical realism, and authentic background that make historical fiction a popular literary genre. Unwillingly uprooted from her Massachusetts home, 12-year-old California Morning Whipple (self-named Lucy) becomes an involuntary citizen of Lucky Diggins. A lifelong dream of her deceased father causes her adventurous mother and siblings to journey by ship to California in 1849. Instead of gold, Lucy finds only tattered tents, no lending library, and rough and boisterous miners. Emotional letters back home reflect Lucy's rebellious, outspoken nature as well as her genuine misery and misgivings. Lucy is slow to admit that the unsettled nature of the western wilderness is the perfect match for her imagination, but her love of reading eventually provides a reason to call California home.

Widely used in literature-based classrooms, historical fiction has become an effective link between social studies and literacy instruction (Farris, 2004; James & Zarillo,

1989; Johnson & Ebert, 1992; Tunnell & Ammon, 1993). The parallel study of historical facts beside a dazzling story set during the same period provides a motivating means of breathing life into the curriculum. Richard Peck's Newbery Award title, *A Year Down Under,* a linked series of candidly crafted vignettes set in rural Illinois during the Great Depression, captures the spirit of the era through Grandma Dawdel, a scheming, feisty old woman surviving in hard times. In addition, the story adds a level of understanding and admiration by a skeptical but increasingly accepting granddaughter. The quality of historical fiction, evidenced by its repeated connections between history and the realities of life,

Historical fiction must be authentically presented, historically accurate, and weave historical detail into a good story. *From* Crispin: The Cross of Lead *by Avi. Copyright © 2002 by Avi. Reprinted by permission of Hyperion Books for Children. All rights reserved.*

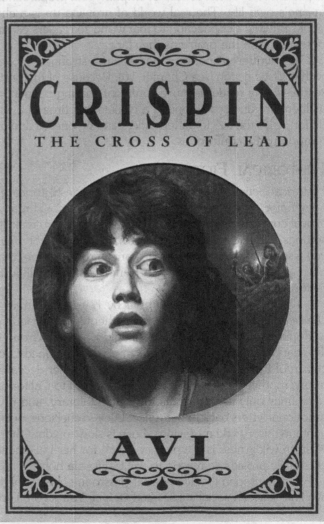

FIGURE 6.3   Book Cluster: Historical fiction

Middle Ages/Early England

Love, D. Anne (2003). *The puppeteer's apprentice*. New York: McElderry. [I]
Sturtevant, Katherine (2006). *A true and faithful narrative*. New York: Farrar, Straus & Giroux. [I/M]

Early America

Carbone, Elisa (2006). *Blood on the river: James Town, 1607*. New York: Viking. [I/M]
Clark, Clara Gillow (2003). *Hill hawk Hattie*. Cambridge, MA: Candlewick. [I]

Westward Movement

Avi (2001). *The secret school*. San Diego: Harcourt Brace. [I]
McCaughrean, Geraldine (2003). *Stop the train!* New York: HarperCollins. [I/M]
Robinet, Harriette Gillem (2003). *Twelve travelers, twenty horses*. New York: Atheneum. [I]

Slavery/Civil War

Lester, Julius (2006). *Time's memory*. New York: Farrar, Straus & Giroux. [I/M]
McMullan, Margaret (2004). *How I found the strong: A civil war story*. Boston: Houghton Mifflin. [I/M]

Immigration

Auch, Mary Jane (2002). *Ashes of roses*. New York: Henry Holt. [I/M]
Cushman, Karen (2002). *Rodzina*. New York: Clarion. [I]
Giff, Patricia Reilly (2004). *A house of tailors*. New York: Random House. [I]
LaFaye, A. (2004). *Worth*. New York: Simon & Schuster. [I/M]
Napoli, Donna (2005). *The king of Mulberry Street*. New York: Random House/Wendy Lamb. [I/M]

Turn of the 20th Century

Peck, Richard (2004). *The teacher's funeral: A comedy in three parts*. New York: Dial. [I/M]
Peck, Richard (2006). *Here lies the librarian*. New York: Dial. [I/M]

Great Depression

Carter, Dorothy (2005). *Grandma's general store: The ark*. Illus. by Thomas B. Allen. New York: Farrar, Straus & Giroux. [I]
Hale, Marian (2004). *The truth about sparrows*. New York: Henry Holt. [I]

World War II/Holocaust

Friedman, D. Dina (2006). *Escaping into the night*. New York: Simon & Schuster. [I/M]
Giff, Patricia Reilly (2005). *Willow run*. New York: Random House. [I/M]
Hesse, Karen (2003). *Aleutian sparrow*. New York: McElderry. [I/M]
Lisle, Janet Taylor (2000). *The art of keeping cool*. New York: Simon & Schuster. [I]
Spinelli, Jerry (2002). *Milkweed*. New York: Knopf. [M]

Civil Rights Movement

Moses, Sheila P. (2004). *The legend of Buddy Bush*. New York: McElderry. [I]

Realistic and Historical Fiction

Countless Internet sites promote reading by encouraging children to locate and select quality literature, engage in interactive literacy-based online activities, and meet favorite authors on the Web.

The Newbery Medal (ALA)

The Newbery Medal is awarded annually to the author of the most distinguished contribution to American literature for children. Although the award is not restricted to realistic and historical fiction, the award has most often been bestowed on these two genres.
http://www.ala.org/ala/alsc/awardsscholarships/literaryawds/newberymedal/newberymedal.htm.

The Scott O'Dell Award

The Scott O'Dell Award for Historical Fiction is awarded annually to a meritorious book published for children or young adults. Scott O'Dell established this award to encourage other writers to focus on historical fiction.
http://www.scottodell.com/odellaward.html

Kids Reads

A great resource for teachers and students who want to learn more about favorite books, series, and authors. Website includes reviews of new titles, interviews with authors, and information on how to contact an author.
http://www.kidsreads.com/authors/authors.asp

Author Spotlight

Published by Houghton Mifflin Company, this site spotlights popular authors such as Chris Van Allsburg and Karen Cushman. Includes literature-based lesson plans and ideas for cross-curricular activities.
http://www.eduplace.com/author/index_flash.html

Book Jackets

An interactive web page created by kids, for kids, which invites students to learn about authors and explore new books.
http://www.bookjackets.com/

Nancy Keane's Children's Literature Webpage

Student may read reviews, explore the many links to children's authors, or participate in book talks on this user-friendly site.
http://www.nancykeane.com

Kid Space at the Internet Public Library

Includes biographical information, frequently asked questions (FAQs), and photos of several well-known children's authors.
www.ipl.org/div/kidspace/askauthor/

makes this genre a welcome choice by both students and their teachers. Through both historical fiction picture books and chapter books, this genre provides a meaningful link to interdisciplinary instruction.

Types of Historical Fiction

Even though all historical fiction tells an energizing story set in a historical time period, variations do exist between types of historical fiction books.

Historically researched with imaginary characters. Most historical fiction is of this type. Set in an authentic period, the invented main character lives amid authentic events, settings, and issues. Katherine Paterson's *Lyddie* remains a memorable literary character as circumstances take her from Vermont to the factory mills of Lowell, Massachusetts. The long, hard hours of factory workers during America's Industrial Revolution are showcased through the eyes of believable characters. Similarly, Paterson's *Jip: His Story* tells a tale of abandonment and hope in Vermont in 1855–1856. Author notes acknowledge research sources that authentically support the writing of these strong examples of historical fiction.

Historical period piece. The historical context is the focus as the social conventions, customs, morals, and values of the historical period are showcased around a character. The thriving years of the Erie Canal set the stage for Jim Murphy's *Desperate Journey* set in 1848 when canals were a means to speed settlers to their destinations westward. When this story takes place, the "Big Ditch" was home and workplace to over 20,000 people—a hardworking, colorful collection of people who helped shape

America's destiny. Maps, an introduction, researched information, and a glossary attest to the historical authenticity of this title as the author weaves history with the thrilling adventure of Maggie Haggerty in a story of courage and family bonds.

Time travel. Contemporary characters are transported to the past as time travel sets them in another historical context. The character lives through actual events and returns to the present with a deeper understanding of history. Elvira Woodruff's *The Orphan of Ellis Island* transports Dominic Cantori from a class visit to Ellis Island back to Italy in 1908 as he unlocks the doors to his past. After the author visited the museum at Ellis Island, she sensed the importance of family in history and used this time travel adventure to reinforce her message. Often classified as a type of fantasy (see Chapter 5), the heavy historical emphasis of some titles comfortably places these books in the historical fiction genre as well.

Personal chronicle. The author actually experienced a historical period and writes about his or her own life through authentic memories or documented journal entries. The reader relives moments from the author's life, usually as a child, and learns about growing up and living in a particular historical period. Laura Ingalls Wilder's Little House series takes the reader to a bygone time yet documents the simple pleasures and joys of growing up on the prairie.

Children's Literature Web Guide
http://www.ucalgary.ca/~dkbrown/authors.html
Provides an extensive list of web links to author's personal websites and author/illustrator site maintained by fans, scholars, and readers.

Carol Hurst's Children's Literature Site
http://www.carolhurst.com/authors/authors.html
Features articles about children's authors, including biographical information, lists of books, and links to other sites with relevant information.

Fiction Authors
Beverly Cleary
The World of Beverly Cleary
http://www.beverlycleary.com/index.html
KidsReads.com—Beverly Cleary
http://www.kidsreads.com/authors/au-cleary-beverly.asp

Scott O'Dell
Scott O'Dell Home Page
http://www.scottodell.com

Pam Muñoz Ryan
Pam Muñoz Ryan: Children's Author
http://www.pammunozryan.com/
Reading Rockets: A Video Interview with Pam Muñoz Ryan
http://www.readingrockets.org/books/interviews/ryan

Christopher Paul Curtis
Christopher Paul Curtis.com
http://www.randomhouse.com/features/christopherpaulcurtis/
KidsReads.com-Christopher Paul Curtis
http://www.kidsreads.com/authors/au-curtis-christopher-paul.asp

Literary Elements in Historical Fiction

Just as this chapter looked at the five literary elements in the context of realistic fiction, so will it view them in the context of historical fiction. An exemplary choice for discussing these elements is Karen Hesse's *Out of the Dust,* the Newbery Medal winner for 1998. The Newbery Medal is awarded annually to the author of the most distinguished contribution to American literature for children. This recent winner exemplifies the effective use of literary elements in writing historical fiction. Although presented in a nontraditional historical format as a novel in free verse, this book captures the spirit of the Depression and the devastated lives of the victims of drought, dust, and poverty.

The **setting** of *Out of the Dust* is Cimarron County, Oklahoma, during the Dust Bowl years of the Great Depression. The book is divided into five sections covering the period from winter 1934 to summer 1935. Each entry is labeled with the exact month and year, making the historical chronology of the weather and economic conditions even more real. The **plot** involves 14-year-old Billie Jo, who is faced with the guilt of accidentally being responsible for the tragic death of her mother and unborn brother. A fire causes tragic burns as well for Billie Jo whose hands are disfigured in the flames. The family's loss and their struggle to deal with inward emotions and the never-ending dust and poverty of the Dust Bowl years form the story line of this historical account of fragile lives in difficult times.

The main **character,** Billie Jo, possesses a passion for playing the piano and loving and respecting her family. The tragic loss of this family compounded by the ghastly ecological conditions cause her to feel isolated, alone, and disconnected from the place she has called home. Yet her attempt to leave her feelings and guilt behind are thwarted as she feels the pull of family, roots, and home. Billie Jo is able to dig deep within to begin anew like so many victims of the terrible Dust Bowl that devastated the Great Plains during the 1930s. The historical account is revealed through her first-person **viewpoint** as the strong voice of "I" shares emotions and unfolding events. The **theme** of this painful account of personal and geographic tragedy is the persistence of the human spirit in desperate times. Not only does the reader learn of the history and vivid conditions of the Oklahoma Dust Bowl, but also the reality of the human will to survive in spite of personal and environmental conditions.

The five literary elements are well represented by Karen Hesse's quality writing and further support the importance of observing, noting, and discussing the role of literary elements in creating quality fictional works. Any Newbery award historical fiction title or any Scott O'Dell award books (see appendix) could be evaluated through a similar literary element lens.

Trends in Historical Fiction

The chapter book has provided the mainstay of the historical fiction genre for decades. Walter Edmonds's *The Matchlock Gun,* Marguerite de Angeli's *Door in the Wall,* Carolyn Reeder's *Shades of Gray,* and Graham Salisbury's *Under the Blood Red Sun* exemplify award-winning titles in chapter book form across a half century. The last decade, however, witnessed some invigorating format additions to the historical fiction genre that appeal to a wider range of readers. Most notable are the historical fiction picture book and historical fiction titles in a series.

The picture book is not entirely new to historical fiction, but many more books are being published today that carry illustrated versions of fictionalized historical events. Based on historical facts, Cynthia Cotton's *Abbie in Stitches* shares the domestic expectations and educational limitations of a young girl in the early 1800s. Barbara Russell's *Maggie's Amerikay* visits the immigrant city of New Orleans and the vibrancy of the ragtime music that surrounds its character. Based on the slave narratives of the WPA of the 1930s, *Night Boat to Freedom* by Margot Theis Raven brings historic voices to life as portrayed in Granny Judith's quilt. Doreen Rappaport's *Freedom River* and Allen Say's *Home of the Brave* share the stories of heroic efforts in authentic contexts in American history.

The picture book format provides a way to introduce the historical fiction genre to younger children. But it also provides an appealing, time-effective means of introducing history to intermediate/middle-level students of history. Connecting humanity to historical times is a strength of the focus of the picture book topic and format for disseminating the personal side of history.

The second trend in historical fiction is the advent of the historical fiction series book. Although series books have been popular in realistic fiction, only recently has historical fiction taken on the series appeal. A quality example of a historical fiction series is the Dear America series, which uses journal entries to deliver historically accurate information about the growth of our country through the words of children. The appeal of journal reading, the American history connections to the elementary social studies curriculum, and the continuing saga of young female characters during various historical periods blend to appeal to intermediate-level readers. The series began with early titles such as Lasky's *A Journey to the New World: The Diary of Patience Whipple* and Gregory's *The Winter of Red Snow: The Revolutionary War Diary of Abigail Jane Stewart* and has continued to Lasky's *Christmas After All: The Great Depression Diary of Minnie Swift*.

The Dear America series has extended to stories of slavery, westward expansion, and immigration and has grown in quality with authors such as Kathryn Lasky, Patricia McKissack, Rodman Philbrick, and Jim Murphy. Hansen's *I Thought My Soul Would Rise and Fly: The Diary of Patsy, a Freed Girl* won a Coretta Scott King honor book award. Each title is authenticated with historical notes, author notes, archival photographs, maps, recipes, sheet music, and other indications of life during the historical period. With increased popularity, the series has branched out with the My Name Is America series, which focuses on male characters including Denenberg's *The Journal of William Thomas Emerson: A Revolutionary War Patriot* and Philbrick's *The Journal of Douglas Allen Deeds: The Donner Party Expedition*. Written at a lower reading level, the My America series includes McMullan's *As Far as I Can See: Meg's Prairie Diary* and has inspired reading of historical fiction in second to third grades. The Royal Diaries series includes titles such as Gregory's *Catherine: The Great Journey/Russia, 1743*, as well as "diaries" of Elizabeth and Victoria. The series appeal with titles tied to history has led to their use in classrooms, and they are popular items on library shelves.

EVALUATING QUALITY HISTORICAL FICTION

First presented in 1984, the Scott O'Dell Award is given to the author of a distinguished work of historical fiction written for children or adolescent readers (Rochman, 2004). The award was originated by Scott O'Dell, author of quality historical fiction including *Island of the Blue Dolphins, Sing Down the Moon,* and *Sarah Bishop.* Winners of this award constitute a sound starting point for selecting

Literary Legend

Historical Fiction Author

The name **Scott O'Dell** (1898–1989) is virtually synonymous with children's historical fiction. Although he did not publish his first novel until he was 62, he made an immediate impact by winning the Newbery Medal for *Island of the Blue Dolphins,* published in 1960. This exceptional first novel was noteworthy for its strong Native American protagonist, Karana, and for its true story of survival on an isolated island. The novel was the first of almost 30 novels in which O'Dell typically used young first-person narrators to bring history to life for young readers. These protagonists interacted with a wide array of historical figures, from Moctezuma and Sacagawea to St. Francis of Assisi and Kit Carson. O'Dell's ideas for his novel came from his historical and biographical readings, and from stories he heard during his travels.

Many of his novels allow readers to see history from viewpoints traditionally left out of textbooks. For example, *Sing Down the Moon* is told by Bright Morning, a young Navaho woman who shares her thoughts and feelings as she experiences the Long Walk, a forced journey of 10,000 Navahos from their homes to imprisonment at Fort Sumner, New Mexico. O'Dell's desire to see the history of the New World, in particular, continue to be told in fiction is reflected in the creation of the Scott O'Dell Award for Historical Fiction. This award has helped assure that Scott O'Dell's combined love of history and fiction continues to be passed down to inquisitive children everywhere.

(1960). *Island of the blue dolphins.* Boston: Houghton Mifflin.

(1966). *The king's fifth.* Boston: Houghton Mifflin.

(1967). *The black pearl.* Boston: Houghton Mifflin.

(1969). *Journey to Jericho.* Boston: Houghton Mifflin.

(1970). *Sing down the moon.* Boston: Houghton Mifflin.

(1980). *Sarah Bishop.* Boston: Houghton Mifflin.

(1981). *The feathered serpent.* Boston: Houghton Mifflin.

(1985). *The road to Damietta.* Boston: Houghton Mifflin.

(1986). *Streams to the river, river to the sea.* Boston: Houghton Mifflin.

(1989). *My name is not Angelica.* Boston: Houghton Mifflin.

the best of the genre. Recent winners provide many of the examples throughout this chapter.

Although historical fiction must first and foremost deliver a good story, several specific criteria should be considered in judging the best of this genre. Parallel examples from Avi's *Crispin: The Cross of Lead,* 1994 Newbery Medal book, and its sequel, *Crispin: At the Edge of the World,* connect to each criteria to better reflect the quality of this genre of literature.

History should be authentically presented.   No attempt should be made to shelter the reader from the realities of the time period. The reality of city living habits of medieval times (street garbage, sleeping on straw, street performances) shared in *Crispin* replicate the feudal system hierarchy and the authentic life surrounding it. Likewise, the language of the period, although brief and direct, reflects the lack of education in the times.

Historical accuracy must be a priority.   Historical fiction is grounded in historical fact and authenticity must be preserved. Fictitious characters and contrived conversations abound, but the context must truly reflect the times. Crispin's journey through the English countryside during the 14th century reflects the small walled towns of feudalism and the adjacent peasant villages. Children illegitimately born of royal blood often had their heritage disguised to prevent them from assuming a role in the family tree. Crispin was engaged by Bear's singing and juggling at the town fair. Although partially fictionalized, fairs and entertainment were popular during the Middle Ages, and the event holds true to the happenings of the times.

The story must re-create the times through setting, daily life, and customs.   The reader should be able to visualize the physical surroundings, imagine the clothing, taste the meals, and note the traditions of the times. *Crispin* transports the reader to both the outlaws in the woods and the reality of the cold housing in medieval times. Readers may be surprised by the underlying religious tone of the story, but this is part of medieval times. The thought of Crispin at 13 years of age not knowing his identity may seem disturbing to today's adolescent reader, yet many illegitimate children were indicative of the promiscuous time and the importance of social hierarchy, royal expectations, and customs of the Middle Ages.

The story reveals history through a character of similar age to the reader.   By becoming involved with the protagonist, male or female, the reader generally assimilates history while empathizing with a character. The character's actions, beliefs, and values must be aligned with the time period. The language of the character should be appropriate to the period, including figures of speech that reflect the times. Dialogue must convey a feeling of the period, but it must accomplish this without overwhelming the reader. Thirteen-year-old Crispin's brief speech reflects the language of the period and his servant status during these times. The character and village names reflect English history and royal titles.

The writing style should unobtrusively weave historical detail into a good story.   The reader should be immersed in history without actually realizing that's what is happening. Crispin's unfolding story of seeking his identity provides a historical sequencing and attests to religion's impact on the times, and each chapter reflects the evolving growth and realization as Crispin becomes a young man with royal ties. The challenge of achieving this literary blend is a demanding one and attained by several talented writers who specialize in this genre.

BENEFITS OF HISTORICAL FICTION

Beyond the value of enjoying a well-written story, historical fiction offers these several benefits to the reader:

- Historical fiction presents historical facts through the everyday life of young people living during a particular historical period. Historical facts shared through realistic characters and settings bring history to life for readers (Cianciolo, 1981). *The Apprenticeship of Lucas Whitaker* by Cynthia DeFelice focuses on consumption during the mid-1800s as this scourge leaves Lucas an orphan. As an apprentice to Doc Beecher, Lucas exposes beliefs and attitudes of the day regarding health and witchcraft as he even digs up coffins to ward off the affliction. The extraordinary advances in medical knowledge through the last century stand in stark contrast to the beliefs of this period.

- Historical fiction provides personal interaction with and understanding of the people, places, and events related to a particular historical period. Katherine Paterson's *Jip: His Story* evokes the attitudes and social conditions of the 1850s. The plot revolves around Jip, a gypsy who as an infant fell from a wagon eight years before the story opens. He becomes a resident of the town poor farm and seems doomed to permanent servitude. Jip befriends an elderly man, who is prone to fits of violence and confined to a wooden cage. His growing awareness of the wretched conditions and the concern of a new teacher lead to a startling revelation about Jip's origins. Carefully planned by a master of this genre, this book shares a historical period through outstanding writing.

- Historical fiction provides enjoyment in reading a literary genre steeped in historical accuracy yet focused on strong characters whose lives are set in a historical context. Avi's two-volume *Beyond the Western Sea (Book One: The Escape from Home; Book Two: Lord Kirkle's Money)* tells a fast-paced story based on the escape of Irish emigrants from the Great Famine. A wealth of characters, short chapters, and the talent of Avi as a writer combine to keep the reader involved from start to finish. A superb read-aloud that represents historical fiction at its best, this remarkable saga shares the pleasure and fulfillment of this genre, which can lead to lifelong reading experiences.

READER RESPONSE TO HISTORICAL FICTION

Reader response to historical fiction, typically in the form of chapter books for intermediate/middle-level readers, is through literature conversations and response journals, but especially through character journals, which invite the reader to become a part of history through character identification (see Chapter 10). Choosing either Edward or Simon from Carolyn Reeder's Civil War novel, *Across the Lines,* helps create empathy for people and the situations surrounding this period in American history. Historical fiction begs dramatic reenactments of scenes and dialogue from the text or adaptation to a readers' theater script (see Chapter 12). Honored works of historical fiction, such as Elizabeth Speare's *The Witch of Blackbird Pond,* the Colliers's *My Brother Sam Is Dead,* Avi's *The True Confessions of Charlotte Doyle,* Patricia Beatty's *Charley Skedaddle,* Patricia MacLachlan's *Sarah, Plain and Tall,* Scott O'Dell's *Island of the Blue Dolphins,* and Lois Lowry's *Number the Stars,* provide a chronological look at history that invites written response through reader immersion in another time and another place.

Some of the most honored children's books grace the historical fiction genre. Although seemingly reserved for older readers, many excellent picture books also stand as an introduction to this genre for both younger and older readers. *Henry's Freedom Box* by Ellen Levine and *Moses: When Harriet Tubman Led Her People to Freedom* by Carole Boston Weatherford both share the inspiring challenges of the Underground Railroad and the fictionalized escapes to freedom before the Civil War. These titles invite younger readers into this genre and open literature connections to history in early elementary classrooms.

Well-written historical fiction can help children find their place in the vast framework of history. Quality historical fiction breathes life into history and the curriculum and connects across time with personal feelings and experiences. As children savor historical fiction, they realize that today's events rapidly become a part of tomorrow's history.

ISSUES OF GENDER ROLES

The genres of realistic and historical fiction showcase the increasing trend toward scrutinizing the gender roles of characters in literature. An increasingly large number of books present positive images of girls and women while avoiding stereotypes of young male characters. Susan Lehr's (2001) *Beauty, Brains, and Brawn: The Construction of Gender in Children's Literature*, a collection of essays, reminds teachers of the need to provide alternative roles that present well-rounded male and female characters who have choices and options. It is vital to have books about girls who do things and make things happen (Sprague & Keeling, 2000). Of equal concern are books with male characters who exhibit tenderness and compassion through tears. Considering gender and gender stereotypes and authentic female and male voices in children's literature becomes more important when we realize children's literature provides valid ground for the selection of role models.

Heine et al. (1999) present "Six Characteristics to Consider When Examining Children's Books for Positive Gender Role Models." After considering the quality of the literature itself, the strength of the gender representation becomes a selection issue.

- **Character's personal traits.** Consider the complexity of the character and his or her range of emotions. Reflect on the changes and growth that occur to the character during the book. Enumerate the admirable traits of the character while considering how the character deals with problems and issues.
- **Character's view of issues.** Determine whether the character focuses on gender issues and appropriate actions for females and males. Evaluate whether

he or she is overly conscious of physical attributes. Consider whether the character faces dilemmas that help in coming-of-age or issues that make a difference in the world.

- **Character's method of solving problems.** Determine how the character uses personal strengths to solve problems. Regard the character's initiative and inner strength in dealing with problems. Evaluate the problem-solving strategies used by the characters including seeking help, sharing problems with family and friends, and solving problems through literacy.
- **Character's relationships with others.** Evaluate the healthy relationship the character has with others in the book. Determine if mutual respect, honesty, friendship, and commitment are part of those relationships.
- **Character's departure from traditional stereotypes.** Female role models as characters should avoid being passive, fearful, weak, gentle, giggly, dependent, emotional, or vain. Male characters should move away from being strong, brave, competitive, unemotional, in charge, adventurous, and aggressive.
- **Character's voice for the untraditional role.** Consider how the character might speak for a role not found elsewhere in literature. Support books in which the character represents a cultural, ethnic, or socioeconomic group not typically found in literature.

Fulfilling these characteristics, both female and male role models dominate modern realistic fiction. Tiger Ann Parker in Kimberly Willis Holt's coming-of-age *My Louisiana Sky* embodies these traits. Tiger valiantly confronts the loss of her grandmother, the challenge of her mentally deficient parents, and the changes in her own world. Sistine Bailey shows her feelings as readily as Rob Horton hides his in Kate Di Camillo's *The Tiger Rising*. As they learn to trust their friendship, both share personal memories and heartache that have been locked up for too long. In Jerry Spinelli's *Wringer,* Palmer LaRue reveals his personal struggle to overcome peer pressure and societal expectations and to resolve his own sense of doing what's right. A reluctant student, Jack, finds his voice through journal entries inspired by the persistence and poetic modeling of Miss Stretchberry in Sharon Creech's *Love That Dog.*

Strong male role models abound in historical fiction. In Janet Taylor Lisle's World War II novel, *The Art of Keeping Cool,* Robert confronts his fears of Nazi submarines, a German artist living reclusively outside of town, and his own paternal grandfather. With growing maturity, Robert becomes an observer of his sensitive cousin, Eliot, and finds his own way to deal with the family secret. Crippled Pascal and his brother, Gideon, set off in hopes of claiming the land promised to black soldiers by General Sherman in Harriet Robinet's *Forty Acres and Maybe a Mule.* They soon discover building a better life in the years following the Civil War, a formidable task.

Recent strong female characters in historical fiction might include Jennifer Holm's *Boston Jane* who ventures to the wilderness of the Pacific Northwest. Discovering who she really is, Jane thrives as a fearless, loyal woman of the frontier. Gloria Whelan's *Angel on the Square* features privileged Katya Ivanova caught in a war-torn Russia and challenged to determine her own future. Karen Cushman revealed strong medieval female characters in *Matilda Bone* and *The Midwife's*

Apprentice. She continues her portrait of feisty, independent adolescent girls with *Rodzina,* an overlarge standoffish girl of Polish origin sent off from Chicago on the Orphan Train to pursue an unknown fate.

Teachers have the responsibility to select literature that represents both male and female characters in nonstereotyped roles. Considerations of these roles dominate realistic and historical fiction, yet permeate across all genres—from picture books to fantasy to informational texts. Being aware of the perceptions of characters as role models provides yet another criteria for the selection of the best books for vulnerable readers in constant search of role models.

ISSUES OF CONTROVERSY AND CENSORSHIP

The genres of realistic and historical fiction cannot be mentioned without addressing the responsibility of controversial selection of literature from those genres for individual reading or classroom use. Selection, however, assumes the companion issue of censorship.

> Once upon a time and far away children's books were perceived as simple things, concerned with naughty little rabbits, perplexed toy bears, and fairy princesses. Today they're often viewed as a pernicious enemy with the ability to corrupt impressionable minds and destroy our country. Those who hold this opinion seek then to remove these terrible influences from classrooms and libraries. (McClure, 1995, p. 3)

When teachers and librarians/media center directors believe that children must be exposed to meaningful literature for reading to come alive, they also believe that they must read what is personal and important to them. For many children, those issues include those they confront on a daily basis both in and out of school—divorce, death, disability, substance abuse, physical abuse, cultural differences, nontraditional families, and prejudice. Exposure to books on these topics may lead children to become better readers and better able to cope with issues in their own lives (Dresang, 2003). Sexual orientation also has gained literary attention as numerous books share gay and lesbian characters (Schall & Kauffman, 2003). Yet in well-intentioned efforts to develop sensitivity, respect, and tolerance within the traumatic contexts of children's lives, teachers and librarians may be opening their literary choices to criticism from the community beyond the school (Pavonetti, 2002). In an honest attempt to show children "they are not alone," the issue of censorship becomes an issue for consideration as part of the literature environment in a response-based reading program.

In her introduction to *Battling Dragons,* a collection of authors' voices on issues dealing with censorship, Susan Lehr (1995) points to the growing number of authors writing about the diverse and somewhat frightening experiences of children today and in the past. Episodes from Minfong Ho's *The Clay Marble,* Eve Bunting's *Fly Away Home*, or Paula Fox's *Monkey Island* (Fox, 1991) represent but a few examples of the violence and neglect that real children experience as recaptured in children's literature. "The books provide real and often disturbing views of life, challenging readers to think about issues from which some would rather shelter children" (p. xiii). Whether censors are politically motivated or moved by a sense of morality, they attempt to monitor and control the books children read rather than having reading selection be a matter of personal choice. The commonality among censors (parents, teachers, librarians, community members) is their desire to protect children from influences they perceive as evil or harmful.

Julie Wollman-Bonilla's (1998) study of preservice and inservice teachers' criteria for rejecting works of children's literature from their classrooms are enlightening and, unfortunately, indicative of a conservative attitude observed in the professional teaching community. "[t]eachers commonly objected to texts that reflect gender, ethnic, race, or class perspectives or experiences that differed from their own" (p. 289). These are the three rationales behind text inappropriateness and examples cited in this study:

1. The belief that a text is inappropriate for children because it might frighten or corrupt them by introducing them to things they don't or shouldn't know about. [Examples cited: *Fly Away Home* (Bunting, 1991)—homelessness; *Bridge to Terabithia* (Paterson, 1977)—death; *Smoky Night* (Bunting, 1994)—riots; *Roll of Thunder, Hear My Cry* (Taylor, 1976)—discrimination.]

2. The belief that a text is inappropriate for children because it fails to represent dominant social values or myths. [Examples cited: *Amazing Grace* (Hoffman, 1991)—nontraditional families and improper English; *Tar Beach* (Ringgold, 1991)—struggle for financial security and challenges work ethic as a key to happiness.]

3. The belief that a text is inappropriate for children because it identifies racism or sexism as a social problem. [Examples cited: *Nettie's Trip South* (Turner, 1987)—blacks considered three fifths of a person in the Constitution; *William's Doll* (Zolotow, 1972)—challenges traditional gender roles.]

Wollman-Bonilla (1998) further suggests teachers are quite conscious of their criteria for text rejection yet challenges their thinking on each criterion. Rejecting texts because they might frighten or corrupt actually separates schools and society rather than using schools as a place in which children are taught to act responsibly and exhibit open-mindedness in a diverse world. Using books as a means to uphold mainstream norms does not teach reading as a critical thinking process or recognize that readers construct meaning from their personal backgrounds and experiences. Finally, believing that if they avoid a discussion of racism and sexism, it will go away typically reveals the status quo embedded within these real issues. With a desire to do what is "best" for children, the question still remains: "Who decides what is best for children?" (p. 292).

Ballentine and Hill (2000) invited student response to Sharon Draper's *Forged by Fire* and Christopher Paul Curtis's *The Watsons Go to Birmingham—1963* with second, third, and fourth graders in an attempt to take up books that contain dangerous truths. Similarly, Smith (2002) challenged future teachers to respond to Mildred Taylor's *The Friendship* and Michael Dorris's *Morning Girl*. Read alongside professional articles, these two novels provided a revised view of today's world developed during literature discussion groups. Teacher education programs provide an appropriate environment to coax and stretch preservice teachers beyond mainstream norms and to encourage them to approach reading as a critical thinking process through well-selected literature.

In the school setting, professional guidelines should serve both teachers and librarians in making selections for the classroom or the media center. "Selection" takes a more positive view of literature choices (than censorship) by *including* specific materials, *intending* to advise and educate, and *increasing* access to ideas and information. Collecting reviews from respected professional sources, applying guidelines for literary quality (see Chapters 3–8), and following policy statements to back up choices generally ensures quality literary choices for children.

Selecting quality realistic and historical fiction (and all genres, for that matter) demands that those who decide what is "best" for children recognize their own biases and offset them by providing a balanced program that assists students in becoming both effective readers and lovers of literature. Providing time for discussion and response following the reading of all books may be the most appropriate means of ensuring this needed balance. Building a strong classroom and library/media center collection that represents diversity of thought and peoples through realistic and historical fiction (as well as other genres) should be a priority.

CLOSING THOUGHTS

The genres of realistic and historical fiction hold strong appeal for independent readers in the intermediate/middle-level grades. The appeal often lies in the reality of the characters and the challenging problems in their lives. Whether the setting is contemporary or historical, a fictional character and an involved reader form a strong bond. That bond is often evidenced in oral or written response connections to these powerful genres. Identifying with a character of a similar age seems to draw readers to books. Whether set in a historical context or in hometown/urban contemporary America, these characters face problems, encounter obstacles, and falter in their attempts to grow up. Yet they maintain an admirable persistence, a growing maturity, and a problem-solving capability that provides a role model to the reader.

Teachers need to revere these genres because realistic and historical fiction can change readers in classrooms into lifelong readers. Reading popular authors aloud and portraying male and female characters as role models brings these genres to life at a critical time as children determine their literacy futures. The incredible blend between social studies and historical fiction makes their inclusion viable in interdisciplinary connections. The meaningful relationship between a contemporary character and a reader of realistic fiction makes this genre mandatory as children strive to grow up. The inclusion of realistic fiction and historical fiction ensures an opportunity for growth as a consumer of literature and as a maturing individual.

References

Ballentine, D., & Hill, L. (2000). Teaching beyond "Once upon a time." *Language Arts, 78,* 11–20.

Blaska, J. K. (1996). *Using children's literature to learn about disabilities and illness.* Moorhead, MN: Practical Press.

Cianciolo, P. (1981). Yesterday comes alive for readers of historical fiction. *Language Arts, 59,* 452–462.

Dresang, E. T. (2003). Controversial books and contemporary children. *Journal of Children's Literature, 29,* 20–31.

Farris, P. J., (2004). *Elementary and middle school social studies: An interdisciplinary instructional approach* (4th ed.). New York: McGraw-Hill.

Hancock, M. R. (1996). *State children's choice book awards: Instructional insights through children's literary preferences.* Paper presented at the 41st Annual Convention of the International Reading Association, New Orleans, LA.

Heine, P., Inkster, C., Kazemek, F., Williams, S., Raschke, S., & Stevens, D. (1999). Strong female characters in recent children's literature. *Language Arts, 76,* 427–434.

James, M., & Zarillo, J. (1989). Teaching history with children's literature: A concept-based interdisciplinary approach. *Social Studies, 80,* 153–158.

Johnson, N. M., & Ebert, M. J. (1992). Time travel is possible: Historical fiction and biography— passport to the past. *The Reading Teacher, 45,* 488–495.

Kiefer, B. Z., Hickman, J., & Hepler, S. (2007). *Charlotte Huck's children's literature in the elementary school* (9th ed.). New York: McGraw-Hill.

Landrum, J. (1999/2000). Adolescent novels that feature characters with disabilities: An annotated bibliography. *Journal of Adolescent & Adult Literature, 42,* 284–290.

Landrum, J. (2001). Selecting intermediate novels that feature characters with disabilities. *The Reading Teacher, 55,* 252–258.

Lehr, S. (Ed.) (1995). *Battling dragons: Issues and controversies in children's literature.* Portsmouth, NH: Heinemann.

Lehr, S. (Ed.) (2001). *Beauty, brains, and brawn: The construction of gender in children's literature.* Portsmouth, NH: Heinemann.

McClure, A. (1995). Censorship of children's books. In S. Lehr (Ed.), *Battling dragons: Issues and controversies in children's literature* (pp. 3–25). Portsmouth, NH: Heinemann.

Nodelman, P. (1992). *The pleasures of children's literature.* New York: Longman.

Pavonetti, L. (2002). It seems important that we should have the right to read . . . *Journal of Children's Literature, 28,* 9–15.

Rochman, H. (2004). The Scott O'Dell award for historical fiction. *Book Links, 14,* 40–43.

Schall, J., & Kauffmann, G. (2003). Exploring literature with gay and lesbian characters in the elementary school. *Journal of Children's Literature, 29,* 36–45.

Smith, S. A. (2002). "Would I use this book?" White, female education students examine their beliefs about teaching. *The New Advocate, 15,* 57–66.

Sprague, M. M., & Keeling, K. K. (2000). A library for Ophelia. *Journal of Adolescent & Adult Literature, 43,* 640–647.

Swartz, M. K., & Hendricks, C. G. (2000). Factors that influence the book selection process of students with special needs. *Journal of Adolescent & Adult Literacy, 43,* 608–618.

Tompkins, G. E. (2005). *Language arts: Patterns of practice* (6th ed.). Upper Saddle River, NJ: Merrill/Prentice-Hall.

Tunnell, M. O., & Ammon, R. (1993). *The story of ourselves: Teaching history through children's literature.* Portsmouth, NH: Heinemann.

Wollman-Bonilla, J. E. (1998). Outrageous viewpoints: Teachers' criteria for rejecting works of children's literature. *Language Arts, 75,* 287–295.

Children's Books Cited: Realistic Fiction [P] = K–2; [I] = 3–5; [M] = 6–8

Balliett, Blue (2004). *Chasing Vermeer.* New York: Scholastic. [I]

Birdsall, Jeanne (2005). *The Pendericks: A summer tale of four sisters, two rabbits, and a very interesting boy.* New York: Knopf. [I]

Bunting, Eve (1991). *Fly away home.* Illus. by Ronald Himler. Boston: Clarion/Houghton Mifflin. [P/I]

Bunting, Eve (1994). *Smoky night.* Illus. by David Diaz. San Diego: Harcourt Brace. [P/I]

Byars, Betsy (1985). *Cracker Jackson*. New York: Viking. [I/M]

Cleary, Beverly (1999). *Ramona's world*. Illus. by Alan Tiegreen. New York: Morrow. [P/I]

Clements, Andrew (1996). *Frindle*. Illus. by Brian Selznick. New York: Simon & Schuster. [I]

Clements, Andrew (1999). *The Landry news*. Illus. by Salvatore Murdocca. New York: Simon & Schuster. [I]

Clements, Andrew (2000). *The janitor's boy*. New York: Simon & Schuster. [I]

Clements, Andrew (2001). *The school story*. New York: Simon & Schuster. [I]

Clements, Andrew (2002). *The jacket*. New York: Simon & Schuster. [I]

Clements, Andrew (2005). *Lunch money*. New York: Simon & Schuster. [I]

Creech, Sharon (1994). *Walk two moons*. New York: HarperCollins. [I/M]

Creech, Sharon (1997). *Chasing redbird*. New York: Joanna Cottler/HarperCollins. [I/M]

Creech, Sharon (2001). *Love that dog*. New York: HarperCollins. [I/M]

DeFelice, Cynthia (1998). *The ghost of Fossil Glen*. New York: Farrar, Straus & Giroux. [I]

DeFelice, Cynthia (2004). *The ghost of Cutler Creek*. New York: Farrar, Straus & Giroux. [I]

DeFelice, Cynthia (2005). *The ghost and Mrs. Hobbs*. New York: Farrar, Straus & Giroux. [I]

Di Camillo, Kate (2000). *Because of Winn-Dixie*. Cambridge, MA: Candlewick. [I]

Di Camillo, Kate (2001). *The tiger rising*. Cambridge, MA: Candlewick. [I]

Fox, Paula (1991). *Monkey island*. New York: Orchard. [I]

Gantos, Jack (2003). *Jack adrift: Fourth grade without a clue*. New York: Farrar, Straus & Giroux. [I]

Gardiner, John (1980). *Stone fox*. Illus. by Marcia Sewall. New York: Crowell. [P/I]

Hamilton, Virginia (1999). *Bluish*. New York: Scholastic/Blue Sky. [I]

Hesse, Karen (1994). *Sable*. Illus. by Marcia Sewall. New York: Holt. [P/I]

Hill, Kirkpatrick (1993). *Winter camp*. New York: McElderry Books. [I]

Ho, Minfong (1991). *The clay marble*. New York: Farrar, Straus & Giroux. [I/M]

Hobbs, Will (2001). *Down the Yukon*. New York: Morrow. [M]

Hoffman, Mary (1991). *Amazing Grace*. Illus. by Caroline Binch. New York: Dial. [P/I]

Holt, Kimberly Willis (1998). *My Louisiana sky*. New York: Henry Holt. [I]

Holt, Kimberly Willis (2001). *Dancing in Cadillac light*. New York: Putnam. [I]

Horvath, Polly (2004). *The Pepins and their problems*. New York: Farrar, Straus & Giroux. [I]

Howe, James (2005). *Totally Joe*. New York: Atheneum. [I]

Lisle, Janet Taylor (2000). *The art of keeping cool*. New York: Simon & Schuster. [I]

Lowry, Lois (1999). *Zooman Sam*. Boston: Houghton Mifflin. [P/I]

Mack, Tracy, & Citrin, Michael (2006). *The fall of the amazing Zalindas* (Sherlock Holmes and the Baker Street Irregulars series). New York: Orchard/Scholastic. [I/M]

McDonald, Megan (2004). *Judy Moody, M.D. The doctor is in!* Cambridge, MA: Candlewick Press. [P]

McDonald, Megan (2005). *Stink: The incredible shrinking kid*. Cambridge, MA: Candlewick Press. [P]

Mikaelsen, Ben (2001). *Touching spirit bear*. New York: HarperCollins [I]

Myers, Walter Dean (2000). *Monster*. New York: Harper-Collins. [M]

Naidoo, Beverly (2000). *The other side of truth*. New York: HarperCollins. [I/M]

Naylor, Phyllis Reynolds (1991). *Shiloh*. New York: Atheneum. [I]

Naylor, Phyllis Reynolds (1994). *Alice in-between*. New York: Atheneum. [I]

Naylor, Phyllis Reynolds (1996). *Alice in lace*. New York: Atheneum. [I]

Naylor, Phyllis Reynolds (2006). *Roxie and the hooligans*. New York: Atheneum. [I]

Park, Barbara (1995). *Mick Harte was here*. New York: Apple Soup. [I]

Paterson, Katherine (1977). *Bridge to Terabithia*. New York: Crowell. [I/M]

Paulsen, Gary (1987). *Hatchet*. New York: Bradbury. [I/M]

Paulsen, Gary (1991). *The river.* New York: Delacorte. [I/M]

Paulsen, Gary (1996). *Brian's winter.* New York: Delacorte. [I/M]

Paulsen, Gary (1999). *Brian's return.* New York: Delacorte. [I/M]

Perkins, Lynne Rae (2005). *Criss cross.* New York: Greenwillow. [I/M]

Rawls, Wilson (1961). *Where the red fern grows.* New York: Doubleday. [I/M]

Ringgold, Faith (1991). *Tar beach.* New York: Crown. [P/I]

Rylant, Cynthia (1992). *Missing May.* New York: Orchard Books. [I/M]

Sachar, Louis (1987). *There's a boy in the girl's bathroom.* New York: Knopf. [I]

Spinelli, Jerry (1990). *Maniac Magee.* New York: HarperCollins. [I]

Spinelli, Jerry (1997). *Wringer.* New York: Harper-Collins. [I]

Staples, Suzanne Fisher (1989). *Shabanu: Daughter of the wind.* New York: Knopf. [M]

Staples, Suzanne Fisher (2005). *Under the persimmon tree.* New York: Farrar, Straus & Giroux. [M]

Tolan, Stephanie (2002). *Surviving the Apple-whites.* New York: HarperCollins. [M]

White, Ruth (1996). *Belle Prater's boy.* New York: Farrar, Straus & Giroux. [I/M]

White, Ruth (2004). *Buttermilk hill.* New York: Farrar, Straus & Giroux. [I]

Zolotow, Charlotte (1972). *William's doll.* Illus. by William Pene Du Bois. New York: Harper-Collins. [P]

Children's Books Cited: Historical Fiction

Avi (1990). *The true confessions of Charlotte Doyle.* New York: Orchard Books. [M]

Avi (1996). *Beyond the western sea. Book one: The escape from home.* New York: Orchard Books. [I/M]

Avi (1996). *Beyond the western sea. Book two: Lord Kirkle's money.* New York: Orchard Books. [I/M]

Avi (2002). *Crispin: The cross of lead.* New York: Hyperion. [I/M]

Avi (2006). *Crispin: At the edge of the world.* New York: Hyperion. [I/M]

Beatty, Patricia (1987). *Charley Skedaddle.* New York: Morrow. [I]

Collier, James Lincoln, & Collier, Christopher (1974). *My brother Sam is dead.* Four Winds. [I/M]

Cotton, Cynthia (2006). *Abbie in stitches.* Illus. by Beth Peck. New York: Farrar, Straus & Giroux. [P/I]

Curtis, Christopher Paul (1996). *The Watsons go to Birmingham—1963.* New York: Delacorte. [I/M]

Cushman, Karen (1995). *The midwife's apprentice.* Boston: Clarion. [M]

Cushman, Karen (1996). *The ballad of Lucy Whipple.* Boston: Clarion. [I/M]

Cushman, Karen (2000). *Matilda Bone.* Boston: Clarion. [I/M]

Cushman, Karen (2003). *Rodzina.* New York: Clarion. [I]

de Angeli, Marguerite (1949). *Door in the wall.* New York: Doubleday. [I]

DeFelice, Cynthia (1996). *The apprenticeship of Lucas Whitaker.* New York: Farrar, Straus & Giroux. [I/M]

Denenberg, Barry (1998). *The journal of William Thomas Emerson: A Revolutionary War patriot* (My Name Is America series). New York: Scholastic. [I]

Dorris, Michael (1992). *Morning girl.* New York: Hyperion. [I/M]

Draper, Sharon (1997). *Forged by fire.* New York: Atheneum. [I/M]

Edmonds, Walter (1941). *The matchlock gun.* Illus. by Paul Lantz. New York: Dodd. [I]

Gregory, Kristina (1996). *The winter of red snow: The Revolutionary War diary of Abigail Jane Stewart* (Dear America series). New York: Scholastic. [I]

Gregory, Kristina (2005). *Catherine: The great journey—Russia, 1743* (The Royal Diaries series). New York: Scholastic. [I]

Hansen, Joyce (1997). *I thought my soul would rise and fly: The diary of Patsy, a freed girl* (Dear America series). New York: Scholastic. [I]

Hesse, Karen (1997). *Out of the dust.* New York: Scholastic. [I/M]

Holm, Jennifer L. (2001). *Boston Jane: An adventure.* New York: HarperCollins. [I/M]

Lasky, Kathryn (1996). *A journey to the New World: The diary of Patience Whipple* (Dear America series). New York: Scholastic. [I]

Lasky, Kathryn (2001). *Christmas after all: The Great Depression diary of Minnie Swift* (Dear America series). New York: Scholastic. [I]

Levin, Ellen (2006). *Henry's freedom box: A true story from the Underground Railroad.* Illus. by Kadir Nelson. New York: Scholastic. [P/I]

Lowry, Lois (1989). *Number the stars.* Boston: Houghton Mifflin. [I]

MacLachlan, Patricia (1985). *Sarah, plain and tall.* New York: Harper & Row. [P/I]

McMullan, Kate (2002). *As far as I can see: Meg's prairie diary* (My America series). New York: Scholastic. [P]

Murphy, Jim (2006). *Desperate journey.* New York: Scholastic. [I]

O'Dell, Scott (1960). *Island of the blue dolphins.* Boston: Houghton Mifflin. [I/M]

O'Dell, Scott (1970). *Sing down the moon.* Boston: Houghton Mifflin. [I/M]

O'Dell, Scott (1980). *Sarah Bishop.* Boston: Houghton Mifflin. [I/M]

Paterson, Katherine (1991). *Lyddie.* New York: Dutton. [M]

Paterson, Katherine (1996). *Jip: His story.* New York: Lodestar. [M]

Peck, Richard (2000). *A year down under.* New York: Dial/Penguin Putnam. [I/M]

Philbrick, Rodman (2001). *The journal of Douglas Allen Deeds: The Donner party expedition* (Dear America series). New York: Scholastic. [I/M]

Rappaport, Doreen (2000). *Freedom river.* Illus. by Bryan Collier. New York: Jump at the Sun/Hyperion. [I]

Raven, Margot Theis (2006). *Night boat to freedom.* Illus. by E. B. Lewis. New York: Farrar, Straus & Giroux/Melanie Kroupa. [I]

Reeder, Carolyn (1989). *Shades of gray.* New York: Macmillan. [I/M]

Reeder, Carolyn (1997). *Across the lines.* New York: Atheneum. [I/M]

Robinet, Harriet Gillem (1998). *Forty acres and maybe a mule.* New York: Atheneum. [I]

Russell, Barbara Timberlake (2006). *Maggie's Amerikay.* Illus. by Jim Burke. New York: Farrar, Straus & Giroux. [I]

Salisbury, Graham (1994). *Under the blood red sun.* New York: Delacorte. [I/M]

Say, Allen (2002). *Home of the brave.* Boston: Houghton Mifflin. [I]

Speare, Elizabeth (1958). *The witch of blackbird pond.* Boston: Houghton Mifflin. [M]

Taylor, Mildred (1976). *Roll of thunder, hear my cry.* Illus. by Jerry Pinkney. New York: Dial. [I]

Taylor, Mildred (1987). *The friendship.* New York: Dial. [I]

Turner, Ann (1987). *Nettie's trip South.* Illus. by Ronald Himler. New York: Macmillan. [P/I]

Weatherford, Carole Boston (2006). *Moses: When Harriet Tubman led her people to freedom.* Illus. by Kadir Nelson. New York: Hyperion/ Jump at the Sun. [I]

Whelan, Gloria (2002). *Angel on the square.* New York: HarperCollins. [I]

Wilder, Laura Ingalls (1932/1953). *Little house in the big woods* (Little House series). Illus. by Garth Williams. New York: Harper & Row. [P/I]

Woodruff, Elvira (1997). *The orphan of Ellis Island: A time travel adventure.* New York: Scholastic. [I]

Woodruff, Elvira (1999). *The memory coat.* Illus. by Michael Dooling. New York: Scholastic. [I]

CHAPTER 7

Biography and Informational Books

The Realm of Nonfiction

Martin Luther King, Jr.
Pastor, Speaker, Leader, Lover.
Husband of Coretta Scott.
Who cares deeply about freedom.
Who feels sad when he saw white only signs.
Who needs freedom for black people.
Who gives peace and caring about everyone.
Who fears hate.
Who would like to see black and white children playing together.
Resident of Atlanta, Georgia
A powerful speaker
Martin Luther King, Jr.

Second-grade response to
Martin's Big Words
by Doreen Rappaport

183

Nonfiction literature for children continues to flourish. Not only has nonfiction become more plentiful in numbers published, but it has attained and maintained a high quality of literary distinction with well-written text and superb illustrations or photographs that blend into an adventure in informational reading (Zarnowski, Kerper, & Jensen, 2001). Nonfiction literature consists of the genres of biography (including autobiography, memoirs, fictionalized biography) and informational books (including both informational picture books and informational chapter books). In many classrooms, the well-written and designed nonfiction books available today have taken priority over traditional textbooks as informational resources (Bamford & Kristo, 2003). Nonfiction comfortably builds on the natural curiosity of the learner to inquire, know, and investigate. The informational age of the new millennium continues to deliver an explosion of data most effectively delivered to children through quality children's nonfiction literature.

BIOGRAPHY

A biography shares the life of an authentic person from the past or present, celebrates his or her challenges and accomplishments, and inspires the reader with dedication and determination to lead one's own successful life. Biographies are written about people who have had a positive impact on society, leaving the reader with an optimistic view of his or her potential as a contributor to our society (Zarnowski, 1990).

According to Levstik (1993), elementary students link themselves closely to biographical characters. Biographies enable readers to experience real life by vicariously tapping the experiences of achievers while often providing a historical context for understanding such people's lives. Biography has had a natural appeal to readers and an effective link to all the disciplines through the years. Whereas the serial biographies of the past provided rather dry, formula factual information about famous people, today's biographies present flesh-and-blood individuals, with both strengths and weaknesses, in an entertaining manner. The past decade has given rise to the picture book biography as a means for the primary and intermediate reader (K–5) to engage with this genre. Titles such as Pam Muñoz Ryan's *When Marian Sang: The True Recital of Marian Anderson, the Voice of a Century* and Russell Freedman's *The Voice That Challenged a Nation: Marian Anderson and the Struggle for Equal Rights* become outstanding read-alouds for sharing the biography genre across grade levels and within the curriculum. In addition, authors such as David Adler, Candace Fleming, Kathleen Krull, and Diane Stanley have carried this genre to new heights as they honestly introduce students to the multidimensional human characteristics of famous people in both their public and private lives.

Types of Biography

Biographies can be discussed across four dimensions: (1) the degree of authenticity presented in the text, (2) the amount of coverage of the subject's life, (3) the treatment of a single or multiple subject(s) and (4) the perspective from which a biography is told. Awareness of these organizational categories of biography assists in determining the multilayered facets and possibilities of this genre across the entire curriculum.

Degree of Authenticity

The degree of authenticity relates to the amount of historical accuracy, documentation, and research that is brought to the biographical presentation. Although most biographies are grounded in some degree of authenticity, it is the depth of that authenticity that differentiates biographies from one another.

Factual portrait.   The most authentic type of biography, the factual portrayal supports all factual information through direct documentation of letters, diaries, interviews, and eyewitness accounts. Reliable resource bibliographies and acknowledgments to museums and historical societies often verify that intensive research has taken place. Authentic photographs, verifiable quotations, facsimiles of writing, and original maps can also substantiate the information on the subject.

Lincoln: A Photobiography by Russell Freedman provides the highest quality example of a factual portrait. Not only did this title win a Newbery Medal, it also opened the genre to new attention and exploration by authors and publishers. The book is filled with photographs, letters, diary entries, campaign posters, and other authentic documentation of research into Lincoln's life. An extensive bibliography further documents the author's research, showing that the utmost attention was paid to authentic reporting of factual information through well-written text.

Jean Fritz epitomizes the best of factual portraits. Her early books on figures of American history such as And Then What Happened, Paul Revere? combine humor and dialogue based on a rich foundation of documented factual information. Her later biographies, like Bully for You, Teddy Roosevelt and The Great Little Madison, follow the factual portrait within a chapter book format. Endnotes by the author always verify sources of information and the technical research that supports the comfortable delivery of facts about the lives of great Americans.

Fictional portrait.   Although tied to historical fact, the fictional portrayal reflects the author's creative addition of scenes, dialogue, or thoughts for which there is no documented basis. Based on careful research, the author paints factually grounded scenes through contrived conversation between or among characters. Clever authors skillfully weave fictionalized dialogue around existing facts in a reasonable and believable manner. The degree of fictionalization varies greatly from minor alterations to major changes to accommodate story delivery. Emily Arnold McCully's Marvelous Mattie: How Margaret E. Knight Became an Inventor is structured around pertinent facts about the subject's prowess as a female inventor, but the actual words and thoughts of the character and dialogue between characters are invented by the author. Kathryn Lasky's John Muir: America's First Environmentalist tells the story of this renowned naturalist with adequate facts. However, it is filled with historically assumed textual scenarios and vivid visual reenactments to make the story flow for younger readers.

Biographical fiction.   Some biographies appear to be more fiction than fact, and they are termed biographical fiction. *Shoeless Joe and Black Betsy* by Phil Bildner is a picture book that shares the life of Joe Jackson, the amazing baseball player from the Chicago White Sox, and his relationship with his power-hitting bat. An afterword actually describes the facts surrounding the story, and a page of baseball statistics concludes the text. At first sight, this book shouts biography, but a closer look reveals an excellent example of biographical fiction.

Amount of Coverage

The amount of coverage within the subjects' lives carries a wide range of possibilities while filling a wide range of needs for the reader.

Comprehensive biography.   This type covers the entire life of a subject from birth to death. Comprehensive biographies enable readers to see how the complexities of childhood, academic background, or life experiences can intricately shape the personality of an adult. Typically a chronological journey, the comprehensive account appeals to readers who want or need every fact and detail about a subject from the past. David Adler's picture book biography, *Joe Louis: America's Fighter,* takes the reader from 1914, the year of the boxer's birth, through his early fights, through his glory as world heavyweight champion, and concludes on the day of his death on April 12, 1981. Judith Blook Fradin and Dennis Brindell Fradin's well-documented account of the life of *Jane Addams: Champion of Democracy* brings forth lesser known but comprehensive facts about an American icon's lifetime dedication to improving society.

Partial biography.   Covering only a part of a subject's life, this format is typically selected in biographies for young children that often cover the childhood of their subject. Gene Barretta's *Now & Ben: The Modern Inventions of Benjamin Franklin* tells of its subject not as a statesman but focusing on his creative inventions. Although the end of the book tells of Ben Franklin's contributions to his country, the illustrated biography focuses on the creative accomplishments of Franklin's genius. Frank Keating's *Theodore* tells of selected incidents in the boyhood and adult life of the youngest man ever to be president. Partial biographies also tend to be accounts of living persons whose active lives and varied accomplishments are still evolving.

Single-Subject/Collective Biography

Persons' lives can be shared as single-subject biographies or grouped in a collection of several similar subjects with some common strand in their lives.

Single-subject biography.   In this case, the personality of the selected subject is typically well known, highly respected, and has earned a place in history for his or her accomplishments. The subjects can be scientists, sports figures, explorers, artists, authors, politicians, or simply ordinary people who overcome great adversity. Most biographies in both picture book and chapter book formats today rely on single-subject coverage. Jacqueline Briggs Martin's *Snowflake Bentley* introduces Wilson Bentley, snowflake photographer, from his childhood to his untimely death. The woodcut Caldecott Medal illustrations of Mary Azarian capture rural Vermont and the scientist's persistence. Told through well-developed text in a chapter book format, Candace Fleming's *Our Eleanor: A Scrapbook Look at Eleanor Roosevelt's Remarkable Life* is enhanced by Eleanor's journals, letters, and press releases woven throughout the text telling of her childhood, her marriage to Franklin Delano, her struggles to balance being first lady and sharing her political views, and her endless contributions and awards.

Collective biography. The life stories of several people in one book are connected by a common strand that runs through the subjects' lives. The subjects may be part of the same profession or follow the same passion. Penny Coleman's *Adventurous Women: Eight True Stories About Women who Made a Difference* includes biographical essays about extraordinary women who were bold in confronting obstacles and taking risks in pursuit of diverse goals. Collective biographies such as Alan Govenar's *Extraordinary Ordinary People: Five American Masters of Traditional Arts* serve the purpose of bringing human similarities together for potential comparison and contrast.

Biography series. Many children's authors have become specialists in writing in the biographical genre and have applied their research skills to the lives of several individuals. More than formula writing, the newer series biography may carry a common theme that flows throughout the series. Kathleen Krull's Giants of Science series includes titles on *Leonardo Da*

(continued)

RESOURCES ON THE WEB
Informational Nonfiction

Teachers may turn to the Web to locate quality nonfiction books that suit a wide variety of readers and topics. Begin by browsing these sites with award-winning books.

Orbis Pictus Award for Outstanding Nonfiction for Children (NCTE)
This website provides general information about the annual Orbis Pictus Award for Nonfiction for Children along with links to past winners and honor books.
http://www.ncte.org/elem/awards/orbispictus/106877.htm

ALA Robert F. Sibert Informational Book Award (ALA)
Established by the Association for Library Service to Children, the Robert F. Sibert Informational Book Award is awarded annually to the author of the most distinguished informational book published in English. Includes links to past winners and honor books.
http://www.ala.org/ala/alsc/awardsscholarships/literaryawds/ sibertmedal/Sibert_Medal.htm

Biographical Nonfiction

The following websites provide teachers and students with a wealth of information and resources that may prove helpful when reading and writing biographies. Visit these sites frequently because they are constantly changing and growing.

Biography
The *Biography Channel* allows users to search over 25,000 of the greatest lives, past and present.
http://www.biography.com/

Biography Maker
This user-friendly website provides writing guidelines for questioning, learning, synthesis, and storytelling as the stages of writing an inviting biography.
http://www.bham.wednet.edu/bio/biomaker.htm

Presidents of the United States
The Internet Public Library provides biographical information, election results, notable events, and some points of interest on each of the presidents. Links to biographies, historical documents, audio and video files, and other presidential sites are also included.
http://www.ipl.org/div/potus/

The History Channel
In addition to a wealth of articles, biographies, video clips, and speeches, this History Channel site provides teachers with resources including study guides, instructional ideas, and a free newsletter.
http://www.history.com/

(Continued)
Nonfiction Authors
Russell Freedman
Children's Literature: Meet Authors & Illustrators
http://www.childrenslit.com/f_freedman.html
Scholastic's Authors & Books: Russell Freedman's Biography
http://books.scholastic.com/teachers/authorsandbooks/ authorstudies/authorhome.jsp?authorID=2146&&displayName =Biography
Russell Freedom Webcast (Library of Congress)
http://www.loc.gov/today/cyberlc/feature_wdesc.php?rec=3428

Andrea Warren
Andrea Warren Home Page
http://andreawarren.com/
Meet the Author: Andrea Warren
http://www.eduplace.com/kids/hmr/mtai/warren.html

Jim Murphy
Jim Murphy: Making History Come Alive
http://www.jimmurphybooks.com/
The Children's Book Council, Meet the Author: Jim Murphy
http://www.cbcbooks.org/cbcmagazine/meet/jim_murphy.html

David A. Adler
David A. Adler: Author of fiction and nonfiction books for young readers
http://www.davidaadler.com/

Vinci, Isaac Newton, and *Sigmund Freud.* David Adler's picture book series on famous Americans includes *A Picture Book of Samuel Adams* and *A Picture Book of Dwight David Eisenhower.* The Childhood of Famous American series, including *Arthur Ashe: Young Tennis Champion* by Paul Mantell, has brought the biography genre in a simple chapter book format to upper primary readers for almost 70 years. The Childhood of World Figures paperback series now includes figures such as *Leonardo Da Vinci: Young Artist, Writer, and Inventor* by George Stanley. Although biographical series have typically been frowned on as formula writing, today's series reflect a higher quality of writing and greater selectivity of subjects to share with children.

Biographical Perspectives

Biographies can also differ in the perspective from which the stories of people's lives are told.

Autobiography. Told, and usually written by the subject of the book, an autobiography is a first-person account of a subject's life. It is likely to be near factual in delivery as a person reflects on the true details of the joys and sorrows of his or her own life. Autobiographies tend to be highly personalized, leaving the reader with an emotional perspective on events in the subject's life. *Through My Eyes* by Ruby Bridges reveals the courage and inspiration of a 6-year-old Ruby during school integration in 1960 in New Orleans. Supported by authentic photographs and news articles, Ruby moves the hearts and opens the minds of readers who watch her enter William Frantz Elementary School protected by federal marshals. Almost 50 years later, the reader feels the sting of racial prejudice in our nation. The first-person voice of the writer provides a powerful testimony of a person's life to the reader.

Memoir. Related to autobiography is a memoir, a record of events based on the writer's own observations. In children's books, this is often a retrospective account that focuses on a memorable or tragic event in the author's life. *Good Fortune: My Journey to Gold Mountain* by Li Keng Wong shares her 7-year-old memory of embarking on a trip from southern China to America on foot, by train, and by boat against America's strict Chinese immigration laws. Anita Lobel's *No Pretty*

Pictures: A Child of War, personal narration brings to life the childhood nightmare in Nazi-occupied Poland. The trauma of her life, her subsequent capture and brief imprisonment in Auschwitz concentration camp, and her ultimate escape to freedom unfold through written memories. *The Story of My Life: An Afghan Girl on the Other Side of the Sky* interweaves Farah Ahmedi's childhood in Afghanistan where she steps on a land mine on her way to school with an epic journey toward an American adolescence in Chicago. Often written as a chronology or diary, the memoir is characterized by the strong, emotional first-person voice of one who relives the memory through writing.

Narrated biography.   The most common type of biography is that told by an author through a third-person voice. The voice is one of authority and is aided by research and documentation that makes the delivery of information believable. This is also the likely writing style of a child when asked to share biographical information on a subject.

Russell Freedman's *The Adventures of Marco Polo* reflects the narrated style of writing in children's biography. The narrated style overrides the traditional bland expository mode while delivering facts to children through motivating text supported by the strong voice of the author. Listen while reading a reflective portion on the opening page of this quality title:

> As Marco Polo lay dying, friends and relatives gathered anxiously by his bedside and begged him to confess. They pleaded with him to tell the truth, to renounce his exaggerations and lies, so he might meet his maker with a clear conscience. He was known in some circles as "the man of a million lies." And all because of a book in which he told fantastic tales about his travels and adventures. (p. 5)

Outsider biography.   Often a biography can be told by an individual distanced from the subject. Robert Burleigh's *The Secret of the Great Houdini* tells the story of the master of deception as he mesmerizes a little boy through one of his great escape feats. Sam shares his experiences as he learns that the hard work behind Houdini's illusions represent a goal everyone can attain if they believe in themselves. Another outsider biography is Louise Borden's *Good-bye, Charles Lindbergh,* which focuses on an accidental but true encounter between a boy and the revered aviator. This unique style is quite uncommon but presents an interesting slant on a major figure in the context of the real world rather than isolated from it.

Examining a recent biography to see how the characteristics just discussed apply to quality titles assists us in understanding the quality and depth of this genre. *Duke Ellington: The Piano Prince and His Orchestra,* skillfully written by Andrea Davis Pinkney, is a single-subject fictionalized biography of a great 20th-century composer and pianist. Based almost entirely on fact, the reader follows Duke from his childhood reluctance to play the piano to his dramatic rise to fame at the Cotton Club in Harlem. The author incorporates only a few contrived quotes and statements that cannot be historically documented. For the most part, however, the facts speak clearly through dates and actual events. This book is an example of a partial slice-of-life biography covering the subject's childhood, rise to popularity, and eventual performance

Picture book biographies encourage the genre to be introduced as early as the primary grades or serve as an inspiration at the intermediate and middle levels.

John Muir. *Text copyright © 2006 by Kathryn Lasky. Illustrations copyright © 2006 by Stan Fellows. Reproduced by permission of the publisher Candlewick Press, Inc., Cambridge, MA.*

at Carnegie Hall. The book is intended to highlight Duke's greatest accomplishments, with an additional author's note following the story that reveals other highlights of his career and death in 1974. This is an outstanding picture book biography illustrated with the bright, bold scratchboard renderings of Brian Pinkney that capture the rhythm of Duke's music as he became one of the greatest composers—the King of the Keys, the Piano Prince, The Duke. Picture book biographies like this one have become increasingly popular with even younger children and allow them to be introduced to biography as a genre during the primary grades. Equally praiseworthy is the Pinkney's companion biography, *Ella Fitzgerald: The Tale of a Vocal Virtuosa.*

EVALUATING QUALITY BIOGRAPHY

Because biographies involve real people and their lives, the importance of factual accountability is a major focus of the criteria for quality in this genre.

Accuracy of fact and detail. The top priority in assessing biography must be the historical accuracy of the text and the integrity of the author's presentation. Authors must admit gaps in their research so readers themselves can judge the accuracy of the portrayal. All sides of a subject should be shared, including weaknesses and character faults. A shaded view of a less-than-human character reflects on the honesty and credibility of the author. Although the age of the audience must be considered, the biography needs to focus on accuracy without risking an overglorified portrayal of a subject. The biography should be scanned for author references and acknowledgments to museums, libraries, and individuals who shared expertise on the subject.

The Amazing Life of Benjamin Franklin by James Cross Giblin exemplifies accuracy of fact and detail. A printer, a statesman, an inventor, and a father, Franklin resided in Philadelphia where he played an important role in the American Revolution. His publication of *Poor Richard's Almanack,* his work on scientific experiments, and his appointment as postmaster general make him an intriguing subject for a biography. An author bibliography and source notes acknowledge museums, associations, libraries, and adult definitive biographies for their assistance in collecting factual details and writings of Franklin. An artist's note by Michael Dooling validates his own research at the American Philosophical Society and his travel to Williamsburg and battlegrounds of the Revolutionary War in an attempt to capture 84 years of Franklin's life in a minimal number of paintings. This title exemplifies the best of the genre and the recent trend toward high-quality biography.

Quality writing. The biography genre has soared beyond the formula writing of the Landmark biographies of the 1950s and 1960s. Although children may be interested in a biography subject, they need good writing to motivate them gently through the flow of information. Biographies that overwhelmingly consist of expository text often scare off prospective readers, whereas those that skillfully present biography as story seem to hold their attention.

Barbara Kerley's *The Dinosaurs of Waterhouse Hawkins* exemplifies the quality of writing that captures the determination of a Victorian artist to build life-size models of dinosaurs in both England and New York City. Kerley captures the initial defeats of this lesser-known historical figure, discouraged, but determined to carry on against all odds. Caldecott Honor illustrations by Brian Selznick assist in bringing the text to life.

> Waterhouse carried on with his work, but on May 3, his dream was shattered.
> Vandals broke into his workshop. Wielding sledgehammers, they smashed the dinosaurs. Then they carted the pieces outside and buried them in the park.
> Waterhouse arrived to find chaos: chunks of rubble, mangled wire, plaster shards, and dust. He simply couldn't believe it.
> Waterhouse stumbled outside, only to find mounds of dirt and dinosaur rubble. Two years of his life, utterly ruined. . . .
> Waterhouse staggered away. His dinosaurs were broken, and so was his spirit. (n. p.)*

This quality of writing is becoming more common in biographical portrayals and is certain to inspire children to sample this genre during self-selection and independent reading.

---

*From *The Dinosaurs of Waterhouse Hawkins* by Barbara Kerley. Published by Scholastic Press, a division of Scholastic Inc. Copyright © 2001 by Barbara Kerley. Reprinted by permission.

Contextual immersion. Besides presenting factual information on a subject, the author must surround the reader in the social context of the times. The mention of prominent figures of the times, descriptions of clothing, and timely news events immerse the reader in the social context of the subject's life, thus building a greater sense of understanding and a broader historical perspective. Diane Stanley's biography *Michelangelo* immerses the reader in the historical period of the Italian Renaissance, both through her writing and through her illustrations that showcase the dress, architecture, and sculpture of this period of rebirth through the outstanding art of this Renaissance genius. From the opening map of Italian states to the final pages of authenticated information, this biography transports the reader to an accomplished historical and artistic period.

In light of these three criteria, *York's Adventures with Lewis and Clark: An African American's Part in the Great Expedition* by Rhoda Blumberg exemplifies authenticity, from its inclusion of archival drawings and photographs to the diary entries and letters collected though thorough research. Authenticity is documented through a list of primary works and bibliographic sources, illustration credits, and explanatory endnotes. Quality writing tells the story of York, Clark's slave, who fostered friendly relationships with Native American tribes, making a vital contribution to the expedition's success. Immersion in the reality of paddling boats, lugging provisions, climbing mountains, and building shelters extends the reader's perspective beyond the typical facts of Lewis and Clark through an extensive bibliography for intermediate and middle-school readers.

BENEFITS OF BIOGRAPHY

The benefits of biography begin with the presentation of models of people whose hard work and determination help them overcome obstacles and achieve high goals. Many biographical subjects are ordinary people who accomplish extraordinary deeds, compelling children to build from their own strengths and set high goals for themselves. *Gregor Mendel: The Friar who Grew Peas* by Cheryl Bardoe portrays a child who overcame poverty and obscurity and whose determined sense of scientific inquiry moved him to become the world's first geneticist. Biography models a process of collecting and presenting research on a person. By reading this genre and studying its authors, children become aware of how investigation of multiple resources and transmission of facts through quality writing bring a subject to life for the reader. Dolores Johnson's *Onward: A Photobiography of African-American Polar Explorer Matthew Henson* provides acknowledgments of multiple resources, websites and places to visit, and a strong bibliography for further research.

Biography provides a curricular connection across disciplines. Biographies of figures from science, history, mathematics, the humanities, and the arts enrich the study of these content areas. Peter Sis's *Starry Messenger: Galileo Galilei,* for example, depicts the life of the famous scientist, mathematician, astronomer, philosopher, and physicist, making a natural link to mathematics and science curricula. Barbara Kerley's *The Dinosaurs of Waterhouse Hawkins* represents one man's quest to reproduce accurate sculptures of dinosaurs and also links to these curricular areas.

Doreen Rappaport's *Martin's Big Words: The Life of Dr. Martin Luther King, Jr.* and Pam Muñoz Ryan's *When Marian Sang: The True Recital* of Marian Anderson fit superbly into social studies discussions on the struggle for human equality. Almost all theme explorations should include a biography of a related person such as Louise Borden's *Fly High! The Story of Bessie Coleman* for integrating into a unit on flight.

Biography extends beyond famous Americans to those renowned around the world and increases student awareness of the traits that characterize global leaders, past and present. Students are immersed in different times and different cultures, opening a window on the world of humankind. Diane Stanley's *Saladin* introduces us to an admirable leader of the Middle East, *Joan of Arc* reflects the history of France, and her *Leonardo Da Vinci* transports the reader to Italy's rich Renaissance.

READER RESPONSE TO BIOGRAPHY

Biography presents a wide variety of reader response options for children. Reading several biographies on a single subject can lead to comparison and contrast of a subject's strengths and weaknesses. Such scrutiny may even reveal conflicting information on a subject. Biography can model research as children try their own use of documentation as they compose an autobiography (Zarnowski, 1990) or fictionalized biography (Zarnowski, 1988). Response to biography can take the form of further reading because bibliographies lead children to other sources on a subject. Comparing two biographies on a common subject may bring conflicting facts and viewpoints. Biography is easily coordinated with other content areas and themes. Students even enjoy dressing as the biography subject and sharing their lives in the first-person voice. Chapter 13 suggests several other options as response to biography.

Many possibilities exist as children are exposed to the biography genre. This genre grew tremendously in quality and quantity during the past decade and warrants inclusion for independent reading, read-alouds, research, and reading enjoyment. Even reluctant readers/listeners respond to Walter Dean Myer's *The Greatest: Muhammed Ali* with spontaneity and interest. Perhaps picture book biographies have provided the greatest momentum to the growth of biography as younger readers engage themselves in a genre that has traditionally been focused on older readers. Biography shares quality writing and models of determined, hardworking people that can inspire children to set high goals and achieve success in life.

INFORMATIONAL BOOKS

The quantity and quality of informational books soared in the last decade in response to the huge information explosion, the increased use of factual books across academic curricula, and the high quality and dynamic presentation of knowledge by publishers. Lawrence Pringle (2004), author of over 100 nonfiction books for children, applauds the trend in "nonfiction rising" as the genre flourishes in the new century. Although informational books have traditionally been used exclusively for research, the proliferation of books in this genre has led to an expanded scope in the classroom that includes expository reading, curricular integration, and personal inquiry (Saul & Dieckman, 2005). Yet informational books remain an "untapped goldmine"

(Livingston, Kurkjian, Young, & Pringle, 2004), ripe for personal and curricular discovery and exploration.

Informational books are factual presentations of documented knowledge. Their purpose is to instill information and inquiry in the reader. Informational books cover a wide range of topics in all disciplines, including the sciences, social sciences, and the humanities. Although most informational books are written in expository text to transmit information, many informational books have gained prominence by using a narrative "hybrid" approach to delivering information (Pappas, 2006).

Traditionally, informational books had little or no appeal to teachers beyond their expected use for report writing. In the past few years, however, informational books are used for pleasure reading or selected as a source for a class read-aloud. Sharing informational books with young children has opened the classroom door to an intro-duction to expository text (Palmer & Stewart, 2003; Yopp & Yopp, 2000). Even struggling readers know that informational reading and browsing can be personally fulfilling (Hynes, 2000). Informational books carry the reputation of being increas-ingly user friendly, eye appealing, and reader satisfying. Informational books have gained new respect, well-deserved literary honors, and a growing reputation for quality (Corsaro, 2005; Hunt, 2005). Reputable authors and illustrators, motivating formats, colorful presentations, and creative means of disseminating facts now char-acterize the nonfiction genre.

Types of Informational Books

The following categories of informational books are based on the formats the books use to transmit knowledge to the reader. Outstanding titles exist in all of these formats, and they provide information to children of varying age and reading ability levels.

Informational chapter books. This format features mostly text organized in chapters or sections. Graphics and illustrations supplement the words, and primary information is delivered through the text. Jim Murphy's *An American Plague: The True and Terrifying Story of the Yellow Fever Epidemic of 1793* contains archival drawings and researched accounts of the devastating plague that hit Philadelphia over 200 years ago. The text carries the chronological development of the growing strength of the plague and its paralyzing effect on a heavily populated part of the nation. Divided into well-titled chapters, the book invites both browsing or reading from cover to cover.

Informational picture books. These present factual information in a picture book format. The text and illustrations both play a vital role in contributing to the understanding of the topic. Before the reader's eyes unfolds a visual world of color and a textual world of intriguing information. Lynn Curlee's *Parthenon* combines compelling text with outstanding illustrations that reveal the conception, engineering, planning, construction, and completion of this Greek architectural wonder. His other titles, including *Liberty, Capital*, and *Ballpark*, also pay tribute to the symbols of America built by people.

Photographic essays.   Presentation of information is both through the text and the breathtaking photographs that accompany it. Unlike the picture book, the visual presentation is authentic, either historic, panoramic, or microscopic, with the book offering both visual and textual appeal. Joanne Ryder's *A Pair of Polar Bears: Twin Cubs Find a Home at a the San Diego Zoo* provides video camera and photographic shots of Kalluk and Tatqiq, found orphaned in Alaska, and their adjustment to their new home. Sneed Collard's text and photographs in *The Prairie Builders: Reconstructing America's Lost Grasslands* reveal scientists saving America's tallgrass prairie.

Informational books with a narrative blend.   Several new books present a blend of fact and fiction, with information typically presented in a narrative style. Intended to both inform and entertain, these books lure the avid reader into the informational realm as well as captivate the reluctant reader by surrounding intriguing facts with a motivating text. *An Extraordinary Life: The Story of a Monarch Butterfly* by Laurence Pringle with paintings by Bob Marstall laid the groundwork in the 1990s for hybrid text by personifying a butterfly into a real character and documenting its migrational flight. A decade later, books like Diana Aston and Sylvia Long's *An Egg is Quiet* and Chris Butterworth's *Sea Horse: The Shyest Fish in the Sea* epitomize the literary power of weaving narrative and expository text into an informational book.

Trends in Informational Books

Saul and Dieckman (2005) pointed out several reasons for choosing and using informational books beyond the increased quality and quantity previously mentioned. Their research has provided impetus in the creative inclusion of informational books across the curriculum.

Evidence of research documentation.   Increasingly, informational books have highlighted the authenticity of the knowledge being disseminated to children. Book jackets share biographical information reflecting the expert credentials of authors, illustrators, and photographers. Extended lists of references to document the authenticity of the text are included as well as bibliographies of related children's books for more extensive research. Glossaries, timelines, and maps further extend the research efforts brought to the book. A brief view of Russell Freedman's *Children of the Great Depression* makes the reader aware of the quality and quantity of research that made this book possible. The best informational books actually serve as a model format of high-quality documented research for children.

The growing importance of illustration.   If children's attention is to be captured, information must reach beyond the text. Indeed it is often the colorful illustrations or photographs that motivate a child to delve into the text for additional information. One need only look at the realistic art of Lambert Davis in Cynthia Rylant's *The Journey: Stories of Migration* to realize how children can be captivated

The creation of the *Orbis Pictus* Award for Outstanding Nonfiction for Children marked a milestone in the well-deserved respect given to informational books.
Cover from Children of the Great Depression *by Russell Freedman. Copyright © 2005 by Russell Freedman. Reprinted by permission of Clarion Books, an imprint of Houghton Mifflin Company. All rights reserved.*

and invited into the text by the appeal of visual presentation. The same seems true for the colorful drawings of John Sills in Cathryn Sills's *About Marsupials: A Guide for Children*, which invite young readers into the life of koala bears and kangaroos.

Unconventional formats and approaches.
The ability of the format itself to disseminate information has had a tremendous impact on the popularity of informational books. Cartoon-style art, in particular, seems to capture a growing nonfiction audience. Judith St. George's Caldecott Medal winning *So You Want to Be President?* matches little-known facts on the presidents with the playful caricatures of David Small. Joanna Cole and Bruce Degan's *The Magic School Bus and the Science Fair Expedition* celebrates 20 years of a nonfiction author/illustrator team. Cheryl Harness brings history to life through textual and visual art packed tightly on double-page spreads of *Ghosts of the Civil War*. Alexandra Siy and Dennis Kunkel's electron microscopic photographs in *Mosquito Bite* enhance the presentation format of this awe-inspiring book of larger-than-life perspectives on nature.

Informational books for the very young.
With increased emphasis on early literacy, publishers have simplified advanced topics so they can be shared with younger children. Joy Cowley's *Chameleon, Chameleon* with photos by Nic Bishop provides motivating realism to capture children's natural interest during a read-aloud. Steve Jenkin's *Actual Size* provides conceptual understanding of size through scale models of animals. Authors like Jim Arnosky, Sandra Markle, and Gail Gibbons have targeted this market with quality titles.

Specialized topics. The narrower lens of specific informational books has created a specialized focus on rather obscure but interesting topics. Many books abound on fish, but there is also a book on the life of a single fish titled *The Cod's Tale* by Mark Kurlansky. Broad books on great disasters, for example, have now been narrowed to individual titles like Jim Murphy's *The Great Fire*. Jean Fritz narrowed the entire body of Leonardo da Vinci's artwork to one unfinished sculptured design that has recently become a completed reality—*Leonardo's Horse*, which now stands in Milan, Italy. The specialized topic book often creates a sense of inquiry that allows children to broaden their level of interest to a narrower domain.

Recognition and awards. The creation of the Orbis Pictus Award for Outstanding Nonfiction for Children by the National Council of Teachers of English in 1990 marked a milestone in the respect given to informational books. Established to promote and recognize excellence in the writing of nonfiction for children, this award has brought the informational genre to national attention for teachers. The Robert F. Sibert Informational Book Award was established in 2001 to honor the author of the most distinguished informational book published the previous year. The prestigious awards and honors status have recently been given to Russell Freedman's *Children of the Great Depression* (Orbis Pictus 2006), Sally Walker's *Secrets of a Civil War Submarine: Solving the Mysteries of the H. L. Huntley* (Robert Sibert 2006), and Susan Campbell Bartoletti's *Hitler Youth: Growing Up in Hitler's Shadow* (Orbis Pictus Honor and Newbery Honor 2006).

Children possess a natural curiosity to ask questions and seek answers and the inquiry process has been revitalized through the new appealing books in this genre. As informational trade books take on an increasingly important role in inquiry-based classrooms, the quality and quantity of knowledge they provide children through inviting formats is making a critical impact on both literacy and interdisciplinary instruction.

EVALUATING QUALITY INFORMATIONAL BOOKS

As informational books have gained new respect and an expanded role in the classroom curriculum beyond report writing, this genre has become more intensely scrutinized. The quality of the books being published has actually raised the standards for their selection. Five challenging criteria set the benchmark that informational books must reach to gain high regard in the informational book genre.

Accuracy and authenticity. The standards of correct and documented information begin with the author. Verifying the credentials of the transmission of knowledge does much to ensure the reader that only up-to-date information from an expert in the field is being shared. An example is Seymour Simon, whose countless books on the human body, including *Guts: Our Digestive System*, emphasize his expertise as a teacher, science expert, and award recipient. Expert qualifications, reputation, and previous experiences equate with accuracy of information. Acknowledgments are often bestowed on experts in the field, museum, or professional collections, further documenting validity of information.

Literary Legend

Nonfiction Author

Russell Freedman does not consider what he does to be nonfiction. The term is too broad and suggests bland writing about people and events that lacks the spark to truly draw readers in. A one-time news reporter for the Associated Press, his vivid writing and carefully chosen photographs seemingly allow readers to walk through historical events and talk to living, breathing participants. A diligent researcher who picks relevant topics he is enthusiastic about, Freedman's books are set apart by his unique style of telling the story with both words and photographs. Quotes from firsthand sources give the text life, and each of the more than 100 photographs chosen for a book further enhance the text while giving the readers an additional window into events and lives which might otherwise remain distant. Handpicked by the author, many of these hard-to-find photos have not previously appeared in print.

Freedman's books do not merely "replay" previous accounts of topics ranging from cowboys to child workers, frequently revealing a very different story than readers might expect. For example, he shows that real cowboys had very little in common with their movie counterparts. Overlooked aspects of history, including lives of women, children, and Native Americans, find their authentic voice through Freedman's thorough research and insightful storytelling. The winner of the 1988 Newbery Award for *Lincoln: A Photobiography*, Russell Freedman is a master of biographies that reveal the person behind the myth, as well as fascinating accounts of historical events with contemporary relevance. Through his nearly 50 texts, Freedman has unquestionably achieved his stated goal of making young readers care about history.

(1985). *Cowboys of the wild west*. New York: Clarion.

(1987). *Lincoln: A photobiography*. New York: Clarion.

(1991). *The Wright brothers: How they invented the airplane*. New York: Holiday.

(1995). *Immigrant kids*. New York: Puffin Books.

(1998). *Martha Graham: A dancer's life*. New York: Clarion.

(2004). *The voice that challenged a nation: Marian Anderson and the struggle for equal rights*. New York: Clarion.

(2005). *Children of the great depression*. New York: Clarion.

(2006). *Freedom walkers: The story of the Montgomery bus boycott*. New York: Holiday.

Accuracy of facts is one of the criteria set by the National Science Teacher Association (Outstanding Science Trade Books for Children) and the National Council for the Social Studies (Notable Children's Trade Books) in their yearly selection standards. Information needs to be as up to date as possible at the time of publication because knowledge changes so rapidly. Another related criterion includes the inclusiveness of information. All significant facts must be included and no relevant information should be omitted. Additional criteria related to accuracy and authenticity include stereotypes. In gender issues, women should be readily portrayed as scientists and truck drivers; men should be shown as nurses and beauticians. Ethnic portrayal is also important because scientists, politicians, and inventors span the multicultural mix of our society. Authors should also distinguish between fact and theory with the use of terms like "as far as we know . . ." or "we believe . . ." for sharing unverified statements. Author credentials, acknowledgments to experts in the field, and an indication of the research process further validate this criteria.

Writing style. Informational writing must be clear and direct if facts are to be accurately understood. Yet the qualities of good writing—voice, sentence flow, word choice, visual imagery—are just as important in informational as in narrative text. Reader involvement is a critical factor in delivery style. Where direct expository text is traditional, children are likely to be more engaged by the use of the second-person "you" as Karen Wallace uses it in *Imagine You Are a Crocodile.* Authors might ask direct questions that lead children to speculate, gather information, and guide them toward an answer. Writing in the present tense makes information more accessible and believable as well. Debbie Miller's *Big Alaska,* for example, incorporates imagery through word choice on a journey across the nation's largest state. The use of authentic vocabulary is crucial to informational writing as a glossary of terms is included with Joan Dash's *The Longitude Prize* for those new to seafaring terms. The writing should read aloud well, involve the child, and share information in a meaningful way.

Organization. The structure, or clear order of information, must reflect a meaningful arrangement. Consider the scope of the topic, the structure of the writing. Wendy Pfeiffer's *A Log's Life* relates the cause-and-effect cycle of a dying tree in the forest. Seymour Simon's *Crocodiles & Alligators* naturally chooses a compare/contrast mode for delivering information. Catherine Thimmesh's *Girls Think of Everything* tells stories of inventions created through a problem/solution format. The description mode provides the appropriate format for sharing *Yankee Doodle America: The Spirit of 1776 from A to Z* by Wendell Minor. Sequential order is the choice of Richard Ammon's *An Amish Year*; chronological order is evidenced in Raymond Bial's *Nauvoo: Mormon City on the Mississippi River.*

Access features. This criterion is made evident through chapter titles, headings, and subheadings as indicated in the table of contents, and can also be assessed by reference aids appended to the book. The index, glossaries, bibliography, and appendixes should reflect important terminology, topics, and related material as a part of the book. Ann Bausum's *With Courage and Cloth: Winning the Fight for a Woman's Right to Vote* uses intriguing chapter titles in the table of contents to capture the reader's attention. The sidebars in Jennifer Armstrong's *Photo by Brady* invite the reader to explore the photographic process and imagine "the photo not taken." Shelley Tanaka uses a timeline to share the history of *Mummies: The Newest, Coolest & Creepiest from Around the World.*

A glossary in Robert Burleigh's *Seurat and La Grande Jatte* assists the reader with the infusion of artistic terms. The bibliography of additional sources in James Deem's *Bodies from the Ashes: Life and Death in Ancient Pompeii* leads the reader to additional resources for extended inquiry into this natural disaster. Even captions in Sy Montgomery's *The Tarantula Scientist* provide a quick read in anticipation of more information in the text. Finally, the index in Sy Montgomery's *Quest for the Tree Kangaroo* guides the reader to specific aspects of this expedition.

Visual format. Whether pencil sketches, intricate pen-and-ink drawings, or photographs support the text, visual representations serve to clarify and extend textual information. The suitability of the media for the topic should be considered. For example, Bruce Hiscock's bold vision of *Wings of Light: The Migration of the Yellow Butterfly* by Stephen Swinburne in pastel watercolors does not detract from, but instead enhances, the topic. The same is true for Dorothy Henshaw Patent's *The Buffalo and the Indians,* which uses incredible color photographs to capture the struggle to save and reintroduce endangered buffalo into nature. William Munoz's photographs have captions that relate to the text but provide an additional fact or perspective to the book's content. As with all books, the format should be attractive with meaningful placement of text and pictures, ornamented headings to invite interest, varying type sizes for differing levels of information, enticing endpapers, and adequate margins to avoid information overload.

BENEFITS OF INFORMATIONAL BOOKS

Informational books add a new perspective to the reading realm of children. Their role is an important one as children emerge into independent reading and inquiry-based research.

- Informational books invite children into the world of nonfiction reading for both learning and enjoyment.
- Informational books cover a wealth of topics, so readers can readily locate a title on a subject of immediate interest.
- Informational books become a valuable resource for content area or interdisciplinary instruction, providing different information and perspectives on a topic.
- Informational books can stimulate a child's interest on an unfamiliar topic, thus opening a world of inquiry and beginning a quest of generating questions and pursuing answers.
- Informational books provide a model for conducting research by showing how an expert gathers, evaluates, organizes, and shares information with an audience.

Figure 7.1 reviews a number of outstanding authors/researchers/photographers/illustrators of both biography and informational books for children. In addition to the nonfiction titles mentioned throughout the chapter, this bibliography extends their writing accomplishments to better represent the quantity and quality of outstanding authors of nonfiction for children.

FIGURE 7.1   Book Cluster: Noteworthy nonfiction creators

David Adler (Author and researcher)

(2005). *Joe Louis: America's fighter.* Illus. by Terry Widener. San Diego: Harcourt. [P/I]

(2005). *A picture book of Samuel Adams.* Illus. by Ronald Himler. New York: Holiday House. [P]

(2004). *Enemies of slavery.* Illus. by Donald A. Smith. New York: Holiday House. [I]

(2003). *A picture book of Lewis & Clark.* Illus. by Ronald Himler. New York: Holiday House. [P]

(2002). *A picture book of Dwight David Eisenhower.* New York: Holiday House [P/M]

(2001). *Dr. Martin Luther King, Jr.* New York: Holiday House. [I/M]

(2000). *B. Franklin, printer.* New York: Holiday House. [I/M]

Jim Arnosky (Author and illustrator)

(2006). *Grandfather buffalo.* New York: Putnam. [P]

(2005). *Under the wild western sky.* New York: HarperCollins. [P]

(2005). *Hook, line & sinker: A beginner's guide to fishing, boating, & watching water wildlife.* New York: Scholastic. [I/M]

(2004). *Following the coast.* New York: HarperCollins. [P]

(2002). *All about frogs.* New York: Scholastic. [P]

(2002). *Field trips: Bug hunting, animal tracking, bird watching, and shore walking.* New York: HarperCollins. [P/I]

(2000). *Wild & swampy.* New York: Morrow. [P]

Susan Campbell Bartoletti (Author and researcher)

(2005). *Hitler youth: Growing up in Hitler's shadow.* New York: Scholastic. [I/M]

(2004). *The flagmaker.* Illus. by Claire Nivola. Boston: Houghton Mifflin. [P]

(2001). *Black potatoes: The story of the great Irish famine.* Boston: Houghton Mifflin. [M]

(1999). *Kids on strike.* Boston: Houghton Mifflin. [I/M]

Raymond Bial (Author, researcher, and photographer)

(2005). *Nauvoo: Mormon city on the Mississippi River.* Boston: Houghton Mifflin. [I]

(2004). *Where Washington walked.* New York: Walker. [I]

(2002). *Tenement: Immigrant life on the Lower East Side.* Boston: Houghton Mifflin. [I]

(2001). *Ghost towns of the American West.* Boston: Houghton Mifflin. [I]

(2000). *A handful of dirt.* New York: Walker. [I]

Rhoda Blumberg (Author and researcher)

(2004). *York's adventures with Lewis & Clark: An African American's part in the Great Expedition.* New York: HarperCollins. [I/M]

(2001). *Shipwrecked! The true adventures of a Japanese boy.* Illus. with photographs. New York: HarperCollins. [M]

(1998). *What's the deal? Jefferson, Napoleon, and the Louisiana Purchase.* Washington, DC: National Geographic Society. [I/M]

(1996). *Full speed ahead: The race to build a transcontinental railroad.* Washington, DC: National Geographic. [I/M]

Russell Freedman (Author and researcher)

(2006). *The adventures of Marco Polo.* Illus. by Bagram Ibatoulline. New York: Arthur A. Levine/Scholastic. [I/M]

(2006). *Freedom walkers: The story of the Montgomery bus boycott.* New York: Holiday House. [I]

(continued)

FIGURE 7.1 Continued

(2005). *Children of the Great Depression*. New York: Clarion. [I]

(2004). *The voice that challenged a nation: Marian Anderson and the struggle for equal rights*. New York: Clarion. [I/M]

(2003). *In defense of liberty: The story of America's Bill of Rights*. New York: Holiday House. [I]

(2002). *Confucius: The golden rule*. Illus. by Frederic Clement. New York: Scholastic. [I/M]

(1993). *Eleanor Roosevelt: A life of discovery*. Boston: Clarion. [M]

(1987). *Lincoln: A photobiography*. Boston: Clarion. [I/M]

Jean Fritz (Author and researcher)

(2001). *Leonardo's horse*. Illus. by Hudson Talbott. New York: Putnam. [I]

(1999). *Why not, Lafayette?* New York: Putnam. [I]

(1995). *You want women to vote, Lizzie Stanton?* New York: Putnam. [I]

(1991). *Bully for you, Teddy Roosevelt*. New York: Putnam. [I/M]

(1989). *The great little Madison*. New York: Putnam. [I/M]

(1973). *And then what happened, Paul Revere?* Illus. by Margot Tomes. New York: Coward/McCann. [P/I]

Gail Gibbons (Author and illustrator)

(2006). *Ice cream*. New York: Holiday House. [P]

(2005). *Owls*. New York: Holiday House. [P]

(2005). *Dinosaur discoveries*. New York: Holiday House. [P]

(2002). *Tell me, tree: All about trees for kids*. New York: Little, Brown. [P]

(2002). *The berry book*. New York: Holiday House. [P]

(2001). *Ducks!* New York: Holiday House. [P]

James Cross Giblin (Author and researcher)

(2005). *Good brother, bad brother: The story of Edwin Booth & John Wilkes Booth*. New York: Clarion. [M]

(2004). *Secrets of the sphinx*. New York: Scholastic. [I/M]

(2002). *The life and death of Adolf Hitler*. Boston: Clarion. [M]

(2000). *The amazing life of Benjamin Franklin*. Illus. by Michael Dooling. New York: Scholastic. [I/M]

Kathryn Lasky (Author and researcher) **and Christopher G. Knight** (Photographer)

(2006). *John Muir: America's first environmentalist*. Illus. by Stan Fellows. Cambridge, MA: Candlewick. [P/I]

(2001). *Interrupted journey: Saving endangered sea turtles*. Cambridge, MA: Candlewick. [I/M]

(1997). *The most beautiful roof in the world: Exploring the rainforest canopy*. Photographs by Christopher G. Knight. San Diego: Harcourt Brace. [I]

(1994). *The librarian who measured the earth*. Illus. by Kevin Hawkes. Boston: Little, Brown. [I]

(1993). *Searching for Laura Ingalls: A reader's journey*. With Meribah Knight. New York: Macmillan. [I/M]

Sandra Markle (Author and photographer)

(2006). *Rescues!* Minneapolis, MN: Millbrook. [I]

(2005). *Outside and inside mummies*. New York: Walker. [I]

(2005). *Snakes: Biggest! Littlest!* Photos by Joe McDonald. Honesdale, PA: Boyds Mills Press. [P/I]

FIGURE 7.1   Continued

(2002). *Growing up wild: Penguins.* New York: Atheneum. [P]

(2001). *Outside and inside rats and mice.* New York: Atheneum. [P/I]

(2001). *Growing up wild: Wolves.* New York: Atheneum. [P]

Milton Meltzer (Author and researcher)

(2002). *Ten kings and the worlds they ruled.* New York: Orchard. [M]

(2001). *There comes a time: The struggles for civil rights.* New York: Random House. [M]

(1998). *Ten queens: Portraits of women of power.* New York: Dutton. [M]

(1993). *Lincoln: In his own words.* Illus. by Stephen Alcorn. San Diego: Harcourt Brace. [I/M]

(1992). *The amazing potato.* New York: HarperCollins. [I/M]

Jim Murphy (Author and researcher)

(2003). *Inside the Alamo.* New York: Delacorte. [I/M]

(2003). *An American plague.* New York: Clarion. [I/M]

(2000). *Blizzard: The storm that changed America.* New York: Scholastic. [M]

(1995). *The great fire.* New York: Scholastic. [I/M]

(1993). *Across America on an emigrant train.* Boston: Clarion. [I/M]

Dorothy Henshaw Patent (Author and researcher)

(2006). *The buffalo and the Indians: A shared destiny.* Photographs by William Munoz. New York: Clarion. [I/M]

(2004). *The right dog for the job: Ira's path from service dog to guide dog.* Photographs by William Munoz. New York: Walker. [P/I]

(2004). *Garden of the spirit bear: Life in the great northern rainforest.* Illus. by Deborah Milton. New York: Clarion. [I]

(2003). *Plants on the trail with Lewis & Clark.* Photographs by William Munoz. New York: Clarion. [I/M]

(2000). *The bald eagle returns.* Photographs by William Munoz. Boston: Clarion. [I/M]

Laurence Pringle (Author and researcher)

(2003). *Whales! Strange and wonderful.* Illus. by Meryl Henderson. Honesdale, PA: Boyds Mills Press. [P/I]

(2001). *A dragon in the sky: The story of a green darner dragonfly.* New York: Orchard. [I]

(2001). *Global warming: The threat of Earth's changing climate.* New York: SeaStar. [I]

(2000). *Bats! Strange and wonderful.* Honesdale, PA: Boyds Mills Press.

(1997). *Extraordinary life: The story of a monarch butterfly.* Illus. by Bob Marstall. New York: Orchard Books. [I/M]

(1995). *Fire in the forest: A cycle of growth and renewal.* Paintings by Bob Marstall. New York: Atheneum. [I/M]

Seymour Simon (Author and researcher)

(2006). *Stars.* New York: HarperCollins. [P/I]

(2005). *Guts: Our digestive system.* New York: HarperCollins. [P/I]

(2004). *Cats.* New York: HarperCollins. [P]

(2003). *Spiders.* New York: HarperCollins. [P]

(2002). *Destination: Space.* New York: HarperCollins. [P/I]

(2002). *Seymour Simon's book of trains.* New York: HarperCollins. [P]

(2001). *Animals nobody loves.* New York: Simon & Schuster. [P/I]

(continued)

FIGURE 7.1   Continued

(2000). *Gorillas*. New York: HarperCollins. [P/I]

(1999). *Crocodiles & Alligators*. New York: HarperCollins. [P/I]

Diane Stanley (Author, researcher, and illustrator)

(2002). *Saladin: Noble prince of Islam*. New York: HarperCollins. [I/M]

(2000). *Michelangelo*. New York: HarperCollins. [I/M]

(1998). *Joan of Arc*. New York: Morrow. [I/M]

(1996). *Leonardo da Vinci*. New York: Morrow. [I/M]

(1993). *Charles Dickens: The man who had great expectations*. With Peter Vennema. New York: Morrow. [I/M]

(1992). *Bard of Avon: The story of William Shakespeare*. With Peter Vennema. New York: Morrow. [I/M]

(1990). *Good Queen Bess: The story of Elizabeth I of England*. With Peter Vennema. New York: Four Winds. [I/M]

Jerry Stanley (Author and researcher)

(2003). *Cowboys and longhorns*. New York: Crown. [I/M]

(2000). *Hurry freedom! African Americans in Gold Rush California*. Illus. with photographs. New York: Crown. [I/M]

(1998). *Frontier merchants: Lionel and Barron Jacobs and the Jewish pioneers who settled the West*. New York: Crown. [I/M]

(1994). *I am an American: A true story of Japanese internment*. New York: Crown. [I/M]

(1992). *Children of the Dustbowl: The true story of the school at Weedpatch Camp*. New York: Random. [I/M]

Kate Waters (Author and researcher)

(2001). *Giving thanks: The 1621 harvest feast*. Photographed by Russ Kendall (in cooperation with Plymouth Plantation). New York: Scholastic.

(1996). *On the Mayflower: Voyage of the ship's apprentice and a passenger girl*. Photographs by Russ Kendall. New York: Scholastic. [P/I]

(1996). *Tapenum's day: A Wampanoog Indian boy in Pilgrim times*. Photographs by Russ Kendall. New York: Scholastic.

(1993). *Samuel Eaton's day: A day in the life of a Pilgrim boy*. Photographs by Russ Kendall. New York: Scholastic. [P/I]

(1989). *Sarah Morton's day: A day in the life of a Pilgrim girl*. Photographs by Russ Kendall. New York: Scholastic. [P/I]

READER RESPONSE TO INFORMATIONAL BOOKS

Informational books set the stage for both oral and written response in the forms of readers' theater, written aesthetic response, diary entries, and book selection. Response can even be measured by additional research stimulated by the introduction of an inspiring informational book. The formats of informational books provide models for delivering student research as well. Chapter 13 contains an entire range of prompts and response-based activities focused on informational books.

There is an informational book to arouse and feed each child's area of interest. Whether satisfying an insatiable appetite for dinosaurs, fulfilling a dream to explore the outer limits of the universe, or experiencing the quest to discover new countries and cultures, informational books fulfill personal needs. Because these books account for more than half of library acquisitions and circulation, their importance with children is magnified. With the increased inclusion of informational books, teachers can reach that child who does not readily respond to fiction. Informational books have the power to teach, to inspire, to answer, to stretch, to challenge, and to fulfill. Their current popularity attests to their importance in children's natural inquiry and their need to stretch beyond their own borders. A superlative resource for inquiry-based teachers, informational books have found a permanent home across the elementary/middle-level curriculum.

CLOSING THOUGHTS

Today's biography and informational books reach far beyond the traditional research demands of the classroom. Through read-alouds, choices for independent reading, and as a natural springboard to content area study, children's nonfiction has risen to new heights. The quality and quantity of information delivered through these nonfiction genres makes nonfiction a viable choice for inclusion across the curriculum as well as for reading enjoyment.

As lifelong readers, many literate adults favor nonfiction titles for leisure reading. A renewed emphasis on expository reading has reinvigorated the nonfiction genres. The expository nature of biography and nonfiction demands introduction at an even earlier stage of reading development. The abundance of quality authors and quality works of nonfiction blended with the expertise and enthusiasm of a teacher can move the inclusion of nonfiction across grade levels, and curricular areas can encompass both research and reading to be viewed through both efferent and aesthetic lenses.

References

Bamford, R. A., & Kristo, J. V. (Eds.) (2003). *Making facts come alive: Choosing quality nonfiction literature K–8* (2nd ed.). Norwood, MA: Christopher-Gordon.

Corsaro, J. (2005). Honoring nonfiction: The Robert F. Sibert Medal. *Book Links, 15,* 22–25.

Hunt, J. (2005). Where do all the prizes go? Thoughts on the state of informational books. *The Horn Book, 81,* 439–445.

Hynes, M. (2000). "I read for facts:" Reading nonfiction in a fictional world. *Language Arts, 77,* 485–495.

Levstik, L. S. (1993). "I wanted to be there:" The impact of narrative on children's thinking. In M. O. Tunnell & Ammon, R. (Eds.), *The story of ourselves: Teaching history through children's literature.* Portsmouth, NH: Heinemann.

Livingston, N., Kurkjian, C., Young, T., & Pringle, L. (2004). Nonfiction as literature: An untapped goldmine. *The Reading Teacher, 57,* 582–591.

Palmer, R. G., & Stewart, R. A. (2003). Nonfiction trade book use in primary grades. *The Reading Teacher, 57,* 38–48.

Pappas, C. C. (2006). The information book genre: Its role in integrated science literacy research and practice. *Reading Research Quarterly, 41,* 226–250.

Pringle, L. (2004). Nonfiction rising. *The Reading Teacher, 57,* 588.

Saul, E. W., & Dieckman, D. (2005). Choosing and using information text books. *Reading Research Quarterly, 40,* 502–513.

Yopp, R. H., & Yopp, H. K. (2000). Sharing informational text with young children. *The Reading Teacher, 53,* 410–423.

Zarnowski, M. (1988). Learning about fictionalized biography: A reading and writing approach. *The Reading Teacher, 42,* 136–142.

Zarnowski, M. (1990). *Learning about biographies: A reading-and-writing approach for children*. Urbana, IL: National Council of Teachers of English.

Zarnowski, M., Kerper, R. M., & Jensen, J. M. (Eds.) (2001). *The best in children's nonfiction: Reading, writing, and teaching Orbis Pictus Award Books*. Urbana, IL: National Council of Teachers of English.

Children's Books Cited: Biography [P] = K–2; [I] = 3–5; [M] = 6–8

Adler, David (2002). *A picture book of Dwight David Eisenhower*. New York: Holiday House. [P]

Adler, David (2005). *A picture book of Samuel Adams*. Illus. by John and Alexandra Wallner. New York: Holiday House. [P]

Adler, David (2005). *Joe Louis: America's fighter*. Illus. by Terry Widener. San Diego: Gulliver Books/Harcourt Brace. [P/I]

Ahmedi, Farah (with Tamim Ansary) (2005). *The story of my life: An Afghan girl on the other side of the sky*. New York: Simon & Schuster. [I/M]

Bardoe, Cheryl (2006). *Gregor Mendel: The friar who grew peas*. Illus. by Jos. A. Smith. New York: Abrams Books for Young Readers (in association with The Field Museum). [I]

Barretta, Gene (2006). *Now & Ben: The modern inventions of Benjamin Franklin*. New York: Henry Holt. [P/I]

Bildner, Phil (2002). *Shoeless Joe & Black Betsy*. Illus. by C. F. Payne. New York: Simon & Schuster. [I]

Blumberg, Rhoda (2004). *York's Adventures with Lewis and Clark: An African-American's part in the great expedition*. New York: HarperCollins. [I/M]

Borden, Louise (1998). *Good-bye, Charles Lindbergh*. Illus. by Thomas B. Allen. New York: McElderry Books. [P/I]

Borden, Louise, & Kroeger, Mary Kay (2001). *Fly high! The story of Bessie Coleman*. Illus. by Teresa Flavin. New York: McElderry. [P/I]

Bridges, Ruby (1999). *Through my eyes*. Illus. with photographs. New York: Scholastic. [I/M]

Burleigh, Robert (2002). *The secret of the great Houdini*. Illus. by Leonid Gore. New York: Atheneum. [P/I]

Coleman, Penny (2006). *Adventurous women: Eight true stories about women who made a difference*. New York: Henry Holt. [I/M]

Fleming, Candace (2005). *Our Eleanor: A scrapbook look at Eleanor Roosevelt's remarkable life*. New York: An Anne Schwartz Book/Atheneum. [M]

Fradin, Judith Bloom, & Fradin, Dennis Brindell (2006). *Jane Addams: Champion of democracy*. New York: Clarion. [M]

Freedman, Russell (1987). *Lincoln: A photobiography*. Boston: Clarion. [I/M]

Freedman, Russell (2004). *The voice that challenged a nation: Marian Anderson and the struggle for equal rights*. New York: Clarion. [I/M]

Freedman, Russell (2006). *The adventures of Marco Polo*. Illus. by Bagram Ibatoulline. New York: Arthur A Levine Books/Scholastic [I/M]

Fritz, Jean (1973). *And then what happened, Paul Revere?* Illus. by Margot Tomes. New York: Coward. [I]

Fritz, Jean (1989). *The great little Madison*. New York: Putnam. [I/M]

Fritz, Jean (1991). *Bully for you, Teddy Roosevelt*. Illus. by Mike Wimmer. New York: Putnam. [I/M]

Giblin, James Cross (2000). *The amazing life of Benjamin Franklin*. Illus. by Michael Dooling. New York: Scholastic. [I/M]

Govenar, Alan (2006). *Extraordinary ordinary people: Five American masters of traditional arts*. Cambridge, MA: Candlewick. [I/M]

Johnson, Dolores (2006). *Onward: A photobiography of African-American polar explorer Matthew Henson*. Washington, DC: National Geographic.

Keating, Frank (2006). *Theodore*. Illus. by Mike Wimmer. New York: Simon & Schuster. [P/I]

Kerley, Barbara (2001). *The dinosaurs of Waterhouse Hawkins: An illuminating history of Mr. Waterhouse Hawkins, artist and lecturer*. Illus. by Brian Selznick. New York: Scholastic. [I/M]

Krull, Kathleen (2005). *Leonardo Da Vinci*. Illus. by Boris Kulikov, (Glants of Science series) New York: Viking. [I\M]

Krull, Kathleen (2006), *Isaac Newton*. Illus. by Boris Kulikov. (Giants of Science series). New York: Viking. [I\M]

Krull, Kathleen (2006). *Sigmund Freud*. Illus. by Boris Kulikov. (Giants of Science series). New York: Viking. [I/M]

Lasky, Kathryn (2006). *John Muir: America's first environmentalist*. Illus. by Stan Fellows. Cambridge, MA: Candlewick Press. [P/I]

Lobel, Anita (1998). *No pretty pictures: A child of war*. New York: Greenwillow. [M]

Mantell, Paul (2006). *Arthur Ashe: Young tennis champion* (Childhood of Young American series). New York: Simon & Schuster/Aladdin. [P/I]

Martin, Jacqueline Briggs (1998). *Snowflake Bentley*. Illus. by Mary Azarian. Boston: Houghton Mifflin. [P/I]

McCully, Emily Arnold (2006). *Marvelous Mattie: How Margaret K. Knight became an inventor*. New York: Farrar, Straus & Giroux. [P]

Myers, Walter Dean (2001). *The greatest: Muhammed Ali*. New York: Scholastic. [I/M]

Pinkney, Andrea Davis (1998). *Duke Ellington: The piano prince and his orchestra*. Illus. by Brian Pinkney. New York: Hyperion. [P/I]

Pinkney, Andrea Davis (2002). *Ella Fitzgerald: The tale of a vocal virtuosa*. New York: Jump at the Sun/Hyperion. [P/I]

Rappaport, Doreen (2001). *Martin's big words: The life of Dr. Martin Luther King, Jr.* Illus. by Bryan Collier. New York: Jump at the Sun/Hyperion. [P/I/M]

Ryan, Pam Muñoz (2002). *When Marian Sang: The true recital of Marian Anderson, the voice of a century*. Illus. by Brian Selznick. New York: Scholastic. [I/M]

Sis, Peter (1996). *Starry messenger: Galileo Galilei*. New York: Farrar, Straus & Giroux. [P/M/I]

Stanley, Diane (1996). *Leonardo Da Vinci*. New York: Morrow. [I/M]

Stanley, Diane (1998). *Joan of Arc*. New York: Morrow. [I/M]

Stanley, Diane (2000). *Michelangelo*. New York: HarperCollins. [I/M]

Stanley, Diane (2003). *Saladin*. New York: HarperCollins. [I/M]

Stanley, George (2005). *Leonardo Da Vinci: Young artist, writer, and inventor* (Childhood of World Figures series). New York: Simon & Schuster/Aladdin. [P/I]

Wong, Li Keng (2006). *Good fortune: My journey to Gold Mountain*. Atlanta: Peachtree. [I/M]

Children's Books Cited: Informational Books

Ammon, Richard (2000). *An Amish year*. Illus. by P. Patrick. New York: Atheneum. [P/I]

Armstrong, Jennifer (2005). *Photo by Brady: A picture of the Civil War*. New York: Atheneum. [I/M]

Aston, Diana, & Long, Sylvia (2006). *An egg is quiet*. San Francisco: Chronicle Books. [P]

Bartoletti, Susan Campbell (2005). *Hitler youth: Growing up in Hitler's shadow*. New York: Scholastic. [M]

Bausum, Ann (2004). *With courage and cloth: Winning the fight for a woman's right to vote*. Washington, DC: National Geographic. [I/M]

Bial, Raymond (2006). *Nauvoo: Mormon city on the Mississippi River*. Boston: Houghton Mifflin. [I]

Burleigh, Robert (2004). *Seurat and La Grande Jatte*. New York: Abrams (in association with the Art Institute of Chicago). [I]

Butterworth, Chris (2006). *Sea horse: The shyest fish in the sea*. Illus. by John Lawrence. Cambridge, MA: Candlewick. [P/I]

Cole, Joanna (2006). *The magic school bus and the science fair expedition*. Illus. by Bruce Degan. New York: Scholastic. [I]

Collard III, Sneed B. (2005). *The prairie builders: Reconstructing America's lost grasslands* (Scientists in the Field series). Boston: Houghton Mifflin. [I/M]

Cowley, Joy (2005). *Chameleon, chameleon*. Photos by Nic Bishop. New York: Scholastic.

Curlee, Lynn (2000). *Liberty*. New York: Atheneum. [I/M]

Curlee, Lynn (2003). *Capital*. New York: Atheneum. [I/M]

Curlee, Lynn (2004). *Parthenon*. New York: Atheneum. [I/M]

Curlee, Lynn (2005). *Ballpark*. New York: Atheneum. [I/M]

Dash, Joan (2000). *The longitude prize*. Illus. by Dusan Petricic. New York: Farrar, Straus & Giroux. [I/M]

Deem, James M. (2005). *Bodies from the ash: Life and death in ancient Pompeii*. Boston: Houghton Mifflin. [I/M]

Freedman, Russell (2005). *Children of the Great Depression*. New York: Clarion. [I/M]

Fritz, Jean (2001). *Leonardo's horse*. Illus. by Hudson Talbott. New York: Penguin Putnam. [I]

Harness, Cheryl (2002). *Ghosts of the Civil War*. New York: Simon & Schuster. [I/M]

Jenkins, Steve (2004). *Actual size*. Boston: Houghton Mifflin. [P/I]

Kurlansky, Mark (2001). *The cod's tale*. Illus. by S. D. Schindler. New York: Penguin Putnam. [I/M]

Miller, Debbie S. (2006). *Big Alaska: Journey across America's most amazing state*. Illus. by Jon Van Zyle. New York: Walker. [P/I]

Minor, Wendell (2006). *Yankee Doodle America: The spirit of 1776 from A to Z*. New York: G. P. Putnam's Sons. [P/I]

Montgomeny, Sy (2005). *The tarantula scientist*. Photographs by Nic Bishop. (Scientists, in the Field series). Boston: Houghton Mifflin. [I/M]

Montgomeny, Sy (2006). *Quest for the tree kangaroo: An expedition to the Cloud Forest of New Guinea*. Photographs by Nic Bishop. Boston: Houghton Mifflin. [I/M]

Murphy, Jim (1995). *The great fire*. New York: Scholastic. [I/M]

Murphy, Jim (2003). *An American plague: The true and terrifying story of the yellow fever epidemic of 1793*. Boston: Houghton Mifflin/Clarion. [I/M]

National Council for the Social Studies (NCSS) and the Children's Book Council (CBC). (Annual). Notable Children's Trade Books in the Field of Social Studies. *Social Education*, April/May issue.

National Science Teacher Association (NSTA) and the Children's Book Council (CBC). (Annual). Outstanding Science Trade Books for Children. *Science and Children*, March issue.

Patent, Dorothy Henshaw (2006). *The buffalo and the Indians: A shared destiny*. Photographs by William Munoz. New York: Clarion. [I]

Pfeiffer, Wendy (1997). *A log's life*. Illus. by R. Brickman. New York: Simon & Schuster. [P/I]

Pringle, Laurence (1997). *An extraordinary life: The story of a monarch butterfly*. Illus. by Bob Marstall. New York: Orchard Books. [I/M]

Ryder, Joanne (2006). *A pair of polar bears: Twin cubs find a home at the San Diego Zoo*. New York: Simon & Schuster. [P]

Rylant, Cynthia (2006). *The journey: Stories of migration*. Illus. by Lambert Davis. New York: Blue Sky/Scholastic. [P/I]

Sill, Cathryn (2006). *About marsupials: A guide for children*. Illus. by John Sill. Atlanta: Peachtree. [P/I]

Simon, Seymour (1999). *Crocodiles & alligators*. New York: HarperCollins. [P/I]

Simon, Seymour (2005). *Guts: Our digestive system*. New York: HarperCollins. [P/I]

Siy, Alexandra, & Kunkel, Dennis (2005). *Mosquito bite*. Watertown, MA: Charlesbridge. [P/I]

St. George, Judith (2000). *So you want to be president?* Illus. by David Small. New York: Philomel. [I/M]

Swinburne, Stephen R. (2006). *Wings of light: The migration of the yellow butterfly*. Illus. by Bruce Hiscock. Honesdale, PA: Boyds Mills Press. [P/I]

Tanaka, Shelley (2005). *Mummies: The newest, coolest & creepiest from around the world*. New York: Abrams. [I/M]

Thimmesh, Catherine (2000). *Girls think of everything: Stories of ingenious inventions by women*. Illus. by M. Sweet. Boston: Houghton Mifflin. [I/M]

Walker, Sally M. (2005). *Secrets of a Civil War submarine: Solving the mysteries of the H. L. Huntley*. Minneapolis, MN: Carolrhoda Books. [I/M]

Wallace, Karen (1997). *Imagine you are a crocodile*. Illus. by Mike Bostock. New York: Henry Holt. [P/I]

CHAPTER 8

Multicultural and International Literature

Appreciating Cultural and Global Diversity

Adam thinks he is doing something special with the farmer, but then he realizes that the farmer has abandoned him to the army. I can't imagine how that would feel, thinking that you were going to town for a good reason; then the next minute you are confused and scared. He seems kind of dumb and you can tell he's not a fast thinker.

Adam asks Sergeant Krauter if he can get new boots and he says no, so Adam steals the boots late at night. If my feet were as bad as described, I would do the same. You got to do what you got to do. I also thought it was a smart idea when he made the boots look weathered. (I take back what I said about him being kind of dumb . . .)

I didn't know much about the Napoleonic War. The thing I liked a lot about the book was the way the author described everything. During the whole book, I pictured what it would be like to live through that time and in that place.

Eighth-grade reader response to *An Innocent Soldier* by
Josef Holub (Mildred Batchelder Award 2006)

Multicultural and international literature transport the reader to many lands and survey many cultures as they attempt to share differences among peoples and history of the world. Yet in their showcase of diversity, both multicultural and international literature encourage the recognition of commonalities among humanity. Although cultural contexts and locations change, people retain their sameness, revealing similarities in emotions, commitments, dreams, and expectations.

The text and photographs of Jan Reynolds's *Celebrate! Connections Among Cultures* provides an inspiring look of the cultural traditions and emotional bonds that unite all humanity. The similarities between cultural traditions—gathering together, eating and drinking, playing music and dancing—convince the reader that "We are one human family celebrating life on earth!" (n.p.). Multicultural and international children's literature open the world of all peoples to children by inviting young readers to gain understandings about heritages, beliefs, and values that are, as they may soon discover, not so different from their own. Literature of a diverse culture—African American, Asian American, Latino American, Native American, Middle Eastern—opens the culture's heart to the reading audience, showing the culture's joy and grief, love and hatred, hope and despair, expectations and frustrations, and the effects of living in a society where differences are not always readily accepted (Cai & Bishop, 1994). International literature bridges geographical boundaries and connects readers to the rest of the world (Stan, 2002; Tomlinson, 1998). These literatures provide the connection between the common world cultures of humanity as they serve as a means to transmit history and ideals.

Multicultural literature serves a dual purpose in the lives of children. When a child sees him- or herself—one's own color, one's own heritage, one's own traditions—in a text, he or she feels pride, acceptance, and belonging. During a poetry unit, for example, an African American fourth-grade girl spent her recess in the media center when she discovered Eloise Greenfield was a poet of her culture. She proudly displayed *Honey, I Love* as her peers returned from the playground and kept the book close at hand for the entire week. The other purpose of multicultural literature involves mainstream or "ethnically encapsulated" (Banks, 1988) children. These are readers who often remain isolated in their own world and lack exposure to other colors and cultures. These are the young readers who open their eyes to Lisa Rowe Fraustino's *The Hickory Chair* and Patricia McKissack's *Goin' Someplace Special* and readily identify with their own family members. These are the readers who open their hearts to Evie Thomas, an African American, who must adjust to a new identity when her family is forced to move in Jacqueline Woodson's *Hush.* Exposure to multicultural literature provides both a mirror into one's own world and a door into the culture and lives of others—thus becoming an "instrument of power" (Ching, 2005).

International literature, too, serves a dual purpose for readers. It opens the realm of children's books to some familiar classics as the folktales of the Brothers Grimm, Anne Frank's *The Diary of A Young Girl,* or Christina Bjork's *Linnea in Monet's Garden.* When children read translated stories that they know children in other countries are reading, they feel a connection and a nearness to children around the world, perhaps resulting in a richer, deeper, more empathetic understanding of humanity as adults. International literature transports the reader to unfamiliar global settings to visit new places and new faces. If readers are to gain a global understanding of connections within an international community, children's books may be the perfect place to begin that global relationship (Gebel, 2006).

In this text, multicultural and international literature are not considered genres of literature but mirrors that reflect the story of humankind *across all genres.* Although many multicultural and a few international titles have been included throughout the genre chapters of this text, this chapter provides an opportunity to showcase authors, illustrators, titles, and response connections that share a special purpose in touching the hearts, minds, and souls of readers while broadening their knowledge and experiences about the commonalities of humanity. The chapter is divided into two sections—a complete section on multicultural literature, which has gained a respectful audience in the past two decades, and a developing section on international children's literature, which is gaining a steadily strong and potentially dynamic interest by advocates of children's literature and response.

MULTICULTURAL LITERATURE

Five issues surround multicultural literature and provide an ongoing agenda for discussion on the topic. These issues become the framework for this opening section of the chapter.

- The inclusiveness of various *definitions* of multicultural literature will be clarified.
- The issue of *authenticity,* the "insider" versus the "outsider" author perspective, will be examined.
- *Selection criteria* that encompass or exclude certain titles must be considered.
- The *curricular relevance* of multicultural literature requires a supportive discussion.
- The past, current, and future *availability* of multicultural literature that meets the criteria for authenticity, cultural and historical accuracy, and aesthetic pleasure must be assessed.

The following discussion should broaden your knowledge of these important perspectives on children's literature and provide information to enhance judgment when selecting and naturally including multicultural literature across the curriculum.

Definitions of Multicultural/Multiethnic Literature

Junko Yokota (1993) initially defined multicultural children's literature as "literature that represents any distinct cultural group through accurate portrayal and rich detail" (p. 157). Her definition allows inclusion of not only people of color but other distinct cultural/religious groups as well as European cultural groups. This definition would not only include Walter Dean Myers's *The Harlem Hellfighters,* a regiment of World War I African American soldiers, but also provide for sharing Isaac Millman's autobiographical tale of his childhood efforts to hide his Jewish identity during World War II in *Hidden Child.*

Literary Legend

African American Author

During **Virginia Hamilton**'s lifetime (1936–2002), she received every single award given to writers of children's literature, from the Newbery Award to the Hans Christian Andersen Medal. Keenly aware of the need for African American characters across all genres, Hamilton brought her multicultural vision to realistic fiction, science fiction, and mysteries, as well as numerous picture books, folktales, and nonfiction titles. The fantastic and realistic worlds created in her writing are populated with unforgettable characters such as Zeely, M.C. Huggins, Pretty Pearl, and Justice.

Hamilton lived and wrote on a farm in the tiny Ohio village of Yellow Springs. Given that the farm had been in her family for generations, it is not surprising that so much of her writing focused on African American history and cultural traditions. Hamilton's grandfather was brought to Ohio on the Underground Railroad, and this history is reflected in *The House of Dies Drear*. Her Newbery Award winning novel, *M.C. Higgins, the Great,* also set in Ohio, concerns a family's struggle against the strip mining that threatens the family home. Virginia Hamilton's books (more than 35 in all) form the foundation of a multicultural legacy in children's literature that continues to preserve black history and culture.

(1967). *Zeely.* New York: Scholastic.

(1968). *The house of Dies Drear.* New York: Macmillan.

(1971). *The planet of Junior Brown.* New York: Macmillan.

(1974). *M.C. Higgins, the great.* New York: Macmillan.

(1985). *The people could fly: American black folktales.* Illus. by Leo & Diane Dillon. New York: Knopf.

(1992). *Dryslongo.* Illus. by Jerry Pinkney. San Diego: Harcourt Brace.

(1993). *Many thousand gone: African Americans from slavery to freedom.* Illus. by Leo & Diane Dillon. New York: Knopf.

(1995). *Her stories: African American folktales, fairy tales, and true tales.* Illus. by Leo & Diane Dillon. New York: Blue Sky/Scholastic.

(1999). *Bluish: A novel.* New York: Blue Sky/Scholastic.

(2002). *Time pieces: The book of times.* New York: Blue Sky/Scholastic.

Violet Harris (1992) focused her early definition of multicultural literature in *Teaching Multicultural Literature in Grades K–8* on any group that had marginal status and lacked complete access to mainstream institutions. This label included people of color (African, Asian, Hispanic, Native American), religious minorities (Amish, Jewish), regional cultures (Appalachian, Cajun), people with disabilities (physical, mental), the aged, and, to some extent, women and girls. Using this definition, titles ranging from Margarita Engle's *The Poet Slave of Cuba: A Biography of Juan Francisco Manzano* to Tonya Bolden's *Maritcha: A Nineteeth Century American Girl* would be included.

In her last edition of *Using Multiethnic Literature in the K–8 Classroom,* Harris (1997) narrows her definition and focus by referring to literature exclusively about people of color—African, Asian, Hispanic/Latino, Native American—as "multiethnic literature." However, this chapter moves beyond literature of people of color through mostly "multiicultural literature" while still including "multiethnic" titles that share specific cultures from around the globe. In addition, many of the titles mentioned span more than one culture and present a multiple perspective on people around the world.

Authenticity

For years, scholars have debated the authenticity of multicultural literature written by authors inside and outside the culture. Although most agree that an author need not be of the culture about which he or she is writing, the debate continues among literature experts (Fox & Short, 2003). Most agree that to achieve authenticity, the author must either be of the culture or take on the perspective of other people living in the culture. Unfortunately, few people have the opportunity to live within a culture and note its distinctive nuances. For example, Paul Goble is one of the few authors given genuine recognition for an "outsider" perspective on the Plains Indians (e.g., *Storm Maker's Tipi*) after actually living with Native Americans for more than a decade. Suzanne Fisher Staples spent years as a journalist in Pakistan before writing *Shabanu: Daughter of the Wind* and its sequels. Authors must fill in their own cultural gaps before presuming to bridge cultural gaps for readers.

Cai and Bishop (1994) address the authenticity issue by discussing a hierarchy of multicultural literature based on the inside–outside perspective. **World literature** includes folktales and fiction from non-Western countries or other underrepresented groups outside the United States. This category includes adaptations by both American writers as well as literature directly from root cultures. For example, Geraldine McCaughrean's *The Golden Hoard* includes myths from China and Persia and legends from Wales to Australia. Mary Pope Osborne's *One World, Many Religions* shares the way people worship across the seven major religions of the world.

Cross-cultural literature focuses on the unique experiences of a cultural group written by an author whose ethnic background is outside the culture. The intention of these titles is to foster acceptance of cultural diversity or to encourage constructive intercultural relationships. Doreen Rappaport's trilogy of *No More! Stories and Songs of Slave Resistance, Free at Last: Stories and Songs of Emancipation,* and *Nobody Gonna Turn Me 'Round: Stories and Songs of the Civil Rights Movement* share the history of the authentic voices of those who fought for equality and freedom. Although outside the African American culture, Rappaport's research and authentic words capture the slaves' thirst for freedom and share accounts of their mistreatment and the freeman's struggle to maintain equal rights, creating a compelling, historical portrait of bravery.

Finally, **parallel culture literature** is written by authors from a cultural group who represent the experience and images developed as a result of being acculturated and socialized within the culture itself. A focused example is Walter Dean Myers's *Harlem,* which poetically portrays the sounds, sights, and memories of this section of New York where he was raised. Christopher Myers's collage art resonates strong emotions and adds another dimension to the understanding of this African American urban culture. Although the "inside" perspective is still viewed by most multicultural specialists as the most "authentic," the acceptance of different levels of involvement within a culture broadens the number of books that attain varying degrees of authenticity, thus broadening the spectrum of acceptable quality titles of multicultural literature.

Authenticity reflects accuracy of portrayal. This trait continues as a topic for debate as it now expands to include authentic language as a consideration in determining authenticity (Barrera & Quiroa, 2003). Although this discussion is likely to be ongoing, an awareness of the variable tiers of authenticity may bring some degree of acceptance to a wider span of quality books from authors both inside and outside, yet well-informed about the culture. Although the debate continues, authors from outside a culture are gaining more respect as the accuracy of their books is qualified by their well-informed perspective.

EVALUATING QUALITY MULTICULTURAL LITERATURE

Many teachers and librarians lack confidence in their ability to make informed decisions about multicultural titles, believing they do not have the cultural knowledge to select literature that does not foster stereotypes of a particular group. Although wide reading over time about a particular cultural group will assist in developing cultural sensitivities, they often request assistance in making difficult choices.

A reputable identification of quality multicultural literature comes from book award winners that have been carefully scrutinized by children's literature experts. The Coretta Scott King Award honors outstanding African American authors and illustrators of books for children and young adults (see appendix). Recent winning authors include Julius Lester for *Day of Tears,* Toni Morrison for *Remember: The Journey to School Integration,* and Angela Johnson for *The First Part Last.* Coretta Scott King Award winners for illustration include Bryan Collier for Nikki Giovanni's *Rosa,* Kadir Nelson for Ntozake Shange's *Ellington Was Not a Street,* and Ashley Bryan for *Beautiful Blackbird.*

The Pura Belpré Award (see appendix) honors Latino writers and illustrators whose work best portrays, affirms, and celebrates the Latino cultural experience in the work of literature for youth. A relatively new award, recent winners include authors Viola Canales for *The Tequila Worm,* Julia Alvarez for *Before We Were Free,* Pam Muñoz Ryan for *Esperanza Rising,* and Alma Flor Ada for *Under the Royal Palms: A Childhood in Cuba.* Pura Belpré illustrator awards include Raul Colon for Pat Mora's *Dona Flor,* Yuyi Morales for *Just a Minute,* Susan Guevara for Gary Soto's *Chato and the Party Animals,* and Carmen Lomas Garza for *Magic Windows.*

The Notable Books for a Global Society provides an annual list of outstanding trade books for enhancing student understanding of people and cultures throughout the world (see appendix). The notable multicultural books selected must meet one or more of the following criteria:

1. Portray cultural accuracy and authenticity of characters in terms of:
   a. physical characteristics.
   b. intellectual abilities and problem-solving capabilities.
   c. leadership and cooperative dimensions.
   d. social and economic status.
2. Be rich in cultural details.
3. Honor and celebrate diversity as well as common bonds in humanity.
4. Provide in-depth treatment of cultural issues.
5. Include characters with a cultural group or between two or more cultural groups who interact substantively and authentically.
6. Include members of a "minority" group for a purpose other than filling a "quota."
7. Invite reflection, critical analysis, and response.
8. Demonstrate unique language or style.
9. Meet generally accepted criteria of quality for the genre in which they are written.
10. Have an appealing format and be of endearing quality.

Recent recipients of this honor include Demi's *The Hungry Coat: A Tale of Turkey* (Middle Eastern), Margot Theis Raven's *Circle Unbroken* (African American), Pamela Turner's *Hachiko: The True Story of a Loyal Dog* (Japanese), and Jacqueline Woodson's *Coming on Home Soon* (African American).

Both children's literature and multicultural literacy experts offer general guidelines for evaluating and selecting multicultural literature that meets high standards (Darigan, Tunnell, & Jacobs, 2002; Kiefer, Hepler, & Hickman, 2007). Even criteria for specific cultures assures alignment between children and authentic cultural experiences (Hefflin & Barksdale-Ladd, 2001). All multicultural literature must first and foremost fulfill the same standards for literary traits that are used to scrutinize all types of quality children's literature. In addition, the following criteria blend into a structured template for scrutinizing quality multicultural literature across genres.

Characters

- Characters should authentically reflect the distinct cultural experience of a specific cultural group.
- Names of characters should be culturally authentic, and their personalities should reflect believable attributes.
- Characterization should be true to life and balanced, representing both positive and negative behaviors and traits.
- Perpetuation of cultural stereotypes must be avoided.
- Gender roles within the culture should be portrayed authentically, reflecting the changing roles and status of women and men in cultures.

Settings

- Settings should be representative of and consistent with a historical or contemporary time, place, or situation of a particular culture.
- Factual information describing a historical setting must be accurate in detail.
- Contemporary settings must align with current situations of a cultural group.

Themes

- Themes should be consistent with the values, beliefs, customs, traditions, and conflicts of the specific cultural group.
- Social issues and conflicts related to cultural groups should be treated honestly, accurately, and openly.

Language

- Language should reflect the distinctive vocabulary, style, and patterns of speech of the cultural group.
- Dialect should be natural and blend with plot and characterization while not being perceived as substandard language.
- Language should represent sensitivity to a people; derogatory terms should be excluded unless essential to a conflict or used in historical context.

Illustrations

- Physical characteristics of people of a diverse culture should replicate natural appearance and avoid stereotypes.
- Illustrations should reflect accurate cultural setting.
- Characters should be portrayed as unique individuals within a culture.
- Illustrations should complement and enhance imagery of the story.

The application of these criteria ensures that children of all cultures who see themselves in a book will experience self-worth from the illustrations they view, the words they read, and the characters with whom they identify. A book should fill the reader of another culture with a positive view and clearer understanding of the represented culture. All readers should depart the multicultural reading experience with a more accurate understanding of both themselves and others.

BENEFITS OF MULTICULTURAL LITERATURE

When seeking reasons to include multicultural literature in the classroom, teachers readily define a strong rationale for integration across the curriculum. Benefits of linking multicultural literature to curricular topics abound and result in meaningful instruction. Multicultural literature delivered through varied curricular models is associated with these benefits:

- An understanding of cultural groups (African American, Native American, Latino, Asian American, and others)
- An increased respect among and between members of cultural groups

- A self-understanding from the perspective of members of a cultural group
- A call for social action to assure the equality of cultural groups within our society and around the world

Banks (1989) described a hierarchy of four curricular models for integrating multicultural/multiethnic content into the curriculum. They provide a meaningful framework through which to address possible response-based connections between the reader and multicultural literature. Teachers must view these as models that can be addressed within the existing curriculum, rather than perceiving them as an addendum to the already weighty burden of content-specific curriculum. This discussion serves to link these curricular models with current literature and response-based activities.

The lowest level of the multicultural hierarchy is the **contributions approach,** in which readers read about and discuss ethnic holidays, heroes, and customs. The teacher may read *Martin's Big Words* by Doreen Rappaport to commemorate the birthday of Dr. Martin Luther King or share *Moses: When Harriet Tubman Led Her People to Freedom* by Carole Boston Weatherford during Black History month. Unfortunately, this is the multicultural level at which most classrooms currently function, yet it serves as a springboard for higher-level connections through response. Because biographies so readily fit the contributions approach, biopoems and prompts that address character traits are highly appropriate response connections. Suggesting that students design a bulletin board based on literature titles or research facts on a hero or holiday also extends response. Even basic factual information about cultures and people of culture broadens understanding of a cultural group.

The second level is the **ethnic additive approach,** in which content and themes that reflect other cultures are added to the existing curriculum, maintaining its purpose and structure. Multicultural literature is added to curriculum but not necessarily viewed from a cultural perspective. For example, a kindergarten teacher may read Debbi Chocolate's *Kente Colors* because recognizing colors is a learning outcome. The teacher emphasizes the colors described rather than discussing the culturally distinctive kente cloth. Folktales also abound at this level because they carry the reader to a variety of cultures that share similar stories. A prime example is the multicultural versions of Cinderella ranging from John Steptoe's *Mufaro's Beautiful Daughters,* which carries the reader to Zimbabwe, or Robert San Souci's *Cendrillon,* which is embedded in Caribbean lore. In this scenario, comparison/contrast serves as a higher level interpretive response. The context of culture within the existing curriculum strives to deepen a personal understanding of cultural groups.

The third level, the **transformation approach,** actually changes the structure of the curriculum to enable readers to view problems and themes from the perspective of different ethnic and cultural groups. An appropriate example is a study of Lewis and Clark, the Louisiana Purchase, and the expedition West during the early 1800s. An important part of American history, it has been viewed through the unlikely eyes of York, a black slave who accompanied them on the journey. Laurence Pringle's *American Slave, American Hero: York of the Lewis and Clark Expedition* reveals the perspective of Captain Clark's slave who dared to dream of freedom as he gazed at the vastness of the wilderness yet unexplored. Carolyn Reeder's *Across the Lines*

RESOURCES ON THE WEB
Global Cultures
The Internet provides teachers and students the opportunity to open their doors and invite the outside world into their classrooms. The following websites offer reviews of multicultural international literature and ideas for selecting and using these books in the classroom.

The Mildred L. Batchelder Award (ALA)
This award is given annually to an American publisher for a children's book considered to be the most outstanding of those books originally published in a foreign language in a foreign country, and subsequently translated into English and published in the United States.
http://www.ala.org/ala/alsc/awardsscholarships/literaryawds/ batchelderaward/batchelderaward.htm

Coretta Scott King Author Award (ALA)
This award (or awards) is given to an African American author and an African American illustrator for an outstandingly inspirational and educational contribution. Visit the *Coretta Scott King Book Award* page to learn more about the Coretta Scott King Award, the selection process, and past and present winners and honor books.
http://www.ala.org/ala/emiert/corettascottkingbookawards/ corettascott.htm

The Pura Belpré Award (ALA)
The Pura Belpré Award, is presented to a Latino/Latina writer and illustrator whose work best portrays, affirms, and celebrates the Latino cultural experience in children's literature. Visit this site for more information and links to past and present winners.
http://www.ala.org/ala/alsc/awardsscholarships/literaryawds/ belpremedal/ belprmedal. htm

Multicultural Children's Literature
Complied by the North Central Regional Educational Laboratory, this website offers links to listings and reviews of multicultural children's literature.
http://www.ncrel.org/sdrs/areas/issues/educatrs/presrvce/ pe3lk28.htm

How to Choose the Best Multicultural Books
In this *Scholastic Instructor* online article, teachers will find reviews of multicultural books suitable for grades K–8; advice from authors such as Gary Soto, Floyd Cooper, and Patricia Polacco; and key criteria for selecting books.
http://teacher.scholastic.com/products/instructor/ multicultural.htm

Vandergrift's Children's Literature Page
This site contains links of children's literature that contain realistic stories and also depict positive visual images of children from

reveals the contrasting human sides of the Civil War as Edward, a plantation owner's son, and Simon, his black companion and servant, share their close friendship, different choices, and the demands of the new freedom from alternating points of view. Insights gained through a fresh historical perspective may be gathered in a character journal or a literature response journal. Viewing historical events from an alternative perspective increases self-understanding of cultures through humane cultural literature experiences.

The highest level of Banks's hierarchy is the **social action approach.** Readers are challenged to identify social problems, make decisions, and take action to resolve problems. Identification through literature, critical response analysis, and a plan of action related to cultural differences provide an outstanding outlet for response to literature. The cognitive aspects of reader response (prediction, speculation, problem solving, decision making) become paramount because societal issues are the focus of discussion and personal thought. For example, the issue of racial discrimination can be introduced through Diane Shore and Jessica Alexander's *This Is the Dream.* This picture book highlights places people could not go or things they could not do because of color. Response takes the form of discussing ways in which discrimination still exists and what can be done to alleviate discrimination in our schools, our communities, and our nation. Motivating readers to seek equality for individuals of all cultures reaps both personal and societal benefits.

These four levels of multicultural involvement through literature set high standards and a hierarchical ladder of participation for teachers and students. Teachers often lack confidence to move beyond the first level because their lack of comfort with multicultural literature creates uncertainty about how they can increase its effective use in their classrooms. Banks's categories, supported by a growing knowledge of multicultural titles, provide the sense of direction teachers need for gradual but committed growth to multicultural education.

QUALITY MULTICULTURAL LITERATURE IN THE CLASSROOM

As children of culturally and linguistically diverse backgrounds continue to be a growing portion of our country's population, the need and desire to publish multicultural children's literature remain strong. Strong literature-based programs in our schools demand that children of color have access to literature that is relevant to their own lives and portrays all children, not merely those of the dominant culture. Our growing consciousness of our global society requires that all children be exposed to a multicultural perspective, and multicultural literature provides a means for accomplishing this end.

The quantity and quality of multicultural titles has grown tremendously in the past decade. The fourth edition of *Kaleidoscope,* edited by Hansen-Krening, Aoki, and Mizokawa (2003), contains hundreds of annotations selected from a larger pool of quality books of multiethnic diversity that direct teachers to contemporary issues in books that showcase respect and responsibility. Professional books (Dressel, 2003; Henderson & May, 2005) and recent journal articles (Dressel, 2005; Landt, 2006; Louie, 2005) exist to assist teachers in sharing these titles with children and young adults. Belinda Louie (2006) presents research-based "Guiding Principles" to assist teachers with instructional strategies to enhance student

diverse cultural and ethnic backgrounds. Click on the links: *African-American, Part One A–M; African-American, Part Two M–Z; Asian-American Hispanic-American; Native-American.*
http://www.scils.rutgers.edu/~kvander/ChildrenLit/index.html

International Children's Digital Library
In a joint effort by University of Maryland's Human-Computer Interaction Lab and The Internet Archive, the ICDL brings an extensive library of international children's literature. The site makes hundreds of children's books freely available on the Web at no cost to the user. The books are fully illustrated and in their original languages.
http://www.icdlbooks.org/

Book Box
BookBox is essentially a Web-based jukebox of digital books in languages from around the world. It synchronizes the text, audio, and visual media to create an educational and entertaining reading experience for children.
http://www.bookbox.com/(see also http://www.planetread.org/)

Multicultural Authors
Virginia Hamilton
Virginia Hamilton Official Website
http://www.virginiahamilton.com/
Meet the Author – Virginia Hamilton
http://www.eduplace.com/kids/hmr/mtai/hamilton.html

Gary Soto
The Official Gray Soto Website
http://www.garysoto.com
Meet the Author – Gary Soto
http://www.eduplace.com/kids/hmr/mtai/soto.html

Alma Flor Ada
AlmaFlorAda.com
http://www.almaflorada.com
Meet the Author – Alma Flor Ada
http://www.eduplace.com/kids/tnc/mtai/ada.html

Linda Sue Park
Official Website of Children's Author Linda Sue Park
http://www.lspark.com/
KidsReads.com – Linda Sue Park
http://www.kidsreads.com/authors/au-park-linda-sue.asp

understanding and enjoyment of stories about diverse cultural groups. These principles include the following:

- Check the authenticity of the story.
- Understand the world of the ethnic characters.
- See the world through the characters' perspectives.
- Identify values that shape the characters' conflict-resolution strategies.
- Relate self to the text and critique the portrayal of characters in the text and in popular media.
- Use variants of the same story or collections of stories to help students to build a schema.
- Talk, write, and respond throughout the reading of the multicultural texts. (pp. 438–440)

The cross-cultural possibilities that may result from multicultural units involving these powerful response strategies should motivate and compel children to embrace multicultural literature in the classroom.

READER RESPONSE TO MULTICULTURAL LITERATURE

Response to literature that reflects a multicultural society provides essential opportunities for readers to interact with texts by expressing opinions and reactions to similarities and differences in cultures other than their own. All response activities discussed throughout this entire text are also applicable to multicultural titles. This section of this chapter, however, travels through each genre, citing response connections specific to the genre while providing specific response activities for quality multicultural titles. A genre approach provides an effective means to link reader response and multicultural literature.

Each of the following sections suggests types of response connections to multicultural literature in each genre and is supplemented by a list of quality multicultural titles from the genre. Each bibliographic entry lists a represented culture and the suggested grade level (P, grades K–2; I, grades 3–5; M, grades 6–8) for response connections. A shift in publication beyond the abundance of African American literature toward Latino American literature was apparent during the past few years. Asian American and Native American cultures still seek additional quality authors and illustrators from their respective cultures to contribute to their ethnic literature. The culture of the Middle East is steadily entering this realm of cultural discovery and appreciation.

Response to picture storybooks.   Reader response to multicultural literature may begin with the simple length—but meaningful content—of a multicultural picture storybook. Many of these titles reflect a character of a specific culture but share a universal message. Response begins with a memorable read-aloud followed by response prompts designed to impart a personal response to the book (see Chapter 10). A Chinese American selection such as Lenore Look's *Uncle Peter's Amazing Chinese Wedding* might result in a read-aloud and response that indicates connections between Jenny's life and the reader's own family wedding traditions. The story reflects a strong sense of family, and its message is applicable across cultures.

Children readily connect a sense of family and tradition across cultures.
Reprinted with the permission of Atheneum Books for Young Readers, an imprint of Simon & Schuster Children's Publishing Division from Uncle Peter's Amazing Chinese Wedding *by Lenore Look, illustrated by Yumi Heo. Illustrations copyright © 2006 Yumi Heo.*

A culturally specific read-aloud of Milly Lee's *Landed* results in aesthetic connections reflecting the struggle between the anticipation of a new home in a strange land and constant yearning for one's homeland and cultural heritage. Many children in today's classroom will readily identify with the meaning and message of titles like these. Children may respond to Tamar's *Garden of Happiness* by noting how people of all cultures cooperate to produce an aesthetic garden in an urban neighborhood. Avoiding didacticism, these titles inevitably pull children of all cultures together through common human experiences. Experiential prompts provide the most effective responses to these stories of true to life people of all the colors of the human race. The picture storybooks listed in Figure 8.1 are brief read-alouds, but they have a powerful impact as children of all cultures reflect and connect to their own lives.

Response to traditional literature. The genre that has the power to transport the reader around the entire globe through simple story is traditional literature—myths, legends, and folktales. Whether reading common tales across cultures or following a global journey across continents and cultures, traditional tales provide a valuable source for response to their multicultural nature. Three response goals are paramount in sharing multicultural traditional tales:

1. Identifying visual and verbal cues to the specific culture
2. Identifying intertextual connections and commonalities between and among tales of varying cultures
3. Creating a pleasurable, interesting experience with the literature of another culture

FIGURE 8.1 Book Cluster: Multicultural picture books

African American

Collier, Bryan (2000). *Uptown*. New York: Holt. [P/I]

Daly, Nikki (2001). *What's cooking, Jamela?* Cambridge, MA: Candlewick. [P]

Fraustino, Lisa Rowe (2001). *The hickory* chair. Illus. by Benny Andrews. New York: Scholastic. [P/I]

Grimes, Nikki (2002). *Danitra Brown leaves town*. Illus. by Floyd Cooper. New York: HarperCollins. [P]

Holiday, Billie, & Herzog, Arthur, Jr. (2004). *God bless the child*. Illus. by Jerry Pinkney. New York: Amistad/HarperCollins. [P/I]

Mollel, Tololwa M. (2000). *Subira subira*. Illus. by Linda Saport. Boston: Houghton Mifflin. [P]

Stock, Catherine (2001). *Gugu's house*. New York: Clarion. [P]

Stuve-Bodeen, Stephanie (2002). *Elizabeti's school*. Illus. by Christy Hale. New York: Lee & Low. [P]

Woodson, Jacqueline (2005). *Show way*. Illus. by Hudson Talbott. New York: Putnam. [P/I]

Asian American

Louie, Therese On (2002). *Raymond's perfect present*. Illus. by Suling Wang. New York: Lee & Low.

Namioka, Lensey (2001). *The hungriest boy in the world*. Illus. by Aki Sogabe. New York: Holiday House [P]

Pak, Soyung (1999). *Dear Juno*. Illus. by Susan K. Hartung. New York: Viking. [P]

Say, Allen (1999). *Tea with milk*. Boston: Houghton Mifflin. [P/I]

Say, Allen (2005). *Kamishibai man*. Boston: Houghton Mifflin. [P/I]

Williams, Laura E (2006). *The best winds*. Illus. by Eujin Kim Neilan. Honesdale, PA: Boyds Mills Press. [P/I]

Wong, Janet (2000). *This next new year*. Illus. by Yangsook Choi. New York: Farrar, Straus & Giroux. [P]

Latino American

Ada, Alma Flor (2002). *I love Saturdays y domingos*. Illus. by Elivia Savadier. New York: Atheneum. [P]

Andrews-Goebel, Nancy (2002). *The pot that Juan built*. Illus. by David Diaz. New York: Lee & Low. [P/I]

Bernier-Grand, Carmen T. (2005). *Cesar: !Se, se puende! Yes, we can!* Illus. by David Diaz. New York: Marshall Cavendish. [P/I]

Delacre, Lulu (2005) *Arrorro, Mi Nino: Latino lullabies and gentle games*. New York: Lee & Low. [P]

Elya, Susan Middleton (2006). *Bebe goes shopping*. Illus. by Steven Salerno. San Diego: Harcourt. [P]

Jiminez, Francisco (1998). *La mariposa*. Illus. by Simon Silva. Boston: Houghton Mifflin. [P]

Leiner, Katherine (2001). *Mama does the mambo*. Illus. by Edel Rodriguez. New York: Hyperion. [P/I]

O'Neill, Alexis (2002). *Estela's swap*. Illus. by Enrique O. Sanchez. New York: Lee & Low. [P]

Perez, L. King (2002). *First day in grapes*. Illus. by Robert Casilla. New York: Lee & Low. [P]

Robledo, Honorio (2001). *Nico visits the moon/Nico visita la luna*. El Paso, TX: Cinco Puntos Press. [P]

Ryan, Pam Muñoz (2001). *Mice and beans*. Illus. by Joe Cepeda. New York: Scholastic. [P]

Salas-Porras, Pipina (2001). *El ratoncito pequeño/The little mouse*. Illus. by José Cisneros. El Paso, TX: Cinco Puntos Press. [P]

Soto, Gary (2000) *Chato and the party animals*. Illus. by Susan Guevera. New York: Putnam.

Soto, Gary (2006) *My little car*. Illus. by Pam Pararone. New York: Putnam. [P]

FIGURE 8.1 Continued

> **Native American**
>
> Dengler, Marianna (1996). *The worry stone.* Illus. by Sibyl Graber Gerig. Flagstaff, AZ: Northland/Rising Moon. [I]
> Schick, Eleanor (1996). *My Navajo sister.* New York: Simon & Schuster. [P]
> Van Camp, Richard (1997). *A man called Raven.* Illus. by George Littlechild. New York: Children's Book Press [P/I]

Most traditional tales are published in the picture book format, inviting readers to respond to cultural specifics through both text and illustrations. Children's response might initially focus on the unique apparent differences of a culture—clothing, language, names, homes. With appropriate prompts and teacher planning, children can grow toward a recognition of cultural commonalities—role of family, valued human traits, cleverness and wit, the triumph of good over evil. A sound background of traditional literature deemed important in one's own culture is essential for these higher-level connections to occur between and among cultures.

Because traditional tales have roots in the oral tradition, response to these tales results from oral retellings, storytelling, or dramatic reenactments. Memorable characters, specific themes, and repetitive actions provide structure for response. Huy Voun Lee's *In the Leaves,* a story sharing written Chinese characters, begs response through written replication. Both John Bierhorst's *Is My Friend at Home? Pueblo Fireside Tales* and Joseph Bruchac's *Crazy Horse's Vision* contain the elements for retelling the folktale orally in the primary and intermediate grades. The titles listed in Figure 8.2 celebrate the oral tradition and invite oral and written response.

A common classroom response activity is to compare and contrast variants of traditional tales from various cultures. The 500 variants of Cinderella, for example, differ in name, characters, objects, and settings, but the literary element of theme remains constant and binds various cultures around the world together. An in-depth study and comparative response to Cinderella variants enhance understandings, appreciations, and respect for various cultural groups (Kaminski, 2002; Yang, Siu-Runyan, & Vilscek, 1997). Comparisons among settings, characters' appearances, and cultural values as well as themes provide opportunities for personal response through cultural charts, story maps, or oral discussion. The titles listed in Figure 8.3 are intended for both primary and intermediate levels and provide only a cross section of the cultures that embrace the Cinderella tale. Finally, multicultural traditional tales should be enjoyed aesthetically for the wonderful stories they tell. These are often the stories that stay with the reader long after the read-aloud and the response.

Response to multicultural poetry. Multicultural poetry strikes the same emotional chord within us that all poetry does. Its rhyme and rhythm and its flowing lines appeal to our inner senses. The experiences it shares allow for immediate

FIGURE 8.2 Book Cluster: Multicultural traditional tales

African American

Bryan, Ashley (2002). *Beautiful blackbird.* New York: Atheneum. [P/I]

Burns, Khephra (2001). *Mansa Musa: The lion of Mali.* Illus. by Leo & Diane Dillon. New York: Gulliver. [I/M]

Diakite, Baba Wague (1999). *The hatseller and the monkeys.* New York: Scholastic. [P/I]

Hamilton, Virginia (1995). *Her stories: African American folktales, fairy tales, and true tales.* Illus. by Leo & Diane Dillon. New York: Scholastic. [I/M]

Hamilton, Virginia (1997). *A ring of tricksters: Animal tales from America, the West Indies, and Africa.* Illus. by Barry Moser. New York: Scholastic. [P/I]

Hamilton, Virginia (2004). *The people could fly: The picture book.* Illus. by Leo & Diane Dillon. New York: Knopf. [I/M]

Kimmell, Eric A (2002). *Anansi and the magic stick.* Illus. by Janet Stevens. New York: Holiday House. [P]

Lester, Julius (2005) *The old African.* Illus. by Jerry Pinkney. New York: Dial. [P/I]

Musgrove, Margaret (2001). *The spider weaver: A legend of Kente cloth.* Illus. by Julia Cairns. New York: Scholastic. [P/I]

Asian American

Fu, Shelley (Reteller) (2001). *Ho Yi the archer and other classic Chinese tales.* Illus. by Joseph F. Abboreno. New York: Linnet. [I/M]

Myers, Tim (2000). *Basho and the fox.* Illus. by Oki S. Han. New York: Cavendish. [P/I]

Simonds, Nina, & Swartz, Leslie (2002). *Moonbeams, dumplings, and dragon boats: A treasury of Chinese holiday tales, activities, and recipes.* Illus. by M. So. San Diego: Harcourt. [I]

Latino American

Gerson, Mary-Joan (2001). *Fiesta femenina: Celebrating women in Mexican folktales.* Illus. by Maya Christina Gonzalez. New York: Barefoot. [I/M]

Gonzalez, Lucia M. (1997). *Señor Cat's romance and other favorite stories from Latin America.* Illus. by Lulu Delacre. New York: Scholastic. [P/I]

Montes, Marisa (2000). *Juan Bobo goes to work.* Illus. by Joe Cepeda. New York: HarperCollins. [P]

Native American

Bierhorst, John (Reteller) (2001). *Is my friend at home? Pueblo fireside tales.* Illus. by Wendy Watson. New York: Farrar, Straus & Giroux. [P]

Bruchac, Joseph (2000). *Crazy Horse's vision.* Illus. by S. D. Nelson. New York: Lee & Low. [I]

Bruchac, Joseph, & Bruchac, James (2001). *How chipmunk got his stripes.* Illus. by Joe Aruego and Arlane Dewey. New York: Dial. [P]

Curry, Jane Louise (Reteller) (2001). *The wonderful sky boat and other Native American tales of the Southwest.* New York: McElderry. [I/M]

connections to our own. The carefully selected word choices make us appreciate the power of language. Multicultural poetry, however, inspires all of these authentic responses within the context of a specific culture. Having poems read aloud by a member of a culture makes for a special response experience. The emphatic

FIGURE 8.3   Multicultural versions of the Cinderella tale [all P/I]

Bernhard, Emery (1994). *The girl who wanted to hunt: A Siberian tale*. Illus. by Durga Bernhard. New York: Holiday House.

Brown, Marcia (1971). *Cinderella or the little glass slipper*. New York: Charles Scribner's Sons. (France)

Climo, Shirley (1989). *The Egyptian Cinderella*. Illus. by Ruth Heller. New York: HarperCollins.

Climo, Shirley (1993). *The Korean Cinderella*. Illus. by Ruth Heller. New York: HarperCollins.

Daly, Jude (2000). *Fair, brown and trembling: An Irish Cinderella story*. New York: Farrar, Straus & Giroux.

Hamilton, Virginia (1995). "Catskinella." *In Her stories: African American folktales, fairy tales, and true tales* (pp. 23–27). Illus. by Leo & Diane Dillon. New York: Blue Sky/Scholastic.

Han, Oki S. (1996). *Kongi and Potgi: A Cinderella story from Korea*. Illus. by Stephanie Plunkett. New York: Dial.

Hayes, Joe (Reteller) (2000). *Estrella de Oro/Little Gold Star: A Cinderella cuento retold in Spanish and English*. Illus. by Gloria Osuna Perez and Lucia Angela Perez. El Paso, TX: Cinco Puntos Press.

Hooks, William H. (1987). *Moss gown*. Illus. by Donald Carrick. Boston: Clarion. (N. Carolina)

Huck, Charlotte (1989). *Princess Furball*. Illus. by Anita Lobel. New York: Greenwillow. (Germany)

Jacobs, Joseph (1989). *Tattercoats*. Illus. by Margot Tomes. New York: Putnam. (England)

Louie, Ai-Ling (1982). *Yeh-shen: A Cinderella story from China*. Illus. by Ed Young. New York: Philomel Books.

Martin, Rafe (1992). *The rough-face girl*. Illus. by David Shannon. New York: Putnam. (Algonquin/Native American)

Pollock, Penny (1996). *The turkey girl*. Illus. by Ed Young. Boston: Little, Brown. (Zuni/Native American)

San Souci, Robert D. (1989). *The talking eggs*. Illus. by Jerry Pinkney. New York: Dial. (Louisiana)

San Souci, Robert D. (1994). *Sootface: An Ojibwa Cinderella story*. Illus. by Daniel San Souci. New York: Bantam Doubleday Doll. (Native American)

San Souci, Robert D. (Reteller). (2000). *Little Gold Star: A Spanish American Cinderella tale*. Illus. by Sergio Martinez. New York: HarperCollins.

San Souci, Robert D. (2001). *Cendrillon: A Caribbean Cinderella*. Illus. by Brian Pinkney. New York: Simon & Schuster.

Schroeder, Alan (1997). *Smoky Mountain Rose: An Appalachian Cinderella*. Illus. by Brad Sneed. New York: Dial.

Silverman, Erica (1999). *Raisel's riddle*. Illus. by Susan Graber. New York: Farrar, Straus & Giroux.

Steptoe, John (1987). *Mufaro's beautiful daughter: An African tale*. New York: Lothrop, Lee & Shepard.

Wilson, Barbara Ker (1993). *Wishbones: A folk tale from China*. Illus. by Meilo So. New York: Bradbury.

Winthrop, Elizabeth (1991). *Vasilissa the beautiful: A Russian folktale*. Illus. by Alexander Koshkin. New York: HarperCollins.

articulation, appropriate pauses, and authentic dialect of an African American or Hispanic American voice brings special life and light to the poetry presentation.

Children's responses to multicultural poetry begin with the oral connection. Nikki Grimes wrote and Cozbi A. Cabrera illustrated *Thanks a Million*. Acrylic illustrations showcase 16 poems ranging from haiku to rebus to riddle that remind us how wonderful it is to share a simple "thank you" for those things for which we

The rhyme and rhythm of multicultural poetry invites choral reading and oral connections to the reader's own life. *From* Thanks a Million *by Nikki Grimes, jacket art © 2006 by Cozbi A. Cabrera. Used by permission of HarperCollins Publishers.*

Poems by NIKKI GRIMES *Pictures by* COZBI A. CABRERA

Thanks a Million

are grateful. Children will readily respond to the illustrations and well-written poems that pay tribute to the simple things in life that are special. Stories of their own "thank you's" to personal heroes will abound as children respond to the prompt "What/who does this poem remind you of in your own life?" Grimes's selection of poems sensitively portrays all kinds of appreciation, so no child will feel excluded from the discussion.

Intermediate readers especially want to become a part of the poem through choral reading. Providing a cultural read-aloud model followed by direct participation may itself provide a cultural response as children attempt to match rhythm, tempo, and the authentic language of the poem. For example, Lissette Norman's *My Feet Are Laughing* contains the title poem that encourages dialogue to flow from the lips of the reader. The words offer an invitation to learn more about the African American culture, and that appreciation itself becomes a response.

Response to multicultural poetry can also be extended through an artistic response. As children examine the intriguing mixed-media constructions in Brian Swann's *Touching the Distance: Native American Riddle-Poems,* they can share the solutions to the riddles through their own art. Emotions of middle-school students can be captured through artwork in response to Philippe Lardy's symbolic representations of Marilyn Nelson's sonnets in *A Wreath for Emmett Till*. Oral discussion on the meaning or messages of poems can bring about cultural understandings, but the beauty and distinction of a multicultural poem lies in its use of language to capture the values, priorities, and visions of a culture (see Figure 8.4). An appreciation of and response to the special language of poetry would be a desired response at any age level.

FIGURE 8.4   Book Cluster: Multicultural poetry

African American

Dunbar, Paul Laurence (2000). *Jump back, honey.* Illus. by A. Bryan, C. Buard, J. Spivey Gilchrist, B. Pinkney, J. Pinkney, and Faith Ringgold. New York: Hyperion. [I/M]
Medina, Tony (2002). *Love to Langston.* Illus. by R. Gregory Christie. New York: Lee & Low. [I/M]
Muse, Daphne (2006). *The entrance place of wonders: Poems of the Harlem Renaissance.* Illus. by Charlotte Riley-Webb. New York: Abrams. [P/I]
Nelson, Marilyn (2001). *Carver: A life in poems.* Asheville, NC: Front Street. [M]
Nikola-Lisa, W. (2006). *How we are smart.* Illus. by Sean Qualls. New York: Lee & Low. [I/M]
Tadjo, Veronique (Ed.) (2004). *Talking drums: A selection of poems from Africa south of the Sahara.* New York: Bloomsbury. [I/M]

Asian American

Cheng, Andrea (2005). *Shanghai messenger.* Illus. by Ed Young. New York: Lee & Low. [I/M]
Gollub, Matthew (1998). *Cool melons—Turn to frogs! The life and poems of Issa.* Illus. by Kazuko G. Stone. New York: Lee & Low. [P/I]
Mak, Kam (2002). *My Chinatown: One year in poems.* New York: HarperCollins. [I/M]
Young, Ed (2005). *Beyond the great mountains: A visual poem about China.* San Francisco: Chronicle Books. [I/M]

Latino American

Alarcon, Francisco X. (2001). *Iguanas in the snow and other winter poems/Iguanas en la nieve y otros poemas de invierno.* Illus. by Maya Christina Gonzales. San Francisco: Children's Book Press. [I]
Carlson, Lori Marie (1998). *Sol a sol: Bilingual poems.* Illus. by Emily Lisker. New York: Henry Holt. [P]
Medina, Jane (1999). *My name is Jorge: On both sides of the river.* (Poems in English and Spanish) Illus. by Fabricio Vanden Broeck. Honesdale, PA: Boyds Mills/Wordsong. [I/M]
Stevens, Ilan (2001). *Wáchale! Poetry and prose about growing up Latino in America.* Chicago: Cricket Books. [I/M]

Native American

Begay, Shonto (1995). *Navajo: Visions and voices across the mesa.* New York: Scholastic. [M]
Philip, Neil (Ed.). (1996). *Native American poems.* Photographs by Edward S. Curtis. New York: Viking. [I]
Swann, Brian (1998). *Touching the distance: Native American riddle-poems.* Illus. by Maria Rendon. San Diego: Harcourt Brace. [P]

Response to realistic fiction. The straightforward appeal of characters' personalities and authentic actions in multicultural realistic fiction invite personal connections and reader response. Primarily chapter books, these multicultural titles lend themselves naturally to literature response journals (see Chapter 10) for the intermediate/middle-level reader. They invite spontaneous, ongoing response as the story unfolds and the character develops.

Minimal research has been conducted comparing responses of mainstream readers and readers of a specific culture to multicultural literature. Realistic fiction, however, provides an avenue for response by readers from both within and from those outside the culture. Adolescents will respond openly to Carolyn Marsden's *Moon Runner* or Janet McDonald's *Brother Hood,* both set in urban settings. Sharing these perspectives in literature conversations or in peer sharing sessions might open readers' minds to varying perspectives on a cultural incident or set of values. Because of their contemporary settings and characters close to the age of readers, the appeal of this genre, especially to the grade 5–8 student, is apparent. The realistic fiction titles listed in Figure 8.5 contain the level of emotion and conflict that inspire heartfelt response.

Response to historical fiction. Historical fiction provides an excellent backdrop through which one can experience the life of a character in another historical time and place. A character journal (see Chapter 10) supplies an effective means for taking on the guise of a character and experiencing life from a historical perspective. Multicultural literature provides an additional layer to this simulated experience. The reader not only takes on the persona of the character but also attempts to acquire the perspective of a cultural character, feeling the devastation of war, the ache of discrimination, or the scar of prejudice. The character journal in no way equates the experience of the reader with that of the cultural character. It does, however, attempt to bring a varied perspective to the reader that might otherwise be missed or dismissed during reading. In Julius Lester's *Time's Memory,* the reader is challenge to relive the slave experience. The written response to a culturally defined historical novel enhances the perspective with which historical events and characters may be viewed by the outside culture. A dramatic reenactment or readers' theater script of several of the emotional scenes in the titles listed in Figure 8.6 creates emotional responses to both historical events and human attitudes as well as to literature.

Response to biography/autobiography. The lives of ethnically diverse individuals outside the mainstream culture stand as an inspiration to readers from both within and without a cultural group. People of all cultures show ambition to personally succeed, determination to contribute to a better world, skills to lead armies to victory, and the desire to uncover the secrets of science. The valued personal qualities of the human race are exemplified through people of all cultures. Exposure to biography across cultures is vital for all children. For years, a steady diet of mainstream heroes took precedence over a cultural mix of heroes and heroines.

FIGURE 8.5   Book Cluster: Multicultural realistic fiction

African American

Flake, Sharon G. (2004). *Who am I without him? Short stories about girls and the boys in their lives.*
    New York: Jump at the Sun/Hyperion. [M]
Grimes, Nikki (2003). *Bronx masquerade.* New York: Dial. [M]
Haskins, James (1998). *Moaning bones: African American ghost stories.* New York: Lothrop. [P/I]
Myers, Walter Dean (2000). *145th Street: Short stories.* New York: Delacorte. [M]
Naidoo, Beverly (2001). *The other side of truth.* New York: HarperCollins. [I/M]

Asian American

Lin, Grace (2006). *The year of the dog.* New York: Little, Brown. [I]
Marsden, Carolyn (2004). *Silk umbrellas.* Cambridge, MA: Candlewick. [I]
Na, An (2001). *A step from heaven.* Asheville, NC: Front Street. [M]
Yep, Laurence (2002). *When the circus comes to town.* Illus. by Suling Wang. New York:
    HarperCollins. [I]

Latino American

Delacre, Lulu (2000). *Salsa stories.* New York: Scholastic. [M]
Jaramillo, Ann (2006). *La Linea.* New York: Roaring Brook. [I/M]
Johnston, Tony (2001). *Any small goodness: A novel of the barrio.* Illus. by Raul Colon. New York:
    Scholastic. [I/M]
Martinez, Victor (1996). *Parrot in the oven/Mi vida.* New York: HarperCollins. [I/M]
Soto, Gary (1997). *Buried onions.* New York: Harcourt. [M]

Native American

Bruchac, Joseph (2001). *Skeleton man.* New York: HarperCollins. [M]
Mikaelson, Ben (2001). *Touching Spirit Bear.* New York: HarperCollins. [M]

Multicultural

Fleischman, Paul (1997). *Seedfolks.* New York: HarperCollins. [M]

A concerted effort must be made to include multicultural biographies throughout the entire curriculum, avoiding tokenism by showcasing them throughout the entire school year. Consider the fairness and importance to each child, whatever his or her color, of seeing himself or herself as part of the true account of a famous person of his or her race, ethnic group, color, or culture.

Response to biographical accounts of multicultural lives should focus both on personal traits and cultural contributions of the subject (see Figure 8.7). A biopoem composition following the reading of a Rosa Parks, Nelson Mandela, Jim Thorpe, or Langston Hughes biography reflects personal, historical, and cultural contributions

FIGURE 8.6 Book Cluster: Multicultural historical fiction

African American

Curtis, Christopher Paul (1999). *Bud, not Buddy.* New York: Delacorte. [I]
Moses, Sheila (2004). *The legend of Buddy Bush.* New York: McElderry. [I]
Robinet, Harriette Gillem (2000). *Walking to the bus-rider blues.* New York: Atheneum. [I]
Taylor, Mildred (2001). *The land.* New York: Phyllis Fogelman. [I/M]

Asian American

Park, Linda Sue (2001). *A single shard.* New York: Clarion. [I]
Park, Linda Sue (2002). *When my name was Keoko.* New York: Clarion. [I/M]
Park, Linda Sue (2004). *The firekeeper's son.* New York: Clarion. [I]
Yep, Laurence (2000). *Dream soul.* New York: HarperCollins. [I]
Yin (2001). *Coolies.* Illus. by Chris K. Soentpiet. New York: Philomel. [I]

Latino American

Osa, Nancy (2003). *Cuba 15.* New York: Delacorte. [M]
Ryan, Pam Muñoz (2000). Esperanza rising. New York: Scholastic. [I/M]

Native American

Bruchac, Joseph (2005). *Code talker: A novel about the Navajo Marines in WWII.* New York: Dial. [M]
Carvell, Marlene (2005). *Sweetgrass basket.* New York: Dutton. [I/M]
Cooney, Caroline (2001). *The ransom of Mercy Carter.* New York: Delacorte. [M]
Erdrich, Louise (1999). *The birchbark house.* New York: Hyperion. [I/M]
Erdrich, Louise (2005). *The game of silence.* New York: HarperCollins. [I/M]

(see Chapter 13). More importantly, it reflects the personal strengths that all people require to make a difference in our world. The commonalities of the human spirit are paramount to cultural differences and are reflected through biographical response.

Response to nonfiction books. Nonfiction titles that extend knowledge about cultural groups provide a factual addition to information on a culture. Historical understandings and aesthetic interactions are enriched through the informational perspective on a topic. Response to informational books moves beyond efferent knowledge toward aesthetic connections to people of color and cultural experiences. Ann Bausum's *Freedom Riders: John Lewis and Jim Zwerg on the Front Lines of the Civil Rights Movement* not only provides factual information on the black and white perspectives of the 1960s, but it touches the reader's heart aesthetically because both men possess common needs, goals, and hope for equal rights for the future. Reading informational texts efferently builds factual background, and reader response to informational text builds aesthetic empathy and greater understanding of the human element that links all colors and cultures. The titles in Figure 8.8 reflect the growing quality and diversity of nonfiction related to multicultural topics.

FIGURE 8.7   Book Cluster: Multicultural biography/autobiography

African American

Adler, David A. (2007). *Satchel Paige: Don't look back.* Illus. by Terry Widener. San Diego: Harcourt. [P/I]

Bridges, Ruby (1999). *Through my eyes.* Illus. with photographs. New York: Scholastic. [I/M]

Cline-Ransome, Lesa (2000). *Satchel Paige.* Illus. by James E. Ransome. New York: Simon & Schuster. [I]

Myers, Walter Dean (2001). *The greatest: Muhammad Ali.* New York: Scholastic. [I/M]

Myers, Walter Dean (2001). *Bad boy: A memoir.* New York: HarperCollins. [I/M]

Pinkney, Andrea Davis (2000). *Let it shine: Stories of black women freedom fighters.* Illus. by Stephen Alcorn. San Diego: Harcourt Brace. [I/M]

Rappaport, Doreen (2001). *Martin's big words: The life of Dr. Martin Luther King, Jr.* Illus. by Brian Collier. New York: Jump at the Sun/Hyperion. [P/I/M]

Turner, Glennette Tilley (2006). *An apple for Harriet Tubman.* Illus. by Susan Keeter. Morton Grove, IL: Albert Whitman. [P/I]

Asian American

Burleigh, Robert (2006). *Tiger of the snows: Tenzing Norgay—the boy whose dream was Everest.* Illus. by Ed. Young. New York: Atheneum. [I/M]

Mochizuki, Ken (2006). *Be water, my friend: The early years of Bruce Lee.* Illus. by Dom Lee. New York: Lee & Low. [I/M]

Wong, Li Keng (2006). *Good fortune: My journey to Gold Mountain.* Atlanta, GA: Peachtree.

Yoo, Paula (2005). *Sixteen years in sixteen seconds: The Sammy Lee story.* Illus. by Dom Lee. New York: Lee & Low. [I]

Latino American

Chambers, Veronica (2005). *Celia Cruz, queen of salsa.* Illus. by Julle Maren. New York: Dial. [I]

Jiminez, Francisco (1998). *The circuit: Stories from the life of a migrant child.* Albuquerque, NM: University of New Mexico Press. [M]

Jiminez, Francisco (2001). *Breaking through.* Boston: Houghton Mifflin. [I/M]

Native American

Brown, Don (2006). *Bright path: Young Jim Thorpe.* New Milford, CT: Roaring Brook Press. [P/I]

Bruchac, Joseph (2006). *Jim Thorpe: Original all-American.* New York: Dial. [M]

Crow, Joseph Medicine (2006). *Counting Coup: Becoming a Crow chief on the reservation and beyond.* Washington, DC: National Geographic. [I/M]

Marrin, Albert (2000). *Sitting Bull and his world.* New York: Dutton. [I/M]

Tallchief, Maria (with Rosemary Wells) (1999). *Tallchief: America's prima ballerina.* Illus. by Gary Kelley. New York: Viking. [I]

Middle Eastern

Brown, Tricia (2006). *Salaam: A Muslim American boy's story.* Photos by Ken Cardwell. New York: Henry Holt. [P/I]

Demi (2003). *Mohammed.* New York: McElderry. [I/M]

Winters, Jeanette (2006). *The librarian of Basra: A true story from Iraq.* San Diego: Harcourt. [P/I]

FIGURE 8.8 Book Cluster: Multicultural nonfiction

African

Onyefulu, Ifeoma (1996). *Ogbo: Sharing life in an African village.* San Diego: Gulliver Books/Harcourt Brace. [I]

Williams, Mary (2005). *Brothers in hope: The story of the lost boys of Sudan.* Illus. by R. Gregory Christie. New York: Lee & Low. [I]

African American

Barboza, Steven (1994). *Door of no return: The legend of Goree Island. New York:* Cobblehill/Dutton. [I/M]

Fradin, Dennis Brindell (2000). *Bound for the North Star: True stories of fugitive slaves.* New York: Clarion. [I/M]

Hamilton, Virginia (1993). *Many thousand gone: African Americans from slavery to freedom.* Illus. by Leo & Diane Dillon. New York: Knopf. [I/M]

McKissack, Patricia C., & McKissack, Frederick L. (1994). *Christmas in the big house, Christmas in the quarters.* Illus. by John Thompson. New York: Scholastic. [I/M]

Schlissel, Lillian (1995). *Black frontiers: A history of African American heroes in the old West.* New York: Simon & Schuster. [I/M]

Stanley, Jerry (2001). *Hurry freedom! African Americans in Gold Rush California.* Illus. with photographs. New York: Crown. [I/M]

Asian

Blumberg, Rhoda (2001). *Shipwrecked! The true adventures of a Japanese boy.* New York: HarperCollins. [I/M]

O'Conner, Jane (2002). *The emperor's silent army: Terracotta warriors of ancient China.* New York: Viking. [I/M]

Hispanic American

Ashabranner, Brent (1996). *Our beckoning borders: Illegal immigration in America.* Photographs by Paul Conklin. New York: Cobblehill/Dutton. [I/M]

Hoyt-Goldsmith, Diane (1994). *Day of the dead: A Mexican-American celebration.* Photographs by Lawrence Migdale. New York: Holiday House. [I]

Japanese American

Cooper, Michael L. (2000). *Fighting for honor: Japanese Americans and World War II.* New York: Clarion. [I/M]

Oppenheim, Joanne (2006). *Dear Miss Breed: True stories of the Japanese American incarceration during World War II and the librarian who made a difference.* New York: Scholastic. [M]

Stanley, Jerry (1994). *I am an American: A true story of Japanese internment.* New York: Crown. [I/M]

Latino American

Ancona, George (1998). *Barrio: Jose's neighborhood.* San Diego: Harcourt Brace. [P/I]

Freedman, Russell (2001). *In the days of the vaqueros: America's first true cowboys.* Boston: Clarion. [I/M]

FIGURE 8.8   Continued

Hoyt-Goldsmith, Diane (1999). *Las Posadas: A Hispanic Christmas celebration.* Photos by Lawrence
    Migdale. New York: Holiday House.
King, Elizabeth (1998). *Quinceañera: Celebrating fifteen.* New York: Dutton. [M]
Sandler, Martin W. (2001). *Vaqueros: America's first cowmen.* New York: Henry Holt. [I/M]

Middle East

Frank, Mitch (2005). *Understanding the Holy Land: Questions about the Israeli-Palestinian conflict.*
    New York: Viking. [M]
Macauley, David (2003). *Mosque.* Boston: Houghton Mifflin. [I/M]

Native American

Cooper, Michael (1999). *Indian school: Teaching the white man's way.* New York: Clarion. [I/M]
Philip, Neil (2006). *The great circle: A history of the first nations.* New York: Clarion. [M]
Waldman, Neil (2001). *Wounded Knee.* New York: Atheneum. [M]
Yue, Charlotte, & Yue, David (2000). *The wigwam and the longhouse.* Boston: Houghton Mifflin. [I]

INTERNATIONAL LITERATURE

The current emphasis for children to become aware global citizens has generated an
increasing openness to and curiosity about international literature. Carl Tomlinson's
(1998) *Children's Books from Other Countries* was the first book to make available
a compilation of annotations of books published outside the United States. International literature is defined as "that body of books originally published for children in
a country other than the United States in a language of that country and later published in this country" (Tomlinson, 1998, p. 4). In the narrowest sense, international
literature includes all genres of literature divided into two categories:

- Books originally written in a language other than English and subsequently
  translated into English (e.g., Christina Bjork's *Linnea in Monet's Garden*—
  originally published in Sweden) (see Figure 8.9)
- Books originally written in English but in a country other than the United
  States (e.g., J. K. Rowling's *Harry Potter & the Sorcerer's Stone*—originally
  published in England; Mem Fox's *Wilfred Gordon McDonald Partridge*—
  originally published in Australia) (see Figure 8.10)

A third prospective category includes an undefined area bordering on international literature. Books originally published in the United States for children of this
country, but whose characters and settings are international, abound. Books like Ted
Lewin's *The Storytellers,* Naomi Shahab Nye's *19 Varieties of Gazelle: Poems of
the Middle East,* and Diane Hoyt-Goldsmith's *Celebrating Ramadan* carry the
reader to other countries, but the books were originally published in the United
States. Chapter books such as Alice Mead's *Girl of Kosovo* or Richard Moser's

FIGURE 8.9 Book Cluster: Translated international children's literature

Anno, Mitsumasa (1978/1992). *Anno's journey.* New York: Philomel. (Originally published by Fukuinkan Shoten in Japan)

Beck, Martine (1990). *The wedding of brown bear and white bear.* Illus. by Marie H. Henry. Translated by Aliyah Morgenstern. New York: Little, Brown. (Originally published in France)

Bredsdorff, Bodil (2004). *The crow-girl: The children of crow cave.* Translated from Danish by Faith Ingwersen. New York: Farrar, Straus, & Giroux.

Bjork, Christina (1987). *Linnea in Monet's garden.* Translated by Joan Sandin. Illus. by Lena Anderson. (Originally published in Sweden)

Bjork, Christina (1999). *Vendela in Venice.* Illus. by Inga-Karin Eriksson. Translated by Patricia Crompton. Stockholm/New York: R & S. (Originally published in Sweden)

Buchholz, Quint (1999). *The collector of moments.* Translated by Peter F. Niemeyer. New York: Farrar, Straus & Giroux. (Originally published in Germany)

Carmi, Daniella (2000). *Samir and Yonatan.* Translated from Hebrew by Yael Lotan. New York: Scholastic. (Originally published in Israel)

Ellabbad, Mohieddin (2006). *The illustrator's notebook.* Translated from Arabic by Sarah Quinn. Groundswood.

Funke, Cornelia (2002). *The thief lord.* Translated by Olive Latsch. New York: The Chicken House/Scholastic (Originally published in Germany)

Gallaz, Christophe (1985). *Rose Blanche.* Illus. by Roberto Innocenti. Translated by Martha Covington and Richard Graglia. Creative Education. (Originally published in France)

Garcia, Laura Gallego (2005). *The legend of the wandering king.* Translated from Spanish by Dan Bellm. New York: Arthur Levine/Scholastic.

Ho, Minfong (compiler) (1996). *Maples in the mist: Children's poems from the Tang Dynasty.* Translated by Mingfong Ho. Illus. by Jean & Mou-sein Tseng. New York: Lothrop, Lee & Shepard. (Originally published in China)

Holub, Joseph (1998). *The robber and me.* Translated by Elizabeth D. Crawford. New York: Henry Holt. (Originally published in Germany)

Maruki, Toshi (1982). *Hiroshima no pika.* Translated by Kurita-Bando Literary Agency. New York: Lothrop, Lee & Shepard. (Originally published in Japan)

Orlev, Uri (1991). *The man from the other side.* Translated from Hebrew by Hillel Halkin. Boston: Houghton Mifflin. (Originally published in Israel)

Orlev, Uri (2003). *Run, boy, run.* Translated from Hebrew by Hillel Halkin. Boston: Houghton Mifflin.

Quintana, Anton (1999). *The baboon king.* Translated by John Nieuwenhuizen. New York: Walker. (Originally published in Dutch in the Netherlands)

Stolz, Joelle (2004). *The shadows of Ghadames.* Translated from French by Catherine Temerson. New York: Delacorte.

Varmer, Jhordia (2005). *Hans Christian Andersen: His fairy tale life.* Illus. by Lilian Brogger. Translated from Danish by Tina Nunnally. Toronto: Groundswood.

Zenatti, Valerie (2005). *When I was a soldier.* Translated from French by Adriana Hunter. New York: Bloomsbury.

Zazoo invite the reader into new locations and new cultures yet are not considered international literature in the purest sense. Many of these titles have been included in genre chapters, but they are being compiled and viewed in this potential category that transports the reader to global settings with global characters. Susan Stan's (2002)

FIGURE 8.10   Book Cluster: International books originally published in English in another country

Ahlberg, Janet, & Ahlberg, A. (1986). *The jolly postman and other people's letters.* Illus. by Janet Ahlberg. Boston: Little, Brown (UK)

Almond, David (1999). *Skellig.* New York: Delacorte. (UK)

Baker, Jeannie (1991). *Window.* New York: Greenwillow. (Australia)

Browne, Anthony (1990). *Gorilla.* New York: Knopf. (UK)

Dahl, Roald (1988). *Matilda.* Illus. by Quentin Blake. New York: Viking. (UK)

Ekoomiak, Normee (1990). *Arctic memories.* New York: Henry Holt. (Canada)

Fox, Mem (1985). *Wilfrid Gordon McDonald Partridge.* Illus. by Julie Vivas. La Jolla, CA: Kane/Miller. (Australia)

Hoffman, Mary (1991). *Amazing Grace.* Illus. by Caroline Binch. New York: Dial. (UK)

Hutchins, Pat (1986). *The doorbell rang.* New York: Greenwillow. (UK)

Ibbotson, Eva (2002). *Journey to the river sea.* New York: Dutton. (UK)

Jacques, Brian (1986). *Redwall.* New York: Philomel. (UK)

Mahy, Margaret (1987). *17 kings and 42 elephants.* Illus. by Patricia McCarthy. New York: Dial. (New Zealand)

McNaughton, Colin (1997). *Oops!* San Diego: Harcourt. (UK)

Montgomery, Hugh (2002). *The voyage of the Arctic tern.* Illus. by Nick Poullis. Cambridge, MA: Candlewick. (UK)

Rowling, J. K. (1998). *Harry Potter and the sorcerer's stone.* New York: Scholastic. (UK)

Waddell, Martin (1992). *Can't you sleep, Little Bear?* Illus. by Barbara Firth. Cambridge, MA: Candlewick Press. (UK)

Willliams, Sue (1990). *I went walking.* Illus. by Julie Vivas. San Diego: Harcourt. (Australia)

Wojciechowski, Susan (1995). *The Christmas miracle of Jonathan Toomey.* Illus. By P. J. Lynch. New York: Walker. (Co-published by USA and UK)

The World Through Children's Books and Doris Gebel's (2006) *Crossing Boundaries with Children's Books* organize books geographically by world region and country as well as featuring internationally published literature.

EVALUATING QUALITY INTERNATIONAL LITERATURE

Because knowledge of international children's literature is limited and the number of translated children's books is minimal, teachers and their prospective readers must look to the experts for advice and opinions on quality titles. The United States Board on Books for Young People (USBBY) and its parent organization, the International Board on Books for Young People (IBBY), champion the cause of international literature for children. IBBY is committed to promoting international understanding and world peace through children's books. There are 62 member nations headquartered in Basel, Switzerland. Overall, those involved with children and books should look to international awards to begin their understanding of quality international children's literature.

The Hans Christian Andersen Medal, sponsored by IBBY since 1956, is the most prestigious children's book award in the world. Awarded every two years, it is presented to a living author and illustrator whose complete works have made the most important international contributions to children's literature (see appendix). Author winners include Margaret Mahy (New Zealand), Martin Waddell (Ireland), Aidan Chambers (United Kingdom), Ana Maria Machado (Brazil), Katherine Paterson (United States), Uri Orlev (Israel), and Virginia Hamilton (United States). Illustrator winners include Quentin Blake (United Kingdom), Anthony Browne (United Kingdom), Tomi Ungerer (France), Klaus Ensikat (Germany), and Mitsumasa Anno (Japan). Early winners with whom teachers may have some familiarity are Astrid Lindgren (*Pippi Longstocking*—Sweden) and Meindert DeJong (*The Wheel on the School*—U.S. Newbery Award).

The Mildred L. Batchelder Award is given to the publisher of a children's book that has been translated into English in the previous year and originally appeared in a country other than the United States. Sponsored by the American Library Association, recent winners include Josef Holub's *An Innocent Soldier* (translated from the German by Michael Hoffman), which tells of a young farmhand's experience as a soldier during Napoleon's invasion of Russia in 1811. A Batchelder Honor book for younger children is *Nicolas* by Rene Goscinny (translated from the French by Anthea Bell), which introduces American children to the hilarious escapades of a schoolboy and his classmates in an all-boys' school. If a teacher wants to become familiar with the best translated international children's books available in this country, the Batchelder Award list is the best place to begin (see appendix).

Bookbird: A Journal of International Children's Literature is the journal of IBBY, containing articles and opinion pieces, national book award listings, and important new children's literature reviews. The IBBY Honour List is published every two years and provides a catalog of outstanding recently published books, recommended by IBBY member nations as suitable for publication in other languages. The Honour List is credited with increasing the number of translations and foreign editions of excellent children's books.

Librarians might also become aware of publishers of international children's titles. These are some publishers known for their support of international children's literature:

- Candlewick Press (brings British authors and illustrators to the United States).
- Farrar, Straus & Giroux (distributes through an agreement with Raben and Sjogren, the largest Swedish publisher of children's books).
- Front Street Publishers (translations from the Dutch).
- Kane/Miller Book Publishers (specializes in translated children's books from around the world).
- North-South Books (English imprint of Nord-Sud Verlag, the Swiss children's book publisher).
- Simon & Schuster (publishes picture books and chapter books from other English-speaking countries and translated chapter books). Margaret K. McElderry, imprint of this publisher, is recognized for her leadership in bringing international children's books to the United States.
- Tundra Books (specializes in Canadian, Native American, and French/English titles).

BENEFITS OF INTERNATIONAL LITERATURE

The nature of an expanding global society requires teachers to share literature that expands the literary scenario to an international venue. The value of international children's books in developing an increased understanding for world cultures is unquestionable. Expanding the reading environment to characters from other cultures, settings in other countries, and issues from other cultures fosters a broader perspective beyond reading to a deeper appreciation of the world in which we live. Benefits from reading international literature include increased understanding and cultural growth in these areas.

- The history, traditions, and people of other countries come alive through literature.
- A truer view of life through the eyes of individual characters paints a more understandable perspective and appreciation of the world than television and newspapers.
- Intriguing stories build interest in global people and places, thus creating a deeper understanding and appreciation of the geography and history embedded in the school curriculum.
- Books written by a native of an international setting give authenticity and an international perspective to the existing curriculum.
- International children's books often present language diversity, thus giving authentic insights into the use of foreign language to build respect and pride in one's own heritage.
- The treasured stories of children around the world can be enjoyed by our readers as they develop shared experiences and increase their global perspective. (Tomlinson, 1998)

From David Almond's *Fire Eaters* to Anthony Browne's *Gorilla* (United Kingdom), from Jeannie Baker's *The Hidden Forest* to Mem Fox's *Wilfred Gordon McDonald Partridge* (Australia), readers experience English language in new settings and situation. From Christina Bjork's *Vendela in Venice* to Cornelia Funke's *The Thief Lord*, readers are transported to a European setting for vicarious experiences in Venice, Italy. From Suzanne Fisher Staples's *Under the Persimmon Tree* (Pakistan) to Uri Orlev's *Run, Boy, Run* (Israel), readers gain a fresh perspective on the Middle East. A new generation of "readers of the world" will thrive and deepen their cultural appreciation for global diversity through the growing body of international children's books.

READER RESPONSE TO INTERNATIONAL LITERATURE

Children can become engaged with international children's books in the same effective ways teachers share all quality literature. They should be given opportunities to respond to them through prompts, written journals, drama, extended reading by the same author, author studies, and other effective response opportunities. Because they may seem new and different, teachers must show interest and passion in promoting these stories so children will be willing to try them.

Tomlinson (1998) suggests that teachers can assist in the introduction of international children's literature into the classroom curriculum in the following ways:

- Read international books aloud. Because children may be reluctant to select these for independent reading, they may learn to love them through read-alouds.
- Share international literature through book talks. Show locations of origin on a map and note similarities between international books.
- Display international books in the classroom or the school library.
- List characters and locate settings on maps to assist with differences in international stories.
- Introduce foreign words or terms before reading the book. Pronouncing correctly is ideal but not a necessity. If the story is engaging, the new words will not bother children nor interfere with comprehension.
- Integrate international books with thematic units in social studies or history (e.g., *Rose Blanche* by Christophe Gallaz and Roberto Innocenti–Switzerland, set in World War II Germany).
- Encourage students to research countries in which international literature is set.
- Emphasize both the similarities and differences in book characters' lives with those of readers.
- Create an author or illustrator study of an international author or illustrator (e.g., Anthony Browne).
- Introduce an international pen pal/key pal program as children from two countries read and respond to an international title.

Teachers can become more familiar with international children's books by reading other sources written about this topic. Freeman and Lehman's (2001) *Global Perspectives in Children's Literature* and Hazel Rochman's (1993) *Against Borders: Promoting Books for a Multicultural World* will assist in stretching limited knowledge of global publications by extending boundaries for reading to international literature. This section is intended to whet your appetite for the potential and promise of international literature in the K–8 classroom.

CLOSING THOUGHTS

Multicultural literature celebrates the diversity of the people who represent our communities, our country, and our world. Its inclusion in the curriculum needs to be natural, sincere, and elevated to its proper level of importance. Although multicultural children's literature focuses on literature by and about people who are underrepresented in the school curriculum, we still have a long way to go in believing that multicultural literature should be about all people. In our own honest response to choosing multicultural literature, we must look for authenticity in character, setting, language, clothing, and action. Stereotypes remain pervasive, and the number of books produced about people of color still remains comparatively small.

International literature serves as a vehicle for learning more about the world, thus holding the promise of preserving and extending world peace. Teachers must promote more engagement with translated books, books published in English in other countries, and even titles published in the United States but having foreign characters and settings. Abolishing borders for reading is a way of extending knowledge about the similarities between people of different countries rather than focusing on their differences. Teachers should be challenged to read international children's literature and share its promise of understanding with young readers who will soon grow to be citizens of the world.

The link between multicultural and international literature and aesthetic response might contribute to the building of understandings beyond one's personal realm of experience. As readers, we can move beyond being expressions of our own culture. Readers can transcend culture and begin to understand others and their feelings toward others more clearly. Exposure to multicultural and international children's literature enriched by the challenge of honest response challenges children to share their feelings, including fears and misunderstandings. Response causes us to view the human side of all nations, to think more clearly, and to handle our feelings toward others. Multicultural and international literature provide a means for opening more honest discussions about the oneness of humanity and the equality of all people.

References

Banks, J. A. (1988). *Multicultural education: Issues and perspectives.* Boston: Allyn & Bacon.

Banks, J. A. (1989). Multicultural education: Characteristics and goals. In J. A. Banks & C. A. M. Banks (Eds.), *Multicultural education: Issues and perspectives* (pp. 2–26). Needham Heights, MA: Allyn & Bacon.

Barrera, R. B., & Quiroa, R. E. (2003). The use of Spanish in Latino children's literature in English: What makes for cultural authenticity? In D. L. Fox & K. G. Short (Eds.), *Stories matter: The complexity of cultural authenticity in children's literature* (pp. 247–268). Urbana, IL: National Council of Teachers of English.

Bookbird: A journal of international children's literature. Basel, Switzerland: International Board on Books for Young People. (Published quarterly)

Cai, M., & Bishop, R. (1994). Multicultural literature for children: Towards a clarification of the concept. In A. Dyson & C. Genishi (Eds.), *The need for story: Cultural diversity in classroom and community* (pp. 57–71). Urbana, IL: National Council of Teachers of English.

Ching, S. H. D. (2005). Multicultural children's literature as an instrument of power. *Language Arts, 83,* 128–136.

Darigan, D. L., Tunnell, M. O., & Jacobs, J. S. (2002). *Children's literature: Engaging teachers and children in good books.* Upper Saddle River, NJ: Prentice Hall/Merrill.

Dressel, J. (2003). *Teaching and learning about multicultural literature: Students reading outside their culture in a middle school classroom.* Newark, DE: International Reading Association.

Dressel, J. (2005). Personal response and social responsibility: Responses of middle school students to multicultural literature. *The Reading Teacher, 58,* 750–764.

Fox, D. L., & Short, K. G. (Eds.) (2003). *Stories matter: The complexity of cultural authenticity in children's literature.* Urbana, IL: National Council of Teachers of English.

Freeman, E. B., & Lehman, B. A. (2001). *Global perspectives in children's literature.* Boston: Allyn & Bacon.

Gebel, D. J. (Ed.) (2006). *Crossing boundaries with children's books.* Lanham, MD: Scarecrow Press.

Hansen-Krening, N., Aoki, E. M., & Mizokawa, D. T. (Eds.) (2003). *Kaleidoscope: A multicultural booklist for grades K–8* (4th ed.). Urbana, IL: National Council of Teachers of English.

Harris, V. (Ed.) (1992). *Teaching multicultural literature in grades K–8*. Norwood, MA: Christopher-Gordon.

Harris, V. (Ed.) (1997). *Using multiethnic literature in the K–8 classroom*. Norwood, MA: Christopher-Gordon.

Hefflin, B. R., & Barksdale-Ladd, M. A. (2001). African American children's literature that helps children find themselves: Selection guidelines for K–3. *The Reading Teacher, 54*, 810–819.

Henderson, D., & May, J. (2005). *Exploring culturally diverse literature with children and adolescents*. Boston: Pearson.

Kaminski, R. A. (2002). Cinderella to Rodolphus. *The Dragon Lode, 20*, 31–36.

Kiefer, B. Z., Hepler, S., & Hickman, J. (2007). *Charlotte Huck's children's literature* (9th ed.). Boston: McGraw-Hill.

Landt, S. M. (2006). Multicultural literature and young adolescents: A kaleidoscope of opportunity. *Journal of Adolescent & Adult Literacy, 49*, 690–697.

Louie, B. Y. (2005). Development of empathetic responses with multicultural literature. *Journal of Adolescent and Adult Literacy, 48*, 566–578.

Louie, B. Y. (2006). Guiding principles for teaching multicultural literature. *The Reading Teacher, 59*, 438–448.

Rochman, H. (1993). *Against borders: Promoting books for a multicultural world*. Chicago: American Library Association.

Stan, S. (Ed.) (2002). *The world through children's books*. Lanham, MD: Scarecrow Press.

Tomlinson, C. M. (Ed.) (1998). *Children's books from other countries*. Lanham, MD: Scarecrow Press.

Yang, S., Siu-Runyan, Y., & Vilscek, E. (1997). Stories of Cinderella from around the world. *The Dragon Lode, 15*, 9–15.

Yokota, J. (1993). Issues in selecting multicultural children's literature. *Language Arts, 70*, 156–167.

Children's Books Cited [P] = K–2; [I] = 3–5; [M] = 6–8

Ada, Alma Flor (1998). *Under the royal palms: A childhood in Cuba*. New York: Atheneum. [I/M]

Almond, David (2003). *The fire eaters*. New York: Delacorte. [M]

Alvarez, Julia (2002). *Before we were free*. New York: Knopf. [M]

Baker, Jeannie (2000). *The hidden forest*. New York: Greenwillow. [P]

Bausum, Ann (2006). *Freedom riders: John Lewis and Jim Zwerg on the front lines of the Civil Rights Movement*. Washington, DC: National Geographic. [I/M]

Bierhorst, Joseph (2001). *Is my friend at home? Pueblo fireside tales*. Illus. by Wendy Watson. New York: Farrar, Straus & Giroux. [P/I]

Bjork, Christina (1987). *Linnea in Monet's garden*. Illus. by Lena Anderson. Translated from the Swedish by Joan Sandin. New York: R & S. [I]

Bjork, Christina (1999). *Vendela in Venice*. Illus. by Inga-Karin Eriksson. Translated from the Swedish by Patricia Crampton. New York: R & S/Farrar, Straus & Giroux. [I/M]

Bolden, Tonya (2005). *Maritcha: A nineteenth century American girl*. New York: Abrams. [I/M]

Browne, Anthony (1985). *Gorilla*. New York: Knopf. [P]

Bruchac, Joseph (2000). *Crazy Horse's vision*. Illus. by S. D. Nelson. New York: Lee & Low. [I]

Bryan, Ashley (2003). *Beautiful blackbird*. New York: Atheneum. [P]

Canales, Viola (2005). *The tequila worm*. New York: Random House/Wendy Lamb. [M]

Chocolate, Debbi (1996). *Kente colors*. Illus. by John Ward. New York: Walker. [P]

DeJong, Meindert (1954). *The wheel on the school*. Illus. by Maurice Sendak. New York: Harper. [I]

Demi (2004). *The hungry coat: A tale from Turkey*. New York: McElderry. [P/I]

Engle, Margarita (2006). *The poet slave of Cuba: A biography of Juan Francisco Manzano*. Illus. by Sean Qualls. New York: Henry Holt. [I/M]

Fox, Mem (1985). *Wilfred Gordon McDonald Partridge.* Illus. by Julie Vivas. La Jolla, CA: Kane/Miller. [P/I]

Frank, Anne (1967). *Anne Frank: The diary of a young girl.* Translated from the Dutch by B. M. Mooyaart. New York: Doubleday. [M]

Fraustino, Lisa Rowe (2001). *The hickory chair.* Illus. by Benny Andrews. New York: Scholastic. [P/I]

Funke, Cornelia (2002). *The thief lord.* Translated from the German by Oliver Latsch. New York: Scholastic. [I]

Gallaz, Christophe, and Roberto Innocenti (1985). *Rose Blanche.* Translated from the French by Martha Coventry and Richard Graglia. Mankato, MN: Creative Education. [I/M]

Garza, Carmen Lomas (1999). *Magic windows: Cut paper art and stories.* New York: Children's Book Press. [P/I]

Giovanni, Nikki (2005). *Rosa.* Illus. by Bryan Collier. New York: Henry Holt. [P/I]

Goble, Paul (2001). *Storm Maker's Tipi.* New York: Atheneum. [I]

Goscinny, Rene (2005). *Nicholas.* Illus. by Jean-Jacques Sempe. Translated from the French by Anthea Bell. New York: Phaedon Press Limited. [P/I]

Greenfield, Eloise (1978). *Honey, I love: And other poems.* Illus. by Leo & Diane Dillon. New York: Harper & Row. [P/I]

Grimes, Nikki (2006). *Thanks a million.* Illus. by Cozbi A. Cabrera. New York: Greenwillow/Harper Collins. [P/I]

Holub, Josef (2005). *An innocent soldier.* Translated from the German by Michael Hoffman. New York: Arthur A. Levine. [M]

Hoyt-Goldsmith, Diane (2001). *Celebrating Ramadan/Ramadan al-muazzam.* New York: Holiday House. [I/M]

Johnson, Angela (2004). *The first part last.* New York: Simon & Schuster. [M]

Lee, Huy Voun (2005). *In the leaves.* New York: Henry Holt. [P/I]

Lee, Milly (2006). *Landed.* Illus. by Yangsook Choi. New York: Farrar, Straus & Giroux. [I]

Lester, Julius (2005). *Day of tears: A novel in dialogue.* New York: Jump at the Sun/Hyperion. [M]

Lester, Julius (2006). *Time's memory.* New York: Farrar, Straus & Giroux. [M]

Lewin, Ted (1998). *The storytellers.* New York: Lothrop, Lee & Sheperd. [I]

Lindgren, Astrid (1950). *Pippi Longstocking.* Illus. by Louis Glanzman. Translated by Florence Lamborn. New York: Viking. [P/I]

Look, Lenore (2006). *Uncle Peter's amazing Chinese wedding.* Illus. by Yumi Heo. New York: Atheneum. [P/I]

Marsden, Carolyn (2005). *Moon runner.* Cambridge, MA: Candlewick. [I]

McCaughrean, Geraldine (1995). *The golden hoard: Myths and legends of the world.* New York: McElderry. [I/M]

McDonald, Janet (2004). *Brother hood.* New York: Farrar, Straus & Giroux. [M]

McKissack, Patricia C. (2001). *Goin' someplace special.* Illus. by Jerry Pinkney. New York: Atheneum. [P/I/M]

Mead, Alice (2001). *Girl of Kosovo.* New York: Farrar, Straus & Giroux. [I]

Millman, Isaac (2006). *Hidden child.* Farrar, Straus & Giroux. [I/M]

Mora, Pat (2005). *Dona Flor: A tall tale about a giant woman with a great big heart.* Illus. by Raul Colon. New York: Knopf. [P/I]

Morales, Yuyi (2003). *Just a minute: A trickster tale and counting book.* San Francisco: Chronicle. [P]

Morrison, Toni (2004). *Remember: The journey to school integration.* Boston: Houghton Mifflin. [I/M]

Mosher, Richard (2001). *Zazoo.* New York: Clarion. [M]

Myers, Walter Dean (1997). *Harlem.* Illus. by Christopher Myers. New York: Scholastic. [I/M]

Myers, Walter Dean (and Bill Miles) (2006). *The Harlem Hellfighters: When pride met courage.* New York: HarperCollins. [M]

Nelson, Marilyn (2005). *A wreath for Emmett Till.* Illus. by Philippe Lardy. Boston: Houghton Mifflin. [M]

Norman, Lissette (2006). *My feet are laughing.* Illus. by Frank Morrison. New York: Farrar, Straus, & Giroux. [I]

Nye, Naomi Shahib (2002). *19 varieties of gazelle: Poems of the Middle East.* New York: Greenwillow. [M]

Orlev, Uri (2003). *Run, boy, run.* Translated by Hillel Halkin. Boston: Houghton Mifflin. [M]

Osborne, Mary Pope (1996). *One world, many religions: The way we worship.* Illus. with photographs. New York: Knopf. [I/M]

Pringle, Laurence (2006). *American slave, American hero: York of the Lewis and Clark expedition.* Illus. by Cornelius Van Wright & Ying-Hwa Hu. Honesdale, PA: Calkins Creek Books. [I/M]

Rappaport, Doreen (2001). *Martin's big words: The life of Dr. Martin Luther King, Jr.* Illus. by Bryan Collier. New York: Jump at the Sun/Hyperion. [P/I/M]

Rappaport, Doreen (2002). *No More! Stories and songs of slave resistance.* Illus. by Shane W. Evans. Cambridge, MA: Candlewick. [I/M]

Rappaport, Doreen (2004). *Free at last! Stories and songs of emancipation.* Illus. by Shane W. Evans. Cambridge, MA: Candlewick. [I/M]

Rappaport, Doreen (2006). *Nobody gonna turn me 'round: Stories and songs of the Civil Rights movement.* Illus. by Shane W. Evans. Cambridge, MA: Candlewick. [I/M]

Raven, Margot Theis (2004). *Circle unbroken.* Illus. by E. B. Lewis. New York: Farrar, Straus & Giroux. [P/I]

Reeder, Carolyn (1997). *Across the lines.* New York: Atheneum. [I/M]

Reynolds, Jan (2006). *Celebrate! Connections among cultures.* New York: Lee & Low. [P]

Rowling, J. K. (1998). *Harry Potter and the sorcerer's stone.* New York: Scholastic. [I/M]

Ryan, Pam Muñoz (2000). *Esperanza rising.* New York: Scholastic. [I/M]

Ryan, Pam Muñoz (2004). *Becoming Naomi Leon.* New York: Scholastic. [I/M]

San Souci, Robert D. (2001) *Cendrillon: A Caribbean Cinderella.* Illus. by Brian Pinkney. New York: Simon & Schuster. [P/I]

Seigelson, Kim L. (1999). *In the time of the drums.* Illus. by Brian Pinkney. New York: Jump at the Sun/Hyperion. [P/I]

Shange, Ntozake (2004). *Ellington was not a street.* Illus. by Kadir Nelson. New York: Simon & Schuster.

Shore, Diane Z., & Alexander, J. (2006). *This is the dream.* Illus. by James Ransome. New York: HarperCollins. [P/I]

Soto, Gary (2000). *Chato and the party animals.* Illus. by Susan Guevara. New York: Putnam. [P]

Staples, Suzanne Fisher (1989). *Shabanu: Daughter of the wind.* New York: Knopf. [M]

Staples, Suzanne Fisher (2005). *Under the persimmon tree.* New York: Farrar, Straus & Giroux. [M]

Steptoe, John (1987). *Mufaro's beautiful daughters: An African tale.* New York: Lothrop, Lee & Shepard. [P/I]

Swann, Brian (1998). *Touching the distance: Native American riddle-poems.* Illus. by Maria Rendon. San Diego: Browndeer Press/Harcourt Brace. [P/I]

Tamar, Erika (1996). *Garden of Happiness.* Illus. by Barbara Lambase. San Diego: Harcourt Brace. [P/I]

Turner, Pamela S. (2004). *Hachiko: The true story of a loyal dog.* Illus. by Yan Mascimbene. Boston: Houghton Mifflin. [I]

Weatherford, Carole Boston (2006). *Moses: When Harriet Tubman led her people to freedom.* Illus. by Kadir Nelson. New York: Jump in the Sun/Hyperion. [P/I/M]

Woodson, Jacqueline (2001). *The other side.* Illus. by E. B. Lewis. New York: Putnam. [P/I]

Woodson, Jacqueline (2002). *Hush.* New York: Putnam. [I/M]

Woodson, Jacqueline (2004). *Coming on home soon.* Illus. by E. B. Lewis. New York: Putnam, [P/I]

PART III

Celebrating Response Connections

PART III   RESPONSE CONNECTIONS TO THE **IRA/NCTE** *STANDARDS FOR THE ENGLISH LANGUAGE ARTS*

- Students apply a wide range of strategies to **comprehend, interpret, evaluate, and appreciate texts.** They draw on their **prior experience,** their **interactions with other readers and writers,** their **knowledge** of word meaning and **of other texts,** their word identification strategies, and their **understanding of textual features.**
- Students **adjust their use of spoken, written, and visual language to communicate effectively** with a variety of audiences and for different purposes.
- Students **employ a wide range of strategies as they write** and **use different writing process elements** appropriately **to communicate with different audiences for a variety of purposes.**
- Students use a variety of **technological** and information **resources** to gather and synthesize information and **to create and communicate knowledge.**
- Students participate as **knowledgeable, reflective, creative, and critical members of a variety of literacy communities.**
- Students **use spoken, written, and visual language** to accomplish their own purposes.

Building on the sound knowledge of literary genres acquired in the previous section of this text, Part III of *A Celebration of Literature and Response* showcases the reader's personal response engagement with literature. No children's literature title truly exists without the response of the reader—the lump in the throat, the grin of delight, the tear in the eye, the spontaneity of applause. The desire to connect personal lives to literary experiences forms the framework of reader response. Although these connections have been somewhat minimalized in teaching settings, Louise Rosenblatt (1978) reawakened teachers to the importance of the reader in the literature-response engagement. The interaction between the literature and the reader creates the unique response that text seeks to elicit through meaningful modes of expression. Part III of this text, therefore, attends to the critical role of the reader of children's literature and the value of personal response through direct engagement and connection with the text.

Chapter 9 presents a developmental approach to the oral response to literature. From first responses to storybook reading in the home environment to interactive storybook reading in the primary classroom, children learn to voice their honest emotions and enthusiasm for literature through talk. As oral expression and literary experiences grow, informal literature discussions including retellings and storytelling ensue. Eventually, structured guidelines and roles for literature conversations formalize and encourage an open forum for oral response in classroom settings. Even technology combines with literature as online literature discussions create a new medium for conversation about books.

Chapter 10 suggests an approach that transitions the reader developmentally from oral to written response. As readers gain adeptness with writing as a mode of personal expression, both prompted and unstructured literature response journals become an important vehicle for response. Numerous examples of the voices of teachers and children provide evidence of the power of written response to literature.

Building on the uniqueness of written response, Chapter 11 honors the model and role of literature in a young writer's apprenticeship. Even inexperienced writers utilize patterned or predictable books, fairy-tale variants, and various writing connections as springboards to their own early writing experiences. For maturing young authors, literature serves as a model of the ideas, organization, voice, word choice, sentence fluency, and conventions that gradually emerge in their own creative written ventures. Abundant links between literature and types/traits of writing provide books that model the writing craft.

Although oral and written responses seem to dominate response to literature in classrooms, the expressive arts share an additional option for creative response in Chapter 12. Drama, art, and music provide opportunities to revisit and reengage with the text through movement, readers' theater, and puppetry or through varied art medium/techniques and musical performance/selection.

Finally, Chapter 13 emphasizes the challenge and possibility of blending efferent and aesthetic response to nonfiction literature. Traditionally reserved for seeking efferent information, nonfiction has the potential to elicit aesthetic response to read-alouds, biographical formats, photographic essays, and informational picture books. This unheralded context for response invites readers to fling their arms wide to incorporate response to the nonfiction genre. The recently explored potential of response to nonfiction provides a unique challenge to both teachers and readers.

Janet Hickman (1995) supports the "not by chance" planning and nurturing of children's responses to literature by "teachers who consistently provide multiple avenues to reading and responding." The breadth of response options in Part III provides a diverse menu from which the reader or teacher may choose the response engagement that best captures the special transaction with a unique title from the vast store of children's literature.

Hickman, J. (1995). Not by chance: Creating classrooms that invite responses to literature. In N. L. Roser & M. G. Martinez (Eds.), *Book talk and beyond: Children and teachers respond to literature* (pp. 3–9). Newark, DE: International Reading Association.

Rosenblatt, L. M. (1978). *The reader, the text, the poem: The transactional theory of a literary work.* Carbondale: Southern Illinois University Press.

CHAPTER 9

Talking About Books
From Oral Response to Literature Conversations

ERIN (Discussion Leader):	Brick and Mariel reflect the period of the 1940s in New York. What evidence did you find that made this novel a "period piece"?
JENNA (Vocabulary Enricher):	Let me begin. I had to figure out what "pageboy" hair and "Chiclet" teeth were from my own grandmother. I phoned her since these were new terms to me. She told me a pageboy haircut was mid-length with a turned-under look—no curls or layers. Chiclets were a brand of gum in pieces with white-coated rectangles the size of large teeth. No question—these terms belonged to the 1940s.
JOHN (Literary Luminary):	Loretta quoted President Franklin D. Roosevelt when she said "The only thing we have to fear is fear itself." Let me read that passage to you (and John reads page 41 of the text aloud).
ERIN (Discussion Leader):	Any other hints on the past from this title?
BRIAN: (Illustrator):	Well, what about the Brooklyn Dodgers? They are now the Los Angeles Dodgers.

Look at my visual reflection on the over-all book (shows drawing). You'll see historic Ebbetts Field in the shadow of New York skyscrapers.

LIZ (Summarizer): *When I look at your drawing, Brian, I wondered if anyone else noticed those small pictures that opened each chapter. If the chapter was set in New York, you see the baseball park. If it occurred on the apple farm in rural New York state, you see the farmhouse and orchard. Big Apple, Little Apple! That's clever! It helped me keep the story straight as it unfolded chapter by chapter.*

Literature Conversation of Five Preservice Teachers about *All the Way Home* by Patricia Reilly Giff

The most natural response to literature, either read aloud or independently savored, is to talk about it. Primary children can't wait to share their spontaneous reactions, their personal connections, or their likes or dislikes following the reading of a book. Intermediate/middle-level readers look forward to verbal interactions with a teacher and peers—an opportunity to voice their opinions while gaining new perspectives from other readers. These natural responses capture the individualized response to literature through the oral medium. Oral responses can be shared between two individuals, within a small group, or among an entire class. Oral response is spontaneous and builds strong oral communication skills while allowing for the risk taking and uniqueness encouraged by reader response.

This chapter presents a developmental perspective on oral response to literature. Beginning with early childhood, literature encounters include repetition, language exploration, and interactive participation. Retellings and simple storytelling provide additional oral avenues for developing a sense of story and practicing oral language skills as response to literature. Gradually, open-ended prompts provide primary children with a flexible framework to extend their oral response. By the intermediate level, readers enjoy the freedom of literature conversations in which they are encouraged to share thoughts, opinions, feelings, and reactions with peers through oral discussion. Technology encourages online literature conversations that waver between oral conversations and written response. This chapter's emphasis on the development of oral response showcases the importance of the verbal response mode in building a strong basis for sharing understandings and interactions with literature.

MEMORABLE LITERATURE ENCOUNTERS: EARLY CHILDHOOD (PREK–K)

Memorable early experiences with literature inspire young children toward lifelong reading. Rather than assigning a passive role to the listener, astute teachers choose literature that encourages active engagement. Active involvement in the early reading process can genuinely motivate an emergent learner toward becoming an independent reader. Making reading memorable through participation in literature moves reading and the reader toward a positive lifelong experience. Active involvement through literature begins with insightful oral response to quality read-alouds (Beck & McKeown, 2001). The teacher read-aloud provides a gentle group setting for sharing the story and eliciting response. In its earliest stage, oral response to literature may focus on the language of literature. Young children warm to repeated phrases, the rhyme and rhythm of words, and the enjoyment that oral language brings.

Listen to the Language of Literature

The language of children's literature provides an essential resource for the acquisition, development, and enrichment of oral language in young children. Savoring the language of literature and reveling in rhyming texts are productive ways in which literature contributes to early language enrichment. These are the books whose alliterative titles and texts flow off the tongue and are pure fun to repeat— Petr Horacek's *Silly Suzy Goose* and Pamela Duncan Edwards's *The Worryworts*. These are the titles whose texts are written in playful language and provide word choices that invite exploration—Tony DiTerlizzi's *G Is for One Gzonk! An Alpha-Number-Bet Book* and Brian Cleary's *Hairy, Scary, Ordinary: What Is an Adjective?* These are the poetic picture storybooks that revel in simple rhyme and demand repetition—Cheryl Hudson's *Hands Can* and Bill Martin, Jr.'s *Panda Bear, Panda Bear, What Do You See?* These are the concept books that introduce the alphabet, numbers, and the basic concepts that form a foundation for further learning—Nancy Tafuri's *Five Little Chicks* and Simms Taback's Caldecott winning *There Was an Old Lady Who Swallowed a Fly*. These are the multicultural titles that share the beauty of a second language and culture—Kelly Cunnane's *For You Are a Kenyan Child* and Lois Ehlert's *Cuckoo/Cucú*. These language-focused titles beg children to experiment with language—to listen, to engage, to create. All of the following books and response-related activities provide the necessary precursors that build emergent readers and early oral response.

Listen to the language that invites play.   The natural response of young children as they listen to alliterative language is to repeat it over and over and over again. As a kindergarten teacher reads aloud Bill Martin and John Archambault's *Chicka Chicka Boom Boom,* the children started chanting the phrase. Not only was it fun to say, it had lasting power as well. As they retreated to the playground for recess, many of them skipped as they chanted the memorable phrase and shrieks of "chicka chicka boom boom" echoed from the swing set for the next week. Children naturally love language, and language-based participation invites language practice and exploration. Thus begins oral response to literature.

A similar response proved true for another group of kindergartners whose teacher was reading Uri Shulevitz's *So Sleepy Story*. The repetition of "sleepy" proved magical for a house and its contents when awakened by drifting music and for the students who used the word *sleepy* continuously throughout the day in hopes of applying its special power to classroom objects. Later in the day, the amusing story of Phyllis Root's *Rattletrap Car* engaged the same children as they thrilled to the sound of "razzleberry dazzleberry, snazzleberry fizz" and imitated the sounds of "wappity bappity, lumpety bumpety, clinkety clankety." The desire to play with the language of literature captures the enjoyment of the wonder of words and encourages spontaneous response to language itself.

Listen to the language of rhyme.

Picture storybooks written in rhyme contain the language of literature that appeals to young children and encourages early oral response. The natural response to rhyme is to identify it, chant it, and even create it. Imagine an energetic multiage primary classroom magically converted to a barnyard during a reading of Denise Fleming's *Barnyard Banter*. Listen to the rhyming text

> Donkeys in the paddock, hee, haw, haw
> Crows in the cornfield, caw, caw, caw
> Crickets in the stone wall, chirp, chirp, chirp!
> Frogs in the farm pond, burp, burp, burp.*

Superimposed as a guessing game is the repeated phrase "*But where's goose?*" which is eagerly screamed on cue by participants who also willingly join in the honking at the end of the story. Active involvement creates a foundation for emergent oral response to literature.

---

*Excerpt from *Barnyard Banter* by Denise Fleming. Copyright © 1994 by Denise Fleming. Reprinted by permission of Henry Holt and Company, LLC.

RESOURCES ON THE WEB

Online literature conversations lend themselves to integration of technology. Meeting the needs and resources of almost any contexts and users, electronic communications are available in multiple forms, including e-mail exchanges, threaded discussions, and online chats.

E-mail Exchanges
E-mail technology is readily available and allows teachers and students innovative opportunities to facilitate literature conversations between readers in different classrooms. E-mail partnerships (often referred to as Keypals or Webpals) can be established between classmates or students from different locations around the world. Pairs of preservice teachers and elementary-school students may also produce rich conversations about literature. Students may contact a favorite author by accessing the author's e-mail link, a common feature on author websites. To establish e-mail partnerships from around the world, visit ePALS.com (www.epals.com).

Threaded Discussions
A threaded discussion is simply a chronological listing of participants' comments (with their names linked to their comments). Using an electronic message board, groups of readers participate in literature discussions asynchronously—meaning not simultaneously, but rather at their own time. The asynchronous context allows each reader to reflect on the text, consider peer responses, and contribute to the discussion without the risk of being interrupted by group members.

Online Chats
In an online chat room, groups of readers participate in synchronous, or real-time, discussion. When a reader posts a message or response to literature to a chat room, every other user who is viewing the chat room Web page sees the message and can respond immediately. Just like in a face-to-face conversation, but without the physical presence, participants can "speak" at any time.

In *Summer Sun Risin'*, author W. Nikola-Lisa creates a beautiful day for a child from opening "Wake up, little one—summer sun's a'risin'" to the closing "Summer sun's a'sleepin' only stars overhead." Rhythmic text and first person reflections in Marie Bradby's *Once Upon a Farm* bring familiarity to language while children enjoy repeating and smiling as they share their spontaneous responses.

The Role of the Big Book in Early Oral Response

For more than two decades, both teachers and researchers have advocated the inclusion of the big book format in children's early engagement with literature (Combs, 1987; Slaughter, 1983; Trachtenburg & Ferruggia, 1989). A big book is an enlarged version of an authentic piece of children's literature that makes both illustrations and text highly visible to the child during a read-aloud event. Often referred to as a "shared reading experience" (Holdaway, 1982), the big book reading event replicates the lap-reading time many children have sadly never experienced at home. The warmth and closeness to a picture book in a read-aloud setting encourages children to note the connection between the teacher's voice and the printed word as he or she points to the text during this experience (Strickland, 1988). Gradual "reading" participation becomes both an early type of oral response to literature and a milestone in emergent literacy.

Many popular titles of children's books with predictable text that invite reading participation are available in big book formats. For the novice teacher, a word of caution is necessary. All big books, unfortunately, are not authentic literature. The popularity of the big book format has encouraged publishers to create predictable texts released in big book format. In full support of authentic literature-based instruction, always check the library to locate the hardback trade book version of the big book. If the text and illustrations are the same, you have likely located an authentic big book from real literature. The authenticity factor gains importance as children excitedly discover the "real book" version in the library for later independent reading.

Big book engagement leads to early oral response. Whether children are simply joining in on repetitive phrases or actually making sound/symbol relationships on the road to becoming a reader, the big book format invites response. It continues to play a meaningful role both in the development of the emergent reader and in the foundational aspects of early reader response.

ORAL RESPONSE PROMPTS: PRIMARY-GRADE RESPONSE (K–2)

Young children's spontaneous thoughts and oral reactions to read-aloud books foster highly valued engagement and response to literature (Sipe, 2002). But teachers may introduce a more structured, yet open-ended approach to encourage thought and expand response offerings. The use of open-ended reader response prompts following a read-aloud event invites readers to focus, feel, connect, and relate literature. Some response purists voice opposition to the notion of teacher-initiated prompts as distorting the natural response process. Yet experience with children in classroom-based research illustrates the power of the prompt in challenging children to stretch their thinking without distorting their natural response to a book.

A reader response prompt can be defined as an open-ended question designed to encourage the reader/listener to respond at the end of a read-aloud event. Unlike a traditional closed-end comprehension question, a reader response prompt has no predetermined right or wrong answer. The response lies within each child and each response is expected to be unique. David Bleich (1978) improvised three prompts, which provide the basis for responding orally to any piece of literature at any level:

- What did you notice in the story?
- How did the story make you feel?
- What does the story remind you of from your own life?

These at first appear quite simple, but they actually open vistas of response to children that otherwise might be left unexplored. Kelly (1990) used these prompts with third graders over an entire school year and documented remarkable growth in quality, quantity, and depth of oral response. At first, children responded to these three prompts following teacher read-alouds. Later on, these prompts guided discussion for independent reading. Initially, many respondents seem confused by the prompts because they are quite different from the narrowly focused comprehension questions to which they may have become accustomed. With some teacher modeling and with experience over time, these prompts become internalized. Teachers no longer need to state the prompts—they automatically become the framework for oral response.

As children grow in response to the three basic prompts, teachers may choose to pose other open-ended prompts to their students. These continue to invite individual response and encourage independent thought. Additional response prompts may include the following:

- What special meaning or message does the story have for you?
- What did you like or dislike about the story?
- What was the most important part of the story?
- What would it feel like to be (name a character)?
- Who have you known that was like (name a character)?
- What have you experienced that was like what (name a character) experienced?
- What do you think will happen to (name a character) in the future?
- What else do you have to say about what we've just read?

Although these prompts lead young children toward more extensive oral response sharing, they should *not* become a standard routine following each read-aloud. A knowledgeable teacher familiar with each book title will realize that a few specific prompts lend themselves to a particular title, whereas others might elicit thoughts more effectively from another book. A steady diet of the same prompts can become just as inhibiting as closed-end comprehension questions at the end of a basal reader story. Choose prompts wisely, ascertain their connectedness to the literature, and present the prompts effectively and in a nonthreatening format.

Teachers can enhance oral response by providing a consistent environment in which book talk is valued. Not only must children be given ample time to talk during formal oral sharing, but they must be provided time for informal responses as well. When they arrive in the morning, when they get ready to go home, and the many times between are all appropriate times to talk about books. Response is not built through a drill-and-practice routine but through a natural environment of acceptance of unique thoughts and responses to the literature that is read to them or that they read independently.

INTERACTIVE STORYBOOK READING: PRIMARY-GRADE RESPONSE (K–2)

Teachers differ in their read-aloud styles and in the amount of dialogue in which they engage children during and after reading (Martinez & Teale, 1993). All children, but especially those who enter school with limited storybook reading experience, benefit from interactive read-alouds (Klesius & Griffith, 1996). Intended to build language and literacy understanding with young children, interactive read-alouds also encourage oral responses to literature. As teachers read stories interactively, they encourage children to interact orally with the text, their peers, and the teacher during, rather than following, the read-aloud. During interactive reading, teachers pose questions that lead readers to make sense of the text while eliciting aesthetic, personal response (Koblitz, 2002). This process facilitates a child's growing ability to orally respond to a story.

The process of using ongoing conversation during a read-aloud without distracting from the story is more challenging than it may appear. Barrentine (1996) suggests selecting "a high-interest picture book with rich language, absorbing plots, lively characters and multiple layers of meaning" (p. 41). Fisher, Flood, Lapp, and Frey (2004) identified seven components of an effective interactive read-aloud:

1. *Text selection* should be based on the interests and needs of the reading audience. Include award winners and those books to which children can connect their own lives.
2. *Preview and practice* to determine where to pause effectively for questions, how to best model fluency, and where to incorporate personal response.
3. *Clear purpose* establishes the "why" of listening to increase the attention of the children.
4. *Fluent reading* models the best of reading aloud with conventional pronunciation of characters names and flawless flow of plot.
5. *Animation and expression* should be planned and executed to assist listeners in becoming engaged through changing voice, hand gestures, facial expressions, and props.
6. *Response-based discussion* to the text before, during, and after the read-aloud should balance aesthetic and efferent responses for comprehension and personal connections.
7. *Independent reading and writing* meaningfully connected to the read-aloud should be planned for subsequent activities during the day. Include journal prompts or selecting books related by author or topic.

Karma Wilson's *Bear's New Friend*, well suited for a light interactive read-aloud, is a story in rhyme, a predictable book, and a woodland summer adventure. The bright, spirited illustrations by Jane Chapman assist in inviting children into the story.

Books with predictable text and repetitive language foster interactive storybook reading.
Reprinted with the permission of Margaret K. McElderry Books, an imprint of Simon & Schuster Children's Publishing Division from Bear's New Friend *by Karma Wilson, illustrated by Jane Chapman. Jacket illustration copyright © 2006 by Jane Chapman.*

The predictability of the story and the repetition of phrases guide the interactive framework of the read-aloud. The story begins: "In the woods, in the sun/on a hot summer day, / Bear feels an itching/to head out and play." The pattern set by the text quickly allows children to note the various types of animals and the repeated phrase ("And the bear asks 'Who?'"). Teacher prompts can help the children predict the next animal to attempt to perplex Bear. Children can join in on well-chosen alliterative language for each critter ("Howdy Ho") and on a repeated phrase ("And the bear asks 'Who?'") that marks the turning of the page. Small groups can take the time to count the forest inhabitants featured on each page. Words/phrases describing the animal actions (peering, rustling, trembling) can be discussed for vocabulary building. Predicting the final ending means listening to the text and observing the colorful illustrations throughout the read-aloud.

Not every read-aloud justifies an interactive approach, but the interactive read-aloud does consistently engage students with literature and encourage response throughout a read-aloud, rather than limiting response to a retrospective nature. Phyllis Root's *One Duck Stuck,* Doreen Cronin's *Click Clack Moo* and *Giggle, Giggle, Quack,* and Judy Hindley's *Do Like a Duck Does!* provide optimal introduction to this early mode of response.

This section addresses reading aloud to young children, but the power of read-alouds for children in the intermediate and middle-school grades is optimal for reader response (Albright & Ariail, 2005; Serafini & Giorgis, 2003). Although the read-aloud may lose some of its direct interactive nature, the power of response within the read-aloud event holds strong potential at these levels.

RETELLING: BEYOND COMPREHENSION TO ORAL RESPONSE

For years, reading followed by retelling has been used as an oral response mechanism for assessing comprehension or as an instructional tool to facilitate readers' understanding of the reading process (Morrow, 1986). More recently, retelling has been viewed as a device to collect reader response to literature through oral language. Retellings are a powerful departure from recall questions, and, with teacher encouragement, reflect personal meaning-making. Retellings can personalize a story by drawing on sense of story, personal experience, and feelings and reactions to a story. Retelling may be aided by visual representations in younger children, but they still share the individual voice and style of the reader and draw from the personal interaction with text.

Morrow (1986) found that repeated retellings have a positive effect on the future oral dictation of original stories as children improve their story sense and knowledge of story elements. Retellings provide the opportunity to express understanding in a nonthreatening way. Whereas traditional comprehension questions may set children up for failure, retelling challenges children to state everything they remember in their own words without the threat of being wrong. Encouragement and praise is given for details, story elements, and personal reactions that are included. Over time, personal improvement through retellings becomes evident, and growth in meaning-making and oral articulation are the ultimate outcome.

Several titles lend themselves to retelling because of both story structure and repetition. Bernard Waber's *Bearsie Bear and the Surprise Sleepover Party* contains the perfect elements for successful retelling. Characters' names like Cowsie Cow and Moosie Moose are easily remembered. Repetitive scenes of knocks on the door and requests to stay overnight form a pattern for the reteller. Repetitive dialogue (e.g., "Good night!" "Piggie Pig may sleep over") also provides confidence for new story retellers. Remembering that Porkie Porcupine initially has a different fate than the other animals reveals comprehension. The oral inflections of dialogue, the changing voices of characters, and the revealed reaction to the story ending provide meaningful outlets for oral response through a retelling.

Teachers should be aware of the following elements in considering level of performance of retellings or in modeling their own retelling.

Setting	Begins story with an introduction.
	Includes time and place of story.
Character	Names main character.
	Names some secondary characters.
Problem	States the main problem in the story.
Episodes	Recalls episodes in the story.
	Sequences episodes properly.
Solution	Identifies the solution to the problem.
	Provides story ending.

Avi's *Things that Sometimes Happen: Very Short Stories for Little Listeners* includes minimal characters and a simple plot as an effective way to begin the retelling process even with kindergartners. The use of retellings to improve the quality and the understanding of story elements is convincing, especially when monitored over time.

STORYTELLING AS RESPONSE: RETAINING ORAL TRADITIONS

Although being loosely linked to retellings, the art of storytelling is built on personal response to literature. Storytelling differs from retelling because of its creative nature. Not only is a story being told, but the drama and language behind the story add an important dimension to the personal response. This oral response mode seems particularly well suited to intermediate-level students who might share their oral talent with primary-level students in their school setting.

Tailypo, retold by Jan Wahl, is a scary tale set in the bayou country of Louisiana. The storytelling strength of the story lies in the characters (old man, monster, and dogs), in the setting (cabin in the marshy woods), and in the repeated words ("Tailypo, Tailypo, all I want is my tailypo."). This story was told by a sixth grader to second graders, and their response included gasps, giggles, oohs and aahs, and genuine fear. Like retelling, storytelling retains most of the language and story structure of the original text. Portions may be deleted, but characteristic vocabulary, introduction, description of setting, and repetitive phrases are retained in their original form. Storytelling includes performance response because the storyteller often sets the mood through lighting, engages interest through props, and captures the audience through vocal intonations. Although storytelling preparation can be time consuming, its presentation as an individual oral response to literature not only showcases an individual mode of response but allows younger listeners to appreciate the classic oral tradition of literature.

Books that might be used for storytelling as oral response typically belong to the genre of traditional tales because of their oral tradition. Verna Aardema's *Anansi Does the Impossible: An Ashanti Tale* revisits the beloved trickster spider as he and his wife outsmart the Sky God and win back the folktales of their people. A storytelling prior to a fourth-grade class's unit on folktales would be a motivating opening to an exciting genre study. Similarly, storytelling Steven Kellogg's contemporary version of *The Three Little Pigs* (Percy, Pete, and Prudence) will prove successful for an older student who shares it with a group of first graders who have just read the original version. Giggles are ensured as Tempesto the wolf bellows, "Open up, Pork Chop! Or I'll huff and I'll puff and I'll flatten this dump!"

A Native American storytelling might include John Bierhorst's *Is My Friend at Home? Pueblo Fireside Tales.* These seven interconnected stories include brief tales that reveal how Coyote got his ears, how Bee learned to fly, and why Mouse walks softly. These *pourquoi* tales can be told by second-grade book buddies to their older peers. Many picture books share stories in a sequential framework, include strong dialogue, and contain excellent descriptions that can be savored and expressed in the storytelling mode of response.

LITERATURE CONVERSATIONS: TALKING ABOUT BOOKS

As children enter both early and advanced stages of independent reading, teachers strive to provide more experiences of reading wonderful books and talking about them with others. Small groups of students with similar interests read and discuss picture books, short chapter books, and full-length chapter books, using a higher level of thinking to discuss and respond to what they have read. Initially called grand conversations (Peterson & Eeds, 1990), these small discussion groups explore "rough draft understandings" (Short & Pierce, 1990) of literature with other readers. More recently, literature conversations take the form of book bistros (Kasten & Wilfong, 2005), literature circles (Daniels, 2002), dialogic discussion (Adler, Rougle, Kaiser, & Caughlan, 2004; Doyle, 2006), and online discussion (Carico & Logan, 2004).

Literature conversation groups are based on the belief that reading is a transactional process as students bring meaning to and take meaning from the text. Built on aesthetic response to literature, students engage in collaborative listening, thinking, and understanding as dialogue leads participants to new perspectives on a book. They generally are composed of only four to six students who ideally, over time, build a dining room table style of conversation to response sessions (Atwell, 1987/1998). A sense of community and an acceptance of risk taking are necessary components that lead to the success of literature conversations. Because there are no correct responses in a conversation, the session must be viewed as dialogue among readers rather than the fulfillment of a teacher-generated agenda. Honesty and personal impressions are valued, honored, and used as a springboard for ongoing discussion.

Owens (1995) suggests a sound rationale for utilizing literature conversations as a support framework for sharing and celebrating response. She justifies the inclusion of literature conversations as oral response because they:

- promote a love for literature and build positive attitudes toward reading
- reflect a constructivist, child-centered model of literacy
- encourage extensive and intensive reading
- invite natural discussions that lead to student inquiry and critical thinking
- support diverse response to texts
- foster interaction and collaboration
- provide choice and encourage responsibility
- expose children to literature from multiple perspectives
- nurture reflection and self-evaluation (p. 3)

Classic research (Eeds & Wells, 1989; Lehman & Scharer, 1996) and more current studies on the inclusion of literature conversations in a response-based reading program point to progress in literacy, literary, and social outcomes (Allen, Moller, & Stroup, 2003; Brevig, 2006; Kooy, 2003; Long & Gove, 2003). These classroom-based studies highlight the potential of literature conversations to improve the ability to communicate personal thoughts about literature, become a critical listener and speaker, and keep an open mind to new perspectives on a literary text.

Literature Conversations with Young Children (1–2)

Many teachers of young children assume that literature conversations are only for intermediate- and middle-level readers. Although adjustments must be made for developmental levels and reading capabilities in the lower primary grades, the tasks of exploring meaning and engaging in conversations about literature are still paramount. Although a facilitator (parent, intern, upper-grade student) is necessary with young children, the teacher steps back and allows personal thoughts to provide the script of the conversation.

The first adaptation of the primary-level literature conversation begins with book selection. Because most first- and second-grade students are unable to read substantive picture books on their own, the literature conversation typically begins with a teacher read-aloud. The book should be read at least two times so children are better prepared to absorb its content and establish their personalized response. With repeated readings, many of the children are able to read the book independently by the day of the scheduled literature conversation. Children should be asked to draw their response to the book and to bookmark a favorite part in preparation for the small group discussion.

The importance of rereading or revisiting old favorites for literature conversations with young children cannot be stressed enough. Understandings are difficult to articulate on a first reading, and multiple readings improve the quality of discussions. A whole-class literature conversation serves as a model and conceptual foundation before moving to small groups. With short attention spans and a strong desire to talk, four children seems the optimal size.

Young children may begin literature conversations by talking about favorite parts of the book and relating the story to experiences from their own lives. From there they move on to elaborations of their own drawings in response to the story. A teacher, student intern, or adult facilitator is necessary with young conversationalists to assist in focusing on specific issues and building the framework of the decision. Myers (2005) suggests cleverly titled roles for kindergarten discussions—Princess Storyteller, Clara Clarifier, Quincy Questioner, and the Wizard. Raphael, Florio-Ruane, George, Hasty, and Highfield (2004) provide a framework for literature discussion in the primary grades by simultaneously addressing standards and promoting a love of reading.

With significant modeling and the selection of appropriate titles to discuss, young children can succeed in talking about literature in a small group format. Literature-based teachers report the success of literature conversations in their primary classrooms (Frank, Dixon, and Brandts, 2001; Jewell & Pratt, 1999; Roller & Beed, 1994) and strongly encourage their peers to venture into this oral response realm with younger children. Martinez-Roldan and Lopez-Robertson (1999/2000) report success initiating literature circles in a first-grade bilingual classroom.

Not all picture books, not even those that are our own favorites, will sustain literature conversations. Here are some important criteria:

- A well-crafted story with meaningful theme
- Sufficient depth to provide discussion
- The inclusion of memorable language
- Diverse characters in real-world situations

Figure 9.1 lists the thought-provoking titles necessary to stimulate natural response in a literature conversation with young readers.

Literature Conversations: Intermediate (3–5) and Middle Levels (6–8)

As independence in reading grows, so too grows the quality of talk linked to literature conversations. Cognitive development and social growth provide additional support to the small group conversation. Whether referred to as literature circles (Daniels, 2002), book clubs (Raphael, Florio-Ruane, & George, 2001), or grand conversations (Eeds & Wells, 1989), talk provides rehearsal for communicating thought and building comprehension.

Not all books intended for intermediate/middle-level readers will sustain literature conversations. Figure 9.1 titles draw from criteria suggested by Dianne Monson (1995). She imparts three questions to scrutinize appropriate literature for response discussion:

1. Does the book succeed in arousing my emotions and will it arouse children's emotions?
2. Is the book well written?
3. Is the book meaningful? (p. 113)

Sharing these suggested titles as read-alouds or as independent reading options will stimulate and impart critical thinking and authentic response in readers.

Although young children require more guidance, many older students are capable of and eager to facilitate a literature conversation independently. With proper modeling and experience, literature conversations often include the following oral engagements and response. They typically proceed in the designated order with common lulls between each stage of conversational development:

- Impressions and personal responses to the book (favorite parts, initial enjoyment of the book)
- Connections to personal experiences and other book titles (text-to-life and text-to-text connections)
- Specific conversational focus (critical dialogue, careful consideration of others' thoughts, focus on specific aspect of the book)
- Expansion and textual support of personal responses and building off of participant comments
- Determination of focus for next meeting (a starting point for the next day's conversation)

FIGURE 9.1   Book Cluster: Titles that stimulate literature conversations

Grades 1–2

Arnold, Marsha Diane (2000). *The bravest of us all*. Illus. by Brad Sneed. New York: Dial.
Bradby, Marie (2000). *Momma, where are you from?* Illus. by Chris K. Soentpiet. New York: Orchard.
Bynum, Jane (2006). *Nutmeg & Barley: A budding friendship*. Cambridge, MA: Candlewick.
Cruise, Robin (2006). *Little mama forgets*. Illus. by Stacy Dressen-McQueen. New York: Farrar, Straus & Giroux.
Kvanosky, Laura M. (2004). *Frank & Izzy set sail*. Cambridge, MA: Candlewick.
McClintock, B. (2006). *Adele & Simon*. New York: Farrar, Straus & Giroux.
Napoli, Donna Jo. (2001). *Albert*. Illus. by Jim LaMarche. San Diego: Harcourt Brace.
Nivola, Claire A. (2002). *The forest*. New York: Farrar, Straus & Giroux.
Polacco, Patricia (2001). *Mr. Lincoln's way*. New York: Philomel.
Stevenson, Robert L. (2006). *The moon*. Illus. by Tracy Campbell Pearson. New York: Farrar, Straus & Giroux.
Wilson, Karma (2006). *Moose tracks!* Illus. by Jack E. Davis. New York: McElderry.
Woodson, Jacqueline (2001). *The other side*. Illus. by E. B. Lewis. New York: Putnam.
Yangsook, Choi (2001). *The name jar*. New York: Knopf.

Grades 3–5

Clements, Andrew (2000). *The Landry news*. New York: Atheneum.
DiCamillo, Kate (2006). *The miraculous journey of Edward Tulane*. Cambridge, MA: Candlewick.
Fraustino, Lisa Rowe (2001). *The hickory chair*. Illus. by Benny Andrews. New York: Scholastic.
Giff, Patricia Reilly (2001). *All the way home*. New York: Delacorte.
Gutman, Dan (2006). *The homework machine*. New York: Simon & Schuster.
Hahn, Mary Downing (2001). *Anna on the farm*. New York: Clarion.
Henkes, Kevin (2003). *Olive's ocean*. New York: HarperCollins.
Hesse, Karen (1998). *just Juice*. New York: Scholastic.
Holt, Kimberly Willis (1998). *My Louisiana sky*. New York: Henry Holt.
Hopkinson, Deborah (2003). *Girl wonder: A baseball story in nine innings*. Illus. by Terry Widener. New York: Simon & Schuster.
Lin, Grace (2006). *The year of the dog*. New York: Little, Brown.
Lynch, Chris (2000). *Gold dust*. New York: HarperCollins.
McKissack, Patricia C., & Moss, Onawumi Jean (2005). *Precious and the Boo Hag*. Illus. by Kyrsten Broken. New York: Atheneum.
Naylor, Phyllis Reynolds (2006). *Roxie and the hooligans*. New York: Simon & Schuster.
Taylor, Mildred (1990). *Mississippi bridge*. New York: Bantam.
Williams, Vera B (2001). *Amber was brave, Essie was smart*. New York: Greenwillow.

Grades 6–8

Blackwood, Gary (1998). *The Shakespeare stealer*. New York: Dutton.
Grimes, Nikki (2006). *The road to Paris*. New York: Putnam.
Hesse, Karen (2001). *Witness*. New York: Scholastic.
Jaramillo, Ann (2006). *La Linea*. New York: Roaring Brook Press.
Johnston, Tony (2001). *Any small goodness: A novel of the barrio*. New York: Scholastic.
Kadohota, Cynthia (2006). *Weedflower*. New York: Atheneum.

(continued)

FIGURE 9.1 Continued

Larson, Kirby (2006). *Hattie big sky.* New York: Delacorte.
Lowry, Lois (1993). *The giver.* Boston: Houghton Mifflin.
Naidoo, Beverly (2001). *The other side of truth.* New York: HarperCollins.
Paterson, Katherine (2006). *Bread and roses, too.* New York: Clarion.
Peck, Richard (1998). *A long way from Chicago: A novel in stories.* New York: Dial.
Philbrick, Rodman (2000). *The last book in the universe.* New York: Scholastic.
Sachar, Louis (1998). *Holes.* New York: Farrar, Straus & Giroux.
Staples, Suzanne Fisher (1989). *Shabanu: Daughter of the wind.* New York: Knopf.
Taylor, Mildred (2001). *The land.* New York: Putnam.

In many cases, however, teachers quickly discover that turning students loose to talk about books requires more structure and organization. To keep older students on the task of reader response, roles may be assigned that focus on sharing response without limiting or inhibiting the freedom it demands. Daniels (2002) describes these six possible roles that students can assume within a grand conversation group:

1. The *discussion director,* who makes certain the group has brought along questions for the discussion and helps keep the group focused on the purpose of the discussion
2. The *literary luminary,* who locates sections of the book that read aloud well or provide deeper insight into the discussion
3. The *connector,* who specifically looks for connections between the book and the real-world experiences of the readers
4. The *illustrator,* who creates any type of visual or graphic representation to describe what has been read
5. The *vocabulary enricher,* who looks for important word choices that enrich the writing or deepen the understanding of the reader
6. The *summarizer,* who wraps up the reading for the day by assimilating the discussion and making a final statement as the group comes to closure

These roles may also be viewed as directed responses to literature because each student focuses on a specific aspect of the literature experience. Although the group contains the same students over a period of time, the roles rotate to share responsibilities, create response possibilities, and maintain interest.

Another means of keeping students on task is to provide guidelines for conversational response (see Figure 9.2). Prepared by the teacher for a specific title, the guidelines serve to facilitate oral response *only* when other personal responses have been exhausted. They provide a road map for conversation or a model for an introductory level of discussion. Experienced groups may never need these springboards for response, but novice conversationalists are likely to depend heavily on them to sustain talk for 20 to 30 minutes.

Documented success with literature conversations in the intermediate/middle-level setting was first reported by Keegan and Shrake (1991) and Nystrand, Gamoran,

FIGURE 9.2   *Crispin: The Cross of Lead* (Avi, 2002 Newbery Medal book):
Literature conversation guidelines

- Discuss these characters for their strengths, weaknesses, triumphs, and downfalls.

    Crispin   Bear   Aycliffe   Lord Furnival   Father Quinel

- If this book were to be made into a movie, who do you envision playing these roles?
- Discuss the story setting/period in terms of the following aspects of life in England in the Middle Ages.

    the role of religion   serfdom   town life   royal birthright

- Locate and respond to your favorite passage.
- How did you feel when you realized Crispin was of royal blood?
- What meaning or message about "self-identity" do you gain from this book?
- What will happen to Crispin when the book ends?
- What did you like/dislike about the book? How would you change it?
- How did you react to:
    Crispin's escape from the village
    Cerdic's advice about his escape
    Crispin's seeing the two dead men shortly after leaving the village
    Crispin's sacred oath to Bear
    Crispin's early thought that Bear is "crazy"
    Bear winning Crispin's trust
    The cross of lead

Read a response from your journal in which you:
- Use a quote from the book
- Talk to a character
- Judge a character
- Give advice to a character
- Indicate questions or confusion
- Make a text-to-text connection
- Make a text-to-life connection
- Laugh out loud
- Feel tears roll from your eyes

and Heck (1993). Extended research at this level indicates even more promise of literature conversation as a successful format for discussion (Almasi, O'Flahavan, & Ayra, 2001; Carrico, 2001; Evans, 2002; Hill, Schlick-Noe, & King, 2003; Johnson, 2000; Kasten & Wilfong, 2005; Moller, 2004, Whitin, 2005). Raphael, Florio-Ruane, and George (2001) provide an organizational framework for book clubs to encompass reader response groups as part of overall literacy instruction.

The greatest challenge to most educators is the changing role of the teacher, who must relinquish rights to directing a discussion. Eeds and Peterson (1991) refer to the role of "teacher as curator" (p. 118), who must collect response, nurture it, and delight in the independent thoughts of readers. The role of the teacher is often described as "scaffolding" (Maloch, 2002, 2004) during the discussion or "coaching"

(Bacon, 2005; O'Flahavan, 1994/1995) before and after the conversation. Teachers strive to balance between retaining some control of the social and interpretive dimensions of response and relinquishing total control to students. Too much teacher participation subverts authenticity of response, particularly with older students. Teachers, therefore, must learn to listen instead of talk while still providing verbal support and direction when students demonstrate that they need it (Short, Kaufman, Kaser, Kahn, & Crawford, 1999).

Online Literature Conversations

In preparing students for their literacy futures, teachers should challenge their own instructional practices by integrating technology into the literacy curriculum (Wepner, Valmont, & Thurlow, 2000). The goal is not to replace children's oral responses to literature but to extend their literature conversation online through the use of technology. Studies about programs in which preservice teachers and elementary school students exchanged e-mails as online conversations about literature indicate the value of modeled online talk about books in elementary reader comprehension (Leu & Leu, 2000; McKeon, 1999). In particular, the keypal project (Larson, 2002) presents a valuable tool for modeling reader response and aspects of technology.

Prior to embarking on an online literature conversation, the students should experience ample oral response conversations. Even the use of written response journals (Chapter 10) prepares them for the online conversation. Guided by teacher modeling of rich response options, students likely have previously shared thoughts in formal and informal literature conversations. Learning how confidently to share opinions and interpretations with others is a critical precursor to the online conversation. Because of the confidentiality of response and the insecurities of the Internet, all online conversations should be conducted through a teacher's e-mail address. Parents must be informed of the project and be made aware of the channeling of all e-mail responses through the teacher's account. Larson (2002) has also prepared guidelines for preservice teachers in implementing the keypal project (see Figure 9.3).

Titles that have worked well with keypal projects include Christopher Paul Curtis's *Bud, Not Buddy,* Karen Hesse's *just Juice,* Kate DiCamillo's *Because of Winn-Dixie,* Kirkpatrick Hill's *The Year of Miss Agnes,* and Linda Sue Park's *A Single Shard.* Preservice teachers will have previously read these in a children's literature course or a reading/language arts methods course. Elementary children will respond three times during an ongoing reading of the text. Figure 9.4 provides a sample of an ongoing online conversation based on responses to *Because of Winn-Dixie* that illustrate the questions, the predictions, the personal connections, and the textual connections that occur as readers "talk" about books online.

The online literature conversation optimally blends reader response and technology as a medium for literature discussions. Preservice queries and comments challenge critical thinking and enhanced comprehension. Discussions encourage text-to-life and text-to-text connections. Timely responses and the retention of privacy by the teacher seem essential in a successful project. Of course, keypal projects could be implemented between several classrooms in the same school, between grade-level classrooms in the same district, and even between children in schools in other states. Even more challenging would be the opportunity to discuss titles set in international locations, such as *A Single*

FIGURE 9.3   Guidelines for online literature conversations*

Goals
- The elementary school students will develop partnerships with preservice teachers to exchange responses electronically to literature.
- The students will demonstrate skills needed to read and respond to literature.
- The students will effectively create and communicate through media conversations.

Expectations of Preservice Teachers
- Be knowledgeable about the content of the literature.
- Reply to a minimum of three e-mails in a professional and timely manner.
- Respect and honor confidentiality guidelines.

Responding to Your Elementary School Keypal
- Establish a supportive and encouraging environment in which your keypal feels free to express thoughts about literature.
- Include thought-provoking questions to challenge your keypal to think critically about the book's characters and events.
- Encourage responses through text-to-text and text-to-life connections.
- Send all keypal responses to the classroom teacher's e-mail address with the keypal's first name and book title on the subject line. Write back using the "reply" command.

Shard, with children in Korea. The possibilities appear endless as technology provides a bridge for conversation between young people across the globe.

CLOSING THOUGHTS

The developmental trail of oral response to literature begins with children's early read-aloud events in which they respond to language, repetition, and the joy of memorable literature experiences. As they begin school, oral response to literature gains a more structured, intentional nature as teachers insert prompts both during and after stories to create interactive storybook reading and retrospective reflections on books. Retellings and storytellings provide structured frameworks for emerging oral response. Literature conversations provide a group format for sharing response. Although young children require some modeling and guidance, older students revel in the freedom of open conversations on literature. Through designated roles, the use of guidelines, or teacher scaffolding in a natural sharing configuration, readers learn to become listeners and build meaning through valued shared perspectives on literature. Even online conversations provide a means to communicate electronically about literature.

The advantages of oral response to literature include its spontaneity, its developmental nature, and its time efficiency. While focusing on communication skills, oral response also demands listening to the responses of others to enhance one's own interactions with the text. Oral response should *not* be limited to young children based on their lack of reading proficiency or developmental difficulty with written

---

*Adapted from Larson, L. (2002). The Keypal Project: Integrating literature response and technology. *Kansas Journal of Reading, 18*, 57–62.

FIGURE 9.4 Sample of a preservice teacher/fifth-grader online literature conversation

From:	Mrs. Larson/Dawn
To:	David
Date:	11/08/02 10:09 AM
Subject:	Because of Winn-Dixie

Dear David,

Hi, my name is Dawn. My favorite books are the Little House series by Laura Ingalls Wilder. I feel nervous about doing this keypal project because this is the first time I've ever done something like this.

I selected to read Because of Winn-Dixie because I like dogs and it sounds very interesting to read. I think the book was easy to get into because once you read the preview on the back of the book, I knew it was going to be interesting. Opal is easy to relate to because Opal took Winn-Dixie home. I would take a stray animal home and find a good home for it. . . . . . The part that made me laugh was when Winn-Dixie showed his teeth like he was smiling. I think that Opal will be able to keep Winn-Dixie because her dad is a preacher and he cares about animals. Why is Opal called by her middle name instead of her first name? The book reminds me of the movie Annie because Annie wants to keep a dog she found on the street and Annie is an orphan. . . . . Why is this story about a dog? I used to have a pet hamster named Fefe but she died. When she was alive I treated her like a friend.

Sincerely, Dawn

From:	David
To:	Mrs. Larson/Dawn
Date:	11/09/02 8:42PM
RE:	Keypal Response 1

Dawn,

I have never done anything like this either, but I am excited because I think we will both learn something new from each other. I recently read The Lord of the Rings trilogy by J. R. R. Tolkien. I really enjoyed these books. I also really enjoy reading different nonfiction books.

I also appreciated the description of Winn-Dixie smiling. That really makes you fall in love with this dog even if you can't see her. What feelings do you have for Opal? Do you know of people in similar experiences (moving to a new place and struggling to find new friends)? I never had to move to a new place when I was younger. I believe that would have been a very tough transition. Did you catch it toward the beginning of Chapter 2 where Opal explains that her daddy called her by her middle name, which belonged to her mother. I think this is significant in illustrating the love that her daddy had for her mother.

The book reminds me of my life during middle school. We had a stray dog show up at our farm. We kept her and before long she had seven puppies. We still have the original dog. It was so much fun to have a dog during that stage of my life. I believe the friendship aspects a dog provides really enhance this story.

FIGURE 9.4 Continued

What do you think about Opal calling her daddy "the preacher"? . . . . Why did the preacher not want to tell Opal about her mother? I really enjoyed it toward the end of Chapter 3 and the beginning of Chapter 4 as "the preacher" tells Opal more about her mother. I believe this serves as a comfort to Opal.

Enjoy the next several chapters.
David

To: David
From: Mrs. Larson/Dawn
Date: 11/16/02 10:34 AM
Subject: RE: Keypal Response 2

Dear David, Hi it's Dawn!

Thank you for responding to my first e-mail. Your first e-mail helped me understand the book more because now that I know that Opal probably doesn't want her name so she has her mother's name. I enjoyed getting my first response because I'd never got e-mail from someone before. I have read to Chapter 15 so far. The book is making me feel happy so far because Opal made a friend and she got invited to a party . . . . The book surprised me when Opal got invited to the birthday party. The part of the book when Winn-Dixie was in the store I think is irritating that the manager was screaming and yelling about Winn-Dixie being in the store. I think Opal will find her mother because Opal might go looking for her mother because she has clues about her mother and she sort of knows what her mom looks like. . . . . I think Opal calls her dad Preacher instead of dad because people always call her dad preacher and it got stuck in her head and calls him preacher because he is a preacher. My predictions are coming true that Opal gets to keep Winn-Dixie. Why does Opal want to be invited to a five-year-old birthday party? The book is easier now that I know what is going on more.

Opal reminds me of my friend Gracieanne because Gracieanne cares about animals like Opal does. The book reminds me of the movie Harry Potter because Harry doesn't have a mom or dad, but Opal has a dad but he is busy all the time and her mom left her when she was three. A kid in my class just moved here and she is making new friends. The preacher did not want to tell Opal about her mother because he was afraid she would say something like why didn't you tell me earlier. I feel sad for Opal that her mom left her when she was only three.

Sincerely,
Dawn

To: Mrs. Larson / Dawn
From: David
Date: 11/17/02 3:44 PM
Subject: Keypal Response 2

Hi Dawn,

I am glad that you are enjoying this book. I know you are really thinking about the events of the story, which I believe will enhance your enjoyment of the book.

(continued)

FIGURE 9.4 Continued

I agree with you that it is nice to see Opal invited to a party. I believe she is excited about this because it is the first acceptance by other children she has experienced since moving. What was your first impression of Gloria Dump? Are there any people in your neighborhood that people shy away from because of their appearance? I really enjoy reading about all of Opal's different friends. They are such unique characters. The pet store scene where all the animals run around outside of the cages painted a funny picture in my mind. I can't imagine trying to catch all those animals. Do you have any predictions about what Otis was in jail for? I was really surprised when he told Opal he had been in jail. He kind of made me nervous after that because I wasn't sure what kind of things he had done to get in jail.

One thing that I found intriguing was Gloria's memory tree. I really appreciated the message it presented. I think Gloria had some great advice for Opal. What can you learn from this scene between Opal and Gloria in Chapter 14?

You are getting into a section now where you will learn more about Amanda. As you learn more, think about how you would act in her situation. Would you be known as pinch-faced Dawn or smiley Dawn? This section of the text really illustrates the struggles people of all ages go through. It reminds me of the necessity of making the best of bad situations so that I am not known as pinch-faced David.

Enjoy the remaining chapters of the book.
David

To:	David
From:	Mrs. Larson / Dawn
Date:	11/24/02 10:09 AM
Subject	Keypal Response 3

Dear David,

Hi, it's Dawn. I have finished the book. Thank you for writing to me and helping me understand the book more now that I know what's going on. The book did not end the way I thought it would because Opal did not find her mother and I thought she would. . . . . Opal is still my favorite character because she still cares about animals. The book reminds me of Bud, Not Buddy because Bud doesn't have a mom or dad and Opal has a dad but he is really busy and her mom left her when she was three and she feels like an orphan and Bud is an orphan.

I think you should read the book Frindle because it is really funny and it is about a kid named Nick that makes up the word Frindle. I think that the author should make a sequel to Because of Winn-Dixie because I want to see if Opal ever finds her mother. I think that Opal should find her mother in the sequel . . . . . I think that her dad will pay attention more to Opal because he cares about her more. I think the Dewey boys will be really good friends with Opal. I thought Gloria was going to be mean because the Dewey boy said she was. I already read the part why Otis was in jail but before I read that part I thought he went to jail cause he stole something. I have an old lady who lives on my street and she is shy. I would not be known as pinch-faced Dawn because I would remember the good times not the bad. I learned not to be afraid of your fears. I am looking forward to your final response.

Your keypal, Dawn

FIGURE 9.4 Continued

To: Mrs. Larson / Dawn
From: David
Date: 11/25/02 5:57PM
Subject: Keypal Response 3

Hi Dawn,

I am glad to hear that you finished the book. It sounds like you really enjoyed the book, although it did not turn out as you anticipated. When I read the book I shared your predictions of Opal meeting her mother. However, as the book neared the end I believe that Opal had learned how to make the best of different situations and a reunion with her mother no longer seemed necessary.

I agree that there are strong similarities between this book and Bud, Not Buddy. At times both main characters in these stories seem very mature and independent for their age. I am really glad that you have been thinking about how this book relates to your life. I was especially glad to hear that you would not be known as pinch-faced Dawn. Hopefully, you have thought about some of the people in your neighborhood who would appreciate an extra friend.

You have many great ideas for a sequel. Perhaps you could write several chapters that would act as a sequel. Your chapters would be great because they could include some of the things you want to happen.

I have read Frindle within the past few months. I also really enjoyed it. I appreciated Nick's creativity and his teacher's motives. It has been very enjoyable to communicate with you about this book. Keep reading. Reading has been and continues to be a very important part of my life.

Your keypal, David

response modes. Oral response needs to be encouraged throughout the K–8 classroom as foundations are built through read-alouds, frameworks are established through prompts, and social interactions about books are nurtured through literature conversations. The major mode of reader response for adult readers consists of informal conversation through engagements with other readers. Thus the oral response encourages and preserves the authenticity of response by its very nature and progresses developmentally from simple responses to read-alouds toward mature conversations about literature.

References

Adler, M., Rougle, E., Kaiser, E., & Caughlan, S. (2004). Closing the gap between concept and practice: Toward dialogic discussion in the language arts classroom. *Journal of Adolescent & Adult Literacy, 47,* 312–322.

Albright, L. K., & Ariail, M. (2005). Tapping the potential of teacher read-alouds in middle schools. *Journal of Adolescent & Adult Literacy, 48,* 582–591.

Allen, J., Moller, K. J., & Stroup, D. (2003). "Is this some kind of soap opera?": A tale of two readers across four literature discussion contexts. *Reading & Writing Quarterly, 19,* 225–251.

Almasi, J. F., O'Flahavan, J. F., & Ayra, P. (2001). A comparative analysis of student and teacher development in more and less proficient discussions of literature. *Reading Research Quarterly, 36,* 96–120.

Atwell, N. (1987/1998). *In the middle: Writing, reading, and learning with adolescents.* Portsmouth, NH: Heinemann. (Original work published 1987)

Bacon, S. (2005). Reading coaches: Adapting an intervention model for upper elementary and middle school readers. *Journal of Adolescent & Adult Literacy, 48,* 416–427.

Barrentine, S. J. (1996). Engaging with reading through interactive read-alouds. *The Reading Teacher, 50,* 36–43.

Beck, I. L., & McKeown, M. G. (2001). Text talk: Capturing the benefits of read-aloud experiences for young children. *The Reading Teacher, 55,* 10–20.

Bleich, D. (1978). *Subjective criticism.* Baltimore, MD: Johns Hopkins University Press.

Brevig, L. (2006). Engaging in retrospective reflection. *The Reading Teacher, 59,* 522–530.

Carrico, K. M. (2001). Negotiating meaning in classroom literature discussions. *Journal of Adolescent & Adult Literacy, 44,* 510–518.

Carrico, K. M., & Logan, D. (2004). A generation in cyberspace: Engaging readers through online discussions. *Language Arts, 81,* 293–302.

Combs, M. (1987). Modeling the reading process with enlarged text. *The Reading Teacher, 40,* 422–426.

Daniels, H. (2002). *Literature circles: Voice and choice in book clubs and reading groups* (2nd ed.). York, ME: Stenhouse.

Doyle, B. G. (2006). Promoting emergent literacy and social emotional learning through dialogic reading. *The Reading Teacher, 59,* 554–564.

Eeds, M., & Peterson, R. (1991). Teacher as curator: Learning to talk about literature. *The Reading Teacher, 45,* 118–126.

Eeds, M., & Wells, D. (1989). Grand conversations: An exploration of meaning construction in literature study groups. *Research in the Teaching of English, 23,* 4–29.

Evans, K. S. (2002). Fifth-grade students' perceptions of how they experience literature discussion groups. *Reading Research Quarterly, 37,* 46–69.

Fisher, D., Flood, J., Lapp, D., & Frey, N. (2004). Interactive read-alouds: Is there a common set of implementation practices? *The Reading Teacher, 58,* 8–17.

Frank, C. R., Dixon, C. N., & Brandts, L. R. (2001). Bears, trolls, and pagemasters: Learning about learners in book clubs. *The Reading Teacher, 54,* 448–462.

Hill, B. C., Schlick-Noe, K. L., & King, J. A. (2003). *Literature circles in middle school: One teacher's journey.* Norwood, MA: Christopher-Gordon.

Holdaway, D. (1982, Autumn). Shared book experience: Teaching reading using favorite books. *Theory into Practice,* pp. 293–300.

Jewell, T. A., & Pratt, D. (1999). Literature discussions in the primary grades: Children's thoughtful discourse about books and what teachers can do to make it happen. *The Reading Teacher, 52,* 842–850.

Johnson, H. (2000). "To stand up and say something": "Girls only" literature circles at the middle level. *The New Advocate, 13,* 375–389.

Kasten, W. C., & Wilfong, L. G. (2005). Encouraging independent reading with ambience: The Book Bistro in middle and secondary school classes. *Journal of Adolescent & Adult Literacy, 48,* 656–664.

Keegan, S., & Shrake, K. (1991). Literature study groups: An alternative to ability grouping. *The Reading Teacher, 44,* 542–547.

Kelly, P. R. (1990). Guiding young students' response to literature. *The Reading Teacher, 43,* 464–470.

Klesius, J., & Griffith, P. (1996). Interactive storybook reading for at-risk learners. *The Reading Teacher, 49,* 552–560.

Koblitz, D. (2002). Reading to students as part of genre study. *School Life, 7,* 1–2.

Kooy, M. (2003). Riding the coattails of Harry Potter: Readings, relational learning, and revelations in book clubs. *Journal of Adolescent & Adult Literacy, 47,* 136–145.

Larson, L. C. (2002). The keypal project: Integrating literature response and technology. *Kansas Journal of Reading, 18,* 57–62.

Lehman, B. A., & Scharer, P. (1996). Reading alone, talking together: The role of discussion in developing literary awareness. *The Reading Teacher, 50,* 26–35.

Leu, D. J., & Leu, D. D. (2000). *Teaching with the Internet: Lessons from the classroom* (3rd ed.). Norwood, MA: Christopher-Gordon.

Long, T. W., & Gove, M. K. (2003). How engagement strategies and literature circles promote critical response in a fourth-grade urban classroom. *The Reading Teacher, 57,* 350–361.

Maloch, B. (2002). Scaffolding student talk: One teacher's role in literature discussion groups. *Reading Research Quarterly, 37,* 94–112.

Maloch, B. (2004). One teacher's journey: Transitioning into literature discussion groups. *Language Arts, 81,* 312–322.

Martinez, M. G., & Teale, W. H. (1993). Teacher storybook reading style: A comparison of six teachers. *Research in the Teaching of English, 27,* 175–199.

Martinez Roldan, C. M., & Lopez-Robertson, J. M. (1999/2000). Initiating literature circles in a first-grade bilingual classroom. *The Reading Teacher, 53,* 270–281.

McKeon, C. A. (1999). The nature of children's e-mail in one classroom. *The Reading Teacher, 52,* 698–705.

Moller, K. J. (2004/2005). Creating zones of possibility for struggling readers: A study of one fourth-grader's shifting roles in literature discussions. *Journal of Literacy Research, 36,* 419–460.

Monson, D. (1995). Choosing books for literature circles. In B. Campbell Hill, N. Johnson, & K. L. Schlick Noe (Eds.) *Literature circles and response* (pp. 113–130). Norwood, MA: Christopher Gordon.

Morrow, L. M. (1986). Effects of structural guidance in story retelling on children's dictation of original stories. *Journal of Reading Behavior, 2,* 135–151.

Myers, P. A. (2005). The princess storyteller, Clara clarifier, Quincy questioner, and the wizard: Reciprocal teaching adapted for kindergarten students. *The Reading Teacher, 59,* 314–324.

Nystrand, M., Gamoran, A., & Heck, M. J. (1993). Using small groups for response to and thinking about literature. *English Journal, 82,* 14–22.

O'Flahavan, J. F. (1994/1995). Teacher role options in peer discussion about literature. *The Reading Teacher, 48,* 354–356.

Owens, S. (1995). Treasures in the attic: Building the foundation for literature circles. In B. Campbell Hill, N. J. Johnson, & K. L. Schlick Noe (Eds.) *Literature circles and response* (pp. 1–12). Norwood, MA: Christopher-Gordon.

Peterson, R., & Eeds, M. (1990). *Grand conversations: Literature groups in action.* New York: Scholastic.

Raphael, T. E., Florio-Ruane, S., & George, M. (2001). Book club plus: A conceptual framework to organize literacy instruction. *Language Arts, 79,* 159–168.

Raphael, T. E., Florio-Ruane, S., George, M., Hasty, N. L., & Highfield, K. (2004). *Book club plus: A literacy framework for the primary grades.* Lawrence, MA: Small Planet Communications.

Roller, C. M., & Beed, P. L. (1994). Sometimes the conversations were grand, and sometimes . . . *Language Arts, 71,* 509–515.

Serafini, F., & Giorgis, C. (2003). *Reading aloud and beyond: Fostering the intellectual life with older readers.* Portsmouth, NH: Heinemann.

Short, K., Kaufman, G., Kaser, S., Kahn, L. H., & Crawford, K. M. (1999). "Teacher-watching": Examining teacher talk in literature circles. *Language Arts, 76,* 377–385.

Short, K., & Pierce, K. M. (Eds.) (1990). *Talking about books: Creating literate communities.* Portsmouth, NH: Heinemann.

Sipe, L. R. (2002). Talking back and taking over: Young children's expressive engagement during storybook read-alouds. *The Reading Teacher, 55,* 476–483.

Slaughter, J. P. (1983). Big books for little kids: Another fad or a new approach for teaching beginning reading? *The Reading Teacher, 36,* 758–762.

Strickland, D. S. (1988). Some tips for using big books. *The Reading Teacher, 41,* 966–968.

Trachtenburg, R., & Ferruggia, A. (1989). Big books from little voices: Reaching high risk beginning readers. *The Reading Teacher, 42,* 284–289.

Wepner, S. B., Valmont, W. J., & Thurlow, R. (2000). *Linking literacy and technology: A guide for K–8 classrooms.* Newark, DE: International Reading Association.

Whitin, P. (2005). The interplay of text, talk, and visual representation in expanding literary interpretation. *Research in the Teaching of English, 39,* 365–397.

Children's Books Cited [P] = K–2; [I] = 3–5; [M] = 6–8

Aardema, Verna (1997). *Anansi does the impossible: An Ashanti tale.* Illus. by Lisa Desimini. New York: Atheneum. [I]

Avi (2002). *Things that sometimes happen: Very short stories for little listeners.* Illus. by Marjorie Priceman. New York: Atheneum. [P]

Bierhorst, John (2001). *Is my friend at home? Pueblo fireside tales.* Illus. by Wendy Watson. New York: Farrar, Straus & Giroux. [P/I]

Bradby, Marie (2002). *Once upon a farm.* Illus. by Ted Rand. New York: Orchard. [P]

Cleary, Brian (2000). *Hairy, scary, ordinary: What is an adjective?* Illus. by Jenya Prosmithsky. Minneapolis, MN: Carolrhoda. [P/I]

Cronin, Doreen (2001). *Click clack moo, cows that type.* Illus. by Betsy Lewin. New York: Simon & Schuster. [P]

Cronin, Doreen (2002). *Giggle giggle quack.* Illus. by Betsy Lewin. New York: Simon & Schuster. [P]

Cunnane, Kelly (2006). *For you are a Kenyan child.* Illus. by Ana Juan. New York: Atheneum. [P]

Curtis, Christopher Paul (1999). *Bud, not Buddy.* New York: Delacorte. [I]

DiCamillo, Kate (2000). *Because of Winn-Dixie.* Cambridge, MA: Candlewick Press. [I]

DiTerlizzi, Tony (2006). *G is for gzonk! An alpha-number-bet book.* Cambridge, MA: Candlewick. [P]

Edwards, Pamela Duncan (1999). *The worry-worts.* Illus. by Henry Cole. New York: HarperCollins. [P]

Ehlert, Lois (1997). *Cuckoo/Cucú.* San Diego: Harcourt Brace. [P/I]

Fleming, Denise (1994). *Barnyard banter.* New York: Henry Holt. [P]

Giff, Patricia Reilly (2001). *All the way home.* New York: Delacorte. [I]

Hesse, Karen (1999). *Just Juice.* New York: Scholastic. [I]

Hill, Kirkpatrick (2000). *The year of Miss Agnes.* New York: Atheneum. [I]

Hindley, Judy (2002). *Do like a duck does!* Illus. by Ivan Bates. Cambridge, MA: Candlewick Press. [P]

Horacek, Petr (2006). *Silly Suzy goose.* Cambridge, MA: Candlewick. [P]

Hudson, Cheryl (2003). *Hands can.* Photographs by John Gancis Bourke. Cambridge, MA: Candlewick. [P]

Kellogg, Steven (Reteller) (1997). *The three little pigs.* New York: Morrow. [P]

Martin, Bill, Jr. (2003). *Panda bear, panda bear, what do you see?* Illus. by Eric Carle. New York: Henry Holt. [P]

Martin, Bill, Jr., & Archambault, John (1989). *Chicka chicka boom boom.* Illus. by Lois Ehlert. New York: Simon & Schuster. [P]

Nikola-Lisa, W. (2002). *Summer sun risin'.* Illus. by D. Tate. New York: Lee & Low. [P]

Park, Linda Sue (2001). *A single shard.* New York: Clarion. [I]

Root, Phyllis (1998). *One duck stuck.* Illus. by Jane Chapman. Cambridge, MA: Candlewick Press. [P]

Root, Phyllis (2001). *Rattletrap car.* Illus. by Jill Barton. Cambridge, MA: Candlewick Press. [P]

Shulevitz, Uri (2006). *So sleepy story.* New York: Farrar, Straus & Giroux. [P]

Taback, Simms (1997). *There was an old lady who swallowed a fly.* New York: Viking. [P/I]

Tafuri, Nancy (2006). *Five little chicks.* New York: Simon & Schuster. [P]

Waber, Bernard (1997). *Bearsie Bear and the surprise sleepover party.* Boston: Houghton Mifflin. [P]

Wahl, Jan (1991). *Tailypo.* Illus. by Wil Clay. New York: Henry Holt. [P/I]

Wilson, Karma (2006). *Bear's new friend.* Illus. by Jane Chapman. New York: McElderry Books. [P]

CHAPTER 10

Literature Response Journals

Written Reflections During Reading

Literature Response Journal

p. 63 I've just finished reading about Sklya being back in her children's lives and all of the sporatic and unpredictable things she keeps doing. No one ever knows what her mood will be, so they feel as if they are all walking on eggshells constantly. She can hardly be counted on and I feel frustrated that she just prances into the kids' lives after seven years and doesn't even respect or acknowledge the huge sacrifices Gram has made to raise them.

p. 96 Just reading about Clive and Skyla wanting to take Naomi with them to Las Vegas for a trip sent up immediate red flags. Their manipulative scheming is terrifying because the author has already set up a bond between the reader and the main character. You know if Skyla doesn't spend time with her children now, she will most definitely neglect them in the future. Except then it will be far more devastating because Gram won't be able to come to Naomi's rescue. My appreciation for the grandmother grows with every page of this book.

p. 153 I am doing my best to create the radish carvings in my mind and to form a mental picture of the finished product. Maybe Naomi's father is in the crowd and will want to visit his old friends. How wise Pam Muñoz Ryan was when she wrote this book to incorporate so many Spanish words. This book supports diversity in the classroom beautifully. A culturally and linguistically diverse child would be able to connect with Naomi in many ways.

p. 224 What anxiety and nervousness Naomi must be feeling right now, wondering what will happen when they see the judge and who will gain custody. I can hardly imagine what it would be like for Owen and his sister to be separated. Or what would it be like for Gram? I predict that Naomi will carve something magnificent to symbolize all that she has experienced. It is the way she best expresses herself; it is who she is and projects her cultural roots.

Excerpts from the Literature Response
Journal of a Preservice Teacher for Pam
Muñoz Ryan's *Becoming Naomi Leon*

As you just witnessed, a future teacher's rich personal responses to *Becoming Naomi Leon* were recorded throughout the reading of this title, not retrospectively at the end of the book. As a book is read, fleeting thoughts, reactions, opinions, connections, and predictions flash through the mind of the reader. Once the journey is completed, most of those fleeting ideas cannot be rekindled in their genuine, spontaneous form. In fact, the vital remnants of the reading process are actually lost when response is reserved until after the reading event is completed.

A child's responses to Paula Fox's classic *One-Eyed Cat* are also more context specific and emotionally richer when recorded throughout the text rather than only at the book's conclusion (Hancock, 1992). Compare these responses written during and following the reading of this introspective story of a boy disobediently shooting his gun in the dark of night and hiding the truth from his parents.

Ned your lying again your living a life of lies are you proud? Are you happy? Look at what your doing living a big lie. You can't see me, you can't be me, but I can see you and I can be you and I am so sick living in your lying world.

(Sixth-grade response on p. 102 of *One-Eyed Cat*)

The book wasn't all that boring. It had a happy ending and a psychological theme. I'm surprised he told his mom but it would be hard to keep it a secret that long. I can understand why this is a Newbery honor book.

(Sixth-grade response on the final page of *One-Eyed Cat*)

Whereas the first entry reflects reader involvement and actually speaks to the character, the second entry, written by the same reader, reflects only a bland retrospective overview of the text.

Because the reading process is an ongoing accumulation of plot information, character insights, and personal connections, it is crucial to capture those thoughts throughout the reading journey, rather than waiting until the journey is complete. Written response to literature is the vehicle for accomplishing this task. The written response creates a permanent record of the reader's thoughts before, during, and following the reading. The written record can be drawn on for later discussion, revisiting the book, or as a seed for more extensive writing. The written response deserves particular attention in celebrating the value of response in exposing the individuality of the reader.

The purpose of this chapter is to explore the possibilities of written response across age/grade levels and to encourage literature-based professionals consistently to inspire their students to realize the full potential of this response option. Because response is developmental in nature, a gradual approach to transitioning to the written response is suggested. Categories for both primary and intermediate/middle-level responses are suggested as options and a means of exploring an expanding response potential. Complete guidelines for utilizing literature response journals and introspective character journals also highlight this chapter. Written response establishes the permanence of the reader's passing ideas, enabling him or her to revisit and build from them through continual growth in the understanding of and appreciation for literature.

TRANSITIONING FROM ORAL TO WRITTEN RESPONSE

The written response to literature captures the fleeting thoughts of readers in print, creating a permanent record of the ongoing responses of a reader to literature. Developmentally, written response builds on all of the other response modes and finds itself near the peak of the developmental hierarchy of response. Young children's oral abilities allow them to verbalize response; older students in intermediate and middle grades acquire increasing ability to transfer their spontaneous thoughts and reflections from their heads and hearts to a journal format. This transition from oral to written response can be guided by including structured reading, the use of prompts, and teacher modeling before complete freedom in written response is granted. Some students will make this transition smoothly and effectively, but many will need to take interim steps on the road to independent written response.

Transitioning through picture books. Although the oral response to literature is valued and encouraged, the teacher must provide ways to help students transfer their rich oral responses to written form. The beginning of written response in a journal might be initiated with daily read-alouds of picture books (see Figure 10.1) followed by an open-ended prompt or choice of prompts for journal writing (see discussion of oral prompts in Chapter 9). Initially, allow students to discuss their responses orally, a familiar routine for most. Then request that students capture those

FIGURE 10.1 Book Cluster: Transitions from oral to written response

Picture Books

Avi (2003). *Silent movie*. Illus. by C. B. Mordan. New York: Atheneum. [I]
Bunting, Eve (1994). *Smoky night*. Illus. by David Diaz. San Diego: Harcourt Brace. [P/I]
Bunting, Eve (2004). *My special day at Third Street School*. Illus. by Suzanne Bloom. Honesdale, PA:
    Boyds Mills Press. [P/I]
Curtis, Gavin (1998). *The bat boy and his violin*. Illus. by E. B. Lewis. New York: Simon & Schuster. [P/I]
Gerstein, Mordacai (2003). *The man who walked between the towers*. New York: Roaring Brook. [P/I]
Grimes, Nikki (2002). *Talkin' about Bessie: The story of aviator Elizabeth Coleman*. Illus. by E. B.
    Lewis. New York: Orchard. [P/I]
Hest, Amy (2004). *Mr. George Baker*. Illus. by Jon J. Muth. Cambridge, MA: Candlewick.
Howard, Elizabeth Fitzgerald (2000). *Virgie goes to school with us boys*. Illus. by E. B. Lewis.
    New York: Simon & Schuster. [P/I]
LaMarche, Jim (2000). *The raft*. New York: HarperCollins. [I]
McKissack, Patricia (2000). *The honest to goodness truth*. Illus. by Giselle Potter. New York: Atheneum. [P/I]
Polacco, Patricia (2000). *The butterfly*. New York: Philomel. [I]
Rappaport, Doreen (2001). *Martin's big words: The life of Dr. Martin Luther King, Jr.* Illus. by Bryan
    Collier. New York: Hyperion. [P/I/M]
Recorvits, Helen (2002). *My name is Yoon*. Illus. by Gabi Swiatkowska. New York: Farrar, Straus &
    Giroux. [P/I]
Rosen, Michael (2005). *Michael Rosen' sad book*. Illus. by Quentin Blake. Cambridge, MA:
    Candlewick. [I/M]
Say, Allen (1993). *Grandfather's journey*. Boston: Houghton Mifflin. [P/I]
Turner, Ann (2001). *Abe Lincoln remembers*. Illus. by Wendell Minor. New York: HarperCollins. [P/I]
Woodson, Jacqueline (2004). *Coming on home soon*. Illus. by E. B. Lewis. New York: Putnam. [P/I]

Transitional Chapter Books

Buchanan-Smith, Doris (1973/2005). *A taste of blackberries*. Illus. by Mike Wimmer. HarperCollins. [I]
Dunrea, Oliver (2006). *Hanne's quest*. New York: Philomel. [I]
Gardiner, John (1980). *Stone fox*. New York: HarperCollins. [P/I]
Haas, Jessie (2001). *Runaway radish*. Illus. by Margot Apple. New York: Greenwillow. [P/I]
Hesse, Karen (1994). *Sable*. Illus. by Marcia Sewall. New York: Henry Holt. [P/I]
Hesse, Karen (1999). *Just juice*. Illus. by Robert Andrew Parker. New York: Scholastic. [I]
Look, Lenore (2006). *Ruby Lu, empress of everything*. Illus. by Anne Wilsdorf. New York: Atheneum. [P/I]
Lowry, Lois (2002). *Gooney bird Greene*. Illus. by Middy Thomas. Boston: Houghton Mifflin. [P/I]
Wells, Rosemary (2002). *Wingwalker*. Illus. by Brian Selznick. New York: Hyperion. [I]

Chapter Books

Avi (2001). *The secret school*. New York: Harcourt Brace. [I]
Balliet, Blue (2006). *The Wright 3*. Illus. by Brett Helquist. Scholastic. [I]
Barry, Dave, & Pearson, Ridley (2004). *Peter and the star catchers*. New York: Hyperion. [I/M]
Chodenko, Gennifer (2004). *Al Capone does my shirts*. New York: Putnam. [I/M]
Clements, Andrew (1998). *Frindle*. New York: Simon & Schuster. [I]
Cooper, Susan (1999). *King of shadows*. New York: McElderry. [I]

FIGURE 10.1 Continued

Creech, Sharon (2002). *Ruby Holler*. New York: HarperCollins. [I]
Creech, Sharon (2006). *Replay*. New York: Joanna Cotler/HarperCollins. [I/M]
Gantos, Jack (2000). *Joey Pigza loses control*. New York: Farrar, Straus & Giroux. [I/M]
Hannigan, Katherine (2004). *Ida B*. New York: Greenwillow. [I]
Lowry, Lois (1989). *Number the stars*. Boston: Houghton Mifflin. [I]
Lowry, Lois (2006). *Gossamer*. Boston: Houghton Mifflin. [I/M]
Martin, Ann (2001). *Belle Teal*. New York: Scholastic. [I]
Naylor, Phyllis R (1991). *Shiloh*. New York: Macmillan. [I]
Wiles, D (2001). *Love, Ruby Lavender*. New York: Harcourt Brace. [I]

very thoughts from their minds and hearts on paper. Allow 5 to 8 minutes to write a personal response. Over time, growth will be seen in honesty and depth of response. In fact, students are likely to begin requesting even more time for writing. See Figure 10.8 later in this chapter for examples of children's written responses to David Wiesner's *The Three Pigs*.

Transitioning through chapter books. Teachers may next want to read aloud short chapter books (see transitional chapter book titles in Figure 10.1) to their students each day and follow the read-aloud with response prompts designed exclusively for the read-aloud title. Initially, they may again respond orally and then transfer their oral response to the written form in a journal. Written responses may be read orally the next day before the read-aloud or kept private at the discretion of the student. Teachers may even seek permission to make a few response entries into overhead transparencies to serve as written models of internal thoughts.

Another transitioning model involves teacher composition of a response on an overhead or computer with a projection screen. Immediately following the read-aloud chapter, the teacher can model his or her thoughts by spontaneously composing a journal entry. Attention should be given to flow of reaction with minor concern for conventions. By listening and watching, students hear and witness the response process in action and realize that words can fluently move from their heads to their paper.

Once the students have made the transition from oral to written response, the teacher can facilitate and expand the breadth and depth of the quality of response through varied response prompts (see chapter book titles in Figure 10.1). Some reader response advocates disagree with the use of prompts to extend response, but others have experienced the growth that occurs when prompts encourage various levels of interaction in readers.

TEACHER-CONSTRUCTED PROMPTS

Distinctive response prompts can be used to encourage diverse response at four levels of reader interaction with literature: experiential prompts, aesthetic prompts, cognitive prompts, and interpretive prompts. Either a teacher reads the story aloud,

From Under the Hawthorn Tree *by Marita
Conlon-McKenna. Illustrated by Donald Teskey.
Copyright © 1990. Reprinted by permission of
Holiday House.*

Under the Hawthorn Tree

Marita Conlon-McKenna

Illustrated by Donald Teskey

chapter by chapter, or each student reads the selected book independently. At the
end of selected chapters, students are asked to respond to a teacher-constructed
prompt. The teacher prepares these prompts by appropriately selecting from all four
avenues of reader interaction. The events of particular chapters naturally lend themselves to any one of four prompt types, as discussed next.

Experiential prompts. These are response prompts that elicit prior
knowledge, prior personal experience (text-to-life connections), and prior reading
(text-to-text connections). They focus on what the reader brings to the reading
experience.

- How do you relate this chapter to your own life?
- How does (*name a character*) remind you of someone you know?
- How does (*name a character*) remind you of some other character you've met
  in a book?

Aesthetic prompts.   These are response prompts that elicit feelings, empathy, and character identification. They promote emotional interactions with the text, moving response beyond efferent plot summary.

- How does this chapter make you feel?
- How would you feel if you were (*name a character*) in this situation?
- How would you feel if you were (*name another character*)?

Cognitive prompts.   These are response prompts that encourage solving problems, making predictions, and making inferences about characters and plot development. They require readers to think, brainstorm, create, and construct outcomes.

- What do you think will happen to (*name a character*)?
- If you were (*name a character*), what would you do in this situation?
- What advice would you give (*name a character*) at this point in the story?

Interpretive prompts.   These are response prompts that elicit personal consideration of meaning or message, morals or values, and personal judgment of characters and situations. They call for a degree of higher-level reasoning by requiring an explanation that is often difficult to put into words.

- What meaning or message does this chapter have for you?
- Why do you believe (*name of character*) did or did not make the right choice?
- What do you think the following words mean? (*Quote text*)
- What kind of person do you think (*name of character*) is? How do you know?

These prompts worked particularly well in a study designed and conducted by Hancock (1994, 1995) with children in Ireland and the United States. *Under the Hawthorn Tree* by Marita Conlon-McKenna is set in Ireland in the late 1840s during the height of the Great Famine. Three homeless children (Michael, Eily, and Peggy) escape the workhouse and begin a journey beset with hunger and danger in an attempt to locate their only living relatives in a distant Irish village. The prompt categories formed the framework for this reader response study, which encouraged a multiple perspective on response. The study also explored the ability of children's literature to transcend cultural differences and build humanistic empathy, trust, and understanding while enriching a global perspective of our world.

Figure 10.2 gives a complete overview of the experiential, aesthetic, cognitive, and interpretive prompts designed for varying chapters of *Under the Hawthorn Tree.* Note that the prompts delve into four perspectives of response: (1) background experience, (2) feelings, (3) predictions and problem solving, and (4) personal interpretation and judgment. Although they vary from chapter to chapter, they integrate the four response perspectives throughout the entire book. Sample authentic responses from each category of response from Irish and American children reveal the potential effectiveness of these well-designed open-ended prompts with this book title. The Irish students, although they had experience with literature in

FIGURE 10.2 Response prompts: *Under the Hawthorn Tree*

Experiential Prompts

Response prompts that elicit prior knowledge, life connections, and connections to prior reading
What do you know about the Great Famine in Ireland or what do you think it was? (Prereading)
Of what other book or story that you have read do the events of this story remind you? (Chapter 5)
What does this chapter remind you of from your own life? (Chapter 9)
Although this story takes place a long time ago, why does it still seem so real as we read it today?
    (Chapter 11)
What does this chapter remind you of from your own life? (Chapter 12)

Aesthetic Prompts

Response prompts that elicit feelings, emotional reactions, empathy, and character identification
How do you feel about what is happening to the O'Driscoll family? (Chapter 1)
What would you say to Michael, Eily, and Peggy to ease the pain they feel inside over the death of
    their baby sister Bridget? (Chapter 2)
*"We're Irishmen, and our food is being sent away, grown in Irish soil to feed English bellies, while ours
    are empty and our people starve and die."* How do these words make you feel? (Chapter 10)
How would you feel if you were Michael in his desperate search for help? (Chapter 14)
How did you react to the children's attempts to use any kind of nourishment, even cow's blood, to
    keep them going? (Chapter 15)

Cognitive Prompts

*Response prompts that encourage solving problems, making predictions, and making inferences
    about characters and plot*
What do you think about the children's plans to escape the workhouse? (Chapter 4)
What advice would you give Michael and Eily as they struggle to help their sick little sister Peggy?
    (Chapter 13)
What do you predict will happen now that the children have finally reached Castletaggart?
    (Chapter 16)
Why do you think this author titled this book *Under the Hawthorn Tree*? (Chapter 17)

Interpretive Prompts

*Response prompts that elicit personal consideration of meaning or message, morals or values, and
    personal judgment of characters and situations*
What kind of mother does Mrs. O'Driscoll seem to be? (Chapter 3)
What event will you remember most from this chapter? (Chapter 6)
What special meaning or message does this chapter have for you? (Chapter 7)
"We're still alive. We're tired and hungry and on our own, but we still have each other. . . ." What do
    Eily's words mean to you? (Chapter 8)
*"Those that emigrated to America and Canada brought with them their strength and their courage
    and hope. Those that were left behind struggled to survive and worked to build a country where
    such a disaster could never happen again."* What special meaning do these words have for you?
    (Postreading)

their reading program, had never experienced open-ended prompts. Yet the power of the literature, the thought-provoking prompts, the openness of the teachers, and the honesty of the readers combined to provide authentic testimony to capturing written thoughts on paper. The following samples illustrate this point.

Experiential prompt (prereading/chapter 1). *What do you know about the Great Famine in Ireland or what do you think it was?* Ronan, who lives in County Cork in a small town that still bear the scars of the Great Famine, responded,

The famine years were 1845, 1846 and 1847. Ireland's population decreased by over two million. Over half of those emigrated to other countries. . . . Because of their poverty, most of the Irish people depended on potatoes for food. Irelands potatoe failure was caused by a plant disease called blight. . . . People used to call the people donkey eaters . . . because they ate donkey flesh. . . . My house is three famine cottages put together. . . .

Sophie, also from County Cork, responded with both words and a drawing (see Figure 10.3) to illustrate the experiential schema she brought to the book.

FIGURE 10.3   Response to *Under the Hawthorn Tree,* Chapter 1, by Sophie from Ireland

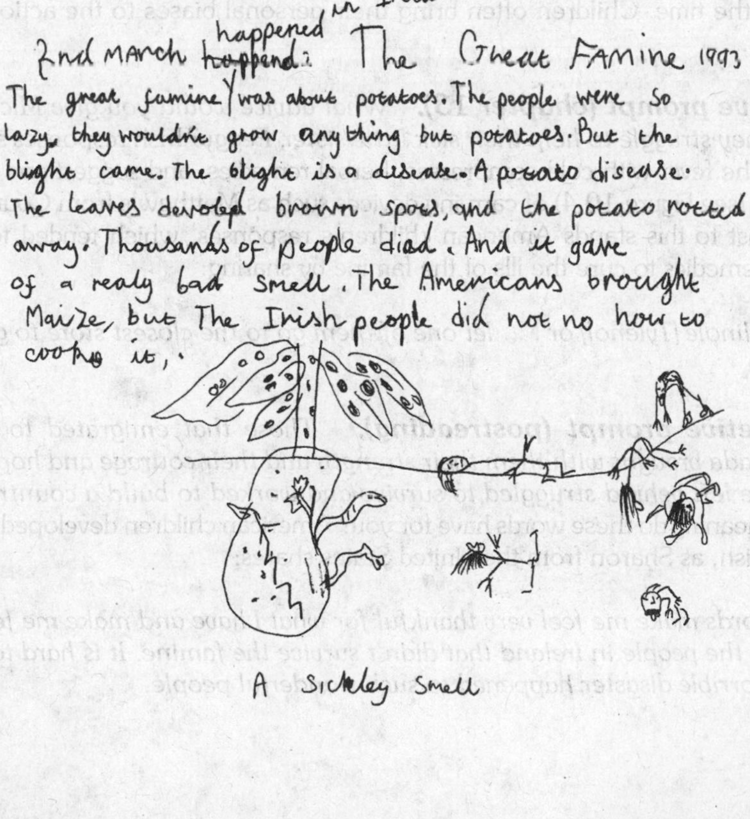

2nd March happened in Ireland it ~~happened:~~ The Great Famine 1993

The great famine was about potatoes. The people were so lazy, they wouldn't grow anything but potatoes. But the blight came. The blight is a disease. A potato disease. The leaves developed brown spots, and the potato rotted away. Thousands of people died. And it gave of a realy bad smell. The Americans brought Maize, but The Irish people did not no how to cook it,

A Sickley Smell

Another child quoted a famine poem in Gaelic,

Pr'tai ar naidin, pra'tai um noin	Potatoes in the morning, potatoes at midday,
Agus da' n-eireoinn i nean-oiche,	And if we got up at midnight,
Pra'tai gheobhainn	We could get potatoes again.

and another related a long tale of mistaken famine death at a local cemetery. The variety of responses to a simple experiential prompt serves as testimony to the individuality of reader response.

Aesthetic prompt (chapter 10). *"We're Irishmen, and our food is being sent away, grown in Irish soil to feed English bellies, while ours are empty and our people starve and die." How do these words make you feel?* Charlotte from Dublin revealed anger at the English and used a "we–they" identification as she responded,

I feel jealous about this. The English taking all our food when we are starving to death. We are dieing and they are probably very healthy, wealthy, and well-off. We are about to die and they have us as slaves so that they don't die.

Noteworthy here is that Irish children do not study the famine formally until their fifth–sixth class. A movement in Irish textbooks and by teachers has arisen to avoid portraying the English as "bad guys" and to instead put the famine in the context of international happenings and to explain the political, social, and cultural attitudes of the time. Children often bring their personal biases to the actions in the literature.

Cognitive prompt (chapter 13). *What advice would you give Michael and Eily as they struggle to help their sick little sister, Peggy?* Irish responses suggested treating the fever with cold compresses, herbal remedies, and suggestions and even drawings (see Figure 10.4) of carrying devices such as Matthew's from County Cork. In contrast to this stands American children's responses, which tended to choose today's remedies to cure the ills of the famine by sharing:

Go get tilinole [Tylenol] or . . . let one of them go to the closest store to get some medicine.

Interpretive prompt (postreading). *"Those that emigrated to America and Canada brought with them their strength and their courage and hope. Those that were left behind struggled to survive and worked to build a country." What special meaning do these words have for you?* American children developed empathy for the Irish, as Sharon from the United States shares:

These words make me feel very thankful for what I have and make me feel very sorry for the people in Ireland that didn't survive the famine. It is hard to believe such a horrible disaster happened to such wonderful people.

FIGURE 10.4 Response to *Under the Hawthorn Tree*, Chapter 13, by Matthew from Ireland

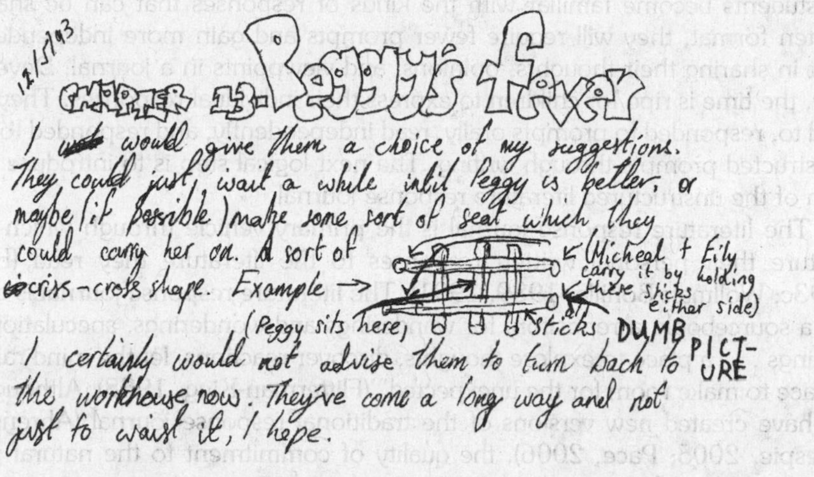

12/5/'03

CHAPTER 13- Peggy's Fever

I would give them a choice of my suggestions.
They could just wait a while until Peggy is better, or
maybe (if possible) make some sort of seat which they
could carry her on. A sort of ← (Micheal + Eily
criss-cross shape. Example →   carry it by holding
                                      these sticks
(Peggy sits here)   sticks DUMB PICTURE   either side)
I certainly would not advise them to turn back to
the workhouse now. They've come a long way and not
just to waist it, I hope.

Stephen from Dublin records a final reflection that projects the religious sentiment that pervades many Irish responses:

[A]nd I'm sad to say that there was so many people who saved our lives by giving their own. I pray that God will enter this country and be with us as we are his children and I know he loved the people in the famine the exzact same way he does now.

These responses inform practitioners of the variety and depth of responses collected from all four avenues of response: experiential, aesthetic, cognitive, and interpretive. These prompts have no right or wrong preconceived answers. Their value lies in personal honesty and a willingness to share innermost thoughts through the written response mode.

Not all books lend themselves to these varied response options, so it is important for the teacher to locate an appropriate book and to design worthwhile prompts. Although *Under the Hawthorn Tree* linked a prompt to each book chapter, it is not necessary to introduce a prompt for all chapters. Be certain the prompts are meaningfully designed and will elicit thoughts worthy of written response. Those who achieve success with this title might be interested to know that there are two sequels: *Wildflower Girl,* which continues the saga of the youngest child who journeys alone to America to start a new life in Boston, and *Fields of Home,* which completes the trilogy.

The potential of prompts to elicit written responses to literature through active reflection and thought should not be underestimated. The prompt categories and related prompts provide a framework or model for many titles. These prompts ask readers to think, to feel, to express, to connect, to predict, to interpret, to relate, to become. The prompts compel the reader to focus on the characters, the dilemmas, the causes, the outcomes, and the implications. Some may view prompts as restrictive, but they exist to serve as facilitators of understanding, feeling, and engagement in literature.

The Literature Response Journal

As students become familiar with the kinds of responses that can be shared in a written format, they will require fewer prompts and gain more independence and trust in sharing their thoughts, opinions, and viewpoints in a journal. Developmentally, the time is ripe for children to express their individual responses. They've been read to, responded to prompts orally, read independently, and responded to teacher-constructed prompts through writing. The next logical step is to introduce the freedom of the unstructured literature response journal.

The literature response journal is the primary vehicle through which students capture their personal written responses to the literature they read (Hancock, 1993c; Wollman-Bonilla, 1989, 1991). The literature response journal is described as "a sourcebook, a repository for wanderings and wonderings, speculations, questionings . . . a place to explore thoughts, discover reactions, let the mind ramble . . . a place to make room for the unexpected" (Flitterman-King, 1988). Although teachers have created new versions of the traditional response journal (Ahrens, 2005; Gillespie, 2005; Pace, 2006), the quality of commitment to the natural response process remains firm in capturing ongoing thoughts.

The final stage of written response involves independent reading and spontaneous recording of thoughts. Although a natural first step in the response process is to write at the end of each chapter, capable students should be encouraged to respond at any point in the book at which a response enters their mind. This freedom elicits the fullest, richest range of responses. For others who may still have difficulty with such an open-ended request, the guidelines in Figure 10.5 provide direction, focus, and options for sharing written responses through a literature journal. They reflect the openness and freedom of the journal and encourage risk taking and trust. The guidelines provide impetus but do not limit response options.

Exploring Response Options

What kinds of responses can teachers expect students to produce in literature response journals when complete freedom of expression is granted the reader? Several classroom studies have provided information about the types of responses children exhibit to quality literature when reading and responding in a literature journal or reading log. Knowing the response capabilities of varying ages of children assists in teacher expectations of response options. In the studies discussed in the following subsections, the suggested categories must not be considered all inclusive. Children should always be encouraged to explore their own ideas and response styles, even those responses that do not fit these categories. Teachers are encouraged to use these categories as a framework for response options, not a limitation on them.

Primary-Grade Responses

Julie Wollman-Bonilla and Barbara Werchadlo (1995) noted two qualitatively different kinds of responses from ongoing studies of first graders that originated with whole-class journals and narrowed to a research focus on a small group.

FIGURE 10.5 Guidelines for literature response journals*

Guidelines for literature response journals

- *Feel free to write* your innermost feelings, opinions, thoughts, likes, and dislikes. This is your journal. Feel the freedom to express yourself and your personal responses to reading through it.
- *Take the time to write* down anything that you are thinking while you read. The journal is a way of recording those fleeting thoughts that pass through your mind as you interact with the book. Keep your journal close by and stop to write often, whenever a thought strikes you.
- *Don't worry* about the accuracy of spelling and mechanics in the journal. The content and expression of your personal thoughts should be your primary concern. The journal will not be evaluated for a grade. Relax and share.
- *Record the page number* on which you were reading when you wrote your response. Although it may seem unimportant, you might want to look back to verify your thoughts.
- *One side only* of your spiral notebook paper, please. Expect to read occasional interested comments from your teacher. These comments will not be intended to judge or criticize your reactions, but will create an opportunity for us to "converse" about your thoughts.
- *Relate the book* to your own experiences and share similar moments from your life or from books you have read in the past.
- *Ask questions* while reading to help you make sense of the characters and the unraveling plot. Don't hesitate to wonder why, indicate surprise, or admit confusion. These responses often lead to an emerging understanding of the book.
- *Make predictions* about what you think will happen as the plot unfolds. Validate, invalidate or change those predictions as you proceed in the text. Don't worry about being wrong.
- *Talk to the characters* as you begin to know them. Give them advice to help them. Put yourself in their place and share how you would act in a similar situation. Approve or disapprove of their values, actions, or behavior. Try to figure out what makes them react the way they do.
- *Praise or criticize* the book, the author, or the literary style. Your personal tastes in literature are important and need to be shared.
- *There is no limit* to the types of responses you may write. Your honesty in capturing your thoughts throughout the book is your most valuable contribution to the journal. These guidelines are meant to trigger, not limit, the kinds of things you write. Be yourself and share your personal responses to literature through your journal.

- Text-centered responses (what is happening in the book)
  1. *Retelling.* Recounts text events.
  2. *Understanding characters.* Expresses understanding of characters' thoughts or feelings, either stated or implied in the text.
  3. *Question.* Questions or expresses curiosity about plot or characters' actions.
  4. *Prediction.* Predicts plot or characters' actions.

*From Hancock, M. R. (1993). Exploring and extending personal response through literature journals. *The Reading Teacher, 46*(6), 472. Copyright © 1993 by the International Reading Association. All rights reserved.

- Reader-centered responses (readers' thoughts and feelings about the book and the experience of reading the book)
    1. *Personal reaction.* Expresses students' thoughts or feelings about the text.
    2. *Relating to experience.* Relates text to students' own experiences.
    3. *Self in story.* Expresses students' sense of being in the story or desire to be participating in the story events. (pp. 564–565)

The researchers reported the majority of responses to Dahl's *James and the Giant Peach* in the first two months of school as 83% text centered and 17% reader centered. A small group of four girls continued with the project and a dramatic shift from text centered (29%) to reader centered (71%) occurred during November through May for the case study participants. The study articulates the importance of discussion prior to writing for emergent readers and writers, the challenge involved with some children recording written thoughts even with the encouragement of constructive spelling, and the growth in response quantity and diverse categories over time. The study presents an initial working framework for the potential responses of primary-age children and serves as a guide for classroom teachers. A later study by the same researchers (Wollman-Bonilla & Werchaldo, 1999) showcased the important role of teachers and peers in scaffolding between textual understanding and the child's response.

Through teacher action research, Mary Dekker (1991) reported results of a two-year study of the use of self-selected texts, silent reading, and reading logs as part of her second- and third-grade reading program. Student responses at this age/grade level fell into six categories:

1. *Retelling.* Students tell all or parts of the story they read.
2. *Simple evaluation.* Students write that they liked or disliked the book but do not provide textual information.
3. *Elaborated evaluation.* Students write why they liked the book and provided one or more incidents from the text to describe what they liked.
4. *Personal experience.* Students relate the events in the book to events in their own lives.
5. *Character response.* Students tell what they liked or disliked about particular characters.
6. *Record questions.* Students ask questions about the book itself or ideas the text explored.

Dekker (1991) found that describing response was only one part of her role as response facilitator. She also used her knowledge of types of response to help the students create richer and more varied responses. By valuing book talk and continually demonstrating connections between oral and written response, Dekker's students grew to love literature and appreciate options for response. This practitioner study reflects longitudinal growth of a teacher and her students in the realm of primary-grade reader response. The results validate an earlier study by Diane Barone (1990) about the potential of primary-level students to move beyond comprehension toward aesthetic response. Dekker's categories serve as catalysts for teachers who want to begin but need to set some expectations for themselves while building an awareness of the response potentials of their primary students.

Intermediate/Middle-Level Responses

An extensive case study of written responses of intermediate-level students (Hancock, 1991, 1993c) revealed a variety of rich options of which practitioners need to be made aware. Teachers need to be cognizant of the possible avenues of response before they can assist their students in extending response in personal literature response journals. The following "categories of response" originated from a study of sixth-grade subjects' responses to realistic fiction (Hancock, 1991). They have been adapted and supplemented to include a wider range of students (grades 4 though 8) via a continuing study of reader response through written journals (Hancock, 1993a, 1995). An exploration of these categories and sample responses in each category alert the teacher to the possibilities, not the probabilities, of response.

The categories of response are organized into three response stances of the reader: (1) immersion, (2) self-involvement, and (3) detachment. Each major category and accompanying subcategories are supplemented by examples from authentic journals for Gary Paulsen's *Hatchet,* Katherine Paterson's *The Great Gilly Hopkins,* or Paula Fox's *One-Eyed Cat.*

Immersion categories.   Indicates reader immersion in the text in an attempt to make sense of emerging character and plot.

1. *Understanding.* Responses indicate the reader's current understanding of both character and plot. Responses move beyond summary to reflect a personal interpretation or they may reflect sudden discovery of meaning.

Brian is having trouble taking the death of the pilot.
W. E. doesn't want Gilly to leave that's for sure.
These past few pages show how one lie can lead to a whole series of lies.

RESOURCES ON THE WEB
Electronic Response Journals

Although using paper and pencil has been the primary mode for journaling in the past, the increased use of technology and changing nature of today's students have brought a plethora of innovative approaches to response journaling, including electronic documents and Weblogs. Weblogs, or blogs, are online spaces that provide individuals with his or her own virtual Web spaces for posting of personal responses and commentary.

Blog postings can be read by anyone and responded to instantaneously. To protect students' privacy, teachers may explore blog websites to set up individual blogging accounts with restricted access to outside readers. Once accounts have been created, students receive immediate journaling spaces to support class content, particularly literacy events, and reader response options. Although blogs primarily provide one-way communication, inserting hyperlinks to other blogs or relevant websites support interactive writing and communication. Readers of blogs may add comments to the original postings, supporting open expression and dialogue about the literature.

Utilizing electronic documents (such as Microsoft Word) offer an alternative to Web-based blogs. Electronic documents allow students to post personal commentary, add links, and interact with peers without posting the documents on the Internet.

Blog Software
Blogger.com is a free, easy-to-use website where students can publish their own blogs.
http://www.blogger.com
Live Journal offers free blogging accounts. Upgraded fee-based accounts with more features are also available.
http://www.livejournal.com.
Xanga offers both free accounts and fee-based accounts with upgraded features.
http://www.xanga.com

Helpful Resources for Beginning Bloggers
Blogging? It's Elementary My Dear Watson. This article includes lesson plans and ideas for using blogging in education.
http://www.education-world.com/a_tech/tech/tech217.shtml
Blog Uses in Education. A visual representation of reading and writing blogs.
http://www.edtechpost.ca/gems/matrix2.gif
Blog Basics. Presented by Microsoft, this website offers tips on starting a blog, keeping an online journal, and blogging safely.
http://www.microsoft.com/athome/intouch/onlinejournal.mspx

2. *Character introspection.* Responses indicate the reader's effort to make introspective insights into the feelings, thoughts, and motives for behavior of the characters. Responses reflect a sense of understanding through reasoning but indicate a degree of uncertainty on the part of the reader. They often begin with tentative statements [i.e., "It sounds like . . . ," "He must be . . . ," "She probably . . . ," "I think (*character's name*) . . ."].

I think Brian is having trouble forgetting the divorce.
Trotter is probably ignoring Gilly to get her mad.
It sounds like Ned doesn't like where he lives.

3. *Predicting events.* Responses reflect reader speculation about what will emerge as the text proceeds. These statements often begin with "I bet . . . ," "I guess . . . ," "I think . . . ," "If . . . then." Also included are response statements that validate or invalidate both stated and unstated predictions, serving as a link between prediction and understanding.

If he keeps eating the berries, he will die.
I bet Brian will get his parents together. They will probably work together to find him.
The parents didn't get together. (invalidates earlier prediction)
I didn't think she'd steal the money.

4. *Questioning.* Responses reflect a lack of complete understanding or a questioning of text. They may reflect puzzlement indicated by "I wonder why . . . ," "I can't tell." Questions may reflect confusion. Statements that begin "I can't believe . . . ," "I'm surprised . . . ," "I didn't know . . . ," may reflect doubt or disbelief in the reader's attempt to comprehend the text.

I wonder if the pilot is all eaten up by now.
This is weird. Why does Brian have the flu? You don't normally throw up water.
What do they mean by "When the ax dropped"?

Self-involvement categories. Reflects responses that exhibit personal involvement with character and plot in which the reader vicariously becomes the character, becomes part of the plot or setting, or puts himself or herself in place of the character in the book's action.

5. *Character identification.* Responses show the reader has achieved a sense of personal identification with the character through statements like, "If I were . . . ," "I probably would/wouldn't. . . ." Empathetic identification such as, "I know how he feels . . . ," "I feel sorry for . . ." or sharing a related experience from the reader's life may also occur. Directly addressing the character or giving advice also indicates involvement.

For Pete's sake, Brian, tell me what you know.
If I were Ned, I'd get that thought out of my head.
Poor Gilly. I gues that's the way it is if your a foster child.
I experience the same, lawyers, yelling, and fighting.

6. *Character assessment.* Responses indicate the reader's judgment of the actions and values of the character measured against his or her own personal standards of behavior. Evaluative terms such as traits of the character (e.g., smart, dumb, nice, mean) and distinctive expression of likes or dislikes may appear. Responses may also reflect perception of growth or change such as, "She's starting to . . . ," "He's beginning to . . ."

> *Brian is very unintelligent he ate the berries with the pits and now he's sick serves him right.*
> *I like Gilly. She says what she thinks.*
> *Brian is starting to change for the good. He is very responsible at times.*

7. *Story involvement.* Responses indicate the reader's personal involvement in the story and resulting reaction to setting, theme, actions, or sensory aspects of the story. Evaluative terms (e.g., "disgusting," "cool," "weird") often reflect this interaction. Responses may reflect personal satisfaction or dissatisfaction with the unfolding events of the story. Active or passive anticipation of reading might be shared by "I can't wait . . . ," "Do I have to go on?"

> *I just lost my appetite. Brian eating turtle eggs. Raw eggs at that.*
> *It would be nice to live on a hill with a view in a big old house.*
> *I can't wait to get to the part where he shoots the cat.*
> *Disgusting. Absolutely disgustingly chilling. Gross! Gross! Gross!*

Detachment categories. Responses indicate that the reader detaches from the book in order to evaluate literature or to contemplate his or her perspective on reading/writing.

8. *Literary evaluation.* Responses indicate the reader's evaluation of all or part of the book. They may indicate praise or criticism of the author, writing style, literary genre, or ability to maintain reader interest. Responses may compare or contrast the book, author, or genre to others known to the reader (includes text-to-text connections).

> *These were boring pages because all they talked about was fish.*
> *I don't think the author should have Gilly use swear words.*
> *This is so realistic. I love it.*

9. *Reader/writer digressions.* Responses indicate the wanderings of the reader's mind while he or she interacts with the text, often showing thoughts outside the context of the book. They may include references to the act of reading, the literature response journal, the nature of the reading/writing environment, or simply digressive statements (includes text-to-life connections).

> *I think I'd like to go backpacking. My mom did with her sister when she was younger.*
> *I know people say you can't hear a book, but I sort of can. Like you can hear almost anything that is said.*

*I have found something out about the responses. I write the most when there
is some kind of action in the story.
I'm sick of writing right now. I'll write again at the end of the chapter.*

Teacher knowledge of response categories provides an informative framework for encouraging all that response can offer. Be aware that not all children will be comfortable with or capable of all types of response. The goal should not be to include all types of response but to expand the number and kinds of individual response options over time. Continuous, encouraging feedback with some directive, but not demanding, comments helps lead children to fulfill their own unique response potential and develop a characteristic response style.

Ongoing research in reader response reports the use of a variety of response formats, including journals, in response to multicultural literature (Lehr & Thompson, 2000), resulting in a thematic framework for categorizing response. Visual response to literature continues to initiate further research as students interpret text visually through graphic organizers and artistic expression (Hubbard, Winterbourne, & Ostrow, 1996; Whitin, 2005).

EXTENDING RESPONSE THROUGH WRITTEN FEEDBACK

Perhaps the most powerful component of the literature response journal is the written feedback that a teacher provides on an intermittent basis to each student (Hancock, 1993b). Written feedback sustains the journal writing process through comments valuing personal response to a book. Eager students anticipate the daily/weekly return of their journals, savoring the rich personal comments of the teacher. Particularly early in the literature response journal experience, students need to know that they are on the right track, that their honest responses are valued, and that responses deserve to be shared. The teacher needs to react to the literature response journal as often as possible—at least three times per week at first. Writing in the margins of the journal works for some teachers; others believe sticky notes keep the journal in the handwritten control of the reader.

A common pitfall of response journals is that students become limited by the type of response they are willing to try. Unaware of the multiplicity of response options to literature, they take the safe road and continue what has worked for them in the past. A talented, informed teacher, however, can skillfully identify some options that might be open to each reader. These categories of response then become options for possible exploration by a student.

During the early stages of response journal writing, teacher comments tend to be reinforcing, nondirective, and encouraging. They inspire the reader to reflect, to connect, and to continue to share innermost thoughts and feelings. Subtly, those comments may even model the kinds of responses to which the reader may aspire. For example, an excellent choice for a literature response journal is Sharon Creech's *Chasing Redbird*. Written in short chapters, the format lends itself to intermittent writing. It concerns the character of 13-year-old Zinny Taylor and her struggle to deal with her aunt's death and to find her own identity. In response to a student response journal entry, the teacher may respond,

You really have put yourself into Zinny's situation. You seem to be on the verge of reacting to her decision to clear the trail on her own. What do you think of that decision? Is it what you would do if these circumstances of a loved one's death surrounded your life? Just what is it Zinny is trying to accomplish anyway? I worry about her out there alone, especially if she stays away from home for days at a time. You've really grasped Zinny's adventurous spirit, perhaps because she is really a lot like you, Jennifer.

Jennifer is not required to answer the teacher's questions, but teacher feedback does make her think more deeply and encourages her to identify further with the main character. Her responses are likely to reflect a value judgment on Zinny's decision and perhaps a personal connection to the loss of a special person in her life. Teacher encouragement, not directives, provides powerful momentum to think deeper, share more honestly, and connect story events to one's own life.

Figure 10.6 shares excerpts from an ongoing response journal to Gary Paulsen's *The Haymeadow* by a sixth-grade student. Note the parallel ongoing comments from the teacher that motivate the student to persist, grow, and stretch through response. The development of a comfortable response style begins during the first journal and usually continues to blossom through subsequent journals. Take the time to read the student responses (cursive) and the teacher comments (manuscript) to confirm the difference teacher encouragement made in maintaining the momentum and increasing the depth of response.

Following an initial period of teacher–student confidence building, response partners take on an important role in the feedback process. Self-selected partners may exchange journals at the end of reading workshop to react to partner comments. If this is uncomfortable for specific children, it is important to continue teacher feedback with those individuals. Teachers should always be certain to provide their own feedback once a week, even when the literature response journal process is well in place.

Response provides a unique mode of expression, and a teacher demanding responses in a particular mode may negate the freedom of response. At the same time, well-directed suggestions may lead the student to explore any otherwise unexplored options. A teacher wields powerful influence over a student's initiative to explore and expand response. Students must feel the freedom to accept or reject suggestions offered. The literature response journal is primarily a vehicle for personal expression. When that expression becomes stagnant, however, it is the teacher's responsibility to provide additional ideas for varying the natural response categories. As students in a trusting environment acquire more experience with response, they must feel free to accept or reject suggestions and only internalize response options that feel comfortable to their style of responding (Hancock, 1993b).

Figure 10.7 shares the written responses of third-, fifth-, and sixth-grade students to classic Caldecott and Newbery Medal titles. Only through teacher effort in providing feedback do these children maintain their motivation to respond often and honestly to literature, regardless of grade level. In addition, Figure 10.8 lists several books that work well with literature response journals because of dramatic episodes, memorable

FIGURE 10.6 Literature response journal of a sixth grader to Gary Paulsen's *The Haymeadow* (note teacher feedback)

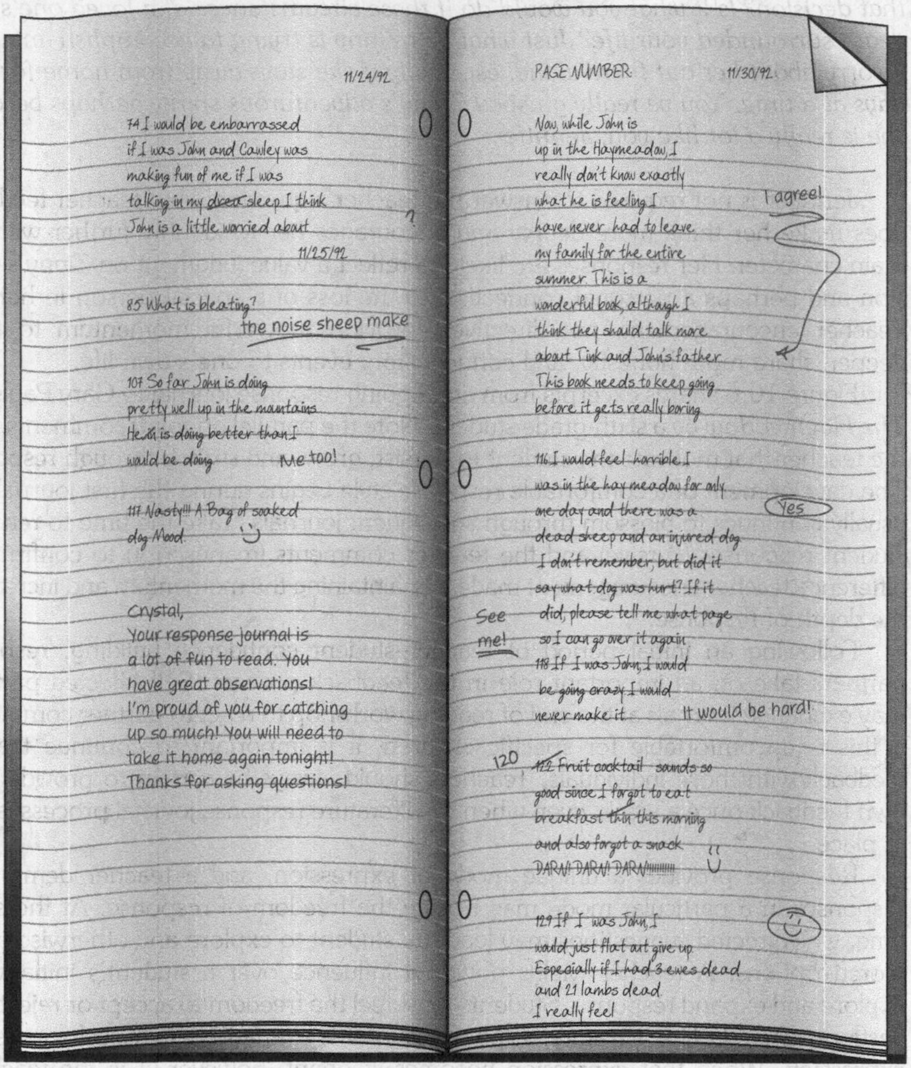

Left page (11/24/92):

74 I would be embarrassed if I was John and Cawley was making fun of me if I was talking in my sleep I think John is a little worried about

11/25/92

85 What is bleating?
    the noise sheep make

107 So far John is doing pretty well up in the mountains His is doing better than I would be doing   Me too!

117 Nasty!!! A Bag of soaked dog food

Crystal,
Your response journal is a lot of fun to read. You have great observations! I'm proud of you for catching up so much! You will need to take it home again tonight! Thanks for asking questions!

Right page (PAGE NUMBER 11/30/92):

Now, while John is up in the Haymeadow, I really don't know exactly what he is feeling I have never had to leave my family for the entire summer. This is a wonderful book, although I think they should talk more about Tink and John's father This book needs to keep going before it gets really boring   I agree!

116 I would feel horrible I was in the hay meadow for only one day and there was a dead sheep and an injured dog I don't remember, but did it say what dog was hurt? If it did, please tell me what page so I can go over it again   Yes
See me!
118 If I was John, I would be going crazy I would never make it   It would be hard!

120 122 Fruit cocktail sounds so good since I forgot to eat breakfast this morning and also forgot a snack DARN! DARN! DARN!!!!!!

129 If I was John, I would not just flat out give up. Especially if I had 5 ewes dead and 21 lambs dead I really feel

characters, and presentation of moral dilemmas. The selection of motivating reading is the first step toward success with response journals.

THE CHARACTER JOURNAL

A steady flow of literature response journals with every book read in a literature-based program is not advised. Just as students turn off to routine worksheets, they can easily tire of the same format of response journal writing. This text introduces several other

FIGURE 10.6   Continued

PAGE NUMBER:

Sorry for John Although
he has taken it very
well. Leary Paulsen is
expressing himself very
well in this book

I like how you changed pen colors!

129-130 I would be really
scared to have to use the rifle.
I would love to have horses like
Speck and Spud, wouldn't ya?
Please answer!

Tell me what you like about
Speck or Spud

I think horse's names express their
personalities and I can just imagine
how they look. Spud is probably a
mottled brown (a giant couch potato?)
& Speck probably looks like it's
splattered with mud!

39 Thank goodness John found
the rifle. I hope there is no
damage to the rifle. Can't wait!!!

140 I wonder what he will clean
the rifle with besides water. It
is going to be hard to get all the
mud and slime out of the rifle.
I am also sure, positive that
John will find a way

Such confidence

PAGE NUMBER: 12-2-92

161 I hate bears. He
is probably really scared.

167 Poor Peg. I don't
know what I would
do if I was John. I
would feel scared and
wouldn't know if
I could handle it

183 Nasty, canned ham. Canned
Bake beans

184 I can't see why he
would say his father is shy

194 I would not want my
father to leave.   *Me either*

195 I like the end
And they rode up the
canyon into the Haymeadow
And the sheep And the Dogs
And the mountains

Yes! Good quote!

I think John made
it really well by himself all alone
Especially at his age. I
hope to read more books by
Gary Paulsen.

response modes that provide a change from written response. If response journals prove popular with students, however, another type of response journal, the character journal, provides a viable format that truly engages the reader in the reading process through a first-person writing stance.

A character journal is a written diary kept by the reader as he or she assumes the role of a character as a book is read. The reader actually becomes the character and keeps an ongoing journal by writing about prominent episodes that occur during specific chapters of a book. The reader writes in the first-person voice of the character,

FIGURE 10.7 Literature response journal entries for Caldecott/Newbery Medal titles

Third graders' prompted response to *The Three Pigs* by David Wiesner (2002 Caldecott Medal)

It was very funny when the dragon was moving. His tail was not because it was in the picture. On one of the pages, the dragon and pigs had alphabet soup. But my favorite part was when the pig rolled the wolf up and made him into an airplane and flew him.

—Logan

I liked The Three Pigs *because when they went into a book, they could get animated. When they came out, they were back to what they looked like before. They had beautiful pictures. And every time they went into a book, they would bring back friends from the book. I really liked the book. It was one of my favorites!*

—Jessica

Fifth graders' prompted response to *A Single Shard* by Linda Sue Park (2002 Newbery Medal)

My favorite part was when Ajimg, Min's wife, said to Tree-ear, "Please come and make this your new home. We will change your name to Hyung-pil." That was the name of their first son who died. That is so nice of her to do that and welcome Tree-ear to their home. He will now learn to make pottery like his new father.

—Emily

All of this book will catch someone's interest, but my favorite part was the breathtaking ending. When Tree-ear arrived back at Min's house his heart shattered like Min's pottery when he found out that Crane-man, his only friend, died. I could feel his rage and disappointment. Then his emotions changed rapidly when he finally had a new family. Tree-ear, now Hyung-pil, is no longer an orphan, but a happy boy. This story has one big lesson. If you want to accomplish something, and once you try hard enough, you should know how much effort you put into it. Even if along the way something blocks your path, or all your hard work shatters in front of you, something good comes out of it, as long as you try.

—Spencer

Sixth graders' open response to *Bud, Not Buddy* by Christopher Paul Curtis (2000 Newbery Medal)

One thing I notice about Bud is he's been raised well and that if he wants to do something he sure will. When he got to Grand Rapids, he was determined to find his daddy. One thing I think is that Mr. C. isn't his daddy, but might know where Bud's daddy really is. I also feel Bud is a courageous and brave young man. Oh, and my favorite part in the stop is when he poured water on Todd's p.j.'s so he'd wet his bed and get his mama all angry! This might be one of my favorite books!

—Ashley

Mr. C. seems to be embarrassed about Bud and will not admit to have left his wife (or some girl he met) alone with a baby. Most of the book has great words and details, except for "woop-zoop-sloop." It sounds just really annoying and dumb. I think that maybe Mr. C. will like Bud a little, but not too much. Since he knows that his demanding nature drove his daughter that died away, the last sentence may be correct.

—Quint

I have felt like Bud in that you don't always know if someone's joking or serious. If you question them and they're joking they laugh and if they're serious they get mad. That is how this book reminds me of my life. I think Bud will make peace with Herman E. Calloway after Herman gets over Bud's mother. I think Bud will play his saxophone with the band—or should I say Sleepy LaBone!

—Bridget

FIGURE 10.8   Book Cluster: Inviting literature response journals

Alexander, Lloyd (2001). *The gawgon and the boy.* New York: Dutton. [I/M]
Avi (1990). *The true confessions of Charlotte Doyle.* New York: Orchard Books. [I/M]
Avi (2002). *Crispin: The cross of lead.* New York: Hyperion. [I]
Balliett, Blue (2004). *Chasing Vermeer.* New York: Scholastic.[I]
Birney, Berry G. (2005). *The seven wonders of Sassafras Springs.* New York: Atheneum.[I]
Conlon-McKenna, Marita (1990). *Under the hawthorn tree.* New York: Holiday House. [I]
Curtis, Christopher Paul (1999). *Bud, not Buddy.* New York: Delacorte. [I]
Cushman, Karen (1994). *Catherine, called Birdy.* Boston: Clarion. [M]
Cushman, Karen (2003). *Rudzina.* New York: Clarion. [I]
Fenner, Carolyn (1995). *Yolanda's genius.* New York: McElderry Books. [I]
Fleischman, Paul (1997). *Seedfolks.* New York: HarperCollins. [M]
Gwaltney, Doris (2006). *Homebound.* New York: Simon & Schuster. [I/M]
Harnett, Sonya (2001). *Thursday's child.* Cambridge, MA: Candlewick Press. [I/M]
Hess, Amy (2007). *Remembering Mrs. Rossi.* Illus. by Heather Maione. Cambridge, MA: Candlewick. [I]
Hesse, Karen (1992). *Letters from Rifka.* New York: Holt. [I]
Hobbs, Will (2001). *Down the Yukon.* New York: HarperCollins. [I/M]
Holm, Jennifer (2001). *Boston Jane.* New York: HarperCollins. [I/M]
Holt, Kimberly (2001). *Dancing in Cadillac light.* New York: Putnam. [I/M]
Lowry, Lois (1995). *The giver.* Boston: Houghton Mifflin. [M]
Lowry, Lois (2000). *Gathering blue.* Boston: Houghton Mifflin.
Lyon, George Ella (2002). *Gina. Jamie. Father. Bear.* New York: Atheneum. [M]
Moses, Shelia P. (2004). *The legend of Billy Bush.* New York: McElderry. [I]
Naylor, Phyllis Reynolds (2005). *Polo's mother.* Illus. by Alan Daniel. New York: Atheneum. [I]
Park, Linda Sue (2001). *A single shard.* New York: Clarion. [I]
Park, Linda Sue (2002). *When my name was Keoka: A novel of Korea in World War II.* New York: Clarion. [I/M]
Paterson, Katherine (2002). *The same stuff as stars.* New York: Clarion. [I]
Paulsen, Gary (1987). *Hatchet.* New York: Delacorte. [I]
Philbrick, Rodman (2004). *The young man and the sea.* New York: Schoalstic. [M]
Robinet, Harriette Gillem (2000). *Walking to the bus-rider blues.* New York: Atheneum. [I]
Ryan, Pam Muñoz (2001). *Esperanza rising.* New York: Scholastic. [I/M]
Smith, D. James (2005). *The boys of San Joaquin.* New York: Atheneum. [M]
Staples, Suzanne Fisher (1989). *Shabanu: Daughter of the wind.* New York: Knopf. [M]
Wiles, Deborah (2005). *Each little bird that sings.* San Diego: Gulliver/Harcourt. [I]

sharing his or her thoughts, feelings, trepidations, and responses to the unfolding events of the book. A character journal compels the reader to climb under the character's skin, to walk in the character's shoes, and to realize the character's joys and frustrations. Simultaneously, the character journal encourages reflection as the reader thinks, judges, and weighs the actions, emotions, and reaction of the character against his or her own standards and behavior (Hancock, 1993a).

Purposefully, the character journal serves as a mode for recording the interactive process of reading and writing and promoting character involvement during the reading of literature. Because the journal is written from a character's point of view, the reader becomes the character and vicariously lives through the experiences and emotions of the story. Specific benefits of the journal include the ability to:

- Attain a high level of involvement with the literature read. The character journal sustains a personalized reading transaction enhanced by taking on the persona of the character, discouraging a distanced reading stance.
- Sustain a personal interest in the outcome of the story. With a greater stake in the unraveling plot, the events not only happen to the character but to the reader as well.
- Experience growth as an interactive reader by becoming a part of the book. As both an active participant in reading and an engaged spectator, the reader realizes that an inside stance in reading enhances the literature experience itself.
- Gain a deeper sense of story and appreciation for literature. Deeper immersion in reading through character stance may contribute to the reader's levels of understanding and enjoyment.
- Attain a deeper understanding of characters of different cultures, genders, ages, and times. Sharing the fate of characters encourages the reader to challenge or clarify his or her own beliefs and choices resulting in insights into one's own self.

Not all book titles and genres work with the character journal format of response. Careful selection can make the difference between outstanding responses and mediocre response. Several criteria assist in choosing a book to partner with the character journal.

- The age of the main character must be similar to the age of the readers. The closer the age, the greater the level of involvement. Stated simply, 12-year-olds want to read about and identify with 12- to 14-year-olds. They want to walk in the shoes of a character similar to their immediate or approaching age.
- The main character must be strongly portrayed and evidence growing maturity as the book unfolds. The same principles for defining a strongly portrayed character can be applied here. If readers are indeed to grow in an understanding of themselves, the character must continuously question, likely falter, but ultimately move ahead and learn from an experience.
- The plot must unfold through a series of highly emotional events compelling the reader to become involved. A balance of character introspection and action events blended with anticipation and momentum results in stronger reader participation.
- The text must be written in the third person so that conversion to the first-person response as character retains originality. First-person accounts of first-person texts usually result in repetition and summary. First-person responses to third-person writing, however, cultivate original entries filled with honesty and emotion.
- The text may be written with multiple characters or narrator viewpoints (Hornik, 2006), allowing for choice of contrasting perspectives depending on choice of narrator or character.

FIGURE 10.9   Book Cluster: Inviting character journal response

Bauer, Joan (2002). *Stand tall.* New York: Putnam. [I/M]
Canales, Viola (2005). *The tequila worm.* New York: Wendy Lamb/Random House. [M]
Clements, Andrew (2002). *A week in the woods.* New York: Simon & Schuster. [I]
DeFelice, Cynthia (1998). *The ghost of fossil glen.* New York: Farrar, Straus & Giroux. [I]
Di Camillo, Kate (2002). *The tiger rising.* Cambridge, MA: Candlewick. [I]
Doling, Katharine (2004). *January 2005. San Diego:* Harcourt. [M]
Graff, Nancy Price (2005).*Taking wing.* New York: Clarion. [I/M]
Hahn, Mary Downing (1991). *Stepping on the cracks.* Boston: Clarion. [I/M]
Hill, Kirkpatrick (1990). *Toughboy and Sister.* New York: Macmillan. [I]
Janeczko, Paul (2004). *Worlds afire.* Cambridge, MA: Candlewick. [I/M]
Ketchum, Liza (2005). *Where the great hawk flies.* New York: Clarion. [I/M]
Kurtz, Jane (2001). *Jakarta missing.* New York: Greenwillow. [I/M]
Paterson, Katherine (1991). *Lyddie.* New York: Lodestar. [M]
Paulsen, Gary (1992). *The haymeadow.* New York: Delacorte. [I/M]
Pearsall, Shelley (2002). *Trouble don't last.* New York: Knopf. [I]
Salisbury, Graham (2005). *Eyes of the emperor.* New York: Wendy Lamb/Random House. [M]
Spinelli, Jerry (1990). *Maniac Magee.* New York: HarperCollins. [I]
Tolan, Stephanie (2002). *Surviving the Applewhites.* New York: HarperCollins. [I/M]

Figure 10.9 highlights literature that invites first-person response through a character journal. These books reflect the criteria listed and invite the reader to step into the shoes of the character and project his or her narrative voice. Some titles reflect multiple narrators or alternating character points of view.

A study by Hancock (1993a) was instrumental in exploring, defining, and stylizing the journal as part of a literature-based reading program. Two books that fit the criteria given earlier include Will Hobbs's *Bearstone* and Katherine Paterson's *Lyddie. Bearstone* is a coming-of-age story of a lonely 14-year-old Native American foster child in search of his own identity, who learns to love and be loved by an aging Colorado rancher.

To see how the first-person voice of the writer enters third-person context of the writing, evidence Beth's response to Cloyd's irresponsible, but emotional revenge on his foster parent:

Well, I showed him. I took that saw . . . and cut every stupid, monster like, precious peach tree of his. Everyone I cut I thought of the sweet revenge I was getting. . . . I wanted the death of those trees to be slow and painful not just for the trees but for Walter too. I want Walter to pay for the hurt he caused me . . . I want him to watch the trees die and know it's his fault. . . .

Lyddie is historical fiction about the harsh life and adult responsibilities of a 13-year-old factory girl in Lowell, Massachusetts, in 1843 as she struggles to earn

FIGURE 10.10 Student guidelines for a character journal*

- Become the main character and record your thoughts, feelings, and reflections in your journal through the character's voice.
- Write the chapter number to which your journal entry refers in the left margin.
- Choose one episode from each chapter to relive in your written journal entry.
- Write on only the front side of each page in your journal. Your teacher (or partner) will comment back to you as you become the main character.
- There are no right or wrong entries for the character journal. Your journal will be unique. Find a style of first-person writing that feels comfortable to you.
- Don't be concerned about spelling/mechanics. Expressing your thoughts in the voice of the character through involvement in the book is your main objective.
- Feel free to write whatever you are thinking as you become the character. One of the unique features of the journal is the freedom it allows. You may say the things you feel in the role of the character.
- Use parentheses ( ) following your character entry to express your own personal thoughts on the actions, motives, decisions, or feelings of the character. Use this option as a means of being and expressing yourself.
- Remember: Write the thoughts and feelings of the character as you live through the episodes of the book with him or her. Put yourself in the mind and heart of that character and write what you, as the main character, think and feel.

money to save her family farm. The harassing attentions of the boss at the mill toward Lyddie were expressed by Justin, who was able empathetically to identify with Lyddie's distress:

That day was hot. I started feeling sick. I couldn't wait to go to bed. My head hurt. But Mr. Marden told me to wait when all the girls left. I was with him all alone. I was to disy to understand anything. He put his hands on me. He was saying something but I couldn't understand him. I didn't know what he was trying to do. Whatever it was I wasn't going to put up with it. I stomped on his foot and ran out of there.

Getting into the character is hard work; it can, in fact, be emotionally draining. Yet the strong characterization of these titles brought the students back to this level of intensity repeatedly throughout their reading.

The guidelines in Figure 10.10 assist students as they embark on character journals for the first time. Involvement in the life of a literary character provides an opportunity for readers to respond to the lives of others and an invitation to reflect on their own emerging identities.

---

*From Hancock, M. R. (1993). Character journals: Initiating involvement and identification through literature. *Journal of Reading, 37*, 45. Copyright © 1993 by the International Reading Association. All rights reserved.

Responding to Character Journals

To sustain the motivation needed to maintain the intense involvement expressed in the character journal, the teacher (or peer) needs to respond intermittently in writing to character journal entries. The comments serve two purposes: (1) to ensure the reader that he or she is responding as the character and (2) to address the reader as the main character as complete character involvement and identification evolve. Although the need for encouragement declines, students anticipate teacher/peer comments each day before continuing the reading and responding process.

Note these comments constructed as teacher feedback to a reader/responder. Notice how the student is addressed as herself, and subsequently addressed as the main character as reader involvement becomes ever apparent in response entries.

Carrie,

(Chapter 1)

You have already become Lyddie as you take charge of the bear incident. Already you are showing your empathetic nature when you refer to your mama's "condition" at the end of the entry. You'll have no trouble becoming Lyddie. You are already feeling and thinking like her.

Lyddie,

(Chapter 8)

You've been through so many changes. Now a new job! You express your fear of failing so intensely. It's not bad enough to have to learn the tricks of the trade in the factory, but now you have that unending noise to bear. Running the loom is a real challenge. But think of all you've been through and how far you've come. You're a factory girl now!

As with all journals, the enthusiasm and effort for the character journal can be sustained when the respondents know that someone cares about and appreciates their level of involvement.

Reading in the guise of a literary character, feeling his or her emotions, joys and fears, and reflecting on one's own identity provide a meaningful experience unavailable in a traditional reading program. Not only do character journals result in well-written, emotionally packed entries, but the first-person response process results in a level of involvement previously unknown to many readers.

CLOSING THOUGHTS

Written response to literature provides an excellent means to record those transient thoughts that flow through the mind of the reader during the act of reading. They provide documentation of the personal transaction between reader and text as a permanent record of a journey through literature. Readers who have completed several literature response journals over time claim that the response journal process stays in their heads even when reading independently. Children report more continuous reflective reading throughout a book as a result of engagement in this process.

Of all the benefits of written responses to literature, perhaps the long-term one that stands out the most is that written response causes the child to become a more reflective reader. Forcing oneself to stop reading, to capture a thought on paper, and to reenter the text with a personal commitment creates lifelong readers. The conversation that results between the reader and the journal writing continues on in the reader's mind even after the pencil leaves the paper. Meaning-making is enhanced through the power of the written response. The written response mode is time consuming and requires commitment and feedback if it is to succeed. Yet the treasure of reading and revisiting the documented flow of thoughts captured during the reading event makes this a response mode to inspire and appreciate in readers.

References

Ahrens, B. C. (2005). Finding a new way: Reinventing a sixth-grade reading program. *Journal of Adolescent & Adult Literacy, 48,* 642–654.

Barone, D. (1990). The written response of young children: Beyond comprehension to story understanding. *The New Advocate, 3,* 49–56.

Dekker, M. M. (1991). Books, reading, and response: A teacher-researcher tells a story. *The New Advocate, 4,* 37–46.

Flitterman-King, S. (1988). The role of the response journal in active reading. *The Quarterly of the National Writing Project and the Center for the Study of Writing, 10,* 4–11.

Gillespie, J. (2005). "It would be fun to do it again:" Multigenre response to literature. *Journal of Adolescent & Adult Literacy, 48,* 678–684.

Hancock, M. R. (1991). *A case study investigation of the process and content of sixth-grade literature response journals.* Unpublished doctoral dissertation, Northern Illinois University.

Hancock, M. R. (1992). Literature response journals: Insights beyond the printed page. *Language Arts, 69,* 36–42.

Hancock, M. R. (1993a). Character journals: Initiating involvement and identification through literature. *Journal of Reading, 37,* 42–50.

Hancock, M. R. (1993b). Exploring and extending personal response through literature journals. *The Reading Teacher, 46,* 466–474.

Hancock, M. R. (1993c). Exploring the meaning-making process through the content of literature response journals: A case study investigation. *Research in the Teaching of English, 27,* 335–368.

Hancock, M. R. (1994). *Reader response across the sea: Irish and American children respond to literature.* Paper presented at the 39th annual convention of the International Reading Association, Toronto, Canada.

Hancock, M. R. (1995). Discovering common bonds: Linking Ireland and America through literature. *Children's Books in Ireland (Journal of the Children's Literature Association of Ireland), 12,* 17–18.

Hornik, L. M. (2006). Two sides (or more) to every story: Books with multiple narrators. *Book Links, 15*(5), 26–30.

Hubbard, R. S., Winterbourne, N., & Ostrow, J. (1996). Visual responses to literature: Imagination through images. *The New Advocate, 9,* 309–323.

Lehr, S., & Thompson, D. L. (2000). The dynamic nature of response: Children reading and responding to *Maniac Magee* and *The Friendship. The Reading Teacher, 53,* 480–493.

Pace, B. G. (2006). Between response and interpretation: Ideological becoming and literacy events in critical readings of literature. *Journal of Adolescent & Adult Literacy, 49,* 584–594.

Whitin, P. E. (2005). The interplay of text, talk, and visual representation in expanding literacy interpretation. *Research in the Teaching of English, 39,* 365–397.

Wollman-Bonilla, J. E. (1989). Reading journals: Invitations to participate in literature. *The Reading Teacher, 43,* 112–120.

Wollman-Bonilla, J. E. (1991). *Response journals: Inviting students to think and write about literature.* New York: Scholastic.

Wollman-Bonilla, J. E., & Werchadlo, B. (1995). Literature response journals in a first-grade classroom. *Language Arts, 72,* 562–570.

Wollman-Bonilla, J. E., & Werchaldo, B. (1999). Teacher and peer roles in scaffolding first-graders' responses to literature. *The Reading Teacher, 52,* 598–607.

Children's Books Cited [P] = K–2; [I] = 3–5; [M] = 6–8

Conlon-McKenna, Marita (1990). *Under the hawthorn tree.* New York: Holiday House. [I]

Conlon-McKenna, Marita (1991). *Wildflower girl.* New York: Holiday House. [I]

Conlon-McKenna, Marita (1997). *Fields of home.* New York: Holiday House. [I]

Creech, Sharon (1997). *Chasing redbird.* New York: HarperCollins. [I]

Curtis, Christopher Paul (2001). *Bud, not Buddy.* New York: Delacorte. [I]

Dahl, Roald (1961). *James and the giant peach.* Illus. by Nancy Ekholm Burkert. New York: Knopf. [P/I]

Fox, Paula (1984). *One eyed cat.* New York: Bradbury. [I]

Hobbs, Will (1989). *Bearstone.* New York: Antheneum. [M]

Park, Linda Sue (2001). *A single shard.* New York: Clarion. [I/M]

Paterson, Katherine (1978). *The great Gilly Hopkins.* New York: Crowell. [I/M]

Paterson, Katherine (1991). *Lyddie.* New York: Lodestar. [M]

Paulsen, Gary (1987). *Hatchet.* New York: Bradbury. [I/M]

Paulsen, Gary (1992). *The haymeadow.* New York: Delacorte. [I/M]

Ryan, Pam Muñoz (2000). *Esperanza rising.* New York: Scholastic. [I/M]

Ryan, Pam Muñoz (2004). *Becoming Naomi Leon.* New York: Scholastic. [I/M]

Wiesner, David (2001). *The three pigs.* New York: Clarion. [P/I]

CHAPTER 11

Literature as a Model for Writing
Apprenticing the Author's Craft

Why the Willow Tree Rattles in the Wind

Long, long ago, before the age of the human race, trees were the world's population. There were millions of different species and every tree's name was its kind. There were names we know today like Maple and Oak. There were also names like Billoweed and Crannyrook. Another special thing about the trees was that they were immortal.

Among these trees was a beautiful tree with long leaves and graceful branches. Her name was Willow. She was very cheerful and kind; therefore, she had many friends. Willow treated each one of them like a jewel on a crown.

The trees lived very peaceful until one day. A light breeze blew. But the trees were used to change in the weather. Snow, rain, and wind were all familiar to them so they paid no attention. The breeze turned into a strong wind, then into a violent storm.

Now the trees were afraid and their minds filled with panic. They clung on to the soil digging their roots deep down into the earth. Some were very lucky and survived. Nevertheless, others weren't so lucky and were uprooted and blown into the seas. Willow was one of the fortunate ones to withstand the hurricane, which came to be known as "The Great Breeze."

Though the storm subsided and never occurred again, the remaining handful of trees still wept and moaned for the lost ones. Willow shed a thousand tears for each of her many friends. She would never forget them. That was how many types of trees were wiped out and became extinct.

During the storm, something strange happened. Mother Earth created a phenomenon called humans. When humans and trees first met, they became the best of friends. However, as humans increased in their technology, humans cut down the trees for supplies to build and make things. So now trees can't move since they are too scared to speak or do anything to get the attention of humans.

When the wind or just a breeze blows, Willow, the willow tree, is brave enough to shake her branches to warn her friends about "The Great Breeze."

Sixth-grade myth written in response to reading/
read-alouds of various titles of mythology

The relationship between readers and writers becomes increasingly apparent as children read more literature and write more often in their classrooms. The more one reads, the greater the impact on one's own writing (Barksdale-Ladd & Nedeff, 1997; Hansen, 2001). The more exposure to quality literature, the better the model for one's own writing efforts (Certo, 2004; Dean & Grierson, 2005; Moore-Hart, 2006). The student writing that opens the chapter, for example, was composed by a writer with a rich background in literature. This chapter's intent is to connect readers and writers through exposure to quality literature and invited opportunities to extend literature experiences through writing as a mode of response. Literature serves as a model of literary genres, literary elements, writing styles, and formats for writing. One of the many responses to quality literature is to note the writing craft incorporated in literature and apply that craft to one's own writing. Reading literature for enjoyment is always a priority, but looking beyond the personal meaning of the words to uncover an author's writing skill impacts a reader's own writing efforts (Walmsley & Walp, 1990).

From the time parents first read to a child, a sense of story begins to develop. A sense of standard openings (*Once upon a time . . .*) and optimistic endings (. . . *and they lived happily ever after*) forms the parameters of a child's internalization of story structure. A familiarity with characters—what they look like, how they act, what they say—provides the young child with the critical role of character in story. The setting (. . . *in a deep, dark forest at the edge of the kingdom*) also invites young children into the secrecy and intrigue of literature. These repeated initial exposures to books provide a schema through which future readers will comprehend story in their minds, create story in their imaginations, and even eventually write stories of their own (Applebee, 1980; Golden, 1984). The natural tendency to incorporate literary elements and techniques into their own writing—"literary borrowing" (Lancia, 1997)—is a cumulative response to the reading of literature in which children have engaged during many early years of their lives.

Teachers desiring to motivate young authors may inspire them by reading aloud trade books focused on writing. Roni Schotter's *Nothing Ever Happens on 90th Street,* for example, follows Eva's frustrations in finding a topic for her writing assignment. Not only is the topic right on her own front steps, but her neighbors supply tips to enhance each stage of the writing process. Sharon Creech's *Love That Dog* follows the growth of a reluctant but interested fifth-grade boy on his journey toward becoming a poet. Journal entries document his growing interest, his connections to his own life, and his eventual acceptance of poetry as a means of expression. Figure 11.1 includes titles of a variety of books that serve as a springboard and

FIGURE 11.1 Book Cluster: Inspiring young writers

Codell, Esme Raji (2003). *Sahara special.* New York: Hyperion. [I]

Cofer, Judith Ortiz (2004). *Call me María.* New York: Orchard. [M]

Creech, Sharon (2001). *Love that dog.* New York: HarperCollins. [I]

Donnelly, Jennifer (2003). *A northern light.* San Diego: Harcourt. [M]

Fletcher, Ralph (1998). *Flying solo.* New York: Clarion. [I]

Fletcher, Ralph (2002). *Poetry matters: Writing a poem from the inside out.* New York: HarperCollins. [I/M]

Janeczko, Paul B. (2002). *Seeing the blue between: Advice and inspiration for young poets.* Cambridge, MA: Candlewick Press. [I/M]

Johnson, D. B. (2004). *Henry works.* Boston: Houghton Mifflin. [P]

Lasky, Kathryn (2003). *A voice of her own: The story of Phillis Wheatley, slave poet.* Illus. by Paul Lee. Cambridge, MA: Candlewick Press. [I/M]

Lisle, Janet Taylor (2002). *How I became a writer and Oggie learned to drive.* New York: Philomel. [I]

Polacco, Patricia (1998). *Thank you, Mr. Falker.* New York: Philomel. [I]

Schotter, Roni (1997). *Nothing ever happens on 90th Street.* Illus. by K. Brooker. New York: Orchard. [I/M]

Wersba, Barbara (2005). *Walter: The story of a rat.* Illus. by Donna Diamond. Asheville, NC: Front Street. [P/I]

Winter, Jeanette (2002). *Emily Dickinson's letters to the world.* New York: Farrar, Straus & Giroux. [I/M]

Winter, Jeanette (2003). *Beatrix.* New York:Farrar, Straus & Giroux. [P/I]

Woodson, Jacqueline (2003). *Locomotion.* New York: Putnam. [M]

invitation to the writing craft, either through characters who are writers or through authentic writing experiences.

This chapter covers several areas in which literature is celebrated as a model for writing. The earliest writing of predictable text based on patterned books provides a first experience of literature as a model for writing. Using quality literature for extended writing activities forms the typical core of most school literature-writing connections. Moving beyond these initial experiences, however, children can become true apprentices of the author's craft through both author studies and recognition of writing traits within the titles of their favorite authors. Literature as a model for writing provides high standards as budding writers attempt to share their personal and creative stories through the written response of composition. A child's imaginative or informative writing is a long-term response to literature built on multiple episodes of reading aloud, independent reading, and numerous writing experiences. The cumulative effect of writing calls into play what one knows about the writing craft and blends that knowledge with what one has discovered through a lifetime of encounters with quality literature.

PREDICTABLE BOOKS: AN EFFECTIVE BEGINNING

The youngest children may get their first opportunity at being authors as they collaboratively play a role in writing their own version of a predictable/pattern book (Heald-Taylor, 1987; Rhodes, 1981). A predictable/pattern book is based on a simple idea and enhanced through repetition or patterned elements, making it effective for learning to read as well as for first attempts at story writing. The most well-known classic of this type is Bill Martin's *Brown Bear, Brown Bear, What Do You See?* The title phrase is followed by "I see a red bird looking at me." Subsequent passages use different colored animals but predictably follow the question, "Color/animal, color/animal what do you see?" Children are eager to "write" new phrases, including "I see a black-and-white panda looking at me" or "I see a green dinosaur looking at me." These early attempts at writing within the framework of a patterned book are delightful experiences that build a feeling of confidence and success in writing. At the same time, children are learning to read their own writing. Not only do predictable/pattern books create authors, they reinforce emerging readers. Books like Eric Carle's *The Very Hungry Caterpillar,* Margaret Wise Brown's *Goodnight Moon,* and Denise Fleming's *In the Tall, Tall Grass* provide important early models for emergent literacy.

As children gain confidence in simple pattern books, they move toward those that are a bit more complicated and often take collaboration and planning. Judi Barrett's *Things That Are Most in the World* presents superlatives in a creative pattern. For example, "The jumpiest thing in the world is two thousand two hundred twenty-two toads on a trampoline" (n.p.). A photocopy page at the end of the book invites young authors to fill in the superlative adjective and the accompanying description. Accompanying illustrations visually represent the concept. Intermediate students easily grasp the concept of a cumulative pattern as represented so well in Nancy Andrews-Goebel's *The Pot That Juan Built.* Written in the form of "The House That Jack

FIGURE 11.2   Book Cluster: Predictable/pattern books

Aylesworth, Jim (1994). *My son John.* Illus. by David Frampton. New York: Holt. [P/I]

Blos, Joan (1992). *A seed, a flower, a minute, and hour.* New York: Simon & Schuster. [P]

Brown, Margaret Wise (2002). *My world of color.* Illus. by Loretta Krupinski. New York: Hyperion. [P]

Catalonotto, Peter (2005). *Kitten red, yellow, blue.* New York: Simon & Schuster. [P]

Cousins, Lucy (2005). *Hooray for fish.* Cambridge, MA: Candlewick. [P]

Donaldson, Julia (2006). *One Ted falls out of bed.* Illus. by Anna Currey. New York: Henry Holt. [P]

Falwell, Cathryn (1998). *Word wizard.* New York: Clarion. [P]

Fleming, Denise (1993). *In the small, small pond.* New York: Holt. [P]

Gag, Wanda (1929). *Millions of cats.* New York: Coward-McCann. [P]

Hutchins, Pat (1986). *The doorbell rang.* New York: Greenwillow. [P]

Liao, Jimmy (2006). *The sound of colors: A journey of the imagination.* New York: Little, Brown. [P]

Martin, Bill, Jr. (1991). *Polar bear, polar bear, what do you hear?* Illus. by Eric Carle. New York: Holt. [P]

Martin, Bill, Jr. (1999). *A beasty story.* Illus. by Steven Kellogg. San Diego: Harcourt Brace. [P]

Rockwell, Anne (1999). *Bumblebee, bumblebee, do you know me?* New York: HarperCollins. [P]

Root, Phyllis (2001). *Rattletrap car.* Illus. by Jill Barton. Cambridge, MA: Candlewick. [P]

Schaefer, Lola M. (2000). *This is the sunflower.* Illus. by Donald Crews. New York: Greenwillow. [P]

Scheer, J., & Bileck, M. (1964). *Rain makes applesauce.* New York: Holiday House. [P]

Shannon, George (2005). *White is for blueberry.* Illus. by Laura Dronzek. New York: Greenwillow. [P]

Slate, Joseph (1998). *Miss Bindergarten celebrates the 100th day of kindergarten.* Illus. by Ashley
    Wolff. New York: Dutton. [P]

Taback, Simms (1999). *Joseph had a little overcoat.* New York: Viking. [P]

Van Laan, Nancy (1998). *Little fish, lost.* Illus. by Jane Conteh-Morgan. New York: Atheneum. [P]

Van Laan, Nancy (1998). *So say the little monkeys.* Illus. by Yami Heo. New York: Atheneum. [P]

Williams, Sue (1990). *I went walking.* Illus. by Julie Vivas. San Diego: Harcourt Brace. [P]

Williams, Sue (1998). *Let's go visiting.* Illus. by Julie Vivas. San Diego: Harcourt Brace. [P]

Yolen, Jane (2000). *Off we go!* Illus. by Laurel Molk. New York: Little, Brown. [P]

Built," this cumulative story tells about art forms and Mexican cultures. The textual pattern can inspire older students verbally to recreate the building of the Statue of Liberty, the Eiffel Tower, or their own school building.

Predictable/pattern books abound across age levels, so there is no shortage of possibilities for including them in the primary reading–writing literacy program. Many of these titles are classics because they have proven themselves over time to be children's favorites. Figure 11.2 shares additional titles that invite patterned writing and accompanying illustrations as response to their formats.

LITERATURE AS A SPRINGBOARD FOR WRITING

Some quality books actually serve as a model for writing and beg for written extensions that allow the form or format to be used for the written response. Savoring them first as literature is important. The experience of reading immersion must always precede the actual writing experience. Weaving literature into the writing workshop fosters the reading–writing connection in the literacy classroom (Hancock, 2007).

Wordless Books

Wordless picture books provide a sound source for group writing in the primary grades. Tomie de Paola's *Pancakes for Breakfast* is a favorite of young children. For this book, a teacher adds children's dictated words to a story chart as the class creates a story to accompany the colorful illustrations. Wordless picture books are indeed a natural resource for imaginative writing, especially for older children who can share their texts with their younger peers. Action-packed illustrations and artistic character portrayals provide the seed for plot and character development. Books like Lynd Ward's classic, *The Silver Pony* can result in worthy texts composed in groups or with the dedication of an individual writer. David Wiesner's Caldecott award winner *Flotsam* generates unusual ideas in young writers as they develop words for the memorable illustrations or write a sequel for the rediscovery of the undersea camera by another curious child. Book buddies extending the text in Wiesner's Caldecott award title, *The Three Pigs,* make the book accessible to their younger counterparts. With ample opportunity to peruse the books prior to and during writing, imaginative response generates the words of the child's evolving text. The variety and ingenuity that result once again document the diversity of response. See additional listings in Chapter 3 for wordless picture books that invite writing.

Journal Writing

Teachers who desire students to keep personal journals to capture informal writing experiences need only look to literature models to inspire the journaling process. Opal Whiteley, a foster child living in the lumber camps of the Northwest at the turn of the century, poignantly shares her love of nature through excerpts from the diary she kept when she was 5 and 6 years old. A note from Jane Boulton at the end of the book shares Opal's prowess and persistence at keeping a diary. The reader learns that Opal kept the diary in constructed spelling on the backs of envelopes. She spent many years as a foster child in 19 different lumber camps following the tragic death of her parents. Although Opal hid her treasured diary, a stepsister found it and tore it into "a million pieces," which Opal preserved. When she was 20 years old, Opal met a book publisher who suggested she reproduce her diary in its original form for publication. Opal painstakingly pasted all the scraps of paper together so her eloquent diary could be shared in book form. The selector then issues the following invitation to captivated readers: "And now you may want to start a diary of your own." This informational note, the text of *Only Opal: The Diary of a Young Girl,* and the gentle paintings of Barbara Cooney truly invite children to respond by recording their daily experiences in a journal format.

Sarah Stewart's *The Journey* transports a young Amish girl from her secure rural environment to the dynamic setting of the city of Chicago. Journal entries reveal a growing appreciation for the quietude and security of her home. Similarly, the diary format of Marissa Moss's titles including *Amelia's 6th-Grade Notebook* captures the academic and social realities of a young girl through her written entries and visual representations of daily school episodes. The strong first-person voice of children finds it way naturally into personal journal writing, and these titles model the importance of recording personal experience and feelings. Additional journal and diary titles are listed in Figure 11.3.

FIGURE 11.3   Book Cluster: Springboards for writing

Journal Writing

Creech, Sharon (2000). *The wanderer*. Illus. by David Diaz. New York: HarperCollins. [I]
Cronin, Doreen (2003). *Diary of a worm*. Illus. by Harry Bliss. New York: HarperCollins. [P]
Cronin, Doreen (2005). *Diary of a spider*. Illus. by Harry Bliss. New York: Harper Collins. [P]
Cushman, Karen (1994). *Catherine, called Birdy*. Boston: Clarion. [M]
Foreman, Michael (2006). *Mia's story: A sketchbook of hopes and dreams*. Cambridge, MA: Candlewick. [P/I]
French, Jackie (2003). *Diary of a wombat*. Illus. by Bruce Whatley. New York: Clarion/Haughton Mifflin. [P]
Moss, Marissa (2000). *Hannah's journal: The story of an immigrant girl*. San Diego: Harcourt Brace. [I]
Moss, Marissa (2001). *Rose's journal: The story of a girl in the Great Depression*. San Diego: Harcourt Brace. [I]
Stewart, Sarah (2001). *The journey*. Illus. by David Small. New York: Farrar, Straus & Giroux. [P/I]
Turner, Ann (1997). *Mississippi mud: Three prairie journals*. Illus. by Robert Blake. New York: Harper-Collins. [I]
Webb, Sophie (2004). *Looking for seabirds: Journal from an Alaskan voyage*. Boston: Houghton Mifflin. [I]
Wilson, Laura (2001). *How I survived the Irish Famine: The journal of Mary O'Flynn*. New York: Harper-Collins. [I/M]

Letter/Postcard Formats

Ada, Alma Flor (2001). *With love, Little Red Hen*. Illus. by Leslie Tryon. New York: Atheneum. [P/I]
Cushman, Karen (1996). *The ballad of Lucy Whipple*. Boston: Clarion. [I/M]
Fleming, Candace (2003). *Boxes for Katje*. Illus. by Stacey Dressen-McQueen. New York: Farrar, Straus & Giroux. [P]
Hesse, Karen (1992). *Letters from Rifka*. New York: Holt. [I/M]
MacLachlan, Patricia (1985). *Sarah, plain and tall*. New York: Harper & Row. [P/I]
Stewart, Sarah (1997). *The gardener*. Illus. by David Small. New York: Farrar, Straus & Giroux. [P]
Teague, Mark (2002). *Dear Mrs. LaRue: Letters from obedience school*. New York: Scholastic. [P]
Teague, Mark (2004). *Detective LaRue: Letters from the investigation*. New York: Scholastic. [P]

Fairy-Tale Variants

Ernst, Lisa Campbell (1995). *Little Red Riding Hood: A newfangled prairie tale*. New York: Simon & Schuster. [P/I]
Ernst, Lisa Campbell (2002). *The three spinning fairies: A tale from the Brothers Grimm*. New York: Dutton. [P/I]
Fleming, Candace (2004). *Gator gumbo: A spicy hot tail*. Illus. by Sally Anne Lambert. New York: Farrar, Straus & Giroux. [P/I]
Hartman, Bob (2002). *The wolf who cried boy*. Illus. by Tim Raglin. New York: Putnam. [P]
Hawkins, Colin, & Hawkins, Jacqui (2004). *Fairytale news*. Cambridge, MA: Candlewick. [I]
Lowell, Susan (2000). *Cindy Ellen: A wild western Cinderella*. Illus. by J. Manning. New York: Harper-Collins. [P/I]
Mills, Lauren (2001). *The dog prince*. Illus. by Lauren Mills & Dennis Nolan. New York: Little, Brown. [I]
Moser, Barry (2001). *The three little pigs*. New York: Little, Brown. [P/I]
Osborne, Mary Pope (2000). *Kate and the beanstalk*. Illus. by Giselle Potter. New York: Atheneum. [P/I]
Osborne, Mary Pope (2002). *The brave little seamstress*. Illus. by Giselle Potter. New York: Atheneum. [P/I]

(continued)

FIGURE 11.3 Continued

Osborne, Will, & Osborne, Mary Pope (2005). *Sleeping Bobby*. Illus. by Giselle Potter. New YorK: Atheneum. [I]

Sweet, Melissa (2005). *Carmine: A little more red*. Boston: Houghton Mifflin. [P]

Vaes, Alain (2001). *The princess and the pea*. New York: Little, Brown. [I/M]

Wiesner, David (2001). *The three pigs*. New York: Clarion. [P/I/M]

Special Invitations to Write

Bartoletti, Susan Campbell (2003). *Nobody's noisier than a cat*. Illus. by Beppe Giocobbe. New York: Hyperion. [P] (descriptive writing)

Chaikin, Miriam (2002). *Don't step on the sky: A handful of haiku*. Illus. by Hiroe Nakata. New York: Henry Holt. [P/I] (haiku poetry)

Fisher, Valorie (2003). *Ellsworth's extraordinary electric ears and other amazing alphabet anecdotes*. New York: Atheneum. [P/I] (alliteration)

Leedy, Loreen (2004). *Look at my book: How kids can write and illustrate terrific books*. New York: Holiday House. [I] (writing process)

Orloff, Karen Kaufman (2004). *I wanna iguana*. Illus. by David Catrow. New York: Putnam. [P] (persuasive writing)

Raven, Margot Theis (2004). *Circle unbroken: The story of a basket and its people*. Illus. by E. B. Lewis. New York: Farrar, Straus & Giroux [I] (sequence of events)

Sandin, Joan (2003). *Coyote school news*. New York: Henry Holt. [I] (newsletter articles)

Spinelli, Eileen (2006). *When you are happy*. Illus. by Geraldo Valerion. New York: Simon & Schuster. [P/I] (patterned writing)

Wellington, Monica (2005). *Zinnea's flower garden*. New York: Dutton. [P] (technical writing)

Letter/Postcard Writing

Personal written communication is a standard requirement of the elementary writing curriculum. Books that include letters, postcards, and other forms of written communication serve as models for children's authentic writing experiences. When the Ahlbergs's *The Jolly Postman* was published 20 years ago, teachers warmed to the innovative idea of literature/writing links. *Stringbean's Trip to the Shining Sea* by Vera and Jennifer Williams chronicled Stringbean Coe's cross-country trip through postcards and snapshots while inspiring children to respond by writing and designing their own picture postcards. Books continue to hold the letter-writing model that encourages response in this format. *With Love, Little Red Hen* and other titles by Alma Flor Ada use letter format to transport fairy-tale characters into a story.

Beverly Cleary's memorable *Dear Mr. Henshaw* touches readers as a link to letter writing to authors; Candace Fleming's *Boxes for Katje* incorporates letters between Americans and Europeans following World War II. Literature models abound to model this form and the expectations for responding through written communication formats. Additional titles in which letters/postcards convey the story can be found in Figure 11.3.

FIGURE 11.4 Class chart for ways to transform fairy tales

How can we change a story?

1. We can change the style, from old-fashioned to modern language.
2. We can change or add to the details in the plot (*Somebody and the Three Blairs*).
3. We can change a few of the main events in the plot (Stephen Kellogg's *Chicken Little*).
4. We can keep a few of the main events but change most of the plot (*Sleeping Ugly*).
5. We can change the setting (time and place). If the setting is changed, there will probably need to be many more changes in characters and detail (*Snow White in New York; Ugh*).
6. We can change the point of view (*The True Story of the Three Little Pigs*, told by the wolf).
7. We can change the characters in the story by

   — changing their occupation (*The Principal's New Clothes*)
   — changing their gender (*Prince Cinders*)
   — reversing their roles in the story (*Somebody and the Three Blairs*).

8. We can write a sequel to the original story (*The Frog Prince Continued*).
9. We can keep the words of the original story but change the illustrations (Anthony Browne's *Hansel and Gretel*).

From *Reading Teacher* by Sipe, L. R. Copyright 1993 by International Reading Association. Reproduced with permission of International Reading Association in the format Textbook via Copyright Clearance Center.

Fairy-Tale Variants

Since the appearance of Jon Scieszka's *The True Story of the Three Little Pigs,* an explosion of fairy-tale variants have appeared both in children's book publishing and in classrooms. The point of view shift to the perspective of A. Wolf served as an inspiration and model for children to write their own fairy-tale variants. Titles such as Osborne's *The Brave Little Seamstress* and *Kate and the Beanstalk,* Mills's *The Dog Prince,* and Brett's *The Gingerbread Baby* have further fed the imaginations of children to write their own versions of popular fairy tales. Transforming traditional stories, enjoying modern variants, and creating their own versions reflect enthusiastic responses to literature. Sipe (1993) lists a variety of ways to transform stories. In Figure 11.4 his suggestions allow children individually or as a group to decide how they want to alter the original traditional tale.

Sleeping Bobby by Will and Mary Pope Osborne mirrors the classic Sleeping Beauty tale with a reversed gender perspective. Colin and Jacqui Hawkins's *Fairy Tale News* and *Pirate Treasure Map: A Fairytale Adventure* provide varied formats of including fairy-tale characteristics through a creative perspective. Children's imaginations soar as they respond by renaming characters, twisting the plot, or adding humor to these often familiar tales. Teachers, however, need to recognize that not all children have the original tale in their literary schema, so it is just as important to share an original version alongside the usually humorous variant. The reading–writing connection is apparent and natural in traditional tale transformations as children respond to literature by learning more about the elements of this genre through their own creative writing efforts. Additional fairy-tale variant models can be found in Figure 11.3

Special Invitations to Write

Occasionally, a book invites children to participate in the writing process by writing a sequel, continuing an unfinished story, or naturally updating a format. The premier example of this writing connection is Chris Van Allsburg's classic *The Mysteries of Harris Burdick*. The story introduction, read convincingly aloud, motivates children to write imaginative stories to accompany the 14 mysterious black-and-white illustrations. The brief but interesting captions serve as a stimulus for creative writing. Even reluctant writers are invigorated by the opportunity to respond to these unique visual invitations. The beautiful language of Jane Yolen's *Owl Moon* provides opportunities for extended writing for primary children (Egawa, 1990). Another direct and meaningful writing extension emerges from reading Judith Viorst's title poem from *If I Were in Charge of the World and Other Worries*. Children long to update and personalize the poem based on its original format and message.

A genuine writing invitation from Janet Wong's *You Have to Write* encourages the somewhat reluctant writer that he or she has something to write about, and, because they "have to write," they might as well make it their best. Selecting a topic, playing with words, and writing several drafts bring forth the reality of the hard work of the young author.

Even a reluctant writer can be inspired to follow an authentic experience through the writing process.
Reprinted with the permission of Margaret K. McElderry Books, an imprint of Simon & Schuster Children's Publishing Division from You Have to Write *by Janet S. Wong, illustrated by Teresa Flavin. Jacket illustration copyright © 2002 Teresa Flavin.*

A caution is in order so that writing extensions remain natural responses to literature. Too often well-intentioned teachers warp literature or insist on repeated writing extensions with every literature sharing. The writing connection should flow naturally from the literature. If the desired activity is not authentic and strays away from the literary model, perhaps the literature should merely be enjoyed for its own merits. Preserve the writing experience exclusively for those books with inherent connections to writing because they foster rather than tamper with authentic response.

AUTHOR STUDIES

The most powerful way to introduce students to the writing craft and foster a commitment to writing is to introduce them to the flesh-and-blood authors behind their favorite books. Ideally, a visit to a school by an author would answer typical queries about how he got started, where she gets her ideas, and how long it takes to write a book. Author visits are becoming more common and easier to arrange and facilitate (Darigan, Tunnell, & Jacobs, 2002), but they still remain a dream for most children. But a teacher can, so to speak, bring an author to the classroom through an author study (Peck & Hendershot, 1997). An author study blends biographical information on an author with an intensive exposure to his or her published books. Immersion in background information coupled with familiarity of many works by a single author provide much speculation and inspiration about the writing craft.

Reader response to author studies exhibit themselves in several ways. Children are invited to explore via these tasks:

- Locate and read more books by the author.
- Research further biographical information on the author through books and the Internet.
- E-mail an author.
- Create an author brochure with biographical information and annotations of selected books.
- List similar writing techniques of the author across books.
- Incorporate writing techniques of the author into own writing.
- Compare and contrast author's writing style to other known authors through discussion.

RESOURCES ON THE WEB
Online Book Reviews

The Internet offers countless possibilities for supporting literature-based writing instruction. In response to quality literature, students may use technology to compose and publish their own book reviews. Large bookstores like Amazon.com (*www.amazon.com*) encourage readers to express their opinions about books by submitting their own reviews. Teachers may want to access already published reader reviews to model the purpose for and formats of book reviews.

Follow these steps to inspire and inform aspiring reviewers:

1. Provide each student with an intriguing children's book along with instructions *not* to open the book.
2. Instruct the students to learn as much as possible about their books by reading several online book reviews. Based on these reviews, ask students to form an opinion about his or her book.
3. Allow students time to read their books.
4. After finishing reading their books, ask students to compose their own book reviews. Amazon.com states that the "review should focus on the book's content and context" and that "the best reviews include not only whether you like or dislike the product, but also why."
5. Submit the reviews to the online bookstore. At the bottom of each catalog page on amazon.com is a link called "Write an online review and share your thoughts with other customers." To ensure privacy, a separate Kids' Review Form is available for students younger than 13 that does not request names or e-mail addresses.

FIGURE 11.5 Side-by-side author autobiography/creative works

Byars, Betsy (2002). *Keeper of the doves*. New York: Viking.
Byars, Betsy (1991). *The moon and I*. New York: Morrow.*
Byars, Betsy (1996). *Tornado*. New York: HarperCollins.

Cleary, Beverly (1999). *Ramona's world*. New York: Morrow.
Cleary, Beverly (1988). *A girl from Yamhill: A memoir*. New York: Morrow.
Cleary, Beverly (1991). *Strider*. New York: Morrow.

De Paola, Tomie (2000). *Strega Nona takes a vacation*. New York: Putnam.
De Paola, Tomie (2005). *Now one foot, now the other*. New York: Putnam.
De Paola, Tomie (2005). *Stagestruck*. New York: Putnam.
De Paola, Tomie (2007). *Why?* (A 26 Fairmount Avenue Book). New York: Putnam. See also: *Christmas Remembered* (2006); *I'm Still Scared* (2006); *What a Year* (2003); *Here We All Are* (2001); *26 Fairmount Avenue* (2001).

Florian, Douglas (2001). *Lizards, frogs, and polliwogs*. San Diego: Harcourt.
Florian, Douglas (2005). *See for yourself* (Meet the Authors series). Norwood, MA: Richard C. Owen.
Florian, Douglas (2005). *Zoo's who*. San Diego: Harcourt.
Florian, Douglas (2006). *Handspring*. New York: Greenwillow.

Lowry, Lois (1993). *The giver*. Boston: Houghton Mifflin.
Lowry, Lois (1998). *Looking back: A book of memories*. Boston: Houghton Mifflin.*
Lowry, Lois (2000). *Gathering blue*. Boston: Houghton Mifflin.

Myers, Walter Dean (2001). *Bad boy: A memoir*. New York: HarperCollins.
Myers, Walter Dean (1999). *Monster*. New York: HarperCollins.
Myers, Walter Dean (1996). *Slam!* New York: Scholastic.

Nixon, Joan Lowery (2002). *The making of a writer*. New York: Delacorte.*
Nixon, Joan Lowery (2000). *Nobody's there*. New York: Delacorte.
Nixon, Joan Lowery (2001). *Playing for keeps*. New York: Delacorte.

Paulsen, Gary (2001). *Guts: The true stories behind Hatchet and the Brian books*. New York: Delacorte.*
Paulsen, Gary (1987). *Hatchet*. New York: Bradbury.
Paulsen, Gary (1999). *Brian's return*. (1996). *Brian's winter*. (1991). *The river*. New York: Delacorte.

Naylor, Phyllis Reynolds (1987). *How I came to be a writer*. New York: Simon & Schuster.
Naylor, Phyllis Reynolds (1991). *Shiloh*. New York: Atheneum.
Naylor, Phyllis Reynolds (1996). *Shiloh season*. New York: Atheneum.

Spinelli, Jerry (1989). *Maniac Magee*. Boston: Little, Brown.
Spinelli, Jerry (1997). *Wringer*. New York: HarperCollins.
Spinelli, Jerry (1998). *Knots in my yo-yo string: The autobiography of a kid*. New York: Knopf.*

*Authors share their personal struggles and successes with writing through autobiographies that serve as models of the author's craft.

Reading an autobiography of an author alongside the author's work incorporates an added dimension to an author study and enhances a student perspective on the connection between an author's life and his or her work. For example, a teacher read-aloud of Gary Paulsen's autobiographical *Guts: The True Stories Behind Hatchet and the Brian Books* alongside literature circles on these fictional titles build connections between the author's life experiences, personal emotions, and the survival stories he writes. This idea presents a powerful combination for aspiring writers as they blend the author's life and writing craft with the product of his or her efforts. Figure 11.5 contains numerous suggestions for pairing author autobiography and creative works to be read side by side.

APPRENTICING THE AUTHOR'S CRAFT

In *Author: A True Story,* Helen Lester, author of popular children's books, shares her struggles with writing both as a child and as a successful author. She humorously shares the hurdles that are a part of writing:

> Sometimes writing stories is so HARD for me!
> I can't come up with a single idea,
> and my stories get stuck in the middle
> and I can't think of a title,
> and I have trouble making the changes my
> editor wants me to make,
> and I lose my pencils,
> and I wonder why I'm doing this,
> and I get very very VERY frustrated.*

Writing is hard work, but the reward lies in the accomplishments of bringing ideas of the imagination to the page as written words. Learning the author's craft takes time and multiple models of strong writing. That's why literature plays such a crucial role in helping young writers by providing models that reflect various aspects of the craft of writing.

If response to literature is to include improved student writing, the teacher must guide young writers in an awareness of the craft of writing within the context of quality children's/young adult literature. The six-trait analytic model of writing (Spandel & Stiggins, 2000) provides a framework for discussion of the author's craft. Although intended for analytic assessment of writing, the six traits can also be viewed as areas addressed by effective writers. The six writing traits include ideas and content development, organization, voice, word choice, sentence fluency, and writing conventions. By understanding these traits and seeing their use modeled in authentic published works, student response to literature may be enriched by the use of these traits in their own writing. For example, a student who is aware of Gary Paulsen's use of ellipses in *The Haymeadow* may effectively incorporate this writing convention

---

*From *Author: A True Story* (p. 23) by Helen Lester. Copyright © 1997 by Helen Lester. Reprinted by permission of Houghton Mifflin Company. All rights reserved.

Authors share their personal struggles and successes with writing through biographies that serve as models of the author's craft.

into her or his own survival story. The notion of an opening phrase repeatedly used for dramatic effect like Cynthia Rylant's *When I Was Young in the Mountains* might come to mind when writing one's own personal narrative. Literature provides the models that make readers first, then writers.

An elaboration of each writing trait will assist in understanding the relationship between the trait and a young author's response by the application of each trait in one's own writing (Culham, 2003). The following discussion defines each writing trait, makes suggestions for exposure to and application of the trait, and includes a list of literature that effectively models and reflects use of the trait. Figure 11.6 also provides textual connections to each trait. Children need to become familiar with the terminology of writing. As literature is discussed following its enjoyment (or alongside it in the case of chapter books), these writing traits might be identified and analyzed as components of the writing craft.

Ideas and Content Development

Ideas are the seeds of writing and grow by developing content into story. Young authors always wonder where authors get their ideas and how they turn them into stories. Reading authentic literature and discussing a core idea and its development are essential to understanding this trait. Perhaps idea development is most easily detected in a picture book, such as Patricia McKissack's *Goin' Someplace Special* in which a black child (the author, herself) in Memphis in the 1950s ventures out on a trip to the public library, with "racial alerts" along the way. From simple ideas, based on personal experiences, stories grow.

FIGURE 11.6   Book Cluster: Modeling the author's craft/six-trait writing

Idea and Content Development

Barron, T. A. (2004). *High as a hawk*. Illus. by Ted Lewin. New York: Philomel. [I]

Giff, Patricia Reilly (2001). *All the way home*. New York: Delacorte. [I]

Harrington, Janice N. (2004). *Going north*. Illus. by Jerome Legarrigue. New York: Melanie Kroupa/Farrar, Straus & Giroux. [P/I]

Howard, Elizabeth Fitzgerald (2001). *Virgie goes to school with us boys*. Illus. by E. G. Lewis. New York: Simon & Schuster. [P/I]

McKissack, Patricia (2001). *Goin' someplace special*. Illus. by Jerry Pinkney. New York: Atheneum. [I]

Peck, Richard (2001). *Fair weather*. New York: Dial. [I/M]

Prosek, James (2004). *A good day's fishing*. New York: Simon & Schuster. [P/I]

Organization

Narrative

Avi (2001). *The secret school*. San Diego: Harcourt Brace. [I]

Bierhorst, John (2001). *Is my friend at home? Pueblo fireside tales*. Illus. by Wendy Watson. New York: Farrar, Straus & Giroux. [P]

Fleming, Candace (2004). *Gator gumbo: A spicy hot tale*. Illus. by Sally Anne Lambert. New York: Farrar, Straus & Giroux. [P/I]

High, Linda O. (2000). *Barn savers*. Illus. by Ted Lewin. Honesdale, PA: Boyds Mills Press. [P/I]

Johnson, Angela (2004). *Just like Josh Gibson*. Illus. by Beth Peck. New York: Simon & Schuster. [P/I]

Osborne, Mary Pope (2002). *The brave little seamstress*. Illus. by Giselle Potter. New York: Atheneum. [P/I]

Park, Linda Sue (2001). *A single shard*. New York: Clarion. [I/M]

Tavares, Matt (2004). *Oliver's game*. Cambridge, MA: Candlewick. [I]

Expository

Adler, David (2002). *A picture book of Dwight D. Eisenhower*. New York: Holiday House. (Sequence) [P/I]

Murphy, Jim (2003). *An American plague*. New York: Clarion. [I/M]

Ryder, Joanne (2001). *Little panda*. New York: Simon & Schuster. (Description) [P]

Simon, Seymour (2000). *Crocodiles & alligators*. New York: HarperCollins. (Compare/Contrast) [P/I]

St. George, Judith (2004). *You're on your way, Teddy Roosevelt*. Illus. by Matt Faulkner. New York: Philomel. [P/I]

Voice

Creech, Sharon (2001). *Love that dog*. New York: HarperCollins. [I]

Hoose, Phillip (2001). *We were there, too! Young people in U.S. history*. New York: Farrar, Straus & Giroux. [I/M]

Hopkinson, Deborah (2002). *Under the quilt of night*. *Illus. by* James E. Ransome. New York: Atheneum. [P/I]

Stewart, Sarah (2001). *The journey*. Illus. by David Small. New York: Farrar, Straus & Giroux. [P/I]

Wallace, Karen (2004). *I am a tyrannosaurus*. Illus. by Mike Bostock. New York: Atheneum. [P]

Wells, Rosemary (2002). *Wingwalker*. Illus. by Brian Selznick. New York: Hyperion. [I]

(continued)

FIGURE 11.6 Continued

Word Choice

Banks, Kate (2005). *The great blue house.* Illus. by Georg Hallensleben. New York: Farrar, Straus & Giroux.

Brown, Margaret wise (2002). *My world of color.* Illus. by Loretta Krupinski. New York: Hyperion. [P]

Greenfield, Eloise (2004). *In the land of words: New and selected poems.* Illus. by Jan Spivey Gilchrist. New York: HarperCollins. [P/I]

Heller, Ruth (1989). *Many luscious lollipops.* New York: Grosset & Dunlap. [I]

Hopkins, Lee Bennett (2004). *Wonderful words: Poems about reading, writing, speaking, and listening.* Illus. by Karen Barbour. New York: Simon & Schuster. [P/I]

Leiner, Katherine (2002). *Mama does the mambo.* Illus. by Edel Rodriguez. New York: Hyperion. [I]

Martin, Bill, Jr., & Archambault, John (2002). *I pledge allegiance.* Illus. by Chris Raschka. Cambridge, MA: Candlewick Press. [P/I]

Steig, William (1971). *Amos & Boris.* New York: Farrar, Straus & Giroux. [P/I]

Sentence Fluency

Fleming, Candace (2002). *Muncha! Muncha! Muncha!* Illus. by G. Brian Karas. New York: Atheneum. [P]

Johnson, Angela (2003). *I dream of trains.* Illus. by Loren Long. New York: Simon & Schuster. [I]

Houston, Gloria (1992). *My great Aunt Arizona.* Illus. by Susan C. Lamb. New York: HarperCollins. [I]

Lyon, George Ella (2004). *Weaving the rainbow.* Illus. by Stephanie Anderson. New York: Atheneum. [P]

Rockwell, Ann (1998). *One bean.* Illus. by Megan Halsey. New York: Walker. [P]

Rylant, Cynthia (1982). *When I was young in the mountains.* Illus. by Diane Goode. New York: Dutton. [I]

Conventions

Cronin, Doreen (2002). *Giggle, giggle, quack.* Illus. by Betsy Lewin. New York: Simon & Schuster. [P]

O'Conner, George (2004). *Kapow!* New York: Simon & Schuster. [I]

Pulver, *Robin (2003). Punctuation takes a vacation.* Illus. by Lynn Rowe Reed. New York: Holiday House. [P/I]

Truss, Lynne (2006). *Eats, shoots & leaves: Why commas really do make a difference!* Illus. by Bonnie Timmons. New York: Putnam. [P/I/M]

Many authors report they keep a small notebook handy for writing down ideas, and young authors should be encouraged to do the same. Experiences give rise to ideas that can be developed into stories. Eve Bunting was inspired to write *Fly Away Home* upon witnessing the homeless in a large airport. Because writers seem to write best within the context of familiar settings, children should be allowed to choose their own writing topics based on personal experiences. Patricia Polacco uses her childhood relatives and nostalgic recollections in *Something About Hensley's.* Writers develop stories from small bits and pieces of their own lives. Sharing as many literary connections as possible to demonstrate the seed of an idea will help young writers plant their own seeds for writing.

A graphic organizer or story web also shows how an idea can expand into a story. By having young writers make a web of a favorite book, they can visualize the seed idea and monitor its growth through character and plot development (Bromley, 1996). An event sequence web for Zinnea Taylor's clearing of the Bybanks-Chocton trail in Sharon Creech's *Chasing Redbird* provides visual evidence of how an author stages events as part of plot development. Webs can naturally become a rehearsal outline for a child's own story. Janice Harrington's *Going North* follows a black family's automobile journey from the South to Nebraska accompanied along the way by the uncertainties and concerns of a new home. A graphic organizer of this literary journey would indicate beginning, conflicts, highpoints, roadblocks, and eventual resolutions.

Robert Blake's *The Perfect Spot* provides a model for a web for a young author's own perfect spot. Envision the seed for writing as the name of the place forms the core of the web and descriptions of the sights, sounds, tastes, and feelings surround it with details. The web as a framework for story in both reading and writing illustrates to the young author the importance of a key idea and its development in the creation of story.

Organization

Organization can be described as a well-marked trail that winds its way through a piece of writing so the reader can find the way toward meaning. This trait must be exhibited successfully in both narrative and expository writing if story plot or informational facts are to be delivered in a meaningful, sequential fashion.

Narrative writing. In exploring the structure of narrative writing, it is crucial to read aloud literature that develops the beginning/middle/end concept of story. Read, for example, Ellen Levine's *Henry's Freedom Box,* which follows the harrowing journey of Henry Brown, a slave during the time of the Underground Railroad, in a wooden crate as he mails himself to freedom in the North. The outstanding artwork of Kadir Nelson follows the sequence of events of Henry "Box" Brown's tragic life. Children should also be encouraged to engage in oral, written, or artistic retellings of stories to establish a model for sequence. Sharing authentic literature that delivers a story in sequential order provides additional models to acquire this sense of organization. Application of this sense of organization results in a related response through a child's own application in his or her writing so the reading audience can follow the same type of organized trail.

In addressing organization, literature also models effective leads and conclusions as young writers learn the value of capturing the reader's attention and leading toward a sense of resolution. Opening and closing paragraphs serve as "bookends" to the entire story. Examine the opening paragraphs of *Kira-Kira,* the 2005 Newbery Medal Award title by Cynthia Kadohata, to illustrate a strong lead that entices the reader toward continued reading. This strong opening invites even a reluctant reader to learn more about the relationship between the two Japanese sisters as they adjust to their mobile life in the South.

> My sister, Lynn, taught me my first word: *kira-kira*. I pronounced it *ka-a-ahhh*, but she knew what I meant. *Kira-kira* means "glittering" in Japanese. Lynn told me that when I was a baby, she used to take me onto our empty road at night, where we would lie on our backs and look at the stars while she said over and over, "Katie, say '*kira-kira, kira-kira*.'" I loved that word! When I grew older, I used *kira-kira* to describe everything I liked: the beautiful blue sky, puppies, kittens, butterflies, colored Kleenex. (p. 1)*

As the author seeks closure for her main character and the loss of her sister, she concludes this novel from the 1950s with these words:

> I wish Lynn could have lived to see the sea with us. When we first walked up to the Pacific Ocean, the tears welled up in my eyes and her death seemed near. I don't think anyone understood as well as I did how badly Lynn had longed to walk along the water the way my family and I did that New Year's Day. I hid my tears from my parents. But the water started to make me happy again. Here at the sea—especially at the sea—I could hear my sister's voice in the waves: "*Kira-kira! Kira-kira!*" (p. 244)*

Teach children to appreciate the last lines of books that bring resolution, satisfaction, and closure to the reader. Making the last sentence count leaves the reader with something to think about. This type of model brings high standards to the young writer but supplies varied techniques for responding to those expectations in his or her own writing.

Expository writing. Informational books reflect the internal structure and organization of a second type of writing—expository writing (Moss, 2003). Modeling begins with read-alouds and independent reading of informational books. Noting how information is organized through graphic organizers or outlines provides a visual framework for the delivery of information to the reader. A graphic organizer for Jim Arnosky's *All About Frogs,* for example, begins with the topic of frogs but radiates outward to include packages of information on all aspects of their habitat, mating, eating, and lifespan. Providing graphic organizers or data charts to assemble information obtained through expository reading prepares students for the research process and key organization of expository writing. Researching a topic and organizing details into tables, charts, or webs parallels preparing an outline for a writer as information is transmitted to the reader.

Perhaps the trait of organization is the most important aspect of expository writing. Locating books that describe, sequence, compare and contrast, relate cause and effect, and propose problems and solutions are ideal candidates for models of quality expository writing. Effective leads and concluding sentences carry the same importance in expository as in narrative writing. Lynn Curlee begins and ends *Ballpark* with an enticing opening and promising conclusion. Following the text of the lyrics of "Take Me Out to the Ball Game," the invitation begins,

---

*Reprinted by permission of Atheneum, an imprint of Simon & Schuster Children's Publishing Division from *Kira-Kira* by Cynthia Kadohata. Copyright © 2004 Cynthia Kadohata.

Everyone knows the grand old song. The simple poem and jaunty tune evoke lazy, sunny summer afternoons. Fleecy clouds floating in clear blue skies. Vivid, clipped green grass and colorful advertising signs. Flags and pennants snapping in the breeze. Venders hawking hot dogs and sodas, pretzels and beer. Swelling organ music and the announcer's excited voice booming from loud speakers. The sharp crack of bat solidly meeting ball. The deafening roar of the cheering crowd. It's a day at the ballpark! (p. 1)

Following a tour of America's famous ballparks, players, and events, Curlee concludes:

America's "game of summer" was enjoyed by our grandparents, and it will be enjoyed by our grandchildren. Baseball links us with our past and our future. Now in the twenty-first century there is a new spirit in the air, with a new generation of players, a new generation of fans, and a new generation of ballparks to take their places beside the old. The national pastime looks ahead. Let the game continue.

Play ball! (p. 41)*

Other expository models to which students might respond through modeled writing include Sandra Markle's *Rescues!* (problem–solution), Carla Killough McClafferty's *Something Out of Nothing: Marie Curie and Radium* (cause–effect), Rosalyn Schanzer's *George vs. George: The American Revolution Seen from Both Sides* (compare–contrast), Kelly Milner Halls's *Albino Animals* (description), and Rhoda Blumberg's *York's Adventures with Lewis and Clark* (sequence).

Pointing out organizational skills and strategies in both narrative and expository writing in the context of literature students have read and respect serves to inspire their own writing. The visual example and the application in the context of literature supplies the momentum for budding authors as they try their hands at the art of writing. A natural written response to immersion in quality literature with a focus on the writing craft is the incorporation of best techniques of honored children's authors in one's own writing.

Voice

Voice is best described as the trait that leaves the imprint of the author on a piece. As writers compose, they leave their distinctive fingerprints on their work through a commanding voice projected through their words. The read-aloud or independent reading model of locating literary examples exhibiting a strong element of voice is the most effective way of introducing this writing trait to prospective young authors. Personal voice is best practiced and identified through journal writing (i.e., literature response journals, character journals, personal journals). As young writers hear their own voices in their written words, they begin to carry that voice through to more formal writing assignments.

Locating the author's voice in quality literature is a simple task. If one is fortunate enough to have heard an author speak in person, you can almost hear that author's voice loud and clear as the words propel through your mind. In *Wingwalker*, Rose-mary Wells portrays second grader Reuben, who must leave the peacefulness of small town life in Oklahoma so his father can pursue work during the drought of the Dust Bowl. Cherishing his secure life, Reuben thinks nothing can ever invade his isolated world. Hear the character's voice reveling in this security:

> I liked to look out at the world from our attic window. The land that circled Ambler, Oklahoma, was silky green prairie. Here and there you could spot an oil drilling station with a drilling rig pumping away like a big iron grasshopper.
> I believed that I could see the whole world from that attic window. I believed that nothing in it would ever change but the seasons of the year; that no one ever died except very old people whom I did not know. I was just beginning the second grade.*

Clarification of voice in informational writing becomes a simple task when comparing an encyclopedia entry on the Chicago fire with an opening excerpt from Jim Murphy's Newbery Honor book, *The Great Fire*.

> A shed attached to the barn was already engulfed in flames. . . . Fire ran along the dry grass and leaves, and took hold of a neighbor's fence. The heat from the burning barn, shed, and fence was so hot that the O'Leary's house, forty feet away, began to smolder. Neighbors rushed from their homes, many carrying buckets or pots of water. The sound of music and merrymaking stopped abruptly, replaced by the shout of "FIRE!" It would be a warning cry heard thousands of times during the next thirty-one hours.†

Although both examples would contain facts, dates, and details, the Murphy writing contains the author's voice filled with an overwhelming sense of the power and tenac-ity of this fire. The writing is lively, confident, honest, powerful, knowledgeable, and places the reader at the scene. The author's voice speaks directly to the audience, giving the reader an eyewitness account. The author's voice comes through in every word, and the writing sounds different from the way anyone else would depict the event. Other titles in which authors' voices ring loud and clear include Avi's *The True Confessions of Charlotte Doyle* (first-person historical fiction), Robert Burleigh's *Flight: The Journey of Charles Lindbergh* (third-person narrative), and Paul Fleisch-man's *Bull Run* (first-person historical fiction/multiple characters).

Word Choice

Word choice can be described as the author's selection of precise words that clarify the message and paint pictures in the mind of the reader. Word choice is rich, sharp, vivid vocabulary that uses brisk, fresh adjectives, and sharp, energetic verbs to add momentum to the writing. Although word choices increase the power of the author, they must remain natural, sensible, and meaningful. They are the words that make the reader say, "Aaah, that was a good way to say it!"

---

*From *Wingwalker* by Rosemary Wells. Copyright © 2002 by Rosemary Wells. Published by Hyperion Books for Children. All rights reserved.

†From *The Great Fire* (p. 15). Copyright © 1995 by Jim Murphy. Reprinted by permission of Scholastic, Inc.

Teachers can naturally teach the art of word choice by pointing out exquisite examples ever present in literature read-alouds. Students can also be asked to be aware of effective word choice in their independent reading and take note in a writing notebook of "aaah" words collected from literature. Kevin Henkes presents a masterful example of simple but effective word choice in his tale of a confident mouse who goes off to her first day of school. *Chrysanthemum* is ridiculed by her mouse peers because of her unusual name. As Victoria taunts her with demeaning statements, the author states "Chrysanthemum wilted." Aaah! As the story continues and her beautiful name is even considered for the music teacher's offspring, Henkes writes, "She blushed. She beamed. She bloomed." Aaah! This simple example points out the power of the perfect word in one's writing.

Poetry and alphabet books, in particular, place an emphasis on word choice. Bill Martin, Jr. and John Archambault's *Listen to the Rain* is a poem picture book that uses words to set the stage for the approaching and fleeting rainstorm. The reader initially notes the quiet beginnings of the rain event through a *slow soft sprinkle* and a *drip-drop tinkle*. As the storm hits with increasing force, the reader witnesses the *hurly-burly, topsy-turvy, lashing gnashing* of the torrential winds and the lightning-filled sky. As the storm departs, listeners react to the *quietude* and the *fresh wet silent after-time of rain.*[*] The rich language brings the entire storm, from start to finish, to readers' vivid imaginations. Explore and savor the word choice and language that reminds the reader of the power of words. Not only are vocabularies enriched, but an awareness of the power of words is renewed.

Jerry Spinelli provides an example of snapshot writing in *Maniac Magee* that highlights the importance of detailed words in transmitting a description to the reader. Savor the rich word choices in this description of the infested kitchen.

> [He] had seen some amazing things in his lifetime, but nothing as amazing as that house. . . . Cans and bottles lay all over, along with crusts, peelings, cores, scraps, rinds, wrappers—everything you would normally find in a garbage can, and everywhere there were raisins. . . .
>
> Nothing could be worse than the living and dining rooms, yet the kitchen was. A jar of peanut butter had crashed to the floor; someone had gotten a running start, jumped into it, and skied a brown, one-footed track to the stove. On the table were what appeared to be the remains of an autopsy performed on a large bird, possibly a crow. The refrigerator contained two food groups: mustard and beer. The raisins here were even more abundant. He spotted several of them moving. They weren't raisins; they were roaches.[†]

Models like these provide excellent examples and inspire young writers to incorporate strong word choices as they compose. Perfect word choice doesn't just happen, particularly in a picture book where words are at a minimum. Nor does it happen in chapter books just because words are more plentiful. Word choice should

---

[*]Quotes from *Listen to the Rain* by Bill Martin, Jr. and John Archambault, © 1988 by Bill Martin, Jr. and John Archambault. Reprinted by permission of Henry Holt and Company, LLC.
[†]From *Maniac Magee*. Text copyright © 1990 by Jerry Spinelli. Reprinted by permission of Little, Brown and Company.

be noted, valued, and applauded using quality literature as a model. Students will respond to this writing trait by using "aaah" words in their own writing. In fact, this is probably the trait to which they most easily respond and most quickly flows into their own written work.

Sentence Fluency

When writing is read aloud, sentence fluency becomes evident. Sentence fluency is the smooth rhythm and effortless flow of the words as they leap off the page into the mind of the reader. Sentence fluency evidences itself through variation in sentence length and the use of transitions between paragraphs, pages, or chapters. Sentence fluency clarifies, energizes, and condenses thoughts into a natural flow of ideas. When we say some titles like Kate DiCamillo's *The Miraculous Journey of Edward Tulane* are "meant to be read aloud," we are probably bringing the writing element of sentence fluency into focus.

Sentence length can vary from long and stretchy to short and snappy. Variety brings a read-aloud flow to writing. Angela Johnson uses this technique in *I Dream of Trains*. In this excerpt, the author expresses a boy's dream, first with a short sentence while the text expands to his broader hope for the future though a long, train-like sentence.

> One day, when I am older
> I will leave the cotton behind.
> I'll miss my family and the woods –
> All that made me smile . . . .
>
> But when my time comes for leaving,
> I will take a train and
> remember as I roll away
> what Papa said about Casey
> and his soul-speaking whistles
> and my place in the big wide world.*

This title creates a memorable read-aloud. Response to this writing trait is often seen in young writers' attempts to vary sentence length. Their initial flow may be a bit awkward, but they soon realize that sentence length variation takes planning to be an effective literary device.

Other aspects of sentence fluency might be varying sentence order, repetition of particular sentences, or smooth transitions exemplified in George Ella Lyon's *Weaving the Rainbow*. The rhythm of writing forms an aspect of writing that can be identified in works by children's literature authors and applied in one's own writing.

---

*Reprinted with permission of Simon & Schuster Books for Young Readers, an imprint of Simon & Schuster Children's Publishing Division from *I Dream of Trains* by Angela Johnson. Text copyright © 2003 Angela Johnson.

Once again, the literary model extends into the response mode as young authors incorporate these ideas into their own writing.

Writing Conventions

Writing conventions include all of the things writers add to polish a piece of writing so the other five traits can be appreciated by the reader. In actuality, it is often editors who apply these finishing touches to a literary work. These include spelling, punctuation, mechanics, paragraphing, formatting, and printing. Examining a published page from a child's favorite book is an effective way for that child to realize how important these conventions are to the reader. Although we take correctness for granted as readers, as writers we must work so conventions help clarify the writer's message. Once again, by looking to literature to model conventions, a young writer sees the importance of correctness and, in return, responds by polishing his or her own writing with professional conventions. Literature should not be used as drill and practice for inserting conventions in a page of a book. Pointing out and appreciating the use of punctuation in Judy Hindley's *Do Like a Duck Does!* or Margie Palatini's *The Web Files*, for example, make emergent writers more aware of conventions in the context of writing.

The more authentic literature that surrounds readers, the more writers will respond by applying new techniques and traits to their own quality writing. McElveen and Dierking (2001) provide numerous examples of children's books as models to teach writing skills. Teachers who point out the writing traits of children's authors and who focus on the author's craft alongside book discussion are likely to encourage stronger writing in their own young authors (Wall, 2000).

CLOSING THOUGHTS

Response to literature can be evidenced in the impact of the literary craft on a child's own writing. Surrounding young authors with quality literature is probably the best way to help teach them the art of writing. Whether they hear literature through a read-aloud or experience it in their minds during independent reading, emergent writers, with the guidance of an aware teacher, note literary techniques and slowly emulate them in their own creative works. Young writers internalize writing through literature. Therefore, a child's own writing can be considered a cumulative response to the well-written literature that has surrounded him or her during a childhood of quality reading.

Only selected literature titles are meant to create authentic writing extensions. An overdose of writing extensions weakens the literary response and dishonors the literature. Used selectively and judiciously, well-planned writing extensions can be meaningful and create special literature memories. A growing awareness of children's literature and quality writing assists the teacher in making decisions that assist the young writer, rather than imposing restrictions on him or her.

Children's authors serve as role models for writing. Through biographies and autobiographies they share how ideas emerge, how their childhoods influenced their writing, and how hard work surrounds writing. Young authors begin to view writers as their friends as they familiarize themselves not only with their books but also with characteristics of their writing.

Finally, providing writing models through literature reinforces the reading—writing connection. Because the processes of reading and writing exhibit many parallels, it is only reasonable to place literature at the center of both literary processes. Quality literature can motivate reading, and it can also impact writing. Children respond to literature by reading more, writing with more spirit and interest, and feeling growing pride in the impact of literacy in their lives.

References

Applebee, A. (1980). Children's narratives: New directions. *The Reading Teacher, 34,* 137–142.

Barksdale-Ladd, M. A., & Nedeff, A. R. (1997). The worlds of a reader's mind: Students as authors. *The Reading Teacher, 50,* 564–573.

Bromley, K. D. (1996). *Webbing with literature: Creating story maps with children's books* (2nd ed.). Boston: Allyn & Bacon.

Certo, J. L. (2004). Cold plums and the old men in the water: Let children read and write "great" poetry. *The Reading Teacher, 58,* 266–271.

Culham, R. (2003). *6 + 1 traits of writing: The complete guide.* New York: Scholastic.

Darigan, D. L., Tunnell, M. O., & Jacobs, J. S. (2002). *Children's literature: Engaging teachers and children in good books.* Upper Saddle River, NJ: Prentice Hall/Merrill.

Dean, D., & Grierson, S. (2005). Re-envisioning reading and writing through combined-text picture books. *Journal of Adolescent & Adult Literacy, 48,* 456–468.

Egawa, K. (1990). Harnessing the power of language: First graders' literature engagement with "Owl Moon." *Language Arts, 67,* 582–588.

Golden, J. M. (1984). Children's concept of story in reading and writing. *The Reading Teacher, 37,* 578–584.

Hancock, M. R. (2007). *Language arts: Extending the possibilities.* Upper Saddle River, NJ: Merrill/Prentice Hall.

Hansen, J. (2001). *When writers read* (2nd ed.). Portsmouth, NH: Heinemann.

Heald-Taylor, G. (1987). How to use predictable books for K–2 language arts instruction. *The Reading Teacher, 40,* 656–661.

Lancia, P. J. (1997). Literary borrowing: The effects of literature on children's writing. *The Reading Teacher, 50,* 470–475.

McElveen, S. A., & Dierking, C. C. (2001). Children's books as models to teach writing skills. *The Reading Teacher, 54,* 362–364.

Moore-Hart, M. A. (2006). A writers' camp in action: A community of readers and writers. *The Reading Teacher, 59,* 326-338.

Moss, B. (2003). *Exploring the literature of fact: Children's nonfiction trade books in the elementary classroom.* New York: Guilford.

Peck, J., & Hendershot, J. (1997). Meet *Officer Buckle and Gloria* through their creator's own story. *The Reading Teacher, 50,* 404–408.

Rhodes, L. K. (1981). I can read! Predictable books as resources for reading and writing instruction. *The Reading Teacher, 34,* 511–518.

Sipe, L. R. (1993). Using transformations of traditional stories: Making the reading—writing connection. *The Reading Teacher, 47,* 18–26.

Spandel, V., & Stiggins, R. J. (2000). *Creating writers: Linking writing assessment and instruction* (3rd ed.). White Plains, NY: Longman.

Wall, H. (2000). How do authors do it? Using literature in a writer's workshop. *The New Advocate, 13,* 157–170.

Walmsley, S. A., & Walp, T. P. (1990). Integrating literature and composing into the language arts curriculum: Philosophy and practice. *The Elementary School Journal, 90,* 251–274.

Children's Books Cited [P] = K–2; [I] = 3–5; [M] = 6–8

Ada, Alma Flor (2001). *With love, Little Red Hen*. Illus. by Leslie Tryon. New York: Atheneum. [P/I]

Ahlberg, Janet, & Ahlberg, Allan (1986). *The jolly postman, or other people's letters*. Boston: Little, Brown. [P/I]

Andrews-Goebel, Nancy (2002). *The pot that Juan built*. Illus. by David Diaz. New York: Lee & Low. [P/I]

Arnosky, Jim (2002). *All about frogs*. New York: Scholastic. [P]

Avi (1990). *The true confessions of Charlotte Doyle*. New York: Orchard Books. [M]

Barrett, Judi (1998). *Things that are most in the world*. Illus. by John Nickle. New York: Atheneum. [P/I]

Blake, Robert (1993). *The perfect spot*. New York: Philomel Books. [P/I]

Blumberg, Rhoda (2004). *York's adventures with Lewis & Clark: An African-American's part in the great expedition*. New York: Harper-Collins. [I/M]

Boulton, Jane (Adapter) (1994). *Only Opal: The diary of a young girl*. Illus. by Barbara Cooney. New York: Philomel Books. [I]

Brett, Jan (1999). *The gingerbread baby*. New York: Putnam. [P]

Brown, Margaret Wise (1947). *Goodnight moon*. New York: Harper & Row. [P]

Bunting, Eve (1991). *Fly away home*. Illus. by Ron Himler. Boston: Clarion. [I]

Burleigh, Robert (1991). *Flight: The journey of Charles Lindbergh*. Illus. by Mike Wimmer. New York: Philomel Books. [I]

Carle, Eric (1971). *The very hungry caterpillar*. New York: Crowell. [P]

Cleary, Beverly (1983). *Dear Mr. Henshaw*. New York: Morrow. [I]

Creech, Sharon (1997). *Chasing redbird*. New York: HarperCollins. [I]

Creech, Sharon (2001). *Love that dog*. New York: HarperCollins. [I/M]

Curlee, Lynn (2005). *Ballpark: The story of America's baseball fields*. . New York: Atheneum. [I/M]

de Paola, Tomie (1978). *Pancakes for breakfast*. San Diego: Harcourt Brace. [P]

DiCamillo, Kate (2006). *The miraculous journey of Edward Tulane*. Cambridge, MA: Candlewick. [P/I]

Fleischman, Paul (1993). *Bull run*. Woodcuts by David Frampton. New York: HarperCollins.[I]

Fleming, Denise (1991). *In the tall, tall grass*. New York: Holt. [P]

Fleming, Candace (2003). *Boxes for Katje*. Illus. by Stacey Dressen-McQueen. New York: Farrar, Straus & Giroux. [P/I]

Halls, Kelly Milner (2004). *Albino animals*. Plain City, OH: Derbycreek Publishers. [I/M]

Harrington, Janice N. (2004). *Going north*. Illus. by Jerome Lagarrigue. New York: Farrar, Straus & Giroux. [P/I]

Hawkins, Colin, & Hawkins, Jacqui (2004). *Fairy tale news*. Cambridge, MA: Candlewick. [I]

Hawkins, Colin, & Hawkins, Jacqui (2006). *Pirate treasure map: A fairytale adventure*. Cambridge, MA: Candlewick. [I]

Henkes, Kevin (1992). *Chrysanthemum*. New York: Greenwillow. [P]

Henkes, Kevin (2004). *Kitten's first full moon*. New York: Greenwillow. [P]

Hindley, Judy (2002). *Do like a duck does!* Illus. by Ivan Bates. Cambridge, MA: Candlewick Press. [P]

Johnson, Angela (2003). *I dream of trains*. Illus. by Loren Long. New York: Simon & Schuster. [P/I]

Kadohata, Cynthia (2004). *Kira-kira*. New York: Atheneum. [I]

Lester, Helen (1997). *Author: A true story*. Boston: Houghton Mifflin. [P/I]

Levine, Ellen (2007). *Henry's freedom box: A true story from the Underground Railroad*. Illus. by Kadir Nelson. New York: Scholastic. [I]

Lyon, George Ella (2004). *Weaving the rainbow*. Illus. by Stephanie Anderson. New York: Atheneum. [P]

Markle, Sandra (2006). *Rescues!* Minneapolis: Millbrook. [I/M]

Martin, Bill, Jr. (1983). *Brown bear, brown bear, what do you see?* Illus. by Eric Carle. New York: Holt. [P]

Martin, Bill, Jr., & Archambault, John (1988). *Listen to the rain*. Illus. by J. Endicott. New York: Holt. [P/I]

McClafferty, Carla Killough (2006). *Something out of nothing: Marie Curie and radium.* New York: Farrar, Straus & Giroux. [I/M]

McKissack, Patricia (2001). *Goin' someplace special.* Illus. by Jerry Pinkney. New York: Atheneum. [I]

Mills, Lauren (2001). *The dog prince.* Illus. by Lauren Mills & Dennis Nolan. New York: Little, Brown. [I]

Moss, Marissa (2005). *Amelia's 6th-grade notebook.* New York: Simon & Schuster.[I/M]

Murphy, Jim (1995). *The great fire.* New York: Scholastic. [I/M]

Osborne, Mary Pope (2000). *Kate and the beanstalk.* Illus. by Giselle Potter. New York: Atheneum. [P/I]

Osborne, Mary Pope (2002). *The brave little seamstress.* Illus. by Giselle Potter. New York: Atheneum. [P/I]

Osborne, Will, & Osborne, Mary Pope (2005). *Sleeping Bobby.* Illus. by Giselle Potter. New York: Atheneum. [P/I]

Palatini, Margie (2001). *The web files.* Illus. by Richard Egielski. New York: Hyperion. [P/I]

Paulsen, Gary (1992). *The haymeadow.* New York: Delacorte. [I/M]

Paulsen, Gary (2001). *Guts: The true stories behind Hatchet and the Brian books.* New York: Delacorte. [I/M]

Polacco, Patricia (2006). *Something about Hensley's.* New York: Philomel/Putnam. [I]

Rylant, Cynthia (1982). *When I was young in the mountains.* Illus. by Diane Goode. New York: Dutton. [I]

Schanzer, Rosalyn (2004). *George vs. George: The American Revolution seen from both sides.* Washington, DC: National Geographic. [I/M]

Schotter, Roni (1997). *Nothing ever happens on 90th Street.* Illus. by Kyrsten Brooker. New York: Orchard. [I]

Scieszka, Jon (1989). *The true story of the three little pigs.* Illus. by Lane Smith. New York: Viking. [P/I]

Spinelli, Jerry (1990). *Maniac Magee.* Boston: Little, Brown. [I]

Stewart, Sarah (2001). *The journey.* Illus. by David Small. New York: Farrar, Straus & Giroux. [I]

Van Allsburg, Chris (1984). *The mysteries of Harris Burdick.* Boston: Houghton Mifflin. [I/M]

Viorst, Judith (1981). *If I were in charge of the world and other worries.* New York: Atheneum. [I]

Ward, Lynd (1973). *The silver pony.* Boston: Houghton Mifflin. [I]

Wells, Rosemary (2002). *Wingwalker.* Illus. by Brian Selznick. New York: Hyperion. [I]

Wiesner, David (2001). *The three pigs.* New York: Clarion. [P/I]

Wiesner, David (2006). *Flotsam.* New York: Clarion. [I]

Williams, Vera B., & Williams, Jennifer (1988). *Stringbean's trip to the shining sea.* New York: Greenwillow. [I]

Wong, Janet (2002). *You have to write.* Illus. by Teresa Flavin. New York: McElderry. [P/I/M]

Yolen, Jane (1987). *Owl moon.* Illus. by Jon Schoenherr. New York: Philomel Books. [P]

CHAPTER 12

Drama, Art, and Music
Expressive Arts as Response

I love European art. Every trip to European cities includes a visit to a museum that houses the finest masterpieces in the world—the Uffizi in Florence, the Musée du Louvre in Paris, or the Kunsthistoriche Museum in Vienna. But it is not an art history knowledge that motivates or informs me. It is children's art books that have increased my awareness and appreciation of art by targeting and improving my observational skills.

Look Closer by Caroline Desnoettes takes my hand as the author introduces me to several cherished works of art. For example, Vincent van Gogh's 'Bedroom in Arles' is showcased in its full-page glory but also highlighted with a "slice" of its identifying characteristics. When I flip the page overlay, I uncover a palette of four colors—lavender blue, pinkish gray, ochre yellow, khaki green—the hues form the mood and authenticity of this artwork. When I open another flap on the second page, I am provided six questions that focus on the details of this masterpiece itself. I find myself looking for van Gogh's hat, a self-portrait hanging on the wall, the green glow reflection on the window, the generous paint on the canvas, and the repeated pairs of objects across the piece. If I page to the back of the book, I find an elaborated discussion of the artist and the painting.

When I travel to the Musée d'Orsay, I will know exactly what to observe in van Gogh's masterpiece. And it only took a children's book to open my eyes and my heart to art!

Author response to *Look Closer: Art Masterpieces Through the Ages*
by Caroline Desnoettes

Dramatic, artistic, and musical responses to literature have often been reserved for enrichment and hence unfortunately experienced by only the most academically talented students. The ability to express oneself through dramatic presentation, artistic media, or musical prowess, however, is the preferred mode of response for many children. Integrating the expressive arts into the lives of all children through response to children's literature should be considered a natural part of the culture of childhood. Although oral and written response to literature dominate research and practice in the area of literature-based instruction, the expressive modes of response offer endless possibilities for sharing personal response to children's books (Kruas, 2006; Lamme, 1990; Peck & Virkler, 2006; Yopp & Yopp, 2003). Drama, art, and music have just begun to be more extensively explored as channels and outlets for creative response to literature. As teachers of children with varied learning styles and expressive styles, we must keep our minds open to the stimulating possibilities of children's books that encourage personal response through the expressive arts.

DRAMATIC RESPONSE

Dramatic response to literature emerges as performance and emotion blend into personal expression (Kieff, 2002; Kornfeld & Layden, 2005; Macy, 2004). This mode of response displays itself through dramatic movement, choral readings, readers' theater, puppetry, and plays. Children's literature must be read, listened to, and savored before any form of dramatic response can result. A child must feel a familiarity with the text, establish a kinship with characters, internalize the plot sequence, and develop a joy in the language and style before they can be expected to respond expressively. The lived-through experience of repeated readings of the text prepares the performer for the task at hand. Literature of all genres inspires dramatic response but requires immersion, freedom to be oneself, and a growing sense of confidence before the dramatic response is shared. For younger children, dramatic response is spontaneous and unencumbered. Older children prefer some time for informal rehearsal for collaborative efforts, but expression, not perfection, is always the priority of dramatic response.

Movement and Dance as Dramatic Response

Preschool children possess a natural tendency to move in response to the invitations afforded by literature. Movement as response was identified by Hickman (1983) as a spontaneous response to read-alouds. Young listeners will find it hard to resist Doreen Cronin's invitation to *Wiggle* through its rollicking verse and lively illustrations that feature a targeted movement to imitate. Ball bouncing, jump roping, swinging, and hide-and-seek games provide an international play experience through Jane Yolen's collection of *Street Rhymes Around the World.* Even the youngest children naturally move in response to Margaret Mayo's *Choo Choo Clickety Clack!* This natural invitation and celebration of literature through movement builds a foundation for expanding dramatic response as the child grows in reading and performance ability.

Dance is a form of movement that may exhibit itself as response to literature. *Song and Dance,* a selection of poems by Lee Bennett Hopkins, invites young children to do-si-do to Beverly McLoughland's "Birds' Square Dance" and tap their toes to "From Lines Written for Gene Kelly to Dance To" by Carl Sandburg. Poems like "What Is Jazz?" by Mary O'Neill and "Harlem Night Song" by Langston Hughes should be accompanied by the sound of music and dance. Leo and Diane Dillon's *Rap a Tap Tap: Here's Bojangles* invites tap dancing and music selection and integration.

Margot Fonteyn's *Coppelia* includes a copious endnote describing the original ballet that inspired her story. Music from the ballet by Leo Delibes might accompany a performance by talented dancers in the classroom or community. *I Dreamed I Was a Ballerina* blends Anna Pavlova's life with the paintings of Edgar Degas. Young children may be inspired through *Time for Ballet* by Adele Geras and *On Your Toes: A Ballet ABC* by Rachel Isadora; older children revel in the autobiography of *Tallchief: America's Prima Ballerina* completed with Rosemary Wells. Dance needs to be included as an option for dramatic response, particularly for those children who find it a comfortable means of individual expression.

Choral Reading

A simple but effective outlet for dramatic response exists through the performance medium of choral reading (Yopp & Yopp, 2003). Poetry is the genre that naturally lends itself to this oral sharing of language, expression, and rhythm through dramatic response. Young children have a comfortable affinity with verse, rhyme, riddles, and songs, and older readers revel in the well-chosen language, varied moods, and succinctness of poetry. Just as each child responds to a poem in a unique way, so too does he or she share that unique response through the art of choral reading.

The choral reading response can be delivered in several ways. Choral reading can be orchestrated as individual performance, partner presentations, in small groups, or as a whole class. Stewig's (1981) suggested choral reading formats are discussed next.

Echo reading.   The leader reads each line and the group repeats it. This requires a simple quiet poem where repetition breeds reflection. "Night Garden," the title poem from Janet Wong's *Night Garden,* lends itself to echo reading. (Each line is read by a leader and echoed by the group.)

> Deep in the earth/
> a tangle of roots/
> sends up
> green shoots/
> and dreams grow
> wild,/
> dreams go wild/
> like dandelion weeds,/
> feathery heads/
> alive
> with seeds — /
> And these fine seeds/
> about to sprout/
> race the day/
> to find their place/
> in a welcome mind/
> in an open space/
> in a lonely bed –/
> and they send down roots,/
> and they sprout
> and bloom – /
> in the night garden./*

Paired reading. This mode of choral reading became particularly popular through Paul Fleischman's books, *I Am Phoenix* and *Joyful Noise: Poems for Two Voices,* which invite side-by-side reading by two readers. Children learn to appreciate the sounds, feelings, joy, and magic of poetry through this planned vocal expression experience. Access an excerpt from "Whirligig Beetles," for example, that reflects the magic of dual voices resounding the text. A perfect resource for paired reading is Mary Ann Hoberman's *You Read to Me, I'll Read to You*, in which each short rhymed poem inspires the emergent reader with the joys of literacy.

Small group reading. The class divides, and each group or individual within a group reads part of the poem. The repetition and simplicity of "Can I, Can I Catch the Wind" from Pat Mora's *Confetti* lends itself to this type of reading. Envision a group of seven students, each attaining ownership of a single line with all joining on the final answer to the repeated query.

---

*Reprinted with the permission of Margaret K. McElderry Books, an imprint of Simon & Schuster Children's Publishing Division from *Night Garden* by Janet S. Wong. Text copyright © 2000 Janet S. Wong.

Can I, can I catch the wind, in the morning, catch the wind?
Can I, can I catch the wind, in my two hands, catch the wind?
Can I, can I catch the wind, in my basket, catch the wind?
Can I, can I catch the wind, in my clay pot, catch the wind?
Can I, can I catch the wind, in my tin box, catch the wind?
Can I, can I catch the wind, in my straw hat, catch the wind?
Can I, can I catch the wind, in my bird cage, catch the wind?
Wind, Wind, run and spin, dance and spin, run and spin.*

Cumulative reading.   One student or group reads the first line or stanza as other students or groups join in with additional lines or stanzas. An entire class presentation can emerge from Douglas Florian's seasonal collection *Winter Eyes*, with "Good Bye, Winter" as a single example. The opening lines inspire whole-group reading. The middle of the poem allows for both the individual reader's voice and small groups of readers. The poem's closing celebrates the entire group voice once again.

Children naturally warm to the humorous poetry of Shel Silverstein, Jack Prelutsky, or X. J. Kennedy (Kutiper & Wilson, 1993). Their rhymed nonsense focuses on topics of children's everyday existence to create both personal interest and a need to share. Hear the voices and envision the expression of students who each claim alternate lines of "One Winter Night in August," "Mixed Up School," and "Stevie the Internet Addict" from X. J. Kennedy's *Exploding Gravy: Poems to Make You Laugh*. Prelutsky's collection *Scranimals* inspires intermediate students to play with lines for presentation. For a readily prepared cumulative reading experience, consider Paul Fleischman's *Big Talk: Poems for Four Voices* with middle-level students.

Although humor is a welcome springboard for choral reading, other poetry warrants read-aloud response as well. Interdisciplinary units can address their themes through poetry as choral reading journeys across the curriculum. For example, choral readings of poems about creatures of the sea from Douglas Florian's *In the Swim*, creatures of flight in *On the Wing*, mammals from *Mammalabilia*, or amphibians in *Frogs, Toads and Polliwogs* might effectively be shared by partners to introduce research on creatures of the ocean, air, and land.

Poetry provides the core of the material for choral reading as an isolated or integrated dramatic response activity. Easy to locate and fun for students to arrange and rehearse for presentation, poetry contributes a wealth of material for use in choral reading events. Chapter 5 contains a wealth of quality poetry books to enhance choral reading in the classroom. Not only will students improve oral expression, but their attitude toward the poetry genre is likely to grow stronger through positive group sharing. Figure 12.1 focuses on optimal titles to encourage choral reading.

Readers' Theater

Readers' theater as a dramatic response mode provides an effective means to communicate the language of literature and the joy of reading. Readers' theater defines a

---

*"Can I, Can I Catch the Wind" from *Confetti*. Text copyright © 1996 by Pat Mora. Reprinted by permission of *Lee & Low Books*.

FIGURE 12.1 Choral reading, readers' theater, and puppetry plays

Choral Reading

Hoberman, Mary Ann (2004). *You read to me, I'll read to you: Very short fairy tales to read together.* Illus. by Michael Emberley. New York: Little, Brown. [P]

Hoberman, Mary Ann (2005). *You read to me, I'll read to you: Very short Mother Goose tales to read together.* Illus. by Michael Emberley. New York. Little, Brown. [P]

Hopkins, Lee Bennett (1988). *Side by side: Poems to read together.* Illus. by Hillary Knight. New York: Simon & Schuster. [I]

Hovery, Kate (2004). *Voices of the Trojan War.* Illus. by Leonid Gore. New York: Simon & Schuster. [I/M]

Hudson, Wade (2004). *Powerful words: More than 200 years of extraordinary writings by African Americans* Illus. by Sean Qualls. New York: Scholastic. [I/M]

Lewis, J. Patrick (2005). *Please bury me in the library.* Illus. by Kyle M. Stone. San Diego: Gulliver/Harcourt. [I]

Moses, Sheila P. (2005) *I, Dred Scott: A fictional slave narrative based on the life and legal record of Dred Scott.* Illus. by Bonnie Christiansen. New York: McElderry. [M]

Pinkney, Andrea Davis (2001). *Let it shine! Stories of Black women freedom fighters.* San Diego: Harcourt. [I/M]

Readers' Theater

Borden, Louise (2004). *Sea clocks: The story of longitude.* Illus. by Erik Blegvad. New York: McElderry. [I/M]

Greenfield, Eloise (2005). *The friendly four.* Illus. by Jan Spivey Gilchrist. New York: HarperCollins. [I]

Kelly, Irene (2002). *It's hummingbird's life.* New York: Holiday House.

MacDonald, Amy (1996). *Cousin Ruth's tooth.* Boston: Houghton Mifflin. [P/I]

Van Steenwyk, Elizabeth (2003). *One find day: A radio play.* Illus. by Bill Farnsworth. Grand Rapids, MI: Eerdman's Books for Young Readers. [I/M]

Winters, Kay (2003). *Voices of ancient Egypt.* Illus. by Barry Moser. Washington, DC: National Geographic. [I/M]

Puppetry and Play

Aliki (2005). *A play's the thing.* New York: HarperCollins. [P/I]

Best, Cari (2001). *Shrinking Violet.* Illus. by Giselle Potter. New York: Melanie Kroupa/Farrar, Straus & Giroux. [P/I]

Byars, Betsy (2000). *Me Tarzan.* Illus. by Bill Cigliano. New York: HarperCollins. [I]

De Paola, Tomie (2005). *Stagestruck.* New York: Putnam. [P]

Millman, Isaac (2004). *Moses sees a play.* New York: Frances Foster/Farrar. [P]

Shulman, Mark (2004). *Stella the star.* Illus. by Vincent Nguyen. New York: Walker. [P]

presentation of text that is read aloud expressively and dramatically by two or more readers. The primary emphasis is on reading aloud (as opposed to memorization, action, props, or costumes), but the intent is for the readers to read expressively so they paint an image of the events and actions in the minds of the audience (Flynn, 2004). Although the words come from literature, the expressive response comes from inside the heart of the reader as he or she internalizes both characters and situation. A second-grade performance of Martin Waddell's *Owl Babies,* for example, yields concern, fear, and relief from a trio of baby owls as a mother owl leaves the nest to seek food for her growing family.

Although intended to benefit the reader through smoother reading fluency (Martinez, Roser, & Strecker, 1998/1999), increased sight vocabulary, and improved comprehension, readers' theater as response to literature focuses on other outcomes as well (Morado, Koenig, & Wilson, 1999). Expressiveness of oral reading and individual interpretation of text constitute the core of personal response. Delivery, tone, pitch, and volume become components of expression as the reader strives to share the emotion of the text. Personal interpretation results in individual response as the meaning one derives from the text gives rise to the emotional effort behind the oral interpretation of text (Wolf, 1994).

Teacher-generated scripts provide a preliminary experience for initial efforts at readers' theater with personal expression emphasized as a response mode. A simple starting point for whole-class response is Amy MacDonald's *Cousin Ruth's Tooth*. This humorous story follows the Fister family and friends as they seek a solution for the latest family crisis—a lost tooth. The search efforts of relatives, neighbors, and friends move at a rapid pace to the solution offered by the wise queen. The text easily adapts into a script with minimal roles for about 20 students. The crisp, brief, and fast-paced text abounds with humorous characters and should be introduced as a read-aloud and reread and savored several times before a response performance. Characters are likely to match distinct classroom personalities to bring a read-aloud to life through readers' theater response. A similar romp might be created with MacDonald's earlier title, *Rachel Fister's Blister*.

Success in early ventures into readers' theater is built on selection of quality literature that easily translates into script format. Characteristics of books that work with readers' theater response include:

- Books that are short in length so they can be shared in their entirety
- Books that follow a simple story line
- Books that have three or four main characters
- Books that contain ample dialogue

A Beautiful Feast for a Big King Cat (Archambault & Martin, 1994) provides another scriptable text for a small group readers' theater response. A mischievous bold mouse shielded by his protective mother challenges an arrogant cat. Mouse finds himself in the cat's clutches but plays on the cat's ego to get released and return home safely. The portrayals of the teasing mouse, the arrogant cat, and the protective mother mouse provide for individual response through oral expression. Written entirely in rhymed text, repeated lines also lend the text to small group performance. Varied voices, rhyming text, and interesting characters make this a delightful avenue for response to a children's book.

Older children are capable of adapting books into scripts themselves. In this case, written script combines with expressive response through readers' theater. Picture books may provide a beginning resource at this level with performances shared with younger students. After this simple scriptwriting modeling, students should be challenged to script specific portions of chapter books into a readers' theater format. Because of its motivational value, readers' theater leads to more reading as the audience is inspired to read the original title while the performers seek other books by the same author.

The dramatic verbal portrayal through readers' theater aids comprehension, which seems particularly true through historical connections (Fennessey, 2006; Flynn, 2004; Hancock, 2007; Kornfeld & Leyton, 2005). Phillip Hoose's *We Were There, Too!*

Middle-level students perform readers' theater through books with a cast of memorable characters and distinctive voices. *From* Witness *by Karen Hesse. Jacket art copyright © 2001 by Kim McGillivray. Reprinted by permission of Scholastic, Inc.*

provides opportunities to share unique perspectives of youth throughout U.S. history. Similarly, Sherry Garland's *Voices of the Alamo* unfolds in 16 voices over five centuries. Nameless individuals who occupied and shaped Texas—a Spanish conquistador, a Tejino rancher, a Texas farmer, a Mexican army drummer—speak along with principal players in the 1856 battle including General Santa Anna, Davy Crockett, William Travis, and General Sam Houston. An adapted script of Paul Fleischman's *Bull Run* provides short first-person accounts of the first battle of the Civil War from the changing points of view of eager boys, a worried sister, a general, and a physician. Read aloud selectively and emotionally, the voices of the readers reflect the glory, horror, thrill, and disillusionment of war. This text provides a moving performance that enhances the depth and appreciation of the human perspective of this historical period.

Readers' theater opportunities at the middle-level abound. Karen Hesse's *Witness,* written in prose poetry, utilizes eleven voices, each one revealing the infiltration of the Ku Klux Klan into a small Vermont town in 1924. The cast of characters is distinctive, ranging from unforgettable to despicable. Middle-level students will rise to the challenge of creating voices for these individual perspectives. Paul Fleischman's *Seek* provides a collage of voices and a radio sound portrait as Robert Radrovitz searches for his long-lost father. Fleischman includes performance notes at the book's end and suggests adaptation for readers' theater.

Young and Vardell (1993) also suggest weaving readers' theater and the informational genre into the curriculum. Although the response mode highlights readers' theater, the genre focus is nonfiction. Suggested titles include the *Magic School Bus* series, photo essays of Joan Anderson, and even science books by Seymour Simon. Because this material needs to be rescripted for readers' theater, much of the response lies in the creative, collaborative adaption of expository information to script format.

Kieff (2002) suggests responding to school stories through readers' theater. Titles such as Jack Gantos's *Joey Pigza Swallowed the Key,* Sharon Creech's *Love That Dog,* Andrew Clements's *The Landry News,* and Avi's *The Secret School* provide school-based experiences to inspire script writing through poignant vignettes reflecting school relationships.

In any genre, literature must be the primary focus of the readers' theater response. Children must read the book or have it read aloud to them initially. Immersion in the story and personal interpretation of dialogue is mandatory if the readers' theater is built on genuine response. Scripting, assignment of roles, rehearsal, and staging are all important facets of readers' theater, but its true success as response lies in the interpretive oral reading of literature. Within the freedom to express oneself through the character's words lies the repetitive strength of readers' theater as dramatic response to literature.

Puppetry and Plays

Informal use of puppets in a retelling dramatization of literature provides another means of dramatic response to literature. Puppets provide a means for the inexperienced performer to restate a character's words and let his or her voice portray character traits (Flower & Fortney, 1983). The literature that fits so naturally with puppetry usually contains animal characters who can easily be portrayed through animal puppets. Whether the puppets are purchased furry delights or made from socks or cereal boxes, they provide a medium for dramatic oral response.

Martin Waddell's *Farmer Duck* and *Webster J. Duck* provide ample animal characters for a story reenactment. Karma Wilson's *Bear Snores On* provides a cast of forest animals in their efforts to wake up a hibernating bear. A read-aloud of the story with children responding through the interaction and words of their puppets forms a unique response to literature. Verna Aardema's *Traveling to Tondo: A Tale of the Nkundo of Zaire* is well suited for paper plate masks or stick puppets as animal travelers en route to a wedding are delayed by a series of silly circumstances.

Any retellings of traditional tales, such as *The Little Red Hen* by Jerry Pinkney, contain similar characters and stories that some children already know. Familiarity builds confidence through puppetry. Although children tell the story in their own words, some sense of story aids in their ability to articulate their thoughts in the guise of a puppet. Many Jan Brett books, including *The Mitten,* provide printable masks online at www.janbrett.com. Carlo Collodi's *Pinocchio* has been represented by Ed Young and formatted in theater scenes, making it near ready for an intermediate-level student puppet performance.

Although a minimal number of quality plays have been published during the past decade, a written play script provides a literary base for response (Kruas, 2006; Tortello, 2004). Dominic Catalano's *Frog Went A-Courting: A Musical Play in Six*

Acts provides a familiar tale for performance. A brilliant cast of characters, including Frog, Miss Mouse, Reverend Bug,
and Madam Moth, and brief memorizable
lines are accompanied by music to the
well-known song. The dramatic/musical
response combination would provide a
commendable parent night performance.
Ann Hayes's *Onstage & Backstage at the
Night Owl Theater* offers a behind-the-
scenes look into the world of theater.
Shakespearian performances may be inspired by Marcia Williams's adaptations of
Tales from Shakespeare: Seven Plays
and enhanced by Aliki's *William Shakespeare & the Globe.*

The publishing of Paul Fleischman's
Zap may rejuvenate older students' interest
in play performances from literature. This
script is actually a blending of seven plays
modeled on prime time categorical offerings (mystery, comedy, Shakespearean
drama) linked together with the sound of the
remote control's "zap." Sources of quality
literature in play format provide a solid option for dramatic response to literature.
Joseph Bruchac's *Pushing Up the Sky:
Seven Native American Plays for Children* and Lori Carlson's *You're On! Seven
Plays in English and Spanish* extend multicultural choices for performance.

Drama provides a valid avenue for response, particularly for students with
whom oral performance is a comfortable response mode. Young children delight in
movement response. Ranging from choral reading and readers' theater to puppet
and play performances, children of all ages are invited to express their individuality
in the guise of animal or human characters emerging from literature. At the core of
these dramatic response modes lies quality literature that supplies the words, emotions, characters, and situations that call for this unique interaction with literature.

ARTISTIC RESPONSE TO LITERATURE

Art provides an interesting means for readers to respond to the books they read (Hickman, 1983). Art as response can also spring from illustrator studies, art extensions
from literature, and the relationship of art elements to children's book illustrations.

The responder does not need to be artistically talented to use art as a means of expression. The artistic response to literature may arise as a response to text, to illustrations, to a poem, or even to an art element such as line, space, or color. Although interdisciplinary in nature, the artistic response provides variety in response modes to readers who feel and express themselves through pictures as comfortably as others do through words.

Extending Response Through Art

The primary means to use the artistic mode of response in the classroom lies in art enhancement activities suggested by the teacher. These activities must lie within the literature itself rather than being artificially attached to a book. For example, Diana Pomeroy's *One Potato* and *Wildflower ABC* books illustrate various colorful quantities of vegetables and wildflowers with potato prints. A natural, yet authentic extension includes potato prints presented in counting patterns or ABC shapes. The final two pages of the books actually inform adults about how Pomeroy's prints were completed, suggesting the same procedure for children. Ellen Senisi's *Berry Smudges and Leaf Prints: Finding and Making Colors from Nature* provides connections between nature and art. Art extensions are misused in the classroom context if they are distanced from the book itself. Specific titles such as Paul Fleischman's *Lost: A Story in String* can inspire string pictures. The artistic mode of response appears undervalued because of its overuse in unnatural connections to literature. Many titles provide valid art enhancements that extend the message and memory of the reading experience.

Research points to the value of artistic response for young children (Hubbard, 1996; Madura, 1995). Although written expression is difficult for emerging readers and writers, children can readily share personal connections through drawings. Visual representation as a language art has been reinforced by professional standards (National Council of Teachers of English & International Reading Association, 1996) and should be encouraged and respected as a mode of response for children of any age.

offer resources and information about art, music, sculpture, crafts, origami, graphic design, digital art, and performing arts along with tips for using the expressive arts within literacy instruction.

The Art Institute of Chicago
http://www.artic.edu/artaccess/
The Art Institute of Chicago provides a myriad of online resources for teachers, students, and parents on its "Art Access" page. This website includes lesson plans and projects that relate to the museum's collections while providing teachers with ideas for incorporating artistic response to literature.

Tate Online
http://www.tate.org.uk/
Hosted by the Tate Gallery in London, *Tate Online* makes over 65,000 works of art available online. The link "Tate Learning Page" provides online activities for educators of all grade levels, including suggestions for children's own artwork, lesson plans, and online courses. The link "Kids" provides games, activities, and artistic inspiration for kids. "Young Tate" is an art initiative that offers youth (ages 13 to 25) the opportunity to reach their own conclusions about art.

MUSIC
Creating Music
http://www.creatingmusic.com/
Creatingmusic.com offers children of all ages opportunities to compose music, play with musical performance, and learn new skills though interactive games and puzzles. For students responding to literature through music, this is the place to be.

Sites to See: Music
http://www.educationworld.com/a_tech/sites/sites034. shtml
Education World has compiled this list of music sites that offer resources and information about composers, conductors, and musical instruments. Some sites allow students opportunities to see, hear, play, and compose their own music in response to literature.

Connecting Art Elements and Response

The high quality of artwork represented by the works of children's book illustrators deserves and demands attention and response. Art teachers are beginning to turn toward award-winning illustrators to teach art elements. As studies of an illustrator's works are displayed and their stories read to the children, elements of art are showcased and discussed. A directed response to the illustration as a valued component of literature can be designed to incorporate the art element in a student-created work. The illustrator's work of art serves as a model for response through a child's own application of an element of art. The following examples from an art teacher's lesson plans point out the connection between art elements and artistic response across grade levels.

An elementary art teacher analyzed the media, techniques, and styles of a variety of illustrators for children's books and developed an art lesson for each illustrator selected. Selection of illustrators was based on the unique and diverse characteristics of his or her work. Lessons were developed that allowed each child to identify an illustrator's use of basic art concepts. Students were asked to create their own piece of artwork in response to the characteristics and treatment of art concepts as the illustrator being studied. Figure 12.2 lists illustrators and art concepts across grade

FIGURE 12.2 Book Cluster: Art elements and response

Grade 1: Leo Lionni

Lesson focus: Lionni's mice collage
Media: Torn/cut paper
Art Concepts: Collage; overlapping; paper techniques and usage
Illustrator models:

Lionni, Leo (1967). *Frederick*. New York: Pantheon.
Lionni, Leo (1969). *Alexander and the wind-up mouse*. New York: Pantheon.
Lionni, Leo (1992). *Mr. McMouse*. New York: Knopf.
Lionni, Leo (2005/1970). *Fish is fish*. New York: Knopf.
Lionni, Leo (2006/1975). *Pezzettino*. New York: Knopf.

Grade 2: Eric Carle

Lesson focus: Carle's animal train using simple shapes
Media: Painted paper/tissue paper
Art concepts: Mixed media; using shapes to create form; texture
Illustrator models:

Carle, Eric (1989). *Animals, animals*. New York: Philomel Books.
Carle, Eric (1999). *Dragons, dragons and other creatures that never were*. New York: Philomel.
Carle, Eric (2000). *Does a kangaroo have a mother, too?* New York: HarperCollins.
Carle, Eric (2002). *"Slowly, slowly, slowly" said the sloth*. New York: Philomel.
Carle, Eric (2004). *Mr. Seahorse*. New York: Philomel.
Carle, Eric (2005). *10 little rubber ducks*. New York: HarperCollins.

FIGURE 12.2 Continued

Grade 3: Paul Goble

Lesson focus: Goble's Native American teepee with skies showing value
Media: Crayons/watercolors
Art concepts: Color value; tint and shade; patterns
Illustrator models:

Goble, Paul (1990). *Dream wolf.* New York: Bradbury Press.
Goble, Paul (1992). *Love flute.* New York: Bradbury Press.
Goble, Paul (1999). *Iktomi loses his eyes: A Plains Indian story.* New York: Orchard.
Goble, Paul (2001). *Storm maker's tipi.* New York: Atheneum
Goble, Paul (2003). *Mystic horse.* New York: HarperCollins.
Goble, Paul (2004). *Song of creation.* Grand Rapids, MI: Eerdman's

Grade 4: Peter Parnall

Lesson focus: Parnall's trees
Media: Pencil/colored pencil
Art concepts: Lines; linear quality; contour; restricted palette
Illustrator models:

Baylor, Byrd (1986). *I'm in charge of celebrations.* Illus. by Peter Parnall. New York: Scribner's.
Parnall, Peter (1988). *Apple tree.* New York: Macmillan.
Parnall, Peter (1990). *Woodpile.* New York: Macmillan.
Parnall, Peter (1991). *The rock.* New York: Macmillan.
Parnall, Peter (and Justin Richardson) (2005). *And Tango makes three.* New York: Simon & Schuster.

Grade 5: Patricia Polacco

Lesson focus: Polacco's people
Media: Pencil/colored pencil/marker
Art concepts: Contrasting elements; facial proportions; pattern repetition
Illustrator models:

Polacco, Patricia (1988). *Rechenka's eggs.* New York: Philomel Books.
Polacco, Patricia (1990). *Thunder cake.* New York: Philomel Books.
Polacco, Patricia (1993). *The bee tree.* New York: Philomel.
Polacco, Patricia (2002). *When lightning comes in a jar.* New York: Philomel.
Polacco, Patricia (2004). *John Philip duck.* New York: Philomel.
Polacco, Patricia (2004). *Oh, look.* New York: Philomel.
Polacco, Patricia (2005). *Mommies say "shh".* New York: Philomel.
Polacco, Patricia (2006). *Something about Hensley's.* New York: Philomel.

Grades 6/7/8: Jerry Pinkney

Lesson focus: Pinkney's watercolor flowers
Media: Watercolor
Art concepts: Watercolor techniques—transparent overlays; light to dark
Illustrator models:

McKissack, Patricia (1988). *Mirandy and Brother Wind.* Illus. by Jerry Pinkney. New York: Knopf.
Pinkney, Gloria (1992). *Back home.* Illus. by Jerry Pinkney. New York: Dial Books.
Schroeder, Alan (1996). *Minty: A story of young Harriet Tubman.* Illus. by Jerry Pinkney. New York: Dial.
McKissack, Patricia (2001). *Goin' someplace special.* Illus. by Jerry Pinkney. New York: Atheneum.
Aesop (2002). *Aesop's fables.* Illustrated by Jerry Pinkney. New York: SeaStar.
Holiday, Billie (2004). *God bless the child.* Illus. by Jerry Pinkney. New York: Amistad/HarperCollins.
Pinkney, Jerry (2007). *The little red hen.* New York: Dial.

levels. These art element connections provide masters of children's illustration as models for artistic response. Several books from each illustrator should be read and revisited to further reinforce the model. Viewing videos of artists' techniques (Eric Carle, Patricia Polacco) can further enhance the art value of these lessons.

These art element connections invite children to read text and study illustrations before they express their artistic response. The effective connections among literature, illustrations, and artistic response are evident in these examples. Illustrator studies enhanced by a focus on specific art characteristics bring an awareness of the power of art to the picture book. The artistic response to the art of the picture book brings individual interpretation of art forms to life. Children learn more about observation of art and become keener in their encounters with illustration.

Response to Books About Art and Artists

Language and art intertwine as children explore books in which art is creatively shared. The oral response to art is natural as children browse through books like Lucy Micklethwait's *A Child's Book of Art: Discovering Great Paintings* and *I Spy Shapes in Art* and Richard Muhlberger's Metropolitan Museum of Art series including *What Makes a Monet a Monet?* Claire d'Harcourt's *Masterpieces Up Close* and Jean Sousa's *Faces, Places, and Inner Spaces* are meant to be cherished visually, and the natural verbal response of the child to the artwork should be noted. Caroline Desnoette's *Look Closer: Masterpieces Through the Ages* brings children "up close and personal" in observing art and capturing spontaneous response through rich comments and insights.

Children's books also encourage budding artists. Tomie de Paola's *The Art Lesson* humorously reveals the famed illustrator's own dreams and aspirations of being an artist during his early school experiences. In Monica Wellington's playful *Squeaking of Art,* 10 mice visit imaginary galleries in a museum to learn about some of the world's greatest paintings. Ellen Stoll Walsh's *Mouse Magic* introduces the color wheel and explains primary, secondary, and complementary colors to readers who will be inspired to create their own visual magic with color. *My Name Is Georgia* by Jeanette Winter and *Through Georgia's Eyes* by Rachel Victoria Rodriguez introduce younger readers to the accomplishments of a contemporary artist of the desert southwest. Older children are invited to respond artistically following a visual and textual reading of Greenberg and Jordan's *Vincent van Gogh: Portrait of an Artist* or Susan Goldman Ruben's *The Yellow House: Vincent van Gogh and Paul Gauguin Side by Side.*

Furthermore, children can meet the artists through series books on masters of the art world. The *First Impression* series offers the success of Rembrandt, Chagall, and da Vinci; the *Getting to Know the World's Greatest Artists* series traces the lives of Monet, van Gogh, and Picasso. Imagine spending time with Auguste Renoir accompanying him on a walk down the Seine, on a ride to the French countryside, and lunching in a riverside town. Skira-Venturi's *A Weekend with Renoir* and other titles in this first-person artist series brings the masters to life by virtually having the artist talk to the reader. Robert Burleigh has dignified the world of art for children with *Seurat and La Grande Jatte, Toulouse-Lautrec,* and *Paul Cezanne: A Painter's Journey.*

FIGURE 12.3 Book Cluster: Art and music in literature

Grade 1: Art Connections Through Literature

Arnold, Katya (2005). *Elephants can paint, too!* New York: Atheneum.
Burleigh, Robert (2004). *Seurat and La Grand Jatte.* New York: Abrams.
Burleigh, Robert (2005). *Toulouse-Lautrec: The Moulin Rouge and the city of lights.* New York: Abrams.
Burleigh, Robert (2006). *Paul Cezanne: A painter's journey.* New York: Abrams.
Micklethwaite, Lucy (2005). *I spy shapes in art.* New York: Greenwillow.
Rodriguez, Rachel Victoria (2006). *Through Georgia's eyes.* Illus. by Julie Paschkis. New York: Henry Holt.
Rubin, Susan Goldman (2001). *The yellow house: Vincent van Gogh and Paul Gauguin side by side.* Illus. by Jos. A. Smith. New York: Abrams.
Say, Allen (2005). *Kamishibai man.* Boston: Houghton Mifflin.
Schwartz, Amy (2005). *Begin at the beginning: A little artist learns about life.* New York: HarperCollins.
Waldman, Neil (2006). *Out of the shadows: An artist's journey.* Honesdale, PA: Boyds Mills.
Whelan, Gloria (2004). *Burying the sun.* New York: HarperCollins.

Grade 2: Music Connections Through Literature

Aliki (2003). *Ah, music!* New York: HarperCollins.
Beaumont, Karen (2005). *I ain't gonna paint no more!* Illus. by David Catrow. San Diego: Harcourt Brace.
Cabrera, Jane (2005). *If you're happy and you know it.* New York: Holiday House.
Gollub, Matthew (2002). *Gobble, quick, moo.* Illus. by Judy Love. Santa Rosa, CA: Tortuga Press.
Panahi, H. L. (2005). *Bebop express.* Illus. by Steve Johnson and Lou Fancher. New York: Amistad/HarperCollins.
Roth, Susan L. (2006). *Do re mi: If you can read music, thank Guido d'Arezzo* (In association with Angelo Mafucci). Boston: Houghton Mifflin.
Schulman, Janet (2004). *Sergei Prokofiev's Peter and the Wolf.* Illus. by Peter Malone. New York: Knopf.
Zane, Alexander (2005). *The wheels on the race car.* New York: Orchard.

Artistic fantasy focuses imaginatively on the world of art. Journey with *Linnea in Monet's Garden* by Christina Bjork as illustrations, photographs, and reprints of authentic Monet paintings guide us through the garden at Giverny. Reproductions of Bosch's original works enhance Nancy Willard's *Pish, Posh, Said Hieronymus Bosch,* the tale of a housekeeper driven wild by this 15th-century artist. Take a stroll through the National Gallery of Art in Washington, D.C., as Zadrzynska's *The Girl with a Watering Can* exits her famed Renoir frame and mischievously creates unexpected trouble with 10 famous paintings in the museum collection. Verbal links between the stories and reproduction of paintings of the masters encourage interesting response links between literature and art.

Children's books do foster the artistic response in a variety of ways and play a special role in encouraging this mode of response. Whether the response is creating art, appreciating world-renowned art, or reacting to artists and their work, art is a treasured medium of response for children of all ages and talents. Georgia O'Keeffe stated, "I found I could say things with color and shapes that I couldn't say in any other way—things I had no words for." Teachers are encouraged to value and honor the artistic response to literature because it may provide the most expressive means of reader response for many children. Figure 12.3 lists both art books and music titles that inspire artistic or musical response to literature.

MUSIC AS A RESPONSE TO LITERATURE

Musical response to literature exhibits itself in a variety of guises. Musical response may include singing the lyrics/text of a book, accompanying the reading of a book with musical instruments, selecting music as background for a read-aloud, or celebrating the life of musicians by listening to and appreciating their music. Music tends to be an interdisciplinary response across literary genres as related topics range from show tunes to spirituals, from mountain music to childhood songs, from Mozart to a homemade string band. Trade books that invite readers into the world of music are plentiful but should be scrutinized through four criteria suggested by Fluckinger and Kuhlman (2000):

1. The level of character participation in performing, listening, reading, and/or writing music
2. Evidence of character development because of musical engagement
3. Invitation for aesthetic response
4. Invitation for efferent response by learning about musical elements, instruments, composers, and so on.

Sing a Song

A wealth of picture books uses song lyrics as text (Lamme, 1990; Nespeca, 2005). The rhyming lyrics tell delightful stories and naturally invite reader response through song. Musical response, however, needn't be reserved for music time because music serves as a mode of expression that can be shared across the curriculum. Response is natural, but not perfect, so a few flat notes should not discourage a teacher from encouraging children to break out in song. Mary Ann Hoberman's *Bill Grogan's Goat* and *There Once Was a Man Named Michael Finnigan* and Teri Sloat's *Farmer Brown Goes Round and Round* contain musical scores. Yet the words are meant for singing either on or off key.

On a more serious note, Jeanette Winter's *Follow the Drinking Gourd* provides a connection to the subject of slavery and the underground railroad. The lyrics of the simple folk song, sung by slaves, carry the directions north to freedom. Although the words powerfully stand alone, the slow drone of the music tells of the long tired struggle of the slaves for freedom. Accompanying the book is the music that begs to be played and sung for an even richer understanding of the plight of slavery. Most music teachers welcome an opportunity to integrate lessons with the classroom teacher, so teachers should take the initiative to communicate their requests.

Integrating books like these into the curriculum and planning for musical response can only enhance a topic of study. Other titles stand alone as sound literature with the natural response link to music. A literature-based music teacher will be alert to these titles and be ready to collaborate with the classroom teacher. But the classroom teacher does not need to wait for a music teacher to elicit musical response. Opening this avenue of response to literature reaches a special group of talented students who may resist other response modes while welcoming music.

Surround Literature with Music

Several books beg to be accompanied by music. Imagine Rimski-Korsakov's "The Flight of the Bumblebee" playing quietly behind the read-aloud of Jan Brett's *Berlioz the Bear.* Listen to the overture from Rossini's opera to accompany Leonard Everett Fisher's *William Tell.* Place the piano sound of *Duke Ellington* and the voice of *Ella Fitzgerald* behind a read-aloud of these Andrea Davis Pinkney/Brian Pinkney biographical masterpieces. A CD accompanies *Gershwin's Rhapsody in Blue* by Anna Calenza, as the reader learns the background behind the concerto. The musical mode of reader response exhibits itself not through musical performance but through the thoughts inspired by the blend of text and music. Whether those thoughts are kept private or shared orally, they often result in the desire to listen to the musical work repeatedly, to learn more about a musician's life, or to recognize or introduce classical music.

Fictionalized biographies of musicians call for an introduction to their creations through their music. Accompanying the reading of these books with the well-known music of the composers connects literature and music effectively. Mozart, for example, may be introduced through Catherine Brighton's *Mozart: Scenes from the Childhood of a Great Composer* or Lisl Weil's *Wolferl,* which covers the first six years of Mozart's life. The sounds of Mozart can readily surround Peter Sis's *Play, Mozart, Play!* and Stephen Costanza's *Mozart Finds a Melody.* Judith Cherniak's edited poems in *Carnival of the Animals* blend with the music of Saint-Saens. Bach's Brandenburg concertos accompany Jeanette Winter's *Sebastian: A Book About Bach;* the sounds of opera radiate against the backdrop of Leontyne Price's *Aida,* and the music of composer Charles Ives surrounds *What Charlie Heard* by Modicai Gerstein.

Children also are profoundly talented at selecting music to accompany books they may be reading. A media specialist helped children locate music to supplement *The Maestro Plays* by Bill Martin, Jr., as the sounds were recorded on CD-ROM to blend with the text of this piece of children's literature. Capture the nostalgia of Woody Guthrie's music that accompanies *My Dolly, Bling Blang,* and *Howdi Do* on CDs. For young children, Anne Hayes's *Meet the Orchestra* has animals introducing various instruments as the orchestra warms up for a performance led by the king of the jungle. Older students could easily identify and play appropriate music to highlight each instrument and select a symphonic melody for the jungle performance. Insert the sounds of a fiddle behind a read-aloud of Marianna Dengler's *Fiddlin' Sam.* Musical sounds strategically placed will bring this unusual history of music to life. Some popular chapter books might deserve musical background during some of their most intense moments. Just as movies are backed by well-composed scores, readalouds might be enhanced by locating appropriate music to accompany dramatic episodes in favorite chapter books.

Another option for musical response to literature is to place the instruments, handmade or homemade, into the hands of the children as they respond in accompaniment to the story. Besides Philemon Sturges's alternative version of an old favorite in *She'll Be Comin' Round the Mountain,* this book invites musical participation with instruments. Fiddles, spoons, guitars, and banjos may provide the background sounds to turn this participatory read-aloud into a memorable musical response experience. The same is true for Aliki's *Ah, Music!* The African American spiritual is showcased in *All Night, All Day* by Ashley Bryan, which contains musical accompaniments. You can almost hear Walter Dean Myers's *The Blues of Flats Brown* and the jazz of Alan Schroeder's *Satchmo's Blues* as instruments reveal the music of Memphis and New Orleans jazz. Music as an accompaniment for literature provides another illustration of how music, literature, and response form a complementary blend in exposing and motivating children through the music that carries an expressive language of its own.

CLOSING THOUGHTS

The expressive modes of response through dramatic, artistic, and musical performance can be easily overshadowed by the consistent use of oral language and writing as the dominant reader response modes. Short, Kauffman, and Kahn (2000) encourage response across multiple sign systems to assist children in broader thinking and creative reflection, extension of ideas, and aesthetic understanding and new perspectives about life and literature. To attain a balance in reader response to literature and to address the needs of all types of learners, the dramatic, artistic, and musical response must be invited, offered, and celebrated as a valuable response option. Just as emotions are captured through words for some learners, others find expression in the performance media. A classroom that encourages choice and exploration of a variety of response modes is more likely to create lifelong readers.

To reach children with varying expressive talents, teachers need to design literature experiences that open the door to performance response through drama, art, and music. Those who feel less talented in these areas should enlist the help of art, music, or drama teachers to build confidence and comfort in the joy these responses bring to children. Taking advantage of the wealth of books that naturally extend themselves into these response modes will assist in reaching all children in a cross-curricular context. Teachers are encouraged to open their minds to the unlimited possibilities of children's books that celebrate involvement in literature through the fine arts.

References

Fennessey, S. (2006). Using theater games to enhance language arts learning. *The Reading Teacher, 59,* 688–690.

Flower, C., & Fortney, A. (1983). *Puppets—methods and materials.* New York: Davis.

Fluckinger, J., & Kuhlman, W. D. (2000). When human needs are met with music: Children's books share possibilities. *Journal of Children's Literature, 26,* 55–60.

Flynn, R. M. (2004). Curriculum-based readers theater: Setting the stage for reading and retention. *The Reading Teacher, 58,* 360–365.

Hancock, M. R. (2007). Another time, another place: Bringing social studies to life through literature. In P. J. Farris (Ed.), *Elementary and middle school social studies: An interdisciplinary multicultural approach* (5th ed., pp. 349–386). Long Grove, IL: Waveland Press.

Hickman, J. (1983). Everything considered: Response to literature in an elementary school setting. *Journal of Research and Development in Education, 16,* 8–13.

Hubbard, R. S. (1996). Visual responses to literature: Imagination through images. *The New Advocate, 9,* 309–323.

Kieff, J. (2002). Voices from the school yard: Responding to school stories through readers' theater. *Journal of Children's Literature, 28*, 80–87.

Kornfeld, J., & Leyden, G. (2005). Acting out: Literature, drama, and connecting with history. *The Reading Teacher, 59*, 230–238.

Kruas, J. A. (2006). Playing the play: What the children want. *Language Arts, 83*, 413–421.

Kutiper, K., & Wilson, P. (1993). Updating poetry preferences: A look at the poetry children really like. *The Reading Teacher, 47*, 28–35.

Lamme, L. L. (1990). Exploring the world of music through picture books. *The Reading Teacher, 44*, 294–300.

Macy, L. (2004). A novel study through drama. *The Reading Teacher, 58*, 240–248.

Madura, S. (1995). The line and texture of aesthetic response: Primary children study authors and illustrators. *The Reading Teacher, 49*, 110–118.

Martinez, M., Roser, N. L., & Strecker, S. (1998/1999). "I never thought I could be a star": A readers theatre ticket to fluency. *The Reading Teacher, 52*, 326–334.

Morado, C., Koenig, R., & Wilson, A. (1999). Miniperformances, many stars! Playing with stories. *The Reading Teacher, 53*, 116–123.

National Council of Teachers of English and International Reading Association. (1996). *Standards for the English language arts*. Urbana, IL, and Newark, DE: Author.

Nespeca, S. M. (2005). Books to sing: Song-based picture books. *Book Links, 14*, 17–20.

Peck, S. M., & Virkler, A. J. (2006). Reading in the shadows: Extending literacy skills through shadow-puppet theater. *The Reading Teacher, 59*, 786–795.

Short, K. G., Kauffman, G., & Kahn, L. H. (2000). "I just want to draw": Responding to literature across multiple sign systems. *The Reading Teacher, 54*, 160–171.

Stewig, J. (1981). Choral speaking: Who has the time? Why take the time? *Childhood Education, 57*, 25–29.

Tortello, R. (2004). Tableaux vivants in the literature classroom. *The Reading Teacher, 58*, 206–208.

Wolf, S. A. (1994). Learning to act/acting to learn: Children as actors, critics, and characters in classroom theatre. *Research in the Teaching of English, 28*, 7–44.

Yopp, R. H., & Yopp, H. K. (2003). Time with text. *The Reading Teacher, 57*, 284–287.

Young, T. A., & Vardell, S. (1993). Weaving readers theatre and nonfiction into the curriculum. *The Reading Teacher, 46*, 396–406.

Children's Books Cited [P] = K–2; [I] = 3–5; [M] = 6–8

Aardema, Verna (1991). *Traveling to Tondo: A tale of the Nkundo of Zaire*. Illus. by Will Hillenbrand. New York: Knopf. [P/I]

Aliki (1999). *William Shakespeare & the Globe*. New York: HarperCollins. [I/M]

Aliki (2003). *Ah, music!* New York: HarperCollins. [P]

Archambault, John, & Martin, Bill, Jr. (1994). *A beautiful feast for a big king cat*. Illus. by Bruce Degen. New York: HarperCollins. [P]

Avi (2001). *The secret school*. San Diego: Harcourt. [I]

Bjork, Christina (1987). *Linnea in Monet's garden*. Illus. by Lena Anderson. New York: R & S Books. [I]

Brett, Jan (1988). *The mitten*. New York: Putnam. [P]

Brett, Jan (1991). *Berlioz the bear*. New York: Putnam. [P]

Brighton, Catherine (1990). *Mozart: Scenes from the childhood of a great composer*. New York: Doubleday. [P/I]

Bruchac, Joseph (2000). *Pushing up the sky: Seven Native American plays for children*. Illus. by T. Flavin. New York: Dial. [I]

Bryan, Ashley (1991). *All night, all day: A child's first book of African-American spirituals*. Musical arrangement by David Manning Thomas. New York: Atheneum. [P/I]

Burleigh, Robert (2004). *Seurat and La Grande Jatte*. New York: Abrams. [I/M]

Burleigh, Robert (2005). *Toulouse-Lautrec: The Moulin Rouge and the city of lights*. New York: Abrams. [I/M]

Burleigh, Robert (2006). *Paul Cezanne: A painter's journey*. New York: Abrams. [I/M]

Calenza, Anna Harwell (2006). *Gershwin's rhapsody in blue*. Illus. by Jo Ann E. Kitchet. Watertown, MA: Charlesbridge. [I/M]

Carlson, Lori Marie (Selector) (1999). *You're on! Seven plays in English and Spanish*. New York: Morrow. [I/M]

Catalano, Dominic (1998). *Frog went a-courting: A musical play in six acts*. Honesdale, PA: Boyds Mills Press. [P]

Cherniak, Judith (Ed.) (2006). *Carnival of the animals: Poems inspired by Saint-Saens' music*. Illus. by Satoshi Kitamura. Cambridge, MA: Candlewick. (CD included) [P/I]

Clements, Andrew (1999). *The Landry News*. New York: Simon & Schuster. [I]

Collodi, C. (1996). *Pinocchio*. Adapted and illustrated by Ed Young. New York: Philomel Books. [I/M]

Costanza, Stephen (2004). *Mozart finds a melody*. New York: Henry Holt. [P]

Creech, Sharon (2001). *Love that dog*. New York: HarperCollins. [I]

Cronin, Doreen (2005). *Wiggle*. Illus. by Scott Menchin, New York: Atheneum. [P]

de Paola, Tomie (1989). *The art lesson*. New York: Putnam. [P]

d'Harcourt, Claire (2006). *Masterpieces up close: Western painting from the 14th to 20th centuries*. San Francisco: Chronicle Books. [I/M]

Dengler, Marianna (1999). *Fiddlin' Sam*. Illus. by Sibyl Graber Geig. Flagstaff, Az: Rising Moon. [P/I]

Desnoettes, Caroline (2006). *Look closer: Art masterpieces through the ages*. New York: Walker. [P/I/M]

Dillon, Leo & Diane (2003). *Rap a tap tap: Here's Bojangles—Think of that*. New York: Blue Sky/Scholastic. [P/I]

Fisher, Leonard Everett (1996). *William Tell*. New York: Farrar, Straus & Giroux. [I]

Fleischman, Paul (1985). *I am Phoenix: Poems for two voices*. Illus. by K. Nutt. New York: Harper & Row. [I/M]

Fleischman, Paul (1988). *Joyful noise: Poems for two voices*. Illus. by E. Beddows. New York: Harper & Row. [I/M]

Fleischman, Paul (1993). *Bull run*. Woodcuts by David Frampton. New York: Harper-Collins. [I/M]

Fleischman, Paul (2000). *Lost! A story in string*. Illus. by C. B. Mordan. New York: Henry Holt. [P/I]

Fleischman, Paul (2000). *Big talk: Poems for four voices*. Illus. by B. Giacobbe. Cambridge, MA: Candlewick. [I/M]

Fleischman, Paul (2001). *Seek*. Chicago: Cricket. [M]

Fleischman, Paul (2005). *Zap*. Cambridge, MA: Candlewick. [M]

Florian, Douglas (1997). *In the swim*. Paintings by Doug Florian. San Diego: Harcourt Brace. [I/M]

Florian, Douglas (1998). *On the wing*. San Diego: Harcourt Brace. [I/M]

Florian, Douglas (1999). *Winter eyes*. New York: Greenwillow. [P/I]

Florian, Douglas (2000). *Mammalabilia*. San Diego: Harcourt Brace. [I/M]

Florian, Douglas (2001). *Frogs, toads and polliwogs*. San Diego: Harcourt Brace. [I/M]

Fonteyn, Margot (1998). *Coppelia*. Paintings by Steve Johnson & Lou Fancher. San Diego: Gulliver Books/Harcourt Brace. [I]

Gantos, Jack (1998). *Joey Pigza swallowed the key*. New York: Farrar, Straus & Giroux. [I]

Garland, Sherry (2000). *Voices from the Alamo*. Illus. by Ron Himler. New York: Scholastic. [I]

Geras, Adele (2004). *Time for ballet*. Illus. by Shelagh McNicholas. New York: Dial. [P]

Gerstein, Mordicai (2002). *What Charlie heard*. New York: Farrar, Straus & Giroux. [I]

Greenberg, Jan, & Jordan, Sandra (2001). *Vincent van Gogh: Portrait of an artist*. New York: Delacorte. [I/M]

Guthrie, Woody (2000). *Bling blang*. Illus. by Vladimir Radunsky. Cambridge, MA: Candlewick. [P]

Guthrie, Woody (2000). *Howdi do*. Illus. by Vladimir Radunsky. Cambridge, MA: Candlewick. [P]

Guthrie, Woody (2001). *My dolly*. Illus. by Vladimir Radunsky. Cambridge, MA: Candlewick. [P]

Hayes, Ann (1991). *Meet the orchestra*. Illus. by Karmen Thompson. San Diego: Harcourt Brace. [P]

Hayes, Ann (1997). *Onstage & backstage at the Night Owl Theater.* Illus. by Karmen Thompson. San Diego: Harcourt Brace. [I]

Hesse, Karen (2001). *Witness.* New York: Scholastic.

Hoberman, Mary Ann (2001). *You read to me, I'll read to you: Very short stories to read together.* Illus. by M. Emberley. Boston: Little, Brown. [P/I]

Hoberman, Mary Ann (2001). *There once was a man named Michael Finnigan.* Illus. by Nadine Westcott. New York: Little, Brown. [P]

Hoberman, Mary Ann (2002). *Bill Grogan's goat.* Illus. by Nadine Westcott. New York: Little, Brown. [P]

Hoose, Phillip (2001). *We were there, too! Young people in U.S. history.* New York: Farrar, Straus & Giroux. [I/M]

Hopkins, Lee Bennett (1997). *Song and dance.* New York: Simon & Schuster. [P]

Isadora, Rachel (2003). *On your toes: A ballet ABC.* New York: Greenwillow. [P]

Kennedy, X. J. (2002). *Exploding gravy: Poems to make you laugh.* Illus. by Joy Allen. Boston: Little, Brown. [P/I]

MacDonald, Amy (1990). *Rachel Fister's blister.* Illus. by Marjorie Priceman. Boston: Houghton Mifflin. [I]

MacDonald, Amy (1996). *Cousin Ruth's tooth.* Illus. by Marjorie. Priceman. Boston: Houghton Mifflin. [I]

Martin, Bill, Jr. (1994). *The maestro plays.* Illus. by Vladimir Radunsky. New York: Henry Holt. [P]

Mayo, Margaret (2005). *Choo choo clickety clack!* Illus. by Alex Ayliffe. Minneapolis: Carolrhoda. [P]

Micklethwait, Lucy (1999). *A child's book of art: Discovering great paintings.* New York: Dorling Kindersley. [I/M]

Micklewait, Lucy (2005). *I spy shapes in art.* New York: Greenwillow. [P/I/M]

Mora, Pat (1996). *Confetti: Poems for children.* Illus. by Enrique O. Sanchez. New York: Lee & Low Books. [P/I]

Muhlberger, Richard (2002). *What makes a Monet a Monet?* New York: Metropolitan Museum of Art. [I/M]

Myers, Walter Dean (2000). *The blues of Flats Brown.* Illus. by N. Laden. New York: Holiday House. [P/I]

Pavlova, Anna (2001). *I dreamed I was a ballerina.* Paintings by Edgar Degas. New York: Atheneum. [P/I]

Pinkney, Andrea Davis (1998). *Duke Ellington: The piano prince and his orchestra.* Illus. by Brian Pinkney. New York: Hyperion. [I/M]

Pinkney, Andrea Davis (2002). *Ella Fitzgerald: The tale of a vocal virtuosa.* Illus. by Brian Pinkney. New York: Hyperion. [I/M]

Pinkney, Jerry (2007). *The little red hen.* New York: Dial. [P]

Pomeroy, Diana (1996). *One potato.* San Diego: Harcourt Brace. [P]

Pomeroy, Diana (1997). *Wildflower ABC.* San Diego: Harcourt Brace. [P]

Prelutsky, Jack (2002). *Scranimals.* New York: Greenwillow. [I]

Rodriguez, Rachel Victoria (2006). *Through Georgia's eyes.* Illus. by Julle Paschkis. New York: Holt. [P/I]

Rubin, Susan Goldman (2001). *The yellow house: Vincent van Gogh and Paul Cezanne side by side.* Illus by Jos. A. Smith. New York: Abrams. [I]

Schroeder, Alan (1996). *Satchmo's blues.* Illus. by Floyd Cooper. New York: Doubleday. [I]

Senisi, Ellen B. (2001). *Berry smudges and leaf prints: Finding and making colors from nature.* New York: Dutton. [P/I/M]

Sis, Peter (2006). *Play, Mozart, play!* New York: Greenwillow. [P]

Skira-Venturi, Rosabianca (1990). *A weekend with Renoir* (A Weekend with Artists series). Boston: Rizzoli. [I/M]

Sloat, Teri (1999). *Farmer Brown goes round and round.* Illus. by Nadine Westcott. New York: DK. [P]

Sousa, Jean (2006). *Faces, places, and inner spaces: A guide to looking at art.* New York: Abrams (in association with the Art Institute of Chicago). [P/I/M]

Sturges, Philemon (2004). *She'll be comin' 'round the mountain.* Illus. by Ashley Wolff. New York: Little, Brown. [P/I]

Tallchief, Maria (with Rosemary Wells) (1999). *Tallchief: America's prima ballerina.* Illus. by Gary Kelley. New York: Viking. [I]

Venezia, Mike (1990). *Monet* (Getting to Know the World's Greatest Artists series). Danbury, CT: Children's Press. [I/M]

Waddell, Martin (1991). *Farmer duck*. Cambridge, MA: Candlewick Press. [P]

Waddell, Martin (1992). *Owl babies*. Illus. by Patrick Benson. Cambridge, MA: Candlewick Press. [P]

Waddell, Martin (2001). *Webster J. Duck*. Illus. by David Parkins. Cambridge, MA: Candlewick. [P]

Walsh, Ellen Stoll (2000). *Mouse magic*. San Diego: Harcourt Brace. [P]

Weil, Lisl (1991). *Wolferl: The first six years in the life of Wolfgang Amadeus Mozart, 1756–1762*. New York: Holiday House. [P/I]

Wellington, Monica (2000). *Squeaking of art: The mice go to the museum*. New York: Dutton. [P]

Willard, Nancy (1991). *Pish, posh, said Hieronymus Bosch*. Illus. by Leo & Diane Dillon. San Diego: Harcourt Brace. [I/M]

Williams, Marcia (Adapter) (1998). *Tales from Shakespeare: Seven plays*. Cambridge, MA: Candlewick. [I/M]

Wilson, Karma (2002). *Bear snores on*. Illus. by Jane Chapman. New York. McElderry. [P]

Winter, Jeanette (1988). *Follow the drinking gourd*. New York: Knopf. [I/M]

Winter, Jeanette (1998). *My name is Georgia: A portrait*. San Diego: Harcourt Brace. [P/I]

Winter, Jeanette (1999). *Sebastian: A book about Bach*. San Diego: Harcourt Brace. [P/I]

Wong, Janet (2000). *Night garden*. New York: McElderry. [P/I]

Yolen, Jane (1992). *Street rhymes around the world*. Illus. by 17 international artists. Honesdale, PA: Boyds Mills Press. [P]

Zadrzynska, Ewa (1990). *The girl with a watering can*. New York: Chamelon. [I]

CHAPTER 13

Response to Nonfiction

Blending Efferent and Aesthetic Response

My grandpa and grandma lived in Glen Elder and Cawker City when the Dust Bowl hit. Grandpa was 17 years old and a high school senior; Grandma was 18 years old and a teacher in Tipton. Grandma taught 17 children from all eight grades, and she can still name them! She would have to send them home every time there was a sighting of a dust cloud. My great-grandfather was a farmer and could not grow any crops because of the dust. In their house, they would put wet cloths on windows and every open place. At night, the family members would put wet cloths over their mouths. The next morning, there could be dust piles as high as snowdrifts or fence posts.

Grandpa said one of the dust storms lasted for twelve hours! You couldn't see two feet in front of your face from the dust. If you were outside, you would follow the barbed wire fence to get home. When the dust cloud would come, it would move very slowly. The cloud would be red from the Oklahoma dust, but when it arrived in Kansas, it turned a smoky color. Dust would get into all the vehicles and they would not even work.

> *My grandpa and grandma were happy when the rain came, but all the dust on the ground caused it to make puddles, not soak into the ground. Grandpa says that all of the houses standing today that were in the Dust Bowl still have dust that sifted into the cracks almost two inches thick.*
>
> Sixth-grade response to Jerry Stanley's
> *Children of the Dust Bowl* from an interview with grandparents.

On the shelves of elementary/middle-level library media centers lies an emerging literary genre rescued from decades of restricted use. Nonfiction books, including informational books and biography, often limited to a research tool in the past, have experienced a resurgence in the last decade as the demands for this genre have nurtured its growth far beyond its former role. Teachers browse the shelves to locate an informational read-aloud, children scan nonfiction choices for independent reading, and aesthetic response to informational titles becomes a reality in the classroom. The informational picture book or picture book biography, in particular, has echoed the reverberations of the expanding publication of children's nonfiction literature in the past decade. The appeal of the picture book format and the ability of quality text to transfer our ever-growing body of knowledge to children support the blossoming of this genre. Teachers and media specialists are challenged to create a new vision for the informational book by exploring afresh, moving it beyond a traditional research tool, and considering its potential as a valid option for reading and responding.

Children's literature advocates and researchers have collectively explored the complexities of selection and the countless possibilities of using nonfiction in the elementary curriculum (Bamford & Kristo, 2003; Kristo & Bamford, 2004; Moss, 2003), and documented the diverse options of response to nonfiction (Vardell, 1996; Vardell & Copeland, 1992). The potential for including nonfiction read-alouds as part of a balanced read-aloud program (Doiron, 1994; Moss, 1995; Yopp & Yopp, 2000) and the recognition that primary children can process exploratory texts (Palmer & Stewart, 2003, 2005; Richgels, 2002; Tower, 2002) point to expanded use in the school program. Nonfiction literature has even become the focus of responding in literature circles (Daniels, 2002; Johnson & Freedman, 2005; Stien & Beed, 2004) and for sharing facts through informational picture books in the English as a Second Language (ESL) classroom (Hadaway & Mundy, 1999). The growing body of knowledge of expository text structure has expanded the need for the reader to internalize the strategies of reading nonfiction (Moss, 2004; Yopp & Yopp, 2004). The quantity of informational books has met this new demand and the quality has paralleled this growth. The availability of quality informational books for children of both elementary and middle-level programs makes it a natural choice to include within the reading program and in interdisciplinary instruction.

This chapter takes an innovative look at response options for the nonfiction book in a literature-based classroom. From read-alouds to independent reading, from author studies to authentic accounts, from personal connections to biography, to aesthetic response to nonfiction, informational books provide a fresh tool for integrated instruction. Reader response to nonfiction is the major focus of this chapter. To illustrate that reader response can move beyond its typical embedded fictional stature, authentic written responses of sixth-grade students to selected nonfiction titles (Hancock, 1994) are interspersed throughout the chapter as support for aesthetic response to nonfiction.

NONFICTION: INFORMATIONAL BOOKS AND BIOGRAPHY

A children's nonfiction book is a factual representation of information in a well-written format, often illustrated with photographs or drawings. The text and visual images both play an important role in contributing to the understanding of a topic. Books in this genre are further enhanced and documented by accurate glossaries, timeline chronologies, extended bibliographies, informative captions, related maps, useful indexes, and the expert credentials of authors, illustrators, and photographers. The breadth of the nonfiction genre spans the curriculum and integrates traditional areas. Before the reader's eyes unfolds a visual world of color and a textual world of well-documented information. See Chapter 7 for an overview of biography and informational genres as an introduction to nonfiction.

Although informational books are typically located in the nonfiction section of the school or public library, a large number find their way to the picture book shelves because they are identified by format rather than content. This particular type is referred to here as an *informational picture book,* a special type of informational book whose inviting format and well-written text appeals to younger students. Both traditional informational books and informational picture books are shared with respect to their potential use for response-based activities. Biography also takes the form of both chapter books and biographical picture books and is included in the realm of nonfiction.

Read-Aloud Informational Books

To a great degree, teachers have almost exclusively chosen fictional chapter and picture book titles for class read-alouds. Although their students savored their read-aloud voices and the imaginary happenings of the stories, they were unknowingly being sheltered from a literary genre that has great appeal to readers of all ages. Teachers who select informational books as read-alouds take the first step in informing the reader of the respectability and acceptability of these books as a choice for independent reading. Although many children eventually become adult readers of nonfiction, this genre has remained unexplored until recently as a read-aloud option in many classrooms. The natural curiosity of primary students fosters a sense of inquiry through nonfiction titles especially geared to younger children (Moss, Leone, & Dippilo, 1997). If our goal is to create lifelong readers, it is wise to open wide this previously guarded research genre for variety in read-alouds and personal reading choices.

In an effort to overcome the stereotype of nonfiction books as boring and mundane, Doiron (1994) suggests several criteria for a suitable nonfiction read-aloud selection:

- Identify quality authors who share their subjects with clarity, authority, and a direct writing style.
- Look for an inviting presentation that attracts the reader's initial curiosity but gradually leads to independent thinking and additional inquiry.
- Focus on the language of fact presented in a memorable voice that will motivate and hold the reader's attention.

Reading for information can be an enjoyable experience that touches both the efferent needs of the mind and the aesthetic realms of the heart.

The same recommendations for reading aloud quality fiction also apply to reading aloud quality nonfiction books. Here are some specific tips related to nonfiction adapted from suggestions by Doiron (1994):

- Provide background information on the book topic prior to the read-aloud by sharing an artifact, conducting an experiment, or discussing the subject.
- Take advantage of the ability of the genre to generate interest and inquiry by allowing children to become active participants through questions and explanations.
- Focus on the author and illustrator, pointing out documentation of factual accuracy, publication date, format style, and speculating on research procedures for acquiring information.
- Select an appropriate chapter, a small section, or important excerpts from longer chapter books. Not all informational books are meant to be read in their entirety. Provide access to the book for students' further independent reading.
- Choose nonfiction books on a variety of topics to reflect a wide range of appeal to readers.
- Use informational picture books to bridge the reading of fiction and nonfiction as narrative language transmits informative facts.

An exemplary read-aloud for young children that fits these criteria is Kay Winters's *Tiger Trail*. Written in the first-person thoughts of a tiger, the author engages children in becoming the main character—the tigress—as the listener, as this powerful cat cares for her two newborn kits, then stalks and grasps a wild boar in her powerful jaws. The strength of the book also lies both in its dramatic first and last lines, "I am the tigress. I walk alone." (n. p.), and in Laura Regan's realistic oil paintings. This powerful text/illustration connection transforms the reader into an observer role and reader response lies in experiencing the day in the guise of this predator.

An outstanding example of an informational picture book read-aloud for older children is Lynn Curlee's *Seven Wonders of the Ancient World*. Written as expository descriptive text, this fact-based tale reveals these mysterious masterpieces of human achievement, including the Great Pyramid at Giza, the Collossus of Rhodes, and the Hanging Gardens of Babylon. During the read-aloud, the older listener can ponder the lingering response prompt, "What purposes did these wonders have for

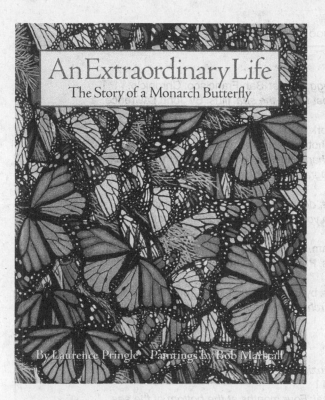

By Laurence Pringle   Paintings by Bob Marstall

Many informational books are written in narrative and capture student interest during read-alouds.

Book cover from An Extraordinary Life: The Story of a Monarch Butterfly. *Illustration copyright © 1997 by Bob Marstall. Reprinted by permission of Orchard Books, an imprint of Scholastic Inc.*

the societies that built them?" Written as brief chapters, the book allows for brief daily read-alouds, culminating in a final day of active response as the class considers the marvels of our own modern age that might be unearthed by archeologists in the far distant future.

An outstanding example of an informational picture book read-aloud for older children is Laurence Pringle's *An Extraordinary Life: The Story of a Monarch Butterfly*. This title won the Orbis Pictus Award in 1998 as the best nonfiction book of the year for children. Written in narrative, this fact-based tale follows the amazing journey of Danaus, a monarch butterfly, from her emergence as a caterpillar in a Massachusetts hayfield, through her metamorphosis into a butterfly, and culminates in her flight south, her mating, and her return migration in spring. Weighing only a fifteenth of an ounce, Danaus flies more than 2,500 miles surrounded by dangers from weather, predators, and humans. Written as four chapters, the book allows for daily read-alouds culminating in a final day of active response as the class sets up an environment for raising monarch butterflies guided by information from the book.

Figure 13.1 provides a list of read-aloud nonfiction books that epitomizes the quality and quantity of books available to capture student reading interest through the informational genre. By reading these titles aloud and probing response through appropriate prompts, students begin to respond to informational text aesthetically. Rather than limiting response to efferent information, they actually interact personally with the text, eliciting personal feelings, reactions, and opinions about a topic.

FIGURE 13.1   Book Cluster: Nonfiction books to read aloud

Primary Grades

Aston, Diana Huts, & Long, Sylvia (2006). *An egg is quiet.* San Francisco: Chronicle. [P]

Butterworth, Chris (2006). *Sea horse: The shyest fish in the sea.* Illus. By John Lawrence. Cambridge, MA: Candlewick. [P/I]

Cowley, Joy (1999). *Red-eyed tree frog.* New York: Scholastic. [P]

Cowley, Joy (2004). *Chameleon, chameleon.* Photos by Nic Bishop. New York: Scholastic. [P]

Helfer, Ralph (2006). *The world's greatest elephant.* Illus. by Ted Lewin. New York: Philomel. [P/I]

Horenstein, Henry (1999). *A is for . . . ? A photographer's alphabet of animals.* San Diego: Harcourt Brace. [P]

Jenkins, Steve (1998). *Hottest, coldest, highest, deepest.* Boston: Houghton Mifflin. [P]

Jenkins, Steve, & Page, Robin (2003). *What do you do with a tail like this?* Boston: Houghton Mifflin. [P]

Karas, Brian (2005). *On earth.* New York: Putnam. [P]

Petersen, Cris (2006). *Fantastic farm machines.* Photos by David R. Lindquist. Honesdale, PA: Boyds Mills Press. [P/I]

Sayre, April Pulley (2001). *Dig, wait, listen.* Illus. by Barbara Bash. New York: Greenwillow. [P]

Singer, Marilyn (2000). *On the same day in March: A tour of the world's weather.* New York: HarperCollins. [P]

Illustrated/Photographed Books

Burleigh, Robert (2006). *Tiger of the snows: Tenzing Norgay. The boy whose dream was Everest.* Illus. by Ed Young. New York: Atheneum. [I]

Dewey, Jennifer Owings (2001). *Antarctic journal: Four months at the bottom of the sea.* New York: HarperCollins. [I]

Hatkoff, Isabella, Hatkoff, Craig, & Kahumbu, Paula (2006). *Owen & Mzee: The true story of a remarkable friendship.* New York: Scholastic. [P/I]

Markle, Sandra (2006). *Rescues!* Minneapolis: Lerner/Millbrook. [I/M]

Marrin, Albert (2006). *Oh, rats! The story of rats and people.* Illus. by C. B. Mordan. New York: Dutton. [I/M]

McLimans, David (2006). *Gone wild: An endangered wildlife alphabet.* New York: Walker. [I/M]

Montgomery, Sy (2001). *The man-eating tigers of Sunbardans.* Boston: Houghton Mifflin. [I/M]

O'Conner, Jane (2002). *The emperor's silent army: Terracotta warriors of ancient China.* New York: Viking. [I/M]

Robbins, Ken (2001). *Thunder on the plains: The story of the American buffalo.* New York: Atheneum. [I]

Siebert, Diane (2003). *Rhyolite: The true story of a ghost town.* Illus. by David Frampton. New York: Clarion. [I]

Turner, Pamela S. (2004). *Hachiko: The true story of a loyal dog.* Illus. by Yan Nascimbene. Boston: Houghton Mifflin. [I]

Chapter Books

Freedman, Russell (2001). *In the days of the vaqueros: America's first true cowboys.* New York: Clarion. [I/M]

Freedman, Russell (2006). *Freedom walkers: The story of the Montgomery bus boycott.* New York: Holiday House. [I]

FIGURE 13.1 Continued

Marrin, Albert (2006). *Saving the buffalo.* New York: Scholastic. [I/M]

McClafferty, Crla Killough (2006). *Something out of nothing: Marie Curie and radium.* New York: Farrar, Straus & Giroux. [M]

Murphy, Jim (2002). *An American plague: The true and terrifying story of the Yellow Fever Epidemic of 1793.* New York: Clarion. [I/M]

Schlosser, Eric, & Wilson, Charles (2006). *Chew on this: Everything you don't want to know about fast food.* Boston: Houghton Mifflin. [I/M]

Informational Author/Illustrator Studies

Just as literature-based instruction supports students becoming informed about the real lives of authors, so too does it challenge the investigative capabilities of those who compile, write, and illustrate informational books. The insatiable quest for information lures individuals from professional careers and sends them to the far reaches of the earth to acquire knowledge to share with children through words, illustrations, or photographs. The spirit of discovery and research that motivates these authors and artists sparks interest in their books and models the inquiry process for students' own quests for answers.

A noteworthy example of a subject for an informational author/illustrator study is Diane Stanley, who has painstakingly traveled, researched, and illustrated superb picture book biographies of *Saladin: The Noble Prince of Islam*, *Michelangelo, Joan of Arc, Leonardo da Vinci, Cleopatra, Charles Dickens, The Bard of Avon: The Story of William Shakespeare*, and *Good Queen Bess*. Stanley, a former medical illustrator, found her artistic strength in realism as she portrays authentic moments from the lives of her subjects. With the growing historical expertise, she is able to share interesting biographical information acquired via extensive travel and library research through both elegant language and revealing illustrations.

Figure 13.2 represents a teacher-prepared author study of historian and Newbery Honor and Orbis Pictus award winning informational author, Jim Murphy. Noteworthy for *The Great Fire* and *Across America on an Emigrant Train*, Murphy continues to explore history through well-chosen documentation and authentic photographs from archival resources. Responding to the research expertise and techniques of informational authors provides a valid model for personal research. Other informational author/illustrators for focused study include Leonard Everett Fisher, Russell Freedman, Jean Craighead George, Gail Gibbons, Diane Hoyt-Goldsmith, Kathryn Lasky, Patricia Lauber, Sandra Markle, Laurence Pringle, and Seymour Simon. Teachers may prepare and share these author studies, and students are also encouraged to research, compile, and present their own informational author studies as a viable response to literature. The blending of biographical information, authentic nonfiction literature, and student response to process and content creates an interesting response format.

FIGURE 13.2 A teacher-prepared author study

Jim Murphy: Illuminator of History

Biographical Information:
Born: September 25,1947, in Newark, New Jersey
Education: BA Rutgers University, 1970
Work-Related Experience: Editorial secretary to managing editor, Seabury Press, Inc (Clarion Books) 1970–1978
Author: Over 25 Nonfiction & fiction titles, 1978–present. Winner of the Newbery Honor and Orbis Pictus Awards
Current Home: Maplewood, New Jersey

Selected Nonfiction by Jim Murphy

Murphy, J. (2002). *An American plague: The true and terrifying story of the Yellow Fever Epidemic of 1793*. New York: Clarion.
Murphy, J. (2000). *Pick & shovel poet: The journeys of Pascal D'Angelo*. New York: Clarion.
Murphy, J. (2000). *Blizzard*. New York: Scholastic.
Murphy, J. (1998). *Gone-a-whaling*. New York: Clarion.
Murphy, J. (1996). *A young patriot: The American Revolution as experienced by one boy*. New York: Clarion.
Murphy, J. (1995). *The great fire*. New York: Scholastic.
Murphy, J. (1993). *Across America on an emigrant train*. New York: Clarion.
Murphy, J. (1992). *The long road to Gettysburg*. New York: Clarion.
Murphy, J. (1990). *The boys' war: Confederate and Union soldiers talk about the Civil War*. New York: Clarion.
Murphy, J. (1984). *Tractors: From yesterday's steam wagons to today's turbo-charged giants*. Philadelphia: Lippincott.
Murphy, J. (1983). *Two hundred years of bicycles*. New York: Harper.
Murphy, J. (1978). *Weird and wacky inventions*. New York: Crown.

Also by the author:
Murphy, J. (2006). *Desperate journey*. New York: Scholastic.
Murphy, J. (1998). *The journal of James Edmond Pease: A Civil War Union soldier (My Name Is America series)*. New York: Scholastic.
Murphy, J. (1998). *West to the land of plenty. The diary of Teresa Angelino Viscardi (My Name Is America series)*. New York: Scholastic.

Resources:
_____(2000). Website *http://www.amazon.com*
Commire, A. (Ed.). (1993). *Something about the author, 77*, 139–142.
Kerper, R. (2000). Excavating voices, illuminating history: A conversation with Jim Murphy. *The New Advocate, 13*, 117–127.
_____ (1996). *Seventh junior book of authors* (pp. 233–34). New York: H. W. Wilson.
Vandergrift, K. (2000). *http://www.scils.rutgers.edu/special/kay/Murphy.html*

FIGURE 13.2   Continued

Comments by Jim Murphy

Children weren't just observers of our history. They were actual participants and sometimes did amazing and heroic things.

I became interested in the idea of writing nonfiction history based on firsthand accounts, and began collecting journals, diaries, and letters—materials in which a person's "voice" told about past events.

When I get my photographs, one of the first things I do is take out my magnifying glass and go over each photograph inch by inch, just to see if there's something in there that could be missed with a quick glance. I round up the photographs very early in the process, even before I write. I often use them to write visual scenes. . . . There is a whole world within them.

Teaching Idea: **The Boys' War** *by Jim Murphy:*

Write a letter home explaining in detail what your experiences have been so far. Although you will mostly write about the food situation, you should also discuss your feelings about the Civil War and your life in camp. You may address the letter to your parents or other relatives or friends. Use your imagination! You should use proper letter form. Use descriptive language that helps the reader picture your life in their minds.

Lotta Larson, 6th-grade teacher
Marlatt Elementary School

READER RESPONSE TO NONFICTION

Response stands at the threshold of informational books just as it does with narrative titles. Although it might be expected that efferent response would predominate natural reactions to informational books, documentation indicates that readers do respond aesthetically to nonfiction (Coleman, 2007). The same rich mixture of responses is available for the reader's transaction with nonfiction. Particularly with texts that lie midway on the continuum of aesthetic and efferent, readers may choose a stance that fluctuates between these two realms of response.

Response to Informational Picture Books in the Primary Grades

Much recent research has focused on the use of nonfiction with younger children and their ability to respond to information through reading, writing, and personal forms of response. Because primary teachers incorporate units or themes into their teaching, the inclusion of nonfiction is a natural fit for blending early reading, response, and content learning. For some children, the benefits of reading and responding to non-narrative text may be the best path to overall literacy, particularly boys and struggling readers and writers (Caswell & Duke, 1998; Saul & Dieckmann, 2005).

Manduran (2000) reported on her own preschool daughter's "response episodes" (p. 392) outside of book-sharing time. She notes response expressed as casual conversation, reevaluation of facts, complex thinking, life/literature connections, and as personal inquiry. Richgels (2002) supports using informational books in kindergarten as both content knowledge and an impetus to emergent literacy. He suggests using a blend of informational books with other functional literacy (labels, recipes, posters, calendars) and with picture storybook reading. Reading to learn (efferent) and reading for pleasure (aesthetic) can result in blended responses. Pappas (1991) found that kindergartners actually preferred the informational books over the storybooks she presented them. For example, young children may genuinely respond to April Sayre's *The Bumblebee Queen,* the story of a queen bee's journey of finding a nest, gathering nectar, laying eggs, and tending her colony through the seasons. Primary children respond to Joy Cowley's *Chameleon, Chameleon* through improvisation, art, and emergent writing in informational journals.

Recent research supports blending learning to read and reading to learn in the primary grades. Informational reading is not the domain of only proficient readers. Just watch and listen as children respond to Jim Arnosky's *All About Turtles* or Gail Gibbons's *Apples* in a primary setting. Read (2001) shared case studies of her first and second graders to document how young children, read, write, and respond to information. Duthie (1994) reported that her first graders gained confidence and comfort with nonfiction as a genre. In fact, their own published nonfiction, written in response to immersion to the genre, reflected unique aspects and characteristics of nonfiction.

Current research strongly supports exposing young children to nonfiction and inviting them to respond to it in kind. If lack of experience with non-narrative texts may lead to poor performance in reading and writing expository text in later grades, then the nonfiction experience in the primary grades may provide a stronger foundation on which to build a nonfiction schema. Refer back to Figure 13.1 which lists several of the newest titles appropriate for the primary (K–2) student.

RESOURCES ON THE WEB
Nonfiction Book Reviews with Presentation Software

As a response option to nonfiction books, students may engage in technology-based projects to share the reading experience with others. Microsoft PowerPoint and similar presentation software typically include a range of capabilities in one user-friendly package. Features such as multimedia elements, hyperlinks, animation, display options, and ready-to-use templates are common and encourage student creativity and unique transaction with the literature. Students can create a series of digital slides to support an oral book review of a nonfiction selection visually following this format:

Slide 1: Title slide including title of presentation and student's name, date, etc.

Slide 2: Bibliographical information about the literature reviewed (title, publisher, author, illustrator, publishing year, etc.)

Slide 3: Introduction of nonfiction topic ("This book is about . . .")

Slides 4–7: Sharing of information of nonfiction topic. May include illustrations, list of interesting facts, diagrams, hyperlinks to websites or electronic documents, digital photographs or video clips, audio files, etc.)

Slide 8: Personal opinion about the book ("I like/dislike this book because . . .")

Slide 9: Information about the author. May include digital photographs, biographical information, hyperlinks to author's website, list of author's published works, etc.)

Slide 10: Reader recommendation ("You should read this book because . . .")

Slide 11: Information about the reviewer. May include student's biographical information, list of other books he or she likes, hobbies, etc.

Response to Informational Picture Books
in the Intermediate Grades

An example of the aesthetic response to an informational picture book includes a patriotic response to the memorable text of Katherine Lee Bates's, *America the Beautiful.* The text provides an opportunity to revisit the simple but stately words that portray our great land while acquiring information about our natural treasures. Each eloquent line is matched to a majestic illustration by Neil Waldman of one of America's natural wonders, enhanced at the book's end by identification and additional information on each sight. After a teacher read-aloud, Martha selected an important phrase and explained its significance.

"For amber waves of grain." That phrase reminds me of where I live, the great plains. Kansas's nickname is the breadbasket of America. It is like the wide wonderful pastures of wheat we have in Kansas. When the wind blows the wheat, it looks like long waves from the ocean . . .

The quality of writing in informational books has improved dramatically in the past few years and contributes to the quality of reader response. No longer is informational text dominated by the encyclopedic delivery of dull factual information. The presentation has been heightened by quality authors whose flow of language to the reader's ear greatly enhances the conveyance of knowledge. Moving from strained expository text to riveting portrayal of factual events nudges the reader toward the aesthetic side of the response continuum. An outstanding example is Robert Burleigh's *Flight* (1991), which shares the portrayal of Lindbergh's struggle to stay awake during his cross Atlantic flight by textually placing the reader in the cockpit with this American hero. Savor this excerpt based on Lindbergh's journal during his 33 ½-hour flight from New York to Paris:

> To sleep is to die!
> These are some of the things he does to stay awake:
> He leans his face near the open window to feel the cold air.
> He holds his eyelids up with his fingers to keep them from closing.
> He remembers growing up on a farm in Minnesota.
> He remembers being a trick pilot, and walking out on a plane's wings.
> He remembers the people in St. Louis who paid for this plane.
> Sometimes he takes a sip of water from his canteen.
> He also has five chicken sandwiches with him. That is all the food he has brought.
> But he eats nothing. It is easier to stay awake on an empty stomach.*

---

*From *Flight: The Journey of Charles Lindbergh* (pp. 16–17) by Robert Burleigh. Copyright © 1991 by Robert Burleigh, text. Used by permission of Philomel Books, a division of Penguin Young Readers Group, a member of Penguin Group (USA) Inc., 345 Hudson Street, New York, NY 10014. All rights reserved.

Following the reading of this book, Heather responds to this aesthetic blend of text and illustrations:

It . . . really makes you feel as though you were in that cramped cockpit with no sleep. The pictures really tell you how he feels, like when the illustrator uses dark colors, he's tired or there's bad weather. The words made it very colorful though. You can tell how he feels: sad, tired, lonely, happy, worried— everything. It was very descriptive.

Examples of other texts that weave language and illustrations in an informational context include Albert Marrin's dramatic text in *Oh, Rats! The Story of Rats and People* with the art of C. B. Mordan. Also consider the biographical humor of Shauna Corey's *You Forgot Your Skirt, Amelia Bloomer!* and Deborah Hopkinson's *Fannie in the Kitchen.* Patricia and Frederic McKissack's *Christmas in the Big House, Christmas in the Quarters* with oil paintings by John Thompson remains a classic informational picture book selection. These titles not only read aloud exceedingly well, but they also suggest informational books as a valid reader response option for students.

Response to Biography

Biographies have advanced far beyond the carbon-copy accounts of presidents and explorers traditionally formatted in dull serialized chapter books. Today's well-written visual accounts of impressive individuals cover figures from the worlds of science, literature, politics, and history. These books become viable options for reader response as the reader soars beyond facts to an identification with and understanding of personal and professional traits of the subject. The blend of dynamic text and, in many cases, vivid visual interpretation adds a new dimension to these biographies.

For example, Catherine read Pam Muñoz Ryan's *When Marian Sang,* a picture book biography of the challenges faced by Marian Anderson. She was asked to reflect on what part of Ms. Anderson's personality reminded her of herself. She maturely proclaimed,

I am persistent in all that I do. When I want to accomplish something and hit a road block, I still am determined to forge ahead. Marian Anderson fought the racial inequalities of her time. Thank goodness her supporters came to her performance outdoors in Washington, DC. I believe my friends and family will always support me and I, too, will succeed.

Open-ended prompts that might be used to assist children in responding to biographies allude to connections between portrayal and personality, greatest accomplishments and disappointments of the subject, and emulation of personality traits in one's own life.

- What did you notice about (*name subject of biography*)?
- What part of (*name subject*) personality reminds you of yourself?
- What part of (*name subject*) life do you find to be an accomplishment?
- What part of (*name subject*) life do you find to be a disappointment?
- What part of (*name subject*) personality would you like to emulate in your own life?

These prompts invite a connected dimension between the life of the reader and the subject of the biography.

Another response option for biography includes responding to the biographical subject by writing a bio-poem (Danielson, 1989). The format of the poem includes the following structure and response:

Line 1:   First name of biographical subject
Line 2:   Four adjectives or phrases describing the subject
Line 3:   Husband/wife/sibling/child of . . .
Line 4:   Lover of . . . (three things or people)
Line 5:   Who feels . . . (three emotions)
Line 6:   Who fears . . . (three things)
Line 7:   Who would like to . . . (three things)
Line 8:   Resident of . . . (city/state/country)
Line 9:   Last name of biographical subject

After reading James Cross Giblin's *Charles A. Lindbergh: A Human Hero,* Richard wrote the following bio-poem in response to the courage and perseverance of its subject.

Lone Eagle
Lillian and Eva were his half-sisters.
Courageous, adventurous, American hero
Who loved to soar in the wide open spaces,
Who loved his estranged parents, and
Who loved loved his faithful flying machine.
Who liked to tinker, ride his motorcycle, barnstorm.
Who got angry at the thought of failing, the misleading shapes of the clouds,
And the crazy crowds clawing all over his plane.
Who hoped the fog would clear, that daylight would come,
And, for a moment, his flight would never end.
Resident of the skies,
Lucky Lindy.

Picture book biographies invite readers to respond to the life of the biographical subject through the structured yet creative formula of a bio-poem. *From* Snowflake Bentley *by Jacqueline Briggs Martin, illustrated by Mary Azarian. Jacket art copyright © 1998 by Mary Azarian. Reprinted by permission of Houghton Mifflin Company. All rights reserved.*

SNOWFLAKE BENTLEY

Jacqueline Briggs Martin   *Illustrated by* Mary Azarian

After reading *Snowflake Bentley* by Jacqueline Briggs Martin, Diana wrote the following bio-poem to respond to the delicate dedication of this scientist and photographer:

Wilson

Younger brother of Charlie

Outdoor enthusiast, farmer, snowflake authority

Who loves snow falling on his mittens,

Drifting in the dried grass of the barren fields,

Sticking to the dark metal handle of the barn door.

Who likes to use his microscope

To observe the tiny miracles

Created by nature.

Who fears that he will never find a way

To save snowflakes

So others can see their intricate patterns.

Who gets angry when the delicate icy crystals melt or evaporate,

Robbing humanity of their wonder,

Without a trace of their existence.

Who hopes his camera will one day

Capture their extraordinary beauty

Preserving their unique designs.

Resident of Jericho, Vermont

Bentley

FIGURE 13.3   Book Cluster: Picture book biographies for inspiring bio-poems

Adler, David A. (2005). *Joe Louis: America's fighter.* Illus. by Terry Widener. San Diego: Harcourt Brace. [P/I]

Anderson, M. T. (2001). *Handel: Who knew what he liked.* Illus. by Kevin Hawkes. Cambridge, MA: Candlewick. [I]

Bardoe, Cheryl (2006). *Gregory Mendel: The friar who grew peas.* Illus by Jos. A. Smith. New York: Abrams. [P/I]

Bildner, Phil (2002). *Shoeless Joe & Black Bet*sy. Illus. by C. F. Payne. New York: Simon & Schuster. [I]

Borden, Louise, & Kroeger, Mary Ann (2001). *Fly high! The story of Bessie Coleman.* Illus. by Teresa Flavin. New York: McElderry. [I]

Byrd, Robert (2003). *Leonardo: Beautiful dreamer.* New York: Dutton. [I]

Curlee, Lynn (2000). *Liberty.* New York: Atheneum. [I]

Giblin, James Cross (2000) *The amazing life of Benjamin Franklin.* Illus. by Michael Dooling. New York: Scholastic. [I/M]

Keating, Frank (2006). *Theodore.* Illus. by Mike Wimmer. New York: Simon & Schuster.

Lasky, Kathryn (2006). *John Muir: America's first environmentalist.* Illus. by Stan Fellows. Cambridge, MA: Candlewick. [P/I]

McCully, Emily Arnold (2006). *Marvelous Mattie: How Margaret E. Knight became an inventor.* New York: Farrar, Straus & Giroux. [I]

Nelson, S. D. (2006). *Quiet hero: The Ira Hayes story.* New York: Lee & Low. [I]

Pinkney, Andrea Davis (2002) *Ella Fitzgerald: The tale of a vocal virtuosa.* Illus. by Brian Pinkney. New York: Hyperion. [I/M]

Ryan, Pam Muñoz (2002). *When Marian sang: True recital of Marian Anderson, voice of the century.* Illus. by Brian Selznick. New York: Scholastic. [I/M]

Walover, Alexandra (2006). *Lucy Maud Montgomery.* New York: Holiday House. [I]

Winter, Jeanette (2005). *The librarian of Bosra: A true story from Iraq.* San Diego: Harcourt. [P/I]

This poetic form provides an interesting format as a child reads and responds to the life, personality, values, and contributions of historical and current biographical subjects. Figure 13.3 lists several picture book biographies providing impetus for bio-poems.

Response to Authentic Accounts

One trend in informational books is to present authentic words, accounts, and documentation of actual people and places in history. The first-person voice of these books brings the individual and the event to life as words and pictures become reality in the reader's mind. Phillip Hoose's *We Were There, Too! Young People in U.S. History* tells the role that young people have played in the making of our nation. Based largely on primary sources—first-person accounts, journals, and interviews—it highlights the accomplishments of over 70 young people of diverse cultures. Because the first-person voice is a strong one for both writing and oral sharing, students enjoy assuming the role of an observer of history.

Responding to young people of varied cultures reinforces the contributions of all people to America's great history. One of these individuals showcased in Hoose's volume, 9-year-old Johnny Clem, became the poster boy of the North during the Civil War. That poster covers the jacket of Jim Murphy's *The Boys' War: Confederate and Union Soldiers Talk About the Civil War.* A sixth-grade class responded to the authentic voice in this book by writing a letter home in the persona of the young Union soldier. Students were invited to share their wartime experiences from lack of food to their feelings about war. Based on information gleaned from the informational text of *The Boys' War,* one sixth-grade boy responded:

March 5, 1862

Dear Pa,

The food here is horrid. Nothing but salt pork, beans, turnips, and hardtack. We hardly get any food anyway with the battles and all. 20 men have been arrested for foraging food but I successfully gathered 50 pounds of honey over the five times I've tried. I've also killed two deer and desiccated the meat.

The battles are bloody. I don't want to talk of them. What I want is to forget them. But I'll tell you this much. I almost got killed. Here's what happened. I was running toward the enemy when one of them fired at my head at the same time. I tripped, so the bullet missed me.

Well, got to go. Love you, Pa.

Sincerely,

Joe Williams

Gripping accounts of discovery and expeditions are also brought to life through extraordinarily researched informational books. These books transport readers to another time and place and offer them the thrill of becoming an active, involved member of a team of explorers in search of a new world, an ancient civilization, or a sunken ship. Jennifer Armstrong's *Shipwreck at the Bottom of the World: The Extraordinary True Story of Shackleton and the Endurance* won the 1999 Orbis Pictus Award for Outstanding Nonfiction. Photographs and well-written text motivate readers to become an active part of an exciting adventure. Sy Montgomery's *Quest for the Tree Kangaroo: An Expedition to the Cloud Forest of New Guinea,* the 2007 Orbis Pictus Award title, and Catherine Thimmesh's *Team Moon: How 400,000 People Landed Apollo 11 on the Moon,* the 2007 Robert Siebert Award title, provide similar intense exploratory experiences. These titles take the reader into a forest habitat and a space environment, present and past. Although the outcome is known in both books, these dramatic expeditions provide opportunities for response through simulated journals.

Response to these first-person accounts might also be in the form of a first-person dramatization as an eyewitness to a piece of history. Because the first-person voice is a strong one for both writing and oral sharing, students enjoy assuming the role of an observer of history. These authentic accounts provide an amazing motivation to both reluctant and avid readers as they share the voice of history as it unfolds.

Response to Photographic Essays

The complexities of science become easier to visualize and understand with informational books that explain and extend our knowledge of life itself. Microscopic photographs that magnify the tiniest creatures and plants or satellite photos that capture the far reaches of outer space motivate further reading and understanding. Barrett and Marantz (1989) suggest that photographs as an illustrative medium be honored with respect and admiration in informational contexts. When provided classroom access to various photographed titles, sixth-grade students readily chose them for independent reading (Hancock, 2007). They responded to the following prompts that focused their attention on the research and preparation that goes into making a photographed informational book:

- How would this book be different if written 10 years sooner?
- How would this book be different if written 10 years later?
- Which photographs do you wish you had taken yourself? Why?
- Compare this book with another book on the same topic that uses drawings rather than photography. Which is better and why?
- What process would the author/photographer use to gather and present this information?
- If you interviewed the author/photographer, what questions would you ask?
- What did you learn from the photographs that you didn't learn from the text?
- What is the most important word in the text to you? Why?

These prompts open unexplored territory to readers of informational books who might never have thought about these ideas. Thinking about the process of writing/photographing an informational book gives the reader an added dimension of response. Responding to how a book is composed gives insights into the research process itself.

After reading Seymour Simon's *Venus* (1992), students were asked to determine what steps the author/photographer took to gather and present the information and photographs:

I think he contacted NASA and asked if they would give him pictures of different parts of Venus . . . so he could . . . make the story good to the reader. (Nick)

He probably researched the planets too and went to the library. He probably interviewed top scientists and astronauts. Then he wrote a book about the planets. (Martha)

A sequential, photographic study of *Jack-in-the-Pulpit* (Wexler, 1993) elicited this response from Cindy:

To get all of this information it would take a few years. . . . A photographer would have to spend a lot of time to take pictures of the plants as they grow through the years. First they'd have to start with the plant's birth, to its death, and after death. An author would have to do the same. They'd have to keep a close eye on it to get every single piece of information as possible.

The value of both text and photographs as supporting tools for acquiring knowledge should be emphasized. While reading Patricia Lauber's spectacular *Summer of*

Fire: Yellowstone 1988, Scott was asked to contemplate what he gleaned from the photographs that he didn't learn from the text. He responded,

I remember more pictures than I do facts. Yellowstone's prettier than it sounds. . . . Sometimes a picture can tell more than the words, like on page 15 or 17, where you can actually see and feel the fire.

Students might exhibit response by actually blending photography and research in preparing their own photographic essay on topics such as wildflowers, insects, or a history of their community. Photography and text as either the inspiration for response or as a response to sharing information on a topic provide the visual support that appeals to many readers of informational books. Explore the titles of Seymour Simon (*Animals Nobody Loves*) and Dorothy Henshaw Patent (*Animals on the Trail with Lewis and Clark*) to witness the power of photographs to elicit response.

Response to Nonfiction Through a Multigenre Research Project

Although Melinda Putz (2006) introduces a varied approach to a research project at the secondary level, the Multigenre Research Project can readily be adjusted to the intermediate and middle levels of instruction. Students are asked to gather literature-based and Web-based information on a person, place, or event, but they are also challenged to share that information creatively through a variety of traditional writing genres. These formats include recipes, advertisements, obituaries, driver's licenses, greeting cards, advice columns, diaries, news articles, graphic organizers, and lists. Students locate a strong number of literature titles related to their topics, and new information will be shared through each piece of writing.

For example, a student focusing on Vincent van Gogh may read Jan Greenberg and Sandra Jordan's *Vincent van Gogh* chapter biography and create a detailed timeline for one genre sharing. That same student may access the picture book *The Yellow House: Vincent van Gogh and Paul Gauguin, Side by Side* by Susan Goldman Rubin and construct a transcript of a conversation between van Gogh and Gauguin during their time together in Provence. Tying this project together is a theme that helps provide transitions from one genre piece to the next. For van Gogh, it could be examples of his well-known artworks or quotes from his own impressions of his artwork.

Each project also includes endnotes and a works cited list to assure recognition of literature and Web citations. The project is packaged in a scrapbook, dossier, catalog, container, or whatever format suits the self-chosen topic. The genres serve as an opportunity for creative aesthetic and efferent writings in response to a topic of the reader/researcher's own interest. The abundance of nonfiction books on selected topics and related websites provide a sound foundation for the knowledge to be shared through creative and varied writing venues. Teachers should be encouraged to read *A Teacher's Guide to the Multigenre Research Project* (Putz, 2006) to explore this open-ended literature-based option that successfully bypasses the traditional informational report.

Response to Nonfiction Through a Literary Nonfiction Anthology

A literary nonfiction anthology encourages the intermediate and middle-level reader to explore and consider personal choices in nonfiction. Literary nonfiction is informational text written in a style that incorporates both the magic of language and characteristics of quality writing while effectively engaging the reader in both the aesthetic and efferent realms (Hancock, 2001). From their vast initial selections, they will choose those that deem special recognition and inclusion in the literary nonfiction anthology.

As with all effective teaching, the teacher needs to model literary examples of quality nonfiction writing. Figure 13.4 defines elements and techniques of literary nonfiction and lists sample titles that teachers can use to keep expectations high for final anthology selections.

Built over a period of time and surrounded by reading, discriminating, and decision making, a literary nonfiction anthology contains a teacher-designated number of books (variable by grade level), book information, an annotation, a quote from the book reflecting quality writing, distinctive features of the book, and a reason for selection (or curricular connection for preservice/inservice teachers). Students browse the nonfiction section of the library to focus on books about personal interests, heroes/heroines, or award-winning nonfiction authors.

Figure 13.5 shares both the contents and a single-page selection from a teacher's literary nonfiction anthology created and aligned with the National Science Education Standards. The quality of titles and the curricular alignment remind educators of the important role of quality nonfiction literature.

CLOSING THOUGHTS

Nonfiction literature fosters both a literacy and a learning experience. The pleasures of factual literature are obtained both by information gathering and savoring the creative manner in which information is shared through this genre. As teachers naturally select special fiction to share with readers, they must also show selectivity in the informational books they choose to share. Quality nonfiction can hook and motivate children to read just as fiction inspires them. Reading aloud informational books helps balance expository and narrative text as children broaden their sense of sharing information alongside their developing sense of story. Read-aloud nonfiction solicits reader response at both the efferent and aesthetic levels. Spontaneous interaction is frequently the basis of response as questions, speculations, related personal experiences, and natural inquiry take hold during oral discussion.

Fifteen years ago, Vardell and Copeland (1992) referred to "the great gift of the genre"— to develop critical thinking so readers become actively involved in processing

FIGURE 13.4 Book Cluster: Literary nonfiction

Characteristics and Techniques of Literary Nonfiction

Dynamic Titles. A magical invitation to read nonfiction comes from the creative use of enticing titles, both of a book and its chapters, that draws the reader into the web of information. See the chapter titles in the following books:

Hoose, Phillip (2004) *The race to save the lord God bird.* New York: Farrar, Straus & Giroux. [M]

Murphy, Jim (2000). *Blizzard! The storm that changed America.* New York: Scholastic. [I/M]

Wechster, Doug (1999). *Bizarre birds:* Honesdale, PA: Boyds Mille Press. [P/I]

Invested Interest in the Topic. The author conveys an underlying reason for extensive investigation that reflects commitment to the research process and passion about the subjects.

Lewin, Ted & Betsy (1999). *Gorilla walk.* New York: Lothrop, Lee & Shepard. [P/I]

Myers, Walter Dean (2001). *The greatest: Muhammad Ali.* New York: Scholastic. [I/M]

Rubin, Susan Goldman with Weissberger, Ela (2006). *The cat with the yellow star: Coming of age in Terezin.* New York: Holiday House. [I/M]

Effective Word Choice. The magic of language breathes life into facts, and well-chosen words blend into visual images and memorable informational text.

Hopkinson, Deborah (2006). *Up before daybreak: Cotton and people in America.* New York: Scholastic. [I]

London, Jonathan (2000). *Panther: Shadow of the swamp.* Illus. by Paul Morin. Cambridge, MA: Candlewick Press. [P]

Miller, Debbie S. (2000). *River of life.* Illus. by Jon Van Zyle. New York: Clarion. [P/I]

Sentence Flow. The use of a variety of sentence patterns to awaken the engagement of the reader and to capture the aesthetic tone of information as it is read aloud or independently.

Borden, Louise, & Kroeger, Mary Kay (2001). *Fly High! The story of Bessie Coleman.* Illus. by Teresa Flavin. New York: Margaret K. McElderry. [P/I]

Burleigh, Robert (1998). Black whiteness: *Admiral Byrd alone in the Antarctic.* Illus. by Walter Lyon Krudrop. New York: Atheneum. [I]

Marrin, Albert (2006). *Saving the buffalo.* New York: Scholastic. [I/M]

Rockwell, Anne (1998). *One bean.* Illus. by Megan Halsey. San Diego: Harcourt Brace. [P]

Compelling Voice. The voices of the author and other contributors provide authenticity and strength to the facts and convince the reader of the power of the topic itself.

Bridges, Ruby (1999). *Through my eyes.* New York: Scholastic. [I/M]

Freedman, Russell (2005). *Children of the Great Depression.* New York: Clarion. [I]

Montgomery, Sy (2001). *The man-eating tigers of Sunbardans.* Boston: Houghton Mifflin. [I]

Philip, Neil (2000). *A braid of lives: Native American childhood.* New York: Clarion. [I/M]

Inviting Leads. The introduction or opening pages capture the curiosity of readers and entice them to move on as they question, wonder, and become intrigued by the topic.

Armstrong, Jennifer (1998). *Shipwreck at the bottom of the world: The extraordinary true story of Shackleton and the Endurance.* New York: Crown. [I/M]

Arnosky, Jim (2000). *All about turtles.* New York: Scholastic. [P]

Freedman, Russell (2004). *The voice that challenged a nation: Marian Anderson and the struggle for equal rights.* New York: Clarion. [I/M]

Robbins, Ken (2001). *Thunder on the plains: The story of the American buffalo.* New York: Atheneum. [P/I]

FIGURE 13.4   Continued

> ***Thought-Provoking Conclusions.*** Final paragraphs leave the reader with lingering thoughts and inquiries and often inspire further discussion or investigation.
>
> Bial, Raymond (1999). *One-room school.* Boston: Houghton Mifflin. [I/M]
>
> Curlee, Lynn (2000). *Liberty.* New York: Atheneum. [I/M]
>
> Warren, Andrea (2004). *Escape from Saigon: How a Vietnam War veteran became an American boy.* New York: Farrar, Straus & Giroux. [I/M]
>
> ***Revelation of the Lesser-Known Fact.*** In the deluge of information on a topic, one lesser-known fact may become the one that is savored and remembered as it is revealed through a lively narrative account.
>
> Blumberg, Rhoda (2004). *York's adventures with Lewis and Clark: An African-American's part in the great expedition.* New York: HarperCollins. [I/M]
>
> Fisher, Leonard Everett (1999). *Alexander Graham Bell.* New York: Atheneum. [P/I]
>
> Stanley, Diane (2000). *Michelangelo.* New York: HarperCollins. [I/M]
>
> St. George, Judith. (2000). *So you want to be president.* Illus. by David Small. New York: Philomel. [P/I]
>
> ***Relation of Facts to Reader Experience.*** Relating facts directly to reader knowledge assists in making them understandable and meaningful.
>
> Brimmer, Larry Dane (2004). *Subway: The story of tunnels, tubes, and tracks.* Honesdale, PA: Boyds Mills. [I]
>
> Markle, Sandra (2001). *Growing up wild: Wolves.* New York: Atheneum. [P]
>
> Ryder, Joanne (2001). *Little panda: The world welcomes Hua Mei at the San Diego Zoo.* New York: Simon & Schuster. [P]
>
> ***Visual Vignettes.*** Important information can be impressively and meaningfully displayed in language-rich charts, tables, and notes. Technical display and visual literacy are powerful resources for transforming information.
>
> Blacklock, Dyan (2004). *The Roman army: The legendary soldiers who created an empire.* Illus. by David Kennet. New York: Walker. [I/M]
>
> Dewey, Jennifer Owings (2001). *Antarctic journal: Four months at the bottom of the world.* New York: HarperCollins. [P/I]
>
> Giblin, James Cross (2000). *The amazing life of Benjamin Franklin.* Illus. by Michael Dooling. New York: Scholastic. [I/M]
>
> Harness, Cheryl (2001). *Remember the ladies: 100 great American women.* New York: HarperCollins. [I/M]

information and less accepting of the written word. Literary quality, variety, and appeal are the hallmark of the new informational book, and reader response ranges from spontaneous response to modeling the style of literature for presenting research, to inquiry-based discussions. The gift of the genre still lies in both the literary and stylistic quality that now habitually graces informational books as well as its power to incite the thinking abilities and curiosity of the reader. The natural desire to respond to new information, to relate it to prior knowledge, and the need to formulate new inquiries continue to bridge nonfiction books and reader response.

FIGURE 13.5 Nonfiction literary anthology—table of contents and sample selection

Table of Contents
Literary Nonfiction Anthology for the National Science Education Standards

Content Standard A: Science as Inquiry
Content Standard B: Physical Science
Content Standard C: Life Science
Content Standard D: Earth and Space Science
Content Standard E: Science and Technology
Content Standard F: Science in Personal and Social Perspectives
Content Standard G: History and Nature of Science

Biography: (history and nature of science)
Snowflake Bentley by Jacqueline Briggs Martin   p. 1
The Dinosaurs of Waterhouse Hawkins by Barbara Kerley   p. 2

Physical Science: (force/motion, energy, matter, magnetism, electricity, light, sound)
A Drop of Water by Walter Wick   p. 3
The Magic School Bus Gets a Bright Idea by Joanna Cole   p. 4

Life Science: (animals, plants, human body, heredity, genetics)
An Extraordinary Life by Laurence Pringle   p. 5
Tell Me, Tree by Gail Gibbons   p. 6

Earth/Space Science: (geology, weather, ocean, volcanoes, solar system, space exploration)
A Handful of Dirt by Raymond Bial   p. 7
Ultimate Field Trip: Blasting Off to Space Academy by Susan Goodman   p. 8

Current Issues in Science: (technological, medical, ecological)
Interrupted Journey: Saving Endangered Sea Turtles by Kathryn Lasky   p. 9
Tropical Rainforest by Anita Ganeri   p. 10

Wick, Walter (1997). *A Drop of Water.* New York: Scholastic.
Annotation:

The spectacular photographs capture water in various stages of movement as Wick explores such topics as surface tension, capillary action, condensation, and evaporation. Readers can examine the changing space of water as it falls from a faucet, soap bubbles reflecting light, and water as steam, ice, and snowflakes. Explorations and experiments dispersed throughout the book help clarify the concept being presented.

Quote from Book:

"And water is precious. Without it, not a single living thing could survive. No plants would grow, not even one blade of grass. No animal would roam the earth, not even a spider. But somewhere in the world right now, snow drifts on a mountaintop and rain falls in a valley. And all around us, we are reminded of the never ending journey of a drop of water" (p. 37).

FIGURE 13.5 Continued

Distinctive Features:

Vocabulary words are italicized within the text and defined. Bold headings introduce each section. The book ends with additional information about each experiment and encourages students to think of their own experiments. It also has some final notes entitled "About This Book" where Wick acknowledges the assistance of W. A. Bentley's techniques when photographing the snowflakes. Also included in this section is a testimony that the photographs have not been altered. The need for this disclaimer demonstrates how incredible the photographs are! The end pages are a rich blue.

Curricular Connections:

- Art: photographs
- Math: patterns and shapes
- Science: properties of water
- Science Processes: experiments
- Literacy: Boston Globe-Horn Book Award for Nonfiction (1997 Winner)

Connected Titles (Physical Science): (force/motion, matter, energy)

Wells, R. (1995). *What's smaller than a pygmy shrew?* Illinois: A. Whitman.
Robbins, K. (1994). *Water.* New York: Holt.
Robbins, K. (1993). *Power Machines.* New York: Holt.
Robbins, K. (1991). *Bridges.* New York: Dial Books.
Curlee, L. (2001). *Brooklyn Bridge.* New York: Simon & Schuster.

References

Bamford, R. A., & Kristo, J. V. (Eds.) (2003). *Making facts come alive: Choosing quality nonfiction literature K–8* (2nd ed.). Norwood, MA: Christopher-Gordon.

Barrett, T., & Marantz, K. (1989). Photographs as illustrations. *The New Advocate, 2,* 227–238.

Caswell, L. J., & Duke, N. K. (1998). Non-narrative as a catalyst for literary development. *Language Arts, 75,* 108–117.

Daniels, H. (2002). Expository text in literature circles. *Voices from the Middle, 9,* 7–14.

Danielson, K. (1989). Helping history come alive with literature. *Social Studies, 80,* 65–68.

Doiron, R. (1994). Using nonfiction in a read-aloud program: Letting the facts speak for themselves. *The Reading Teacher, 47,* 616–624.

Duthie, C. (1994). Nonfiction: A genre study for the primary classroom. *Language Arts, 71,* 588–595.

Hadaway, N. L., & Mundy, J. (1999). Children's informational picture books visit a secondary ESL classroom. *Journal of Adolescent & Adult Literacy, 42,* 464–474.

Hancock, M. R. (1994). *The 3Rs of informational picture books: Responding, reflecting, and researching.* Paper presented at the National Council of Teachers of English spring conference, Portland, OR.

Hancock, M. R. (2001). *Children's literary nonfiction: Discovering the magic of language in informational text.* Paper presented at the National Council of Teachers spring conference, Birmingham, AL.

Hancock, M. R. (2007). Another time, another place: Bringing social studies to life through literature. In P. J. Farris (Ed.), *Elementary and middle school social studies: An interdisciplinary, multicultural approach* (5th ed., pp. 349–386). Long Grove, IL: Waveland Press.

Hoffman, J. V. (1992). Critical reading/thinking across the curriculum: Using I-charts to support learning. *Language Arts, 69,* 121–127.

Johnson, H., & Freedman, L. (2005). *Content area literature circles: Using discussion for learning across the curriculum.* Norwood, MA: Christopher-Gordon.

Kristo, J. V., & Bamford, R. A. (2004). *Nonfiction in focus: A comprehensive framework for helping students become independent readers and writers of nonfiction, K–6.* New York: Scholastic.

Manduran, I. (2000). "Playing possum": A young child's responses to information books. *Language Arts, 77,* 391–397.

Moss, B. (1995). Using children's nonfiction trade-books as read-alouds. *Language Arts, 72,* 122–126.

Moss, B. (2003). *Exploring the literature of fact: Children's nonfiction trade books in the elementary classroom.* New York: Guilford.

Moss, B. (2004). Teaching expository text structures through information trade book retellings. *The Reading Teacher, 57,* 710–718.

Moss, B., Leone, S., & Dippilo, M. (1997). Exploring the literature of fact: Linking reading and writing through information trade books. *Language Arts, 74,* 418–429.

Palmer, R. G., & Stewart, R. A. (2003). Nonfiction trade book use in primary grades. *The Reading Teacher, 57,* 38–48.

Palmer, R. G., & Stewart, R. A. (2005). Models for using nonfiction in the primary grades. *The Reading Teacher, 58,* 426–434.

Pappas, C. C. (1991). Fostering full access to literacy by including information books. *Language Arts, 68,* 449–462.

Putz, M. (2006). *A teacher's guide to the multigenre research project: Everything you need to get started.* Portsmouth, NH: Heinemann.

Read, S. (2001). "Kid mice hunt for their selfs": First and second graders' writing research. *Language Arts, 78,* 333–342.

Richgels, D. J. (2002). Informational texts in kindergarten. *The Reading Teacher, 55,* 586–595.

Saul, E. W., & Dieckman, D. (2005). Choosing and using information text books. *Reading Research Quarterly, 40,* 502–513.

Stien, D., & Beed, P. L. (2004). Bridging the gap between fiction and nonfiction in the literature circle setting. *The Reading Teacher, 57,* 510–518.

Tower, C. (2002). It's a snake, you guys! *Research in the Teaching of English, 37,* 55–88.

Vardell, S. M. (1996). The language of facts: Using nonfiction books to support language growth. In A. A. McClure & J. V. Kristo (Eds.), *Books that invite talk, wonder, and play* (pp. 59–77). Urbana, IL: National Council of Teachers of English.

Vardell, S. M., & Copeland, K. A. (1992). Reading aloud and responding to nonfiction: Let's talk about it. In E. B. Freeman & D. G. Person (Eds.), *Using nonfiction trade books in the elementary classroom: From ants to zeppelins* (pp. 76–85). Urbana, IL: National Council of Teachers of English.

Yopp, R. H., & Yopp, H. K. (2000). Sharing informational text with young children. *The Reading Teacher, 53,* 410–423.

Yopp, R. H., & Yopp, H. K. (2004). Preview-predict-confirm: Thinking about the language and content of informational text. *The Reading Teacher, 58,* 79–83.

Children's Books Cited [P] = K–2; [I] = 3–5; [M] = 6–8

Arnosky, Jim (2001). *All about turtles*. New York: Scholastic. [P]

Armstrong, Jennifer (1998). *Shipwreck at the bottom of the world: The extraordinary true story of Shackleton and the Endurance*. New York: Crown. [I/M]

Bates, Katherine L. (1993). *America the beautiful*. Illus. by Neil Waldman. New York: Atheneum. [P/I]

Burleigh, Robert (1991). *Flight: The journey of Charles Lindbergh*. Illus. by Mike Wimmer. New York: Philomel Books. [I/M]

Corey, Shauna (2000). *You forgot your skirt, Amelia Bloomer!* Illus. by Chesley McLaren. New York: Scholastic. [P/I]

Cowley, Joy (2004). *Chameleon, chameleon*. Photos by Nic Bishop. New York: Scholastic. [P]

Curlee, Lynn (2002). *Seven wonders of the ancient world*. New York: Atheneum. [I/M]

Gibbons, Gail (2002). *Apples*. New York: Holiday House. [P]

Giblin, James Cross (1997). *Charles A. Lindbergh: A human hero*. New York: Clarion. [I]

Greenberg, Jan, & Jordan, Sandra (2002). *Vincent van Gogh: Portrait of the artist*. New York: Delacorte. [I/M]

Hoose, Phillip (2001). *We were there, too! Young people in U.S. history*. New York: Farrar, Straus & Giroux. [I/M]

Hopkinson, Deborah (2001). *Fannie in the kitchen*. Illus. by Nancy Carpenter. New York: Atheneum. [I]

Lauber, Patricia (1991). *Summer of fire: Yellowstone 1988*. New York: Orchard Books. [I]

Marrin, Albert (2006). *Oh, rats! The story of rats and people*. Illus. by C. B. Mordan. New York: Dutton. [I/M]

Martin, Jacqueline Briggs (1998). *Snowflake Bentley*. Boston: Houghton Mifflin. [P/I]

McKissack, Patricia C., & McKissack, Frederick L. (1994). *Christmas in the big house, Christmas in the quarters*. Illus. by John Thompson. New York: Scholastic. [I/M]

Montgomery, Sy (2006). *Quest for the tree kangaroo: An expedition to the Cloud Forest of New Guinea* (Scientists in the Field series). Photographs by Nic Bishop. Boston: Houghton Mifflin. [I/M]

Murphy, Jim (1990). *The boys' war: Confederate and Union soldiers talk about the Civil War*. New York: Clarion. [I/M]

Murphy, Jim (1993). *Across America on an emigrant train*. New York: Clarion. [I/M]

Murphy, Jim (1995). *The great fire*. New York: Scholastic. [I/M]

Patent, Dorothy Henshaw (2002). *Animals on the trail with Lewis & Clark*. Photographs by William Munoz. New York: Clarion. [I/M]

Pringle, Laurence (1997). *An extraordinary life: The story of a monarch butterfly*. Illus. by Bob Marstall. New York: Orchard Books. [I/M]

Rubin, Susan Goldman (2001). *The yellow house: Vincent van Gogh and Paul Gauguin, side by side*. Illus. by Jos. A. Smith. New York: Abrams. [I]

Ryan, Pam Muñoz (2002). *When Marian sang: True recital of Marian Anderson*. Illus. by Brian Selznick. New York: Scholastic. [P/I]

Sayre, April Pulley (2001). *The bumblebee queen*. Illus. by Patricia J. Wynne. Watertown, MA: Charlesbridge. [P/I]

Simon, Seymour (1992). *Venus*. New York: Morrow. [P/I]

Simon, Seymour (2001). *Animals nobody loves*. New York: SeaStar. [P/I]

Stanley, Diane (1996). *Leonardo da Vinci*. New York: Morrow. [I/M]

Stanley, Diane (1998). *Joan of Arc*. New York: Morrow. [I/M]

Stanley, Diane (2000). *Michelangelo*. New York: HarperCollins. [I/M]

Stanley, Diane (2003). *Saladin: Prince of Islam*. New York: HarperCollins. [I/M]

Stanley, Diane, & Vennema, Peter (1991). *Good Queen Bess: The story of Elizabeth I of England*. New York: Four Winds/Simon & Schuster. [I/M]

Stanley, Diane, & Vennema, Peter (1992). *The Bard of Avon: The story of William Shakespeare*. New York: Morrow. [I/M]

Stanley, Diane, & Vennema, Peter (1993). *Charles Dickens: The man who had great expectations*. New York: Morrow. [I/M]

Stanley, Diane, & Vennema, Peter (1994). *Cleopatra*. New York: Morrow. [I/M]

Stanley, Jerry (1992). *Children of the Dust Bowl: The true story of the school at Weedpatch Camp.* New York: Random House. [I/M]

Thimmesh, Catherine (2006). *Team moon: How 400,000 people landed Apollo 11 on the moon.* Boston: Houghton Mifflin. [I/M]

Wexler, Jerome (1993). *Jack-in-the-pulpit.* New York: Dutton. [P/I]

Winters, Kay (2001). *Tiger trail.* Illus. by Laura Regan. New York: Simon & Schuster. [P]

PART IV

Celebrating Intertextual and Interdisciplinary Connections

Response-based links to children's literature through oral response, written journals, and drama/art/music activities provide continuously satisfying reader response connections to literature. Yet perhaps one of the most gratifying appeals of children's literature for teachers and a most meaningful connection for children moves beyond response to individual books. The creative blending of multiple titles of children's literature around a single theme, across both literary genres and

377

academic disciplines, and even incorporating technology provides literature-based connections that make learning relevant to the real world.

Once teachers and readers become adept at varied response options to literature, the challenge exists to plan and implement interdisciplinary response-based units built on quality children's books. Part IV of *A Celebration of Literature and Response* focuses on planning, implementing, and responding to the following:

- Literature clusters (a selective collection of books across genres and disciplines related to a single theme)
- Theme explorations (a vast offering of books across genres and disciplines related to a single higher-level concept or theme through interconnected subthemes)
- Twin texts/technology (an exclusive trio of a fiction title, a nonfiction title, and a related Internet website)

Teachers' increasing knowledge of literature and students' growing confidence with reader response enable them to move beyond isolated response activities to experience the natural thematic nature of higher-level inquiry that results from the creative blending of children's books through an interdisciplinary focus that may include technology. In the age of accountability, less time is afforded to content area study. Themes blending content and literature help integrate literacy effectively into science, social studies, and mathematics.

Chapter 14 supportively guides preservice and inservice teachers through the process of creating literature clusters and theme explorations by sharing tips on these tasks:

1. Selecting a topic
2. Locating literature
3. Utilizing professional resources
4. Designing response-based instruction
5. Implementing an interdisciplinary blend of literature-based activities in the classroom

Lists and graphic organizers of literature clusters and theme explorations enhance this chapter while providing a model for individually planned thematic interdisciplinary instruction. In particular, detailed reflections and advice during each stage of the planning process authenticate the challenge and satisfaction of effectively blending literature across genres and disciplines. Examples of whole-class, small group, and individualized response-based connections provide further guidance for creating unique literature-based interdisciplinary instruction. In addition, a simplified trio of twin texts (fiction and nonfiction) blended with an Internet website provide multiple perspectives on a single theme.

Throughout the implementation of a brief literature cluster, long-term theme exploration, or twin text/technology trio, children respond to literature in ways that help them make connections to the real world. Indeed, the challenge of connecting literature and responses through interdisciplinary connections may result in some of the most meaningful teaching and response-based inquiry and learning that occurs in a literature-based classroom. Adding a pinch of technology reveals that literature and technology can mutually exist in a dynamic world and both can be enhanced by the other.

CHAPTER 14

Interdisciplinary and Intertextual Connections

Response Through Literature Clusters, Theme Explorations, and Twin Texts/Technology

I sat on my office floor and piled high the literature offerings. I don't remember how the hours flew by as I absorbed myself in reading, appreciating, viewing, and perusing the varied genres I had collected related to my theme. I began to group the books in piles that were eventually to become subthemes. A few titles were difficult to categorize, but most of them immediately belonged and connected to other related titles. After manipulating, assigning, and rethinking literature placement, I had eight piles of books towering at my feet. It was then that I paused and realized that the reading, the touching, the turning, and the shifting were actually my response to the literature I had collected. The organization and the designation of subthemes was, in reality, a personal response to the books I was planning to share with children.

Author's reflections on planning her first theme exploration on immigration

Sharing children's literature in a classroom one quality book at a time effectively supports literacy and content area instruction. Inviting children to respond to isolated titles encourages varying modes of response often suggested by the book itself. Yet literature has the power to contribute even more to the broader scope of a child's learning. Creatively blending pieces of literature across genres, authors, and related disciplines enhances the connectedness of literature and content knowledge. Designing classroom instruction based on related titles and planning an array of response-based literature activities associated with them provide a solid base for effective teaching with the new literacies (Castek, Bevans-Mangelson, & Goldstone, 2006; Gambrell, 2005; Labbo, 2005; Leu, Castek, Henry, Coiro, & McMullan, 2004).

This chapter introduces a sequential means to blend literature across genres for interdisciplinary instruction. The process of locating, balancing, and blending related literature for thematic teaching is presented in two stages. First, literature clusters (Hancock, 1997) form a first step in integrating a variety of book titles on a single theme. Books from all literary genres keyed to a single topic provide the basis for instruction of facts and meaningful response-based activities. Second, theme explorations (Weaver, Chaston, & Peterson, 1993) form a longer range view of instruction because a broad-based theme encompasses several subthemes in the form of literature clusters. Together the subthemes and quality children's books blend, connect, relate, and combine into an integrated instructional mode for effective literacy and interdisciplinary instruction. Third, twin texts meet technology in blended trios of information from three perspectives—fiction, nonfiction, and an Internet website (Camp, 2000; Hancock, 2002, 2004). Figure 14.1 characterizes the instructional models of literature clusters, theme explorations, and twin texts/technology. The list assists in pointing out similarities and differences among these three literature-based response-oriented modes of instruction.

To aid in modeling the process of planning and teaching through literature clusters, theme explorations, and twin texts/technology, this chapter contains several graphic organizers, annotated bibliographies, and lists of literature-based response activities as the core of interdisciplinary instruction. These examples and the accompanying procedures for creating them serve as models for planning and implementing thematic interdisciplinary teaching at the primary, intermediate, and middle levels of instruction. Whether based in science (Collard, 2003; Ebbers, 2002; Kaser, 2001; Rice, 2002; Smolkin & Donovan, 2005), social studies (Fuhler, Farris, & Nelson, 2006; Kieff, 2001; McMahon, Gordy, & Strop, 2001; Roser & Keehn, 2002; Wolk, 2004), or mathematics (Hunsader, 2004; Moyer, 2000; Ward, 2005; Whitin & Whitin, 2001), literature lends itself to meaningful thematic blending. Effectively weaving and balancing literature across all genres (with a gentle infusion of technology) provides the essential connections between the narrative, expository, and poetic voices that cause real learning and understanding to occur (Bedford, 2005; Soalt, 2005).

CREATING LITERATURE CLUSTERS

As teachers attempt to include literature across the curriculum, it is crucial to realize that all genres of literature can contribute to conceptual understanding. Confining a science unit to informational books on weather can limit a child's curiosity for and

FIGURE 14.1   Comparison/contrast of literature clusters, theme explorations, and twin texts/technology

Literature Clusters	Theme Explorations	Twin Texts/Technology
Eight to 12 titles that support a curricular topic	Twenty-five or more titles related to an interdisciplinary broad-based theme	One fiction title, one nonfiction title, and one related website
Blends narrative, expository, and poetic voices of literature	Blends narrative, expository, and poetic voices of literature	Blends narrative, expository, and website informational voices
Includes books selected from several literary genres	Includes books from virtually all literary genres	Includes fiction, nonfiction, and related informational website
Basis for aesthetic and efferent response	Basis for aesthetic and efferent response	Basis for aesthetic and efferent response
Planned for read-aloud and whole-group response-based activities	Planned for whole-group, small group, and individual response-based activities	Planned for whole-group, small group, and individual response-based activities
Shared during a 1- to 2-week period during content area scheduled time	Shared across language arts/curricular scheduled time for 2 to 6 weeks (often an entire quarter or school year)	Shared during a 1-week period as an abbreviated unit
Used in a single-classroom configuration	Used in multiage settings or through collaborative teaching/planning	Used in a single classroom configuration or as a cross-grade level study
Building block of a theme exploration	Composed of four to six related literature clusters	Introduction to linking fiction/nonfiction/technology
Enhances response-based instruction and literature-based learning	Enhances response-based instruction, integration of content, inquiry learning, and literature-based learning	Enhances comparative response-based instruction and literature/technology-based learning

understanding of meteorological concepts. Expanding the literary coverage on weather to include folktales explaining weather phenomenon, picture storybooks set in differing weather conditions, and poetry that captures the natural wonder of weather phenomena entices children to learn. Learners relate weather to their own lives, enhance their knowledge base and depth of understanding, and broaden their perceptions beyond factual information.

The means for reaching this depth of conceptual development is literature. The literature must be grouped into meaningful clusters of books that allow children to see the connections among factual, fictional, and poetic perspectives on a topic. A literature cluster is defined as a blend of quality children's trade books chosen from a variety of literary genres that contain narrative, expository, and poetic perspectives on

FIGURE 14.2 Literature Cluster: Deserts

Arnosky, Jim (2005). *Under the wild western sky*. New York: HarperCollins.

Baylor, Byrd (1986). *I'm in charge of celebrations*. Illus. by Peter Parnall. New York: Scribners.

Davies, Nicola (2005). *Deserts*. Boston: Kingfisher.

Dunphy, Madeline (1995). *Here is the southwestern desert*. Illus. by Anne Coe. New York: Hyperion.

Geisert, Bonnie (2001). *Desert town*. Illus. by Arthur Geisert. Boston: Houghton Mifflin.

Guiberson, Brenda Z. (1991). *Cactus hotel*. Illus. by Megan Lloyd. New York: Holt.

Johnston, Tony (1995). *Alice Nizzy Nazzy: The witch of Santa Fe*. Illus. by T. de Paola. New York: Putnam.

Johnston, Tony (2000). *Desert song*. Illus. by Ed Young. San Francisco: Sierra Club.

Kessler, Cristina (1995). *One night: A story from the desert*. Illus. by Ian Schoenherr. New York: Philomel Books.

London, Jonathan (1997). *Ali: Child of the desert*. Illus. by Ted Lewin. New York: Lothrop, Lee & Shepard.

Mora, Pat (1994). *Listen to the desert/Oye al desierto*. Illus..by F. Mora. Boston: Clarion.

Sandler, Michael (2006). *Deserts: Surviving in the Sahara*. New York: Bearport Publishing.

Sayre, April Pulley (2001). *Dig, wait, listen: A desert toad's tale*. Illus. by Barbara Bash. New York: Greenwillow.

Stevens, Janet, & Crummel, Susan Stevens (2005). *Jackalope*. Illus. by Janet Stevens. San Diego: Harcourt.

Wright-Frierson, Virginia (1996). *A desert scrapbook: Dawn to dusk in the Sonoran Desert*. New York: Simon & Schuster.

Yolen, Jane (1996). *Welcome to the sea of sand*. Illus. by Laura Regan. New York: Putnam.

a concept or theme. The goal of a literature cluster is to blend trade books across genres through varying perspectives that address a single topic in an effort to enhance both instruction and learning (Hancock, 1997).

A science/social studies example best illustrates the creation and relevance of a literature cluster about the desert. Although this topic is often covered in intermediate science units, the topic begs to be stretched beyond factual information. Examine the list of related titles shown in Figure 14.2, note their specific genre, and sense the creative blend of varied perspectives on the topic of deserts to be used with children from second through fourth grades. This list of books contains multicultural titles, informational picture books, poem picture books, folktale variants, a cumulative tale, and a literature classic. Besides exposing children to the vast array of genres focused on a single topic, the varied perspectives on desert information provide the learner with a multitude of information.

The poetic perspective of literature often provides the impetus for a themed study. Jane Yolen's *Welcome to the Sea of Sand* or Tony Johnston's *Desert Song* provide an opening read-aloud with sensory descriptions of the "sea of sand." These descriptions enhance visual images and inspire connections and inquiries in the learner. The cumulative pattern nature of Dunphy's *Here Is the Southwestern Desert* opens the door to a choral reading performance with voices added as additional information is introduced. Not only are the students learning facts, they are also gaining an understanding of the interrelatedness of desert inhabitants. The desert speaks in the language of its creatures and natural surroundings in Mora's *Listen to the Desert/Oye al Desierto* in which desert sounds are shared in both English and Spanish. Set in the southwestern desert, Baylor's *I'm in Charge of Celebrations* illuminates the wonders of the desert as a triple rainbow, an encounter with a coyote, and a view of falling stars inspire the author's poetic response to this unique ecosystem.

Factual information and the roots of research can be delivered through interesting book formats. Wright-Frierson's *A Desert Scrapbook, Cactus Hotel,* and Sandler's *Deserts: Surviving in the Sahara* are informational titles that provide a format for drawing, labeling, organizing, and describing desert flora and fauna. A multitude of other information titles displayed in the classroom become resources for individual animal, plant, or geographic reports.

For a connected light fictional touch, read-alouds of Johnston's *Alice Nizzy Nazzy,* a southwestern version of the Russian Baba Yaga tale, and *Jackalope* by Stevens and Crummel may initiate a discussion on the role of the desert in the tales, the factual foundations in each tale, and the location of other world folktales set in a desert environment. The narrative voice of a desert animal in Sayre's *Dig, Wait, Listen: A Desert Toad's Tale* blends with a world perspective from Kessler's *One Night* in which a young Tuareg nomadic boy, Mohammed, faces an adventure while watching a grazing herd of goats one night on the Sahara Desert. The beauty and mystery of the desert of this multicultural selection moves the reader beyond the limited perspective of the American southwestern desert to a global sense of arid regions.

A literature cluster can be implemented as an isolated unit or used as an enhancement to textbook instruction. The books can be shared through read-alouds by the teacher or multiple copies may be made available to groups of students for independent reading. The cluster may be shared during content area instructional time or woven into a reading/language arts block so as to address both literacy and knowledge. The most important aspect of a literature cluster is its ability to blend literary genre through narrative, expository, and poetic voices with the student absorbing multiple perspectives—aesthetic and efferent—on a topic. Beyond the informational focus of traditional units lies the importance of connecting facts to feelings, appreciation, and insights that personalize and enhance learning.

Benefits of Literature Clusters

The desert model clarifies the importance of blending literary genres in a content area lesson to relate the narrative, expository, and poetic voices of literature on a single topic. The range of literature takes the unit far from the traditional content area base to an interdisciplinary approach steeped in language. Consider the benefits of such an approach to literature-based instruction in the content areas.

Children are exposed to all literary genres.   Their exposure to narrative, expository, and poetic voices not only varies informational perspectives but provides models for reading and writing in these three modes. Literature clusters are in and of themselves interdisciplinary; they are contrived to extend content area learning into the language arts.

Literature clusters contain multiage possibilities. Because cluster selections make the literary experience—rather than a grade-level match—a priority, literature clusters appeal to a wide range of age and ability levels. In fact, they provide a sound base for interdisciplinary instruction in multiage configurations.

Literature clusters provide a broader vision of a topic. Unlike traditional textbook instruction, children are encouraged to connect learning within a cluster as they detect relationships, compare factual and fictional perspectives, and revel in the language arts/literature enhancement of the informational base. As learners accumulate a medley of literature clusters throughout the school year, they even begin to connect learning between clusters. As their exposure to and familiarity with literature increases, children begin to create connections between clusters. For example, a science-based cluster on deserts might later connect to a social studies–based cluster on Egypt.

Literature clusters naturally connect fact and fiction for both enjoyment and learning. Their greatest strength lies in their ability to create lifelong readers. Through exposure to all literary genres, readers find comfort and satisfaction in a wide variety of books. In addition to building content area knowledge, they are immersed in a multiplicity of books, which fosters their desire to read and contributes to their future as lifelong readers.

Literature clusters create natural opportunities for reader response. As books across genres are shared, response-based activities meaningfully match specific titles. Readers' theater, extended writing, graphic organizers, choral reading, and literature response journals extend the themed literature into varied response modes.

Creating a Literature Cluster

What resources can be used for creating literature clusters? What steps does a teacher take to blend books intentionally from all literary genres? Several suggestions and sequential steps make the process challenging, fulfilling, and functional.

Determine a theme. A theme for a literature cluster finds its roots in the curriculum guide or the interests of the students. It can grow from a topic currently being studied, focus on one aspect of a topic under study, or be an original, freshly conceived topic that has never been investigated before. It can be broad if the intent is to pursue it in depth through further clusters, or it can be narrow and limit itself to a short survey of a topic.

Locate a core book. As a teacher begins to view literature on the designated topic, he or she can usually locate a book that truly appeals to one's taste, sparks imagination, and relates to the topic at hand. This title might be considered the core book. Read it to get an introduction to the topic and to activate the flow of related literature titles. Plan a potential opening activity for your theme based on this book. Although no other literature may have been collected at this point, the core book serves as an inspiration for finding, accessing, and linking related literature to the topic. For example, Mary Newell DePalmo's *A Grand Old Tree* sparks interest in an exploration of trees because of its potential to inspire the reader/listener to appreciate the value and longevity of trees in our environment. Or Debbie Miller's *Are Trees Alive?* might be just what it takes to get upper-primary students enthusiastic about a "How do We Connect to our Environment?" theme. Often a children's literature title might actually be creative enough to generate the theme for an entire cluster. A core book naturally generates the teacher's enthusiasm for the possibilities of the literature, the framework of the theme, and the related activities that will accompany the literature cluster.

Conduct a library search. Use general subject descriptors to access related book titles in your school or public library. The verso page of your core book provides additional subject descriptors that might result in further titles. The importance of these descriptors in stretching the literature search cannot be underestimated. With most libraries online—and often linked with other schools, the public library, and a university children's collection—this process is invigorating as well as challenging.

Brainstorm with teachers and media specialists. Two minds are better than one when you attempt to brainstorm literature that might be related to a potential theme. Locate those professionals who know children's literature well. It is amazing what can be derived from a 10-minute session with people who appreciate and know children's books. Literature clusters taught in multiaged classrooms already have a team of professionals in place for this brainstorming session. Keep in mind the breadth of all literary genres throughout your brainstorming. A common tendency is to locate informational texts readily with little thought given to a possible fantasy connection, a multicultural focus, and the importance of biography to almost every topic.

Access professional resources. Teachers are often surprised by how much of the brainstorming has already been done for them by professional experts in children's literature. Two helpful resources for creating literature clusters are *Book Links,* a journal of the American Library Association that focuses on thematically related titles across genres, and *The Reading Teacher,* a journal of the International Reading Association that consistently has a monthly column, "Children's Books," which reviews children's literature in an interdisciplinary mode by focusing on a single topic (Kurkjian, Livingston, & Young, 2004–2006). These sources often guide the teacher not only to titles that relate well to a theme but also to the highest quality literature.

Design response-based instruction to accompany the literature. Determine which books will be shared through read-alouds, which will be available as multiple copies for independent reading, and which will be resources for research. Review reader response modes to plan varied response activities or to allow for student-selected response-based projects.

Implement the literature cluster as the basis of instruction. Typically housed in a content area time slot or woven into reading/writing blocks, the literature cluster should relate to the topic and strive for connectedness between books and information. Blending aesthetic and efferent response to a theme results in a higher-level learning experience.

Literature clusters provide the perfect balance of fiction and nonfiction, imaginative and informative, narrative and expository, matter-of-fact and poetic. They challenge readers to sample all literary genres and synthesize them into a meaningful and memorable understanding of a topic. Clusters of related literature broaden the scope of study, immerse the learner, and evoke natural curiosity and further inquiry. Although these clusters stand alone as an introduction to a topic, they also form the foundation of theme explorations, discussed next. The art of creating literature clusters establishes a model for blending literature clusters into the larger scope of a theme exploration. In a special way, the creation of literature clusters encompasses an educator's response to the literature she or he knows will open a new level of inquiry to the learner. Literature clusters form an intertextual link that challenges teachers to absorb children's literature, relate titles to each other, and take a first step toward understanding the interdisciplinary ramifications of children's books across the curriculum.

Sample Literature Clusters

The next few pages of this chapter contain several models of literature clusters built on the open-ended topics of trees, journeys, and the Middle East. Although the bases of these clusters lie in the language arts, science, and social studies, the literature itself blends varied voices and genres into a meaningful introduction to each topic. These clusters serve as models and are meant to inspire the creation of literature clusters on topics for your curriculum.

Examine each sample cluster for (1) quality literature, (2) a genre blend, (3) an interdisciplinary focus, and (4) narrative, expository, and poetic perspectives. Determine a core book with personal appeal that will initiate interest in the topic. Distinguish between teacher read-alouds and independent reading titles. Connect appropriate books to both spontaneous and teacher-initiated response-based activities. Supplement additional titles that instinctively come to mind. Appreciate the high-quality literature and the blended perspective of the literature cluster itself. Imagine and match reader response to individual titles as well as to the total package of literature. Consider teacher enthusiasm in sharing these titles as an introduction to a curricular theme. Finally, celebrate the connectedness of learning created by quality literature across literary genres that captures blended voices on a topic.

The three literature clusters included in this chapter provide a model for blending literature on a single theme across literary genres. Spreading the topic of trees across disciplines is the goal of "The Life and Legend of Trees" (Figure 14.3). At a more abstract level, "Journeys Within and Apart" (Figure 14.4) creatively explores a broad view of journeys of animals, people, and those that occur within ourselves. A "Cultural Study: The Middle East" (Figure 14.5) focuses on the history, geography, social structure, legends, and religion of this little-known but newsworthy part of the

FIGURE 14.3   Literature Cluster: The life and legend of trees

Arnosky, Jim (1992). *Crinkleroot's guide to knowing the trees.* New York: Bradbury. INFORMATIONAL
    Crinkleroot teaches the reader to identify trees, determine their age, and respect them as homes
    for animals.

DePalmo, Mary Newell (2005). *A grand old tree.* New York: Arthur A. Levine/*Scholastic.* PICTURE BOOK
    Documents the life of a tree and all it gives humanity.

Gibbons, Gail (2002). *Tell me tree: All about trees for kids.* Boston: Little, Brown. INFORMATIONAL
    A visual display of basic information about trees told through text, illustrations, sidebar information,
    and labeled diagrams.

Levine, Ellen (1995). *The tree that would not die.* Illus. by Ted Rand. New York: Scholastic.
    HISTORICAL FICTION
    The Treaty Oak of Austin, Texas, tells America's history through its own voice during its 400-year life span.

Levy, Constance (1994). *A tree place and other poems.* Illus. by R. Sabuda. New York: McElderry
    Books. POETRY
    Forty small poems celebrate nature from inchworms and cicadas to forests and volcanoes.

Locke, Deborah (2004). *Forest.* New York: DK Publishing. INFORMATIONAL
    Introductory characteristics of forests around the world, the plants and animals that populate them,
    and their endangerment.

Locker, Thomas, & Candace Christiansen (1995). *Sky tree: Seeing science through art.* Illus. by
    T. Locker. New York: HarperCollins. PICTURE BOOK
    Locker's luminous paintings ask readers to consider a tree's seasonal changes from an artist's
    perspective.

Lyon, George Ella (1989). *A B Cedar: An alphabet of trees.* Illus. by Tom Parker. New York: Orchard
    Books. ABC CLASSIC
    Alphabet book introducing leaves and tree identification and classification.

Miller, Debbie S. (2002). *Are trees alive?* Illus. by Stacey Schuett. New York: Walker & Company.
    INFORMATIONAL
    An introduction to trees that compares parts of a tree to parts of a human body with illustrations
    and brief descriptions of trees found around the world.

Montgomery, Sy (2006). *Quest for the tree kangaroo: An expedition in the Cloud Forest of New Guinea.*
    Photographs by Nic Bishop. Boston: Houghton Mifflin. INFORMATIONAL
    A scientific journey that showcases the search for this little-known marsupial in this isolated paradise.

Pringle, Laurence (1994). *Fire in the forest: A cycle of growth and renewal.* Paintings by B. Marstall.
    New York: Atheneum. INFORMATIONAL
    Fire is a friend to the forest as it recycles organic matter, provides new food sources for wildlife,
    and clears the way for a new generation of trees and plants. View a forested landscape before,
    during, and after a fire.

Rex, Adam (2006). *Tree-ring circus.* San Diego: Harcourt. PICTURE BOOK
    Cumulative tale in which a tree becomes a hiding place for animals, a runaway clown, and even an
    elephant.

Van Laan, Nancy (1998). *The magic bean tree: A legend from Argentina.* Illus. by Beatriz Vidal. Boston:
    Houghton Mifflin. FOLKTALE
    A young Quechuan boy sets out on his own to bring the rains back to his parched homeland and is
    rewarded by a gift of carob beans that come to be prized across Argentina.

Yarbrough, Camille (1996). *The little tree growin' in the shade.* Illus. by T. Geter. New York: Putnam.
    MULTICULTURAL
    The Tree of Life grew in Africa, but a branch was broken off when millions of Africans were
    captured and brought as slaves to America. That branch took root and grew into a little tree
    nourished by the richness of the culture the people had brought with them. Spirituals and oral
    tradition bring this culture to the reader.

FIGURE 14.4 Literature Cluster: Journeys within and apart

Balgassi, Haemi (1996). *Peacebound trains.* Illus. by Chris K. Soentpiet. Boston: Clarion. HISTORICAL FICTION/MULTICULTURAL
   Poetic language and exquisite paintings evoke the people who fled Korea and a special grandmother and granddaughter relationship.

Bunting, Eve (1996). *Train to somewhere.* Illus. by Ron Himler. Boston: Clarion. HISTORICAL FICTION
   The story of the Orphan Train told by Marianne, one of a group of 14 children journeying from New York across the Midwest in 1878. Marianne is the one nobody wants but she is finally adopted by an elderly couple.

Cunningham, David (1996). *A crow's journey.* Morton Grove, IL: Albert Whitman. POETRY
   Where does the mountain snow go in spring? Through the journey of a crow, we follow the melted water from stream to waterfall, through a trout pool and a meadow, until it meets the sea.

Fisher Staples, Suzanne (1996). *Dangerous skies.* New York: Farrar, Straus & Giroux. REALISTIC FICTION
   This journey of friendship between a white boy and a black girl leads to murder, betrayal, and breaks the reader's heart as it confronts issues of racism and hypocrisy that continue to plague our country.

Fleischman, Paul (1996/2006). *Dateline: Troy.* Collages by G. Frankfeldt and G. Morrow. Cambridge, MA: Candlewick Press. INFORMATIONAL
   The author juxtaposes his compelling retelling of the Trojan War with newspaper clippings of modern events from World War I to the Gulf War. *The Trojan War is still being fought. Simply open a newspaper. . . .*

Friedman, D. Dina (2006). *Escaping into the night.* New York: Simon & Schuster. HISTORICAL FICTION Holina Rudowsk journeys from her Polish ghetto to a secret underground forest encampment in the woods, saving several thousands of Jews from the Nazis.

Hunt, Jonathan (1996). *Leif's saga: A viking tale.* New York: Simon & Schuster. FOLKTALE
   Based on the Icelandic oral histories of Leif Ericksson, this tale tells of gripping challenges, lost dreams, and renewed hope. Illustrations are filled with historical detail, costumes, geography, and architecture.

Lasky, Kathryn (2000). *The journal of Augustus Pelletier: The Lewis & Clark expedition.* New York: Scholastic. HISTORICAL FICTION
   A fictional journey kept by 12-year-old Augustus Pelletier, the youngest member of Lewis and Clark's Corps of Discovery.

Myers, Laurie (2002). *Lewis and Clark and me: A dog's tale.* Illus. by Michael Dooling. New York: Henry Holt. HISTORICAL FICTION
   Seaman, Meriwether Lewis's Newfoundland dog, describes Lewis and Clark's expedition, which he accompanied from St. Louis to the Pacific Ocean.

Nye, Naomi Shahib (2000). *Come with me: Poems for a journey.* Illus. by Dan Yaccarino. New York: Greenwillow. POETRY
   A collection of poems including "Secrets," "When You Come to a Corner," and "Come With Me."

Rupp, Rebecca (2006). *Journey to the blue moon (in which time is lost and then found again).* Cambridge, MA: Candlewick. FANTASY
   A chance encounter with a mysterious lady leads to a spaceship ride to the full Blue Moon, a world where all lost items go, awaiting to be found.

Waldman, Neil (2006). *Out of the shadows; An artist's journey.* Honesdale, PA: Boyds Mills Press. AUTOBIOGRAPHY
   A treasure book from a Russian art museum springboards the journey for four children who survived a turbulent childhood, yet grew up to be renowned artists, writers, and teachers.

FIGURE 14.4 Continued

Webb, Sophie (2004). *Looking for seabirds: Journal from an Alaskan voyage*. Boston: Houghton Mifflin. INFORMATIONAL
> The diary of a journey in search of seabirds contains written observations and detailed sketches of a variety of Aleutian seabirds, vulnerable to disturbances in ocean ecology.

Wulf, Linda Press (2006). *The night of the burning: Devorah's story*. New York: Farrar, Straus & Giroux. HISTORICAL FICTION
> Devorah and her sister, Neshama, are the sole survivors of a post–World War II attack on their Polish village. They take a long journey as orphans to the safety of Cape Jewish Orphanage in South Africa where they learn to be happy again.

Yolen, Jane (2004). *The perfect wizard: Hans Christian Andersen*. Illus. by Dennis Nolan. New York: Dutton. BIOGRAPHY
> The lifelong journey of the great fairy tale writer whose self-doubt and insecurities traveled with him through a lifetime of writing that reflected his own life's experiences.

FIGURE 14.5 Literature Cluster: Cultural study of the Middle East

Cultural Study: The Middle East

Ben-Ezer, Ehud (1997). *Hosni the dreamer: An Arabian tale*. Illus. by Uri Schulevitz. New York: Farrar, Straus & Giroux. PICTURE BOOK
> Hosni, a desert shepherd, finally realizes his dream of traveling to the city where he spends his gold dinar in a way that changes his life forever.

Fletcher, Susan (1998). *Shadow spinner*. New York: Atheneum. HISTORICAL FICTION
> Crippled Marjan joins the Sultan's harem in ancient Persia. She gathers stories for Queen Shaharazad to save her life.

Haskins, Jim (1987). *Count your way through the Arab world*. Illus. by Dana Gustafson. Minneapolis, MN: Carolrhoda. INFORMATIONAL
> Arabic numerals from 1 to 10 introduce concepts about Arab countries and culture.

Heide, Florence Parry, & Gilliland, Judith Heide (1998). *The house of wisdom*. Illus. by Mary Grandpre. New York: DK Ink. PICTURE BOOK
> Ishaq, the son of the chief translator to the Caliph of ancient Baghdad, travels the world in search of precious books and manuscripts. He brings them back to the great library known as the House of Wisdom.

Khan, Aisha Karen (2003). *What you will see inside a mosque*. Photos by Aaron Pepis. Woodstock, VT: Skylights Paths Publishing. INFORMATIONAL
> Introduction to the Muslim faith through a visit to a Middle Eastern mosque.

Lewin, Ted (1996). *Market!* New York: Lothrop, Lee & Sheperd. PICTURE BOOK
> Describes the dynamic characteristics of world markets including those in the Middle East.

McCauley, David (2003). *Mosque*. Boston: Houghton Mifflin. INFORMATIONAL
> Methods and materials used to design and construct a mosque in the late 16th century in Turkey. Through a fictional story, readers learn how these monumental structures are built and how they function within the society they serve.

Napoli, Donna Jo (2000). *Beast*. New York: Atheneum. FOLKTALE
> Elaboration on the table of Beauty and the Beast told from the point of view of the beast and set in Persia.

(continued)

FIGURE 14.5 Continued

Nye, Naomi Shahib (1997). *Habibi.* New York: Simon & Schuster. REALISTIC FICTION
Lyzanne Abboud, her younger brother, and parents move from St. Louis to a new home between Jerusalem and Palestine to the village where her father was born. They face many changes and must deal with the tensions between Jews and Palestinians.

Orlev, Uri (1991). *The man from the other side.* Translated from Hebrew by Hillel Halkin. New York: Houghton Mifflin. REALISTIC FICTION
The relationship of the Israeli/Palestinian characters presented in a quality work of international literature. Recipient of the Mildred Batchelder Award.

Stanley, Diane (2002). *Saladin: Noble prince of Islam.* New York: HarperCollins. BIOGRAPHY
The story of the heroic 12th-century ruler with a focus on the geographical, historical, and religious issues still at the root of today's conflicts. Glorious paintings mirror Islamic artwork.

Staples, Suzanne Fisher (2005). *Under the persimmon tree.* New York: Farrar, Straus & Giroux. REALISTIC FICTION
During the 2001 Afghan War, the lives of Janmal, a young Afghan rebel, and Nusrat, an American Muslim teacher, intersect at a school in Peshawar, Pakistan.

Steele, Philip (2006). *The Middle East.* New York: Kingfisher. INFORMATIONAL
Captures the richness and diversity and the sociological and historical complexities of this region. Religion, resources, history, politics, and current affairs of each country. Includes excellent websites.

Yolen, Jane (1995). *O Jerusalem.* Illus. by John Thompson. New York: Scholastic. POETRY
Poetry written to celebrate the 3,000-year anniversary of the founding of Jerusalem. This holy place for three religions—Judaism, Christianity, and Islam—is enhanced through stirring poetry and evocative paintings.

world. These sample clusters should generate fresh ideas for blending books across genres on a single topic.

BUILDING THEME EXPLORATIONS: A RESPONSE-BASED PROCESS

One of the most effective literature-based techniques for integrating the elementary/middle-level curriculum is through theme explorations. Theme exploration describes a means of organizing instruction around a broad-based theme and connected subthemes rather than around content areas. By teaching through theme exploration, it is possible to integrate instruction, use quality children's literature, and implement response-based activities in a meaningful way across curricular areas.

Theme explorations have gained popularity as the amount of knowledge we seek to disseminate as teachers has become overwhelming. No longer can we teach the entire content curriculum. It appears far more productive to teach the process of exploring quality themes rather than delivering quantified, superficial content area information. Theme explorations are motivating to both teachers and students because they encourage the pursuit of ideas more thoroughly to develop a deeper, rather than a broader, understanding. Their connectedness results in students developing an awareness of relationships among, between, and across ideas. The relevance of the relationship of learning across disciplines offers an added dimension to learning (Shanahan, Robinson, & Schneider, 1995).

The term *theme exploration* (Weaver et al., 1993) must be differentiated from the more traditional meaning of "thematic units." Theme explorations move beyond topic coverage to dynamic ideals. For example, food may be a topic, but the role of food as a contributor to quality of life in our global society is a theme. With traditional primary-level topics (penguins, bears, apples, friendship) the curriculum is unnaturally stretched to allow content area activities related to each content area. In doing so, content areas that do not realistically connect are forced to work. Theme explorations, however, allow for a deeper examination of ideas and ideals through quality literature that encourages response and thinking at higher levels. For example, the adaptation of animals to climate is a broader-based theme that encompasses penguins and polar bears.

Theme explorations even raise the possibility of new ideas being introduced to students that are not even considered in a traditional isolated subject curriculum. If content areas don't fit, there is no mandate to include them as part of the theme exploration. Arrangements can be made for pursuing them independently of the theme. In teachers' zeal to pull all content areas together, we often overdo and create more irrelevant connections than intellectual gain. Theme exploration provides the flexibility and freedom to bring more intellectually stimulating ideas, meaningful literature, and related response-based activities to interdisciplinary instruction.

The process of constructing a theme exploration consists of six major steps:

1. Choosing a broad-based theme
2. Brainstorming related children's literature
3. Locating additional children's literature
4. Creating a graphic web reflecting connectedness between main theme and related subthemes
5. Planning literature-based response activities designed for whole-class, small group, and individual learning
6. Sharing the theme exploration in the classroom

Looking at each step in detail assists us in the design, planning, and implementation of classroom theme explorations. Personal reflections during the evolution of the author's theme exploration should assist readers with insights into the theme exploration process as well as the final instructional product. "Tracing the Fabric of Our Nation Through Story," interspersed throughout the following discussion, provides a model theme exploration. Refer to the graphic organizer (Figure 14.6), the bibliography (Figure 14.7) and the response-based activities (Figure 14.8) as you internalize the process of creating an interdisciplinary themed exploration.

Choosing a Theme

Choosing a theme is the first and unquestionably the most important step in theme exploration. Choosing a broad theme, an innovative question, or a motivating issue can make the difference between a mediocre and a powerful theme exploration. The theme must be broad enough to incorporate several trade book genres and response-based activities but not so broad as to lose the connectedness between elements or subthemes. Because choice is considered an aspect of response, teachers must open

Tracing the Fabric of Our Nation Through Story

A Theme Exploration of Immigration in America: Past and Present

Immigrant Children: Alone and Apart

A Coal Miner's Bride: The Diary of Anetka Kaminska (Bartoletti)
Dear America Series
Wildflower Girl (Conlon-McKenna)
Read-aloud/Irish immigration/great famine
Immigrant Kids (Freedman)
Compare/contrast lives of children then/now
Kids at Work (Freedman)
Write stories from photographs/discuss issue of children's rights
Letters from Rifka (Hesse)
Class set/literature response journal
Dear Emma (Hurwitz)
Hannah's journal: The story of an immigrant girl (Moss)

The New Immigrants: 1965–Present

Voices from the fields: Children of migrant farm workers tell their stories (Atkin)
Informational
Friends from the Other Side (Anzaldua)
Discussion of illegal immigrants as people
A Day's Work (Bunting)
Read-aloud/discuss immigrant work ethic
The Lotus Seed (Garland)
The color of home. (Hoffman)
Picture book
Who Belongs Here? An American Story (Knight)
Discussion of current immigration issues/locate the new immigrant's homelands on a map
Invite a Vietnamese immigrant to speak to the class
Breaking through (Jiminez)
Biography
My Chinatown: One year in poems (Mak)
Poetry
A step from heaven (Na)
Realistic fiction
Lights on the River (Resh)
Research migrant workers' role in your state
Any small goodness: A novel of the barrio (Johnston)
Realistic fiction

Voices of Grandparents: Stories to Be Remembered

How I Became an American (Gundisch)
Was Dreaming to Come to America (Lawlor)
Oral history/readers the atre
The Always Prayer Shawl (Oberman)
Ethnic traditions in America
New Hope (Sorenson)
Storytelling
My Grandmother's Journey (Cech)
Grandfather's Journey (Say)
Stories from grandparents/oral history

The Reluctant Immigrants: African Americans and Slave Trade

Door of No Return (Barboza)
Study of those who came to America against their own will. Issues/history/impact
The Slave Dancer (Fox)
Read-aloud/literature response journal
Many Thousand Gone (Hamilton)
Read-aloud reflections/discussion of forced slavery and cruelty
No More! Stories and Songs of Slave Resistance (Rappaport)

Ellis Island: The Refuge of Our Teeming Shore (1840–1910)

Ellis Island: Gateway to the World (Fisher)
Nonfiction read-aloud to open theme exploration
Ellis Island: New Hope in a New Land (Jacobs)
Research and statistics on immigration process
An Ellis Island Christmas (Leighton)
Reflections: Christmas away from home
If Your Name Was Changed at Ellis Island (Levine)
Research on your own heritage
Land of Hope (Ellis Island Series)
Literature response journal
Sarah, Also Known as Hannah (Ross)
Immigration papers/prepare graphs and charts

The War Immigrants: Victims of Prejudice (1917–1950s)

Leaving for America (Bresnick-Perry)
Connect to own experience—moving
Molly's Pilgrim/Make a Wish Molly (Cohen)
Diversity at school—personal connections
I Am an American (Stanley)
Discuss issue of Japanese internment
The Bracelet (Uchida)
Read-aloud about Japanese internment
Tales from Gold Mountain (Yee)
Discussion of prejudice/cultural differences
The Star Fisher (Yep)
Literature response/grand conversation

Across America: Immigrants in Quest of a New Home

The Orphan Trains (Fry)
Research on the trains through the Plains states
Charlotte's Rose (Cannon)
The Morning Chair (Joosse)
Favorite possessions/writing extension
Across America on an Emigrant Train (Murphy)
Map the 3,000-mile trip across the continent
Clouds of Terror (Welch)
Text for reluctant readers
Klara's New World (Winter)
Family traditions from the Old World

FIGURE 14.6 Theme exploration graphic organizer for immigration

FIGURE 14.7   Theme exploration: Immigration

Enhanced bibliography of children's books:
Tracing the Fabric of Our Nation Through Story

Ellis Island: The Refuge of our Teeming Shore (1840–1910)

Avi (2002). *Silent movie.* Illus. by C. B. Mordan. New York: Atheneum. [I]

Bartone, Elisa (1993). *Peppe the lamplighter.* Illus. by Ted Lewin. New York: Lothrop, Lee & Shepard. [P/I]

Bial, Raymond (2002) *Tenement: Immigrant life on the Lower East Side.* Boston: Houghton Mifflin. [I]

Hopkinson, Deborah (2003). *Shutting out the sky: Life in the tenements of New York, 1880–1924.* New York: Orchard. [I]

Leighton, Maxinne Rhea (1992). *An Ellis Island Christmas.* Illus. by Dennis Nolan. New York: Viking. [P/I]

Levine, Ellen (1992). *If your name was changed at Ellis Island.* Illus. by W. Parmenter. New York: Scholastic. [I]

Nixon, Joan Lowery (1994). *Land of dreams.* (Ellis Island series). New York: Delacorte Press. [I/M]
Also see: *Land of promise* (Irish) and *Land of hope* (Russian)

Ross, Lillian Hammer (1994). *Sarah, also known as Hannah.* Illus. by H. Cogancherry. Morton Grove, IL: Whitman. [I]

Sandler, Martin W. (2004). *Island of hope: The story of Ellis Island and the journey to America.* New York: Scholastic. [I/M]

Across America: Immigrants in Quest of a New Home

Cannon, Ann Edwards (2002). *Charlotte's Rose.* New York: Wendy Lamb Books. [M]

Fry, Annette R. (1994). *The orphan trains* (American Event series). New York: Macmillan. [I/M]

Glaser, Linda (2005). *Bridge to America: Based on a true story.* Boston: Houghton Mifflin. [I/M]

Joosse, Barbara M. (1995). *The morning chair.* Illus. by M. Sewall. Boston: Clarion. [P]

Murphy, Jim (1993). *Across America on an emigrant train.* Boston: Clarion. [I/M]

Sandler, Martin W. (1995). *Immigrants: A Library of Congress book.* Photos. New York: HarperCollins. [I/M]

Winter, Jeanette (1992). *Klara's new world.* New York: Knopf. [P/I]

Immigrant Children: Alone and Apart

Bartoletti, Susan Campbell (2000). *A coal miner's bride: The diary of Anetka Kaminska* (Dear America series). New York: Scholastic. [I]

Brown, Don (2003). *Kid Blink beats the world.* New York: Roaring Brook. [P/I]

Freedman, Russell (1980). *Immigrant kids.* Illus. with photographs. New York: E. P. Dutton. [I/M]

Freedman, Russell (1994). *Kids at work: Lewis Hine and the crusade against child labor.* Boston: Clarion. [I/M]

Hesse, Karen (1992). *Letters from Rifka.* New York: Holt. [I/M]

Lee, Milly (2006). *Landed.* New York: Farrar, Straus & Giroux. [P/I]

Moss, Marissa (2000). *Hannah's journal: The story of an immigrant girl.* San Diego: Harcourt Brace. [I]

Napoli, Donna Jo (2005). *The king of Mulberry Street.* New York: Wendy Lamb. [I/M]

Paterson, Katherine (2006). *Bread and roses, too.* New York: Clarion. [I/M]

Steig, William (2003). *When everybody wore a hat.* New York: HarperCollins. [P]

(continued)

FIGURE 14.7   Continued

Voices of Our Grandparents: Stories to Be Remembered

Cech, John (1991). *My grandmother's journey.* Illus. by S. McGinley-Nally. New York: Bradbury. [P/I]

Gundisch, Karin (2001). *How I became an American.* Chicago, IL: Cricket Books. [I]

Lawlor, Veronica (1995). *I was dreaming to come to America.* New York: Viking. [I/M]

Oberman, Sheldon (1994). *The always prayer shawl.* Illus. by Ted Lewin. Honesdale, PA: Boyds Mills Press. [P/I]

Recorvits, Helen (2006). *Yoon and the Christmas mitten.* Illus. by Gabi Swiatkowska. New York: Farrar, Straus & Giroux. [P/I]

Say, Allen (1993). *Grandfather's journey.* Boston: Houghton Mifflin. Caldecott Medal 1994. [P/I]

Sorenson, Henri (1995). *New Hope.* Illus. by Ted Lewin. New York: Lothrop, Lee & Shepard. [P/I]

The War Immigrants: Victims of Prejudice (1917–1950s)

Bresnick-Perry, Roslyn (1992). *Leaving for America.* Illus. by Mira Reisberg. Emeryville, CA: Children's Book Press. [P/I]

Cohen, Barbara (1983). *Molly's pilgrim.* Illus. by M. Deraney. New York: Lothrop, Lee & Shepard. [P]

Cohen, Barbara (1994). *Make a wish, Molly.* Illus. by Jan Naimo Jones. New York: Doubleday. [P]

Stanley, Jerry (1994). *I am an American: A true story of Japanese internment.* Illus. with photos. New York: Crown. [I/M]

Uchida, Yoshiko (1994). *The bracelet.* New York: Putnam. [I]

Yee, Paul (1989). *Tales from Gold Mountain: Stories of the Chinese in the New World.* New York: Macmillan [I/M]

The New Immigrants: Mexico, Central America, South Korea, China, and the Middle East (1965–Present)

Anzaldua, Gloria (1993). *Friends from the other side.* Illus. by Consuelo Mendez. Emeryville, CA: Children's Book Press. [I]

Atkin, S. Beth (1993). *Voices from the fields: Children of migrant farm workers tell their stories.* Boston: Little, Brown. [M]

Bunting, Eve (1988). *How many days to America? A Thanksgiving story.* Boston: Clarion. [P/I]

Bunting, Eve (1994). *A day's work.* Illus. by R. Himler. Boston: Clarion. [P/I]

Bunting, Eve (2006). *One green apple.* Illus. by Ted Lewin. New York: Clarion. [P/I]

Carlson, Lori M (Ed.) (1994). *Cool salsa: Bilingual poems on growing up Latino in the United States.* New York: Fawcett. [M]

Hoffman, Mary (2002). *The color of home.* New York: Phyllis Fogelman/Penguin Putnam. [P]

Jimenez, Francisco (2001). *Breaking through.* New York: Houghton Mifflin. [M]

Johnston, Tony (2001). *Any small goodness: A novel of the barrio.* New York: Scholastic. [I/M]

Mak, Kam (2002). *My Chinatown: One year in poems.* New York:HarperCollins. [P/I]

Na, An (2001). *A step from heaven.* Asheville, NC:Front Street. [M]

Resh, Jane (1994). *Lights on the river.* Illus. by M. Dooling. New York: Hyperion. [P/I]

The Reluctant Immigrants: African Americans and the Slave Trade

Barboza, Steven (1994). *Door of no return: The legend of Goree Island.* Photos. New York: Cobble-hill/Dutton. [I/M]

(continued)

FIGURE 14.7   Continued

Fox, Paula (1973). *The slave dancer.* New York: Bradbury. [I/M]

Hamilton, Virginia (1993). *Many thousand gone: African Americans from slavery to freedom.* New York: Knopf. [I/M]

Rappaport, Doreen (2002). *No more! Stories and songs of slave resistance.* Illus. by Shane W. Evans. Cambridge, MA: Candlewick Press. [I/M]

Rappaport, Doreen (2003). *Free at last: Stories and songs of emancipation.* Illus. by Shane W. Evans. Cambridge, MA: Candlewick. [I/M]

Celebrating the Fabric of our Nation: Reflective Thoughts

Gunning, Monica (2004). *America, my new home: Poems.* Illus. by Ken Condon. Honesdale, PA: Boyds Mills Press. [I]

Hamanaka, Sheila (1994). *All the colors of the earth.* New York: Morrow. [P]

Hoobler, Dorothy, & Hoobler, Thomas (2003). *We are Americans: Voices of the immigrant experience.* New York: Scholastic. [I/M]

Hopkins, Lee Bennett (Compiler) (1994). Hand in hand: An American history through poetry. Illus. by Peter Fiore. New York: Simon & Schuster. [P/I/M]

Testa, Maria. (2005). *Something about America.* Cambridge, MA: Candlewick. [I]

Whipple, Laura (Compiler) (1994). *Celebrating America: A collection of poems and images of the American spirit.* In association with the Art Institute of Chicago. New York: Philomel Books. [P/I/M]

possibilities for choosing themes to students. Their apparent interest and motivation can influence the selection and direction the theme exploration takes. Theme explorations may spring from curricular topics but are handled in a more creative mode than textbook delivery of instruction. A few examples of theme exploration titles such as "That Was Then/ This Is Now: Exploring Change," "It's a Jungle Out There," "The Road to Freedom," and "Making a Difference" provide sound examples of the various types of thematic journeys on which students and teachers might embark.

The reading of Karen Hesse's Letters from Rifka brought back nostalgic recollections of my own grandparents who came to America from Czechoslovakia and Germany through Ellis Island. Thoughts of a theme exploration on immigration grew but were limited by my own narrow perspective on European immigration. As I began to talk to colleagues and children and explore existing literature about this theme, broadening possibilities came to mind. What about the new wave of immigrants? What about the unwelcomed reaction to Japanese immigrants during World War II? What about those immigrants who journeyed across the prairies of America to the West? My narrow focus of immigration began to grow, and I felt energized as the prospect of locating literature and designing instruction from that literature seemed possible. After countless attempts at theme titles, "Tracing the Fabric of Our Nation Through Story" was born as a theme exploration title that inspired, directed, connected, and broadened the topic of immigration.

FIGURE 14.8   Theme exploration response activities

Suggested Activities:

Tracing the Fabric of Our Nation Through Story

Individual

Keep a literature response journal as you read one of the many chapter books on immigrants (e.g., *Letters from Rifka,* Ellis Island series). Share your innermost thoughts and feelings about leaving a homeland, family, and friends to come to a new life in America.

Keep a character journal—a first-person account of coming to America—while reading *Wildflower Girl.* Write from the point of view of Peggy as she leaves Ireland, travels on a coffin ship, arrives alone in Boston, and obtains a job as a domestic helper. Include the feelings and thoughts going through her/your mind as her tale unfolds.

Collect photographs from your own family history. Interview family members about the photos and tape-record the interview. Use your notes in compiling a fact-based story to accompany the photograph.

Write a poem that reflects the feelings and thoughts of immigrants about leaving their homeland and coming to a strange, new world in America—either in the past or today.

Small Group

Use oral storytelling to present books told through the voices of grandparents who tell their stories of immigration and finding a home in America, i.e., *New Hope, In America, The Always Prayer Shawl.*

Use a readers' theater format to present dramatic readings from *I Was Dreaming to Come to America.* Let the book spark an interest in oral history and the worthy task of documenting history through first-hand accounts.

Read *Friends from the Other Side* in both English and Spanish. Discuss the issue of illegal immigration.

Research one of the many European ethnic groups that came to America through Ellis Island (i.e., Irish, German, Russians, Scandinavians). Discover why they left, when they came, where they settled, and what their ethnic group has added to the fabric of our nation. Record any statistics you might find on a class chart.

Research the plight of immigrant children, both in the cities and those who traveled west on the orphan trains. Compare/contrast life of children today with life of early immigrant children.

Research one of the "new immigrants" from Vietnam, Cambodia, Korea, Mexico, or the Caribbean. Discover why they left, when they came, where they settled, and what their ethnic group adds to the fabric of our nation.

Investigate immigration laws from 1840–1910 and compare them with today's immigration laws. What changes have taken place? Why? Why do we have so many "illegal aliens" today? What should we do in our country to address this issue?

Research migrant workers' role in America. Read *A Day's Work* and *Lights on the River* to demonstrate the work ethic of the new immigrant.

Conduct a "grand conversation" on the books you have been reading about immigration. What are some consistent facts that keep reappearing? What have you learned that you didn't know before? What questions still need to be answered?

Whole Class

Read *Who Belongs Here? An American Story* as an introduction to the issues surrounding immigration. Use the questions in the text to spark discussion.

FIGURE 14.8 Continued

> Invite a person from the community to the classroom to discuss their own (or their parents') immigration to America. Brainstorm a list of questions prior to their presentation. Write a thank-you note for their time and sharing.
>
> Compile and laminate a class scrapbook of immigration photographs and written stories from members of the class.
>
> Celebrate an ethnic cooking day with food from your own culture—German, Hispanic, English, Irish, Scandinavian, etc. Share group reports on each ethnic group and share the wonderful culinary delights as a culminating theme activity.
>
> Make a "quilt" that depicts the many pieces of America that are bound together by the common thread of immigration—America as the land of opportunity and an appreciation of the cultures that make up the fabric of our nation.

Brainstorming and Locating Literature

Literature is a major factor in the direction and scope of the theme. This step is often the most invigorating part of the planning stage for the theme exploration because it does involve the heartbeat of the theme exploration—children's literature. The goal is to locate literature across all literary genres: picture books, traditional/folktales, informational books, historical fiction, biography/autobiography, poetry, realistic fiction, fantasy, and multicultural literature. Although connections to some genres dominate, time and persistence will allow meaningful books from almost all genres to be highlighted for the theme. Don't be too discerning when choosing a preliminary selection of related books. Brainstorm as many titles as you can. Meet with a multiage group of teachers and get input from titles they deem appropriate. Consult with the library/media center director. Ask the children what books come to mind. This initial brainstorming opens the mind to possibilities for connected subthemes and also honors related literature. The initial inclusion of a particular book title or a series of books may actually shape the theme.

This stage must be open minded and open ended. Too often we limit our scope by following traditional connections to themes. Avoid going to the card catalog, the bookshelves, or the computer subject guide initially. Let the collaborative effort of colleagues and children stretch the possibilities that energize the theme exploration.

I began with those titles that were foremost in my mind—titles I had just read, recently seen in bookstores, or read reviews about. I looked to old favorites that had always provided the core of study on this topic. I was reinspired by Emma Lazarus's poetic inscription on the Statue of Liberty and shed a tear as I really looked at photographs in Russell Freedman's Immigrant Kids *for the first time. The local librarian suggested Jerry Stanley's* I Am an American *and a colleague shared a copy of Eve Bunting's* A Day's Work. *Suddenly the theme exploration was bigger than European immigration; it expanded to include Japanese Americans and the new wave of immigrants from Mexico and*

Southeast Asia. I was overwhelmed by where this simple theme could take us, but comforted by the fact that the literature was plentiful, of high quality, and accessible.

Locating Additional Literature

After the initial bookstorming session, library and literature resources should be consulted to extend the related theme literature. Expand the scope and criteria to include both new books as well as classic titles that might contain related information and a desirable style of delivery. Consult the following resources as your literary repertoire continues to grow:

- School district online catalog
- Public library online catalog
- *Subject Guide to Books in Print* (use subject descriptors suggested in other books on the topic)
- *Book Links* (American Library Association), www.ala.org/ BookLinks
- Bookstore websites: www.amazon.com or www.barnesandnoble.com

Continue to keep in mind the priority of locating a blend of all literary genres. Surprisingly, poetry does exist on the designated theme, and biographies span the disciplines. Continue to search until the possibilities slow and connections become stretched instead of meaningful. At this point, the theme exploration collection might number between 50 and 100 books. Although all of these may not provide a primary focus for your theme, many can be used for related independent research and reading by your students.

Time flew by as I sat in front of the library computer screen plugging in descriptors from books I had located. New entries brought new titles and new possibilities for subthemes. I pulled up titles related to grandparents and westward movement. The orphan trains and Mexican Americans elicited many new titles. Several issues of Book Links *provided additional listings of related literature. I was amazed that biography, poetry, and picture books had effectively invaded a theme I was sure was dominated by historical fiction. I located, recalled, and eventually handled over 70 books that showed promise for read-alouds, independent reading selections, research, and response.*

Absorbing the Literature

Read, enjoy, savor, learn, connect, grow, and design your theme exploration from the literature itself. Although reading all of the books is impossible, begin to identify books by genre, to locate possible read-alouds, to devise tentative response-based activities, and to sort and clarify the direction of the theme. Inherent connections between and among titles will become apparent. Spread the books out on a table or floor and begin to organize them in a meaningful way. Move them around, eliminate some, add others, but remain open minded and let the literature direct thought and evolving subthemes. Do a quick check of literary genres. Don't force books to fit the theme, but attempt to include at least six genres in your theme exploration. In this preliminary immersion stage, the teacher is actually responding to literature by creatively linking and extending the theme to related subthemes. Connecting book titles, planning innovative response activities, and reading the literature are all fertile soil for teachers' personal responses. Reread this chapter's opening reflection to recapture the process of organizing the literature into meaningful subthemes. Focus on the immigration bibliography to internalize this process (see Figure 14.7).

Creating a Visual Image of the Theme Exploration

With all of the literature surrounding the theme, the need for a graphic organizer is apparent. To get the webbing process started, sort the literature into four to six related subthemes. Bring in a colleague or a few students to prevent you from being locked into traditional modes. As connections become apparent, books will be linked in related subtheme categories and new connections will begin to emerge.

As the graphic organizer begins to take shape, focus more definitely on potential response-based activities with particular books. Designate a core book and related activity as a springboard for the exploration. Consider a class set of a chapter book title for a reading workshop. Note the potential of informational titles for independent research topics and presentations. Identify possible titles for drama, art, and musical extensions.

The graphic organizer is intended to be an extended theme exploration lesson plan. When complete, it will contain the creative title of the theme exploration, motivating titles of four to six meaningfully related subthemes, lists of literature related to those subthemes, and response-based activities related to particular pieces of literature. In viewing the graphic organizer, innovative organization, motivating presentation, quality literature, and meaningful literature-based activities are apparent (see Figure 14.8). Books span at least six literary genres, so fictional, factual, and poetic perspectives on the theme are present. Interdisciplinary presentation of the thematic focus becomes clearer and teacher confidence in the planning is evident. Teachers might choose to share the graphic organizer with each student (bulletin board or handout) so they can visualize the connectedness of subthemes to the main theme. Many teachers also like to include students in the theme planning at this stage. Children see the connections in learning differently than adults and often provide important input at this point in the theme exploration planning.

This next step seemed to flow naturally from the piles that lay before me. The books themselves formed a graphic web. My task was simply to transfer the breadth of this theme to a graphic representation on paper. The titling of subthemes came surprisingly swiftly, and a reaffirmation of books across many literary genres was reassuring. Stirrings of response-based connections soared in my mind and it was difficult to pick up a book without thinking of a meaningful response connection. Many informational titles begged to be researched, and a few promised dramatic presentation. Although a lack of personal adeptness with the word processor slowed the visual image of the web, the relatedness of the literature to the theme and the connectedness of the subthemes were continuously and emphatically present.

Response-Based Connections to Literature

Finalizing the response-based connections to literature is an important part of the process. Although gathering and organizing the literature is crucial to the success of the theme exploration, the response-based connections will provide the literacy base to this unique delivery of instruction. A mixture of whole-class, small group, and individual response activities should be devised (see Figure 14.8). The response modes should be varied and include some listening to read-alouds, some oral prompting or free discussion, personal written response, and some interactive art, music, or performance activities. Special attention should be given to the opening literature and response because it provides the motivation and inquiry for the entire theme exploration. The culminating activity and final sharing of literature is of equal import because it serves to synthesize, connect, and evaluate the thinking and learning as a result of the theme exploration. This response-based focus to the theme exploration can include research, the writing of mathematical problems, hands-on science, or oral history interviews. The interdisciplinary strength of the theme exploration must be utilized and the response possibilities across disciplines must be explored.

Aside from reveling in the literature, I admit to thoroughly enjoying planning the response-based connections to literature. Mandatory was a literature response journal to Karen Hesse's Letters from Rifka *(4th–5th grade) or Katherine Paterson's* Bread and Roses, Too *(6th–8th grade). Hadn't that book enthralled me as I completed it in a single reading session? A grand conversation on* We Are Americans: Voices of the Immigrant Experience *was likely to initiate personal connections and experiences for students. Sandler's* Island of Hope: The Story of Ellis Island and the Journey to America *presented an informational read-aloud with facts and photos to open our minds and hearts to immigrants. A dramatic reenactment of Lee's* Landed *and a readers' theater from the words of immigrants and their families in Lawlor's* I Was Dreaming to Come to America *inspired me and the evolving exploration. They were not stretches; they were meaningful response options created by themed literature. They would connect the students aesthetically in a relevant way to the message and ideals of this theme exploration.*

Sharing the Theme Exploration with Children

The apex of gathering, reading, inventing, and planning is the actual implementation of the theme exploration in the classroom. Theme explorations can be pursued throughout the entire school day, but they are most often shared in half-day formats with the other half day being used for supplemental instruction that does not meaningfully fit the theme. Mini-portfolios to house theme-related projects, research, and response are useful. Although initial theme explorations may span a two-week period, many experienced teachers see them stretching across a nine-week quarter or, in a few cases, across the entire school year. This type of authentic instruction requires time for planning and accessing materials, but the quality of learning and comprehension justifies the investment (Bergeron & Rudenga, 1996; Soalt, 2005). The joy of this type of teaching comes in the delivery of meaningful instruction through which responses to literature include both an efferent and an aesthetic understanding of a theme or concept. The enjoyment of reading and learning must never be forgotten, especially in an age of accountability where long-term goals are often hidden in the shadow of short-term test gains.

Benefits of Theme Explorations

Literature-based, response-centered theme explorations benefit both teachers and learners as they revitalize instruction and energize the classroom. This interdisciplinary style of teaching and learning scores these tremendous advantages over traditional instruction:

- Teachers are challenged by the opportunity to plan creatively and teach through literature collected on a broad-based theme.
- Teachers gain confidence in teaching the required curriculum through a unique interdisciplinary approach to learning.
- Teachers personally respond to literature through their own creative selection and blending of quality titles related to a broad-based theme.
- Students realize a natural connectedness to learning rather than viewing content as being related to isolated topics.
- Students experience a wide range of literature across genres that connects the factual, fictional, and poetic perspectives on a theme.
- Students experienced genuine, meaningful response-based activities centralized on a theme.
- Students accept the challenge of higher-level thinking and initiate research inquiry into related aspects of the theme.
- Teachers and students become immersed in quality literature across genres that piques their motivation to read, to learn, and to respond.

Figure 14.9 through 14.12 illustrate four models that provide visual and literature cues for creating theme explorations. The graphic organizers contain ideas for theme titles and subthemes and a visual blend of literature across genres, and they are grouped developmentally for sharing with students.

"Whatever the Weather, We'll Weather It Together" (Figure 14.9) explores the wonder of weather across all seasons in a K–1 setting. A typical second-third grade global theme on food is enhanced by "Flavor the World" (Figure 14.10) as food become the topic for fictional and factual investigation of the tastes of the world. Fourth/fifth graders take a literacy journey to the southern states as "Gram, Tell Me More . . ." (Figure 14.11) explores the culture and the history of the South. Sixth, seventh, and eighth graders delight in "The Freedom Struggle" (Figure 14.12) as the historical periods come to life. These graphic organizers and related literature are the authentic efforts of classroom teachers who felt invigorated and challenged by an integrated, literature-based means for delivering interdisciplinary instruction. These

FIGURE 14.9   Theme Exploration: Whatever the Weather, We'll Weather It Together [P]

Whatever the Weather, We'll Weather It Together

What Is Weather?

Cloudy with a Chance of Meatballs (Barrett, 1978)
Pickles to Pittsburgh (Barrett, 1997)
If Frogs Made the Weather (Bauer, 2005)
Weather Words and What They Mean (Gibbons, 1990)
W Is for Wind: A Weather Alphabet (Michaels, 2005)
Weather (Simon, 1993)

Weather Seasoned With Change

The Great Blue House (Banks, 2005)
Leaf Man (Ehlert, 2005)
Wake Up, It's Spring! (Ernst, 2004)
In the Leaves (Lee, 2005)
Summertime Waltz (Payne, 2005)
Mouse's First Spring (Thompson, 2005)
A Child's Calendar (Updike, 1965, 1999)

It's Raining, It's Pouring

Little Cloud (Carle, 1996)
Peach Heaven (Choi, 2004)
The Cloud Book (de Paola, 1975)
And Then It Rained (Dragonwagon, 2003)
Come On, Rain! (Hesse, 1999)
The Puddle (McPhail, 1998)
Big Brown Bear Goes to Town (McPhail, 2006)
The Rain Came Down (Shannon, 2000)
It Looked Like Spilt Milk (Shaw, 1947)
Elsina's Clouds (Winter, 2004)

Don't Know Why There's No Sun Up in the Sky

The Bravest of Us All (Arnold, 2000)
The Story of Lightning and Thunder (Bryan, 1993)
Storms and People (Bundey, 2001)
Aesop's Fables (Kent, 1991)
A House by the River (Miller, 1997)
Thunder Cake (Polacco, 1990)
Walter Was Worried (Seeger, 2005)
When the Wind Bears Go Dancing (Stone, 1997)

Let It Snow, Let It Snow, Let It Snow!

Snow Moon (Brunelle, 2005)
Snow Ponies (Cotten, 2001)
Winter Eyes (Florian, 1999)
Mouse's First Snow (Johnson, 2006)
Snow Sounds (Johnson, 2006)
Snow Family (Kirk, 2000)
The Snowflake Sisters (Lewis, 2003)
Snow (Shulevitz, 1998)
Snow, Snow: Winter Poems for Children
    (Yolen, 1998)

FIGURE 14.10   Theme Exploration: Flavor the World [P/I]

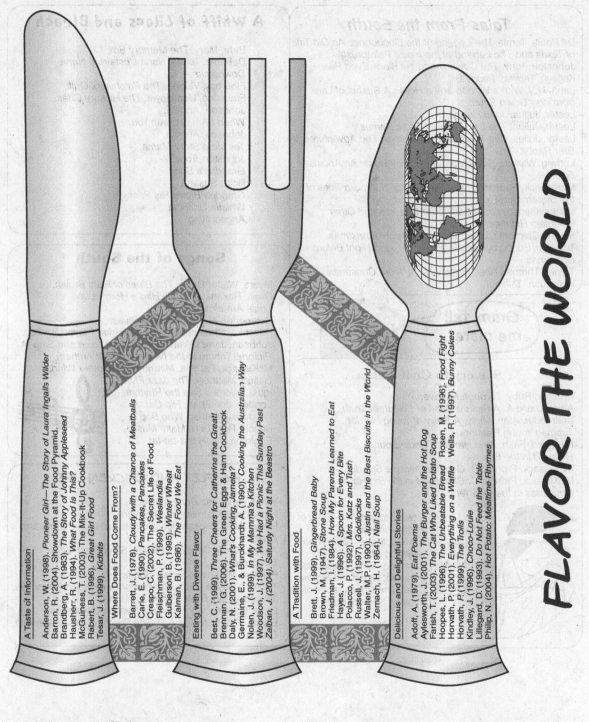

FLAVOR THE WORLD

A Taste of Information

Anderson, W. (1998). *Pioneer Girl—The Story of Laura Ingalls Wilder*
Barron, R. (2004). *Showdown at the Food Pyramid.*
Brandberg, A. (1963). *The Story of Johnny Appleseed*
Hausherr, R. (1994). *What Food Is This?*
McGuiness, T. (2003). *The Mix-It-Up Cookbook*
Rabert, B. (1996). *Great Girl Food*
Tesar, J. (1999). *Kidbits*

Where Does Food Come From?

Barrett, J. (1978). *Cloudy with a Chance of Meatballs*
Carle, E. (1990). *Pancakes, Pancakes*
Crespo, C. (2002). *The Secret Life of Food*
Fleischman, P. (1999). *Weslandia*
Gulberson, B. (1995). *Winter Wheat*
Kalman, B. (1986). *The Food We Eat*

Eating with Diverse Flavor

Best, C. (1999). *Three Cheers for Catherine the Great!*
Brennan, G. (2006). *The Green Eggs & Ham Cookbook*
Daly, N. (2001). *What's Cooking, Jamela?*
Germaine, E., & Burckhardt, A. (1990). *Cooking the Australian Way*
Nolen, J. (1999). *In My Mamma's Kitchen*
Woodson, J. (1997). *We Had a Picnic This Sunday Past*
Zalban, J. (2004). *Saturday Night at the Beastro*

A Tradition with Food

Brett, J. (1999). *Gingerbread Baby*
Brown, M. (1947). *Stone Soup*
Friedman, I. (1984). *How My Parents Learned to Eat*
Hayes, J. (1996). *A Spoon for Every Bite*
Polacco, P. (1992). *Mrs. Katz and Tush*
Russell, J. (1997). *Goldilocks*
Walter, M.P. (1990). *Justin and the Best Biscuits in the World*
Zemach, H. (1964). *Nail Soup*

Delicious and Delightful Stories

Adoff, A. (1979). *Eat Poems*
Aylesworth, J. (2001). *The Burger and the Hot Dog*
Farish, T. (2003). *The Cat Who Liked Potato Soup*
Hoopes, L. (1996). *The Unbeatable Bread*   Rosen, M. (1936). *Food Fight*
Horvath, P. (2001). *Everything on a Waffle*   Wells, R. (1997). *Bunny Cakes*
Horvath, P. (1999). *The Trolls*
Kindley, J. (1996). *Choco-Louie*
Lillegard, D. (1993). *Do Not Feed the Table*
Philip, N. (2004). *Hot Potato: Mealtime Rhymes*

FIGURE 14.11 Theme Exploration: Gram, Tell Me More. . . : Reflections on the South [I]

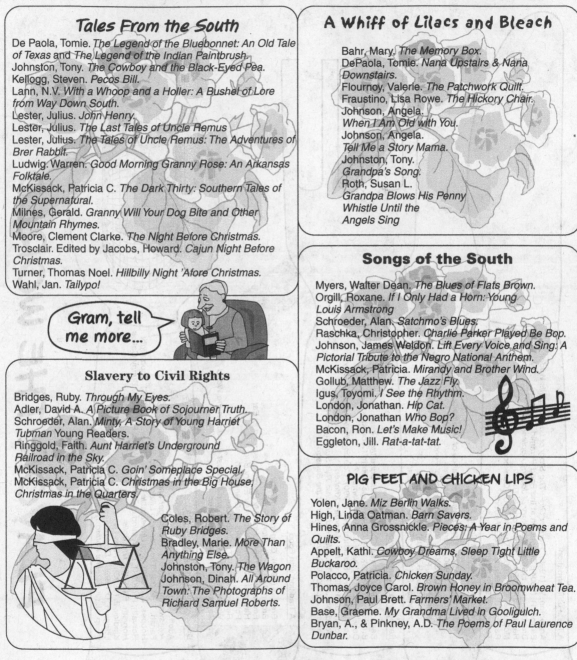

Tales From the South

De Paola, Tomie. *The Legend of the Bluebonnet: An Old Tale of Texas* and *The Legend of the Indian Paintbrush.*
Johnston, Tony. *The Cowboy and the Black-Eyed Pea.*
Kellogg, Steven. *Pecos Bill.*
Lann, N.V. *With a Whoop and a Holler: A Bushel of Lore from Way Down South.*
Lester, Julius. *John Henry.*
Lester, Julius. *The Last Tales of Uncle Remus*
Lester, Julius. *The Tales of Uncle Remus: The Adventures of Brer Rabbit.*
Ludwig. Warren. *Good Morning Granny Rose: An Arkansas Folktale.*
McKissack, Patricia C. *The Dark Thirty: Southern Tales of the Supernatural.*
Milnes, Gerald. *Granny Will Your Dog Bite and Other Mountain Rhymes.*
Moore, Clement Clarke. *The Night Before Christmas.*
Trosclair. Edited by Jacobs, Howard. *Cajun Night Before Christmas.*
Turner, Thomas Noel. *Hillbilly Night 'Afore Christmas.*
Wahl, Jan. *Tailypo!*

Gram, tell me more...

A Whiff of Lilacs and Bleach

Bahr, Mary. *The Memory Box.*
DePaola, Tomie. *Nana Upstairs & Nana Downstairs.*
Flournoy, Valerie. *The Patchwork Quilt.*
Fraustino, Lisa Rowe. *The Hickory Chair.*
Johnson, Angela. *When I Am Old with You.*
Johnson, Angela. *Tell Me a Story Mama.*
Johnston, Tony. *Grandpa's Song.*
Roth, Susan L. *Grandpa Blows His Penny Whistle Until the Angels Sing*

Songs of the South

Myers, Walter Dean. *The Blues of Flats Brown.*
Orgill, Roxane. *If I Only Had a Horn: Young Louis Armstrong*
Schroeder, Alan. *Satchmo's Blues.*
Raschka, Christopher. *Charlie Parker Played Be Bop.*
Johnson, James Weldon. *Lift Every Voice and Sing: A Pictorial Tribute to the Negro National Anthem.*
McKissack, Patricia. *Mirandy and Brother Wind.*
Gollub, Matthew. *The Jazz Fly.*
Igus, Toyomi. *I See the Rhythm.*
London, Jonathan. *Hip Cat.*
London, Jonathan *Who Bop?*
Bacon, Ron. *Let's Make Music!*
Eggleton, Jill. *Rat-a-tat-tat.*

Slavery to Civil Rights

Bridges, Ruby. *Through My Eyes.*
Adler, David A. *A Picture Book of Sojourner Truth.*
Schroeder, Alan. *Minty, A Story of Young Harriet Tubman* Young Readers.
Ringgold, Faith. *Aunt Harriet's Underground Railroad in the Sky.*
McKissack, Patricia C. *Goin' Someplace Special.*
McKissack, Patricia C. *Christmas in the Big House, Christmas in the Quarters.*

Coles, Robert. *The Story of Ruby Bridges.*
Bradley, Marie. *More Than Anything Else.*
Johnston, Tony. *The Wagon*
Johnson, Dinah. *All Around Town: The Photographs of Richard Samuel Roberts.*

PIG FEET AND CHICKEN LIPS

Yolen, Jane. *Miz Berlin Walks.*
High, Linda Oatman. *Barn Savers.*
Hines, Anna Grossnickle. *Pieces: A Year in Poems and Quilts.*
Appelt, Kathi. *Cowboy Dreams, Sleep Tight Little Buckaroo.*
Polacco, Patricia. *Chicken Sunday.*
Thomas, Joyce Carol. *Brown Honey in Broomwheat Tea.*
Johnson, Paul Brett. *Farmers' Market.*
Base, Graeme. *My Grandma Lived in Gooligulch.*
Bryan, A., & Pinkney, A.D. *The Poems of Paul Laurence Dunbar.*

FIGURE 14.12   Theme Exploration: The Freedom Struggle [I/M]

The Freedom Struggle
(Freedom For Us All)

A Place Called Freedom (Sanders, 1997)

The Fight for Freedom
(The American Revolution, The Civil War)

The Blue and the Gray (Bunting, 1996)
The Amazing Life of Benjamin Franklin (Cross, 2000)
Everyon's Revolution (Fleming, 2006)
*Give Me Liberty!: The Story of the Declaration of
    Independence* (Freedman, 2000)
The Silent Witness (Friedman, 2005)
Across Five Aprils (Hunt, 1964)
*Dear Ellen Bee: A Civil War Scrapbook of Two Union
    Spies* (Lyons, 2000)
*The Boy's War: Confederate and Union Soldiers Talk
    About the Civil War* (Murphy, 1990)
A Young Patriot (Murphy, 1996)
United No More: Stories of the Civil War (Rappaport, 2006)
*Geoge vs. George: The American Revolution as Seen from
    Both Sides* (Schanzer, 2004)

Guaranteed Freedoms
(The Bill of Rights)

An Amish Year (Ammon, 2000)
Nothing But the Truth (Avi, 1991)
The True Confessions of Charlotte Doyle
    (Avi, 1990)
Toliver's Secret (Brady, 1976)
Sleds on Boston Common (Borden, 2000)
The Landry News (Clements, 1999)
1791–1991 The Bill of Rights and Beyond
    (1991)
Thunder at Gettysburg (Gauch, 1975)
*A Long Way to Go: A Story of Women's
    Right to Vote* (Oneal, 1990)
The Gold Cadillac (Taylor, 1987)
Constitution Translated for Kids (Travis, 2006)

Let Freedom Ring
(Symbols of Freedom)

Liberty! (Drummond, 2002)
Fireworks, Picnics, and Flags (Giblin, 1983)
Sweet Clara and the Freedom Quilt
    (Hopkinson, 1993)
The Wagon (Johnston, 1996)
*Famous Illustrated Speeches and Documents:
    The Pledge of Allegiance* (Kallen, 1994)
Walt Whiteman: Words for America (Kerley, 2004)
*The Story of the Star-Spangled Banner, By the
    Dawn's Early Light* (Kroll, 1994)
The Gettysburg Address (Lincoln, 1995)
Yankee Doodle America (Minor, 2006)
The Flag We Love (Ryan, 1996)
The Memory Coat (Woodruff, 1999)

Individual Freedom
(Equal for All)

*Feedom Riders: John Lewis & Jim Zwerg
    on the Front Lines of the Civil Rights
    Movement* (Bausam, 2006)
More Than Anything Else
    (Bradley, 1995)
Through My Eyes (Bridges, 1999)
White Socks Only (Coleman, 1996)
*Freedom Walkers: The Story of the
    Montgomery Bus Boycott*
    (Freedman, 2006)
Paperboy (Holland, 1999)
Virgie Goes to School with Us Boys
    (Howard, 2000)
Run Away Home (McKassack, 1997)
My Dream of Martin Luther King
    (Ringgold, 1995)
*Freedom on the Menu: Greensboro
    Sit-Ins* (Weatherford, 2004)

Personal Freedom
(Choices)

The Bravest of Us All (Arnold, 2000)
Train to Somewhere (Bunting, 1996)
Because of Winn-Dixie (DiCamillo, 2000)
Grandmother's Pigeon (Erdich, 1996)
Out of the Dust (Hesse, 1997)
Amber on the Mountain (Johnston, 1994)
Boom Town (Levitin, 1998)
Holes (Sachar, 1998)
Maniac Magee (Spinelli, 1990)
The Other Side (Woodson, 2001)

Pink and Say (Polacco, 1994)

examples serve as inspiration not limitation on the power of literature to create effective interdisciplinary instruction through theme explorations.

TWIN TEXTS MEET TECHNOLOGY

This chapter may inspire teachers to gather literature across genres to address a topic or theme. Teaching with fiction and nonfiction on a particular theme inspires teachers to blend the dual perspectives of narrative and expository text into a meaningful, interconnected understanding of that theme (Camp, 2000). This section of this chapter, however, invites teachers to stretch an additional layer by exploring the use of technology to provide an additional perspective to this blend. Instead of viewing technology as as an intrusion, an infringement, or a threat to the reading of children's literature, teachers need to take a fresh look at this innovative gateway through which literature and technology can mutually exist in a changing educational setting for enhanced understanding (Hancock, 2000).

Blending twin texts and technology showcases the optimal balance of nonfiction and fiction on the same topic with an internet website for the purpose of opening a new gateway to learning, one that merges both efferent and aesthetic reading with viewing and visual representation. Quality websites that enhance inquiry and learning, virtual visits to museums, and abundant access to related information provide a window into the visual world of the Internet (Karchmer, 2000; Livingston & Kurkjian, 2004; Pinkney, 2000). Figure 14.13 provides a visual overview of the blending of these three perspectives as they weave informational print, fictional print, and visual information together through literature and technology.

FIGURE 14.13 Twin texts meet technology model

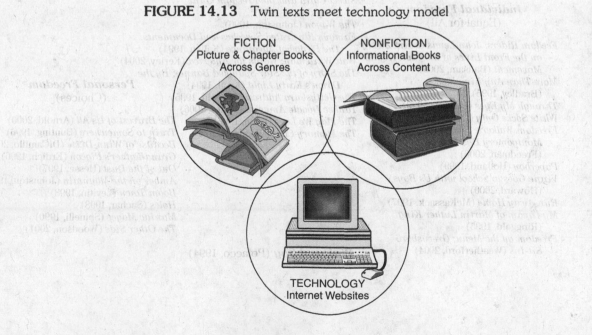

FICTION
Picture & Chapter Books
Across Genres

NONFICTION
Informational Books
Across Content

TECHNOLOGY
Internet Websites

An example may best explain this triad of learning. Imagine fourth-grade students independently reading Laura Ingalls Wilder's titles, including *On the Banks of Plum Creek,* as literature circle selections. Simultaneously, the classroom teacher is reading aloud Kathryn Lasky and Meribah Knight's *Searching for Laura Ingalls Wilder: A Reader's Journey* to gain current information on the authentic preserved Wilder homes across several states. In addition, the teacher plans a visit to the school computer lab to access the home site link (http://www. lauraingallswilder.com) to witness Laura's travels across Wisconsin, Kansas, Minnesota, South Dakota, and Missouri. Additional links to the Laura Ingalls Wilder Museum provide more visual connections to her authentic homes across the prairie. The fictional story is enhanced by the informational journey, and the reader is further stimulated by the visual aspects of the website. Three perspectives on learning—fiction, nonfiction, and technology—succeed in enhancing understanding and provide an even broader view for reader response.

Twin texts and technology assume a variety of delivery methods to students. In the primary grades, teachers may share fiction and nonfiction through read-alouds or shared reading and visit a website beforehand for their own prior knowledge or afterward as a student activity to generate response. In the intermediate grades, the teacher may read aloud the nonfiction title while the students read from a class set of the fictional title. The website may be incorporated before, during, or after reading to generate prior knowledge, provide a visual connection, or stimulate a response built on fact and fiction. The middle school setting may incorporate the website as a prereading activity with independent reading of both nonfiction and fiction or as a

RESOURCES ON THE WEB
Web-Based Projects

Turning to the Internet for an additional dimension to fiction and nonfiction reading experiences may seem like a natural literacy response options for many teachers and students. To ensure quality instruction and responsible viewing of the Internet, teachers should carefully select and preview appropriate sites. The sites listed offer suggestions for extending Russell Freedman's *Children of the Great Depression* (2005) and Karen Hesse's *Out of the Dust* (1997) through Internet-based projects and activites.

TrackStar
http://trackstar.4teachers.org/trackstar/

TrackStrar provides a good starting point for Web-based lessons and activities. Teachers may create an online lesson called a *track* by entering their collected websites (URLs) into a TrackStar and add annotations for their students. In addition to creating a new track, teachers may utilize tracks already made by other educators. For example, a "great depression" keyword search on *TrackStar* yielded over 19,000 already-made tracks; searching for "dust bowl" produced an additional 550 hits. As always, teachers should preview and evaluate all sites before directing their students to a track.

Scholastic Online Activities
http://teacher.scholastic.com/activities/index_grades35.htm

Scholastic offers a large selection of interactive online activities that relate to interdisciplinary content areas. One of many social studies activities, students can learn firsthand about the Great Depression by reading authentic diary excerpts, making arts and crafts, writing their own journal entries, and designing the interior in a period home. This site also offers a transcript of an in-depth interview with Karen Hesse in which the author discusses the research and process involved in writing *Out of the Dust.*

America from the Great Depression to World War II
http://memory.loc.gov/ammem/fsowhome.html

Presented by the Library of Congress, the images in the Farm Security Administration-Office of War Information Collection are among the most famous documentary photographs ever produced. Students can view over 160,000 black-and-white photos and 1,600 colored images depicting Americans in every part of the nation during the Great Depression and the Dust Bowl.

In addition to viewing websites and participating in online activities, students may create their own "virtual guide" to a selection of literature. In response to *Children of the Great Depression* and *Out of the Dust,* students may locate Internet sites they feel would enhance the reading experience by providing prior knowledge or explaining concepts relating to the book, providing a guide for peers interested in these books. Students may share their collection of links through a hyperlinked Microsoft Word document or a few PowerPoint slides.

concluding activity to evaluate the connections between factual and fictional information. The potential flexibility of these configurations provides new approaches and higher-level thinking to the existing literature program.

Benefits to the Learner

The blending of nonfiction, fiction, and an Internet website abounds with outstanding benefits to the teacher and the learner. The following lengthy list provides evidence of the impact of blending these three perspectives in a single week of reading. Any of the titles or the website may:

- Activate prior knowledge
- Facilitate extended learning response-based activities
- Result in enhanced comprehension
- Provide multiple perspectives on a single topic
- Generate higher-level connections between information or sources
- Extend learning through viewing and visual representation of a topic
- Elicit both aesthetic and efferent responses to both fact and fiction
- Accentuate the differences between fact and fiction
- Provide multiple sources for evaluating information
- Set the stage for authentic reading motivation
- Enhance interdisciplinary teaching and learning (Hancock, 2002)

Twin Texts and Technology Across Disciplines

The process of blending fiction, nonfiction and a related website exists across all content area disciplines. The examples shared in Figure 14.14 provide triads for topics related to social studies and science. In addition, twin texts and technology can extend to biographical investigations in social studies, science, and even the arts. The possibilities are endless as the quality of educational websites and quality children's literature across nonfiction and fiction blend into teaching scenarios for enhanced understanding.

Teachers are encouraged to select a favorite textset (typically fiction) and try a nonfiction read-aloud alongside its independent reading. Locate a website that provides a visual enhancement of related information. Elicit both efferent and aesthetic response though a response-based computer lab activity. The power of technology to work alongside children's literature will become clear as it stretches the visual aspects of learning toward reader response to literature.

CLOSING THOUGHTS

Initially, the possibilities for literature clusters, theme explorations, and twin texts/technology may seem restricted by the school curriculum, but literature as the basis of sound teaching actually allows traditional topics to be covered in a creative, interrelated manner. In some cases, literature clusters and theme explorations are limited only by the creativity of teachers and the accessibility of titles. Twin texts seem to connect spontaneously and credible websites are readily accessed, even by inexperienced technology educators. Whereas some teachers will be ready to take the plunge and voice total commitment to this type of instruction, others might want to

FIGURE 14.14 Twin texts meet technology: A quick walk through American history (1870–2001)

Western Settlement

Nonfiction: Lasky, Kathryn, & Knight, Meribah (1993). *Searching for Laura Ingalls Wilder: A reader's journey*. Photographs by Christopher Knight. New York: Macmillan.

Fiction: Wilder, Laura Ingalls (1953). *On the banks of Plum Creek*. Illus, by Garth Williams. New York: HarperCollins.

Website: *www.lauraingallswilder.com/ homesites* provides a detailed guide to the *Little House* series country provides links to the actual homesites in Wisconsin, Kansas, Iowa, South Dakota, and Missouri as well as the Laura Ingalls Wilder Museum in Walnut Grove, Minnesota.

Immigration

Nonfiction: Hopkinson, Deborah (2003). *Shutting out the sky: Life in the tenements New York, 1880–1924*. New York: Orchard.

Fiction: Auch, Mary Jane (2002). *Ashes of roses*. New York: Henry Holt.

Website: *http://www.tenement.org* provides a virtual tour of a tenement located at 97 Orchard Street in New York City. The site allows the viewer to enter the building that housed 7,000 tenants between 1863 and 1935. Additional information on diseases, sweatshops, and other facts of tenement life.

Flight

Nonfiction: Old, Wendie C. (2002). *To fly: The story of the Wright brothers*. Illus. by Robert Andrew Parker. New York: Clarion.

Fiction: Grimes, Nikki (2002). *Talkin' about Bessie: The story of aviator Elizabeth Coleman*. Illus. by E. B. Lewis. New York: Orchard.

Website: *http://www.nasm.si.edu/ wrightbrothers* is located on the National Air and Space Museum (division of the Smithsonian Institution) website. "The Wright Brothers: The Invention of the Aerial Age" provides biographical information, insights into invention, and a gallery of early aircraft. Interactive experiments and activities enhance the events of Kitty Hawk, North Carolina, over 100 years ago.

Great Depression

Nonfiction: Freedom, Russell (2006). *Children of the Great Depression*. New York: Clarion.

Fiction: Henderson, Ailenn Kilgore (2004). *Hard times for Jake Smith: A story of the Depression Era*. Milkweed.

Website: *http://learning.loc.gov/learn/features/timeline/depwwii/depress depress.html* Learning Page in the American Memory section of the Library of Congress website that links information on the Great Depression with photo archives and authentic documents.

World War II and D-Day

Nonfiction: Tanaka, Shelley (2004). *D-Day: They fought to free Europe from Hitler's tyranny*. Illus. by David Craig. New York: Hyperion.

Fiction: Myers, Walter Dean (1999). *The journal of Scott Pendleton Collins, a World War II solider, Normandy, France, 1944*. New York: Scholastic.

(continued)

FIGURE 14.14 Continued

Website: *http://www.pbs.org/wgbh/amex/dday* is the PBS American Experience website that shares basic maps and timelines of D-Day as well as providing links to letters GIs sent home, contents of paratroopers' packs, and additional facts about the Normandy invasion.

Holocaust

Nonfiction: Warren, Andrea (2001). *Surviving Hitler: A boy in the Nazi death camps.* New York: HarperCollins.

Fiction: Spinelli, Jerry (2003). *Milkweed.* New York: Knopf.

Website: *http://www.ushmm.com/museum/exhibit* is the website of the National Holocaust Memorial Museum. Especially for middle-school students are "Life in Shadows" and "Anne Frank, the Writer." Artifact galleries bring the reality of the death camps and the children and adults who lost their lives during World War II.

Civil Rights Movement

Nonfiction: Freedman, Russell (2006). *Freedom walkers: The story of the Mongomery bus boycott.* New York: Holiday House.

Fiction: Robinet, Harriette Gillem (2000). *Walking to the bus-rider blues.* New York: Simon & Schuster.

Website: *http://www.usm.edu/crdp* is the Civil Rights Documentation Project website. It offers oral history and audio clips and transcripts of civil rights movement participants.

Vietnam War

Nonfiction: Warren, Andrea (2004). *Escape from Saigon: How a Vietnam war orphan became an American boy.* New York: Farrar, Straus & Giroux.

Fiction: Myers, Walter Dean (2002). *Patrol: An American soldier in Vietnam.* Illus. by Ann Grifalconi. New York: HarperCollins.

Website: *http://www.pbs.org/wgbh/amex/Vietnam* shares a powerful visual and textual overview of this undeclared war, including a timeline, videoclips, and personal reflections on veterans.

September 11, 2001

Nonfiction: Hampton, Wilborn (2003). *September 11, 2001: Attack on New York City.* Cambridge, MA: Candlewick.

Fiction: Gerstein, Mordicai (2003). *The man who walked between the towers.* Brookfield, CT: Roaring Brook Press.

Website: *http://www. september11news.com* contains the archives of photos, graphics, and images from 9/11 and related events of this unforgettable day.

Adapted from Hancock, M. R. (2004). Recent history in threes: Nonfiction, fiction, and the web. *Book Links, 14,* 6–11.

work progressively with literature clusters, building some degree of success and affirmation before moving on to more comprehensive theme explorations. Interspersed might be twin texts as a viable link to technology.

These types of literature-based interdisciplinary instruction provide diverse opportunities for reader response to quality literature. The challenge of reading across genres in conjunction with the gaining of an understanding of broad conceptual ideas makes this type of instruction highly valuable to both the professional educator of children and the recipients of lifelong literacy and learning. The added value of Internet websites further enhances the efferent and aesthetic experience of exploring a topic though multiple lenses across literary genres, literature, and technology.

References

Bedford, A. W. (2005). From *Charlotte's Web* to the World Wide Web: The impact of the Internet on the field of children's literature. *Journal of Children's Literature, 31*, 11–17.

Bergeron, B. S., & Rudenga, E. A. (1996). Seeking authenticity: What is "real" about thematic literacy instruction? *The Reading Teacher, 49*, 544–551.

Camp, D. (2000). It takes two: Teaching with twin texts of fact and fiction. *The Reading Teacher, 53*, 400–408.

Castek, J., Bevans-Mangelson, J., & Goldstone, B. (2006). Reading adventures online: Five ways to introduce the new literacies of the Internet through children's literature. *The Reading Teacher, 59*, 714–728.

Collard, S. B. (2003). Using science books to teach literacy—and save the planet. *The Reading Teacher, 57*, 280–283.

Ebbers, M. (2002). Science text sets: Using genres to promote literacy and inquiry. *Language Arts, 80*, 40–50.

Fuhler, C. J., Farris, P. J., & Nelson, P. A. (2006). Building literacy skills across the curriculum: Forging connections with the past through artifacts. *The Reading Teacher, 59*, 646–659.

Gambrell, L. B. (2005). Reading literature, reading text, reading the Internet: The times they are a'changing. *The Reading Teacher, 58*, 588–591.

Hancock, M. R. (1997). *Literature clusters: Balancing narrative, expository, and poetic voices for effective interdisciplinary learning.* Paper presented at the 42nd Annual Convention of the International Reading Association.

Hancock, M. R. (2000). The survival of the book in a megabyte world: Children's literature in the new millennium. *Journal of Children's Literature, 26*, 8–16.

Hancock, M. R. (2002). *Twin texts meet technology: Gateway to enhanced inquiry and comprehension.* Paper presented at the 47th Annual Convention of the International Reading Association.

Hancock, M. R. (2004). Recent history in threes: Nonfiction, fiction, and the web. *Book Links, 14*, 6–11.

Hunsader, P. D. (2004). Mathematics trade books: Establishing their value and assessing their quality. *The Reading Teacher, 57*, 618–629.

Karchmer, R. (2000). Using the Internet and children's literature to support interdisciplinary instruction. *The Reading Teacher, 54*, 100–104.

Kaser, S. (2001). Searching the heavens with children's literature: A design for teaching science. *Language Arts, 78*, 348–356.

Kieff, J. (2001). Fostering images of intergenerational relationships through literature clusters. *Journal of Children's Literature, 27*, 61–68.

Kurkjian, C., Livingston, N., & Young, T. (2004–2006). Children's books (monthly column). *The Reading Teacher,* (Vols. 57–59).

Labbo, L. D. (2005). Books and computer response activities that support literacy development. *The Reading Teacher, 59*, 288–292.

Leu, D. J., Castek, J., Henry, L. A., Coiro, J., & McMullan, M. (2004). The lessons that children teach us: Integrating children's literature and the new literacies of the Internet. *The Reading Teacher, 57*, 496–503.

Livingston, N., & Kurkjian, C. (2004). Literature links: Expanding ways of knowing. *The Reading Teacher, 58,* 110–118.

McMahon, S. I., Gordy, L., & Strop, J. (2001). Dilemmas to manage: Developing a balanced, integrated unit of study of the civil rights movement. *The New Advocate, 14,* 251–263.

Moyer, P. S. (2000). Communicating mathematically: Children's literature as a natural connection. *The Reading Teacher, 54,* 246–255.

Pinkney, A. D. (2000). Books and megabytes: Good friends in an information age. *The New Advocate, 13,* 43–49.

Rice, D. C. (2002). Using trade books in teaching elementary science: Facts and fallacies. *The Reading Teacher, 55,* 552–565.

Roser, N. L., & Keehn, S. (2002). Fostering thought, talk, and inquiry: Linking literature and social studies. *The Reading Teacher, 55,* 416–426.

Shanahan, T., Robinson, B., & Schneider, M. (1995). Integrating curriculum: Avoiding some of the pitfalls of thematic units. *The Reading Teacher, 48,* 718–719.

Smolkin, L. B., & Donavan, C. A. (2005). Looking closely at a science trade book: Gail Gibbons and multimodal literacy. *Language Arts, 83,* 52–62.

Soalt, J. (2005). Bringing together fictional and informational texts to improve comprehension. *The Reading Teacher, 58,* 680–683.

Ward, R. A. (2005). Using children's literature to inspire K–8 preservice teachers' future mathematics pedagogy. *The Reading Teacher, 59,* 132–143.

Weaver, C., Chaston, J., & Peterson, S. (1993). *Theme exploration: A voyage of discovery.* Portsmouth, NH: Heinemann.

Whitin, D., & Whitin, P. (2001). What counts in math-related books for children. *Journal of Children's Literature, 27,* 49–55.

Wolk, S. (2004). Using picture books to teach for democracy. *Language Arts, 82,* 26–35.

Children's Books Cited

All children's books cited in this chapter are referenced in the literature clusters, theme explorations, and twin text/technology figures interspersed throughout.

PART V

Celebrating Response Growth Through Assessment

Throughout *A Celebration of Literature and Response,* each chapter has shared the genuine joy and promise of literature-based, response-filled classrooms. Yet the documentation of the craft of reading and personal related response remains a vital issue in literature-based instruction. The ongoing collection of reading accomplishments and response connections in a literature-based classroom attains importance in a society that demands accountability. Although our hearts warm to literature and our faces smile at the spontaneous words of a child's response, assessment must indicate that a response-based classroom contributes to both the art and the craft of lifelong reading.

Part V of *A Celebration of Literature and Response* focuses on authentic documentation of reader response to literature. Authentic assessment builds on the authentic happenings in the classroom—reading and responding to literature. Because response does not readily equate into a number or letter grade, there must be justifiable assessment alternatives that indicate the evolving nature of the reading process and the quality of reader response over time.

Chapter 15 overflows with sample instruments and assessment tools for documenting reader response to literature, including checklists, rubrics, and response categorization schemes. Multiple perspectives on assessing literature response journals and literature circles provide assessment alternatives to be shared with students and parents. Elements of a response portfolio become visible evidence of growth in breadth of response options and quality of response as students collect, select, and reflect on their ongoing literary readings and responses.

Teachers must address the needs of assessment within a literature-based classroom. Because students deserve to celebrate their response successes, authentic assessment provides a means to keep account of reading achievements and response connections. These assessment tools produce convincing short-term evidence for parents, administrators, and readers themselves. They also support reader transactions with literature as an optimal goal of creating lifelong readers who read and respond on both aesthetic and efferent levels each time they pick up a book and make it their own through response. In a political climate of highlighting test scores, educators need to remember long-term goals involving personal transactions through a lifelong relationship with reading literature.

As this textbook draws to a close, it seems critical to address the often neglected aspect of response-based assessment in a literature-rich classroom. The numerous and multifaceted authentic assessment options presented in this chapter collectively and convincingly reflect the strength of literature in enhancing literacy instruction and the power of response to capture the uniqueness of the individual reader.

CHAPTER 15

Documenting
Response to Literature
Authentic Perspectives

> *I believe that if you surround children with books, give a reader choice in selecting the "right" title, and provide time and space for entering "the reading zone" (Atwell, 2006), you will create lifelong readers who capture the joy of reading and the personal connection of reader response. The No Child Left Behind legislation has caused many teachers to abandon their love of literature and turn rigidly to teaching test-related literacy skills. Fear of test scores brings out the worse in teachers as they forget why we really became teachers. If you provide ample time to practice the art of reading, the joy of reading will dominate, and readers will ultimately score well on test scores at state and national levels. If you teach reading skills and strategies, however, readers may score just fine on the reading tests, but they are likely never to experience the wonder and appreciation of being lifelong readers.*
>
> *When parents and readers come to school for academic conferences, my students showcase a portfolio brimming with evidence of their reading and response. Lists of books, journal entries, literature-based writing models, and self-assessments during literature conversations all reflect the*

intensity and depth of readers (and writers) in my class. Even those who struggle with reading are proud to show parents the number and kinds of books they read during a quarter of the year, with personal artifacts to reflect their connections to those titles.

I vow to never forget the ultimate goal of creating lifelong readers who celebrate and value the joy of reading. Authentic reading moves far beyond test scores to an in-depth relationship with a book that is established through teacher encouragement of personal response to literature.

Sixth-grade teacher conversation
in author's office, February 1, 2007

Active involvement in response-based literature activities in an elementary/middle-level classroom provides a rich experience for students but an assessment challenge for teachers. Although many books, research-based articles, and teacher-action research reports applaud the benefits of literature-based instruction and reader response activities, few address the important issue of assessment of response. If confident teachers align their literature-based philosophies with response-based expressions of personal interactions with books, they must also align meaningful assessment with that focus and allow their teaching to be informed by that assessment. National testing mandates loom over empowered teachers who are unwilling to take a backward step from their literature-based successes. This chapter strives to share an assortment of assessment standards and tools designed for reader response-based activities at a variety of age levels. They range from observations to accountability logs, from rubrics to checklists, from self-evaluation to peer evaluation, and from portfolio documentation to program evaluation.

PRINCIPLES OF ASSESSMENT

In focusing on assessment of response-based literature interactions, basic principles of assessment should be introduced and connected to a response-based philosophy of learning. Support for response-based assessment is grounded in a framework based on several basic principles of assessment (Tierney, Carter, & Desai, 1991). These principles serve as a critical reminder that literacy accountability must not focus on the limited perspective of a test score but must be targeted toward reader-centered literacy.

1. *Assessment should be centered in the classroom.* While reading and responding to literature occur both inside and outside the school setting,

assessment should focus on what occurs in the academic setting. Personal transactions with literature are genuinely influenced by experiences outside the classroom; however, assessment should be on literature shared and responses made in the academic setting.

2. *Assessment should be consistent with curricular goals.* Because aesthetic teaching and response-based learning are grounded in a teaching philosophy that values literature and the unique response of each individual, curricular goals are most likely to focus on individual choice, interests, and performance. If the goals focus on creating lifelong readers and learners through literature, not just yearly test performance, there is likely to be a valid connection between curriculum and assessment.

3. *Assessment must be consistent with what is known about human learning.* The uniqueness of the individual learner, the importance of growth over time, the measurement of an individual against his or her own progress, and the importance of choice in learning are essential building blocks of literature-based and response-based learning. Rather than measuring readers against a national norm, the individuality of the learner is respected and individual growth is monitored and celebrated over time.

4. *Assessment must be comprehensive and balanced.* Response based activities must expand to include literature from across all literary genres and to include all modes of response. Limiting a response experience to a teacher's favorite genre and a comfortable mode of responding does little to enhance and broaden learning. A comprehensive diet of literature across genres, as guided by national and state standards, shared across the curriculum and rotating suggestions of varied response-based activities will provide the comprehensive balance suggested by this principle.

5. *Literature and response-based experiences must be numerous and multifaceted, leading to profiles of growth over time.* Assessments must be qualitative as well as quantitative. In other words, keeping track of numbers of books and kinds of responses is important, but this must be supplemented by data on quality and depth of response and the various literature experiences. Response assessment must reflect the constructivist nature of meaning-making so comprehension is analyzed within the personal transaction with literature. Assessment may be accomplished through individual or collaborative means. Most important perhaps, and in contract to test accountability, is that assessment be noncompetitive and each respondent to literature be assessed on her or his own growth, exploration of response options, and special talents in interactions with trade books.

6. *Assessment guides and improves instruction and learning.* Our role as teachers is to document the evolving development of response and to identify a student's strengths and weaknesses in response to literature. Assessment guides and improves instruction. Our role as teachers is to empower students with the freedom to respond, to model response mechanisms, and to sharpen

our own observations of response and increase our confidence in them. Assessment monitors the outcomes of a response-based literature program. Our role as teachers is to document a student as reader and respondent to literature to share with others while determining program strengths and weaknesses for further instructional planning.

A study by Bauer and Garcia (2002) investigated the link between a classroom teacher's implementation of alternative assessment and classroom instruction. The assessment changes that the teacher made actually led to higher quality student-centered instruction. The ongoing knowledge of individual students' reading and writing increased as students self-selected reading materials, self-evaluated, and shared personal interpretations. Providing them greater voice in their literacy development seems to result from the implementation of alternative assessment tools in a literature-based setting. Damico (2005) showcases a broader, comprehensive model of literacy assessment during literature-based instruction and discussion. Johnston (2005) reinforces the need to prepare readers of the new literacies who are resilient, flexible, self-directed, and collaborative. With these findings in mind, take note of the variety of suggestions for authentic assessment, self-documentation, and self-evaluation suggested throughout this chapter.

ASSESSMENT OF RESPONSE-BASED ACTIVITIES

The International Reading Association and National Council of Teachers of English Joint Task Force on Assessment (IRA/NCTE, 1994) prepared a list of standards for the assessment of reading and writing. Drawing from these standards with literary response as a basis for assessment, the following standards should guide assessment of response-based celebrations of literature.

The literature tastes and response-based preferences of students are paramount in assessment. Assessment needs to address what students *do* read and how they *do* respond, rather than what they do *not* accomplish. Immediate teacher feedback is critical to response modes. Specific comments need to be delivered in a timely fashion. Because individual response is not suited to standardized assessment, "the most powerful assessments of students are likely to be those that occur in the daily activity of the classroom" (IRA/NCTE, 1994, p. 15). Allowing reflection on the reader's own literature choices and related response, planning for evaluation of their own growth in reading and response, and setting goals for future literary experiences and response to that literature are mandatory ongoing portions of response-based reading assessment.

The primary purpose of response-based assessment is to improve teaching and learning. The central function of assessment is not to prove whether teaching and learning have occurred, but to improve the quality of the literacy experience for the learner and to increase the likelihood that the learner will become a lifelong reader who naturally views literature as an aesthetic experience.

On one hand, the teacher assumes a facilitator role in a response-based classroom and must be certain that a blend of literary genres, a variety of response modes, and ample opportunity for response are provided. On the other hand, the teacher must document the ways in which the student is growing in appreciation of literature, attitude toward reading, and personal interaction with literature. If our goals are to create lifelong literate individuals, both our program and our students' response progress must be monitored and reflected on continuously by both teacher and reader.

Response-based assessments must recognize and reflect the intellectual and social complexity of literacy and the role of school, home, and society in literacy development.   Reader response captures the experiences of the reader in the broader sense of a literate community because it is the product and culmination of experiences in life and literacy that bring the unique transaction to books. The interactive roles of school, home, and society are honored in a response-based classroom because aesthetic teaching philosophy acknowledges and respects learning beyond the classroom walls.

Response-based assessment must be fair and equitable.   Response must be judged on an individual basis free of gender, cultural, ethnic, religious, linguistic, physical, and socioeconomic bias. It is indeed the mixture of these factors that makes each child a unique reader and respondent. Because the common denominator of reader response is the individual reader, inequitable judgment is less likely to occur in response-based assessment because each reader's thoughts and reactions are individually valued.

The teacher is the most important agent of response-based assessment.   In the past, society valued and invested in testing and devalued the information that teachers gained daily about student learning. Professionals have gained in stature as society begins to come to terms with the knowledge each teacher holds about each child. For teachers to become more effective agents of response-based assessment, they must read and respond themselves. They must discuss the books they read, write their own reflective responses, and share their thoughts and feelings. Only through an understanding of their own response mechanisms can they assess the literary response of their students.

The response-based assessment process should involve multiple perspectives and sources of data.   Limiting reader-response assessment to a singular response product shortchanges the reader. Teachers need to triangulate sources of response by acquiring products of various modes of response (written, oral, artistic) and validating them through informal interviews and formal observations. The reliability of response-based assessment will improve when there are multiple opportunities to observe and discuss response to varied literary selections.

Parents must be involved as active, essential participants in a response-based assessment process. Parent involvement might include the following:

- Becoming knowledgeable about reader response and its relationship to literature across the curriculum
- Actively participating in the assessment process by commenting on response-based performance
- Contributing knowledge of their children as readers and responders in the home environment
- Seeking ways to become more encouraging of their child's development as a reader and responder to literature

Ongoing communication and reporting procedures between school and home should enable parents to talk in productive ways about their children and their literature and response experiences.

Although these standards are adapted from broader perspectives on reading and writing, they do provide a parallel framework for meeting the new challenge of creating and implementing response-based assessments. The instruments, checklists, and suggestions in this chapter evolve from the considerations given about assessment. Other accountability systems are in place across the nation, but these are the assessments focused on creating lifelong readers, far beyond a single test performance.

TOOLS FOR DOCUMENTING READER RESPONSE

The purpose of this section is to address the needs of practitioners who support a response-based literature program in their classrooms. The need to assess and document response as a means of literacy development is likely in most schools. Elaborating on the lifelong implication of reader response to literature may be enough for those who encompass its philosophy, but the reality of assessment retains a strong presence in our educational institutions.

This section suggests a variety of formats—checklists, anecdotal records, graphs, categories, hierarchies—with which to assess multiple dimensions of response. From oral response to written response, from self-assessment to program evaluation, these suggestions provide a much requested component to round out the capabilities of reader response as a reflection of learning.

Response Checklists: Monitoring the Program and the Individual

A response-based literature program should be built on outcomes of engaging in reading and response. Two forms provide checklists of both programs and individual student performance. A teacher can use response-based literature program opportunities (Figure 15.1) to assess response activity offerings within a program context. Updating and monitoring of the checklist encourage a mix of response modes as part of the total literature program. As a teacher notes limited response options in a

FIGURE 15.1 Form for monitoring response program*

Teacher Documentation of Response-Based Literature Program Opportunities						
Teacher _____ Grade/Age _____						
Assessment Period _____						

	Date	Book Title	Date	Book Title	Date	Book Title
Listening Behavior						
Physical response						
Spontaneous response						
Participatory response						
Contact with Books						
Browsing and choosing						
Attention to books						
Proximity to books						
Impulse to Share						
Reading together						
Telling about a book						
Sharing a discovery						
Sharing connections to other books						
Sharing connections to own experiences						
Actions and Drama						
Echoing the action						
Dramatic play						
Readers' theater						
Art, Music, and Constructed Products						
Visual representation (drawing)						
Constructions						
Culinary response						
Musical response						
Oral Response						
Retelling/storytelling						
Literature conversations						
Prompted response						
Written Response						
Literature response journals						
Literature as a model for writing						

*Categories based on: Hickman, J. (1981). A new perspective on response to literature: Research in an elementary classroom setting. *Research in the Teaching of English, 15,* 343–354.

particular area, he or she can make a conscious effort to improve instruction by providing broader response options.

The student engagement profile (Figure 15.2), in contrast, is used to monitor an individual student's level of involvement in response modes. Dependent on response offerings, the teacher documents indications of respondent performance across several response modes. A small area for comments allows minimal space for professional notes or book titles.

A checklist of reader responses to teacher-generated prompts (Figure 15.3) focuses on the development of both oral and written responses to literature. Applicable to both primary and intermediate students, the checklist monitors progress and growth in communicating thoughts and feelings to read-alouds or independently read literature. The checklist implies developmental levels of response to aesthetic, experiential, interpretive, and cognitive prompts. The checklist can be used over a designated period of time by dating and recording the observed growth in response of an individual student. At the same time, teachers can monitor their use of prompt types and the individual's performance over time through the response continuum— emerging, developing, maturing. Teachers may determine how effectively they are addressing variety in prompts to stimulate continuous response development.

Teacher Anecdotal Records

Each teacher needs to keep a notebook containing anecdotal records acquired from his or her observational perspective. This becomes particularly important with primary children where teacher-written records of spontaneous response document valuable evidence of daily response growth. Dated mailing labels are suggested as teachers or participant observers (student teachers, paraprofessionals, inclusion teachers) record daily anecdotal notes on read-aloud responses, sharing time comments, literature circles, and so on. These events could be audio- or videotaped, but then the tapes require transcription for individual students. That task can easily become backlogged and overwhelming, so on-the-spot anecdotal records seem to be more effective. The mailing labels should be transferred daily to the teacher notebook containing observational sheets for each child. As they are accumulated by date, a sequential account of growing response may become evident. These records, as a necessary supplement to the student response portfolio (discussed later in this chapter), provide strong support for response documentation.

Daily Reading Logs and Literature Response Files

As early primary-level children (grades K–2) read individual picture books, informational picture books, or transitional chapter books, they should be asked to record a brief list of the books they read (Hill & Ruptic, 1994) (Figure 15.4). For older students (grades 3–6), the daily reading log shown in Figure 15.5 (Hill & Ruptic, 1994), provides for a brief response on a daily basis.

For many teachers, a response file could be dated, handwritten on index cards, or entered into a computer file. Not only does this file serve as a series of written responses to literature, but it keeps track of the number of books and genres of

FIGURE 15.2   Form for monitoring student response involvement*

Student Engagement Profile: Response-Based Literature Program		
Student name _____ Grade/Age _____		
	Date(s) observed	Teacher Comment

Listening Behavior
 	
    Physical response
    Spontaneous response
    Participatory response		

Contact with Books
 	
    Browsing and choosing
    Attention to books
    Proximity to books		

Impulse to Share
 	
    Reading together
    Telling about a book
    Sharing a discovery
    Sharing connections to other books
    Sharing connections to own experiences		

Actions and Drama
 	
    Echoing the action
    Dramatic play
    Readers' theater		

Art, Music, and Constructed Products
 	
    Visual representation (drawing)
    Constructions
    Culinary response
    Musical response		

Oral Response
 	
    Retelling/storytelling
    Literature conversations
    Prompted response		

Written Response
 	
    Literature response journals
    Literature as a model for writing		

---

*Categories based on: Hickman, J. (1981). A new perspective on response to literature: Research in an elementary classroom setting. *Research in the Teaching of English, 15,* 343–354.

FIGURE 15.3 Form for assessing student responses to prompts

Reader Responses to Teacher-Generated Prompts

Name _____ Grade/Age _____

Book Title(s) _____ Oral _____ Written _____

_____

E = Emerging Response
   Response minimally connects text to focus of prompt.
   Response reflects slight degree of honesty or emotional impact.

D = Developing Response
   Response adequately connects text to focus of prompt.
   Response reflects some degree of honesty and emotional impact.

M = Maturing Response
   Response substantially connects text to focus of the prompt.
   Response reflects complete honesty and emotional impact.

	Date(s) of Evidence	Quality
		E D M
AESTHETIC PROMPTS		
How does this book make you feel?		E D M
How would you feel if you were (*character*)?		E D M
EXPERIENTIAL PROMPTS		
How does this book remind you of your own life?		E D M
How does (*character*) remind you of someone you know?		E D M
How does (*character's*) actions remind you of another book?		E D M
INTERPRETIVE PROMPTS		
What did you notice in this book?		E D M
What meaning or message does the book have for you?		E D M
What do these words mean to you?		E D M
What kind of person do you think (*character*) is?		E D M
COGNITIVE PROMPTS		
What do you think will happen to (*character*)?		E D M
If you were (*character*), what would you do?		E D M
What advice would you give (*character*)?		E D M

FIGURE 15.4   Reading log for grades K–2*

📖 📖 📖 📖 📖 📖   READING LOG   📖 📖 📖 📖 📖 📖

Name _____   Term _____

Date Completed	Title of Book	Author

literature being explored. Teachers might model sample responses of their own or share other children's former responses on overhead transparencies. Here are some subjective guidelines used for ongoing response assessment:

- Depth, honesty, sincerity, and personal voice in response
- Level of personal involvement with text
- Willingness to explore and expand new response options
- Willingness to share authentic thoughts and feelings through writing
- Growth of response over a significant period of time

Responses should be submitted on an ongoing basis throughout an assessment period. Teacher comments would affirm, suggest, or attempt to stretch (but not force) the kinds and quality of response. Model responses can also be shared during whole

*Source: From *Practical Aspects of Authentic Assessment: Putting the Pieces Together* by Bonnie Campbell Hill and Cynthia Ruptic. Reprinted by permission of Christopher-Gordon Publishers, Inc.

FIGURE 15.5 Daily reading log for grades 3–6*

DAILY READING LOG			
Name			Title
Date Started	Date Finished		Author
Date	Pages Read	Event(s)	Response/Prediction

class mini-lessons on enhancing response. The entire file is submitted at the end of the assessment period with a main criteria of growth and development of response style over the assigned time. A narrative evaluation is the key assessment and could be attached to a rubric or point system if a mandated score or grade is necessary.

ASSESSING LITERATURE RESPONSE JOURNALS

As intermediate-level readers (grades 3–5) and middle-level students (grades 6–8) respond to longer chapter books across genres, it is important that their journals capture responses throughout the entire active reading process. This means not only capturing thoughts at the book's conclusion, but, more importantly, recording ongoing response throughout the entire reading process. Therefore, the response base will be much longer and in depth than the brief authentic response to a picture book from a younger child. This facilitates the need for a more intricate assessment tool to determine growth of response of higher quality and perhaps greater quantity.

---

*Source: From *Practical Aspects of Authentic Assessment: Putting the Pieces Together* by Bonnie Campbell Hill and Cynthia Ruptic. Reprinted by permission of Christopher-Gordon Publishers, Inc.

Self-Assessment and Teacher Feedback

The first vehicle for achieving, sustaining, and providing impetus to the power of written response to literature is the teacher comment. It is vital that student response be recognized, encouraged, and expanded periodically. To ensure both teacher and peer comments to literature response journals, a simple system of colored circle stickers (red/blue/green/yellow/orange) is suggested. The teacher designs a schema for labeling various response perspectives. Students label several responses according to this scheme. A sample system might include:

- Blue sticker(s) = a response that captures your deepest interaction with the text; teacher will read and respond to it.
- Yellow sticker(s) = another powerful response; a peer or reading partner will respond to it.
- Green sticker(s) = a response that reflects a text-to-life connection (usually a newly introduced response category is the focus).
- Orange sticker(s) = a response that reflects a prediction or anticipation of the unfolding text (or any other category for a secondary focus).
- Red sticker(s) = a response that reflects reader involvement with a character.

By applying the stickers, the students are actually rereading and self-assessing while categorizing their responses. The teacher's (or peer's) task is tapered to reading and responding to targeted responses. This allows time to share a few significant responses rather than numerous, brief, often less meaningful ones. Figure 15.6 reveals several excerpts from a preservice teacher's journal in response to *Letters from Rifka* by Karen Hesse. Read the entries, note the colored stickers that categorize responses, and focus on teacher feedback in this context.

This system can be adapted for readers from upper primary grades through middle-level grades. The color code can be used over two or three literature books or changed with the reading of each book. Older readers can even devise their own coded system for teacher/peer comments. The benefits to the reader include periodic quality feedback and the opportunity to reread and self-evaluate one's own responses. The benefits to peer readers is the opportunity to read another student's response for variety and extension of one's own response style. Finally, the benefits to the teacher include an opportunity to engage in ongoing assessment of response with an emphasis on quality, not quantity feedback.

Literature Response Journal Rubric

Another form of authentic assessment is a rubric designed for literature response journals. The rubric differentiates response performance by listing characteristics of respondents at each stage of evolving response—novice, emerging, maturing, and self-directed responder. As noted in Figure 15.7, the rubric is built on an evolving continuum associated more with response experience than with age or ability.

The rubric is intended for readers from fourth through eighth grade who engage in the literature response journal process (aligned with Chapter 10 of this text) primarily with realistic fiction or historical fiction books. Four stages of response should

FIGURE 15.6   Literature response journal: Self-assessment and teacher feedback

PAGE NO. | 1

Well-written

Strong interaction with the text.

Letters from Rifka : Responses

PREPARED BY
DATE

September 2, 1919

(YELLOW)

Russia: This entry made me feel both angry and sorry for Rifka. It is hard for me to believe that Rifka's parents put so much responsibility and danger on her. I know that they are trying to save their son but in so doing, they are putting their only daughter's life on the line. Why did the son leave the army anyway? Didn't he know what would happen to his family if he was caught? Later in the entry I felt scared for Rifka. The way the guards were looking at her and touching her hair made me feel almost disgusted inside. This is just a little girl!

Do you think 5th graders will react in a similar way? How will adolescents view this scene?

September 2, 1919

(GREEN)

Russia: At the end of this entry when Rifka is saying good-bye to her home, to her family, and to her past life. I could really relate to her. I have moved many times and can remember the way I felt on moving day. One time that really sticks out in my mind was when I was only five years old. My family was moving from Barstow CA to Rowland Heights, CA because my dad had gotten transferred. I remember being very upset and thinking that all of my things were going to be left behind with the house. I of course was not placed in a dangerous position like Rifka and her family but I was still scared because I wasn't sure what lay ahead for me.

Excellent text to-life Connection that builds empathy toward this character.

Would this be a point to bring up with your students? Today's society is so mobile.

November 27, 1919

en route to Warsaw: The events in this entry made me cringe. The thought of touching someone's hair that hasn't been washed for such a long time and seeing all of these scabs on her head is aweful. What is wrong with this girl? Is she going to die? What will become of her baby? I can't imagine being as strong as Rifka. Even after seeing this girl's scalp Rifka still fixed her hair. It makes me worry about the type of person I am. If I had been in her place I would have somehow excused myself rather than touch this sick girl. How did Rifka become so honorable?

I wanted to warn Rifka. Kindness is great, but it backfires on her here.

discourage the use of a letter grade for each developing stage. Letter grades are never suggested for use with response journals, but growth over time from one developmental category to the next is to be expected.

A *novice responder* is just beginning to experiment with the response process. He or she can be a younger student or a student who has never been challenged to

FIGURE 15.6   Continued

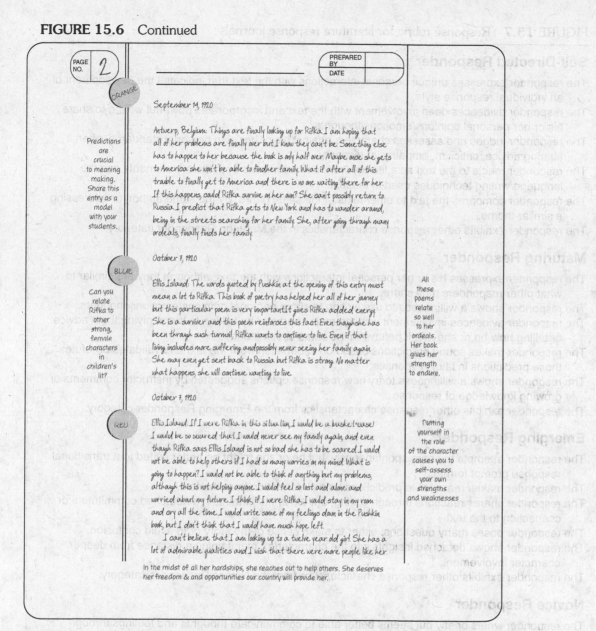

PAGE NO. 2

PREPARED BY
DATE

ORANGE

Predictions are crucial to meaning making. Share this entry as a model with your students.

September 14, 1920

Antwerp, Belgium: Things are finally looking up for Rifka. I am hoping that all of her problems are finally over but I know they can't be. Something else has to happen to her because the book is only half over. Maybe once she gets to America she won't be able to find her family. What if after all of this trouble to finally get to America and there is no one waiting there for her. If this happens, could Rifka survive on her own? She can't possibly return to Russia. I predict that Rifka gets to New York and has to wander around, being in the streets searching for her family. She, after going through many ordeals, finally finds her family.

BLUE

Can you relate Rifka to other strong, female characters in children's lit?

October 7, 1920

Ellis Island: The words quoted by Pushkin at the opening of this entry must mean a lot to Rifka. This book of poetry has helped her all of her journey but this particular poem is very important. It gives Rifka added energy. She is a survivor and this poem reinforces this fact. Even though she has been through such turmoil, Rifka wants to continue to live. Even if that living includes more suffering and possibly never seeing her family again. She may even get sent back to Russia but Rifka is strong. No matter what happens, she will continue wanting to live.

All these poems relate so well to her ordeals. Her book gives her strength to endure.

RED

October 7, 1920

Ellis Island: If I were Rifka in this situation, I would be a basket-case! I would be so scared that I would never see my family again, and even though Rifka says Ellis Island is not so bad she has to be scared I would not be able to help others if I had so many worries on my mind. What is going to happen? I would not be able to think of anything but my problems, although this is not helping anyone. I would feel so lost and alone, and worried about my future. I think, if I were Rifka, I would stay in my room and cry all the time. I would write some of my feelings down in the Pushkin book, but I don't think that I would have much hope left.

I can't believe that I am looking up to a twelve year old girl. She has a lot of admirable qualities and I wish that there were more people like her.

Putting yourself in the role of the character causes you to self-assess your own strengths and weaknesses

In the midst of all her hardships, she reaches out to help others. She deserves her freedom & and opportunities our country will provide her.

respond to literature before. Responses may verge on retelling or plot summary, and they are typically brief and tend to occur at the end of, rather than intermittently, throughout the chapter. Most literature response journal candidates begin their development at this level, but noteworthy encouraging comments from teachers and gradual developmental stances assuredly move them up the rubric.

The *emerging responder* holds promise and gradual growth in his or her journal. Although commitment to the response process is still questionable, the responder

FIGURE 15.7 Response rubric for literature response journals

Self-Directed Responder

The responder expresses unique personal interactions with the text that indicates the development of an individual response style.

The responder evidences deep involvement with the text and incorporates powerful writing to share his or her personal opinions/emotions/thoughts.

The responder judges and assesses characters against his or her own personal standards, often sharing advice, criticism, empathy, or disparity.

The responder reacts to the text as a literary work and addresses both literary elements and the language/writing techniques used in the text.

The responder compares the text to other texts of the same genre, by the same author, or addressing a similar theme.

The responder exhibits other response characteristics in the Maturing Responder category.

Maturing Responder

The responder expresses his or her personal interactions with the text, although they are similar to what other responders may share.

The responder shows a willingness to use writing to share personal opinions/emotions/thoughts.

The responder evidences involvement with the main character by talking to them, giving them advice, or telling how he or she might behave in the same circumstance.

The responder makes sound predictions based on information from the text and validates or refutes those predictions in later responses.

The responder shows a willingness to try new response options suggested by instructor comments or growing knowledge of response.

The responder exhibits other response characteristics from the Emerging Responder category.

Emerging Responder

The responder attempts to share spontaneously, but he or she might be better suited to a transitional response prompt format.

The responder makes reasonable predictions using information from the text.

The responder shares reactions through writing, but the entries maintain a detached commitment or connection to the text.

The responder poses many questions, either to make sense of the story or to avoid confusion.

The responder shows detached insights into the character(s), maintaining a distance from deeper character involvement.

The responder exhibits other response characteristics from the Novice Responder category.

Novice Responder

The responder writes briefly but seems better able to communicate thoughts and feelings through oral response.

The responder writes a number of brief responses that merely fulfills an assignment, rather than sharing a commitment to the text and characters.

The responder summarizes, mostly retelling the story, rather than interacting with it.

The responder indicates a sense of comprehension but rarely exhibits or indicates personal involvement in the text.

The responder expresses frustration with the reading/writing format of the response journal.

might be better guided by teacher-initiated response prompts rather than the free response process. Given time and encouragement, the emerging responder will grow, stretch, and explore response options while indicating a stronger involvement with character and story.

The *maturing responder* is characterized by a willingness to explore response options and to increase engagement in reading. Responses become more varied, often lengthier, genuinely spontaneous, and more deeply emotional. The reader indicates involvement with the characters and even indicates a stake in the outcome of the book. Meaning-making becomes evident as predictions and queries lead to a fuller understanding of the text. Although responses may parallel those of other readers of the same response stature, they are beginning to reflect individuality of thought and someone who is on the verge of becoming a self-directed responder.

The *self-directed responder* expresses highly unique, emotional responses to characters and situations in literature. This independent level is characterized by reading and responding aesthetically across literary genres and becoming adept at intertextual connections as a broader scope of reading is reached. Personal opinions and character assessment against personal standards are common, and an identifiable individual response style emerges. At this level of response accomplishment, the reader continues to respond in her or his mind even if the thoughts are not recorded in a journal. The response process has become completely comfortable and internalized as part of the active process involved in full reading engagement. Readers/responders who reach this level are likely to develop into lifelong readers who continue to respond to literature in their minds and hearts as adults.

This rubric should be adjusted to better suit the developmental levels of readers in a particular classroom. Simplification of the rubric stretches its use to younger children while still maintaining the prime characteristics of respondents to literature.

Categorizing Response to Literature

Teachers and students in upper intermediate/middle-level grades can serve as monitors of evolving response styles in written journals by categorizing response entries. By coding and graphing written responses to literature, a teacher/student can determine which response options dominate a journal, which response options are being explored, and which response options likely need introduction, modeling, or encouragement. Although the process is time consuming, it provides a visual presentation of written response showing most shared and least attempted response options to a particular book. The purpose is not to obtain an even graph across columns, for to expect that is to distort the individuality of response. The purpose is to verify differences of responses to books of different literary genres, to designate primary response categories over several books, and to determine categories that need yet to be explored.

The categories of response to literature shown in Figure 15.8 are adapted from Hancock (1993), whose research was based on intermediate/middle-level journals in response to realistic fiction. (See Chapter 11 as a reminder of those categories and rich responses that exemplify each.) Note the description for additional response options—it encourages unique response options rather than limiting them to the list.

FIGURE 15.8 Categories of response to literature*

Understanding

Responses indicate the reader's current understanding of character or plot. While bordering on summary, the response may reflect a personal interpretation of the story.

Character Introspection

Responses indicate the reader's effort to project insight into the feelings, thoughts, and motives for behavior of the character. (It sounds like. . . . He must be. . . . She probably. . . .)

Predicting Events

Responses reflect the reader's speculations about what will emerge as the text proceeds. This type of response includes validation or invalidation of previous predictions. (I bet. . . . I think. . . . If. . . . then. . . .)

Questioning

Responses reflect a lack of complete understanding of what is evolving in the text. (I wonder why. . . . I can't tell. . . .)

Character Identification

Responses indicate the reader has achieved a sense of kinship with the character by putting him/herself in the character's role. (If I were. . . . I would. . . .)

Text-to-Life Connections

Responses share a connection between the plot or character and the reader's own life.

Character Assessment

Responses indicate the reader's judgment of the actions or values of the character measured against his/her own personal values or standards of behavior.

Story Involvement

Responses indicate the reader's personal reactions to the setting, theme, events, or sensory aspects of the text.

Literary Elements

Responses reflect a knowledge of literary elements that are weighed against other authors, other texts, or other reading/writing experiences.

Text-to-Text Connections

Responses share a connection between the current text and one or more texts that are a part of the reader's literary repertoire.

Reader/Writer Digressions

Responses indicate the wanderings of the respondent's mind while he/she interacts with the text.

Additional Response Options

Response options must not be limited by the categories listed above. Respondents must be encouraged and allowed to expand these categories through natural response modes.

---

*Categories adapted from Hancock, M. R. (1993). Exploring the meaning-making process through the content of literature response journals. *Research in the Teaching of English, 27,* 335–368.

Expect and encourage those to be added to the table and the graph. As students reread their journal entries, they code the type of response they have made. In cases of longer entries, more than one type of response may be applied. The accuracy does not come in placing one's entry into the "correct" category. The usefulness comes in the coder/student being consistent with the placement within categories. After coding, the coded categories are transferred to a graph and filled in (Figure 15.9). The visual representation provides an overview of categories of written response to literature. Although there is value in the visual image itself, its application to future

FIGURE 15.9   Graph for categorization of responses

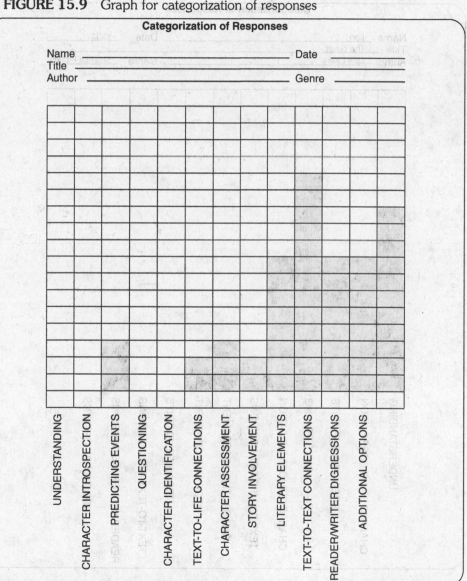

response is the true benefit of implementing this assessment procedure. Two examples, accompanied by narrative overviews, assist in justifying the value of this assessment procedure.

As a seventh grader, Lori's categorized and graphed responses to Lois Lowry's *The Giver* (Figure 15.10) show intense immersion in the text with predictions and questioning as critical components of this science fiction response. Lori, however, does not attempt to judge, support, or refute Jonas's decisions or his relationship to Gabriel, a

FIGURE 15.10 Visual representation of response to *The Giver*: Lori

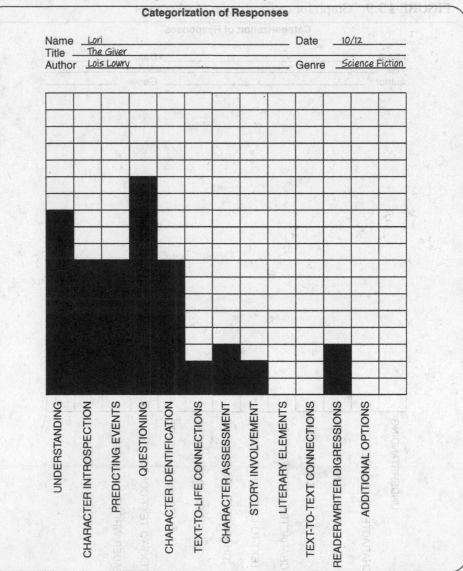

foster child. For the most part, Lori bypasses the opportunity to make connections between Jonas's fate and decisions in her own life. Her involvement with plot may have caused her to forgo response to Lowry's literary elements of a setting devoid of color or characters devoid of free choice. Lori, like so many students, has had little experience with the science fiction genre, perhaps explaining a lack of text-to-text connections.

Daniel's graphic representation (Figure 15.11) indicates a difference in response patterns. Although he questions his way through the book, he avoids predictions. As

FIGURE 15.11   Visual representation of response to *The Giver:* Daniel

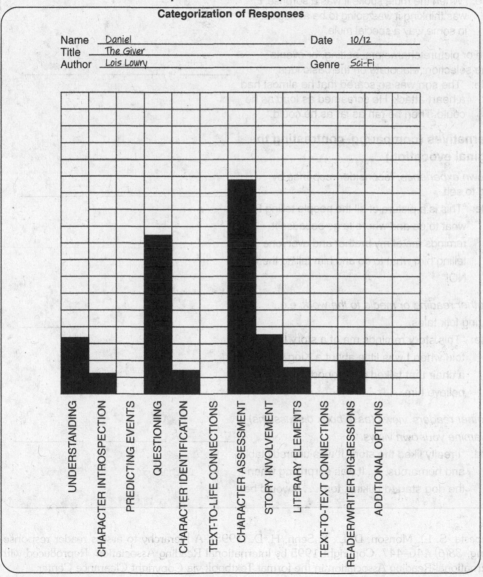

Categorization of Responses

Name   Daniel   Date   10/12
Title   The Giver
Author   Lois Lowry   Genre   Sci-Fi

UNDERSTANDING
CHARACTER INTROSPECTION
PREDICTING EVENTS
QUESTIONING
CHARACTER IDENTIFICATION
TEXT-TO-LIFE CONNECTIONS
CHARACTER ASSESSMENT
STORY INVOLVEMENT
LITERARY ELEMENTS
TEXT-TO-TEXT CONNECTIONS
READER/WRITER DIGRESSIONS
ADDITIONAL OPTIONS

FIGURE 15.12   A taxonomy of aesthetic response*

	Minimal	Moderate	Complete

0. Efferent response.
    Example: "The main characters in the story are the
              talking mule, the talking dog, the boy, and
              his father."

Stage 1: Evocation

1. Relive the experience: reexperience what happened
    as you read; includes acting out, telling, rereading a
    part that you, the reader, choose to reread.
    Example: "When the mule spoke it was a surprise. I
              was thinking it was going to be a magical or
              in some way a special mule."

2. Imagine or picture characters, setting, or events
    from the selection; elaborate on the basic idea.
    Example: "The son was so scared that he almost had
              a heart attack. He screamed as loud as he
              could. Then he ran as far as he could."

**Stage 2: Alternatives (comparing, contrasting the
           original evocation)**

3. *Apply own experience:* reconsider response by
    relating to self.
    Example: "This is a picture of all the people telling Bill
              what to do and where to go because it
              reminds me of my brother and everyone
              telling him what to do and him telling them
              NO!"

4. *Apply other reading or media to the work:* e.g.,
    comparing folk tales.
    Example: "This story reminds me of a story I was
              told when I was little about a King who had
              a chair that talked and nobody would
              believe him. . . ."

5. *Apply other readers' views (as in book discussions)
    or reexamine your own views.*
    Example: "I really liked the story. It was unpredictable
              and humorous. . . . It was surprising when
              the dog started talking, too. . . . It would be

*Source: From Sebesta, S. L., Monson, D. L., & Senn, H. D. (1995). A hierarchy to assess reader response. *Journal of Reading, 38(6)* 446–447. Copyright 1995 by International Reading Association. Reproduced with permission of International Reading Association in the format Textbook via Copyright Clearance Center.

FIGURE 15.12 Continued

great to be able to talk to animals and have them talk back."

6. *Reexamine text from other perspectives:* including hypothesizing, considering another point of view, extrapolating.

    Example: "I wonder why the mule hadn't talked before now? Why did he wait so long to say he was sick of being yelled at?"

Stage 3: Reflective Thinking (thematic level, requiring generalization and application)

7. *Interpretation:* generalize about the meaning of the literary experience, with application to the reader's own life, hence extending #3 to application.

    Example: "Finding out what animals thought would change the world. There may not be anymore eating beef or poultry. Yikes! I love a good leg of chicken."

Stage 4: Evaluation (classified only as aesthetic if the above categories have been met)

8. *Evaluating what you got from the transaction.*

    Example: "If I were the boy I wouldn't trip out. I would go and talk to the animals. What harm can talking to a mule do? Most people chat with their pets anyways. It wouldn't make much difference if the pet talked back. It would actually be nice."

9. *Evaluating the "goodness" of the work itself:* In regard to criteria set by the reader.

    Example: "I think this story really does not have any other point beside the fact that things are not always what they seem. Writing about this donkey might be a lot easier if the story was longer and more thought provoking."

with many readers, he doesn't want those predictions to be wrong, so he avoids putting them in print. Daniel is quick to judge, support, and encourage Jonas in his decisions, but he rarely identifies with the character or speculates on his feelings or thoughts. Although a science fiction character, Jonas carries qualities of most early adolescents, and readers might be expected to identify with those traits. A consistent lack of text-to-text connections reveals a classroom void of experience with this genre.

    Because it would be impossible to conduct this process on every response journal for every reader, it is to the teacher's advantage to model the procedure to students using one of his or her own response journals on an overhead projector. In addition, the modeling might continue by using a volunteer's response journal. Debating categorical placement is not an issue. As long as the coder is consistent in designating categories, the overall purpose will be fulfilled. Students may keep these graphs in portfolios as a part of their assessment and can even present them to the teacher (and parents) for self-evaluation during a conference. The importance of categorizing and graphing responses becomes apparent in assessing response over time. Four graphs, dated and displayed side by side, show expansion of response and familiarity with literature. The visual imaging of response through categorical placement is time consuming, but it should be considered if response variation and exploration are valued, encouraged, and respected.

Hierarchy of Reader Response (Grades 4–8)

Sebesta, Monson, and Senn (1995) developed, refined, and researched a taxonomy of aesthetic response for assessing and interpreting developmental response in grades 4 through 10. Figure 15.12 presents developmentally four stages of aesthetic response and allows the assessor to determine the degree (minimal, moderate, complete) to which the reader expresses each category. Note the realistic inclusion of an efferent stage, which merely reflects summary or repetition of the story, not an emotional interaction with the text.

Stage 1, *Evocation,* focuses on reliving the experience of the text or imagining or picturing literary elements (character, setting, plot events). Stage 2, *Alternatives,* exhibits itself through text-to-life connections, text-to-text connections, and exploration of personal and interpersonal perspectives on the text. Stage 3 rises to the application level of *Reflective thinking,* which highlights personal interpretation of the text. Stage 4, *Evaluation,* forms the pinnacle of aesthetic response as the reader assesses the text within his or her own transaction and evaluates the quality of the work reflective of one's own preset criteria for quality literature.

The researchers found that students in the lower grades "tended to respond more often at the evocation and alternative levels, while the majority of the reflective thinking and evaluation responses came from students in the upper grades" (Sebesta et al., 1995, p. 449). This suggests that response tends to be developmental and provides a tool to assess aesthetic response over time and across grade levels. It also provides a scope and sequence for expanding the response horizons of individual readers/responders over time.

This suggested hierarchy documents individual and class development in reader response and focuses teachers on instruction. The researchers, however, caution teachers to avoid strong dependence on the categories for creating response prompts or comprehension-like questions. "Aesthetic stance . . . is more fluid and emergent than this, and perhaps more holistic than categorical" (Sebesta et al., 1995, p. 450). Those who use the taxonomy for categorization should not expect every response to fit in a distinct category. Response-based teachers must not lose sight of seeking the totally original response that defies categorization. That, indeed, exemplifies the premise of aesthetic response.

ASSESSING LITERATURE CONVERSATIONS

If literature conversations are reader response centered, then an authentic assessment of this oral response sharing format must also be response centered, rather than text centered. Teachers who weave conversations into their classrooms find a

FIGURE 15.13   Literature circle self-evaluation: Primary grades (K–2)*

LITERATURE CIRCLE SELF-EVALUATION

Name _____   Date _____

Title _____

1. I read my book	yes	no
2. I marked places in my book	yes	no
3. I brought my book on Monday	yes	no
4. I shared my book with others	yes	no
5. I thought this book was:		

Not So Good   O.K.   Very Good

FIGURE 15.14   Literature circle self-evaluation: Intermediate grades (3–5)*

LITERATURE CIRCLE SELF-EVALUATION

Name _____   Date _____

Title _____

What did I do well today during our literature circle meeting? (asked good questions, listened actively, responded to others, reread, took a risk, compared the book to my experiences, compared the book to another book)

_____
_____
_____
_____
_____
_____
_____

What do I still need to work on during literature circle meetings?

_____
_____
_____
_____
_____
_____

*Source: From "Literature Circles: Assessment and Evaluation" by Bonnie Campbell Hill. In *Literature Circles and Response* by Bonnie Campbell Hill, Nancy J. Johnson, & Katherine L. Schlick Noe. Copyright © 1995. Reprinted by permission of Christopher-Gordon Publishers, Inc.

FIGURE 15.15   Peer assessment of a grand conversation/literature circle: Middle level (6–8)*

Peer-Assessment of a Grand Conversation/Literature Circle

Book Title _____   Date _____

Author _____   Focus _____

Names of Participants

Preparation

    Read the assigned chapter book
    Prepared literature response journal entries
    Noted book excerpts to share
    Prepared critical thinking questions for discussion

Participation

    Read-aloud response entries from journal
    Posed challenging questions to the group
    Used text to support/clarify
    Made inferences from the text
    Referred to the author's craft
    Shared intertextual connections
    Shared text-to-life connections
    Elicited responses from other group members
    Kept an open mind to the contributions of others
    Maintained a professional conversational demeanor

*Denotes person completing form.

---

*Source: Adapted from *Practical Aspects of Authentic Assessment: Putting the Pieces Together* by Bonnie Campbell Hill and Cynthia Ruptic. Reprinted by permission of Christopher-Gordon Publishers, Inc.

need to assess reading attitudes, reading preparation, levels of response, and amount and range of reading.

For primary-grade literature conversations, Hill (1995) suggests a simple self-evaluation that allows young children to assess preliminary responsibilities as a member of a literature circle (Figure 15.13). As children enter early intermediate grades, a literature self-reflection (Hill, 1995), Figure 15.14, is more appropriate because it requires written self-evaluations. Figure 15.15 is an adaptation of a form used by Hill and Ruptic (1994) in attempting to monitor literature conversations at the grade 6 to 8 levels. The form not only assesses the quality and types of response generated during discussion, but it also allows for both self- and peer evaluation.

The emphasis in literature conversation assessment is self-reflection, which meshes well with the philosophy on reader response. Each individual provides the most thorough understanding of their group responsibilities, response capabilities, and contributions to discussion. Just as a reader is responsible for sharing unique responses through reflection, so too does self-reflection play an important role in assessment.

A READER RESPONSE PORTFOLIO

A portfolio is defined as a collection of a student's work, in different stages of development, that reveals strengths and weaknesses and allows both the student and the teacher to evaluate progress (Tierney et al., 1991). A reader response portfolio, on a narrower scope, is defined as a collection of a student's responses to literature across literary genres and through varying modes of response that reveals a unique and developing response style allowing for both student reflection and teacher narrative assessment.

The reader response portfolio is built on the guiding principles of a portfolio approach to literacy assessment. First, a response portfolio is anchored in *authenticity*. Real evidence or real response is reflected in the portfolio content. All artifacts arise in the aesthetic classroom setting and are products of interactions with authentic children's literature. Second, reader response assessment is a *continuous, ongoing process*. Because response styles are constantly growing and changing, portfolio documentation forms a dated record of evolving response to a variety of literary genres through a variety of response modes. Third, reader response assessment within a portfolio is *multidimensional*. Because response modes encompass oral and written response as well as dramatic and artistic response, the portfolio artifacts are likely to include a variety of formats beyond literature response journals. Finally, portfolio assessment for response must provide *interactive reflection* by both reader and teacher so personal goals may be set. The consistent nature of teacher feedback, readers' narrative evaluations of their own response, and a response conference support these criteria.

No single observation of literature discussion, no single entry from a response journal, no single art form, no single written product built on a literature model can capture the overall authentic, continuous, multidimensional, interactive nature of sound portfolio assessment. The fit between reader response and portfolio documentation is a natural one that supports the uniqueness of the individual learner yet monitors aspects of growth and refinement of reading material choice and response style.

Elements of a Reader Response Portfolio

The multiplicity of items that might be placed in a reader response portfolio is only limited by the assignments of the teacher and the ingenuity and creativity of the responder. These are the two overlying criteria for each artifact: (1) response is based on authentic children's literature; and (2) response reflects a genuine, unique, personal perspective on that literature.

The response documentation may take forms such as these:

- **Literature response file.** Selected brief entries from the reading of picture books, transitional chapter books, or chapter books.
- **Literature response journal.** A notebook or photocopied entries from individual journals.
- **Audiotape.** Recorded conversations (or transcripts) from read-alouds or literature conversations highlighting the individual's oral response and/or interactions with other readers.
- **Videotape.** Performance documentation of response to literature that is likely to include a play, a readers' theater presentation, movement, or musical performance.
- **Photographs.** Documentation of constructions, three-dimensional projects, murals, or presentations resulting from a response to literature.
- **Artwork.** Any original artistic response to literature including drawing, painting, sculpture, or book illustration.
- **Book list.** A list of books read and responded to including date, author, title, illustrator (if applicable), publisher, genre, and response mode chosen for response to each title.
- **Book graph.** A bar graph that records books read and responded to organized by literary genre.
- **Response checklist.** A list that records modes of literary response to literature (e.g., oral, written journals, written product, artistic, music, cooking, sharing).
- **Categorized graphs.** Graphs of response journal entries over several books.

This list is not inclusive, but it does provide an idea of the many options for portfolio inclusion. Although it might be adjusted depending on classroom response options at various age/grade levels, it does show the value of accumulating a variety of artifacts as documentation of response growth and future potential.

Stages of Response Portfolio Development

The four stages of *collection, selection, reflection,* and *projection* that apply to general academic portfolios should be applied to the response-based portfolio as well. Readers can collect all of their responses over a period of time and include them in the portfolio in their different forms.

At scheduled intervals, the selection process causes students to apply self-evaluative techniques to determine which response documentation will remain in the portfolio and which will be excluded. This can be determined by two factors: predetermined standards or numerical criteria with self-selection as a primary factor. Guidelines set by the teacher may require evidence of the following:

- Written response to literature that best reflects growing response style
- Oral response to literature that reflects your ability to contribute to group discussions on literature

- Art or musical or dramatic response documentation through a performance product
- Responder's favorite response
- Responder's choice

Numerical choice simply involves students including a designated number of responses, but student choice is paramount in either selection process.

Whether requirements are imposed or choice is dominant, the third aspect of portfolio assessment is reflection. The reader/responder must include a written reflection on each selection including the following:

1. Why did I choose the response artifact?
2. How does the response artifact reflects the literature read?
3. What does the artifact indicate about my growing confidence to respond to literature?

The personal reflection is most important and should never be eliminated from the portfolio assessment process. Self-reflection reveals personal insights into growth in appreciation of literature and in one's own response to what is read.

The final aspect of portfolio assessment is projection or goal setting. This is jointly managed by the teacher and the student through a portfolio conference. Readers should focus on these three areas of concern:

1. Am I reading books across a variety of genres?
2. Am I responding to books through a variety of response modes?
3. Am I growing in depth and breadth in response to literature?

Goals can be set in all of these areas. Reading across genres can be addressed

---

RESOURCES ON THE WEB
Electronic Response Portfolios

An electronic portfolio, or e-portfolio, uses electronic technologies to support and facilitate teachers and students as they move through the states of collection, selection, reflection, and projection of response-based portfolio artifacts. Electronic portfolios may be created with common software such as Microsoft Office (including Word or Power Point), Adobe Acrobat, or Web page editors (such as Dreamweaver or Front Page). To create portfolios with these tools does not require immediate Internet access, although they may be posted to the Internet at a later time. Teachers may prefer to publish portfolios on CD-recordable discs that can easily be shared with parents. Alternatively, social networking sites and electronic communication tools that emphasize online collaboration and sharing among users provide options for creating and publishing interactive electronic portfolios directly on the Internet.

A variety of artifacts may be included in the e-portfolio. Similar to a traditional reader response portfolio, two criteria guide the selection process of each artifact: (1) response is based on authentic children's literature, and (2) response reflects a unique perspective on the literary selection. Fueled by creative teachers and students, the possibilities of electronic portfolios are endless. Elements of an electronic reader response portfolio may include:

- **Electronic response journals.** Hyperlinks to electronic response journals including personal blogs or electronic documents (see Chapter 10).
- **Information about authors and illustrators.** Hyperlinks to author and illustrator websites.
- **Information about the literature.** Hyperlinks to websites that relate to or extends a book's content or context.
- **Sound files.** Sound files including recorded conversations of literature conversations, music, or personal commentary that highlight individual response and/or interactions with other readers.
- **Artwork.** Scanned images of artistic response to literature, including drawing, painting, book illustrations, or art projects created with KidPix or other drawing programs.
- **Digital photographs and images.** Visual documentations of individual response projects.
- **Digital video recordings.** Performance-based documentation of response to literature through literature conversations, readers' theater, oral presentations, or musical performances.
- **Book list.** A list or database of books read and responded to, including the title, author, date, and chosen response mode.
- **Graphs.** Visual representations (produced in Microsoft Excel or other software program) of books read and responded to by literary genre, author, or response categories.

by stating which literary genres need to be encountered through future reading. The goal is not for readers to forsake their favorite kinds of books but to ensure exposure to all genres to some degree. Response modes can be addressed by looking for voids in type of response. If a reader is only responding through writing, a goal should be set to explore other options that might otherwise be avoided or dismissed. The purpose once again is not to forsake a favorite mode of response but to ensure exposure to various modes of response. Goals can enhance response in a favored mode but also reach toward new options as well. The goals must be jointly set, but those sincerely set by the reader are most likely to be realized.

The reader response portfolio should be shared at a parent/teacher/student conference because it indicates growth in reading, appreciation of literature, and the ability to share personal interactions with books read. Providing an extended view of the reading process, it documents the individuality rather than standardization of the child as reader and responder. The list of books, the graph of genres, and the graph of response modes visually show parents the amount and types of books read and the variety of response modes experienced as an extension of the reading experience. Sharing of individual oral, written, dramatic, or artistic responses reflects the multiple talents of students in communicating personal thoughts and innermost feelings. The reader response portfolio moves assessment far beyond the reading test battery scores in comprehension, vocabulary, and decoding skills. The response portfolio reflects the potential of a reader to become involved in a lifetime of rich literary encounters long after the school experience concludes. Reading as a matter of choice rather than to fulfill a requirement is a valid measure of the growth of a child as a reader.

CLOSING THOUGHTS

Because accountability is a reality in a response-based literature program, teachers must meet the challenge of assessment and documentation of reader response to literature. Perhaps the single most important concern of inservice teachers is literature-based assessment. They feel pressure from administrators and parents to "prove" that children are really learning through literature. This chapter provides a variety of tools to assist the teacher and the reader in documenting response that reflects growth over time. The principles of authentic assessment provide the foundation for checklists, categories of response, a hierarchy of response, and reader response portfolios. Other tools provide a means for assessment to inform instruction through checklists of prompts, response activities, and insightful anecdotal records. Response accountability moves far beyond test performance. Reader response documentation provides a richer, deeper perspective on the ongoing growth and potential of a lifelong reader.

If a response-based view of literature is to be legitimized as part of a balanced reading program, the necessity of meaningful assessment must be addressed. Most advocates of Louise Rosenblatt believe that lifelong reading is an intangible outcome of reader response to literature in the elementary school, but they must show documented evidence of short-term gains and provide specific examples that indicate meaning-making and personal reflection are taking place. Although this type of assessment is certainly more time consuming to collect and assimilate than traditional types of assessment, it should be part of a balanced literacy assessment program for K–8 students. This chapter's offerings attempt to supply educators with tools to assist in this challenging task. These assessment suggestions produce convincing evidence to support what we instinctively know happens to children when they are given the freedom to read and are encouraged in their personal transactions with literature.

References

Atwell, Nancie (2006). *The reading zone: How to help kids become skilled, passionate, habitual, critical readers.* New York: Scholastic Professional Books.

Bauer, E. B., & Garcia, G. E. (2002). Lessons from a classroom teacher's use of alternative literacy assessment. *Research in the Teaching of English, 36,* 462–494.

Damico, J. S. (2005). Multiple dimensions of literacy and conceptions of readers: Toward a more expansive view of accountability. *The Reading Teacher, 58,* 644–652.

Hancock, M. R. (1993). Exploring the meaning-making process through the content of literature response journals: A case study investigation. *Research in the Teaching of English, 27,* 335–368.

Hill, B. C. (1995). Literature circles: Assessment and evaluation. In B. C. Hill, N. J. Johnson, & K. L. Schlick Noe (Eds.) *Literature circles and response* (pp. 167–198). Norwood, MA: Christopher-Gordon.

Hill, B. C., & Ruptic, C. (1994). *Practical aspects of authentic assessment: Putting the pieces together.* Norwood, MA: Christopher-Gordon.

International Reading Association and the National Council of Teachers of English (1994). *Standards for the assessment of reading and writing.* Newark, DE and Urbana, IL: Author.

Johnston, P. (2005). Literacy assessment and the future. *The Reading Teacher, 58,* 684–686.

Sebesta, S. L., Monson, D. L., & Senn, H. D. (1995). A hierarchy to assess reader response. *Journal of Reading, 38,* 444–450.

Tierney, R., Carter, M., & Desai, L. (1991). *Portfolio assessment in the reading-writing classroom.* Norwood, MA: Christopher-Gordon.

Children's Books Cited [P] = K–2; [I] = 3–5; [M] = 6–8

Hesse, Karen (1992). *Letters from Rifka.* New York: Holt. [I]

Lowry, Lois (1993). *The giver.* Boston: Houghton Mifflin. [M]

Epilogue
Continuing the Celebration

I am not under the illusion that the schools alone can change society. However, I can reaffirm the belief uttered so many years ago: We teachers of language and literature have a crucial role to play as educators and citizens. We phrase our goals as fostering the growth of the capacity for personally meaningful, self-critical literary experience. The educational process that achieves this aim most effectively will serve a broader purpose, the nurturing of men and women capable of building a fully democratic society. The prospect is invigorating! (Rosenblatt, 1990, p. 107)

Throughout your journey through *A Celebration of Literature and Response*, you have been immersed in an enormous amount of information about children's literature and children as readers and respondents to literature. You have been introduced to a philosophy of literature-based instruction with reader response at its core. By reading and responding to some of the quality literature shared throughout these pages and by actively becoming involved in some of the response-based activities suggested throughout the text, you have grown in your knowledge of both books and readers. But the celebration has only just begun as you take your expertise to real readers in real classrooms with real literature as the focus of learning.

Whether you go forth as a preservice teacher, a student intern, a first-year teacher, or an experienced practitioner, you have much to celebrate as you carry this information to children in a classroom setting. How have you enriched your response-based, literature expertise to ensure the celebration will continue with children? With judicious reading and response to this text, you have likely assumed the following knowledge base:

- Understanding of Louise Rosenblatt's transactional theory of reader response, efferent and aesthetic response, and short- and long-term impact of literature and response on children as readers and critical thinkers.
- Knowledge of the varied response options across developmental levels and the need to nurture response potential in your classroom.
- Recognition of an aesthetic teaching philosophy and its focus, acceptance, and encouragement of the expression of unique interactions with literature by and among individual readers.
- Knowledge of hundreds of children's books and literary genres to enhance literacy experiences throughout the school day and across an entire elementary K–8 spectrum.
- Familiarity with oral response to literature, including spontaneous read-aloud response, the use of prompts to elicit unique response, and the enhancement of oral response through literature conversations.
- Confidence in the power of the written response to literature, both through literature response journals and through literature as a model for writing.
- Appreciation for responses built on the fine arts of drama, art, and music as an option for sharing responses to literature.
- Ability to connect and blend literature across genres into an effective knowledge base for interdisciplinary instruction.
- Integration and blending of literature and technology as mutually beneficial possibilities for preparing children for their literacy futures.
- Understanding of authentic assessment tools as a means to monitor and document growth in reader response to literature over time.
- Ability to articulate the connection among reader response theory, children's literature, and the critical role of the reader in creating lifelong learners and critical thinking citizens in a democratic society.

> In any reading, many personal, textual, and contextual factors will at any moment influence which of these aspects a reader will pay attention to. A reading event is like a journey. Some reader . . . may be focusing mainly on what he is to remember after the reading journey is over. Another may be focused on just enjoying the journey itself, mainly paying attention to the ideas, scenes, characters, and feelings lived through during the actual reading. Another, without a clear purpose, may end with a blurred, shallow impression. (Rosenblatt, 2005, pp. x–xi)

Reading *A Celebration of Literature and Response* is an "event" that has hopefully been an inspiring personal and professional journey for you as a reader and a teacher. Rather than a "blurred" vision of literature in the classroom, you have now attained a clear vision, far beyond text itself, toward implementation of literature-based ideas.

You are invited to begin your own celebration of literature and response with children as you focus on the application of philosophy, literature, and response in an instructional setting. Open your eyes to all the ways in which readers respond to literature in your classroom and build from that foundation. Take these quality children's books and share them with children throughout the day and across the curriculum. Try developmentally appropriate response-based activities with children hungry for an opportunity to express their reactions to literature. Vary your menu of response activities to capture the interest and abilities of diverse learners. Add a component to your assessment package that focuses on documentation of growth of response. Make connections between your own state standards and the literature-based activities you have experienced through this text. Only when the contents and spirit of this book are carried to real children in real classrooms can the genuine celebration of literature and response begin.

As you move beyond this text into the world of children, literature, and teaching, your professional journey must continue. What can you do to continue your growth in children's literature and reader response to literature? Consider these suggestions:

- Read children's literature. Build a wide repertoire of books to sustain interest and excitement in literature-based teaching. Read across genres, across authors, and include multicultural books.
- Be aware of book awards and lists (see the appendix), anticipate their announcement, and add them to your media center collection.
- Read professional review journals (see chapter references) regularly to update your knowledge of new books for children.
- Read professional journals in reading, language arts, and children's literature for continued research-based connections to the classroom.
- Access up-to-date information on children's authors and newly published titles on the Internet.
- Explore dynamic ways to integrate literature and technology as a means of literacy instruction and a communicative means of sharing personal reflections and interpretations.
- Attend professional meetings with a focus on literature in the classroom.
- Conduct teacher action research in your own classroom on response-based activities or children's responses to particular genres or titles.
- Share books, response, and excitement with other teaching professionals. Spread the enjoyment of literature and response throughout your school and district.

As you move beyond *A Celebration of Literature and Response,* take with you a passion for quality children's literature, the power of response, and the impact of teaching children. You can't create lifelong readers if you lack a genuine enthusiasm for children's literature. You can't expect responses to grow if you are not open to risk taking and a belief in the uniqueness of the individual reader. And you can't impact children as readers if you don't bring energy, commitment, and dedication to the classroom. When these essentials are in place, you are ready to move on with quality literature, unique response, and enthusiastic readers as the foundation of your teaching.

My belief in the importance of the schools in a democracy has not only evolved but increased throughout the years. In 1938, democracy was being threatened by forces and ideologies from outside. Today, I believe it is again seriously threatened by converging forces from within. From local schools to state standards to Supreme Court cases, education has become an arena for this ideological struggle. . . . Of course, the schools cannot do the whole job, but they are essential. We are already overburdened as teachers, yet as citizens we need to promote and defend the social, economic, and political conditions that make it possible for us to carry on our democratic tasks in the classroom. (Rosenblatt, 1999, p. 169)

Cause the celebration of literature and response to continue!

Rosenblatt, L. M. (1990). Retrospect. In Farrell, E. J., & Squire, J. R. (Eds.) *Transactions with literature: A fifty-year perspective* (pp. 97–107). Urbana, IL: National Council of Teachers of English.

Rosenblatt, L. M. (with N. J. Karolides) (1999). Theory and practice: An interview with Louise M. Rosenblatt. *Language Arts, 77,* 158–170.

Rosenblatt, L. M. (2005). *Making meaning with texts: Selected essays.* Portsmouth, NH: Heinemann.

APPENDIX

Children's Book Awards and Recognition

The Caldecott Medal

Named in honor of the 19th-century English illustrator Randolph Caldecott, this medal is presented annually to the illustrator of the most distinguished American picture book for children published during the preceding year. A number of honor books may also be named by the selection committee. Sponsored by the Association for Library Service to Children, a division of the American Library Association, eligibility for this award is limited to U.S. citizens and residents.

2007 *Flotsam* by David Wiesner. Clarion.

Honor Books: *Gone Wild: An Endangered Animal Alphabet* by David McLimans. Walker. *Moses: When Harriet Tubman Led Her People to Freedom* by Carole Boston Weatherford. Illus. by Kadir Nelson. Hyperion/Jump at the Sun.

2006 *The Hello, Good-bye Window* by Norton Juster. Illus. by Chris Raschka. Hyperion.

Honor Books: *Rosa* by Nikki Giovanni. Illus. by Bryan Collier. Holt. *Zen Shorts* by John J. Muth. Scholastic. *Hot Air: The (Mostly) True Story of the First Hot-Air Balloon Ride* by Marjorie Priceman. Atheneum. *Song of the Water Boatman and Other Pond Poems* by Joyce Sidman. Illus. by Beckie Prange. Houghton Mifflin.

2005   *Kitten's First Full Moon* by Kevin Henkes. Greenwillow.

Honor Books: *The Red Book* by Barbara Lehman. Houghton Mifflin. *Coming on Home Soon* by Jacqueline Woodson. Illus. by E. B. Lewis. Putnam. *Knuffle Bunny: A Cautionary Tale* by Mo Willems. Hyperion.

2004   *The Man Who Walked Between the Towers* by Mordecai Gerstein. Roaring Brook.

Honor Books: *Ella Sarah Gets Dressed* by Margaret Chodos-Irvine. Harcourt. *What Do You Do with a Tail Like This?* by Steve Jenkins and Robin Page. Houghton Mifflin. *Don't Let the Pigeon Drive the Bus* by Mo Willems. Hyperion.

2003   *My Friend Rabbit* by Eric Rohmann. Millbrook Press.

Honor Books: *The Spider and the Fly* by Mary Howitt. Illus. by Tony DiTerlizzi. Simon & Schuster. *Hondo & Fabian* by Peter McCarty. Holt. *Noah's Ark* by Jerry Pinkney. North-South Books.

2002   *The Three Pigs* by David Wiesner. Clarion.

Honor Books: *The Dinosaurs of Waterhouse Hawkins: An Illuminating History of Mr. Waterhouse Hawkins, Artist and Lecturer* by Barbara Kerley. Illus. by Brian Selznick. Scholastic. *Martin's Big Words: The Life of Dr. Martin Luther King, Jr.* by Doreen Rappaport. Illus. by Bryan Collier. Hyperion. *The Stray Dog* by Marc Simont. HarperCollins.

2001   *So You Want to Be President?* by Judith St. George. Illus. by David Small. Philomel.

Honor Books: *Casey at the Bat: A Ballad of the Republic Sung in the Year 1888* by Ernest L. Thayer. Illus. by Christopher Bing. Handprint. *Click, Clack, Moo: Cows That Type* by Doreen Cronin. Illus. by Betsy Lewin. Simon & Schuster. *Olivia* by Ian Falconer. Atheneum.

2000   *Joseph Had a Little Overcoat* by Simms Taback. Viking.

Honor Books: *When Sophie Gets Angry—Really, Really Angry* by Molly Bang. Scholastic. *A Child's Calendar* by John Updike. Illus. by Trina Schart Hyman. Holiday House. *The Ugly Duckling* adapted and illustrated by Jerry Pinkney. Morrow. *Sector 7* by David Wiesner. Clarion.

1999   *Snowflake Bentley* by Jacqueline Briggs Martin. Illus. by Mary Azarian. Houghton Mifflin.

Honor Books: *Duke Ellington* by Andrea Davis Pinkney. Illus. by Brian Pinkney. Hyperion. *No, David!* by David Shannon. Blue Sky/Scholastic. *Snow* by Uri Shulevitz. Farrar, Straus & Giroux. *Tibet: Through the Red Box* by Peter Sis. Farrar, Straus & Giroux.

1998   *Rapunzel* by Paul O. Zelinsky. Dutton.

> **Honor Books:** *The Gardener* by Sarah Stewart. Illus. by David Small. Farrar, Straus & Giroux. *Harlem* by Walter Dean Myers. Illus. by Christopher Myers. Scholastic. *There Was an Old Lady Who Swallowed a Fly* by Simms Taback. Viking.

1997   *Golem* by David Wisniewski. Clarion.

> **Honor Books:** *Hush! A Thai Lullaby* by Minfong Ho. Illus. by Holly Meade. Orchard. *The Graphic Alphabet* by Neal Porter. Illus. by David Pelletier. Orchard. *The Paperboy* by Dave Pilkey. Orchard. *Starry Messenger: Galileo Galilei* by Peter Sis. Farrar, Straus & Giroux.

1996   *Officer Buckle and Gloria* by Peggy Rathmann. Putnam.

> **Honor Books:** *Alphabet City* by Stephen Johnson. Viking. *Zin! Zin! Zin! a Violin* by Lloyd Moss. Simon & Schuster. Illus. by Marjorie Priceman. Simon & Schuster. *The Faithful Friend* by Robert D. San Souci. Illus. by Brian Pinkney. Simon & Schuster. *Tops and Bottoms* by Janet Stevens. Harcourt.

1995   *Smoky Night* by Eve Bunting. Illus. by David Diaz. Harcourt.

> **Honor Books:** *Swamp Angel* by Anne Isaacs. Illus. by Paul O. Zelinsky. Dutton. *John Henry* by Julius Lester. Illus. by Jerry Pinkney. Dial. *Time Flies* by Eric Rohmann. Crown.

1994   *Grandfather's Journey* by Allen Say. Houghton Mifflin.

> **Honor Books:** *Peppe the Lamplighter* by Elisa Barone. Illus. by Ted Lewin. Lothrop. *In the Small, Small Pond* by Denise Fleming. Holt. *Owen* by Kevin Henkes. Greenwillow. *Raven: A Trickster Tale from the Pacific Northwest* by Gerald McDermott. Harcourt. *Yo! Yes?* by Chris Raschka. Orchard.

1993   *Mirette on the High Wire* by Emily Arnold McCully. Putnam.

> **Honor Books:** *Seven Blind Mice* by Ed Young. Philomel. *The Stinky Cheese Man and Other Fairly Stupid Tales* by Jon Scieszka. Illus. by Lane Smith. Viking. *Working Cotton* by Sherley Anne Williams. Illus. by Carole Byard. Harcourt.

1992   *Tuesday* by David Wiesner. Clarion.

> **Honor Book:** *Tar Beach* by Faith Ringgold. Crown.

1991   *Black and White* by David McCaulay. Houghton Mifflin.

> **Honor Books:** *Puss'n Boots* by Charles Perrault. Illus. by Fred. Marcellino. Farrar, Straus & Giroux, *"More, More, More," Said the Baby: 3 Love Stories* by Vera B. Williams. Greenwillow.

1990   *Lon Po Po: A Red Riding Hood Tale from China* translated and illustrated by Ed Young. Philomel.

Honor Books: *Hershel and the Hanukkah Goblins* by Eric Kimmel. Illus. by Trina Schart Hyman. Holiday House. *The Talking Eggs* adapted by Robert D. San Souci. Illus. by Jerry Pinkney. Dial. *Bill Peet: An Autobiography* by Bill Peet. Houghton Mifflin. *Color Zoo* by Lois Ehlert. Lippincott.

1989   *Song and Dance Man* by Karen Ackerman. Illus. by Stephen Gammell. Knopf.

Honor Books: *Free Fall* by David Wiesner. Lothrop. *Goldilocks and the Three Bears* retold and illustrated by James Marshall. Dial. *Mirandy and Brother Wind* by Patricia McKissack. Illus. by Jerry Pinkney. Knopf. *The Boy of the Three-Year Nap* by Diane Snyder. Illus. by Allen Say. Houghton Mifflin.

1988   *Owl Moon* by Jane Yolen. Illus. by John Schoenherr. Philomel.

Honor Book: *Mufaro's Beautiful Daughters* retold by John Steptoe. Lothrop.

1987   *Hey, Al* by Arthur Yorinks. Illus. by Richard Egielski. Farrar, Straus & Giroux.

Honor Books: *The Village of Round and Square Houses* by Ann Grifalconi. Little, Brown. *Alphabatics* by Suse MacDonald. Bradbury. *Rumpelstiltskin* retold and illustrated by Paul O. Zelinsky. Dutton.

1986   *The Polar Express* by Chris Van Allsburg. Houghton Mifflin.

Honor Books: *The Relatives Came* by Cynthia Rylant. Illus. by Stephen Gammell. Bradbury. *King Bidgood's in the Bathtub* by Audrey Wood. Illus. by Don Wood. Harcourt.

1985   *Saint George and the Dragon* adapted by Margaret Hodges. Illus. by Trina Schart Hyman. Little, Brown.

Honor Books: *Hansel and Gretel* adapted by Rika Lesser. Illus. by Paul O. Zelinsky. Dodd. *The Story of Jumping Mouse* retold and illustrated by John Steptoe. Lothrop. *Have You Seen My Duckling?* by Nancy Tafuri. Greenwillow.

1984   *The Glorious Flight: Across the Channel with Louis Blériot,* by Alice and Martin Provensen. Viking.

Honor Books: *Ten, Nine, Eight* by Molly Bang. Greenwillow. *Little Red Riding Hood* by the Brothers Grimm. Retold and illustrated by Trina Schart Hyman. Holiday House.

1983   *Shadow* by Blaise Cendrars. Translated and illustrated by Marcia Brown. Scribner's.

Honor Books: *When I Was Young in the Mountains* by Cynthia Rylant. Illus. by Diane Goode. Dutton. *A Chair for My Mother* by Vera B. Williams. Greenwillow.

1982   *Jumanji* by Chris Van Allsburg. Houghton Mifflin.

Honor Books: *Visit to William Blake's Inn: Poems for Innocent and Experienced Travelers* by Nancy Willard. Illus. by Alice and Martin Provensen.

Harcourt. *Where the Buffaloes Begin* by Olaf Baker. Illus. by Stephen Gammell. *On Market Street* by Arnold Lobel. Illus. by Anita Lobel. Greenwillow. *Outside Over There* by Maurice Sendak. Harper.

1981   *Fables* by Arnold Lobel. Harper.

Honor Books: *The Bremen-Town Musicians* retold and illustrated by Ilse Plume. Doubleday. *The Grey Lady and the Strawberry Snatcher* by Molly Bang. Four Winds. *Mice Twice* by Joseph Low. Atheneum. *Truck* by Donald Crews. Greenwillow.

1980   *Ox-Cart Man* by Donald Hall. Illus. by Barbara Cooney. Viking.

Honor Books: *Ben's Trumpet* by Rachel Isadora. Greenwillow. *The Treasure* by Uri Schulevitz. Farrar, Straus & Giroux. *The Garden of Abdul Gasazi* by Chris Van Allsburg. Houghton Mifflin.

1979   *The Girl Who Loved Wild Horses* by Paul Goble. Bradbury.

Honor Books: *Freight Train* by Donald Crews. Greenwillow. *The Way to Start a Day* by Byrd Baylor. Illus. by Peter Parnall. Scribner's.

1978   *Noah's Ark* by Peter Spier. Doubleday.

Honor Books: *Castle* by David McCaulay. Houghton Mifflin. *It Could Always Be Worse* retold and illustrated by Margot Zemach. Farrar, Straus & Giroux.

1977   *Ashanti to Zulu: African Traditions* by Margaret Musgrove. Illus. by Leo and Diane Dillon. Dial.

Honor Books: *The Amazing Bone* by William Steig. Farrar, Straus & Giroux. *The Contest* by Nonny Hogrogian. Greenwillow. *Fish for Supper* by M. B. Goffstein. Dial. *The Golem: A Jewish Legend* retold and illus. by Beverly Brodsky McDermott. Lippincott. *Hawk, I'm Your Brother* by Byrd Baylor. Illus. by Peter Parnall. Scribner's.

1976   *Why Mosquitoes Buzz in People's Ears* retold by Verna Aardema. Illus. by Leo and Diane Dillon. Dial.

Honor Books: *The Desert Is Theirs* by Byrd Baylor. Illus. by Peter Parnall. Scribner's. *Strega Nona* retold and illustrated by Tomie de Paola. Prentice Hall.

1975   *Arrow to the Sun* adapted and illustrated by Gerald McDermott. Viking.

Honor Book: *Jambo Means Hello: Swahili Alphabet Book* by Muriel Feelings. Illus. by Tom Feelings. Dial.

1974   *Duffy and the Devil* retold by Harve Zemach. Illus. by Margot Zemach. Farrar, Straus & Giroux.

Honor Books: *Three Jovial Huntsmen* adapted and illustrated by Susan Jeffers. Bradbury. *Cathedral: The Story of Its Construction* by David McCaulay. Houghton Mifflin.

1973   *The Funny Little Woman* retold by Arlene Mosel. Illus. by Blair Lent. Dutton.

Honor Books: *Hosie's Alphabet* by Hosea Baskin, Tobias Baskin, and Lisa Baskin. Illus. by Leonard Baskin. Viking. *When Clay Sings* by Byrd Baylor. Illus. by Tom Bahti. Scribner's. *Snow-White and the Seven Dwarfs* by the Brothers Grimm. Translated by Randall Jarrell. Illus. by Nancy Ekholm Burkert. Farrar, Straus & Giroux. *Anansi the Spider: A Tale from the Ashanti* adapted and illustrated by Gerald McDermott. Holt.

1972   *One Fine Day* by Nonny Hogrogian. Macmillan.

Honor Books: *If All the Seas Were One Sea* by Janina Domanska. Macmillan. *Moja Means One: Swahili Counting Book* by Muriel Feelings. Illus. by Tom Feelings. Dial. *Hildilid's Night* by Cheli Duran Ryan. Illus. by Arnold Lobel. Macmillan.

1971   *A Story, a Story: An African Tale* by Gail E. Haley. Atheneum.

Honor Books: *The Angry Moon* retold by William Sleator. Illus. by Blair Lent. Atlantic/Little, Brown. *Frog and Toad Are Friends* by Arnold Lobel. Harper. *In the Night Kitchen* by Maurice Sendak. Harper.

1970   *Sylvester and the Magic Pebble* by William Steig. Windmill.

Honor Books: *Goggles!* by Ezra Jack Keats. Macmillan. *Alexander and the Wind-Up Mouse* by Leo Lionni. Pantheon. *Pop Corn and Ma Goodness* by Edna Mitchell Preston. Illus. by Robert Andrew Parker. Viking. *Thy Friend, Obadiah* by Brinton Turkle. Viking. *The Judge: An Untrue Tale* by Harve Zemach. Illus. by Margot Zemach. Farrar, Straus & Giroux.

1969   *The Fool of the World and the Flying Ship: A Russian Tale* by Arthur Ransome. Illus. by Uri Schulevitz. Farrar, Straus & Giroux.

Honor Book: *Why the Sun and the Moon Live in the Sky: An African Folktale* by Elphinstone Dayrell. Illus. by Blair Lent. Houghton Mifflin.

1968   *Drummer Hoff* adapted by Barbara Emberley. Illus. by Ed Emberley. Prentice Hall.

Honor Books: *Frederick* by Leo Lionni. Pantheon. *Seashore Story* by Taro Yashima. Viking. *The Emperor and the Kite* by Jane Yolen. Illus. by Ed Young. World.

1967   *Sam, Bangs and Moonshine* by Evaline Ness. Holt.

Honor Book: *One Wide River to Cross* adapted by Barbara Emberley. Illus. by Ed Emberley. Prentice Hall.

1966   *Always Room for One More* by Sorche Nic Leodhas (pseudonym for Leclaire Alger). Illus. by Nonny Hogrogian. Holt.

Honor Books: *Hide and Seek Fog* by Alvin Tresselt. Illus. by Roger Duvoisin. Lothrop. *Just Me* by Marie Hall Ets. Viking. *Tom Tit Tot* adapted by Joseph Jacobs. Illus. by Evaline Ness. Scribner's.

1965   *May I Bring a Friend?* by Beatrice Schenk de Regniers. Illus. by Beni Montresor. Atheneum.

Honor Books: *Rain Makes Applesauce* by Julian Scheer. Illus. by Marvin Bileck. Holiday House. *The Wave* by Margaret Hodges. Illus. by Blair Lent. Houghton Mifflin. *A Pocketful of Cricket* by Rebecca Caudill. Illus. by Evaline Ness. Holt.

1964   *Where the Wild Things Are* by Maurice Sendak. Harper.

Honor Books: *Swimmy* by Leo Lionni. Pantheon. *All in the Morning Early* by Sorche Nic Leodhas (pseudonym for Leclaire Alger). Illus. by Evaline Ness. Holt. *Mother Goose and Nursery Rhymes* by Philip Reed. Atheneum.

1963   *The Snowy Day* by Ezra Jack Keats. Viking.

Honor Books: *The Sun Is a Golden Earring* by Natalia Belting. Illus. by Bernarda Bryson. Holt. *Mr. Rabbit and the Lovely Present* by Charlotte Zolotow. Illus. by Maurice Sendak. Harper.

1962   *Once a Mouse* retold by Marcia Brown. Scribner's.

Honor Books: *The Fox Went Out on a Chilly Night: An Old Song* by Peter Spier. Doubleday. *Little Bear's Visit* by Else Minarik. Illus. by Maurice Sendak. Harper. *The Day We Saw the Sun Come Up* by Alice Goudey. Illus. by Adrienne Adams. Scribner's.

1961   *Baboushka and the Three Kings* by Ruth Robbins. Illus. by Nicolas Sidjakov. Parnassus.

Honor Book: *Inch by Inch* by Leo Lionni. Obolensky.

1960   *Nine Days to Christmas* by Marie Hall Ets and Aurora Labastida. Illus. by Marie Hall Ets. Viking.

Honor Books: *Houses from the Sea* by Alice E. Goudey. Illus. by Adrienne Adams. Scribner's. *The Moon Jumpers* by Janice May Udry. Illus. by Maurice Sendak. Harper.

1959   *Chanticleer and the Fox* by Chaucer. Adapted and illustrated by Barbara Cooney. Crowell.

Honor Books: *The House That Jack Built ("La Maison Que Jacques a Bâtie"): A Picture Book in Two Languages* by Antonio Frasconi. Harcourt. *What Do You Say, Dear? A Book of Manners for All Occasions* by Sesyle Joslin. Illus. by Maurice Sendak. Scott. *Umbrella* by Taro Yashima. Viking.

1958   *Time of Wonder* by Robert McCloskey. Viking.

Honor Books: *Fly High, Fly Low* by Don Freeman. Viking. *Anatole and the Cat* by Eve Titus. Illus. by Paul Galdone. McGraw.

1957   *A Tree Is Nice* by Janice May Udry. Illus. by Marc Simont. Harper.

Honor Books: *Mr. Penny's Race Horse* by Marie Hall Ets. Viking. *1 Is One* by Tasha Tudor. Walck. *Anatole* by Eve Titus. Illus. by Paul Galdone. McGraw.

Gillespie and the Guards by Benjamin Elkin. Illus. by James Daugherty. Viking. *Lion* by William Pène du Bois. Viking.

1956 *Frog Went A-Courtin'* retold by John Langstaff. Illus. by Feodor Rojankovsky. Harcourt.

Honor Books: *Play with Me* by Marie Hall Ets. Viking. *Crow Boy* by Taro Yashima. Viking.

1955 *Cinderella, or the Little Glass Slipper* by Charles Perrault. Translated and illustrated by Marcia Brown. Scribner's.

Honor Books: *Book of Nursery and Mother Goose Rhymes* compiled and illustrated by Marguerite de Angeli. Doubleday. *Wheel on the Chimney* by Margaret Wise Brown. Illus. by Tibor Gergely. Lippincott. *The Thanksgiving Story* by Alice Dalgliesh. Illus. by Helen Sewell. Scribner's.

1954 *Madeline's Rescue* by Ludwig Bemelmans. Viking.

Honor Books: *Journey Cake, Ho!* by Ruth Sawyer. Illus. by Robert McCloskey. Viking. *When Will the World Be Mine?* by Miriam Schlein. Illus. by Jean Charlot. Scott. *The Steadfast Tin Soldier* by Hans Christian Andersen. Translated by M. R. James. Illus. by Marcia Brown. Scribner's. *A Very Special House* by Ruth Krauss. Illus. by Maurice Sendak. Harper. *Green Eyes* by Abe Birnbaum. Capitol.

1953 *The Biggest Bear* by Lynd Ward. Houghton Mifflin.

Honor Books: *Puss in Boots.* Translated and illustrated by Marcia Brown. Scribner's. *One Morning in Maine* by Robert McCloskey. Viking. *Ape in a Cape: An Alphabet of Odd Animals* by Fritz Eichenberg. Harcourt. *The Storm Book* by Charlotte Zolotow. Illus. by Margaret Bloy Graham. Harper. *Five Little Monkeys* by Juliet Kepes. Houghton Mifflin.

1952 *Finders Keepers* by Will (pseudonym for William Lipkind). Illus. by Nicolas (pseudonym for Nicolas Mordvinoff). Harcourt.

Honor Books: *Mr. T. W. Anthony Woo* by Marie Hall Ets. Viking. *Skipper John's Cook* by Marcia Brown. Scribner's. *All Falling Down* by Gene Zion. Illus. by Margaret Bloy Graham. Harper. *Bear Party* by William Pène du Bois. Viking. *Feather Mountain* by Elizabeth Olds. Houghton Mifflin.

1951 *The Egg Tree* by Katherine Milhous. Scribner's.

Honor Books: *Dick Whittington and His Cat.* Translated and illustrated by Marcia Brown. Scribner's. *The Two Reds* by Will (pseudonym for William Lipkind). Illus. by Nicolas (pseudonym for Nicolas Mordvinoff). Harcourt. *If I Ran the Zoo* by Dr. Seuss (pseudonym for Theodor Geisel). Random. *T-Bone, the Baby-Sitter* by Clare Turlay Newberry. Harper. *The Most Wonderful Doll in the World* by Phyllis McGinley. Illus. by Helen Stone. Lippincott.

1950 *Song of the Swallows* by Leo Politi. Scribner's.

Honor Books: *America's Ethan Allen* by Stewart Holbrook. Illus. by Lynd Ward. Houghton Mifflin. *The Wild Birthday Cake* by Lavinia R. Davis. Illus. by

Hildegard Woodward. Doubleday. *The Happy Day* by Ruth Krauss. Illus. by Marc Simont. Harper. *Henry-Fisherman* by Marcia Brown. Scribner's. *Bartholomew and the Oobleck* by Dr. Seuss (pseudonym for Theodor Geisel). Random.

1949   *The Big Snow* by Berta and Elmer Hader. Macmillan.

Honor Books: *Blueberries for Sal* by Robert McCloskey. Viking. *All Around Town* by Phyllis McGinley. Illus. by Helen Stone. Lippincott. *Juanita* by Leo Politi. Scribner's. *Fish in the Air* by Kurt Wiese. Viking.

1948   *White Snow, Bright Snow* by Alvin Tresselt. Illus. by Roger Duvoisin. Lothrop.

Honor Books: *Stone Soup: An Old Tale* by Marcia Brown. Scribner's. *McElligot's Pool* by Dr. Seuss (pseudonym for Theodor Geisel). Random. *Bambino the Clown* by George Schreiber. Viking. *Roger and the Fox* by Lavinia Davis. Illus. by Hildegard Woodward. Doubleday. *Song of Robin Hood* edited by Anne Malcolmson. Illus. by Virginia Lee Burton. Houghton Mifflin.

1947   *The Little Island* by Golden MacDonald. Illus. by Leonard Weisgard. Doubleday.

Honor Books: *Rain Drop Splash* by Alvin Tresselt. Illus. by Leonard Weisgard. Lothrop. *Boats on the River* by Marjorie Flack. Illus. by Jay Hyde Barnum. Viking. *Timothy Turtle* by Al Graham. Illus. by Tony Palazzo. Viking. *Pedro, the Angel of Olvera Street* by Leo Politi. Scribner's. *Sing in Praise: A Collection of the Best Loved Hymns* by Opal Wheeler. Illus. by Marjorie Torrey. Dutton.

1946   *The Rooster Crows* selected and illustrated by Maud and Miska Petersham. Macmillan.

Honor Books: *Little Lost Lamb* by Golden MacDonald. Illus. by Leonard Weisgard. Doubleday. *Sing Mother Goose* by Opal Wheeler. Illus. by Marjorie Torrey. Dutton. *My Mother Is the Most Beautiful Woman in the World* retold by Becky Reyher. Illus. by Ruth Gannett. Lothrop. *You Can Write Chinese* by Kurt Wiese. Viking.

1945   *Prayer for a Child* by Rachel Field. Illus. by Elizabeth Orton Jones. Macmillan.

Honor Books: *Mother Goose: Seventy-Seven Verses with Pictures.* Illus. by Tasha Tudor. Walck. *In the Forest* by Marie Hall Ets. Viking. *Yonie Wondernose* by Marguerite de Angeli. Doubleday. *The Christmas Anna Angel* by Ruth Sawyer. Illus. by Kate Seredy. Viking.

1944   *Many Moons* by James Thurber. Illus. by Louis Slobodkin. Harcourt.

Honor Books: *Small Rain: Verses from the Bible.* Text arranged from the Bible by Jessie Orton Jones. Illus. by Elizabeth Orton Jones. Viking. *Pierre Pigeon* by Lee Kingman. Illus. by Arnold Edwin Bare. Houghton Mifflin. *The Mighty Hunter* by Berta and Elmer Hader. Macmillan. *A Child's Good Night Book* by Margaret Wise Brown. Illus. by Jean Charlot. Scott. *Good Luck Horse* by Chih-Yi Chan. Illus. by Plato Chan. Whittlesey.

1943   *The Little House* by Virginia Lee Burton. Houghton Mifflin.

Honor Books: *Dash and Dart* by Mary and Conrad Buff. Viking. *Marshmallow* by Clare Turlay Newberry. Harper.

1942 *Make Way for Ducklings* by Robert McCloskey. Viking.

> **Honor Books:** *An American ABC* by Maud and Miska Petersham. Macmillan. *In My Mother's House* by Ann Nolan Clark. Illus. by Velino Herrera. Viking. *Paddle-to-the-Sea* by Holling Clancy Holling. Houghton Mifflin. *Nothing at All* by Wanda Gág. Coward-McCann.

1941 *They Were Strong and Good* by Robert Lawson. Viking.

> **Honor Book:** *April's Kittens* by Clare Turlay Newberry. Harper.

1940 *Abraham Lincoln* by Ingri d'Aulaire and Edgar Parin d'Aulaire. Doubleday.

> **Honor Books:** *Cock-a-Doodle-Doo* by Berta and Elmer Hader. Macmillan. *Madeline* by Ludwig Bemelmans. Viking. *The Ageless Story* by Lauren Ford. Dodd.

1939 *Mei Li* by Thomas Handforth. Doubleday.

> **Honor Books:** *The Forest Pool* by Laura Adams Armer. McKay/Longmans. *Wee Gillis* by Munro Leaf. Illus. by Robert Lawson. Viking. *Snow White and the Seven Dwarfs*. Translated and illustrated by Wanda Gág. Coward-McCann. *Barkis* by Clare Turlay Newberry. Harper. *Andy and the Lion* by James Daugherty. Viking.

1938 *Animals of the Bible, a Picture Book*. Text selected from the King James *Bible* by Helen Dean Fish. Illus. by Dorothy P. Lathrop. Lippincott.

> **Honor Books:** *Seven Simeons: A Russian Tale* by Boris Artzybasheff. Viking. *Four and Twenty Blackbirds* compiled by Helen Dean Fish. Illus. by Robert Lawson. Stokes/Lippincott.

The Newbery Medal

Named for 18th-century British bookseller John Newbery, this medal is presented annually to the author of the most distinguished contribution to American literature for children published in the preceding year. A number of honor books may also be named by the selection committee. Sponsored by the Association for Library Service to Children, a division of the American Library Association, eligibility is limited to U.S. citizens and residents.

2007 *The Higher Power of Lucky* by Susan Patron. Illus. by Matt Phelan. Simon & Schuster.

> **Honor Books:** *Penny from Heaven* by Jennifer L. Holm. Random House. *Hattie Big Sky* by Kirby Larson. Delacorte. *Rules* by Cynthia Lord. Scholastic.

2006 *Criss Cross* by Lynne Rae Perkins. Greenwillow.

> **Honor Books:** *Whittington* by Alan Armstrong. Random House. *Hitler Youth: Growing Up in Hitler's Shadow* by Susan Campbell Bartoletti. Scholastic. *Princess Academy* by Shannon Hale. Bloomsbury. *Show Way* by Jacqueline Woodson. Putnam.

2005   *Kira-Kira* by Cynthia Kadohata. Atheneum.

Honor Books: *Al Capone Does My Shirts* by Gennifer Choldenko. Putnam. *Lizzie Bright and the Buckminster Boy* by Gary D. Schmidt. Clarion. *The Voice That Challenged a Nation: Marian Anderson and the Struggle for Equal Rights* by Russell Freedman. Clarion.

2004   *The Tale of Despereaux: Being the Story of a Mouse, a Princess, Some Soup, and a Spool of Thread* by Kate DiCamillo. Illus. by Timothy Basil Ering. Candlewick.

Honor Books: *Olive's Ocean* by Kevin Henkes. Greenwillow. *An American Plague: The True and Terrifying Story of the Yellow Fever Epidemic of 1793* by Jim Murphy. Clarion.

2003   *Crispin: The Cross of Lead* by Avi. Hyperion.

Honor Books: *The House of the Scorpion* by Nancy Farmer. Atheneum. *Pictures of Hollis Woods* by Patricia Reilly Giff. Random House. *Hoot* by Cary Hiaasen. Knopf. *A Corner of the Universe* by Ann M. Martin. Scholastic. *Surviving the Applewhites* by Stephanie S. Tolan. HarperCollins.

2002   *A Single Shard* by Linda Sue Park. Clarion.

Honor Books: *Everything on a Waffle* by Polly Horvath. Farrar, Straus & Giroux. *Carver: A Life in Poems* by Marilyn Nelson. Front Street.

2001   *A Year Down Under* by Richard Peck. Dial.

Honor Books: *Because of Winn-Dixie* by Kate DiCamillo. Candlewick. *Hope Was Here* by Joan Bauer. Putnam. *Joey Pigza Loses Control* by Jack Gantos. Farrar, Straus & Giroux. *The Wanderer* by Sharon Creech. HarperCollins.

2000   *Bud, Not Buddy* by Christopher Paul Curtis. Delacorte.

Honor Books: *Getting Near to Baby* by Audrey Couloumbis. Putnam. *26 Fairmont Avenue* by Tomie de Paola. Putnam. *Our Only May Amelia* by Jennifer L. Holm. HarperCollins.

1999   *Holes* by Louis Sachar. Farrar, Straus & Giroux.

Honor Book: *A Long Way from Chicago* by Richard Peck. Dial Books for Young Readers.

1998   *Out of the Dust* by Karen Hesse. Scholastic.

Honor Books: *Ella Enchanted* by Gail Carson Levine. HarperCollins. *Lily's Crossing* by Patricia Reilly Giff. Delacorte. *Wringer* by Jerry Spinelli. HarperCollins.

1997   *The View from Saturday* by E. L. Konigsburg. Atheneum.

Honor Books: *A Girl Named Disaster* by Nancy Farmer. Orchard. *Moorchild* by Eloise McGraw. McElderry. *The Thief* by Megan Whalen Turner. Greenwillow. *Belle Prater's Boy* by Ruth White. Farrar, Straus & Giroux.

1996   *The Midwife's Apprentice* by Karen Cushman. Clarion.

Honor Books: *What Jamie Saw* by Carolyn Coman. Front Street. *The Watsons Go to Birmingham—1963* by Christopher Paul Curtis. Delacorte. *Yolanda's Genius* by Carol Fenner. McElderry. *The Great Fire* by Jim Murphy. Scholastic.

1995   *Walk Two Moons* by Sharon Creech. HarperCollins.

Honor Books: *Catherine, Called Birdy* by Karen Cushman. Clarion. *The Ear, the Eye and the Arm* by Nancy Farmer. Orchard.

1994   *The Giver* by Lois Lowry. Houghton Mifflin.

Honor Books: *Crazy Lady* by Jane Leslie Conly. HarperCollins. *Dragon's Gate* by Laurence Yep. HarperCollins. *Eleanor Roosevelt: A Life of Discovery* by Russell Freedman. Clarion.

1993   *Missing May* by Cynthia Rylant. Orchard.

Honor Books: *The Dark-Thirty: Southern Tales of the Supernatural* by Patricia McKissack. Knopf. *Somewhere in the Darkness* by Walter Dean Myers. Scholastic. *What Hearts* by Bruce Brooks. HarperCollins.

1992   *Shiloh* by Phyllis Reynolds Naylor. Atheneum.

Honor Books: *Nothing But the Truth* by Avi. Orchard. *The Wright Brothers: How They Invented the Airplane* by Russell Freedman. Holiday House.

1991   *Maniac Magee* by Jerry Spinelli. Little, Brown.

Honor Book: *The True Confessions of Charlotte Doyle* by Avi. Orchard.

1990   *Number the Stars* by Lois Lowry. Houghton Mifflin.

Honor Books: *Afternoon of the Elves* by Janet Taylor Lisle. Orchard. *Shabanu: Daughter of the Wind* by Suzanne Fisher Staples. Knopf.

1989   *Joyful Noise: Poems for Two Voices* by Paul Fleischman. Harper.

Honor Books: *In the Beginning: Creation Stories from Around the World* by Virginia Hamilton. Harcourt. *Scorpions* by Walter Dean Myers. Harper.

1988   *Lincoln: A Photobiography* by Russell Freedman. Clarion.

Honor Books: *After the Rain* by Norma Fox Mazer. Morrow. *Hatchet* by Gary Paulsen. Bradbury.

1987   *The Whipping Boy* by Sid Fleischman. Greenwillow.

Honor Books: *On My Honor* by Marion Dane Bauer. Clarion. *Volcano: The Eruption and Healing of Mount St. Helens* by Patricia Lauber. Bradbury. *A Fine White Dust* by Cynthia Rylant. Bradbury.

1986 *Sarah, Plain and Tall* by Patricia MacLachlan. Harper.

Honor Books: *Commodore Perry in the Land of the Shogun* by Rhoda Blumberg. Lothrop. *Dogsong* by Gary Paulsen. Bradbury.

1985 *The Hero and the Crown* by Robin McKinley. Greenwillow.

Honor Books: *Like Jake and Me* by Mavis Jukes. Illus. by Lloyd Bloom. Knopf. *The Moves Make the Man* by Bruce Brooks. Harper. *One-Eyed Cat* by Paula Fox. Bradbury.

1984 *Dear Mr. Henshaw* by Beverly Cleary. Morrow.

Honor Books: *The Sign of the Beaver* by Elizabeth George Speare. Houghton Mifflin. *A Solitary Blue* by Cynthia Voigt. Atheneum. *Sugaring Time* by Kathryn Lasky. Photographs by Christopher Knight. Macmillan. *The Wish Giver* by Bill Brittain. Harper.

1983 *Dicey's Song* by Cynthia Voigt. Atheneum.

Honor Books: *The Blue Sword* by Robin McKinley. Greenwillow. *Dr. DeSoto* by William Steig. Farrar. *Graven Images* by Paul Fleischman. Harper. *Homesick: My Own Story* by Jean Fritz. Putnam. *Sweet Whispers, Brother Rush* by Virginia Hamilton. Philomel.

1982 *A Visit to William Blake's Inn: Poems for Innocent and Experienced Travelers* by Nancy Willard. Illus. by Alice and Martin Provensen. Harcourt.

Honor Books: *Ramona Quimby, Age 8* by Beverly Cleary. Morrow. *Upon the Head of the Goat: A Childhood in Hungary, 1939–1944* by Aranka Siegal. Farrar.

1981 *Jacob Have I Loved* by Katherine Paterson. Crowell.

Honor Books: *The Fledgling* by Jane Langton. Harper. *A Ring of Endless Light* by Madeleine L'Engle. Farrar.

1980 *A Gathering of Days: A New England Girl's Journal, 1830–32* by Joan Blos. Scribner's.

Honor Book: *The Road from Home: The Story of an Armenian Girl* by David Kherdian. Greenwillow.

1979 *The Westing Game* by Ellen Raskin. Dutton.

Honor Book: *The Great Gilly Hopkins* by Katherine Paterson. Crowell.

1978 *Bridge to Terabithia* by Katherine Paterson. Crowell.

Honor Books: *Anpao: An American Indian Odyssey* by Jamake Highwater. Lippincott. *Ramona and Her Father* by Beverly Cleary. Morrow.

1977 *Roll of Thunder, Hear My Cry* by Mildred D. Taylor. Dial.

Honor Books: *Abel's Island* by William Steig. Farrar. *A String in the Harp* by Nancy Bond. Atheneum/McElderry.

1976   *The Grey King* by Susan Cooper. Atheneum/McElderry.

Honor Books: *The Hundred Penny Box* by Sharon Bell Mathis. Viking. *Dragonwings* by Lawrence Yep. Harper.

1975   *M. C. Higgins, the Great* by Virginia Hamilton. Macmillan.

Honor Books: *Figgs & Phantoms* by Ellen Raskin. Dutton. *My Brother Sam Is Dead* by James Lincoln Collier and Christopher Collier. Four Winds. *The Perilous Gard* by Elizabeth Marie Pope. Houghton Mifflin. *Philip Hall Likes Me, I Reckon Maybe* by Bette Greene. Dial.

1974   *The Slave Dancer* by Paula Fox. Bradbury.

Honor Book: *The Dark Is Rising* by Susan Cooper. Atheneum/McElderry.

1973   *Julie of the Wolves* by Jean Craighead George. Harper.

Honor Books: *Frog and Toad Together* by Arnold Lobel. Harper. *The Upstairs Room* by Johanna Reiss. Crowell. *The Witches of Worm* by Zilpha Keatley Snyder. Atheneum.

1972   *Mrs. Frisby and the Rats of NIMH* by Robert C. O'Brien. Atheneum.

Honor Books: *Incident at Hawk's Hill* by Allan W. Eckert. Little, Brown. *The Planet of Junior Brown* by Virginia Hamilton. Macmillan. *The Tombs of Atuan* by Ursula K. Le Guin. Atheneum. *Annie and the Old One* by Miska Miles. Little, Brown. *The Headless Cupid* by Zilpha Keatley Snyder. Atheneum.

1971   *Summer of the Swans* by Betsy Byars. Viking.

Honor Books: *Kneeknock Rise* by Natalie Babbitt. Farrar. *Enchantress from the Stars* by Sylvia Louise Engdahl. Atheneum. *Sing Down the Moon* by Scott O'Dell. Houghton Mifflin.

1970   *Sounder* by William H. Armstrong. Harper.

Honor Books: *Our Eddie* by Sulamith Ish-Kishor. Pantheon. *The Many Ways of Seeing: An Introduction to the Pleasure of Art* by Janet Gaylord Moore. World. *Journey Outside* by Mary Q. Steele. Viking.

1969   *The High King* by Lloyd Alexander. Holt.

Honor Books: *To Be a Slave* by Julius Lester. Dial. *When Shlemiel Went to Warsaw and Other Stories* by Isaac Bashevis Singer. Farrar.

1968   *From the Mixed-Up Files of Mrs. Basil E. Frankweiler* by E. L. Konigsburg. Atheneum.

Honor Books: *Jennifer, Hecate, Macbeth, William McKinley, and Me, Elizabeth* by E. L. Konigsburg. Atheneum. *The Black Pearl* by Scott O'Dell. Houghton Mifflin. *The Fearsome Inn* by Isaac Bashevis Singer. Scribner's. *The Egypt Game* by Zilpha Keatley Snyder. Atheneum.

1967   *Up a Road Slowly* by Irene Hunt. Follett.

Honor Books: *The King's Fifth* by Scott O'Dell. Houghton Mifflin. *Zlateh the Goat and Other Stories* by Isaac Bashevis Singer. Harper. *The Jazz Man* by Mary H. Weik. Atheneum.

1966   *I, Juan de Pareja* by Elizabeth Borten de Treviño. Farrar.

Honor Books: *The Black Cauldron* by Lloyd Alexander. Holt. *The Animal Family* by Randall Jarrell. Pantheon. *The Noonday Friends* by Mary Stolz. Harper.

1965   *Shadow of a Bull* by Maia Wojciechowska. Atheneum.

Honor Book: *Across Five Aprils* by Irene Hunt. Follett.

1964   *It's Like This, Cat* by Emily Cheney Neville. Harper.

Honor Books: *Rascal* by Sterling North. Dutton. *The Loner* by Esther Wier. McKay/Longmans.

1963   *A Wrinkle in Time* by Madeleine L'Engle. Farrar.

Honor Books: *Thistle and Thyme* by Sorche Nic Leodhas (pseudonym for Leclaire Alger). Holt. *Men of Athens* by Olivia Coolidge. Houghton Mifflin.

1962   *The Bronze Bow* by Elizabeth George Speare. Houghton Mifflin.

Honor Books: *Frontier Living* by Edwin Tunis. World. *The Golden Goblet* by Eloise J. McGraw. Coward. *Belling the Tiger* by Mary Stolz. Harper.

1961   *Island of the Blue Dolphins* by Scott O'Dell. Houghton Mifflin.

Honor Books: *America Moves Forward* by Gerald Johnson. Morrow. *Old Ramon* by Jack Schaefer. Houghton Mifflin. *The Cricket in Times Square* by George Selden. Farrar.

1960   *Onion John* by Joseph Krumgold. Illus. by Symeon Shimin. Crowell.

Honor Books: *My Side of the Mountain* by Jean George. Dutton. *America Is Born* by Gerald Johnson. Morrow. *The Gammage Cup* by Carol Kendall. Harcourt.

1959   *The Witch of Blackbird Pond* by Elizabeth George Speare. Houghton Mifflin.

Honor Books: *The Family Under the Bridge* by Natalie S. Carlson. Harper. *Along Came a Dog* by Meindert DeJong. Harper. *Chucaro: Wild Pony of the Pampa* by Francis Kalnay. Harcourt. *The Perilous Road* by William O. Steele. Harcourt.

1958   *Rifles for Watie* by Harold Keith. Illus. by Peter Burchard. Crowell.

Honor Books: *The Horsecatcher* by Mari Sandoz. Westminster. *Gone-Away Lake* by Elizabeth Enright. Harcourt. *The Great Wheel* by Robert Lawson. Viking. *Tom Paine, Freedom's Apostle* by Leo Gurko. Crowell.

1957 *Miracles on Maple Hill* by Virginia Sorensen. Illus. by Beth and Joe Krush. Harcourt.

Honor Books: *Old Yeller* by Fred Gipson. Harper. *The House of Sixty Fathers* by Meindert DeJong. Harper. *Mr. Justice Holmes* by Clara I. Judson. Follett. *The Corn Grows Ripe* by Dorothy Rhoads. Viking. *The Black Fox of Lorne* by Marguerite de Angeli. Doubleday.

1956 *Carry on, Mr. Bowditch* by Jean Lee Latham. Houghton Mifflin.

Honor Books: *The Golden Name Day* by Jennie D. Lindquist. Harper. *The Secret River* by Marjorie Kinnan Rawlings. Scribner's. *Men, Microscopes and Living Things* by Katherine B. Shippen. Viking.

1955 *The Wheel on the School* by Meindert DeJong. Illus. by Maurice Sendak. Harper.

Honor Books: *The Courage of Sarah Noble* by Alice Dalgliesh. Scribner's. *Banner in the Sky* by James Ramsey Ullman. Lippincott.

1954 *And Now Miguel* by Joseph Krumgold. Illus. by Jean Charlot. Crowell.

Honor Books: *All Alone* by Claire Huchet Bishop. Viking. *Shadrach* by Meindert DeJong. Harper. *Hurry Home, Candy* by Meindert DeJong. Harper. *Theodore Roosevelt, Fighting Patriot* by Clara I. Judson. Follett. *Magic Maize* by Mary and Conrad Buff. Houghton Mifflin.

1953 *Secret of the Andes* by Ann Nolan Clark. Illus. by Jean Charlot. Viking.

Honor Books: *Charlotte's Web* by E. B. White. Harper. *Moccasin Trail* by Eloise J. McGraw. Coward-McCann. *Red Sails to Capri* by Ann Weil. Viking. *The Bears on Hemlock Mountain* by Alice Dalgliesh. Scribner's. *Birthdays of Freedom, Vol. 1* by Genevieve Foster. Scribner's.

1952 *Ginger Pye* by Eleanor Estes. Harcourt.

Honor Books: *Americans Before Columbus* by Elizabeth Chesley Baity. Viking. *Minn of the Mississippi* by Holling Clancy Holling. Houghton Mifflin. *The Defender* by Nicholas Kalashnikoff. Scribner's. *The Light at Tern Rock* by Julia L. Sauer. Viking. *The Apple and the Arrow* by Mary and Conrad Buff. Houghton Mifflin.

1951 *Amos Fortune, Free Man* by Elizabeth Yates. Illus. by Nora Unwin. Dutton.

Honor Books: *Better Known as Johnny Appleseed* by Mabel Leigh Hunt. Lippincott. *Gandhi, Fighter Without a Sword* by Jeanette Eaton. Morrow. *Abraham Lincoln, Friend of the People* by Clara I. Judson. Follett. *The Story of Appleby Capple* by Anne Parrish. Harper.

1950 *The Door in the Wall* by Marguerite de Angeli. Doubleday.

Honor Books: *Tree of Freedom* by Rebecca Caudill. Viking. *The Blue Cat of Castle Town* by Catherine Coblentz. McKay/Longmans. *Kildee House* by

Rutherford Montgomery. Doubleday. *George Washington* by Genevieve Foster. Scribner's. *Song of the Pines* by Walter and Marion Havighurst. Holt.

1949   *King of the Wind* by Marguerite Henry. Illus. by Wesley Dennis. Rand.

Honor Books: *Seabird* by Holling Clancy Holling. Houghton Mifflin. *Daughter of the Mountains* by Louise Rankin. Viking. *My Father's Dragon* by Ruth S. Gannett. Random. *Story of the Negro* by Arna Bontemps. Knopf.

1948   *The Twenty-One Balloons* by William Pène du Bois. Lothrop.

Honor Books: *Pancakes-Paris* by Claire Huchet Bishop. Viking. *Li Lun, Lad of Courage* by Carolyn Treffinger. Abingdon. *The Quaint and Curious Quest of Johnny Longfoot, The Shoe-King's Son* by Catherine Besterman. Bobbs-Merrill. *The Cow-Tail Switch, and Other West African Stories* by Harold Courlander and George Herzog. Holt. *Misty of Chincoteague* by Marguerite Henry. Illus. by Wesley Dennis. Rand.

1947   *Miss Hickory* by Carolyn Sherwin Bailey. Illus. by Ruth Gannett. Viking.

Honor Books: *The Wonderful Year* by Nancy Barnes. Messner. *The Big Tree* by Mary and Conrad Buff. Viking. *The Heavenly Tenants* by William Maxwell. Harper. *The Avion My Uncle Flew* by Cyrus Fisher. Appleton. *The Hidden Treasure of Glaston* by Eleanore M. Jewett. Viking.

1946   *Strawberry Girl* by Lois Lenski. Lippincott.

Honor Books: *Justin Morgan Had a Horse* by Marguerite Henry. Follett. *The Moved-Outers* by Florence Crannell Means. Houghton Mifflin. *Bhimsa, the Dancing Bear* by Christine Weston. Scribner's. *New Found World* by Katherine B. Shippen. Viking.

1945   *Rabbit Hill* by Robert Lawson. Viking.

Honor Books: *The Hundred Dresses* by Eleanor Estes. Harcourt. *The Silver Pencil* by Alice Dalgliesh. Schribner's. *Abraham Lincoln's World* by Genevieve Foster. Scribner's. *Lone Journey: The Life of Roger Williams* by Jeanette Eaton. Illus. by Woodi Ishmael. Harcourt.

1944   *Johnny Tremain* by Esther Forbes. Illus. by Lynd Ward. Houghton Mifflin.

Honor Books: *These Happy Golden Years* by Laura Ingalls Wilder. Harper. *Fog Magic* by Julia L. Sauer. Viking. *Rufus M.* by Eleanor Estes. Harcourt. *Mountain Born* by Elizabeth Yates. Coward-McCann.

1943   *Adam of the Road* by Elizabeth Janet Gray. Illus. by Robert Lawson. Viking.

Honor Books: *The Middle Moffat* by Eleanor Estes. Harcourt. *"Have You Seen Tom Thumb?"* by Mabel Leigh Hunt. Lippincott.

1942   *The Matchlock Gun* by Walter D. Edmonds. Illus. by Paul Lantz. Dodd.

Honor Books: *Little Town on the Prairie* by Laura Ingalls Wilder. Harper. *George Washington's World* by Genevieve Foster. Scribner's.

Indian Captive: The Story of Mary Jemison by Lois Lenski. Lippincott. *Down Ryton Water* by Eva Roe Gaggin. Illus. by Elmer Hader. Viking.

1941   *Call It Courage* by Armstrong Sperry. Macmillan.

Honor Books: *Blue Willow* by Doris Gates. Viking. *Young Mac of Fort Vancouver* by Mary Jane Carr. Crowell. *The Long Winter* by Laura Ingalls Wilder. Harper. *Nansen* by Anna Gertrude Hall. Viking.

1940   *Daniel Boone* by James H. Daugherty. Viking.

Honor Books: *The Singing Tree* by Kate Seredy. Viking. *Runner of the Mountain Tops* by Mabel L. Robinson. Random. *By the Shores of Silver Lake* by Laura Ingalls Wilder. Harper. *Boy with a Pack* by Stephen W. Meader. Harcourt.

1939   *Thimble Summer* by Elizabeth Enright. Holt.

Honor Books: *Leader by Destiny: George Washington, Man and Patriot* by Jeanette Eaton. Harcourt. *Penn* by Elizabeth Janet Gray. Viking. *Nino* by Valenti Angelo. Viking. *"Hello, the Boat!"* by Phyllis Crawford. Holt. *Mr. Popper's Penguins* by Richard and Florence Atwater. Little, Brown.

1938   *The White Stag* by Kate Seredy. Viking.

Honor Books: *Bright Island* by Mabel L. Robinson. Random. *Pecos Bill* by James Cloyd Bowman. Little, Brown. *On the Banks of Plum Creek* by Laura Ingalls Wilder. Harper.

1937   *Roller Skates* by Ruth Sawyer. Illus. by Valenti Angelo. Viking.

Honor Books: *Phoebe Fairchild: Her Book* by Lois Lenski. Lippincott. *Whistler's Van* by Idwal Jones. Viking. *The Golden Basket* by Ludwig Bemelmans. Viking. *Winterbound* by Margery Bianco. Viking. *Audubon* by Constance Rourke. Harcourt. *The Codfish Musket* by Agnes D. Hewes. Doubleday.

1936   *Caddie Woodlawn* by Carol Ryrie Brink. Illus. by Kate Seredy. Macmillan.

Honor Books: *Honk: The Moose* by Phil Strong. Illus. by Kurt Wiese. Dodd. *The Good Master* by Kate Seredy. Viking. *Young Walter Scott* by Elizabeth Janet Gray. Viking. *All Sail Set* by Armstrong Sperry. Winston.

1935   *Dobry* by Monica Shannon. Illus. by Atanas Katchamakoff. Viking.

Honor Books: *The Pageant of Chinese History* by Elizabeth Seeger. McKay/Longmans. *Davy Crockett* by Constance Rourke. Harcourt. *A Day on Skates: The Story of a Dutch Picnic* by Hilda Van Stockum. Harper.

1934   *Invincible Louisa: The Story of the Author of "Little Women"* by Cornelia Meigs. Little, Brown.

Honor Books: *The Forgotten Daughter* by Caroline Dale Snedeker. Doubleday. *Swords of Steel* by Elsie Singmaster. Houghton Mifflin. *ABC Bunny* by Wanda

Gág. Coward-McCann. *Winged Girl of Knossos* by Erick Berry. Appleton. *New Land* by Sarah L. Schmidt. McBride. *The Apprentice of Florence* by Anne Kyle. Houghton Mifflin. *The Big Tree of Bunlahy: Stories of My Own Countryside* by Padraic Colum. Illus. by Jack Yeats. Macmillan. *Glory of the Seas* by Agnes D. Hewes. Illus. by N. C. Wyeth. Knopf.

1933 *Young Fu of the Upper Yangtze* by Elizabeth Foreman Lewis. Illus. by Kurt Wiese. Holt.

Honor Books: *Swift Rivers* by Cornelia Meigs. Little, Brown. *The Railroad to Freedom* by Hildegarde Swift. Harcourt. *Children of the Soil* by Nora Burglon. Doubleday.

1932 *Waterless Mountain* by Laura Adams Armer. Illus. by Sidney Armer and Laura Adams Armer. McKay/Longmans.

Honor Books: *The Fairy Circus* by Dorothy Lathrop. Macmillan. *Calico Bush* by Rachel Field. Macmillan. *Boy of the South Seas* by Eunice Tietjens. Coward-McCann. *Out of the Flame* by Eloise Lownsbery. McKay/Longmans. *Jane's Island* by Marjorie Hill Alee. Houghton Mifflin. *The Truce of the Wolf and Other Tales of Old Italy* by Mary Gould Davis. Harcourt.

1931 *The Cat Who Went to Heaven* by Elizabeth Coatsworth. Illus. by Lynd Ward. Macmillan.

Honor Books: *Floating Island* by Anne Parrish. Harper. *The Dark Star of Itza* by Alida Malkus. Harcourt. *Queer Person* by Ralph Hubbard. Doubleday. *Mountains Are Free* by Julia Davis Adams. Dutton. *Spice and the Devil's Cave* by Agnes D. Hewes. Knopf. *Meggy McIntosh* by Elizabeth Janet Gray. Doubleday. *Garram the Hunter: A Boy of the Hill Tribes* by Herbert Best. Illus. by Allena Best (Erick Berry). Doubleday. *Ood-Le-Uk, The Wanderer* by Alice Lide and Margaret Johansen. Illus. by Raymond Lufkin. Little, Brown.

1930 *Hitty: Her First Hundred Years* by Rachel Field. Illus. by Dorothy P. Lathrop. Macmillan.

Honor Books: *The Tangle-Coated Horse and Other Tales: Episodes from the Fionn Saga* by Ella Young. Illus. by Vera Brock. Longmans. *Vaino: A Boy of New Finland* by Julia Davis Adams. Illus. by Lempi Ostman. Dutton. *Pran of Albania* by Elizabeth C. Miller. Doubleday. *The Jumping-Off Place* by Marian Hurd McNeely. McKay/Longmans. *A Daughter of the Seine* by Jeanette Eaton. Harper. *Little Blacknose* by Hildegarde Hoyt Swift. Illus. by Lynd Ward. Harcourt.

1929 *The Trumpeter of Krakow* by Eric P. Kelly. Illus. by Angela Pruszynska. Macmillan.

Honor Books: *The Pigtail of Ah Lee Ben Loo* by John Bennett. McKay/Longmans. *Millions of Cats* by Wanda Gág. Coward-McCann. *The Boy Who Was* by Grace T. Hallock. Dutton. *Clearing Weather* by Cornelia Meigs. Little, Brown. *The Runaway Papoose* by Grace P. Moon. Doubleday. *Tod of the Fens* by Eleanor Whitney. Macmillan.

1928 *Gay-Neck, The Story of a Pigeon* by Dhan Gopal Mukerji. Illus. by Boris Artzybasheff. Dutton.

Honor Books: *The Wonder Smith and His Son* by Ella Young. McKay/Longmans. *Downright Dencey* by Caroline Dale Snedeker. Doubleday.

1927 *Smoky, the Cowhorse* by Will James. Scribner's. (No record of the runners-up.)

1926 *Shen of the Sea* by Arthur Bowie Chrisman. Illus. by Else Hasselriis. Dutton.

Honor Book: *The Voyagers* by Padraic Colum. Macmillan.

1925 *Tales from Silver Lands* by Charles J. Finger. Illus. by Paul Honoré. Doubleday.

Honor Books: *Nicholas* by Anne Carroll Moore. Putnam. *Dream Coach* by Anne and Dillwyn Parrish. Macmillan.

1924 *The Dark Frigate* by Charles Boardman Hawes. Little, Brown. (No record of the honor books.)

1923 *The Voyages of Doctor Dolittle* by Hugh Lofting. Lippincott. (No record of the honor books.)

1922 *The Story of Mankind* by Hendrik Willem Van Loon. Liveright.

Honor Books: *The Great Quest* by Charles Boardman Hawes. Little, Brown. *Cedric the Forester* by Bernard G. Marshall. Appleton. *The Old Tobacco Shop* by William Bowen. Macmillan. *The Golden Fleece and the Heroes Who Lived Before Achilles* by Padraic Colum. Macmillan. *Windy Hill* by Cornelia Meigs. Macmillan.

Coretta Scott King Awards

The award commemorates Dr. Martin Luther King, Jr., and his wife, Coretta Scott King, for their work in promoting world peace and brotherhood. Since 1974, one African American author and one African American illustrator have been honored for outstanding inspirational and educational contributions to children's literature and young people for books published during the previous year. The awards are sponsored by the Social Responsibilities Roundtable of the American Library Association.

2007 Author: *Copper Sun* by Sharon Draper. Atheneum/Simon & Schuster.

Illustrator: *Moses: When Harriet Tubman Led Her People to Freedom* by Carole Boston Weatherford. Illus. by Kadir Nelson. Jump at the Sun/Hyperion.

2006 Author: *Day of Tears: A Novel in Dialogue* by Julius Lester. Hyperion/Jump at the Sun.

Illustrator: *Rosa* by Nikki Giovanni. Illus. by Bryan Collier. Henry Holt.

2005   Author: *Remember: The Journey to School Integration* by Toni Morrison.
Houghton Mifflin.

Illustrator: *Ellington Was Not a Street* by Ntozake Shange. Illus. by Kadir A.
Nelson. Simon & Schuster.

2004   Author: *The First Part Last* by Angela Johnson. Simon & Schuster.

Illustrator: *Beautiful Blackbird* by Ashley Bryan. Atheneum.

2003   Author: *Bronx Masquerade* by Nikki Grimes. Dial.

Illustrator: *Talkin' About Bessie: The Story of Aviator Elizabeth Coleman* by
Nikki Grimes. Illus. by E. B. Lewis. Orchard.

2002   Author: *The Land* by Mildred Taylor. Penguin Putnam.

Illustrator: *Goin' Someplace Special* by Patricia C. McKissack. Illus. by Jerry
Pinkney. Atheneum.

2001   Author: *Miracle Boys* by Jacqueline Woodson. Putnam.

Illustrator: *Uptown* by Bryan Collier. Henry Holt.

2000   Author: *Bud, Not Buddy* by Christopher Paul Curtis. Delacorte.

Illustrator: *In the Time of the Drums* retold by Kim L. Siegelson. Illus. by Brian
Pinkney. Hyperion.

1999   Author: *Heaven* by Angela Johnson. Simon & Schuster.

Illustrator: *i see the rhythm* by Toyomi Igus. Illus. by Michele Wood. Children's
Book Press.

1998   Author: *Forged by Fire* by Sharon M. Draper. Atheneum.

Illustrator: *In Daddy's Arms I Am Tall* by Javaka Steptoe. Lee & Low.

1997   Author: *Slam!* by Walter Dean Myers. Scholastic.

Illustrator: *Minty: A Story of Young Harriet Tubman* by Alan Schroeder. Illus. by
Jerry Pinkney. Dial.

1996   Author: *Her Stories: African American Folktales* by Virginia Hamilton. Illus. by
Leo & Diane Dillon. Blue Sky/Scholastic.

Illustrator: *The Middle Passage: White Ships Black Cargo* by Tom Feelings.
Dial.

1995   Author: *Christmas in the Big House, Christmas in the Quarters* by Patricia
McKissack and Frederick McKissack. Illus. by John Thompson. Scholastic.

Illustrator: *The Creation* by James Weldon Johnson. Illus. by James Ransome.
Holiday.

1994 Author: *Toning the Sweep* by Angela Johnson. Orchard.

Illustrator: *Soul Looks Back in Wonder* compiled and illustrated by Tom Feelings. Dial.

1993 Author: *The Dark-Thirty: Southern Tales of the Supernatural* by Patricia McKissack. Knopf.

Illustrator: *Origins of Life on Earth: An African American Creation Myth* by David A. Anderson. Illus. by Kathleen Atkins Smith. Sight Productions.

1992 Author: *Now Is Your Time! The African-American Struggle for Freedom* by Walter Dean Myers. HarperCollins.

Illustrator: *Tar Beach* by Faith Ringgold. Crown.

1991 Author: *Road to Memphis* by Mildred D. Taylor. Dial.

Illustrator: *Aida* retold by Leontyne Price. Illus. by Leo and Diane Dillon. Harcourt.

1990 Author: *A Long Hard Journey* by Patricia and Frederick McKissack. Walker.

Illustrator: *Nathaniel Talking* by Eloise Greenfield. Illus. by Jan Spivey Gilchrist. Black Butterfly Press.

1989 Author: *Fallen Angels* by Walter D. Myers. Scholastic.

Illustrator: *Mirandy and Brother Wind* by Patricia McKissack. Illus. by Jerry Pinkney. Dragonfly.

1988 Author: *The Friendship* by Mildred D. Taylor. Illus. by Max Ginsberg. Dial.

Illustrator: *Mufaro's Beautiful Daughters: An African Tale* retold and illustrated by John Steptoe. Lothrop.

1987 Author: *Justin and the Best Biscuits in the World* by Mildred Pitts Walter. Lothrop.

Illustrator: *Half Moon and One Whole Star* by Crescent Dragonwagon. Illus. by Jerry Pinkney. Macmillan.

1986 Author: *The People Could Fly: American Black Folktales* by Virginia Hamilton. Knopf.

Illustrator: *Patchwork Quilt* by Valerie Flournoy. Illus. by Jerry Pinkney. Dial.

1985 Author: *Motown and Didi* by Walter Dean Myers. Viking.

Illustrator: No award.

1984 Author: *Everett Anderson's Good-Bye* by Lucille Clifton. Holt.

Illustrator: *My Mama Needs Me* by Mildred Pitts Walter. Illus. by Pat Cummings. Lothrop.

1983   Author: *Sweet Whispers, Brother Rush* by Virginia Hamilton. Philomel.

Illustrator: *Black Child* by Peter Mugabane. Knopf.

1982   Author: *Let the Circle Be Unbroken* by Mildred D. Taylor. Dial.

Illustrator: *Mother Crocodile: An Uncle Amadou Tale from Senegal* adapted by Rosa Guy. Illus. by John Steptoe. Delacorte.

1981   Author: *This Life* by Sidney Poitier. Knopf.

Illustrator: *Beat the Story-Drum, Pum-Pum* by Ashley Bryan. Atheneum.

1980   Author: *The Young Landlords* by Walter Dean Myers. Viking.

Illustrator: *Cornrows* by Camille Yarbrough. Illus. by Carole Bayard. Coward.

1979   Author: *Escape to Freedom* by Ossie Davis. Viking.

Illustrator: *Something on My Mind* by Nikki Grimes. Illus. by Tom Feelings. Dial.

1978   Author: *Africa Dream* by Eloise Greenfield. Day/Crowell.

Illustrator: The same title, illustrated by Carole Bayard.

1977   Author: *The Story of Stevie Wonder* by James Haskins. Lothrop.

Illustrator: No award.

1976   Author: *Duey's Tale* by Pearl Bailey. Harcourt.

Illustrator: No award.

1975   Author: *The Legend of Africana* by Dorothy Robinson. Johnson.

Illustrator: The same title, illustrated by Herbert Temple.

1974   Author: *Ray Charles* by Sharon Bell Mathis. Crowell.

Illustrator: The same title, illustrated by George Ford.

1973   *I Never Had It Made* by Jackie Robinson as told to Alfred Duckett. Putnam.

1972   *17 Black Artists* by Elton C. Fax. Dodd.

1971   *Black Troubador: Langston Hughes* by Charlemae Rollins. Rand.

1970   *Martin Luther King, Jr.: Man of Peace* by Lillie Patterson. Garrard.

Pura Belpré Award

Given biennially, this award is presented to a Latino/Latina writer and illustrator whose work best portrays, affirms, and celebrates the Latino cultural experience in an outstanding work of literature for children and youth. The award is cosponsored by the Association of Library Services to Children, a division of the American Library Association (ALA), and the National

Association to Promote Library Service to the Spanish Speaking, an ALA affiliate. The award is named for Pura Belpré, the first Latina librarian from the New York Public Library.

2006   Narrative: *The Tequila Worm* by Viola Canales. Wendy Lamb/Random House, 2005.

Honor Books: *César: Sí, Se Puede! Yes, We Can!* by Carmen T. Bernier-Grand. Illus. by David Diaz. Marshall Cavendish, 2004. *Dona Flor: A Tall Tale About a Giant Woman with a Great Big Heart* by Pat Mora. Illus. by Raul Colon. Knopf/Random House, 2005.

Illustrator: *Doña Flor: A Tall Tale About a Giant Woman with a Great Big Heart* by Pat Mora. Illus. by Raul Colón. Knopf/Random House, 2005.

Honor Books: *Arrorró, Mi Niño: Latino Lullabies and Gentle Games* selected and illus. by Lulu Delacre. Lee & Low, 2004. *Desar: !Si, Se Puede! Yes, We Can!* by Carmen T. Bernier-Grand. Illus. by David Diaz. Marshall Cavendish, 2004. *My Name Is Celia/Me Llamo Celia: The Life of Celia Cruz/La Vida de Celia Cruz* by Monica Brown. Illus. by Raphael Lopez. Luna Rising/Rising Moon, 2004.

2004   Narrative: *Before We Were Free* by Julia Alvarez. Knopf, 2002.

Honor Books: *Cuba 15* by Nancy Osa. Delacorte, 2003. *My Diary from Here to There/Mi Diario de Aquí Hasta Allá* by Amada Irma Perez. Children's Book Press, 2003.

Illustrator *Just a Minute: A Trickster Tale and Counting Book* by Yuyi Morales. Chronicle Books, 2003.

Honor Books: *First Day in Grapes* by L. King Perez. Illus. by Robert Casilla. Lee & Low, 2002. *The Pot That Juan Built* by Nancy Andrews-Goebel. Illus. by David Diaz. Lee & Low, 2002. *Harvesting Hope: The Story of Cesar Chavez* by Kathleen Krull. Illus. by Yuyi Morales. Harcourt, 2003.

2002   Narrative: *Esperanza Rising* by Pam Muñoz Ryan. Scholastic, 2000.

Honor Book: *Breaking Through* by Francisco Jiminez. Houghton Mifflin, 2001. Illustrator: *Chato and the Party Animals* by Gary Soto. Illus. by Suan Guevera. Putnam, 2000.

Honor Books: *Iguanas in the Snow* by Francisco X. Alarcon. Illus. by Maya Christina Gonzalez. Children's Book Press, 2000. *Juan Bobo Goes to Work* retold by Maris Montes. Illus. by Joe Cepeda. HarperCollins, 2000.

2000   Narrative: *Under the Royal Palms: A Childhood in Cuba* by Alma Flor Ada. Atheneum, 1998.

Honor Books: *From the Bellybutton of the Moon and other Summer Poems / Del Ombligo de La Luna y Otro Poemas de Verano* by Francisco X. Alarcon. Illus. by Maya Christina Gonzalez. Children's Book Press, 1998. *Laughing Out Loud, I Fly: Poems in English and Spanish* by Juan Felipe Herrera. Illus. by Karen Barbour. HarperCollins, 1998.

Illustrator: *Magic Windows: Cut-Paper Art and Stories* by Carmen Lomas Garza. Children's Book Press, 1999.

Honor Books: *Barrio: Jose's Neighborhood* by George Ancona. Harcourt Brace, 1998. *The Secret Stars* by Joseph Slate. Illus. by Felipe Davalos. Marshall Cavendish, 1998. *Mama and Papa Have a Store* by Amelia Lou Carling. Dial, 1998.

1998   Narrative: *Parrot in the Oven: Mi Vida* by Victor Martinez. HarperCollins, 1996.

Honor Books: *Laughing Tomatoes and Other Spring Poems* (Jitomates Risueños y Otros Poemas de Primavera) by Francisco X. Alarcón. Illus. by Maya Christina Gonzales. Children's Book Press, 1997. *Spirits of the High Mesa* by Floyd Martinez. Houston, TX: Arte Público Press, 1997.

Illustrated: *Snapshots from the Wedding* by Gary Soto. Illus. by Stephanie Garcia. Putnam, 1997.

Honor Books: *In My Family/En Mi Familia* by Carmen Lomas Garza. Children's Press, 1996. *The Golden Flower: A Taino Myth from Puerto Rico* by Nina Jaffe. Illus. by Enrique O. Sánchez. Simon & Schuster, 1996. *Gathering the Sun: An Alphabet in Spanish and English* by Alma Flor Ada. Illus. by Simón Silva. Lothrop, 1997.

1996   Narrative: *An Island Like You: Stories of the Barrio* by Judith Ortiz Cofer. Orchard, 1995.

Honor Books: *Baseball in April and Other Stories* by Gary Soto. Harcourt Brace, 1990. Illustrated: *Chato's Kitchen* by Gary Soto. Illus. by Susan Guevara. Putnam, 1995.

Honor Books: *The Bossy Gallito: A Traditional Cuban Folktale.* Retold by Lucia M. Gonzalez. Illus. by Lulu Delacre. Scholastic, 1994. *Pablo Remembers: The Fiesta of the Day of the Dead* written and photographed by George Ancona. Lothrop, 1993. *Family Pictures/Cuadros de Familia* by Carmen Lomas Garza. Children's Book Press, 1990.

Orbis Pictus Award for Outstanding Nonfiction for Children

The Orbis Pictus Award was established by the National Council of Teachers of English in 1989 to promote and recognize excellence in nonfiction writing for children. The name, Orbis Pictus, commemorates the work of Johannes Amos Comenius, *Orbis Pictus—The World in Pictures* (1657), considered to be the first book actually planned for children. Each year, one award book and up to five honor books are named. Criteria for selection include accuracy, content, style, organization, illustration, and format. An annotated list of the winner, honor books, and other outstanding works of nonfiction is published in the November issue of *Language Arts* (NCTE) each year.

2007   *Quest for the Tree Kangaroo: An Expedition to the Cloud Forest of New Guinea* by Sy Montgomery. Photographs by Nic Bishop. Houghton Mifflin.

Honor Books: *Gregory Mendel: The Friar Who Grew Peas* by Cheryl Bardoe. Illus. by Jos. A. Smith. Abrams. *John Muir: America's First Environmentalist* by Kathryn Lasky. Illus. by Stan Fellows. Candlewick. *Something Out of Nothing: Marie Curie and Radium* by Carla Killough McClafferty. Farrar, Straus & Giroux. *Team Moon: How 400,000 People Landed Apollo 11 on the Moon* by Catherine Thimmesh. Houghton Mifflin.

2006   *Children of the Great Depression* by Russell Freedman. Clarion.

Honor Books: *E. R. Vets: Life in an Animal Emergency Room* by Donna Jackson. Houghton Mifflin. *Forbidden Schoolhouse: The True and Dramatic Story of Prudence Crandall and Her Students* by Suzanne Jurmain. Houghton Mifflin. *Genius: A Photobiography of Albert Einstein* by Marfe Ferguson Delano. National Geographic. *Hitler Youth: Growing Up in Hitler's Shadow* by Susan Campbell Bartoletti. Scholastic. *Mosquito Bite* by Alexandara Siy and Dennis Kunkel. Charlesbridge.

2005   *York's Adventures with Lewis & Clark: An African-American's Part in the Great Expedition* by Rhoda Blumberg. HarperCollins.

Honor Books: *Actual Size* by Steve Jenkins. Houghton. *The Race to Save the Lord God Bird* by Phillip Hoose. Farrar, Straus & Giroux. *Secrets of the Sphinx* by James Cross Giblin. Illus. by Bagram Ibatoulline. Scholastic. *Seurat and La Grande Jatte: Connecting the Dots* by Robert Burleigh. Abrams. *The Voice That Challenged a Nation: Marian Anderson and the Struggle for Equal Rights* by Russell Freedman. Clarion.

2004   *An American Plague: The True and Terrifying Story of the Yellow Fever Epidemic of 1793* by Jim Murphy. Clarion.

Honor Books: *Empire State Building: When New York Reached for the Skies* by Elizabeth Mann. Illus. by Alan Witschonke. Mikaya Press. *In Defense of Liberty: The Story of America's Bill of Rights* by Russell Freedman. Holiday House. *Leonardo: Beautiful Dreamer* by Robert Byrd. Dutton. *The Man Who Made Time Travel* by Kathryn Lasky. Illus. by Kevin Hawkes. Farrar, Straus & Giroux. *Shutting Out the Sky: Life in the Tenements of New York, 1880–1924* by Deborah Hopkinson. Orchard.

2003   *When Marian Sang: The True Recital of Marian Anderson—the Voice of a Century* by Pam Muñoz Ryan. Illus. by Brian Selznick. Scholastic.

Honor Books: *Confucius: The Golden Rule* by Russell Freedman. Illus. by Frederic Clement. Arthur A. Levine Books. *Emperor's Silent Army: Terracotta Warriors of Ancient China* by Jane O'Conner. Viking. *Phineas Gage: A Gruesome But True Story About Brain Science* by John Fleischman. Houghton Mifflin. *Tenement: Immigrant Life on the Lower East Side* by Raymond Bial. Houghton Mifflin. *To Fly: The Story of the Wright Brothers* by Wendie C. Old. Illus. by Robert Andrew Parker. Clarion.

2002   *Black Potatoes: The Story of the Great Irish Famine, 1845–1850* by Susan Campbell Bartoletti. Houghton Mifflin.

Honor Books: *The Cod's Tale* by Mark Kurlansky. Illus. by S. D. Schindler. Penguin Putnam. *The Dinosaurs of Waterhouse Hawkins: An Illuminating*

History of Mr. Waterhouse Hawkins. Artist and Lecturer by Barbara Kerley. Illus. by Brian Selznick. Scholastic. *Martin's Big Words: The Life of Dr. Martin Luther King, Jr.* by Doreen Rappaport. Illus. by Bryan Collier. Hyperion.

2001   *Hurry Freedom: African Americans in Gold Rush California* by Jerry Stanley. Crown.

Honor Books: *The Amazing Life of Benjamin Franklin* by James Cross Giblin. Illus. by Michael Dooling. Scholastic. *America's Champion Swimmer: Gertrude Ederle* by David A. Adler. Illus. by Terry Widener. Gulliver. *Michelangelo* by Diane Stanley. HarperCollins. *Osceola: Memories of a Sharecropper's Daughter* by Alan B. Govenar. Illus. by Shane W. Evans. Hyperion. *Wild & Swampy* by Jim Arnosky. HarperCollins.

2000   *Through My Eyes* by Ruby Bridges and Margo Lundell. Scholastic.

Honor Books: *At Her Majesty's Request: An African Princess in Victorian England* by Walter Dean Myers. Scholastic. *Clara Schumann: Piano Virtuosa* by Susanna Reich. Clarion. *Mapping the World* by Sylvia A. Johnson. Atheneum. *The Snake Scientist* by Sy Montgomery. Illus. by Nic Bishop. Houghton Mifflin. *The Top of the World: Climbing Mt. Everest* by Steve Jenkins. Houghton Mifflin.

1999   *Shipwreck at the Bottom of the World: The Extraordinary True Story of Shackleton and the Endurance* by Jennifer Armstrong. Crown.

Honor Books: *Black Whiteness: Admiral Byrd Alone in the Antarctic* by Robert Burleigh. Illus. by Walter Lyon Krudop. Atheneum. *Fossil Feud: The Rivalry of the First American Dinosaur Hunters* by Thom Holmes. Messner. *Hottest, Coldest, Highest, Deepest* by Steve Jenkins. Houghton Mifflin. *No Pretty Pictures: A Child of War* by Anita Lobel. Greenwillow.

1998   *An Extraordinary Life: The Story of a Monarch Butterfly* by Laurence Pringle. Illus. by Bob Marstall. Orchard.

Honor Books: *A Drop of Water: A Book of Science and Wonder* by Walter Wick. Scholastic. *A Tree Is Growing* by Arthur Dorros. Illus. by S. D. Schindler. Scholastic. *Digger: The Tragic Fate of the California Indians from the Missions to the Gold Rush* by Jerry Stanley. Crown. *Charles A. Lindbergh: A Human Hero* by James Cross Giblin. Clarion. *Kennedy Assassinated! The World Mourns: A Reporter's Story* by Wilborn Hampton. Candlewick.

1997   *Leonardo da Vinci* by Diane Stanley. Morrow.

Honor Books: *Full Steam Ahead: The Race to Build a Transcontinental Railroad* by Rhonda Blumberg. National Geographic Society. *The Life and Death of Crazy Horse* by Russell Freedman. Holiday House. *One World, Many Religions: The Ways We Worship* by Mary Pope Osborne. Knopf.

1996   *The Great Fire* by Jim Murphy. Scholastic.

Honor Books: *Rosie the Riveter: Women Working on the Home Front in World War II* by Penny Colman. Crown. *Dolphin Man: Exploring the World of Dolphins.* by Laurence Pringle. Atheneum.

1995   *Safari Beneath the Sea: The Wonder of the North Pacific Coast* by Diane Swanson. Sierra Club Books.

Honor Books: *Wildlife Rescue: The Work of Dr. Kathleen Ramsey* by Jennifer Owings Dewey. Boyds Mills Press. *Kids at Work: Lewis Hine and the Crusade Against Child Labor* by Russell Freedman. Clarion. *Christmas in the Big House, Christmas in the Quarters* by Patricia McKissack and Frederick McKissack. Scholastic.

1994   *Across America on an Emigrant Train* by Jim Murphy. Clarion.

Honor Books: *To the Top of the World: Adventures with Arctic Wolves* by Jim Branderburg. Walker. *Making Sense: Animal Perception and Communication* by Bruce Brooks. Farrar, Straus & Giroux.

1993   *Children of the Dust Bowl: The True Story of the School at Weedpatch Camp* by Jerry Stanley. Crown.

Honor Books: *Talking with Artists* by Pat Cummings. Bradbury Press. *Come Back, Salmon* by Molly Cone. Sierra Club Books.

1992   *Flight: The Journey of Charles Lindbergh* by Robert Burleigh. Illus. by Mike Wimmer. Philomel Books.

Honor Books: *Now Is Your Time! The African American Struggle for Freedom* by Walter Dean Myers. HarperCollins. *Prairie Vision: The Life and Times of Solomon Butcher* by Pam Conrad. HarperCollins.

1991   *Franklin Delano Roosevelt* by Russell Freedman. Clarion.

Honor Books: *Arctic Memories* by Normee Ekoomiak. Holt. *Seeing Earth from Space* by Patricia Lauber. Orchard.

1990   *The Great Little Madison* by Jean Fritz. Putnam.

Honor Books: *The Great American Gold Rush* by Rhoda Blumberg. Bradbury Press. *The News About Dinosaurs* by Patricia Lauber. Bradbury Press.

Robert F. Sibert Informational Book Award

Established in 2001, this annual award is given to the author of the most distinguished informational book published during the preceding year. The award is named in honor of Robert F. Sibert, the long-term president of Bound to Stay Bound Books, Inc. of Jacksonville, Illinois, and is sponsored by the company. ALSC of the American Library Association administers the award.

2007   *Team Moon: How 400,000 People Landed Apollo 11 on the Moon* by Catherine Thimmesh. Houghton Mifflin.

Honor Books: *Freedom Riders: John Lewis and Jim Zwerg on the Front Lines of the Civil Rights Movement* by Ann Bausum. National Geographic. *Quest for the Tree Kangaroo: An Expedition to the Cloud Forest of New Guinea* by Sy

Montgomery. Photographs by Nic Bishop. Houghton Mifflin. *To Dance: A Ballerina's Graphic Novel* by Siena Cherson Siegel. Illus. by Mark Siegel. Simon & Schuster.

2006   *Secrets of a Civil War Submarine: Solving the Mysteries of the H. L. Hunley* by Sally M. Walker. Carolrhoda/Lerner.

       Honor Books: *Hitler Youth: Growing Up in Hitler's Shadow* by Susan Campbell Bartoletti. Scholastic.

2005   *The Voice That Challenged a Nation: Marian Anderson and the Struggle for Equal Rights* by Russell Freedman. Clarion.

       Honor Books: *Walt Whitman: Words for America* by Barbara Kerley. Illus. by Brian Selznick. Scholastic. *The Tarantula Scientist* by Sy Montgomery. Photographs by Nic Bishop. Houghton Mifflin. *Sequoyah: The Cherokee Man Who Gave his People Writing* by James Rumford. Translated into Cherokee by Anna Sixkiller Huckaby. Houghton Mifflin.

2004   *An American Plague: The True and Terrifying Story of the Yellow Fever Epidemic of 1793* by Jim Murphy. Clarion.

       Honor Book: *I Face the Wind* by Vicki Cobb. Illus. by Julia Gorton. HarperCollins.

2003   *The Life and Death of Adolph Hitler* by James Cross Giblin. Clarion.

       Honor Books: *Six Days in October: The Stock Market Crash of 1929* by Karen Blumenthal. Atheneum. *Hole in My Life* by Jack Gantos. Farrar, Straus & Giroux. *Action Jackson* by Jan Greenberg and Sandra Jordan. Illus. by Robert Andrew Parker. Millbrook Press. *When Marian Sang* by Pam Muñoz Ryan. Illus. by Brain Selznick. Scholastic.

2002   *Black Potatoes: The Story of the Great Irish Famine, 1845–1850* by Susan Campbell Bartoletti. Houghton Mifflin.

       Honor Books: *Surviving Hitler: A Boy in the Nazi Death Camps* by Andrea Warren. HarperCollins. *Vincent van Gogh* by Jan Greenberg and Sandra Jordan. Delacorte. *Brooklyn Bridge* by Lynn Curlee. Atheneum.

2001   *Sir Walter Raleigh and the Quest for Eldorado* by Marc Aronson. Clarion.

       Honor Books: *The Longitude Prize* by Joan Dash. Illus. by Dusan Petricic. Farrar, Straus & Giroux. *Blizzard: The Storm That Changed America* by Jim Murphy. Scholastic. *My Season with the Penguins: An Antarctic Journal* by Sophie Webb. Houghton Mifflin. *Pedro and Me: Friendship, Loss, and What I Learned* by Judd Winick. Henry Holt.

Theodor Seuss Geisel Award

The Theodor Seuss Geisel Award, established in 2004, was given annually beginning in 2006 to the author(s) and illustrator(s) of the most distinguished contribution to the body of

American children's literature known as beginning reader books published in the United States during the preceding year. The award recognizes great creativity and imagination in literary and artistic achievements to engage children in reading.

2007   *Zelda and Ivy: The Runaways* by Laura McGee Kvasnosky. Candlewick.

   Honor Books: *Mercy Watson Goes for a Ride* by Kate DiCamillo. Illus. by Chris Van Dusen. Candlewick. *Move Over, Rover!* By Karen Beaumont. Illus. by Jane Dyer. Harcourt. *Not a Box* by Antonette Portis. HarperCollins.

2006   *Henry and Mudge and the Great Grandpas* by Cynthia Rylant. Illus. by Sucie Stevenson. Simon & Schuster.

   Honor Books: *Hi! Fly Guy* by Tedd Arnold. Cartwell/Scholastic. *A Splendid Friend, Indeed* by Suzanne Bloom. Boyds Mills Press. *Cowgirl Kate and Cocoa* by Erica Silverman. Illus. by Betsy Lewin. Harcourt. *Amanda Pig and the Really Hot Day* by Jean Van Leeuwen. Illus. by Ann Schweninger. Dial.

Mildred L. Batchelder Award

This award is given to the publisher of a children's book that has been translated into English in the previous year and originally appeared in a country other than the United States. Given annually since 1968, it is sponsored by the Association for Library Service to Children of the American Library Association. Recent winners include the following:

2007   *Pull of the Ocean* by Jean Claude Mourlevat. Translated from French by Y. Maudet. Delacorte.

2006   *An Innocent Soldier* by Josef Holub. Translated from German by Michael Hofmann. Arthur A. Levine.

2005   *The Shadows of Ghadames* by Joelle Stolz. Translated from French by Catherine Temerson. Delacorte/Random House.

2004   *Run, Boy, Run* by Uri Orlev. Translated from Hebrew by Hillel Halkin. Walter Lorraine/Houghton Mifflin.

2003   *The Thief Lord* by Cornelia Funke. Translated from German by Oliver Latsch. The Chicken House/Scholastic.

2002   *How I Became an American* by Karin Gundisch. Translated from German by James Skofield. Cricket Books.

2001   *Samir and Yonatan* by Daniella Carmi. Translated from Hebrew by Yael Lotan. Scholastic.

2000   *The Baboon King* by Anton Quintana. Translated from Dutch by John Nieuwenhuizen. Walker and Company.

1999   *Thanks to My Mother* by Schoschana Rabinovici. Translated from German by James Skofield. Dial.

1998   *The Robber and Me* by Josef Holub. Translated from German by Elizabeth D. Crawford. Henry Holt.

1997   *The Friends* by Kazumi Yumoto. Translated from Japanese by Cathy Hirano. Farrar, Straus & Giroux.

1996   *The Lady with the Hat* by Uri Orlev. Translated from Hebrew by Hillel Halkin. Houghton.

1995   *The Boys from St. Petri* by Bjarne Reuter. Translated from Danish by Anthea Bell. Dutton.

1994   *The Apprentice* by Pilar Molina Llorente. Translated from Spanish by Robin Longshaw. Farrar, Straus & Giroux.

Andrew Carnegie Medal for Excellence in Video

Established with the support of the Carnegie Corporation of New York, the Carnegie Medal honors an outstanding American video production for children released during the previous year. The video is based on a previously published children's book and is administered by the Association for Library Service to Children (ALSC), a division of the ALA. Recent winning videos include the following:

2007   *Knuffle Bunny* by Mo Willems. Produced by Weston Woods Studios.

2006   *The Man Who Walked Between the Towers* by Mordecai Gerstein. Produced by Michael Sporn Animation and Weston Woods Studios.

2005   *The Dot* by Peter Reynolds. Produced by Weston Woods Studio and Fable Vision.

2004   *Giggle, Giggle, Quack* by Doreen Cronin and Betsy Lewin. Produced by Weston Woods Studios.

2003   *So You Want to Be President?* by Judith St. George and David Small. Produced by Weston Woods Studios.

2002   *My Louisiana Sky* by Kimberly Willis Holt. Produced by Aviator Films and Hyperion Studio.

2001   *Antarctic Antics* by Judy Sierra. Produced by Weston Woods Studios.

2000   *Miss Nelson Has a Field Day* by Harry Allard. Produced by Weston Woods Studios.

Other Children's Literature Awards in the United States
Boston Globe/Horn Book Awards

These awards are presented annually to the creators of three outstanding children's books—an excellent work of fiction, a picture book with outstanding illustrations, and an exceptional work of nonfiction. Jointly sponsored by the Boston Globe and the *Horn Book* magazine, these awards are published on the Fanfare pages of the January/February issue of *Horn Book*.

Edgar Allen Poe Award—Best Juvenile Novel

This award is presented to the author of a mystery novel intended for children. Given annually since 1961, it is sponsored by the Mystery Writers of America.

International Reading Association Children's Book Award

This award honors a children's book by a new author who "shows unusual promise in the children's book field." Given since 1975, it is sponsored by the Institute for Reading Research and administered by the International Reading Association.

Laura Ingalls Wilder Medal

Named after the author of the *Little House* series, this medal is presented every three years (originally every five years) by the American Library Association (Children's Book Division) to an author or illustrator whose books have made a lasting contribution to children's literature. Established in 1954, the selection is restricted to books published in the United States. Winners include James Marshall (2007), Laurence Yep (2005), Eric Carle (2003), Milton Meltzer (2001), Russell Freedman (1998), Virginia Hamilton (1995), Marsha Brown (1992), Elizabeth George Speare (1989), Jean Fritz (1986), Maurice Sendak (1983), Theodor Geisel (Dr. Seuss) (1980), Beverly Cleary (1975), E. B. White (1970), Ruth Sawyer (1965), Clara Ingram Judson (1960), and Laura Ingalls Wilder (1954).

NCTE Excellence in Poetry for Children Award

Established in 1977 by the National Council of Teachers of English, this award honors living U.S. poets whose poetry has contributed substantially to the lives of children. Currently awarded every three years, the recognition is given to a poet for the entire body of writing for children ages 3 through 13. Winners include Nikki Grimes (2006), Mary Ann Hoberman (2003), X. J. Kennedy (2000), Eloise Greenfield (1997), Barbara Juster Esbensen (1994), Valerie Worth (1991), Arnold Adoff (1988), Lilian Moore (1985), John Ciardi (1982), Eve Merriam (1981), Myra Cohn Livingston (1980), Karla Kuskin (1979), Aileen Fisher (1978), and David McCord (1977).

Scott O'Dell Award for Historical Fiction

This award is given to the author of a distinguished work of historical fiction for children or young adults set in the New World and published in English by a U.S. publisher. The award originated with celebrated author Scott O'Dell and is administered and selected by an advisory board chaired by Zena Sutherland. Recent winners include *The Green Glass Sea* by Ellen Klages (2007), *The Game of Silence* by Louise Erdrich (2006), *Worth* by A. La Faye (2005), *The River Between Us* by Richard Peck (2004), *trouble don't last* by Shelley Pearsall (2003), *The Land* by Mildred Taylor (2002), *The Art of Keeping Cool* by Janet Taylor (2001), *Two Suns in the Sky* by Miriam Bat-Ami (2000), *Forty Acres and a Mule* by Harriette Gillem Robinet (1999), *Jip: His Story* by Katherine Paterson (1997), *The Bomb* by Theodore Taylor (1996), *Under the Blood-Red Sun* by Graham Salisbury (1995), *Bull Run* by Paul Fleischman (1994), *Morning Girl* by Michael Dorris (1993), and *Stepping on the Cracks* by Mary Downing Hahn (1992). Other authors include Carolyn Reeder, Patricia Beatty, Scott O'Dell, Patricia MacLachlan, Avi, and Elizabeth George Speare.

State Children's Choice Award Programs

STATE	Title of Award [Grade levels/Categories] Year award founded.
ALABAMA	Emphasis on Reading Award [K–2; 3–5; 6–8] 1980
ARIZONA	Arizona Young Reader's Award [Picture; Chapter; M/YA] 1977
ARKANSAS	Charlie May Simon Children's Book Award [4–6] 1970
CALIFORNIA	California Young Readers Medal [Primary; Interm; MS/JH; YA] 1975
COLORADO	Colorado Children's Book Award [Picture Bk; Junior Novel] 1976
	Colorado Blue Spruce Young Adult Book Award [Young Adult] 1985
CONNECTICUT	Nutmeg Children's Book Award [4–6] 1993
FLORIDA	Sunshine State Young Reader's Award [3–5; 6–8] 1983
GEORGIA	Georgia Picture Storybook Award [K–4] 1976
	Georgia Children's Book Award [4–8] 1968
HAWAII	Nene Award [4–6] 1964
ILLINOIS	Rebecca Caudill Young Reader's Book Award [4–8] 1988
INDIANA	Young Hoosier Book Award [K–3; 4–6; 6–8] 1972
IOWA	Iowa Children's Choice Award [3–6] 1980
	Iowa Teen Award [6–9] 1985
KANSAS	William Allen White Children's Book Award [4–8] 1953
	Bill Martin, Jr. Picture Book Award [K–3] 1996
KENTUCKY	The Bluegrass Award [K–3; 4–8] 1983
MARYLAND	Maryland Children's Book Award 1988
MASSACHUSETTS	Massachusetts Children's Book Award [4–6] 1976
MINNESOTA	Maud Hart Lovelace Book Award [3–8] 1980
MISSOURI	Mark Twain Award [4–8] 1972
MONTANA	Treasure State Award [K–3] 1991
NEBRASKA	Golden Sower Award [K–3; 4–6; Young Adult] 1981
NEVADA	Nevada Young Reader's Award [K–2; 3–5; 6–8; 9–12] 1988

NEW HAMPSHIRE	Great Stone Face Children's Book Award [4–6] 1980
NEW JERSEY	Garden State Children's Book Award [Easy to Read; Younger Nonfiction] 1977
NEW MEXICO	Land of Enchantment Children's Book Award [4–8] 1981
NORTH CAROLINA	North Carolina Children's Book Award [Picture Bk K–3; Jr. Bk 4–6] 1992
NORTH DAKOTA	Flicker Tale Book Award [Picture Bk PreK–3; Juvenile 4–6] 1978
OHIO	Buckeye Children's Book Award [K–2; 3–5] 1981
OKLAHOMA	Sequoyah Children's Book Award [3–6] 1959
	Sequoyah Young Adult Book Award [7–9] 1987
RHODE ISLAND	Rhode Island Children's Book Award [3–6] 1991
SOUTH CAROLINA	South Carolina Children's Book Award [3–6] 1975
	South Carolina Junior Book Award [6–9] 1992
	South Carolina Young Adult Book Award [9–12] 1979
SOUTH DAKOTA	Prairie Pasque Book Award [4–6] 1987
TENNESSEE	Volunteer State Book Award [K–3; 4–6; 7–9YA] 1978
TEXAS	Texas Bluebonnet Award [3–6] 1981
UTAH	Utah Children's Book Award [3–6] 1980
	Utah Children's Informational Book Award [3–6] 1986
	Utah Young Adult Book Award [7–12] 1991
	Utah Children's Picture Book Award [K–3] 1996
VERMONT	Dorothy Canfield Fisher Children's Book Award [4–8] 1957
VIRGINIA	Virginia Young Readers Program [Primary; Elem; MS; HS] 1982
WASHINGTON	Washington Children's Choice Picture Book Award [K–3] 1982
WEST VIRGINIA	West Virginia Children's Book Award [3–6] 1985
WISCONSIN	Golder Archer Award [4–8] 1974
	Little Archer Award [K–3]
WYOMING	Indian Paintbrush Award [4–6] 1986
	Soaring Eagle Book Award [7–12] 1989

ALASKA	Northwest Pacific Reader's Choice Award [Youth 4–8] 1940
IDAHO	Northwest Pacific Reader's Choice Award [Senior 9–12] 1990
MONTANA	Northwest Pacific Reader's Choice Award (see above)
OREGON	Northwest Pacific Reader's Choice Award (see above)
WASHINGTON	Northwest Pacific Reader's Choice Award (see above)
ALBERTA/B.C.	Northwest Pacific Reader's Choice Award (see above)

Other Notable Children's Book Recognitions

Notable Books for a Global Society

The Children's Literature and Reading Special Interest Group of the International Reading Association identifies a yearly list of quality literature published during the previous year and written for grades K through 12 that enhances student understanding of people and cultures throughout the world. Criteria focus on titles that are culturally authentic and rich in cultural details and celebrate both diversity and the common bonds of humanity. An annotated list of the notable titles are published in an issue of *The Reading Teacher* (IRA), and an extended list including teaching suggestions and related books is available in the fall issue of *The Dragon Lode*.

Notable Children's Books

This annual American Library Association list is compiled by the Association of Library Service to Children at the midwinter meeting of the ALA. The titles appear in the March issue of *School Library Journal* and also in the March 15 issue of *Booklist*.

Notable Children's Books in the Language Arts K–8

Sponsored by the Children's Literature Assembly (CLA) of the National Council of Teachers of English (NCTE), this recognition is given to works of fiction, nonfiction, and poetry published during the previous year that meet specific criteria. The books must deal explicitly with language, such as plays on words, word origins, or history of language; demonstrate uniqueness in the use of language or style; or invite child response or participation. An annotated list is published annually in an issue of *Language Arts*, and a list with extended annotations and related titles is published in the fall issue of the *Journal of Children's Literature* (CLA).

Notable Children's Trade Books in the Field of Social Studies

The National Council for the Social Studies (NCSS) in cooperation with the Children's Book Council (CBC) selects notable children's trade books in the field of social studies published during the previous year and primarily written for grades K through 8. Criteria for selection include books that emphasize human relations, represent a diversity of groups and are sensitive to a broad range of cultural experiences, present an original theme or fresh slant on a traditional topic, are easily readable and of high literary quality, and have a pleasing format; and, when appropriate, illustrations that enrich text. Organized by thematic strands, the annotated list is published in the March/April issue of *Social Education* and can be found on the NCSS website: http://ncss.org.

Outstanding Science Trade Books for Children

The National Science Teachers Association (NSTA) in cooperation with the Children's Book Council (CBC) selects outstanding science trade books published during the previous year. Criteria for selection include specific guidelines on both content and presentation. An annotated list is published annually in the March issue of *Science and Children*. Additional information available on this website: http://nsta.org.

Teachers' Choices

Each year the International Reading Association's Teachers' Choices project has identified outstanding U.S. trade books published for children and adolescents that teachers find to be exceptional in curriculum use. Criteria for selection include books that reflect high literary qualities; books that might not be discovered or fully appreciated by children without an introduction by a knowledgeable educator or adult; or books that have potential for use across the curriculum. An annotated list (K–2; 3–5; 6–8) including curriculum connections has been published annually since 1989 in the November issue of *The Reading Teacher* (IRA).

Young Adult Choices

Funded by a grant to the International Reading Association (IRA) and supervised by the association's Literature for Adolescents Committee, this project makes teens (grades 7–12) aware of new literature for young adults and allows them to voice their opinions about books being written for them. Young Adult Choices are published in an annotated bibliography in the November issue of the *Journal of Adolescent & Adult Literacy* (IRA).

Children's Literature Awards Given in Other Countries

Amelia Frances Howard-Gibbon Medal (Canada)

This award is given to the illustrator of an outstanding picture book first published in Canada during the preceding year. Sponsored by the Canadian Library Association since 1971, eligibility is limited to Canadian citizens.

Canadian Library Association Book of the Year for Children (Canada)

This award is given to the author of an outstanding children's book first published in Canada during the preceding year. Given annually since 1947, eligibility for this award is limited to Canadian citizens. Occasionally, a second award is given to an outstanding children's book written in French.

Carnegie Medal (Great Britain)

This award is given to the author of an outstanding children's book first published in the United Kingdom during the preceding year. Given annually since 1937, the Carnegie Medal is sponsored by the British Library Association.

Hans Christian Andersen Prize

This award is given to a living author and, since 1996, to a living illustrator whose works have made significant international contributions to children's literature. Sponsored by the International Board on Books for Young People (IBBY), the award has been given every two years since 1956. Other recent winners include Margaret Mahy/New Zealand (2006),

Martin Waddell/Ireland (2004), Aidan Chambers/UK (2002), Quentin Blake/UK (2002), Anthony Browne/UK (2000), and Ana Maria Machado/Brazil (2000). Winners from the United States include Katherine Paterson (1998), Virginia Hamilton (1992), Paul Fox (1978), Scott O'Dell (1972), Maurice Sendak (1970), and Meindert DeJong (1962).

Kate Greenaway Medal (Great Britain)

This award is given to the illustrator of an outstanding picture book first published in the United Kingdom during the preceding year. Given annually since 1957, it is sponsored by the British Library Association.

Martin Waddell, Ireland (2004), Aidan Chambers, UK (2002), Quentin Blake, UK (2002), Anthony Browne, UK (2000), and Ana Maria Machado, Brazil (2000). Winners from the United States include Katherine Paterson (1998), Virginia Hamilton (1992), Paul Fox (1978), Scott O'Dell (1972), Maurice Sendak (1970), and Meindert DeJong (1962).

Kate Greenaway Medal (Great Britain)

This award is given to the illustrator of an outstanding picture book first published in the United Kingdom during the preceding year. Given annually since 1957, it is sponsored by the British Library Association.

Subject and Author Index

Title/Author/ Illustrator Index